By John Rousmaniere

Instructional Books

A Glossary of Modern Sailing Terms (1976, 1989)
The Annapolis Book of Seamanship (1983, 1989, 1999)
The Student and Instructor Workbook for the Annapolis Book of Seamanship (1984)
The Sailing Lifestyle (1985)
Desirable and Undesirable Characteristics of Offshore Yachts (editor, 1987)
The Illustrated Dictionary of Boating Terms (1998)

History Books

The Luxury Yachts (1981)
America's Cup Book, 1851–1983 (1983)
The Golden Pastime: A New History of Yachting (1986)
The Low Black Schooner: Yacht America, 1851–1945 (1987)
A Picture History of the America's Cup (1989)

Other Books

No Excuse to Lose (with Dennis Conner, 1978)
The Enduring Great Lakes (editor, 1979)
"Fastnet, Force 10" (1980)
The Norton Boater's Log (1997)

Videotapes

The Annapolis Book of Seamanship Video Series
    Volume 1, "Cruising Under Sail"
    Volume 2, "Heavy Weather Sailing"
    Volume 3, "Safety at Sea"
    Volume 4, "Sailboat Navigation"
    Volume 5, "Daysailers: Sailing and Racing"
Powerboat Navigation

The Annapolis Book of Seamanship

by John Rousmaniere
Designed and Illustrated by Mark Smith

Third Revised Edition, 1999

SIMON & SCHUSTER

**Dedicated to my shipmates and to all women and men who follow sea under sail.
Fair winds and fair leads to you all.**

"I found my pulse beating with suppressed excitement as I threw the mooring buoy overboard. It seemed as if that simple action had severed my connection with the life on shore; that I had thereby cut adrift the ties of convention, the unrealities and illusions of cities and crowds; that I was free now, free to go where I chose, to do and to live and to conquer as I liked, to play the game wherein a man's qualities count for more than his appearance."

— Maurice Griffiths, *The Magic of the Swatchways*

Simon & Schuster
Rockefeller Center
1230 Avenue of the Americas, New York, NY 10020

SIMON & SCHUSTER and colophon are registered trademarks
of Simon & Schuster, Inc.

Designed by Mark Smith

Manufactured in the United States of America

10 9 8

Library of Congress Cataloging-in-Publication Data
Rousmaniere, John
The Annapolis book of seamanship / by John Rousmaniere :
illustrated and designed by Mark Smith. — 3rd rev. ed.
p. cm.
Includes bibliographical references (p.) and index.
1. Sailing.   2. Seamanship.   I. Title.
GV811.5.R68   1999
623.88—dc21   99-21737
                              CIP
ISBN-13: 978-0-684-85420-5
ISBN-10:   0-684-85420-1

Contents

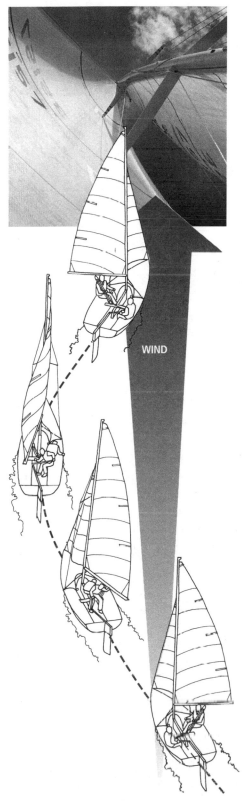

WIND

Contents *continued*

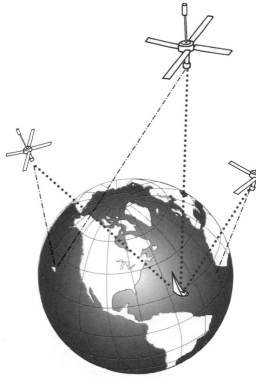

HANDS ON: **How to Read Clouds**

"The face of the sky is our constant, dependable barometer," observes Louis D. Rubin, Sr., in his valuable *The Weather Wizard's Cloud Book.* "Its many 'expressions' tell us what the weather is going to be, when it will change, and to what degree." Here are some hints for predicting weather by reading clouds:

1. Isolated, wispy, white, or very high clouds are indications of fine

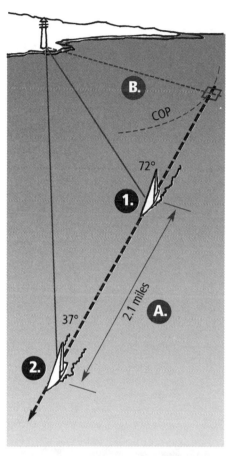

Contents *continued*

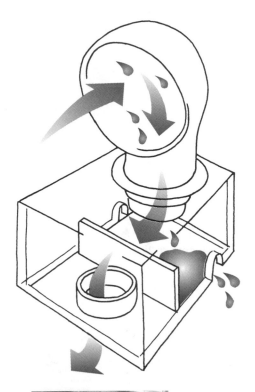

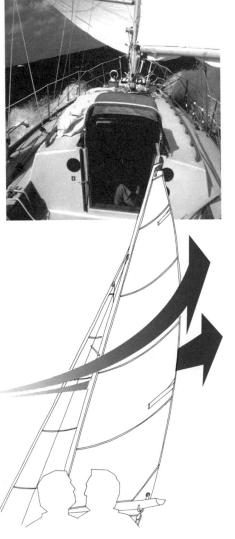

Preface

"Seamanship" has been accurately defined as "The art of sailing, maneuvering, and preserving a ship or a boat in all positions and under all reasonable circumstances." *The Annapolis Book of Seamanship* is intended to cover the fundamental and advanced skills of modern sailing seamanship both thoroughly and in a clear, readable style. This edition of *Annapolis,* the third since 1983, is a major revision. In order to bring the book up to date and make it even more comprehensive, over one-half the work has been revised, and many new topics and features have been introduced. In addition, the design has been modernized and many color illustrations have been added.

New in This Edition. If this edition of *Annapolis* is very different from the original, it is largely because much has changed on the water since 1983. Black buoys are now green, the Global Positioning satellite navigation system (GPS) is almost universally used, and new types of anchors and sails have appeared. In addition safety skills and gear are vastly improved, many more women are commanding boats, and catamarans and trimarans are common where only monohulls used to sail. This is only a sampling from the list of recent developments.

A few of these changes were under way in 1989, when the second edition of *Annapolis* appeared. Ten percent longer than the first edition, it had two new chapters, a complete index (where safety-related topics were highlighted), and several new sections. All the features introduced in that edition remain in this new one, which is substantially changed in many ways. Among the innovations in this new edition are:

Basic skills in early chapters. Fundamental sailing and boathandling skills and gear are introduced in chapters 1, 2, and 3. These topics include important knots, sail trim, the Rules of the Road, heaving-to, and crew-overboard rescue. They are repeated in much greater depth in later chapters, where they are used as foundations for advanced skills.

"Hands On" segments. New here are three dozen special sections, each devoted to a particular seamanship problem and an expert solution. Topics include sending a Mayday distress call, steering by the compass, predicting weather by reading the wind and clouds, tying quick knots, using a cotter pin properly, and safely lighting a galley stove.

More how-to tips. *Annapolis* has always featured easily remembered rules of thumb that guide a crew quickly and successfully through seamanship problems. This edition introduces many new tips while expanding on familiar ones in topics such as trimming sails, selecting an anchor, maneuvering near big ships, and handling heavy weather.

New coverage of multihulls. In this edition we introduce advice on evaluating catamarans and trimarans, on anchoring them, and on handling them under sail (including in storms).

More on emergencies. New material on emergencies, safety, and heavy-weather sailing includes a section on preparing a docked boat for a hurricane. We also have greatly expanded our coverage of crew-overboard rescues and storm tactics.

Equipment updates. We have expanded coverage of the use and care of modern gear and hardware, including radar, GPS, rescue devices, cleats, asymmetrical spinnakers, and engines.

Terminology. In order to add some clarity to the often confusing realm of boating terminology, we define and illustrate major terms when they're first introduced and provide alternative language in parentheses. (Important terms are defined in the glossary.)

Gender. Sailing today is far more inclusive than it was even 16 years ago, and women may be found in most boats, often at the helm. In the numerous examples that we use involving anonymous sailors, to always refer to a sailor as "he" would be inaccurate much of the time and rude all the time. In this edition, the gender generally alternates from example to example. (A boat, however, remains the traditional "she.")

Besides those substantial changes and additions, a multitude of other, smaller modifications keep the book up to date with changing sailing theory, practice, and equipment.

Seamanship and Romance. For all these modern developments, the basic skills and spirit of sailing have not changed at all. Fundamentals of sail trimming, keeping up steerageway, maintaining a dead reckoning plot, and heaving-to are as important now as ever.

As for spirit, sailing remains a blend of romantic adventurousness and careful seamanship. The emphasis here is on the second part of the blend. It is a state of mind called "forehandedness" in the United States Navy. To be forehanded is to be cautious and even pessimistic. A forehanded sailor looks ahead, anticipates the worst, and prepares for it by, among other things, setting and observing standard operating procedures. No place symbolizes this exemplary state of mind and the skills and values of sound seamanship better than Annapolis, Maryland, the home both of the United States Naval Academy and of one of the world's largest and most active fleets of pleasure boats.

Pessimism at first may seem like a weak reason to go sailing. Like most sailors, I came to boats not because I enjoyed naval routine but because the wind in the sails strummed my soul's strings. I felt a bewitching, nervous excitement when I cast off from land. As Maurice Griffiths, a great sailing writer and yacht designer of another era, said in the quote in our dedication, on casting off , "I was free now, free to go where I chose, to do and to live and to conquer as I liked."

That feeling (or the hope for it) must be shared by many if not most readers.

Some, therefore, may think it strange that a major theme of this book is that crews observe the cool cautions of forehandedness and the even colder and less enchanting disciplines of a standard operating procedure (SOP). To cite two examples from the text, there should be policies on board requiring that communications be dryly precise and that certain tasks be done exactly the same way, every time. *Always* refer to compass directions in either magnetic or true degrees, so the navigator and steerer are talking the same language. Always screw in shackle pins from right to left, so you know how to remove gear in the dark without fumbling.

There's not much romance in an SOP. But forehanded preparation liberates you and your crew from worry to enjoy your freedoms. The irony is that you should standardize your techniques in order to best enjoy this free and individualistic pastime. There will be enough adventure out there without any surprises that you and your crew may contribute.

In describing these skills and the equipment to which they are applied, I have tried to be both thorough and clear. This is a book to be *read* as well as *referred to.* The lengthy index should indicate how thorough *Annapolis* is. While compiling and then offering this information, Mark Smith and I have worked to identify and emphasize the fundamentals of seamanship upon which the other principles and skills are based.

Many sailors, unfortunately, are often distracted from the fundamentals by the plethora of boating equipment on the market. The temptation to rely on a piece of hardware, rather than an understanding of how boats are steered, may be difficult to resist. No doubt some new equipment deserves attention. But the issue is whether it deserves to be made the highest priority. At a boat show, safety seminar, or other gathering of sailors, someone inevitably sidles up to the guest speaker and asks, "What about the new Super-XYZ computerized navigation system I've read about in the magazines? Is it really worth an extra $1,000?" The anxiety in the questioner's voice reveals a lack of confidence in sailing ability.

My answer is clear: "Save your money and use it to work on your basic sailing skills. *Go sailing,* preferably in a small boat, where your mistakes are obvious." Mastery of the fundamentals and the application of good habits make for good seamanship. With good seamanship comes the security of knowing that you can meet every challenge. And with security eventually comes a blissful harmony between sailor and boat that, in my experience, cannot be duplicated in any other relationship between a human and an object. This harmony was beautifully described by another classic boating writer, Alfred F. Loomis, when he portrayed a skilled skipper at the helm: "I noticed how much at union with his boat this sailor was, stretched at ease, one arm thrown carelessly along the tiller, head just showing above the gunwale, and face uplifted so that his eyes commanded the luff of the sail."

The experience of and hope for such unity is why we are romantic about boats. It is why we give them (but not our cars and computers) names and personal pronouns. But this harmony between craft and sailor is not natural. It comes with the habitual, intelligent application of the skills and tools of modern sailing seamanship that are the subjects of this book.

John Rousmaniere
February 8, 1999

The Annapolis
Book of Seamanship

CHAPTER 1

The Boat

The idea of sailing a boat upon the sea can seduce even the happiest farmer or mountain climber. There is something about boat and water that sends romance churning in our hearts, and simply the sight of a boat can inspire a reverie. She may be a 15-foot dinghy tied on the roof of a car or a handy cruiser or an America's Cup racer leaping off the cover of a boating magazine. Whatever she is, the boat gleams in our eye, and we find ourselves dreaming, "What if . . . "

Limitless in her poetry, a sailboat is still restricted by the realities of wind and sea. No matter how graceful her lines, tall her mast, strong her rigging, and snug her cabin, a sailboat is tied down (as poetry is not) by her environment. There is no way to avoid the wind's variability, the water's friction, the wave's slap. Many novices have been disappointed, frightened, seasick, or even injured aboard sailboats because they did not accept and learn about these realities and restrictions. Preferring to relax in their dreams, they suffered afloat, and while their souls gloried in their boats' beauty, their bodies ached because they neglected hard practicalities. This book is about those practicalities.

Later in this chapter we'll look at some of those realities, at how wind and sea affect a boat and at how a well-handled boat responds. But first, we will build a foundation by describing the parts of the boat — the wood, fiberglass, metal, cloth, and (increasingly) cutting-edge materials like carbon fiber that, working together, make a boat what she is. As a great seaman, John MacGregor, observed, "The perfection of a yacht's beauty is that nothing should be there for only beauty's sake."

A Note on Terminology. Traditionally, pleasure boats have been grouped in two families: "yachts" are often considered to be longer than about 35 feet, while "boats" are smaller. Some people (including the writer) have enjoyed applying "yacht" as a term of approval to any especially able pleasure boat regardless of its size. But since "yacht" unfortunately has taken on the heavy baggage of social snobbery, in this book "boat" generally will be used to refer to any vessel whose aim is not commercial.

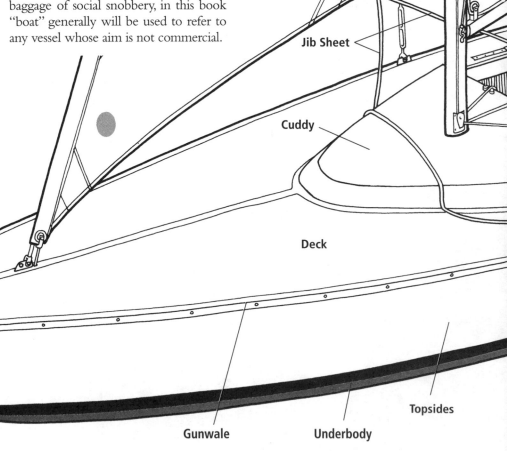

Headstay
Telltale
Spreader
Shroud
Mast
Jib
Jib Sheet
Cuddy
Deck
Bow
Gunwale
Underbody
Topsides

The Parts of a Boat

Each item or part of a boat has a purpose, as we will see in three examples. Our first is the daysailer with a fin keel. Between 18 and 25 feet in length overall (from bow to stern), and weighing between about 1,500 and 3,000 pounds, keel daysailers are available in a number of one-design classes, in which the boats are exactly alike (for example, the Sonar, J-22, Rhodes 19, and Soling). In general appearance keel daysailers are pretty similar, and the example here is a crossbreed of several classes. These boats are found everywhere in America. They race over short courses, go out on day sails (short

sails in daylight), and are used by many sailing schools. These classes also have been used by the pioneering generation of disabled sailors who participate in the Para Olympics.

The hull of the typical daysailer is made of fiberglass, though occasionally you'll come across a wooden boat. The front is the bow, the back is the stern, the top is the deck, the sides are the topsides, and the part below the water is the underbody. There may be a cuddy — a small cabin (room in a boat) offering shelter for the crew (sailors) and their personal gear. The crew sits in or next to the cockpit, a recessed area in the deck. In very small daysailers, the cockpit is only a small foot well. Many cockpits are self-bailing, meaning that water automatically drains out because the sole (floor) is above water level.

The rig consists of the spars and the standing and running rigging. Spars include the mast, which supports the luff (front) of the mainsail, and the boom, which extends the mainsail's foot (bottom) from the mast. The standing rigging consists of wire stays and spreaders (metal struts) that restrain the mast from falling and bending far. The headstay runs from the mast to the bow, the shrouds are stays running to the side decks, and the backstay runs to the stern. Stays and shrouds are usually attached to the boat with turnbuckles, devices with opposed threaded rods that are used to adjust tension in a shroud or stay. The mast is usually aluminum and the stays are usually stainless steel wire. (A few boats have stayless masts that are allowed to bend.) The running rigging includes the halyards that pull up the sails, the sheets, boom vang, traveler, and other lines that shape them, and the blocks (pulleys) that all those lines run through. A line is a length of rope or wire used for a particular purpose in a boat. On many boats, the lines have various colors in order to make identification easier.

The sails are the boat's engine. The jib and the mainsail are the sails found on most boats, although many boats also carry other, more specialized sails. The jib is carried on the headstay. This jib is a working jib; it simply fills the foretriangle, the area between the headstay and the mast. Small boats usually carry only one size jib, but larger boats may carry a working jib plus one or more genoa jibs,

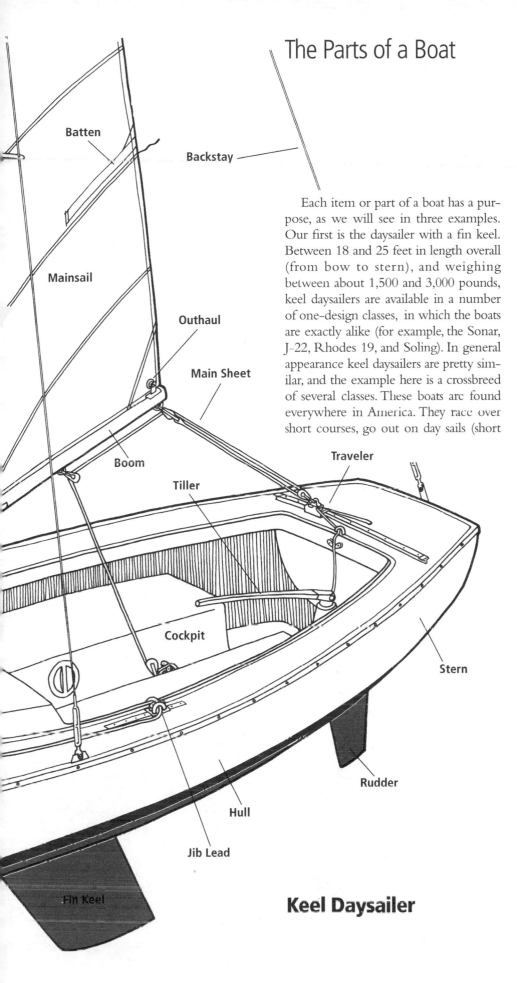

Keel Daysailer

The Parts of a Boat

which overlap the mast. Most sails are constructed of synthetic Dacron cloth. The exception is the spinnaker, a large, colorful nylon balloon- or parachute-shaped sail carried when the wind is aft or abeam (from behind or over the side).

The helm is the tiller (a horizontal rod or pole) or steering wheel with which the helmsman, or steerer, steers the boat.

The appendages (the keel and rudder) are permanent, fixed extensions from the hull's underbody. The rudder, at or near the stern, is turned by the helm and changes the flow of water around the hull in order to turn the boat. The keel performs two important functions. First, it grips the water to keep the boat from slipping sideways (called making leeway). Second, its weight (in lead or iron ballast that accounts for over half the boat's total weight) provides a counter-weight against the side force of the wind, which might make the boat capsize (turn over). A big dif-ference between older and newer boats is keel shape. The fin keel in our example is fairly large, wide, and something like an airplane wing. But on many racing boats (for example, America's Cup boats), the keel is a deep, narrow slat with a heavy bulb of lead ballast at the bottom.

Many daysailers between about 10 and 18 feet have all these features except the fixed keel. Instead, they have a vertically retracting appendage called a centerboard to keep them lightweight and allow them to be beached.

There are more than 500 types of sailboats, and the various parts of the boat are found on each of them in unique combinations. We have looked at a keel daysailer. Now

we'll examine two other, different, and popular types: the 14-foot dinghy and a 30-foot cruiser-racer.

The Dinghy. A dinghy is a small, lightweight boat more lively and responsive than a keel boat and costing less, too. Dinghies range in size from about 8 to 16 feet and weigh between 80 and 250 pounds. Examples include the Optimist, the Vanguard 15, and the Laser, which is one of the world's most popular dinghy classes, numbering over 170,000 boats built. Only 14 feet long and weighing 130 pounds, she is used for sailing instruction, daysailing, and racing at levels as high as the Olympics. While the Laser can sup-port two adults, the boat is primarily sailed as a singlehander, meaning that only one person is on board.

Instead of a heavy metal keel she has a retractable unballasted center-board, weighing just a few pounds, that stops sideslipping. This means

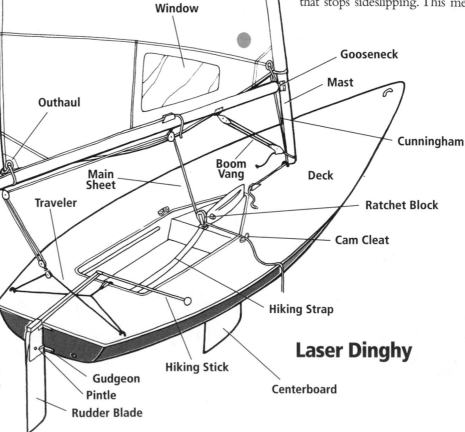

Laser Dinghy

that she's light enough to be hauled out of the water by two people and placed on a car's roof rack. With a sail area of 76 square feet in her mainsail (she has a cat rig, meaning that there is no jib), the Laser is capable of speeds as high as 15 knots in strong winds under capable sailors. (Since 1 knot is a speed of 1 nautical mile an hour, or 1.15 statute mile per hour, this is the equivalent of about 17 MPH.) With no heavy keel as a counterweight, she can capsize (tip over) quickly if not handled well. Since her fiberglass hull is airtight and also contains blocks of foam, the Laser has great buoyancy, and will not only float when capsized but will quickly get sailing again as water drains quickly from her small cockpit. Most keel daysailers also have buoyancy tanks, and so will float after taking large amounts of water aboard. But in their case, the water usually must be laboriously pumped out or bailed out with a bucket.

The Laser's self-bailing footwell is designed not to sit in but to hold the skipper's legs and feet. When the wind pipes up the boat begins to heel (tip), the skipper hooks his feet under a nylon strap in the cockpit called a hiking strap and hikes out, or leans backward to windward (toward the wind), using his weight to lever the boat back upright. Like almost all boats, the Laser sails fastest and most comfortably when she sails flat, with little or no heel. The window in the sail allows the sailor to see other boats when he is hiked out.

The Laser's two appendages are the centerboard and the rudder. The centerboard slides up and down through a slot in the hull, the centerboard trunk. The Laser's centerboard is a version known as a daggerboard. It retracts like a dagger in a sheath. When sailing across or with the wind on the points of sail called the reach and the run, the skipper retracts the centerboard in order to minimize the boat's resistance against the water. Keels cannot be retracted.

Sailing toward the wind's eye on a beat (close-hauled), the sailor leaves the centerboard fully lowered so that its whole area works effectively to resist sideslipping. The other appendage, the rudder, is hooked onto the transom at the stern with pin and socket fittings called pintles and gudgeons. The sailor steers with a tiller. A connecting rod called a hiking stick (or tiller extension) allows him to adjust the tiller even when he is hiking way out.

The Laser's rig is simple. This mast is one of the few that are freestanding, without stays. Unlike most boats, the Laser does not have a halyard for the sail. Instead, a long sock sewn into the sail's luff, or forward (front) edge, is pulled over the mast. The lower forward corner of the sail (the tack) is held down by a short line called the Cunningham, a piece of running rigging (named for its inventor) that is tightened to make a sail flat in fresh winds and loosened to make it full or baggy in light winds. The Laser's Cunningham also keeps the mast in its step (base) if the boat capsizes. Before the mast is stepped, plastic strips called battens are put in slots in the leech (after or back edge) of the sail to keep the leech from flapping.

Once the mast is stepped and the Cunningham is rigged (set up and installed), the sail's clew (after corner) is tied to the boom with a line called the outhaul. Another short line holds the clew close to the boom. Like the Cunningham, the outhaul is tightened in fresh winds and loosened in light winds. The Cunningham and outhaul are sail controls found on almost all boats. So is the boom vang, a tackle (an assembly of rope and blocks, or pulleys, that allow a powerful pull) that runs between the bottom of the mast and the boom. When tightened, the vang flattens the sail and keeps the boom from lifting.

The main sheet is a long line that runs in a tackle from the boom's end to a block on a sideways-running rope traveler, back to the boom, and then forward to the sailor through two other blocks. The second of these blocks is a ratchet block, which has a mechanism that takes some of the load off the sailor's hands.

Because they are light, fast, and prone to capsize, dinghies like the Laser demand full concentration to sail well. On a reach, this Laser's centerboard is raised halfway and her boom vang holds the boom horizontal. The steerer holds the hiking stick firmly but easily so he has full control.

The Parts of a Boat

The Cruiser-Racer. There probably are more cruiser-racers around 30 feet in length than any other type of auxiliaries (sailboats with inboard engines). Almost every builder of cruising boats offers a model in the 28–32 foot range that sleeps four or five people, has a galley (kitchen), and is safe for sailing in protected waters (in lakes, bays, and sounds) or on the ocean near shore. In the right hands and properly equipped, such a boat could take a short offshore overnight passage on an ocean or large lake. The one shown here is a generic boat of moderate displacement (weight) popular on the used-boat market. Weighing about 6,000 pounds and with a sail area of over 425 square feet, she has a large, comfortable cabin in which several people can live for days at a time while cruising, yet she is fast and lively enough to be raced successfully or taken out on pleasurable daysails. While the cruiser-racer may be sailed singlehanded by a talented and

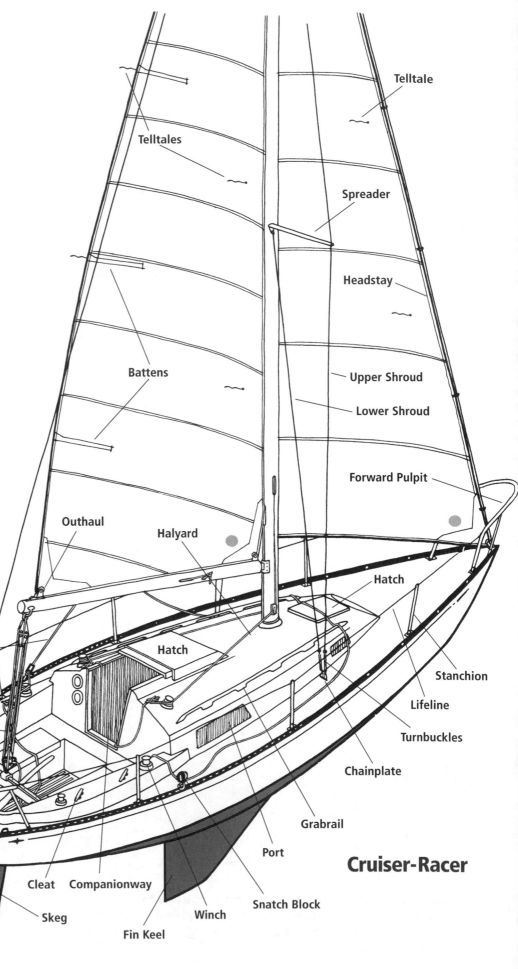

Telltale

Telltales

Spreader

Headstay

Upper Shroud

Lower Shroud

Forward Pulpit

Battens

Outhaul

Halyard

Hatch

Hatch

Jib Sheet

Stanchion

Lifeline

Main Sheet

Turnbuckles

Chainplate

After Pulpit

Grabrail

Traveler

Port

Cruiser-Racer

Rudder

Cleat

Companionway

Snatch Block

Skeg

Winch

Fin Keel

agile sailor, she should go out with a crew of two or more.

To counterbalance her large sail area, the cruiser-racer has a deep, heavy, fixed fin keel. Like the keel, her rudder is also permanently installed. It is controlled by a long tiller or steering wheel in the comfortable cockpit. The cockpit will drain automatically through drain holes in its sole (floor). The tall aluminum mast is permanently stepped in (secured on) a fitting in or on the cabin and supported by stays and spreaders. This boat has a masthead rig, since the jib is hoisted through a block at the masthead, or very top of the mast.

This boat's running rigging is more complicated than the Laser's. Because the crew of this boat can choose from several different size jibs, the blocks through which the jib sheets pass on deck are adjustable so that the jib lead (the angle the sheet makes to the sail) can be optimized. The strong pull of the sheets is too much for a single crew member. Since a tackle like the one on the Laser's main sheet would be too awkward to use on a jib sheet, the sheet is led to a winch. (A winch is a geared drum that is turned by a handle. The combined power of the gears and the handle greatly increases the sailor's pull.) The boat is equipped with winches for the jib sheets and also for the halyards. The main sheet may be a powerful tackle or it may be led to its own winch.

Most of the other important parts of the cruiser-racer are like the Laser's and keel daysailer's. They all have a system for holding up the sail, sheets, an outhaul, a Cunningham, a traveler, and a boom vang for adjusting sail shape. The difference lies in the heft of the gear. Because the boom in the cruiser-racer is heavy, it must be held up when the mainsail is not set, otherwise the boom will drop and injure the crew. Our cruiser-racer solves this dangerous problem with a boom vang that has an integral spring-loaded

Accommodations vary with boat size, type, and purpose. In this small cruiser-racer, the cabin is open. Aft are the galley and head. The vertical strut supports the mast, which is stepped on deck. In most boats, the mast passes through the deck and is stepped on the boat's bottom.

rod that holds the boom up. Alternatively, the boat would have a topping lift — a line from the top of the mast to the end of the boom. By contrast, the day-sailer's and dinghy's booms are so light and easy to handle by an individual crew member that they do not require special gear to support them.

This more complex, larger boom vang on the cruiser-racer illustrates an important point: as boats get longer, their weight, the forces they generate, and their cost all increase exponentially. One rule of thumb is that as the length doubles, the weight and the forces involved are at least cubed. This means that while a 30-footer is only twice as long as a 15-footer, she may weigh as much as eight times more and her sails and sheets may pull eight times harder. In order to handle these forces, sail-handling gear on a cruiser-racer must be much larger and more powerful, adding appreciably to cost. There are exceptions to this rule of thumb. Modern ultra-light displacement racing boats may weigh the same as more traditional boats about half their length, carry the same sail area, and generate the same forces.

In this 40-footer, there's enough room for full separate cabins and plenty of storage space in lockers. Notice the grab holes in the post and the ports that let light below. The galley (foreground) has two sinks and faucets for both fresh and sea water.

Bending on Sails

Bending on the Mainsail. The mainsail on a cruiser-racer usually is left furled (rolled) on the boom, under a cover that protects it from the sun's ultraviolet rays, which degrade Dacron fibers. But we'll show how a mainsail is bent on (rigged). First, make sure that the deck is clean so no grime gets on the sail. This may require hosing or swabbing (mopping) the deck and scrubbing the bottom of your shoes. Now pull the folded mainsail out of its bag and unfold it. There are three corners with cringles (steel rings): the tack,

which is where two corners make a right angle; the clew, where the angle is about 60°; and the head, where the angle is very narrow. First find the tack, the forward lower corner, and the only one where the two edges meet at a right angle. The tack usually is near the sailmaker's label. Next find the foot of the sail, which is the shorter of the two sides

that meet at the tack. At the far end of the foot is the clew, which, like the tack, has a cringle. Along the foot you will find a rope sewed to the sail, called the boltrope, and may find a dozen or more plastic cylinders (called slugs) or metal slides. Starting with the slug or slide nearest the clew, insert them one by one into the groove or onto the track at the top of the boom, being careful that they are not twisted. If there are no slugs or slides, the boltrope itself is slid into a groove in the boom.

When all the slugs are inserted, pull the clew to near the end of the boom. Loosen the outhaul, the line that adjusts the foot of the sail. After inspecting for twists, attach the clew in the outhaul shackle and the tack in the gooseneck fitting at the forward end of the boom

A typical outhaul (above) is connected to a small block and tackle adjusted at the forward end of the boom.

The parts of a mainsail.

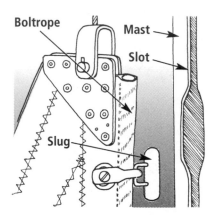

The mainsail's luff is connected to the mast by inserting slugs or the boltrope into the slot, or by putting slides on a track.

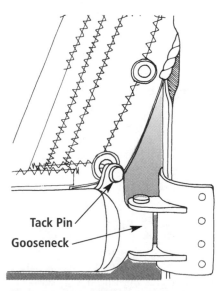

The tack is secured at the gooseneck. Insert the tack pin and other clevis pins from right to left.

using clevis pins (metal pins). The clevis pins are retained by cotter pins (short lengths of wire) or automatic locks. Insert clevis pins from right to left on your boat so you'll be able to quickly unrig sails in an emergency without fumbling around.

Return to the mast and, starting from the tack, work up the luff, making sure it's not twisted. At the head (the top corner), insert the top slug in the groove or the top slide on the track. Insert the other slugs or slides, one by one, then close off the slot with the pin or gate provided in order to keep them from falling off. Inspect the luff to make sure that there are no twisted slugs. The sail is now secure on both boom and mast. If the sail does not have slides or slugs, insert the top of the boltrope in the groove, attach the halyard, and pull the sail up a few inches. Insert the battens in their correct pockets — some are longer than others — and loosely furl the sail on the boom to keep it from blowing around as you finish bending on the sails.

Bending on the Jib. If the jib is not already rigged on a roller-furler, find the jib you want below or in a locker and take it onto the foredeck. Smaller jibs are better on windy days. Pull the sail out of the bag. Like the mainsail it has three corners. Since they may all have approximately the same angle, be careful when rigging. (It helps to mark corners with an indelible pen.) Find the tack, which usually has a small cringle and is near the sailmaker's label. Carry it to the bow, and, facing forward, pull the tack and the luff of the sail through your legs to the headstay. Shackle the tack at the bottom of the headstay. The luff (front edge) may have snaps or hanks that hook onto the headstay. If so, working up the luff from bottom to top, snap them on. They should all go on from the same side. If they face in different directions, the sail is twisted.

On some boats the jibs are not hanked on. Instead, the boltrope on the luff is fed into a groove on the headstay that is much like the groove in the mast. In this case, attach the halyard, insert the boltrope in the groove, and pull the sail up a few inches. (In racing boats there are two grooves and two halyards to allow quick jib changes — one jib goes up while the other is set, then the old sail is lowered.)

When the jib's forward edge is secure, walk aft pulling the clew with you. Locate the jib sheets and lead (pass) them through the appropriate blocks on deck. The proper lead for each jib should be marked with pieces of tape or indelible markings. Tie the ends of the sheets into the jib clew using the bowline knot, described in chapter 5. (The shaking of the jib clew may open a shackle or, worse, cause damage to the boat or injury to a crewmember.)

Her sails furled and secured with sail ties, and her jib halyard connected but kept tight with another tie led to the pulpit, this cruiser-racer can be got under way in minutes. Some boats have roller-furling in the boom or mast or on the headstay.

HANDS ON:
Furling the Smart Way

1. Before furling a sail, first take the precaution of closing all the hatches on the cabin roof so you don't fall through. Serious injuries have resulted from such falls. The famous principle, "One hand for yourself and one for the ship," means that you should be careful as you do ship's work.

2. Flop the whole mainsail over to one side (preferably the leeward, or downwind, side). Working with another crew member, grab the leech in several places and pull it aft as far as possible.

3. Pull the sail away from the boom and shake it so the cloth falls loosely on itself in natural folds. Finally, roll these folds into a sausage and heave it onto the boom, leaning on it to keep it from unrolling.

4. Take several sail ties or stops (lengths of webbing) and loop them tightly around the sail and boom, securing them with bow knots, like the ones tied in shoelaces, so they can be quickly untied.

5. If you're alone you can do the forward part of the sail first, then move aft and go through the procedure again with the after part. When furling, be sure that the battens lie parallel to the boom and not at an angle, for otherwise they'll break and tear the sail.

How Boats Work

Now your boat's rigged and you're ready to cast off and go sailing. Or are you?

It's a seafaring mistake to head out before you know anything about how or why a sailboat works the way she does. Generations of new sailors have figured that since they're perfectly sound, safe drivers despite their ignorance of automotive engineering, there's no reason to understand how a sail works or a boat is steered. The difference is that out at sea there's no state police or AAA to tow

neophytes in when they get into trouble. They also are prisoners of the misguided belief that anybody can tame nature with a few modern gadgets.

The fact is that if you want to enjoy sailing and survive any rough weather you stumble into, you must grasp some important, relatively simple principles. We're covering theory this early because it's important. If you'd prefer to start with some hands-on practicalities, skip to chapter 2 and then come back, but you'll need this information about how boats

work. Some of our discussion will, of necessity, be cut to the bare bones. At times we will use some extreme examples and hands-on teaching aids that might help you visualize the forces at play when a boat sails.

Four Factors and Four Principles. "Every boat is a compromise of four basic factors: seaworthiness, comfort, performance, and cost," writes the designer Ted Brewer in his fine introduction to a book about small boat naval architecture, *Understanding Boat Design*. We will not go into cost, which usually is a function of the other factors (the most expensive boats for their size tend to be either especially heavy, comfortable, seaworthy cruisers or unusually light, intricately built racers). Seaworthiness, comfort, and speed involve several trade-offs in a boat's size and shape in four areas, each involving a technical principle. They are floatation, stability, propulsion, and balance. We have looked generally at the dinghy, keel daysailer, and cruiser-racer. Now let's be more analytical, starting with two very different boats, the lightweight sailboard and the bulky medieval curragh.

The Curragh and the Sailboard. By far the older of these two types of boat is the bulky and surprisingly seaworthy

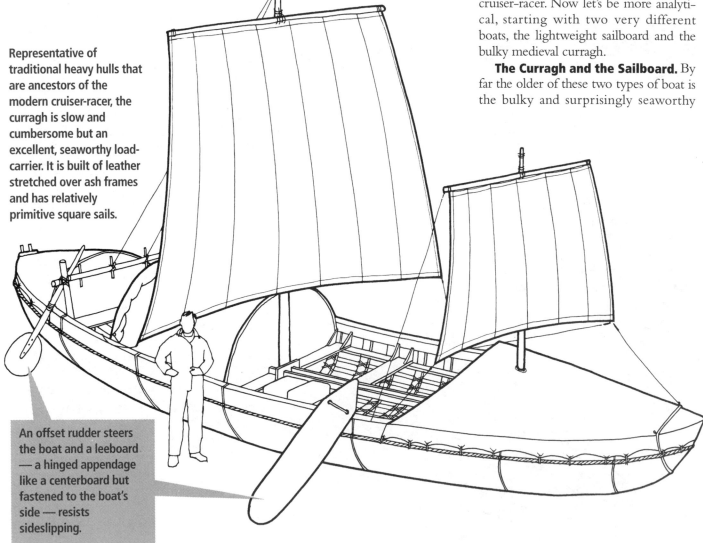

Representative of traditional heavy hulls that are ancestors of the modern cruiser-racer, the curragh is slow and cumbersome but an excellent, seaworthy load-carrier. It is built of leather stretched over ash frames and has relatively primitive square sails.

An offset rudder steers the boat and a leeboard — a hinged appendage like a centerboard but fastened to the boat's side — resists sideslipping.

sailing basket known in Ireland as the curragh (or currach), descended from the ancient coracle. An early form of this sailing vessel appeared in ancient Mesopotamia some 5,000 years ago, making the curragh one of the oldest types of small seafaring vessels known. Because it is fairly easy to build, similar vessels have been used in many cultures. The type is most famous for its appearance in medieval Ireland. According to legend, the Irish monk St. Brendan sailed to America in a curragh in the seventh century AD. The possibility of such a

voyage was proven in 1977 when a crew of five, headed by the explorer Tim Severin, sailed a curragh from Ireland to Newfoundland. The trip was agonizingly slow. *Brendan*, their curragh, rarely sailed faster than about 4 knots, or about 5 MPH. But the tubby boat kept her crew and their gear and food secure and reasonably dry through many icy storms.

Brendan was 36 feet in length overall, from bow to stern. She displaced, or weighed, 4 tons, and she was propelled by oars and about 400 square feet of sail. Cumbersome as she was, she was a superb load-carrier and seaworthy hull.

Where the curragh is ancient, bulky, and slow, the sailboard is modern, slim, and fast. Windsurfing, as this sport is called, was invented in the late 1960s in California by surfers. In fact, a sailboard is a surfboard with a sail and a daggerboard. Ten to 16 feet long, with hulls and rigs weighing well under 100 pounds

soaking wet (which they usually are), sailboards are built of plastic and foam and are sailed singlehanded (with a one-person crew). Sailboards can make over 30 knots (33 MPH) and can sail rings around a curragh.

Despite their dissimilarities, the two boats have much in common. They both are buoyant, resist capsize, move forward under sail, and are steered. But they also have great differences. The older boat's sails are hung from horizontal spars, called yards, secured to two vertical masts. The sailboard's sail is pulled over the mast like a sock and then held out by a split boom called a wishbone. Both boats have appendages that stick down from the hull into the water. On the curragh these are a steering oar in the stern and a hinged leeboard on the side, which creates some side resistance. The sailboard has a daggerboard and another appendage, a small fin called a skeg, that helps keep her on course. Her single crew steers her not with a rudder but by tilting the 70 square-foot sail fore and aft (toward the bow and the stern).

Compared with the boats we looked at earlier, the curragh is a tubbier version of the cruiser-racer and the sailboard is a tippier version of the Laser.

Where the curragh provided relative comfort on long voyages, the sailboard supplies thrills on short outings. The quick, light sailboard was built to carry a single athletic crew at high speeds. The sail is a version of the fore-and-aft rig.

A daggerboard (like a Laser's) and a skeg provide lateral resistance. But there's no rudder because the boat is steered by tilting the sail fore and aft on a universal joint.

Universal Joint

How Boats Work

Flotation: Buoyancy and Displacement. Obviously, an important characteristic that these boats share is that they float. The most basic principle of boat and design is that of flotation: a boat isn't a boat unless she floats. If an object is less dense than the fluid it sits in, it will float. In water, any object will float so long as its total volume (including hull, rig, equipment, crew, and the air between them all) weighs, on average, less than 64 pounds per cubic foot if the water is saline, and 62.2 pounds per cubic foot if it's fresh. If an object with a density of 32 pounds per cubic foot is put in salt water, it will float half in, half out of the water. If its density is 65 pounds per cubic foot, it will be suspended entirely below the water surface.

The weight of a boat is called displacement because when she floats she displaces (pushes aside) a volume of water equal in weight to her own weight. As Archimedes discovered more than 2,200 years ago, an object is buoyed up by a force equal to the weight of the water it displaces. The curragh *Brendan* displaces 4 tons, which means both that the boat weighs 4 tons and that when she is slid into the water she displaces 4 tons of water. Because long tons of 2,240 pounds are used when calculating displacement, *Brendan* displaces (or weighs) 8,960 pounds. She is quite heavy for her size and length, floating about half in and half out of the water. The sailboard, on the other hand, has an extremely light displacement for her length and sits on the water like a leaf. When her sailor comes aboard, she sinks down a few inches. But add the same weight to *Brendan* and she seems not to notice it. The heavy, round curragh, therefore, is a terrific boat for carrying loads.

The curragh is built of materials less

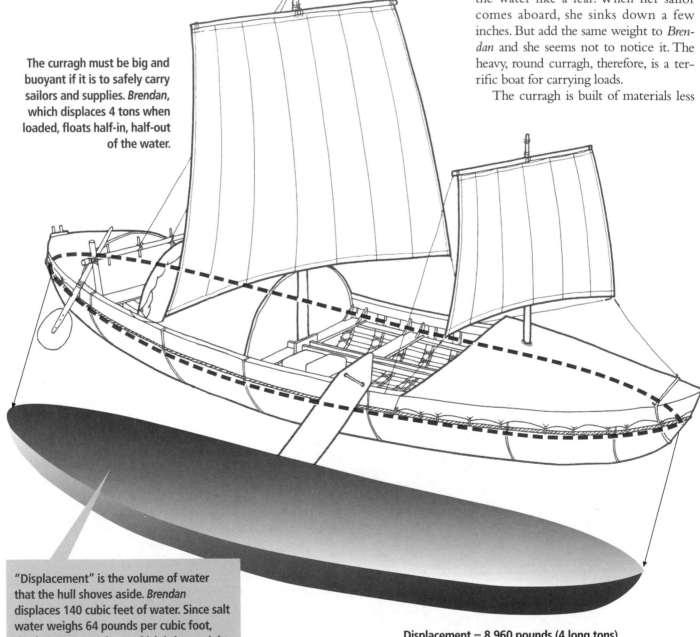

The curragh must be big and buoyant if it is to safely carry sailors and supplies. *Brendan*, which displaces 4 tons when loaded, floats half-in, half-out of the water.

"Displacement" is the volume of water that the hull shoves aside. *Brendan* displaces 140 cubic feet of water. Since salt water weighs 64 pounds per cubic foot, that's 8,960 pounds — which is her weight.

Displacement = 8,960 pounds (4 long tons)
Volume of water displaced = 140 cubic feet

dense than water. Wood is the classic material for boatbuilding because it's strong, easy to work, found everywhere — and because wood floats. (To be exact, almost all woods float. For example, lignum vitae will sink because its density is 78 pounds per cubic foot. It's hard enough to be used in propeller shaft bearings.) *Brendan* was built with frames of ash weighing 41 pounds per cubic foot and sides of leather whose density was 59 pounds per cubic foot. So unless she is overloaded with gear or crew, *Brendan* should float even when swamped (full of water). Other materials also float. The foam in a sailboard weighs less than 2 pounds per cubic foot, but it is quite weak unless it is encapsulated in a plastic shell. A key to a material's usefulness in boat building is its strength per pound. Wood is strong for its weight, and the big load-carrier *Brendan* needs to be strong. Foam usually is much less strong.

Complete with rig and crew, a sailboard displaces about 200 pounds as she skims across the water like a leaf. That's only 3 cubic feet of water spread out along a long, thin underbody.

The vast majority of boats today are constructed of nonbuoyant materials like fiberglass and aluminum. The reason why a boat constructed of these heavier-than-water materials does not sink is that they make up only a small portion of her volume. Because all boats (except sailboards) are vessels that contain the people or objects they carry, they have quantities of empty space, or air, between the sides, deck, and bottom. What counts for buoyancy is the boat's total density, or the average weight per cubic foot of her total volume. Keep it less than 64 pounds per cubic foot, and the boat floats.

Aluminum sheets weigh 165 pounds per cubic foot, so are 2.5 times denser than salt water. Steel, weighing about 490 pounds per cubic foot, is even denser. Both are used to create strong, expensive, custom-built yachts for individual customers. But the best material for building many versions of the same design (stock, or production, boats) is fiberglass, a tough substance composed of glass fibers laid in hardened plastic. The chemical industry calls fiberglass "glass reinforced plastic" or "fiber reinforced plastic," both of which neatly summarize what the material is.

Like most plastics, fiberglass can be easily shaped around molds and therefore is an excellent material for mass production. In some boats, fiberglass is combined with light, exceptionally strong materials such as Kevlar and carbon fiber. Like metal, fiberglass is nonbuoyant, at about 96 pounds per cubic foot weighing half again more than water. Therefore the Laser and other capsizeable fiberglass boats must have watertight buoyancy compartments and built-in foam to keep them from sinking.

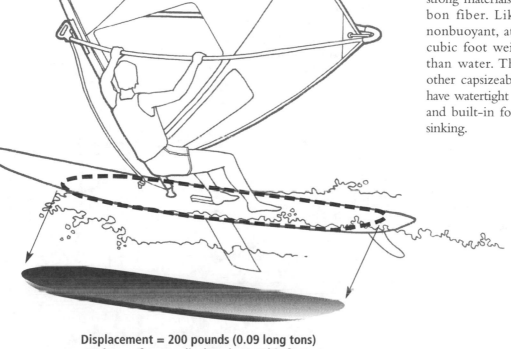

Displacement = 200 pounds (0.09 long tons)
Volume of water displaced = 3 cubic feet

How Boats Work

Buoyancy, Shape, and Purpose. "The design in its entirety should be a frank, vigorous declaration of the use to which the boat is to be put." Those words, written by Norman L. Skene in his classic manual *Elements of Yacht Design*, summarize boat architecture in a nutshell. Just looking at our examples, we can quickly determine what their use is. The tubby, sturdy curragh *Brendan* says "seaworthy." She was built to carry sailors and their equipment long distances, not so much rapidly as safely. St. Brendan was not racing other monks to the new world. He simply wanted to stay dry while he explored the great ocean to the west. The light, flat sail-board and Laser, on the other hand, offer

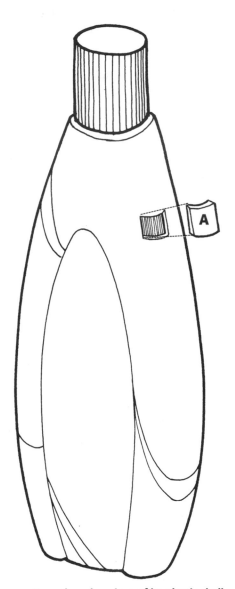

Even though a piece of its plastic shell (A) is more dense than water and will sink, a bottle, like a hull, floats as long as its total density, including the air in it, is less than that of water.

HANDS ON: Bathtub Naval Architecture

The following crude experiment illustrates types of hull shape. In a full bathtub or sink, float two empty bottles, one oblong and the other round. Leave their caps on. First compare the buoyancy of the two bottles. Press down in the middle until you find the spot that, when depressed, pulls the ends down equally. This is the bottle's center of buoyancy. Push down on the ends. The fine-ended oblong bottle, which has less volume at its end than in its middle, will pitch (bob) more readily than the full-ended round bottle. Notice how much more resistant and buoyant the center of the oblong bottle is than its ends. The oblong bottle behaves like a sailboard or Laser hull. It has little buoyancy in its end (or bow) because the sailor rarely goes that far forward. The designer makes the bow just buoyant enough so it doesn't dive under in waves. The middle is much more

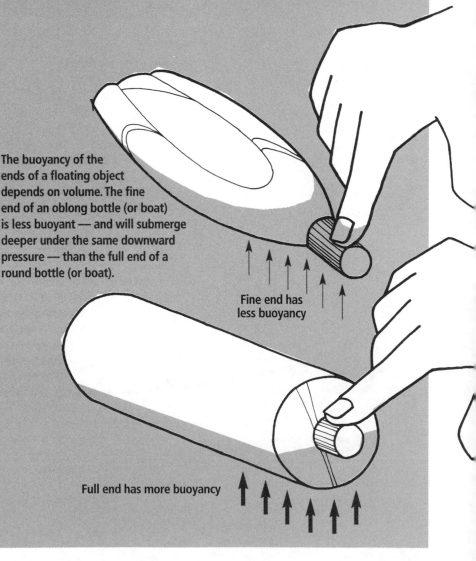

The buoyancy of the ends of a floating object depends on volume. The fine end of an oblong bottle (or boat) is less buoyant — and will submerge deeper under the same downward pressure — than the full end of a round bottle (or boat).

Fine end has less buoyancy

Full end has more buoyancy

no protection at all for their one-person crew — but they do offer thrilling, fast sailing. While *Brendan* could possibly be taken out in the harbor for an afternoon spin or the sailboard might be sailed out into the ocean, most smart people would not buy either boat with those uses in mind.

Many hulls are derived from one of the three shapes we have been looking at. One is very light and flat-bottomed (like the dinghy and sailboard) for fast, short sails in protected waters. Another is moderate in displacement and wedge-bottomed (like the keel daysailer and the cruiser-racer) for somewhat more seaworthiness. And the third is heavy and round-bottomed (like *Brendan*) for long expeditions. A visit to a boatyard when boats are hauled out will give you an idea of these different shapes.

buoyant because that's where the sailor stands or sits. The round bottle is like the curragh *Brendan* and to some extent the cruiser-racer, which require considerable buoyancy in their bows to support the crew, anchors, and other equipment located forward.

Next try to spin the bottles. The flat bottle is more stable and rolls less readily than the round one. Fill the bottles halfway and try to spin them again. The round one should be harder to spin, indicating that heavy boats tip less easily than light ones. The wide, flat-bottomed hull is stable in its way; it resists heeling at an early stage better than the round-bottomed one, but when you push hard on the flat bottle's edge, its initial stability disappears and it will flip over very quickly. While it may have good initial stability (at low angles of heel), it has poor latent stability (at large angles of heel). Once capsized, it will stay that way, while the round boat comes back upright with little effort. The flat-bottomed boat's tendency is to remain upside down — not a good thing when lives are at stake.

With moderate downward pressure, slide the empty oblong bottle sideways across the water surface on its flat side. Then fill it half-way, turn it on its edge, and slide it sideways again. On its side it provides very little grip on the water, behaving just like a sailboard or Laser with the centerboard retracted. But on its edge the flat bottle is like a deep keel boat, with a large lateral surface that resists sideslipping. The lateral plane below the waterline resists the wind's side forces in the sails. The larger the lateral plane and the more efficiently it is shaped, the greater the

resistance will be. As we'll see later on, resistance to side forces is greatest when the boat is moving fast so that the appendage's airfoil shape is best exploited.

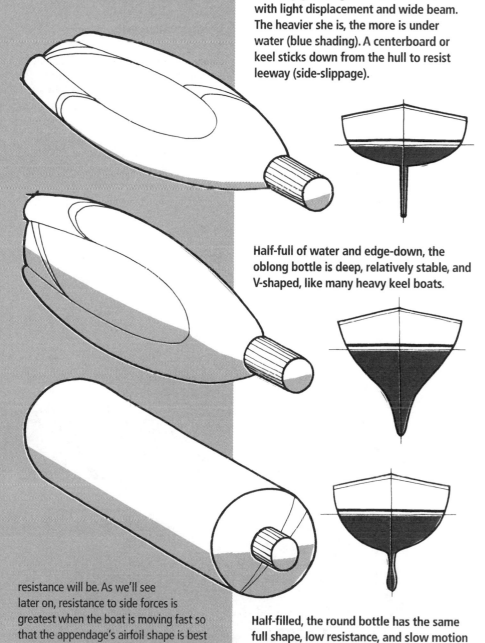

The empty oblong bottle is like a boat with light displacement and wide beam. The heavier she is, the more is under water (blue shading). A centerboard or keel sticks down from the hull to resist leeway (side-slippage).

Half-full of water and edge-down, the oblong bottle is deep, relatively stable, and V-shaped, like many heavy keel boats.

Half-filled, the round bottle has the same full shape, low resistance, and slow motion of a traditional heavy-displacement cruising boat.

How Boats Work

Stability: Pitching, Heeling, and Yawing. Stability is a boat's resistance to forces that threaten to throw her into motion, whether it's up and down (pitching), or side to side (rolling), or tipping her on her side (heeling), or forcing her off course (yawing). Some boats, heavy and designed for going offshore, are stable in all ways. They have full, bulbous bows that don't pitch and long, heavy keels that lever them upright and work like railroad tracks to prevent yawing and keep them on course. While good features to have in a boat in some

situations, such as sailing very long distances with a small crew who care little about reaching a destination quickly, such extreme stability may be counterproductive. Fast boats that are fun to sail are usually unstable in all ways — sometimes violently. The challenge is to match these instabilities to the boat's and the crew's purpose.

As we saw in our improvised bathtub experiments, the round-bottomed shape is more stable than the flat-bottomed one in this way: it is more buoyant in the ends and hence pitches less (although it may roll more). Modern wedge-shaped cruiser-racers generally lie somewhere between the extremes of the dinghy and the curragh. Some relatively heavy-displacement boats may be full-ended in order to accommodate a large forward cabin. Light-displacement boats may be so fine-ended that their bows dig deep into waves. Very heavy boats with bluff bows, on the other hand, may be stopped

by waves that a finer bow slices through.

Heeling. Stability against heeling is the sum of two features, hull form and ballast. The hull form produces form stability. By hull form we mean the cross-sectional (across the hull) shape. As we've seen, a dinghy's or sailboard's wide, flat hull should resist initial heeling better than a round hull. In general, given the same amount of wind and flying the same sails, a wide hull tips less than a narrow one — at first. This is because the center of buoyancy (a locus through which all the buoyancy forces are summarized) has a larger area to travel with a beamy (wide) hull.

When the boat is upright, the center of buoyancy is in the middle of the hull, but as she heels her windward side lifts and her leeward side submerges, the underbody (hull below the water) changes shape, and there is a new center of buoyancy to leeward of the original one. If the center of gravity pulling the

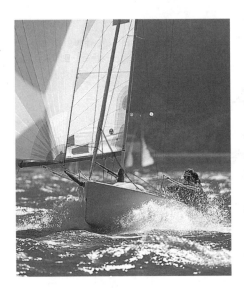

"Different boats for different folks." The heavy long-keeled cruising boat (above) may not be fast, but she has plenty of volume for long-distance cruising. The racing dinghy (upper left) is physically challenging and fast. The cruiser-racer (left) is a compromise between the two extremes — roomy and liveable but, with her fin keel and light displacement, an excellent performer. Each type is excellent for its own purposes.

boat down is to windward of the center of buoyancy, and the center of buoyancy doesn't run out of traveling room as it nears the leeward rail, the boat won't capsize. So a beamy boat provides a larger platform for the center of buoyancy than a narrow boat. This does not mean that beamy boats don't capsize. As we saw in our bathtub experiment, latent

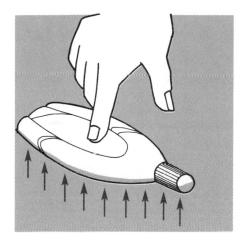

stability — their resistance to tipping over — is less than that of a narrow, deep, heavy hull.

Two kinds of beam are important. One is the extreme beam, or the boat's beam on deck at the widest point. The wider the boat, the greater the initial stability (the most extreme and best example is the multihull, which we will discuss in a few pages). But latent stability, or resistance to capsize at large heel angles, depends far less on wide beam than on deep ballast in a keel. In fact, very wide beam detracts from latent stability. The other kind of beam is waterline beam, or the boat's width at the water level. If the waterline beam is narrow, even a boat with wide extreme beam and tons of ballast will heel quickly in light winds. A home-grown example of the difference between the two beams is the relative ease of tipping a wide-brimmed, small-based salad bowl. A cooking pot whose brim has the

same diameter but whose sides are straight will be much less wobbly.

A wide hull provides stability in part because wide beam allows moveable ballast to be shifted to the windward side, pushing the center of gravity far out from the center of buoyancy. There are two types of moveable ballast. One is the crew hiked out to windward or suspended on trapezes. The heavier the crew and the farther out they hang, the greater is their leverage. The other kind is water ballast. This is water that is pumped into storage tanks on the windward side of beamy offshore racing boats. Many of the large singlehanded (one crew) boats that race around the world and in the ocean today have huge capacity for moveable water ballast.

Form stability is one way to resist heeling, at least at low angles of heel. Then there is the fixed ballast in keel boats that provides latent stability. The lead or iron mass low in the boat starts

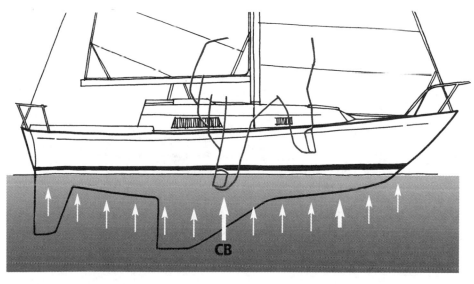

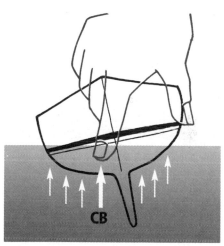

The center of buoyancy (CB) is a locus for all forces keeping the boat afloat. In the bottle, it's where pressing with a finger will push the ends down equally. As the boat heels and the underbody shape changes, the CB shifts. As long as the boat's center of gravity (CG) stays off to the side, the boat will not capsize. Ballast in a keel keeps the CG lower than the CB and provides stability even at large heel angles.

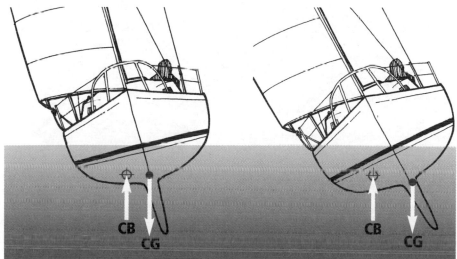

How Boats Work

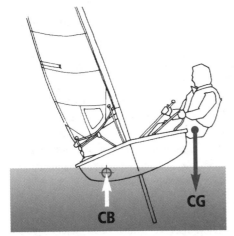

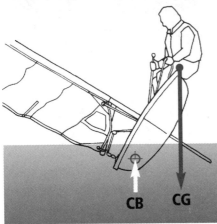

When the center of gravity (CG) gets close to the center of buoyancy (CB), as in the heeled dinghy above, there is little leverage against capsize. This is an example of poor latent stability.

to work once the boat has heeled several degrees, working like a lever against the high side force in the sails. The heavier it is and the lower the ballast lies, the greater is the keel's effect at leveraging the boat back upright. When the ballast is very heavy and deep, the boat does not require much form stability, or wide beam, to keep from heeling.

A ballasted keel's chief contribution is providing latent stability, or resistance to capsize. On one hand, wide, flat boats like the Laser have relatively good initial stability, or resistance at low angles of heel. But when heeled far enough they are like the flat bottle: they will quickly flip right over. On the other hand, a good ballasted keel on a deep boat with

The Westsail 32 cruiser *Sadalsuud* and the outrigger *Slingshot* show two extremes of boat design. The heavy keel boat is relatively stable and roomy but quite slow, while the outrigger (kept on her lines by five men in the pod) has no reason for existence other than to sail fast in smooth water. *Slingshot* was timed at speeds of more than 35 knots, while *Sadalsuud* will do well to make 7 knots.

A bulb or wing keel (above) not only puts ballast lower, but is also formed in a shape that improves water flow over the end of the keel.

a fairly narrow hull may not resist heeling at low angles in light and moderate winds, but it will provide latent stability to prevent capsize. Latent stability is indicated by the range of positive stability, or angle of vanishing stability.

Stability and the Rig. If one way to increase stability is to increase the ballast deep in the keel, another—very different but having the same effect—is to decrease the weight up high, in the rigging. If the rigging is lightened (while not weakening it), stability will increase. For this reason, many boats have very lightweight masts manufactured of carbon fiber, which is stronger for its weight than aluminum. The high cost of carbon fiber keeps this from becoming a broad trend until mass production techniques are developed.

Yawing. When a boat is unstable directionally, she yaws, or wanders off course. Flat-bottomed, light boats like the sailboard are most prone to yawing

Multihulls, like this trimaran, are the fastest sailboats. Their narrow hulls make little resistance and their exceptionally wide beam provides a stable platform for a large sailplan. But because they do not have deep ballasted keels, their center of gravity is high and they have poor latent stability at extreme angles of heel.

and have poor directional stability. They constantly change course in response to the slap of waves or puffs of wind, and the skipper must pay careful attention to the course. The skeg and centerboard provide some directional stability, but the other forces are greater. A deep, heavy hull like the curragh's may cut through the water more steadily. A considerable side force is needed to push her off course. The larger the lateral plane exposed by the underbody, the better the directional stability. (It helps if the keel and rudder are designed and built to good airfoil shapes.) Boats with good directional stability track well and require less attention from the steerer. The trade-off is that when you want to alter course, the tiller or wheel must be turned forcefully and the course alteration may be slow. Turning a boat that yaws slightly is like steering a truck, while turning a boat with poor directional stability is like driving a sports car.

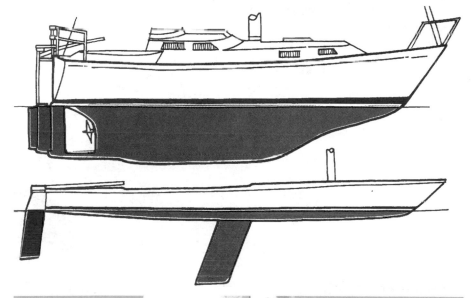

Directional stability depends mainly on the size of the lateral area exposed to the water. A long-keel cruiser will stay on course better than a dinghy.

Like the Laser, there isn't much of a multihull in the water. However, a multihull's extremely narrow hulls help it track straight.

How Boats Work

Propulsion from Sails. When the wind is from behind on a run or broad reach, it works on the sails simply by pushing them. The hull follows along. This is how the old-fashioned square rig on the curragh *Brendan* works. But when the wind is from ahead, square sails work very poorly compared with the fore-and-aft sails like the one on the sailboard and other modern boats. While *Brendan* could sail no closer to the wind than about 70° (and very slowly at that), a modern boat can sail fast at an angle of attack to the wind of less than 40°.

As the wind approaches the boat, it is redirected by the sail and then passes over it, being converted into aerodynamic force forward and to the side (some wind is lost to friction on the sail). One force is a forward driving force parallel to the course sailed. The other is a larger perpendicular force that attempts to push the rig and the boat to the side in both heeling and leeway (side-slippage). Much of this combination of aerodynamic forces is created by suction near the sail's leading edge (luff).

The forward driving force is further developed by two features. One is a well-shaped jib forward of the mast. It and the mainsail function as a single foil, with each enhancing the other, though the jib exerts much more force for its size than the mainsail. The other feature is even air flow across the mainsail from luff to leech, which also requires that the sail be trimmed well. This is why two important indicators when trimming sails are tell-tales on the jib's luff and the mainsail's leech. These telltales should stream aft most of the time, which means there is even air flow over both sides of the sail.

The heeling and leeway side forces are addressed and largely handled by the hull and its appendages. "The sailing craft must be considered as a complex system consisting of two interdependent parts — aerodynamic and hydrodynamic," writes C. A. Marchaj in *Sail Performance*,

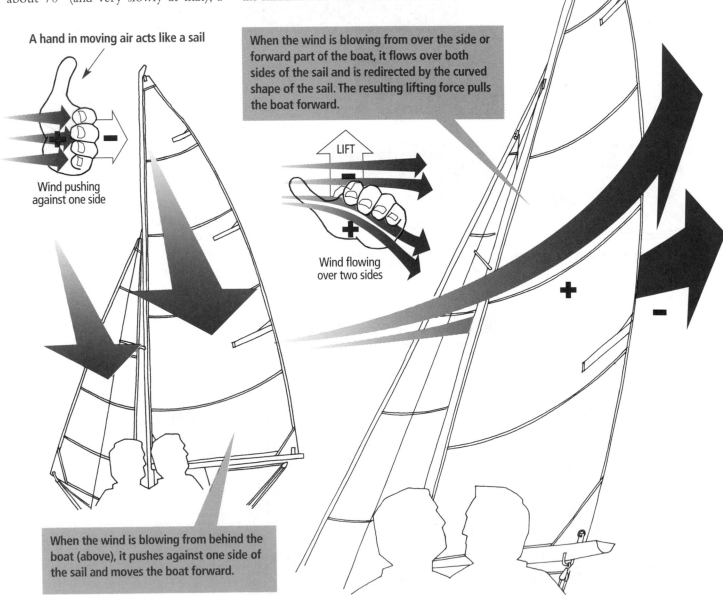

A hand in moving air acts like a sail

Wind pushing against one side

When the wind is blowing from over the side or forward part of the boat, it flows over both sides of the sail and is redirected by the curved shape of the sail. The resulting lifting force pulls the boat forward.

LIFT

Wind flowing over two sides

When the wind is blowing from behind the boat (above), it pushes against one side of the sail and moves the boat forward.

the standard manual of sailing theory. In other words, the sails and hull work together to convert the wind into forward force. The boat's stability (in hull shape and ballast) resists heeling forces, while the shape of her appendages resists leeway. A boat sailing without an appendage will slide mainly to leeward, but if equipped with a well-shaped appendage, she will sail mainly forward while sliding slightly to leeward. As Tom Whidden neatly summarizes the problem in his book *The Art and Science of Sails*, "Without a keel or centerboard, sailboats would be unable to sail above a broad reach."

Think of the sail's side force acting on a well-shaped centerboard, keel, or rudder as like a thumb pushing down on an orange seed: when pressure is applied to the side, the seed squirts forward. A well-shaped appendage has a fairly round leading (forward) edge and its widest point is about one-third of the way back before the appendage tapers to a sharp trailing (back) edge.

This shape is something like the seed's, but what it is most like is that of an airfoil, like a sail or wing. Like a sail, the appendage develops forward push best when the fluid that surrounds it is moving over its surface rapidly and smoothly. This is why it takes so long to get most boats moving fast after they have tacked or made another sharp course alteration. Not until clean, smooth water flow builds along the side of the centerboard or keel does an appendage work efficiently to resist leeway (side-slippage).

The appendages, therefore, transform the side force created by the wind in the sails into a force that both resists side-slippage and makes the boat go forward. This transformation is not perfect. Even at high speed a boat with the wind on her side makes leeway of about 4°. So a beat to windward is a sailing version of a crab's progress across the sand: aim one way, move the other.

The crew's job is to trim the sails so the forward force is maximized and the side force is minimized (so the keel or centerboard doesn't have to do all the work). If they trim (pull in) the sheets too far, the boat will heel and make little or no forward progress. If they ease (let out) the sheets too far, the sails won't

catch enough wind to create any force. As the wind increases, the shape of the sail itself may have to be changed, because a baggy, full sail, while creating more forward force than a flat sail, also creates considerable heeling force that cannot be counterbalanced by the keel or by the hiking crew. (We'll look more closely at sail trim in chapter 3.)

HANDS ON:
Getting a Hand on Wind and Flow

You can get a rough feel for how the wind and water affect foils (sails and appendages) by extending a hand outside the window of a moving car. When the hand is held palm open and flat to the wind, it will be forced back. This is what happens when a boat is running directly before the wind with her sails let all the way out: the wind pushes the sails along and the sails pull the boat with it. Turn the side of your hand toward the front of the car and cup it, making it fuller. As you try different arcs of fullness (on a sail this would be called draft) and different angles of attack to the wind, be sensitive to how the strain on your arm changes. You'll probably feel more force on your palm than on the back of your hand until the hand has an angle of attack of about 45°. At that angle the pressure will begin to be equalized on both sides and you will have to work less hard to keep your arm from flying back. As the angle of attack to the wind continues to sharpen, notice the gradual change in pressure on your hand and arm, until at one point your hand may actually lift up in the direction of the curve. Flatten the arc of your palm and feel the pressure decrease, then gradually make the hand/sail smaller by folding fingers into your palm, "reefing" your hand.

Rudder

Keel

Sail Force

Most of the force generated by a sail is just a bit forward of sideways. Well-shaped appendages — keel, centerboard, skeg, and rudder — convert that side force into forward thrust.

How Boats Work

Balance. After flotation, stability, and propulsion, balance is the fourth of the basic principles. The degree to which the boat is in tune with wind and water, balance is usually measured by how well she sails herself with only a modest helping hand from the person steering. A well-balanced boat steers more easily, sails faster and more comfortably, and is more seaworthy than a poorly balanced boat. Like driving a car with weak shock absorbers or a misaligned front end, sailing a poorly balanced boat is tiring and potentially dangerous.

Unfortunately for their owners, some boats are unbalanced from the moment their designers set pencil to paper. Only major reconstruction can balance their helms and make them competent, seaworthy vessels. But the vast majority of boats are unbalanced only because their crews don't know any better and sail them that way.

The Helm and Rudder. The helm is the tiller or steering wheel that turns the rudder and so changes the boat's course. The helm also corrects imbalances in the boat and her rig. As a rule, if a hull's or a rig's symmetry is destroyed, a boat in motion will tend to swerve from her straight-line course. Just as an automobile's driver first notices an under-inflated tire by feeling the tug of the steering wheel, a boat's steerer first senses that the sails are incorrectly trimmed through the hard pull of the tiller. Knowing how the car or boat should feel when everything is in balance, the driver or steerer can quickly sense when something's awry. He can temporarily correct the imbalance by over-steering against the pull, but soon he'll have to attack the cause of the problem.

As the designer drew and the builder constructed her, the boat should be symmetrical. The starboard side has the same shape as the port side, she sits level in the water without a permanent list, and the water moves around her hull and appendages the same way on both sides. If for some reason there is a built-in asymmetry, then the water will move around one side faster than it does around the other. Sometimes, for example, one side of a keel or centerboard may be flatter than the other side because the fiberglass shell was not carefully shaped. The side with the best airfoil shape will generate more forward thrust than the flat side, so the boat may make less leeway on one tack than on another. Another asymmetry results when the designer and builder miscalculate the weights of gear and fittings and the boat does not float on her lines evenly.

A list, or a heel, immerses one side and raises the other. (When a boat is sailing, the leeward side drops as the windward side lifts.) A level boat will steer straight with the rudder centered, but a heeled boat will tend to head in the direction of the windward, or raised, side. A boat heeled to port will head to starboard unless the helm is adjusted to compensate, and vice versa. Sailors often speak of "cranky" boats that "want" to head one way or the other. Like a wild horse with a bit in its mouth, a sailboat with powerful weather (windward) helm — the tendency to head toward the wind — can be a handful for a steerer. Adjusting the helm only compensates for the asymmetry. It doesn't fix it. Feeling the hard tug, the steerer pulls on the helm to compensate, as though making a turn.

The flaplike rudder impedes the flow of water going past, slowing the boat. If she is simply compensating for an imbalance, the steerer will pull the helm until the asymmetry of the swung rudder balances the asymmetry caused by the imbalance and the boat holds her course. If the steerer wants to alter course, she will hold the helm down or up until the bow has swung onto the new heading. As the stern swings one way, the bow swings the other. To stop the swing, the

Think of the centerboard or keel as a pivot under a balance beam where the mainsail and jib push in opposite directions. When the sails are trimmed right and the hull is heeled just enough, a well-balanced boat should almost sail herself, with about 3° of weather helm.

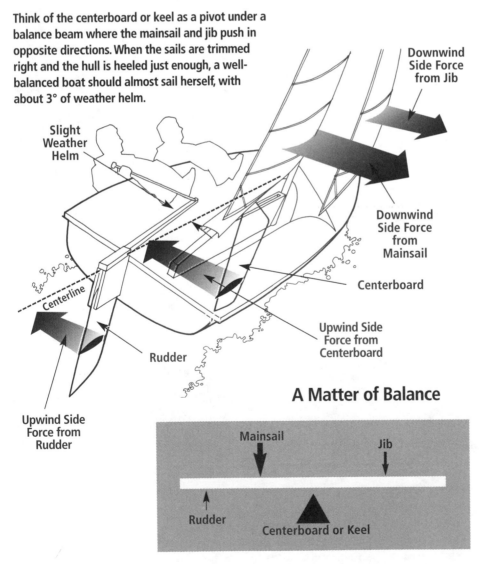

Slight Weather Helm

Downwind Side Force from Jib

Downwind Side Force from Mainsail

Centerboard

Centerline

Upwind Side Force from Centerboard

Rudder

Upwind Side Force from Rudder

A Matter of Balance

Mainsail

Jib

Rudder

Centerboard or Keel

steerer brings the helm back to center. Heavy boats and boats with long keels will have greater directional stability than light boats with short keels, meaning that turns will be slow to start and stop. A large rudder turns a boat more efficiently than a small rudder, but because it blocks more water, it can slow the boat, too, unless the boat is well balanced, with little or no weather helm.

Helm, Rake, and Heel. Weather helm is the boat's tendency to head up and point her bow into the wind or to windward (also called "to weather"). Lee helm is the tendency to bear off and point the bow away from the wind or to leeward. Lee helm usually makes a boat slow and unpredictable, but a slight amount of weather helm improves water flow over the rudder and encourages the steerer to keep sailing closer to the wind. As a rule of thumb, there should be a slight tug of weather helm on the tiller or steering wheel. The rudder should be cocked about 3°, an angle that helps the rudder work at peak efficiency. With the right amount of weather helm, when you let go of the tiller or wheel the boat will fairly quickly swing her bow toward the wind. With too much helm, she will swing up violently; with too little, hardly at all.

The 3° rule, like all general rules around boats, should be observed with discretion. Because heavy boats turn slower than light ones, the same amount of helm will evidence itself differently from boat to boat. And rudder size is important. Boats with relatively small rudders often efficiently carry slightly more weather helm because their rudders make little resistance. Boats with large rudders should carry a little less since it can serve as a brake. If you look over the stern and see a lot of turbulence or even waves behind the rudder, there's too much helm. But if you see no turbulence, there's probably too little.

Much more weather helm is a reliable indication that something is wrong. The sails may be trimmed in too far (especially the mainsail, which tends to twist the boat toward the wind). Or the boat may be heeling too far. Weather helm increases as the boat heels to leeward, partly because of the increased asymmetry of the hull in the water and partly because the sails tilted to leeward twist the rig and boat upwind. If the boat is/

allowed to heel too far, weather helm will exceed the optimum.

Those are temporary problems readily solved by letting the mainsail traveler down a few inches, by easing sheets, or by reefing. But there may be more serious imbalances that may be fixed by moving the mast. When the mast is raked (tilted) aft (toward the stern), weather helm is induced and the boat tends to head up. When it's raked forward, lee helm is induced. Weather helm usually can be decreased by letting off tension on the backstay and tightening the headstay's turnbuckle three or four turns. Do the opposite to increase weather helm. The helm may also be adjusted by moving the mast in its step (the fitting that secures the bottom of the mast). Move the mast aft to increase weather helm and forward to decrease weather helm. (See chapter 17 for a detailed guide to adjusting mast rake.)

Steerageway. A rudder is useless if there is no water flowing over it. Before trying to steer, build up a couple of knots of speed. Once you have steerageway (enough speed to steer with), you can alter course. While waiting for steerageway to build up, keep the helm and rudder centered. Otherwise the rudder will grab the water and act like a brake to slow the boat further and eventually pull her to a halt. Attempt to alter course only when the boat has built up sufficient speed for the rudder to work.

Self-Steering Devices. When the boat is reasonably well balanced so that she'll stay on a straight course with a tug of weather helm, you may rig a self-steering system. The simplest is made by connecting the jib sheet to the tiller or steering wheel through a series of blocks, sometimes using shock cord to hold the helm.

Another kind of self-steerer is the electric automatic pilot, which runs off the batteries and is connected to the steering wheel or tiller with a cable, belt, or rod. The desired heading is set on the instrument, which has an internal compass that keeps the boat on or near course. Because these self-steerers depend on the boat's electrical power, the battery must be charged periodically by running the engine or generator, or by using a trickle charger powered by solar panels, a windmill, or a propeller towed astern. Some automatic pilots may

Self-steering devices such as this wind-powered vane system (above) are often used by long-distance cruisers. Electronic autopilots (below) are extremely effective but require many batteries.

be connected to the GPS electronic navigation system.

A third kind of self-steerer, the wind vane, does not need electricity. It orients the boat to the wind, not the compass. A small sail-like vane on a post over the stern is adjusted to the desired wind angle. It's connected to a flap (called a trim tab) on the trailing edge of the rudder or a small separate rudder. When the boat swings off the desired wind angle, the vane turns the tab or rudder and brings the boat back on course.

Any crew using a self-steerer must still satisfy Rule 5 of the Navigation Rules (rules of the road): "Every vessel shall at all times maintain a proper lookout by sight and hearing."

How Boats Work

Hull Speed and Planing. A boat's speed potential is not unlimited. For one thing, because a strong wind provides as much heeling force as propelling power, a point is finally reached where no amount of lead in the keel or hiking by the crew will keep her sailing fast. Second, as the wind increases, it creates ever-larger waves whose resistance will slow any boat. While an owner can improve his boat's speed potential by giving her a smooth bottom and well-shaped appendages and sails, and by sailing her well, he will inevitably be restricted by those and other limitations.

Heavier boats have a built-in maximum speed called hull speed. These boats are called displacement boats because as they move they are perpetually displacing a new patch of water, which spills out in waves. The opposite to a displacement boat is a planing boat, which can sail on top of the water. A

Displacement keelboats like this classic sloop create waves which ultimately limit the top speed of the boat. Notice how the boat below is sailing in a wave trough of its own making that begins at the bow and ends at the stern. When this happens, a displacement sailboat has theoretically reached its maximum hull speed.

At about ⅓ hull speed, there will be three waves formed along the windward side of a displacement boat.

As the boat accelerates to ½ hull speed, the waves speed up and decrease in number to two.

At hull speed, the boat is creating a single wave the length of her waterline.

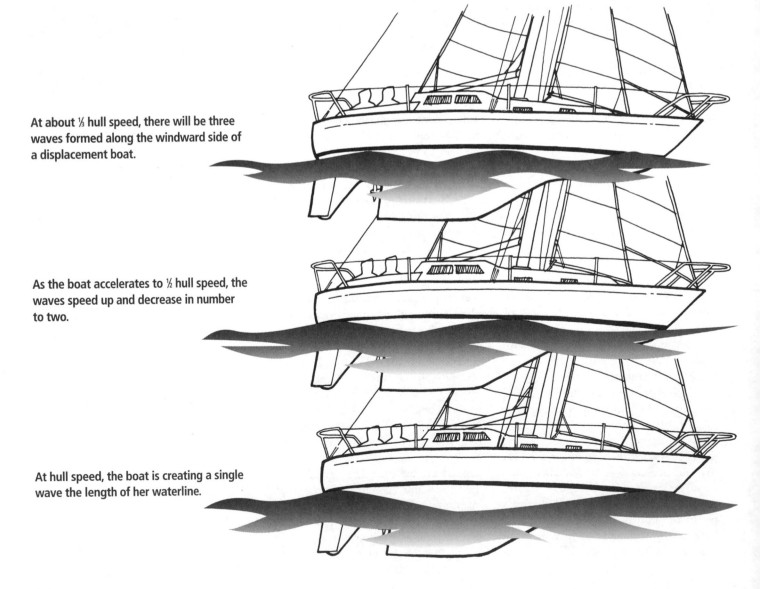

curragh is a displacement boat while a sailboard is a planing boat.

Displacement Boats. As a displacement boat pushes through the water, she makes waves until she reaches a point where she's sitting in the trough between two crests of a wave that she has made, with one crest at her bow and the other at her stern. She is a prisoner of this wave, unable because of her weight to climb on top of it. Her speed, then, is limited by the wave's speed, which is a function of the wave's length. This maximum speed, called hull speed, is the maximum theoretical speed of a displacement, heavy hull. Hull speed is computed by multiplying 1.34 times the square root of the boat's length on the waterline (which is the length of this wave). This rule applies to our model cruiser-racer, our keel daysailer, and the curragh *Brendan*. They

A lightweight dinghy like this Laser is able get up on top of the water and plane. Planing boats regularly exceed their theoretical hull speed.

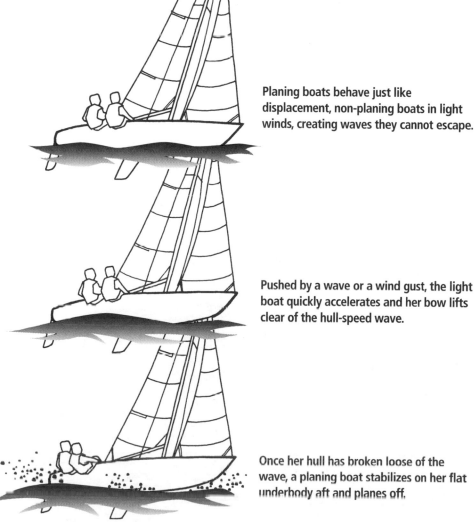

Planing boats behave just like displacement, non-planing boats in light winds, creating waves they cannot escape.

Pushed by a wave or a wind gust, the light boat quickly accelerates and her bow lifts clear of the hull-speed wave.

Once her hull has broken loose of the wave, a planing boat stabilizes on her flat underbody aft and planes off.

will rarely sail faster than hull speed.

Planing Boats. The hull speed restriction applies only to heavy keel boats. Lighter boats with powerful, large sails may be able to lift up and over the forward crest, escape the single-trough wave, and sail much faster than the hull speed. The sailboard can do this. So can the Laser, other dinghies, and the modern ultralight keel daysailers called sport boats. Many of these boats are so light that the total weight of their crews is greater than that of the hull and rig. When those sailors hike on the windward rail, their ballast exerts a large righting moment (leverage) that counters the heeling force on the sails.

In order to get planing, a boat must break out of her wave and skip over the crest at the bow. At low speeds, planing boats work like displacement boats, pushing though the water at low speeds. Given sufficient power by a gust of wind or a following wave, they snap over the bow wave and then, freed from its confinement, speed off on a plane.

We are speaking here of monohulled boats. Multihulls (catamarans and trimarans), which are displacement boats that have many of the characteristics of planing boats, will be discussed later in this chapter.

Why Speed Is Important. Our emphasis on speed may seem surprising. Going fast in a boat may be fun, but many people would not regard it as seamanlike. Yet experienced seamen know that a good turn of speed can be an important safety ingredient. As Colin Mudie, who designed many boats (including *Brendan*), once wrote: "Speed is not only a sensible part of seamanship, it is to a certain extent a satisfactory substitute for some of it." While hot-rodding speed will get you into trouble, quick acceleration and maneuverability can almost always be counted on to get you out of it. Many novice sailors mistakenly buy heavy, slow clunkers because they seem seaworthy. Not only are these boats dull to sail, but they cannot be relied on to make much progress against a strong current or a fresh wind. It's said that a Swedish sailor once spoke of a slow boat that would "go a loooooong vay an' take a looooong time a-gettin' dere, too!"

Boat Dimensions

Boats are described by length, construction material, rig, and type. The Sabre 30 cruiser-racer shown on this page is a class, or identical group, of fiberglass cruising sloops approximately 30 feet in length built by Sabre Yachts in South Casco, Maine. (Some people may refer to her as a "30-foot Sabre.") The plans show her to be modern in appearance, with a tall rig and relatively short fin keel rather than a traditional long keel extending almost from the bow to the rudder. You then would examine her dimensions: her waterline length (which indicates her theoretical hull speed), her beam (a measure of her roominess and stability), her displacement (which suggests her hull shape, light boats being flatter than heavy boats), her ballast (yet another indicator of stability, a high ratio between ballast and displacement indicating good stability), her draft (as a measure both of the amount of water she needs and her ultimate stability), her sail area (an indication of her relative speed and ease of handling), and her sail plan (which tells how the sail area is divided up). The Sabre 30 has these dimensions:

LOA (overall length), 30' 7"

LWL (load waterline length, or the hull's length where it comes out of the water at each end), 25' 6"

Bm. (extreme beam, where the boat is widest), 10' 6"

Disp. (displacement or weight in pounds), 9,400# (lb.)

Ballast (weight in the keel or bilge), 3,800#

The published plans of a cruiser-racer or cruising boat show profile, sail plan, overhead, and cutaway views. In the accommodations plans showing the Sabre 30's interior, you can see the cabins, berths (beds), toilet, lockers (closets), tables, engine, galley (kitchen), and other furnishings and equipment.

Dr. (deepest draft, to the bottom of the keel or centerboard), 5' 3"

SA (sail area in the mainsail and foretriangle, the area between the mast and headstay), 462 sq. ft.

Dimensions are a boat's vital statistics. They may be used with some simple formulas and a pocket calculator to compare boats of similar sizes. On these pages we will apply these formulas to three boats in each of two popular size ranges — around 30 feet and 36 feet LOA. Some of these boats are lightweight high performers looking like the dinghy, some are heavy cruisers in the curragh family, and others are moderate boats falling between those two extremes. Today, most boats are in the middle.

Theoretical hull speed, as we have just seen, is determined by multiplying the square root of the LWL by 1.34. The hull speed of the Sabre 30 here is 6.8 knots.

The ballast/displacement ratio (ballast/disp.), the proportion of displacement that is in ballast (weight in the keel and bilge that counters heeling), indicates the boat's purpose. A ratio lower than about 35 percent may be found in a pure cruising boat, where much of the weight is in living accommodations. One higher than about 45 percent is found in a boat aimed for racing; such boats usually are stripped-out, with few solid bunks and a skimpy galley. In between lie the cruiser-racers like the Sabre 30, whose ratio is 40 percent.

The displacement/length ratio (D/L) is a good indicator of a boat's weight for her size. If her displacement ("D") is light for her length, she's toward the dinghy end of the spectrum — light and flat — rather than the heavy, round curragh end. She's probably fast, bouncy, and tricky to sail, with limited directional stability. "L" in

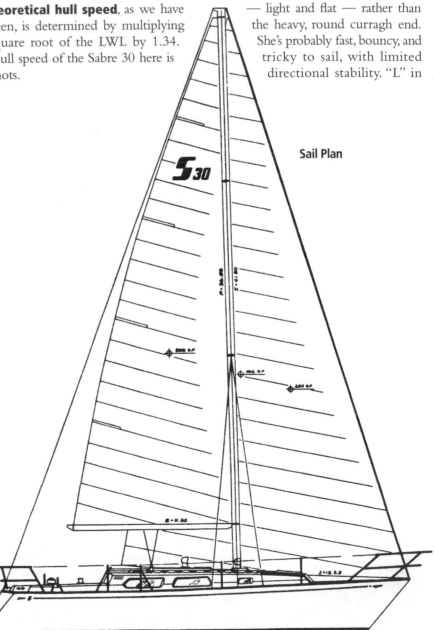

Sail Plan

this formula is length on the waterline, LWL. Here's the formula:

$$D/L = \frac{displacement\ in\ long\ tons}{(.01 \times LWL)^3}$$

The length is cubed to put it in the same dimensional context as displacement, which is a volume (a cubic dimension). Long tons (2,240 lb. per ton) and the constant of .01 make the final product manageable, somewhere between 30 and about 350. The higher the number, the more curragh-like the boat. Boats with a displacement/length ratio over 325 are heavy cruisers. A ratio of 200–325 indicates the boat is a light- to moderate-displacement cruiser or moderate-displacement racer. Anything less than 200 is either a very light-displacement cruiser or a racing boat. A ratio lower than 125 puts a boat in the ultra light-displacement boat (ULDB) category. The D/L for the Sabre 30 works out as follows:

$$D/L = \frac{displacement\ in\ long\ tons}{(.01 \times LWL)^3}$$

$$\frac{9,400/2,240}{(.01 \times 25.5)^3} = \frac{4.20}{.017} = 247$$

With a ratio of 247, the Sabre 30 is in the area of light to moderate displacement.

The sail area/displacement ratio (SA/D) indicates how much sail a boat has relative to her weight. This is the equivalent of a horsepower/weight ratio in an automobile. The higher the number, the more racy the boat or the faster she sails in light wind. Conservative cruising boats have ratios of 10–15, cruiser-racers 16–20, moderate racing boats run from about 21 to 23, and high-performance racers have SA/D ratios above about 24. Here's the formula:

$$SA/D = \frac{sail\ area}{(displ.\ in\ cubic\ feet)^{2/3}}$$

To find displacement in cubic feet,

divide it by 64. To find a number to the ⅔ function, square it and then find its cube root either by trial and error on a calculator or by consulting an engineering manual. For the Sabre 30:

$$SA/D = \frac{sail\ area}{(displ.\ in\ cubic\ feet)^{2/3}}$$

$$\frac{462}{(9,400/64)^{2/3}} = \frac{462}{27.9} = 17$$

An SA/D ratio of 17 puts the Sabre 30 in the cruiser-racer range.

The comparisons with two other boats about her length on the next page indicate that the Sabre 30 is a moderate model falling midway between an extreme cruiser (the Mariner 32) and an extreme racer of the sport boat type (the Melges 30). With her relatively large sail area she will sail well and fast in light to moderate winds (assuming that her bottom is smooth and her sails are shaped well). Yet with her moderate displacement she probably would be more comfortable, if slower, than a very lightweight racing boat. This does not say anything one way or the other about seaworthiness. Very light boats sailed by competent, athletic sailors have gone long distances, and have often participated in long offshore races.

What else do these dimensions tell us? With a deep draft of 5' 3", the Sabre 30 may be a bit long-legged for shallow areas like Chesapeake Bay and Tampa Bay, but she may also have plenty of stability.

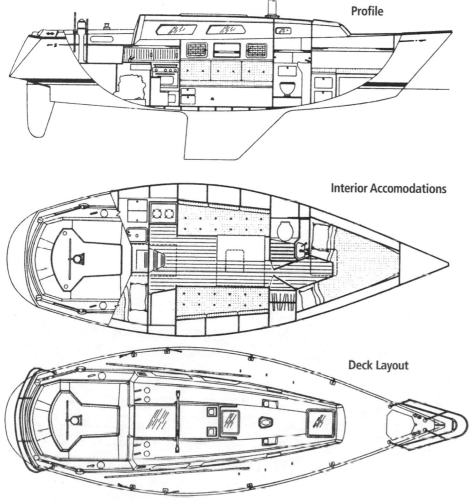

Profile

Interior Accomodations

Deck Layout

Boat Dimensions

Comparing Two 30-Footers. A comparison of two boats about the LOA of the Sabre 30 demonstrates the broad range of boats available, with the Sabre 30 in the middle. The extremely light and high-powered **Melges 30**, built in Wisconsin, is one of the breed of exciting sport boats developed for racing during the 1990s. With extremely high ratios — 75 D/L, 36 SA/D, and 50 percent ballast/disp. — she's a big dinghy with an extremely deep, heavy keel for leverage against her huge rig. She will regularly exceed her theoretical hull speed of 7.2 knots. This is a pure-bred racer. Her small cabin provides minimum accommodations for overnight cruising by a small crew.

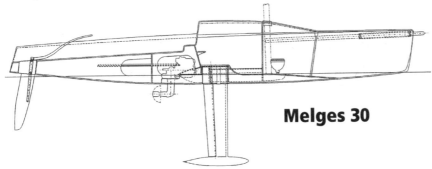

Melges 30

	LOA	LWL	Bm.	Dr.	Disp.	Ballast	SA	Displ./Length	Sail Area/Displ.	Bal./Displ.
Melges 30	31'10"	28'6"	9'10"	7'	3,850#	1,750#	643 sq. ft.	75	36	45%
Mariner 32	31'10"	25'8"	10'	3'8"	12,400#	4,000#	468 sq. ft.	315	14	33%

With a 315 D/L and 14 SA/D, the **Mariner 32** is as pure a traditional cruiser as the Melges 30 is an up-to-date racer. She has a low 33 percent ballast/displacement ratio and a long, shallow keel for cruising in shoal waters. She is not fast, but if properly handled and equipped she should be stable and comfortable in most conditions. Many similar cruisers have been built, like the one shown in the photograph here.

Mariner 32

Comparing Two 36-Footers. The J-105 (the number is her metric length) is built in Rhode Island and used mainly for racing and cruising in coastal waters. She is a light, fast boat. A cruiser-racer, she has berths for four or five people and a galley. Her spinnaker, like the Melges 30's, is set not on the traditional spinnaker pole on the mast but on a long retractable sprit projecting out from her bow.

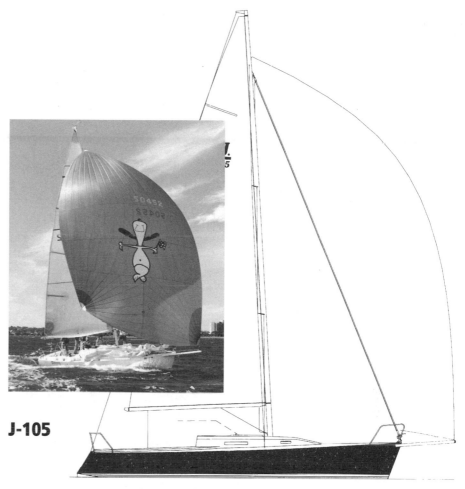

J-105

	LOA	LWL	Bm.	Dr.	Disp.	Ballast	SA	Displ./Length	Sail Area/Displ.	Bal./Displ.
J-105	35'6"	29'6"	11'	6'6"	7,750#	3,400#	577 sq. ft.	135	24	44%
Pacific Seacraft 37	37'11"	27'9"	10'10"	5'6"	16,000#	6,200#	619 sq. ft.	334	16	39%

With a displacement more than twice that of the J-105 on an LWL almost 2 feet shorter, the California-built **Pacific Seacraft 37** is a modern type of offshore cruiser. She is fairly heavy and with full accommodations for living aboard for months at a time, yet carries a large sailplan and considerable ballast in a keel that is a compromise between the cruiser-racer's fin keel and the traditional long keel. A double-ender (with a pointed canoe stern), she has a traditional shippy appearance.

Pacific Seacraft 37

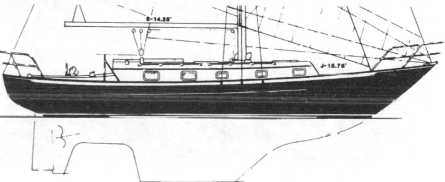

The Lines Plan

The sail plan shows the boat from the side with all the sails she might carry. The Morris 36, designed by Chuck Paine and built in Maine, is a fast cruising boat for coastal waters. While her shape below the water is modern, with a fin keel, her appearance is traditional, with a graceful stern and gradually curving sheer (deck edge). She has a masthead double-headsail cutter rig on which two jibs can be set, one on the headstay and the other on the forestay partway back.

The lines drawn by the naval architect, often with the assistance of a computer, show the boat's shape. In these detailed scale drawings, the boat is sliced into sections across the hull, from bow to stern at the profile (showing buttocks), and from bow to stern from overhead (showing waterlines). In addition, the sail plan shows the positions of the masts,

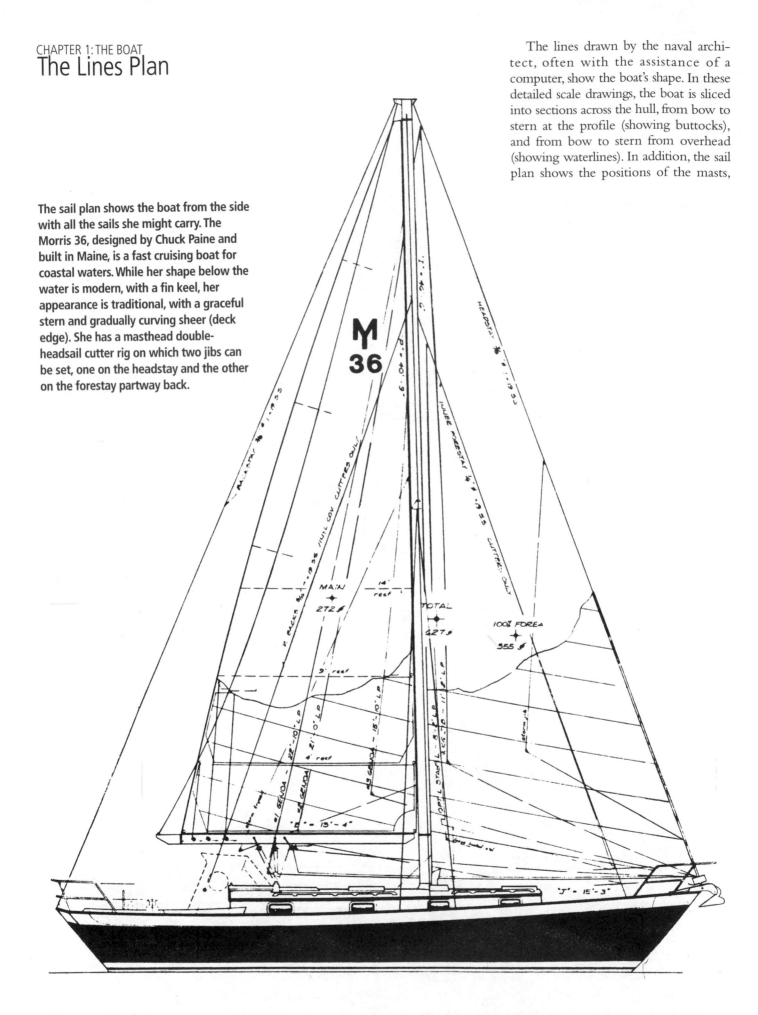

booms, and sails. The designer also draws plans showing deck and interior arrangements, rigging details, and construction. The builder proceeds with construction of either one boat or a plug that will be used to build a series of fiberglass boats.

The Morris 36 is a modern cruiser-racer with a traditional look. Her dimensions are LOA, 36' 3"; LWL, 29' 6"; Bm., 11' 7"; Disp., 16,602#; Ballast, 6,000#; Dr., 5' 6"; S.A., 627 sq. ft. Her ratios put her in the cruiser-racer range: the displacement/length is 288, the sail area/displacement is 16, and the ballast/displacement is 36 percent.

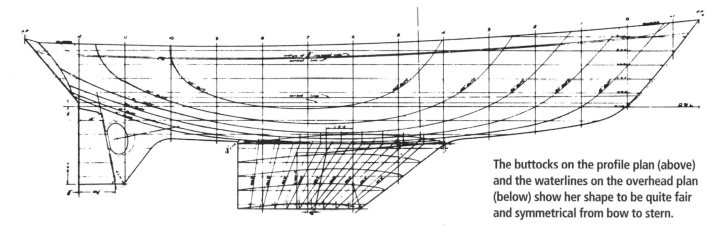

The buttocks on the profile plan (above) and the waterlines on the overhead plan (below) show her shape to be quite fair and symmetrical from bow to stern.

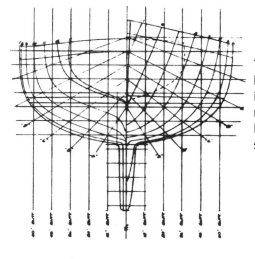

The section plan, which shows how the boat would look if sliced across at regular intervals, shows the Morris 36's deep round-bottomed hull form. The vertical lines are "stations," or places where sections are taken.

The Morris 36's traditional appearance above the water belies her modern lines, with a wide beam, a fin keel, a separate rudder, and a moderate displacement.

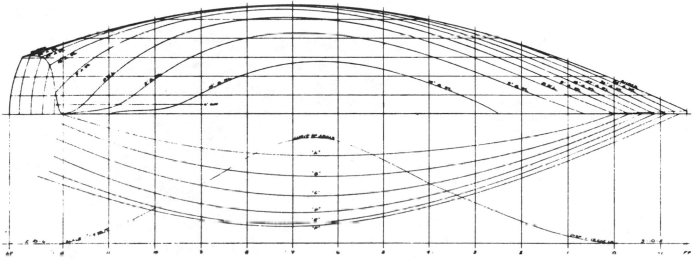

Boat Selection

Boats are successful or unsuccessful, loved or ignored, more for how well they meet the needs of their owners than for any other reason. The "different boats for different folks" rule of thumb reliably makes us tolerant of our own and others' prejudices and needs.

Small Boats. Boats smaller than about 25 feet are inexpensive, and their liveliness makes them enjoyable, excellent developers of sailing talent. A person who is happy sailing alone will like a sailboard, catamaran, or dinghy smaller than about 14 feet. If you like a little company and the water is shallow, two or three people will fit nicely into a center-

Popular types of smaller boats include daysailers with centerboards (above), singlehanded centerboarders (top), racing catamarans (middle), and trailerable cruisers (right). Keel boats can be easily set up for disabled sailors, like this one below with a seat for a paraplegic skipper.

board dinghy or daysailer between 14 and 20 feet. Daysailers (both monohulls and catamarans) and small cruisers for two to five people range from 17 to more than 25 feet. Many of these boats are available in versions that are easily trailerable, meaning that they are pulled in and out of the water on trailers and towed behind automobiles between harbors and home. Although keel boats are more difficult to haul out of the water, they have one big advantage over centerboarders and small catamarans: they are difficult to capsize.

Most of these boats provide little or no shelter for their crews and should always be sailed on protected waters near shore, where the waves are not large and hospitable ports are close at hand.

Cruising Boats. A cruising boat, which can range from about 20 to more than 120 feet, is a boat with sheltered living accommodations. Smaller, lighter boats may be quite suitable for protected waters, where some of them sail very fast, but their ability to sail comfortably and safely offshore in rough weather may be questionable. Larger, heavier boats may be slower but more seaworthy in rough weather out in deep water. This means that if you want to cruise in the ocean or a large lake with the confidence that your boat can handle the roughest weather, you will want to concentrate less on speed than on seaworthiness and seakindliness (the ability to go through big waves in relative comfort). This does not automatically mean that all fast boats are unseaworthy or all heavy boats are seaworthy.

Offshore Design Features. Size and displacement are factors in seaworthiness. A heavy 30-footer may be as seaworthy and stable as a 40-footer of moderate displacement or a light-displacement 50-footer. In addition, a relatively heavy boat will be able to carry more crew, food, fittings, and other weights with less effect on her sailing

The ultralight-displacement sport boat (above) is fast, challenging, and suited for racing in bays and other protected waters. The moderate-displacement cruiser-racer (upper left) can venture offshore a few miles. The heavier cruiser (left) can head farther out if properly prepared and handled.

Boat Selection

ability and trim than a relatively light boat of the same waterline length. One sensible rule of thumb is that for sailing far from shore in rough conditions, a typical moderate-displacement cruiser with a displacement/length ratio of 250–325 should have an overall length of at least 35 feet.

Keel length is something of a shibboleth in conversations about cruising boat design. This is partly because many light-displacement racing boats with very small fin keels and separate rudders have proven to be unseaworthy. However, seaworthiness is a function not only of keel length and rudder placement. A heavy displacement, slow boat with a keel running most of the length of her hull and ending with an attached rudder is not necessarily the most sea-

worthy vessel in extreme conditions. Hull shape, balance, rig, and construction may be equally important. Many seaworthy boats have the same appendage configuration of the Sabre 30, with a moderate-size fin keel and large separate rudder. Still, extremely small keels and rudders don't belong on boats cruising offshore.

Latent (ultimate) stability, or resistance to heel and (ultimately) capsize, is an important concern when choosing a boat to sail offshore and in rough weather. A reliable indicator of a boat's capsizability is her range of positive stability, sometimes called the angle of vanishing stability. This is the angle of heel at which the boat loses the ability to come back upright. At this heel angle, the boat may well capsize.

With her small cockpit and sturdy feel, this Fast Passage 39, designed by Bill Garden, has the characteristics of a good ocean-going boat. She is similar to the Pacific Seacraft 37 that we looked at earlier. Her large keel testifies to fairly heavy displacement and is balanced by a large sail plan in a cutter rig. Her full canoe (pointed) stern gives her a shippy appearance and adds somewhat to her seaworthiness by providing more buoyancy aft. Notice the small cockpit well, which means that less water will be taken aboard if the cockpit is filled by a breaking sea in an ocean storm. The short cockpit also permits more ample accommodations below, with three cabins. Of course, simply having these (or any other) special features does not guarantee that a boat is suitable for going to sea. Any vessel must be properly designed and built, and the rest of the boat must come together as a whole.

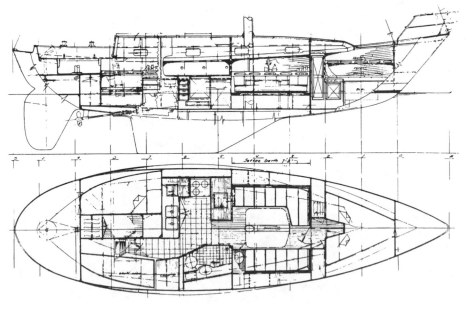

The stability range of a dinghy like the Laser is less than 80°. Once the deck is almost vertical, the boat will flip over. Because these boats are so light, their crews keep them upright by hiking out to windward, which moves the center of gravity upwind and to the side. When they heel about 80°, the crew is almost directly above the center of buoyancy. If they heel another degree, the center of gravity goes from the positive to the negative side. Instead of leveraging the boat upright, it hastens the capsize and the boat flips right over.

But in a keel boat, the center of gravity is deep, and the weight of the ballast in the keel sticking out to the side may raise the stability range to more than 100°, depending on the boat's shape and design features. Very lightweight racing keel boats also depend on crew weight to resist heeling.

If capsize is a problem, so is bringing a boat back upright after she is capsized. The lower the boat's stability range, the more likely she is to remain upside down after a capsize. As a rule of thumb, the minimum for a boat going out in very rough weather in protected waters is about 100°, while the minimum for going offshore is 120°, at which angle of heel the mast lies in the water.

Each boat has her own positive stability range, and it can be calculated by a naval architect from her dimensions, including the location of her center of gravity. Positive stability range increases as boats get heavier, narrower, and deeper, and as their center of gravity is moved lower (for example, by putting more ballast in the bottom of the keel or by adding displacement). Beam is an important factor and should not be extremely large or small. Yacht designer Olin Stephens recommends a rule of thumb involving a ratio between the widest beam on deck and the depth of the hull from the waterline to the top of the keel: "A moderate ratio of beam to hull depth seems ideal," Stephens wrote in Adlard Coles' and Peter Bruce's *Heavy Weather Sailing* (4th edition). Stephens recommended the following rule of thumb: "a beam of not more than three to four times the hull body depth, with a center of gravity low enough to give a positive stability range of 125°."

Buoyancy when capsized or holed is a consideration. Some keel monohulls have watertight bulkheads or large expanses of foam and will float when holed or flooded. While ultimate buoyancy is a definite benefit for people heading out into the ocean (where boats have been sunk by whales and floating containers lost from freighters), living space can be greatly limited. The best alternative is the multihull.

HANDS ON:
The Capsize Screening Formula

A simple way to estimate a boat's resistance to capsize and then to staying upside down after a capsize is to use the capsize screening formula. It was developed in the mid-1980s by the Joint Committee on Safety from Capsizing of the Society of Naval Architects and Marine Engineers and the United States Yacht Racing Union (now the United States Sailing Association). This formula is taken from the book *Desirable and Undesirable Characteristics of Offshore Yachts*, written by the Technical Committee of the Cruising Club of America and edited by the author of this book.

The formula compares the boat's beam with her displacement. If she is unusually beamy or lightweight, she does not do well; if she is relatively narrow or heavy, she does well.

Light-displacement boats may be safe offshore as long as their beams are not too wide.

First, divide the boat's total weight in pounds by 64 to find volume in cubic feet in salt water. Second, find the cube root of that figure. Third, divide the result into the boat's beam . . .

$$\frac{\text{Beam}}{\sqrt[3]{\text{Displacement} \div 64}}$$

If the result is less than 2, then the boat is relatively safe from capsize and remaining upside down. If greater than 2, she is relatively vulnerable. The higher the number, the more vulnerable she is. This is a guideline, not an absolute test, for estimating a boat's ability to recover from a capsize.

Heavy, narrow hulls like this traditional full-keeled sloop are less vulnerable to capsize in extreme sea conditions.

Multihulls

Giant offshore racing catamarans and trimarans have rewritten many of the world's oldest ocean sailing records. This 80-foot catamaran was the first marine vessel (sail or power) to circumnavigate the globe non-stop in under 80 days.

So far, we have been speaking primarily of monohulls, boats with one hull. Multihulls — unsinkable boats with two hulls (catamarans) or three (trimarans) — were invented centuries ago, probably in the Pacific, but it is only since 1970 that they have exploded in popularity around the world in a variety of big and small types. Today multihulls can be found not only sailing off beaches, but also in almost every sailing club, marina, and charter operation.

Multihulls ("multis") have several virtues, one of which, their speed, is well known. A good multihull will outperform a comparably sized monohull in almost all conditions. This speed is the result of their light weight and outstanding initial stability. A 28-foot, 2,700-pound trimaran may have the same 20-foot beam as an 80-foot, 70,000-pound ocean-cruising monohull and sail twice as fast. Beam serves the same function in a multihull as it does in a dinghy: it stands in for ballast. A multi has no ballast and no keel. The stability provided by this wide beam allows multihulls to carry much more sail than a keel monohull of comparable length can safely fly. Although technically a displacement boat because they slice through the water rather than riding on top of it, a catamaran ("cat") or trimaran ("tri") escapes the traditional hull speed trap because their pencil-thin hulls have very little wave-making resistance. Racing daysailing catamarans can average 20+ knots around a race course, while offshore racing cats and tris have set phenominal records for long ocean passages and circumnavigations.

There are other advantages. Multihulls heel very little, if at all. They are unsinkable if capsized, and also can be pulled or driven up on a beach once their centerboards or daggerboards are retracted. Cruising multis (as distinct from their minimalist racing cousins) are exceptionally roomy. The cabins in a good cruising catamaran's hulls and on the broad bridge deck between them offer plenty of shelter and comfort.

Trimarans have most of their living space in the center main hull (the "vaka" in Polynesian terminology), while the two outriggers or floats ("amas") have room for storage.

But no boat is perfect. Their light weight and rapid acceleration can produce a bouncy, quick motion. Because multis must be both strong and light, construction often is expensive. Adding payload has an immediate price in performance. High freeboard for larger accommodations in cruising multihulls creates a wall of windage. A multi's high wetted surface can make her hard to tack and sluggish in light winds unless she has been specifically designed for these conditions.

The simple, nimble Hobie Cat (above) launched a wave of off-the-beach catamarans that brought the excitement of sailing and racing to thousands of non-traditional sailors. In small cats excitement is the draw. Larger cruising cats (below) are gaining popularity due to stability, speed, and ample accomodations.

And multis can capsize. While they have high initial stability due to their beam, they do not have ballasted keels (almost all multihulls have centerboards as appendages). The range of positive stability (angle of vanishing stability) of many catamarans is in the 80–90° range, well under even the most extreme racing monohulls. For trimarans, the stability range may be as low as 85° and as high as 100°. In other words, multis will capsize well before their masts go in the water. At high speed, even a large multihull can capsize almost as quickly as a dinghy.

Once over on her side, a multi may turtle (turn completely over) and lie upside down. While this is not serious for multihull daysailers, this vulnerability is a real consideration for cruising multihulls. As the multihull designer Chris White observes in his book *The Cruising Multihull*, "Capsize is a fact of life. A multihull sailed offshore should be designed, constructed, and sailed to offer the greatest chance of avoiding capsize. But capsize preparation is still essential."

Multihull Types. Multihulls naturally divide into two types, catamarans and trimarans.

Catamarans make up most of the population, since most small multihulls are cats, including the ubiquitous Hobie Cats. These daysailers are lively, fun boats that hone skills and sensitivities for all types of boats. A cat reaches optimum speed when sailed at a slight angle of heel so that her windward hull is just lifting clear of the water. "Flying a hull," as it is called, reduces the boat's wetted surface and friction, but it demands skill and concentration on the crew's part. Flying a hull is limited mostly to small racing cats.

Over 25 feet, there is a growing number of cruising catamarans. Because they have two big hulls, larger cruising catamarans have excellent accommodations for living aboard.

Trimarans appear at about 24 feet. With three hulls, a tri has more wetted surface than a cat of similar size and so in theory is slower if the cat can fly a hull. But with their wider beam, tris are more stable and tend to be more forgiving of mistakes. The ama to leeward provides not only buoyancy as the boat heels but a warning to the crew. When it submerges below the water, it's time to reduce sail. For this reason, while most large (over 35 feet) cruising multihulls are cats, most offshore racing multis, which are sailed aggressively, are trimarans.

Some production trimarans feature amas that fold up next to the hull to allow the boat to be hauled in and out of the water on a trailer. Tris tend to be oriented more toward performance than interior accomodations, in part because they have only one hull big enough to live in.

Displacement/length and sail area/displacement ratios (described earlier) are fair predictors of a catamaran's performance. A racer may have a D/L in the 30–60 range and an SA/D greater than 30. A fast cruiser may have a D/L of 80–100 and an SA/D of 25–30. And a slow cruiser may be in the 100–130 and 15–25 range.

While some boat-handling skills are different, multihull seamanship does not vary from monohull keel boat seamanship in the essentials. Yet the high speed, low latent stability, and rapid acceleration and deceleration of multihulls demand extra vigilance.

Modern folding trimarans deliver a combination of excellent performance, easy handling, and ease of transport. Their shallow draft gains them access to many shoal cruising areas inaccessible to deeper draft keelboats. Folding the amas makes these boats narrow enough to be trailed on highways without special permits.

Construction Materials

Fiberglass is by far the most popular material for building boats (spars are usually made of aluminum). Though not as strong as most types of wood, fiberglass is relatively strong for its weight. Most important, because it is easy to work around molds, it is the best material for building many hulls to the same design. A fiberglass boat starts with a plug — a wooden or plastic hull built to the designer's lines. Plastic female molds of the hull and deck are made from the plug. Sheets of fiberglass strands are laid into the molds and saturated in a gluelike resin, with a releasing agent between the sheets and the molds. Wood or foam blocks are sometimes laid between layers of fiberglass to form a lightweight reinforcing core (fiberglass forms tend to flex and require reinforcement in large flat areas). When the resin has cured, the hull is broken from the mold. The outside layer of the hull, called the gel coat, provides a shiny, attractive surface. Water can creep under the gel coat and cause poxlike blisters than must be ground away with abrasives.

Transverse and longitudinal structural members, called bulkheads and floors, are inserted to stiffen the hull and support the mast and rig. The deck, which was made in its own mold, is then laid over the hull and attached at the rail, or clamp. The bond between the deck and hull is important. If the attachment is weak, the boat will leak at the clamp, or much worse, come apart there under the strain of rough weather. The bond must be reinforced with bolts. Other points to be attentive to when inspecting a fiberglass boat include the way the engine is secured, the strength of the joints between bulkheads and the hull, and the general appearance of fiberglassed areas (if loose strands or extra resin are lying about, the hull may not have been built with care). If you are considering buy-

Fiberglass cruiser-racers at different stages of construction show (left to right) stiffening with a bulkhead, a deck mold, a deck being dropped on a hull, and a two-part hull mold.

ing a boat, you should retain a professional marine surveyor. A satisfactory survey may also be required by an insurance company before it issues a policy on a boat. Names of surveyors may be found in the telephone directory and over the Internet.

While most boats are built of fiberglass, some large custom yachts (built for individual customers) are aluminum or steel, and many small powerboats are built of aluminum, which can be shaped in molds. Both metals require special preparation for use in salt water. Racing and other high-performance boats are built of highly sophisticated, expensive materials such as carbon fiber and Kevlar.

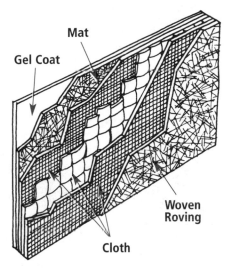

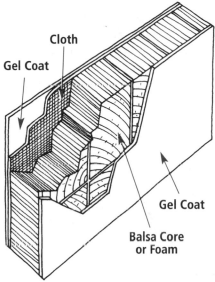

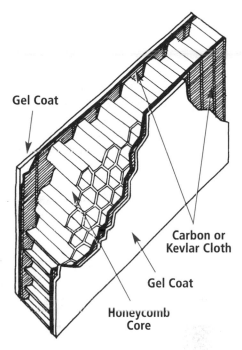

Standard fiberglass construction consists of layers of different types of material chosen for strength and compatibility with resin: (left to right) mat, cloth, woven roving, cloth, and mat. They are laid up in resin one layer at a time under a protective layer called a gel coat.

Balsa wood or foam is sometimes used as a core to provide lightweight stiffening for fiberglass.

Foam and honeycombs also are used in cored construction. Builders may use exotic materials such as carbon fiber and Kevlar to achieve high strength-to-weight ratios.

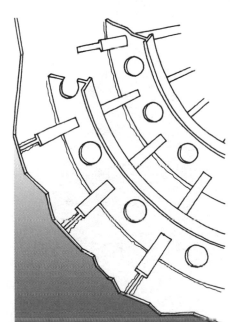

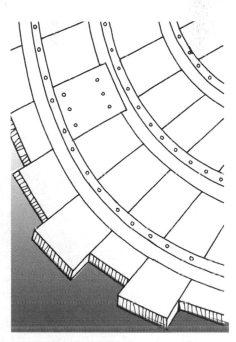

Aluminum construction consists of shaped and welded plates reinforced by frames (here shown with lightening holes that save weight without affecting strength).

Molded plywood and light frames are used in many different types of boats, and many home-built boats are constructed with plywood sheets.

Traditional wood construction, with planks fastened to wooden or metal frames and seams filled with caulking, is heavy but strong.

The Rig

Besides their dimensions, boats are distinguished from one another by rig, the arrangements of sails and masts. The main components of a rig are the mast (supporting the halyards and the front edge of the mainsail), the boom (supporting the bottom edge of the mainsail), the stays (supporting the mast and the jibs), and the sails themselves.

There are six rigs for sailboats, each with its own special characteristics.

The sloop is by far the most popular rig. A sloop has one mast, a boom, one jib (or sometimes two), plus a mainsail. If the jib is hoisted from the top of the mast—and this is the case in most cruising boats — the rig is called **masthead**. However, if the jib is hoisted from anywhere below the top of the mast, the rig is called **fractional**. Most daysailers and some cruising boats have fractional rigs. On many masthead rigs, the jibs are large overlapping genoas, trimmed far aft and in square footage usually larger than the mainsails.

The cutter is a single-masted boat whose mast is stepped almost near the center of the boat. Cutters often carry two relatively small jibs rather than one big one. This is called the cutter rig. The small sails are easier to handle than a genoa. The outer jib is set on the headstay and called the jib, the inner one is set on the forestay and called the forestaysail (or staysail).

The yawl is a divided rig — or a rig with two masts. Divided rigs are used on larger boats to break up the sail plan into

Lateen Rig

Cat-Rigged Dinghy

Sloop-Rigged Dinghy

Sloop-Rigged Catamaran

Gaff-Rigged Catboat

Wishbone Cat Rig

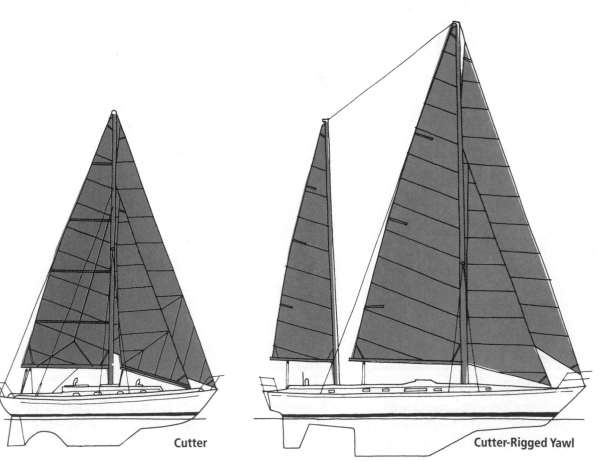

Cutter

Cutter-Rigged Yawl

small, manageable components. The largest sail that can be handled alone by a normal sailor contains 500–600 square feet of cloth. In the yawl rig, a jib and a mainsail are set on the larger, forward mast, called the **mainmast**, and a small sail, the **mizzen,** is set on a small mast stepped way aft, the **mizzenmast.** The mizzenmast in a yawl is stepped aft of the rudder post (the rod on which the rudder hangs). Large light sails called mizzen staysails may be hoisted on the mizzenmast to increase the sail area under certain conditions. A yawl (or any other divided rig, for that matter) may have a masthead or a fractional rig, and also a cutter rig.

The ketch has the same general appearance as the yawl — tall mainmast forward and small mizzenmast aft — except that the mizzenmast is stepped forward of the rudder post and is larger in proportion to the mainmast. The ketch may carry mizzen staysails. Because it breaks down the sail area into three roughly equal areas, the ketch rig has been a favorite for people sailing long distances in large boats.

The schooner, the rig of the great sailing yachts of history, is rarely seen today. It also has a divided rig, but with the forward mast (called the foremast) shorter than the main mast. Between the two masts she may carry a foresail (a small gaff-rigged sail), a staysail, or a large reaching staysail set high and called a gollywobbler.

The cat rig has no jib, and the mast is right up on the bow. Some cat rigs have two masts, usually of equal height.

Rigs may also be categorized by the shape of the mainsail. **The Marconi rig** (Bermudian rig) is the three-sided mainsail or mizzen seen on almost all boats today. The classic four-sided **gaff rig** is still used on some traditional boats. Another type of mainsail that is still seen is the **lateen (sprit) rig,** used on the Sunfish and other small boardboats. This is a three-sided sail supported at the bottom by a boom and at the top by a sprit, or long gaff, all pivoting around the mast. The **wishbone rig,** used on sailboards and some cat rigs, is a pair of curved booms, one on each side of the sail, that hold the clew out from the mast. In addition, there are several **self-tacking rigs** for jibs involving a boom or wishbone on the sail that allows the boat to come about without the crew's having to adjust the jib sheets.

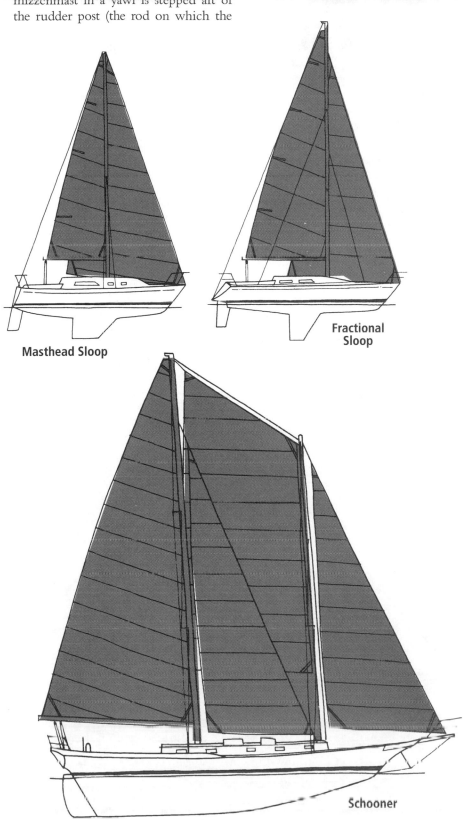

Masthead Sloop

Fractional Sloop

Schooner

Traditional Rigs

While by far the most popular rig today, the three-sided Marconi or Bermudian rig is a relative newcomer, having been developed in small boats in Bermuda in the late 19th century and becoming popular on larger boats only in the 1920s, after engineers developed ways to keep tall masts standing and straight. The Marconi rig derives its name from its great height (compared with the gaff rig) and from the complexity of stays needed to keep it upright — when it appeared, many people thought it looked like one of the tall radio towers built by Guglielmo Marconi.

The gaff, lateen, and other rigs with a third spar aloft date back much further, while the wishbone rig was developed in the early 20th century. The Marconi rig won out over the others because, though more expensive, it is simpler (with only two spars) and usually faster, especially upwind and in rough water because it presents less windage and is less heavy aloft. The claims of a speed benefit have been challenged by some theorists, who perhaps were looking for an argument. It is true that in a reach in fresh winds, the low, wide gaff rig may be faster than the tall, narrow Marconi rig. Traditional rigs have the advantage in one important corner of seamanship: in a blow it is quicker to spill wind by scandalizing (lowering) the outer end of a gaff or strut than by taking the time to reef a Marconi mainsail.

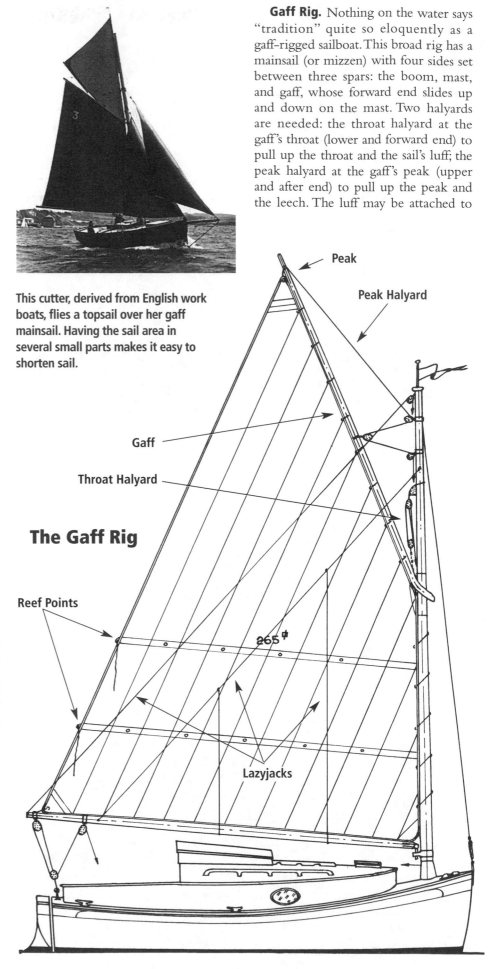

This cutter, derived from English work boats, flies a topsail over her gaff mainsail. Having the sail area in several small parts makes it easy to shorten sail.

Gaff Rig. Nothing on the water says "tradition" quite so eloquently as a gaff-rigged sailboat. This broad rig has a mainsail (or mizzen) with four sides set between three spars: the boom, mast, and gaff, whose forward end slides up and down on the mast. Two halyards are needed: the throat halyard at the gaff's throat (lower and forward end) to pull up the throat and the sail's luff; the peak halyard at the gaff's peak (upper and after end) to pull up the peak and the leech. The luff may be attached to

Peak

Peak Halyard

Gaff

Throat Halyard

The Gaff Rig

Reef Points

265

Lazyjacks

In the gaff rig, the gaff is supported near the mast by the throat halyard and at the end by the peak halyard. To depower the sail, "scandalize" it by dropping the peak. Lazyjacks running from the mast to the middle of the boom hold the boom up and secure the sail when it is lowered.

the mast with slides or with hoops around the mast.

To hoist the sail, pull on both halyards at once until the luff is taut, with slight vertical tension wrinkles. At this point the gaff is horizontal and the sail scandalized (partially filled). You can sit comfortably like this until time to get under way. Then haul on the peak halyard until the peak is cocked up and there are diagonal tension wrinkles across the sail from the peak (the end of the gaff) to the tack.

When the boat is sailing, the gaff falls off to leeward. To decrease the gaff's sag and the mainsail's twist, tighten the peak halyard or rig a vang, which (on the gaff rig) is an adjustable line or tackle leading from the peak down to the windward deck. Tighten the vang to reduce twist in light air and ease it to depower the sail (spill wind) in strong puffs.

To douse a gaff rigged mainsail, after overhauling both halyards to get the kinks out of them, drop the peak slightly, then ease the peak and throat halyards together. The peak should stay cocked up in order to push the throat down the mast. If the sail has lazyjacks (light lines usually rigged from boom to mast to corral the gaff), the sail and gaff will drop neatly onto the boom. Tie a couple of sail stops around the boom, gaff, and sail to keep everything secure.

An advantage of the gaff rig is that because the mast is short, heeling forces are relatively low, even though the heavy gaff is high in the rig. This is one reason most gaff-rigged boats are found in windy areas like San Francisco and Buzzards Bay in southern Massachusetts. But in more moderate conditions, the gaff rig suffers from low performance. A gaff mainsail needs at least 20 percent more sail area than a Marconi mainsail to begin to perform comparably. To increase sail area, many gaff-rigged boats fly large topsails above the gaff.

Because of these and other restrictions, the gaff rig is rarely used except on schooners, cat boats, Friendship sloops, and other classic boats. But of all sailboat rigs, it probably is the most loved. After all, speed is not everything.

Lateen (Sprit) Rig. Found today mainly on Sunfish, the popular little daysailers, this rig may be the parent of the gaff rig. The spar aloft, called the sprit, extends down to the boom forward of the mast. Because the spars are short (usually shorter than the boat itself), a lateen-rigged boat is easily rigged, put away, stowed, and transported with the spars lying on deck. In light air, raise the gaff and boom as far as possible on the mast to catch wind off the water. In fresh air, lower them to drop the center of

Because it's so short, with a mast, boom, and sprit about the same length, the Sunfish's lateen rig is easily stowed and handled.

effort and decrease heeling forces.

Wishbone Rig. This rig is found on sailboards, cat-rigged Nonsuch cruising boats, and some other cruising boats. The wishbone rig uses a triangular sail whose clew is held out from the mast by two curved booms (which look like a chicken's wishbone) on either side of the sail. (Sometimes a single boom is rigged.) This gets rid of the low, swinging boom — the most dangerous object on a sailboat. It also relieves strains on the crew, since the downward thrust of the booms on the sail's clew automatically keeps the leech firm without much pull on the main sheet. On many wishbone-rigged boats, the mast is left freestanding without stays. In a gust, the mast bends to leeward and depowers the sail by spilling wind aloft. On cruising boats, light lines draped under the foot cradle the sail when it is doused.

The wishbone rig is a triangular sail with a unique boom. Because the wishbone pushes down as well as aft, the sail's foot does not lift and there's no need for a boom vang or large main sheet tackle. Loose lines between the wishbones gather the sail when it's doused. The lines in the leech and luff are reefing lines.

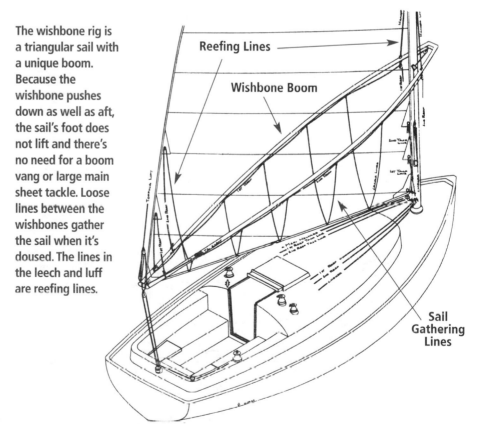

Reefing Lines

Wishbone Boom

Sail Gathering Lines

Sail Furling

Sails are furled (put away) in different ways. Many sails are doused (lowered) onto the boom or deck, where they are flaked in large folds, rolled up, tied down, or put away in bags. Jibs and mainsails may also be rolled up with roller-furlers controlled by lines from the cockpit. Roller-furlers are one of the great blessings of modern sailing.

Full-length battens are popular with cruisers because they help control sail shape, reduce sail flogging and noise, and extend sail life. Another benefit occurs when it's time to drop the mainsail. The battens allow the sail to stack neatly on the boom (see below).

Roller-furling systems (below) reduce the effort and time required to set and stow headsails and make sail-handling safer, as well. The system uses a swivel unit at the head of the jib (right) and a rotating drum at the tack rigged with a furling line that leads back to the cockpit (see below).

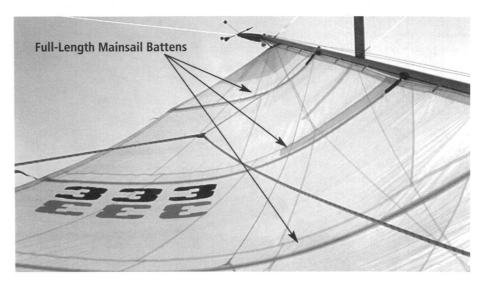

Full-Length Mainsail Battens

Pulling on the furling line rolls up the jib like a vertical window shade. To shield the genoa from the sun's damaging rays while furled, many furling genoas attach sacrificial fabric to the leech and foot of the sail (see below).

Lazyjacks

Most mainsails and some jibs have battens, wooden or fiberglass slats inserted in pockets in the leech (the after edge of the sail) to support the roach (the curved part of the leech) and keep the sail from flapping shapelessly. Traditionally, battens have been about one-quarter the sail's width. Today, however, many if not most sailboats have full-length battens running from leech to luff. Full-length battens are expensive, and may be complicated to rig. But they shape the sail and prevent violent luffing (which can destroy sail fabric). Full-length battens also help the sail stack neatly on the boom when it's lowered. On many boats, lines called lazyjacks are led from the boom up to the mast to cradle the sail as it comes down.

Furling booms (above) and mast furling mainsail systems (below) are most commonly seen on larger yachts, where convenience is worth the added weight, windage, and expense.

HANDS ON: **Boat-Buying Hints**

Since seamanship in its broadest sense means to enjoy and safely use boats, nothing is more important than having the right boat to begin with and using her in a way that is compatible with your skills, resources, and ambitions. Many people underestimate the cost, both in time and money, of maintaining a boat. Boat ownership can be demanding.

Before you go shopping for a new boat, thoroughly erase every romantic notion you have about the sea from your memory. After heaving *Moby Dick* into the garbage can, sit down and have an honest conversation with yourself and your family about what you want out of boating. Make a list of your objectives: fishing (deep-sea or river?), cruising (overnight or around the world?), entertaining (your best friend or your boss?), racing (informal or blood and guts?). If you're interested in cruising, try to anticipate how many berths (beds) you'll need. Find out where you'll be able to store your boat. In some areas waterfront storage is available only for trailerable boats and every marina slip has a six-year waiting list. Will you normally be out in rough weather or calms? On weekends or for months at a time? Will you sail single-handed or with your six sons and their football team?

Next, the tough question: How much boat can you afford? Be realistic. Unlike real estate, boats are not investments. The value of a well-built, well-maintained boat probably will not keep up with inflation. Few people make money on boats, so be sure to relegate your plans to your discretionary and not your retirement account. Before you go shopping, check around with banks and other financial institutions to see what boat loans are available, and at what price. Draw up a preliminary budget based on a hypothetical boat of about the size you're considering, checking with marinas and boatyards to see what their charges may be. As a rule of thumb, annual maintenance costs run about 10 percent of the purchase price. Listings of used boats are carried in boating magazines and at many new-boat sales offices. If you do decide to purchase a used boat, have a marine surveyor examine her thoroughly before you sign the papers.

Here are some typical problems with older boats.

Cruiser-Racer
- ☐ Illegal marine toilet
- ☐ Poorly maintained engine
- ☐ Corroded or loose keel
- ☐ Malfunctioning electronics
- ☐ Air bubbles in compass
- ☐ Wobbly spreaders
- ☐ Bent or dented mast
- ☐ Frayed or worn-out sails
- ☐ Worn halyard sheaves
- ☐ Leaky hatches
- ☐ Kinked rigging
- ☐ Bent or frozen turnbuckles
- ☐ Frayed halyards
- ☐ Leaks along hull/deck joint
- ☐ Bent stanchions
- ☐ Worn pawls on winches
- ☐ Loose "play" in steering
- ☐ Blistered gel coat

Daysailer
- ☐ Warped rudder or centerboard
- ☐ Loose tiller fit
- ☐ Worn pintles or gudgeons
- ☐ Worn hiking strap
- ☐ Frayed sheets or halyards
- ☐ Bent or dented mast or boom
- ☐ Leaky gunwhale
- ☐ Leaky centerboard trunk
- ☐ Elongated screw holes for mounted hardware
- ☐ Flexible hull
- ☐ Worn or frayed sails
- ☐ Bent or frozen turnbuckles
- ☐ Blistered gel coat
- ☐ Scratched or gouged hull

CHAPTER 2

Getting Under Way

Boat handling includes the basic skills of getting under way, understanding wind direction, steering confidently and accurately, trimming the sails properly, and getting back. This chapter addresses those fundamentals, offers some practical tips, and takes you out and back on your first sail. We'll start with the points of sail and then move on to the apparent wind — the wind that the boat helps to create as she moves through the water, and the wind that the skipper and crew trim the sails to.

A theme throughout this chapter is the importance of keeping the boat moving. With steerageway (enough speed to steer efficiently), you control your destiny; without it, you are incapable of maneuvering and at the mercy of wind gusts and current. A rudder is useless when the water is not moving over it.

So you must be moving. If a dinghy or other small boat is stopped by a bad tack or when trying to get under way from the dock or mooring, develop steerageway by sculling, or swinging the helm rhythmically from side to side so the rudder works like a paddle. A larger boat needs a stronger force. The best way to get any boat going under sail from a dead stop is to back the jib (pull it to one side) to swing the bow off, then get her on a close reach with the helm centered so the rudder makes minimum resistance. Trim the sails properly to the wind and in time she will develop steerageway.

THE POINTS OF SAIL

The wind hits a moving sailboat from any one of three general directions: astern, abeam, and ahead. Sailors describe these wind angles as the points of sail, and divide them into two broad categories. One is "off the wind," with the wind coming across the stern (running) or across the side (reaching). The other is "on the wind," with the wind coming over

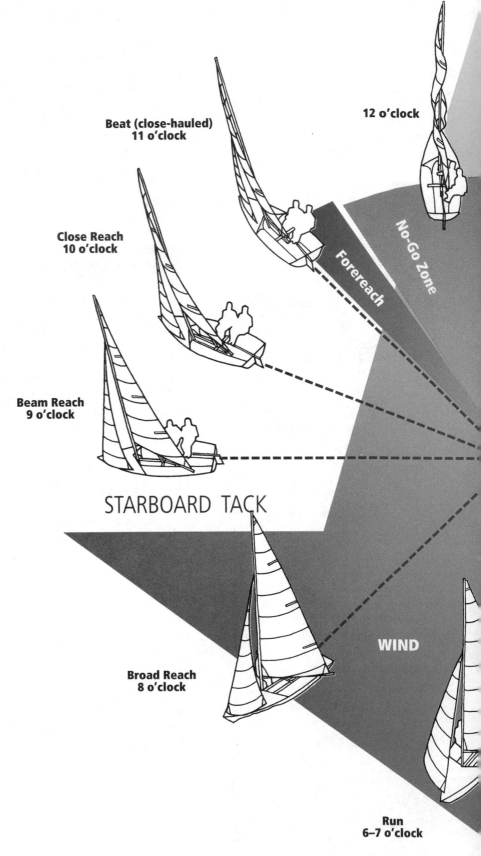

12 o'clock

**Beat (close-hauled)
11 o'clock**

No-Go Zone

Forereach

**Close Reach
10 o'clock**

**Beam Reach
9 o'clock**

STARBOARD TACK

**Broad Reach
8 o'clock**

WIND

**Run
6–7 o'clock**

the bow (beating and forereaching). The points of sail can be shown in a circle either as a pie or a clock where the wind flows from 12 to 6 o'clock.

Running (5 to 7 o'clock) is the most fundamental: turn the stern to the wind and get pushed along. Here the angle of the wind to the sails (the angle of attack) is a broad one.

Reaching (2 to 4 o'clock and 8 to 10 o'clock) occurs when the wind is across the boat. The boat is on a beam reach with the wind coming directly over her beam, or side. Below that, she's sailing on a broad reach, at a broad angle to the wind. Above that she's on a close reach, at a close or narrow angle to the wind. The reach is the fastest point of sail, with the close reach usually being the most fast.

Beating (close-hauled) (1 o'clock and 11 o'clock) lies at about 40° to the wind, although some very close-winded boats may be able to sail as close as 30°. This point of sail is called beating because the boat is bashing into waves rather than running easily with them, and also close-hauled or hard on the wind because sails are trimmed tight.

Above beating, at around 12 o'clock, is an area where the wind's angle of attack is so narrow that the sails fill slightly, if at all. This is the area of forereaching and the no-go zone. **Forereaching (headreaching)** is just above beating. The sails luff (shake) partly, spilling wind, so the boat makes only some headway (speed ahead). Luffing the sails completely is an excellent way to stop a boat. Luffing them a little slows her quickly and makes her motion more comfortable, while still providing enough headway so she can be steered. If you feel out of control, simply ease (let out) the sheets a little or feather (head the boat up into the wind slightly without easing sheets).

The **no-go zone** is just above forereaching. Sometimes called being in the eye of the wind, here the boat is headed directly or almost directly into the wind. A boat may also be described as being head to wind ("head" meaning "bow") or in irons. The sails don't fill at all, the boat has no headway, and she lies helpless and unsteerable.

On any point of sail except when head to wind, the boat is on either the **starboard tack** or the **port tack**. On starboard tack, the wind comes from over the starboard side (the right side when facing forward), the boat heels to the port side, and the sails are trimmed to the port side. On port tack, the wind comes from port (the left side, facing forward), heel is to starboard, and sails are trimmed to starboard.

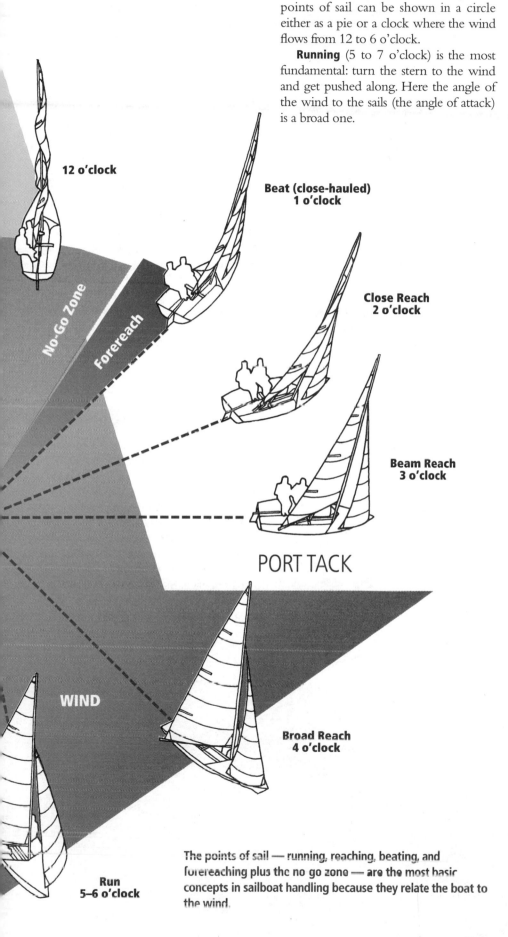

12 o'clock

No-Go Zone

Forereach

**Beat (close-hauled)
1 o'clock**

**Close Reach
2 o'clock**

**Beam Reach
3 o'clock**

PORT TACK

WIND

**Broad Reach
4 o'clock**

**Run
5–6 o'clock**

The points of sail — running, reaching, beating, and forereaching plus the no-go zone — are the most basic concepts in sailboat handling because they relate the boat to the wind.

True Wind and Apparent Wind

The relationship between true wind and apparent wind is illustrated by a bicyclist. His forward motion (gray vector) redirects, decreases, or increases the true wind (black vector) to create a wind that only he feels — the apparent wind (blue vector). The only time when there is no apparent wind is when the bike is stopped.

There are two types of wind. The **true wind** is the wind that blows across the land and water and hits stationary objects like flags on docked boats or perched seagulls (which usually stand facing the wind). This is nature's wind, unaffected by the motion of the objects it hits. But when those objects go into motion, they reshape the true wind and convert it into **apparent wind.** The apparent wind, not the true wind, governs how we trim the sails and which courses we are able to sail. This phenomenon should be familiar to anybody who has pedaled a bicycle in a crosswind. A cyclist making 10 MPH in a 10-MPH crosswind feels the wind not on his ear but on his cheeks. This felt (apparent) wind is stronger and farther ahead than the actual (true) wind because the bike's own speed is augmenting it. Then if the bike heads at 10 MPH directly into a 10-MPH wind, the cyclist not only must

work harder to keep up the 10-MPH speed but feels a 20-MPH wind directly in his face. And if the bike runs at the same speed with a 10-MPH tailwind, the effort would be less and the cyclist feels no wind at all.

The same phenomenon occurs on a moving boat. Using tables or a technique called vector analysis, we can even predict the exact direction and force of the apparent wind so long as we know the boat's speed and heading and the strength and direction of the true wind. It is also possible to solve this simple geometric problem using an electronic calculator programmed with trigonometric functions. (If you know the apparent wind you can use the same techniques to work backward to find the true wind.) Yet precise prediction of apparent wind speed and direction is much less important to the average sailor than a simple understanding of how the forces involved affect

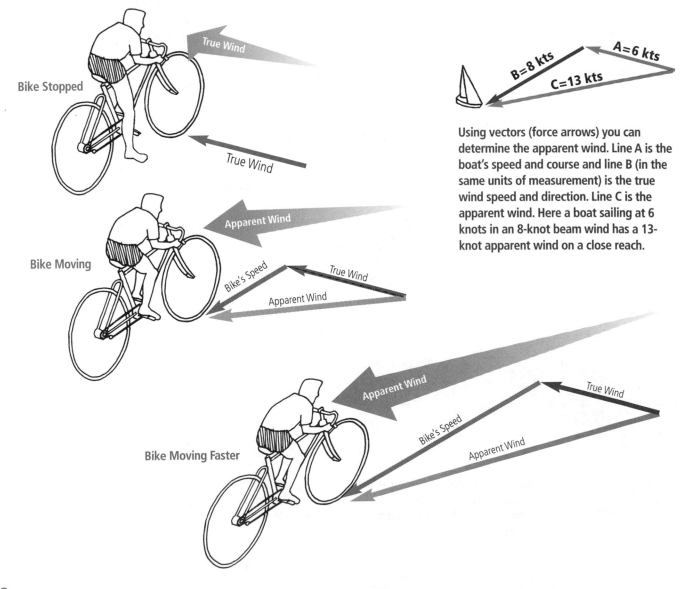

Using vectors (force arrows) you can determine the apparent wind. Line A is the boat's speed and course and line B (in the same units of measurement) is the true wind speed and direction. Line C is the apparent wind. Here a boat sailing at 6 knots in an 8-knot beam wind has a 13-knot apparent wind on a close reach.

the boat on different points of sail. With some experience you'll find that you can predict the angle and velocity to within about 5° and 3 knots. Here are some helpful rules of thumb:

The true wind provides the broad environmental context. The apparent wind is the moving boat's actual wind.

On a reach or a beat, when a boat accelerates the apparent wind will increase and draw forward.

On a run, when a boat accelerates, the apparent wind will decrease and stay in the same direction.

While the apparent wind is the wind the boat sails in, the true wind makes the waves. This means waves usually are at an angle to the apparent wind.

The farther forward the apparent wind draws, the greater are the side forces on the sail that cause heeling and leeway (side-slippage).

Sails work best when the wind flows over them from the luff (front edge) to the leech (back edge) at an apparent wind angle of about 50° (in light wind) to 90° (in strong wind). Therefore, close and beam reaches are the fastest points of sail, and the run (when the wind is at about 170°) and the beat (when it is at about 40°) are slow. When sailing slowly on a run, head up to a broad reach, trim the sails, and allow the wind to flow across the sails. The apparent wind will draw forward quickly and speed you up, often enough to make up for the added distance you'll sail to get to your destination.

When the difference between the boat's speed and the true wind's velocity is great, the apparent wind will not differ much from the true wind. That is, slow boats don't change strong winds very much.

When the boat's speed and the true wind's velocity are close, the apparent wind will be very different from the true wind. In light conditions, even slow boats can have a big effect on the true wind, and fast boats may have radically different apparent winds. Iceboats, racing multihulls, and a few other boats are so fast that they're almost always sailing close-hauled, even when the true wind is way aft. They are said to "make their own wind."

On a beat or a reach, a puff of wind pulls the apparent wind aft, unless it is part of a wind shift. This is because the puff increases the difference between the boat's speed and the true wind's velocity.

Similarly, **a lull in the wind always pulls the apparent wind forward,** again unless it is accompanied by a shift. This is due to the fact that a lull decreases the difference between boat and true wind speeds.

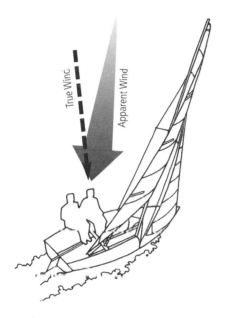

Upwind or on reaches, when the boat accelerates or there is a lull in the true wind, her apparent wind draws forward and she is headed.

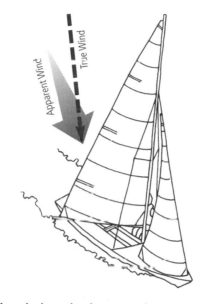

When the boat decelerates or there is a puff, her apparent wind pulls aft and she is lifted. On a run, when she accelerates, her apparent wind decreases.

These Tornado racing catamarans are making at least 12 knots in a true wind of less than 10 knots. With their low resistance, light weight, and high initial stability, multihulls can dramatically increase the apparent wind and pull it forward when sailing on a reach.

Basic Sail Trimming

The wind should flow smoothly across the sails. There are two good visual guides. One is the sail itself, which should not luff (flap) or bubble except at the forward edge of the mainsail, where air flow is broken by the mast. An even more sensitive guide is the telltale. This is a short length of yarn or ribbon sewn on the leech of the mainsail and on both sides of the jib near its luff. The jib telltale on the side the wind is coming from is the

windward telltale; the other is the leeward telltale. The telltales should usually flow approximately straight aft except when you're sailing on a run, directly before the wind. (The exceptions to this rule of thumb will be covered in the next chapter, on sail trim.)

Depending on the point of sail, sails and telltales are used in slightly different

ways in coordination with the helm and the sheets. On a run or reach, the crew sails a steady course and plays (constantly adjusts) the sheets so the telltales stream aft. On a beat, when sailing close-hauled, they cleat the sheet and sail a variable course, steering by (according to) the sails. On any point of sail, in a gusty breeze be prepared to spill wind in a hard puff by quickly easing the sheet a foot or so in order that the sail luffs and the boat does not heel too far or capsize.

Reaching and Running. When sailing off the wind on a reach or run, steering and sail trimming are fairly simple. You set a course and then trim the sails to it, playing the sails.

First, get on a steady course, either by aiming at a stationary object like a buoy or a lighthouse or by sticking to a compass course. Play the sails, trimming and

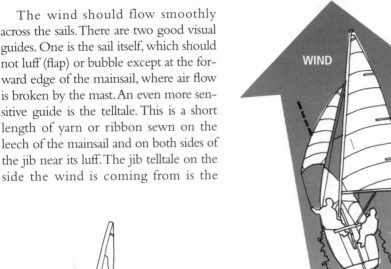

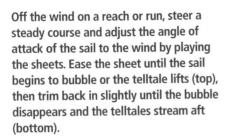

Off the wind on a reach or run, steer a steady course and adjust the angle of attack of the sail to the wind by playing the sheets. Ease the sheet until the sail begins to bubble or the telltale lifts (top), then trim back in slightly until the bubble disappears and the telltales stream aft (bottom).

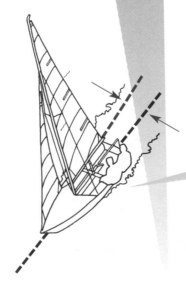

On a run, let the mainsail out all the way with the boom vang just taut, so the boom does not lift. Trim the jib wing-and-wing on the windward side. With almost no side force on the sail the boat will heel to windward unless somebody sits on the leeward side. The telltales should droop since there is no wind flow across the sails.

On a reach, play the sheets to keep the sails from barely luffing. The boom angle to the centerline will be between 20° and 80° depending on the apparent wind direction.

Beating, the main sheet will hold the boom down without help from the boom vang. Trim the sails quite flat, but instead of playing the sheets, change course to keep the sails at the right angle of attack to the wind.

easing them so they are just barely luffing and their telltales are streaming aft. Don't trim them too tight, or the boat will stop dead and heel over too far. And don't ease the sails so far that they're luffing, or they won't work.

Keeping a careful eye on the luff of the sail about halfway up, ease (let out) or trim (pull in) the sheet until the jib's windward telltale lifts or the cloth is just beginning to luff (or bubble). On a sloop or a boat with a divided rig, accurately trim the forwardmost sail first, then trim the after sail or sails. This is because the air flowing off the forward sails affects the ones farther aft.

On a reach, the sail or sails will be between about halfway to three-quarters of the way out. The best guide is the telltale on the windward side or the luffing or bubbling in the sail. Ease the sail out until the bubble appears and the telltales lift, then trim the sail back in a little so the bubble disappears and the telltales stream aft. As you ease the sheets, tighten the mainsail's boom vang to keep the boom approximately horizontal, with the mainsail's leech curving off slightly to leeward. If the leech is straight and the mainsail's telltales are drooping, the vang is too tight. If the leech billows to leeward, the vang is too loose. The greater the apparent wind, the tighter the vang should be — which means that it must be loosened as you head off from a reach to a run.

On a run, the mainsail is all the way out with the boom almost against the leeward shrouds (side stays). Since there is little wind flow across the sails, telltales are not very reliable guides.

A run can be problematical and even dangerous. On runs, boats roll uncomfortably from side to side, and sails may chafe (rub) or tear on the rigging.

Much worse are the dangers of sailing by the lee and suffering an accidental jibe (all-standing jibe). If the wind shifts or the steerer heads off too far, the boat may be caught by the lee (with the wind pushing on the wrong side of the mainsail). Unless the boom is held out by a preventer (a line to the leeward deck), the boat will jibe unintentionally. The wind will heave the sail and boom across the boat violently, surprising and clobbering crewmembers.

So don't run directly before the wind, with it on the stern (at 6 o'clock). Instead, head up slightly to a very broad reach (5 or 7 o'clock) so the wind is slightly on the windward side. (Besides being safer, a broad reach usually is faster, too.)

Beating. You must beat to windward (sail close-hauled) in order to reach a destination in the direction from which the wind is blowing. Instead of sailing a steady course toward a stationary object

This Laser skipper carefully sails by the luff of the sail as he sails on a beat with the sheet cleated.

and playing the sails as the apparent wind shifts, you must change the boat's direction to keep the sails full as the wind direction varies. In altering course, use the luff of the forwardmost sail as a guide. First, pull the sails in almost all the way and keep the boom vang loose. If you are the steerer, sit in a position where you can see the sail luff, and try to keep a very slight bubble in the sail or twitch in the windward telltale. Hold the tiller or wheel firmly but not aggressively. You should be able to make course alterations with short, easy motions of the arm and hand. Don't make large sawing motions. Practice feathering the boat by steering her a few degrees toward the wind. The windward telltales will lift straight up, the bubble will grow, and the sails will luff a few inches back. Then head off (turn the bow away from the wind). And when the bubble disappears and the sail is not luffing at all, head up again (turn the bow toward the wind). These course alterations will be very small — usually no more than about 3°.

A wind change that forces the steerer to head off, called a header, may be caused either by a shift in the direction or a decrease in the velocity of the true wind. On the other hand, a lift, which allows the skipper to head up, is caused by a shift in direction or by an increase in velocity.

The steerer may also use the feel of the wind to help sail close-hauled. Sitting facing forward on the windward side, you will feel the wind on your windward cheekbone when the boat is properly oriented to the apparent wind. If you feel the wind on your mouth, you should head off; if on your ear, you should head up.

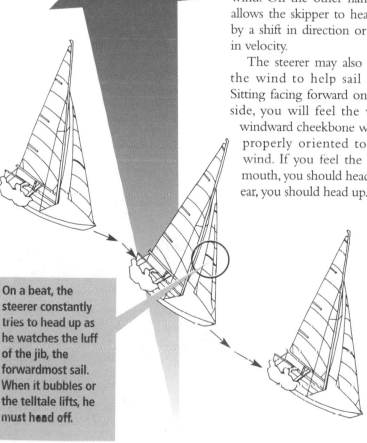

WIND

On a beat, the steerer constantly tries to head up as he watches the luff of the jib, the forwardmost sail. When it bubbles or the telltale lifts, he must head off.

Changing Tacks

A wind shift or necessary course alteration may require a change of tacks. There are two ways to change tacks: tacking by heading up, and jibing by heading off. Both require care, good communications in the crew, and practice.

Tacking (Coming About). Tacking occurs when the boat heads up into the wind, uses her momentum to carry her into and through the no-go zone (eye of the wind), and then heads off with the wind on the other side. The steerer heads up with a strong, fluid shove of the tiller or pull of the wheel. The sails luff partially and then entirely. The bow passes through the wind, and with her helm still over, falls off with the wind on the new side until the sails fill. Heavy keel boats carry considerable momentum and so lose little speed as they tack, so they can be tacked more gently than light centerboarders, with a gradually increasing shove. Light boats must be tacked aggressively so they are not stopped dead (go into irons). Very light dinghies and multihulls may not carry enough momentum to get all the way through the tack. In that case, back the jib (trim it slightly to windward) to pull the bow off while easing the main sheet quite a bit so the mainsail does not work against the jib.

In most boats it does not pay to shove the helm too hard. An abrupt motion will slow the boat drastically as water piles up on the rudder, and the boat may swing over too far and sail beyond the desired new course. During a tack from one close-hauled course to the other, most boats change course about 80°. You can precalculate the compass course on the new tack. Better yet, as the boat completes the tack, keep your eye on the luff of the forwardmost sail and be sensitive to the changing feel of the wind, which should feel the same on your face on the new tack as it did on the other side of your face on the old tack.

It's important that the skipper and crew communicate clearly during a tack. Here are the orders and responses they should use:

Steerer: "Ready about" or "stand by to tack." She should look around to be sure the boat won't tack into another boat or obstruction. The crew meanwhile overhauls the jib sheet to remove kinks and twists, which might jam in blocks, by shaking the line from the cleated part

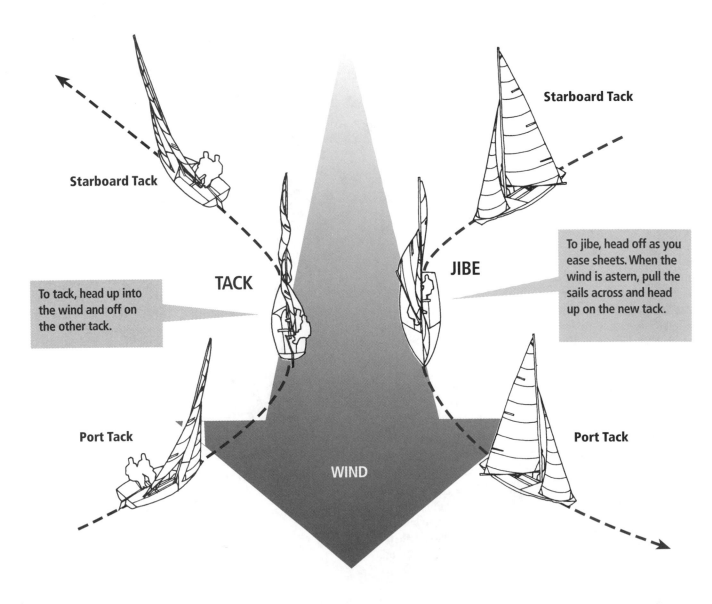

Starboard Tack

Starboard Tack

To jibe, head off as you ease sheets. When the wind is astern, pull the sails across and head up on the new tack.

JIBE

TACK

To tack, head up into the wind and off on the other tack.

Port Tack

Port Tack

WIND

toward the tail. The crew then uncleats the sheet (but holds it), and makes sure no loose gear will tangle in it or the sail.

Crew: "Ready."

Steerer: "Hard a-lee" or "helm's a-lee." This is a signal that the tiller is being pushed to leeward (or that the wheel is being turned to windward). The crew steps or slides across the boat, facing for-ward so he can see the sails clearly. The steerer pushes the tiller or turns the steering wheel firmly. The bow swings up toward the wind and the sail luffs, gradually at first and then completely. The crew casts off the leeward jib sheet and carefully lets the sheet run out through his hands to remove any kinks. Meanwhile he or another crew member pulls in the new leeward jib sheet on the other side.

The jib swings across, the bow passes through the eye of the wind, and the sail flops over on the new leeward side as the jib sheet is trimmed and the steerer slowly brings the helm back, stopping the bow's swing when it has reached about 40° off the wind (the correct angle depends on the boat and condi-tions). The crew meanwhile trims the jib sheet. A mark on the sheet, made with a marking pen, indicates approximately the optimum trim. If the boat is sailing slowly, the jib sheet should be eased out an inch or two, then trimmed to the mark as she accelerates. During the tack, the steerer or crew member eases the main sheet a few inches so that when the boat ends up on the new tack the sail is fairly full, allowing her to acceler-ate back to speed. When there are waves, acceleration may be extremely slow, so be patient before pulling the mainsail back in.

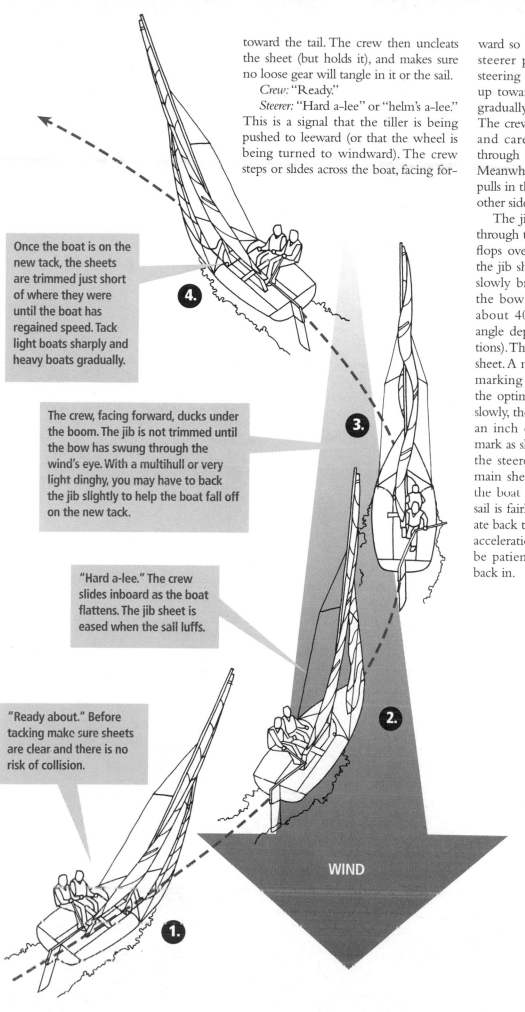

Once the boat is on the new tack, the sheets are trimmed just short of where they were until the boat has regained speed. Tack light boats sharply and heavy boats gradually.

4.

The crew, facing forward, ducks under the boom. The jib is not trimmed until the bow has swung through the wind's eye. With a multihull or very light dinghy, you may have to back the jib slightly to help the boat fall off on the new tack.

3.

"Hard a-lee." The crew slides inboard as the boat flattens. The jib sheet is eased when the sail luffs.

2.

"Ready about." Before tacking make sure sheets are clear and there is no risk of collision.

1.

WIND

Changing Tacks

Jibing. The other way to change tacks is to jibe, by swinging the stern through the eye of the wind as the boat changes course from a run on one tack to a run on the other. Here are the orders and replies:

Steerer: "Stand by to jibe." The crew clears and uncleats the sheets and checks for loose gear. The steerer makes sure she can jibe without risk of a collision.

Crew: "Ready."

Steerer: "Jibe-o." She pulls the tiller to windward (or turns the wheel to leeward) to head off. As the stern swings toward the eye of the wind, a crew member quickly trims the main sheet. (In small boats, the crew may simply grab the boom and swing it across, except in fresh winds when the boom may be allowed to swing across on its own.) The boom will come across sud-

denly, especially in fresh winds, so all crew members should duck.

The jibe should be timed so the boom is trimmed amidships (over the boat's center) just as the stern goes through the eye of the wind. Ease the main sheet quickly on the new tack. Meanwhile the jib is let go and trimmed, much as during a tack.

The steerer heads up to course. Be sure to alert crew members so they are not caught on the wrong side.

The crew may have to pull the boom across or oversteer onto the new tack to bring the mainsail over. After the sails are across, in waves or fresh winds, the steerer heads off sharply for a moment, but not so far that the boat will jibe back. This sharp turn stops the boat's rolling and swing to the new windward side.

"Jibe-o." The sheets are eased as the steerer heads off to a run and then quickly trimmed as the stern swings through the wind's eye.

"Stand by to jibe." The crew checks sheets.

WIND

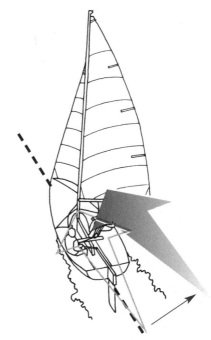

Sailing by the lee, or running with the wind slightly on the wrong side, happens when the boat does not complete a jibe or she heads off too far. There is a constant risk of an accidental, surprise jibe, so the crew must be extremely careful.

Because a jibing boom swings through a larger arc than a tacking boom, it moves very fast unless controlled by tension on the sheet. So jibe carefully and with clear and full communications. To give people time to duck, announce that the boom is coming across the cockpit. Otherwise, heads may be badly hurt. Every jibe must be intentional. In an accidental jibe (all-standing jibe), the crew is always surprised. There may well be injuries, rigging damage, a broach, or a capsize.

Sometimes the mainsail may stay full and not jibe even after the stern has swung through the eye of the wind. To avoid this, oversteer in the new direction by several degrees, sailing slightly higher than the desired new course, until the mainsail comes across under control. Then quickly head off on the new course.

In fresh winds and in waves, boats are very unstable as they come out of jibes. The momentum built up during the swing may roll the boat right over onto her side. A dinghy may capsize, while a keel boat may broach (head up out of control). Some cautious sailors may tack instead of jibe in heavy weather. Another solution is this: just as the boom swings over the centerline and the crew eases the sheet, head off sharply a few degrees for a moment. That helm reversal will stop the turn and bring the boat back upright. Then, once the boat feels steady, head up.

A Bad Tack or Jibe. Sometimes a tack or jibe will leave a boat at her most vulnerable, without any way on and with her beam to the wind. If she isn't moving, she can't be steered. A stopped boat is like a boxer staggering up from the mat. Neither is sturdy enough to withstand a blow, whether a right hook to the jaw or a strong, unexpected gust of wind. The sailor's equivalent of a boxer's low, square crouch is to gain speed until the boat has steerageway. As long as she's going fast enough to be steered, the boat and her rig will absorb much of the wind's blow by translating it into forward drive. But if she's sitting still, the punch will be converted into heeling force.

To gain steerageway in a stopped boat, put the helm amidships (so the rudder doesn't slow the boat) and trim both sails carefully and simultaneously. If you trim the mainsail too far, the boat will head up into the wind. If the jib is overtrimmed, she'll round off and jibe. A bad tack may leave a boat in the no-go zone (in irons, or lying head-to-wind). Stopped dead and with her bow in the wind's eye, she may gather stern way (start to move backward). If so, steer her stern by pushing the tiller in the opposite direction that you want it to aim (or the wheel in the same direction) while also pushing the main boom out to the opposite side. If you want to back down to starboard, push the tiller and boom to port. Once the bow has fallen off far enough to let wind fill the sails, trim the sails slowly until you get steerageway.

The stages of a jibe as demonstrated by these Lasers. Though it's safe in a dinghy, don't let the boom swing across uncontrolled in a larger boat.

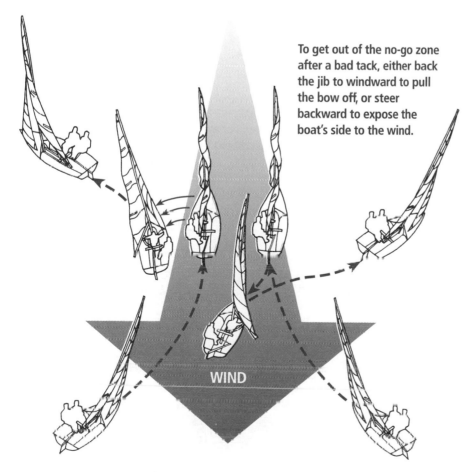

To get out of the no-go zone after a bad tack, either back the jib to windward to pull the bow off, or steer backward to expose the boat's side to the wind.

WIND

Stopping the Boat

"six," tack, turn back, and head off to a broad reach, aiming for a spot about two of your boat's lengths downwind of the target. When nearly downwind of it, head up into the wind, luff the sails, and stop the boat near the target. Six seconds may not be long enough, but in no case should you sail away for longer than 1 minute.

Approach the target in the water with just enough speed for steerageway. If the boat is making more than 2 knots, the person will not be able to hold on. Once alongside, stop the boat by luffing the sails or heaving-to, then throw a line to reach for the person or object.

Crew-overboard rescue will be covered in greater detail in chapter 7.

Just as important as tacking and jibing is the ability to stop the boat near an object in the water. You may need to rescue a crew member who has fallen overboard, recover a hat that has blown over the side, or pick up a mooring. Here are two tactics for stopping the boat after coming back to an object. Both are sailing tactics. You may come back under power but only with the greatest caution, as the propeller may suck in and injure the person.

If a person has gone overboard, your first reaction must be to throw buoyancy (for example, a cockpit cushion) to her or him. The second reaction is to appoint a spotter to point at the victim. The third is to shout encouragement. The fourth is to stay near the victim, and the fifth is to return as quick as you can for the rescue.

The quick-stop is a tight circling maneuver that keeps the boat very near the person or object in the water. You mustn't stray too far, since even small waves screen objects from view. Tack and do several very tight circles around the person. To keep the speed low, the sails must be trimmed tight. It's important that sheets not be touched as the boat tacks and jibes. Allowing the jib to back quickens the turn and slows the boat. Once near the target, head into the wind (the no-go zone) to stop the boat, and throw a line or reach to the person or object.

The reach-and-reach stop (also called the "figure-8" or "6-second stop") is a good technique in many conditions for slow or unmaneuverable boats and in heavy weather for many boats, because there is no jibe. When the person or object goes overboard, quickly alter course to a beam reach and count to six as you sail away, gathering speed. At

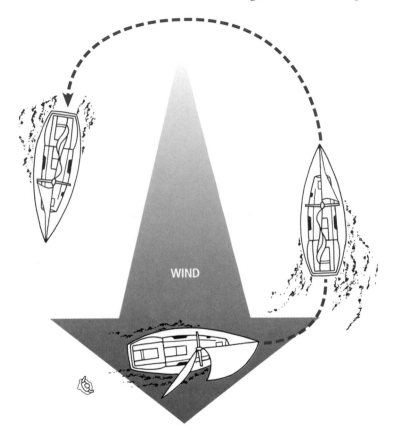

The quick-stop method of stopping the boat near an object or person in the water is a series of tight circles with the sails trimmed flat to slow the boat. Once you have trimmed the sails flat, do not adjust the sheets as the boat tacks and jibes.

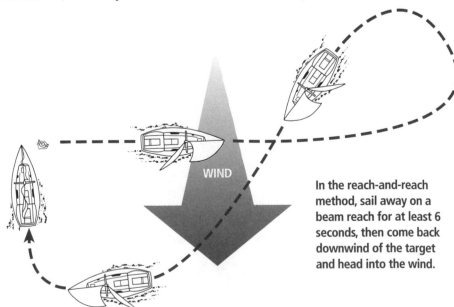

In the reach-and-reach method, sail away on a beam reach for at least 6 seconds, then come back downwind of the target and head into the wind.

Personal and Boat Preparations

Personal Gear. We've had an overview of how a boat shapes the wind and uses it to sail. Now let's get under way. The first step is to properly prepare yourself. Since sailing is a physical activity that requires some flexibility, do some stretches before going aboard. Be forehanded as you plan for the day. Take safety and comfort items suitable for the worst possible conditions. The sultry heat ashore may quickly be wiped away by the wind-chill factor (the effective temperature drops about 1° for every knot of apparent wind). And because the power of the wind increases with the cube of its velocity, the light tug on sheets in a morning calm will become a heavy load in the afternoon breeze. Most of the equipment in the list below will be described in greater detail later. Here we want only to list the essential gear that you should carry with you in a tote or small duffel bag.

A life jacket, or personal flotation device (PFD). Every boat in United States waters is required by law to have a Coast Guard–approved PFD for each person on board, but if you sail frequently, buy and carry your own. The Coast Guard approves two types. One is the non-inflatable PFD, which carries the buoyancy in somewhat bulky foam. The other PFD type is the inflatable, a compact packet or harness until it is inflated. When the wearer goes into the water, she triggers a carbon dioxide cartridge. (Automatic inflation systems are available but were not approved by the Coast Guard in 1999.) Inflatable PFDs cost somewhat more than non-inflatables.

The greater the buoyancy in a PFD, the higher the swimmer's head floats and less likely it is that she will float face-down if unconscious. Buoyancy is listed on sales material. The approved non-inflatable Type III life vest has 15.5 pounds of buoyancy, while the approved inflatable Type III has 22 pounds. Some inflatable and non-inflatable PFDs have

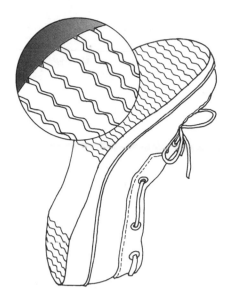

(Above) A non-skid shoe or boot sole has slits that spread to allow the rubber to grip the deck with a squeegee effect.

A USCG-approved non-inflatable Type III life vest provides 15.5 pounds of buoyancy. It may not lift an unconscious person's face clear of the water.

A Coast Guard–approved inflatable Type III PFD provides 22 pounds or more of buoyancy, and is compact enough to wear comfortably when not inflated.

35 pounds, which is ideal. (The average body requires about 8 pounds of buoyancy to float head-up, with the face just clearing the water in smooth conditions.)

Non-skid shoes. In order to prevent slipping and stubbed toes, sailors on boats big enough to walk on should wear boating shoes with non-skid soles. Some brands of general-purpose sneakers grip wet decks effectively. The soles should be white so they don't scuff the deck.

Sun protection includes a baseball cap or wide brimmed hat, high-quality sunglasses, plenty of sun lotion with an SPF (sun protection factor) of 15 or higher, a long-sleeved shirt with a collar, and long trousers. The glare off the water and sails will be intense.

Fluids. Dehydration is a major problem in the sun when you're exerting yourself (and simply holding on in a

Personal and Boat Preparations

moving boat is exercise). Take at least a liter of water for each 4-hour period.

Sailing gloves provide protection for hands that have not yet developed callouses.

Seasickness medication. There are many kinds, and most have side effects. Trial and error is the only reliable method of discovering which works best for you.

Weather protection is often neglected. No matter how hot and dry it is ashore, it probably will be cooler on board. Take at least a fleece jacket (or sweater) plus a windbreaker.

Foul-weather gear is waterproof outer clothing. Since water conducts heat 25 times faster than air, to be warm you must be dry. A water-resistant windbreaker keeps light spray off, but for rain and heavy spray you'll need a foul-weather gear jacket and, perhaps, trousers. Also known as oilskins or slickers, this gear should be yellow, orange, or red so a sailor who has fallen overboard will be quickly spotted in the water. A hat or hood will keep the water off your head and retain heat. Waterproof sea boots with nonskid soles will keep your feet and lower legs dry.

Boat Gear. Many boats are required by law to carry many types of safety equipment beside life jackets. They include fire extinguishers, engine vents, visual and sound distress signals (flares and whistles), and navigation lights for night sailing. Experience has produced good lists of other equipment:

For navigating: binoculars, an accurate compass, local charts, and (in saltwater areas) a tide table.

For safety: the required number of

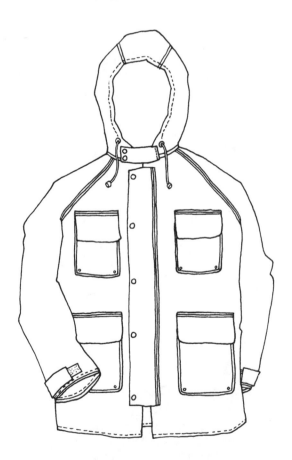
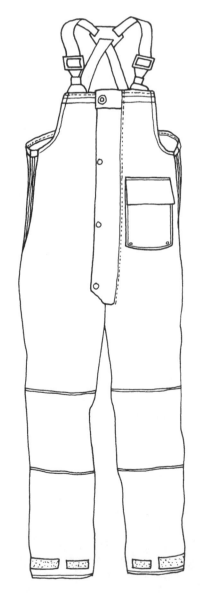

Foul-weather gear comes in many styles. The basic element is the top, with or without a hood. Chest-high bib trousers provide overlapping coverage around the vital organs.

PFDs in good condition, a first-aid kit, a first-aid manual, and at least one bilge pump and bucket.

Miscellaneous: a paddle and at least one waterproof flashlight with spare batteries.

Tools: pliers, screwdrivers that match the heads of screws on board, a crescent wrench, a hammer, a sharp knife, light lubricating oil, waterproof grease, a roll of waterproof tape, and spare shackles, blocks, and cotter pins.

For docking and anchoring: an anchor and at least 100 feet of 3/8-inch (or larger) nylon anchor rode (line), three fenders, and four 20-foot (or longer) lengths of 3/8-inch (or larger) nylon line for docking, towing, and emergencies.

Climbing Aboard. For some people, getting aboard the boat may be the most difficult part of the day. Even when climbing aboard from a marina pier you must make a long step that, if not taken carefully, could turn into an awkward lunge. The best way to get aboard a large, high-sided boat is first to pass up all your baggage and then, with both hands free, put your dignity aside and clamber up as expeditiously as possible on your knees. Plant yourself firmly on the deck before trying to stand, otherwise you may topple backward.

Going aboard a dinghy, rowboat, or other small boat is a double problem: not only must you step down into it from a pier or another boat, but when you get into the dinghy there is little room or stability. The trick here is to keep your weight low, to balance the weight of other people or objects, and to stand and sit on the centerline, the imaginary line running from the middle of the stern to the bow. When stepping into a dinghy, your first foot must immediately go onto the centerline. Stepping onto a rail or on either side of the centerline may skid the dinghy out from under you. Once the first foot is on the centerline, slide down into the boat and sit down as close to the centerline as you can. Don't let go of the pier or other boat unless you're absolutely sure of your footing.

Be equally careful when climbing out of a dinghy. Remember that when someone gets out of one end, the other end will drop suddenly. The best way to unload a dinghy so she stays in trim is first to take cargo or crew from the bow, then from the stern, which (because it's wider) is more buoyant than the bow. Dinghies swamp more quickly when bow-down than when bow-up. Finally, unload the middle. Never make a sudden or unconsidered move in a dinghy.

While a dinghy is being loaded or unloaded, her painter (bow line) should by held by somebody or cleated on the float or the bigger boat. Many dinghy painters are made of polypropylene rope which, because it is buoyant, will not sink and foul propellers. Unfortunately, this rope is also slippery and therefore hard to grip, tie, or cleat securely. Double-check after you secure it. Do not wrap a polypropylene line that is under a load around your wrist or hand because it may cut deeply.

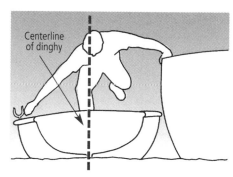

A sailor successfully boards a dinghy from a float, crouching low and stepping into the middle.

Getting Going

Getting under way from a mooring, trailer, or dock (the body of water where a boat lies next to a float or pier) can be either a snap or a disaster, depending on the wind and sea conditions and the crew's skill. Often it's somewhere in between: a frantic, loud panic. It need not be that way if you have practiced and give clear instructions.

Leaving a Mooring. A mooring is connected to an anchor or heavy weight (for example, an engine block) set permanently in the harbor bottom. A buoy holds up the rode (anchor line) which is also connected to a short line called the mooring pendant (pronounced "pennant"), which often has its own small buoy. The pendant connects the boat to the rode.

The crew goes out to their moored boat in a rowboat, a launch, or a shore boat and climbs aboard. They stow their gear, pump out the bilge, rig the sails, and get ready to cast off and go sailing. If they plan to get under way under power, they run the engine blower for at least 4 minutes to vent all fumes from the engine compartment and bilge (a step that is not necessary with diesel engines or with outboard engines). The engine is started. A crewmember looks over the stern at the exhaust pipe to check that cooling water is sputtering out with the exhaust, and the instruments are studied for a few moments to be sure that oil and water pressures are right. The sailors look overboard on both sides and astern for loose lines, which might foul the propeller.

A crewmember goes onto the foredeck to cast off the mooring. If there is a hard pull on the pendant at the bow cleat, the steerer puts the engine into forward gear for a moment so the boat

To avoid sailing around the mooring, hoist the sails only when the bow is directly into the wind, and set the jib last.

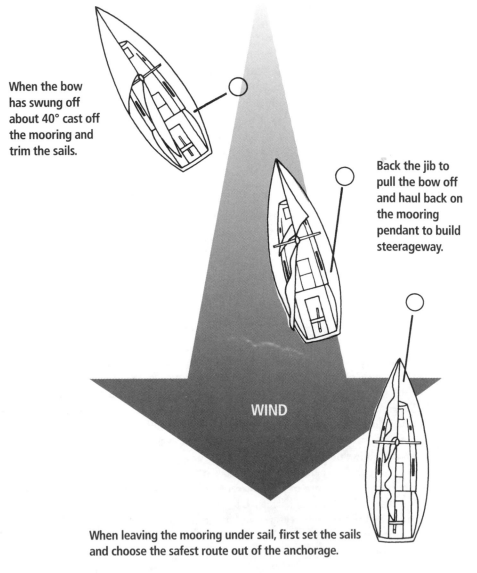

When the bow has swung off about 40° cast off the mooring and trim the sails.

Back the jib to pull the bow off and haul back on the mooring pendant to build steerageway.

When leaving the mooring under sail, first set the sails and choose the safest route out of the anchorage.

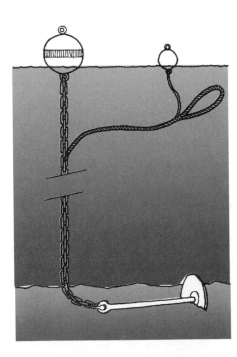

A mooring is a permanently set anchor whose rode (anchor line) is buoyed. The pendant, which is cleated on deck, has its own small buoy.

moves ahead a couple of feet to relieve the strain. The crew lifts the pendant off the cleat and at the steerer's command drops the pendant over the bow with a shout, "She's cast off!" The steerer slowly backs the boat clear of the buoy and pendant, then puts the engine in slow forward gear to power out of the mooring area, keeping the stern and propeller clear of the mooring.

If there's a rowboat or dinghy, it can either be left behind tied to the mooring buoy or towed behind using the painter (bow line). At first the painter should be kept short so the bow almost touches the yacht's stern. That way the dinghy won't tangle with other boats. When the boat is clear of the mooring area, buoys, and other boats, the speed may be increased and the painter let out until the dinghy rides on the crest of the first or second stern wave between 6 and 20 feet astern, depending on the speed.

Leaving a mooring under sail alone is an exercise in seamanship that teaches plenty about boat handling and gives great satisfaction. (If the mooring area is crowded with boats or you feel uncomfortable, use the engine.) The crew goes through almost all the same steps. They will pay special attention to stowing (putting away) personal gear, food, and equipment, since heeling will cause anything that isn't secured to fly around the cabin and cockpit.

Then they bend on the sails (as we described in chapter 1) and hoist them "after sail first," starting with the mizzen if she's a yawl or ketch, then raising the mainsail, and finally unrolling or hoisting the jib just as the crew is about to drop the mooring. The sails should be raised only when the bow is in the eye of the wind. The reason for the "after sail first" rule is that sails toward the stern tend to twist a boat into the wind, while the jib tends to pull her bow off and start the boat sailing around the mooring before she is ready to cast off. With the jib set, there will be a heavy strain on the pendant while the crew tries to cast off. Worse, if the boat starts sailing around the mooring, she may careen into nearby boats.

Hoisting a sail is simple. Remove any sail covers (which keep sails clean and protect them from the destructive rays of the sun), then untie the sail ties (stops, gaskets) that tie the sail to the boom.

Inspect all fittings to be sure that there are no twists and that shackles are securely shut. Make sure the battens are inserted. Tighten the outhaul until there are strain lines along the foot of the mainsail. Attach the halyards and look aloft to make sure they don't foul (wrap around) the spreaders or any other fittings. Uncleat the main sheet and the boom vang, so the boom can rise, but cleat the traveler control lines so the sliding part, called the car, won't bang back and forth. Now pull the halyard with a strong, steady motion while looking aloft to check for tangles. If the halyard is wire with a rope tail (end), wrap the wire around the winch and winch the sail up all the way. Now is the time to pull on sweaters or foul-weather gear if there is any chance that you'll need them.

The boat should be hanging off the mooring head to wind (with her bow pointed into the wind), so the sail will go up easily without filling on either side. Sometimes, however, the tidal or river current may not run parallel to the wind direction and the boat may lie with her bow into the current and her side to the wind. If this happens, the sail will fill on one side, making hoisting difficult and creating a forward force exactly when you don't want to be making way. If this occurs, stop hoisting and steer her into the wind. When the sail luffs completely, quickly pull it all the way up. Its resistance should now keep the boat head-to-wind.

Hoist the after sails first so the bow is into the wind until you're ready to get under way. However, don't leave sails luffing for long since flapping damages the sail cloth. Watch out for the swinging boom.

Cleat the halyard and coil it carefully (as described in chapter 5) so there are no loose lines lying about. (Always neaten up immediately after doing a job. You may not have time later.) If the sail has a boom that is held up by a topping lift, let it out far enough so you can trim the sail tight once you get under way. Now if you're ready to cast off, unroll the jib by trimming what will become the leeward sheet. If the jib is not on a roller-furler, hoist the jib looking aloft, being careful that the sheets are loose so it doesn't fill.

The sails are now set and the skipper should have a plan for sailing out of the mooring area. If the clearest path is to port, he says, "We'll go off on starboard tack. Cast off to starboard." It is important that the crew verbally acknowledge this order so there is no misunderstanding. One crew member goes onto the foredeck and uncleats the mooring pendant. On a big boat or in a fresh wind it may be pulling hard, so he might have to pull on it to gain the few inches needed to lift it off the cleat. When the pendant is uncleated, the crew member snubs it (takes a turn) around the bow cleat to decrease the strain.

The next step can be tricky. The mooring pendant cannot be let go until the boat is on a tack with some steerageway on. If the desired course is to port, she must be got onto starboard tack; if to starboard, onto port tack. In fresh winds the boat may be sailing around the mooring anyway, so the crew waits to cast off the mooring when the boat is on the desired tack. But in light to moderate winds she'll need some help. Back the jib, trimming it to windward, while easing the main sheet most of the way out. The backed jib will pull the bow off to leeward. A small boat may be sculled off a mooring.

As the bow swings off, the crew member on the foredeck quickly frees the mooring pendant from the cleat and the chock (a metal slot on the bow), and

Getting Going

and trailer go back up the ramp. Sailboats launched from a trailer are usually paddled or sculled to a nearby pier before sails are hoisted. Small boats, however, may be sailed off a beach in light winds, but be careful not to drop the rudder or centerboard until the water is deep enough. In an onshore wind (blowing from the water to the land) it may be hard to get away from the land.

Leaving a Pier, Wharf, or Float. A boat can be tied to a pier (a narrow platform sticking out from the land), a wharf (a portion of the shore), or a float (a platform on the water alongside a pier or wharf). Often they are called "docks," although technically the dock is just the body of water that a boat sits in when

pulls it aft along the windward side. Except with large boats, this should shoot her forward to provide a bit of steerageway. As soon as the bow has fallen off about 40°, trim the jib sheet on the leeward side and trim the main sheet. With her sails full, the boat will accelerate.

The skipper should closely supervise all these steps and be ready to stop the process if something goes wrong. For example, if the route out of the mooring area is blocked by other boats, tie up and wait until the way is clear.

Launching from a Trailer. Getting a dinghy or other small boat into the water from a trailer is not difficult in normal, moderate conditions. If you're using a hoist, just make sure that the boat's weight is within its capacity. Push the trailer directly under the hook and have competent people handling the lift-drop controls and the guy ropes. Check carefully for overhead electrical wires, which can be lethal if the mast touches them.

If you're launching on a ramp, rig the boat, bend on the sails, and install the outboard engine (if there is one). Take off the tie-downs but leave the bow restraint secured. Place aboard any equipment that you'll need after the launch. Then slowly back the trailer down the ramp as someone guides the driver with hand signals. Many ramps are built at angles steep enough so that a shallow boat like a dinghy floats off before the car's wheels touch the water. Since salt water can damage the car, a tongue extender may be added to push the trailer several feet farther away.

Once the boat becomes buoyant, unhook the bow restraint, push her off the trailer, and restrain her while the car

When rigging or launching a boat onshore, be very careful to stay away from overhead power lines. If the mast hits or gets near a line, electrical shock can kill or injure sailors working below. A tongue extender on the trailer allows launching with dry car wheels.

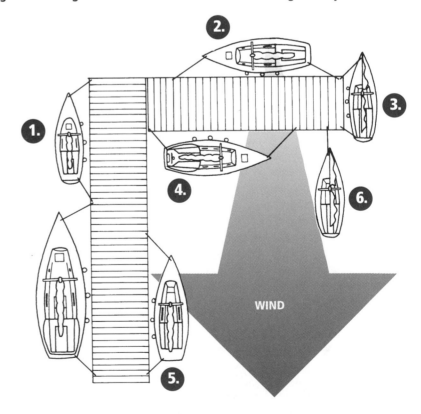

The best way to dock is to lie with the bow into the wind (1, 3, and 5) or on the leeward side of the float (4). On the windward side (2) the boat will be blown onto the float. You can also hang off the float on a bow line (6).

she's tied up. "Docking" is tying up. Given a choice, you want to dock on the leeward side so the wind blows the boat away from the pier, wharf, or float. The wind pressing a boat on the windward side may cause damage and make undocking difficult.

Leaving a dock (undocking) when the boat is on the leeward side of the float is relatively simple. Cast off the lines and head out. But leaving the windward side takes some planning and skill, especially in a strong wind. A small boat should be walked to the edge of the float and shoved off before the sails are hoisted. Larger boats may be taken off under power using fenders to protect her side. Or an anchor may be set upwind and the boat pulled up to the anchor so she hangs head-to-wind. Then sails may be hoisted, the anchor retrieved, and the boat sailed away. Get far away from the pier or float as quickly as you can.

Docking Lines and Fenders. Almost all boats spend some time docked at a float or pier. Boats smaller than 20 feet

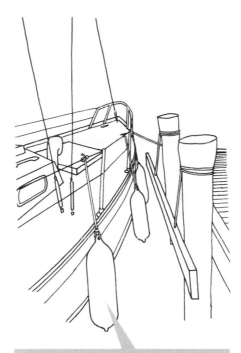

Rubber fenders protect the topsides. A fender board (above) provides a flat bearing surface if the float's side has supporting pilings.

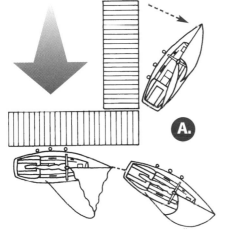

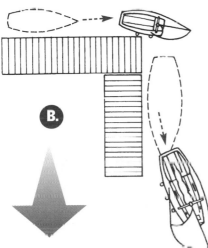

When sailing out of a dock the most important priority is to get away from the float as soon as possible. (A) Use the jib to pull the bow away. (B) Pull the boat along the windward side until her bow is clear, then set the jib. (C) You may have to set an anchor and pull the boat away from the windward side.

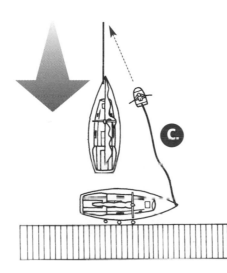

can be secured temporarily with only a bow line running forward and a stern line aft at 45° with moderate tension. The spread restrains the boat from sliding back and forth against the dock. But more docking lines usually are needed (as we'll explain later).

Whenever a boat is lying at (tied to) a float or pier, her topsides should be protected by at least three fenders, the larger the better. These are rubber bumpers hung by lines between the boat's sides and the float. The lines may be tied to a fitting on deck or to the lifelines. Some floats may have canvas-covered pads, but these pads usually are abrasive. An excellent way to spread the load along the fenders is to hang a plank of wood called a fender board horizontally between two fenders and the pier or float. For tying up in dirty water, removable washable covers for fenders may be rigged.

Docking lines should be cut from nylon rope, which provide the stretch that absorbs shocks. (Dacron, used in sheets, stretches very little.) These lines should be sturdy — no smaller than 3/8-inch diameter for 20-footers, and up to 7/8-inch diameter for 50-footers and above. Docking lines should be at least 20 feet long. There are no shackles on a proper docking line, for it's secured to cleats and eyes with splices, wraps, or knots (see chapter 5). Usually, docking lines are laid out so the crew can adjust them without having to go ashore. One way is to dead-end (secure one end) to a cleat or bollard (post) on the float and cleat the line on board with extra line. Another way is to double the line (turn it back) around a cleat or bollard and secure both ends on board. The advantage of doubling is that the line may be cast off without the crew's having to go ashore. If the boat is to be left at the dock for a while, the lines should be arranged so they can be adjusted on the float without anyone having to go aboard.

To tie a boat up properly you need the bow and stern lines plus two spring lines. Springs are intermediate lines laid out in an X shaped pattern to hold the boat against fore and aft surges. The forward spring line runs forward and keeps the boat from surging aft. It is secured on

Getting Going

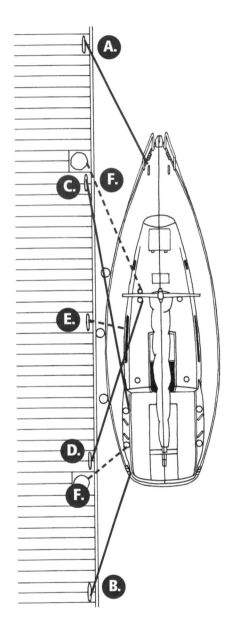

The docking lines are the bow line (A), stern line (B), forward spring (C), after spring (D), and optional breast line (E). In strong winds they should be doubled-up with back-up lines, and additional springs (F) should be rigged. By doubling a docking line you can cast it off from the boat and pull it back on board without assistance on the float. Secure a docking line to a cleat, winch, or other sturdy fitting.

the after part of the boat on a cleat or other sturdy fitting, such as a winch. From that point it runs forward to a cleat or bollard on the float or pier next to the forward part of the boat. The after spring line, which stops forward surges, runs aft from a point on deck near where the forward spring is cleated on the float, to a point on the float near where the forward spring is cleated on deck.

When the springs are equally tensioned, the centerline of the boat will be parallel to the float. If the after spring is tighter, the bow will be held in closer than the stern. If the forward spring is tighter, the stern will pull into the float. When properly rigged, spring lines take almost all the boat's load at the float and the bow and stern lines just restrain the ends from swinging out. In rough weather, additional bow and stern springs should be rigged from different points to reduce the surge back and forth along the float.

An additional docking line that is helpful temporarily is the breast line, which passes from the boat to an attachment point on the float directly alongside. A breast line only provides point-to-point attachment to keep the boat's middle in one position near the float, making it easier for crew to go aboard and ashore.

The spring line is a handy though often overlooked tool for leaving the dock. When used properly, it aims the bow out without having to put a crew member ashore to shove. The principle is that as a boat pulls against a line secured to one end of her hull, the other end swings out. This means that moving astern with the forward spring rigged (and the after spring released) forces the stern into the float and the bow away from it. The farther aft the spring is attached, the closer the stern will be pulled in. To swing the stern out, on the other hand, move forward against the after spring. Once the bow or stern is aimed away from the float, the spring line is cast off and the boat moves out.

Leaving a Slip. Leaving a marina slip is a bit like departing a float, except that a slip has three sides. Because boats usually enter slips bow-first, they must back out. Since reverse gear may be weak, a crew member or two may have to stand on the float and push. Boats without engines will have to be pushed out.

Backing out under power: (1) cast off the stern and bow lines; (2) double the after spring, cast off the forward spring, and power forward slowly; (3) when the stem has swung out, back away from the float.

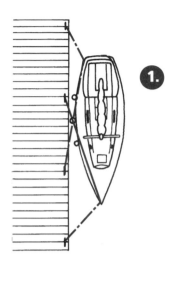

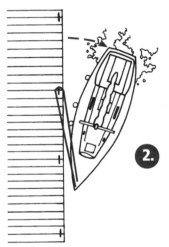

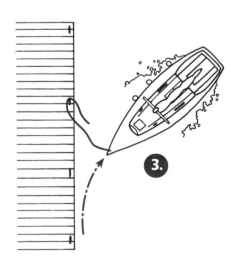

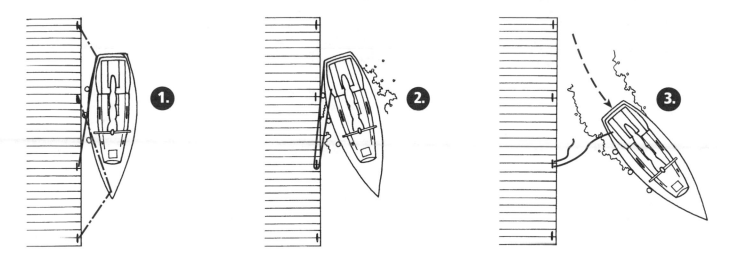

Powering away forward: (1) cast off the stern and bow lines; (2) double the forward spring, cast off the after spring, and back down; (3) when the bow has swung out, shift to forward gear.

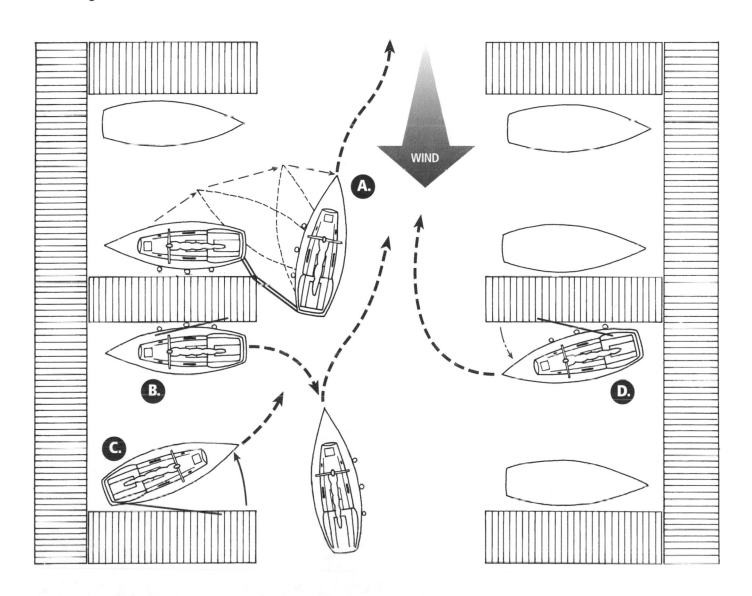

When backing out of a slip, either leave the stern line attached until you're ready to head out into the harbor (A), or go forward against the after spring to swing her stern out before backing down (B). Leaving forward, spring out the bow (C and D).

Boat-Handling Drills

While you're out there enjoying the pleasure of the wind on your face and the feel of control, take time to practice basic skills, like heaving to, with some exercises that will stretch your sailing ability.

Some Safety Tips: First, practice in open water. These drills should be done well away from other boats and from shipping channels and other places where boats are likely to gather.

Keep a lookout, not only for other boats but for rocks, buoys, and land that you may drift down on.

Control the boom. When the mainsail luffs or you change tacks, the boom will swing across at the level of your and your crew's heads. It is a lethal weapon. Control the boom by rigging and using a preventer. This is a line from the boom down and forward to the deck on either side. When the leeward preventer is tensioned, it prevents the boom from swinging across.

Heaving-To. Bringing the boat almost to a stop under sail and leaving her to sail herself is an educational seamanship challenge and, better still, a wonderfully practical tactic. Although often associated with riding out storms, it is used for any number of reasons — to position the boat for a rescue, to ease the motion on a rough passage, to await a change in tide, whatever. The boat is not stopped completely but keeps about 1 knot of gentle steerageway, which absorbs the blows of sea and wind that might smash her if she were lying ahull with no speed on.

There are two ways to heave-to. The traditional way, used usually in strong winds but also effective in other conditions, is to back the jib when the boat is close-hauled or close reaching (or, alternatively, tack without releasing the windward jib sheet). Then adjust the main sheet so the boat jogs along at about 1 knot, steering herself. This does not work well with an overlapping jib, so you may have to roll up the jib partway.

A newer way, which we call the Rod-stop because it was developed by Roderick Stephens, works best in light to fresh winds. On a beam reach, pull the boom all the way forward to the leeward shrouds with a preventer and luff or roll up the jib. Flatten the mainsail with the sail controls. With the mainsail alternately filling on its windward and leeward sides, the boat will make slow, gradual swoops to windward and leeward, usually without a steerer at the helm.

Exercises. Start these exercises in light and medium wind (5–10 knots)

and smooth water, and move up the scale as you gain confidence. Some of these drills may be done under power as well as under sail.

Weaving. On a beam reach (with the wind coming directly across the side), head toward a target — for example, a house on shore or a buoy. Trim the sails so they are just filled (if you ease them a little they will luff) and so the tiller or steering wheel tugs slightly. Then start a series of slow weaves, one every half-minute, to either side of the target. Head off to a broad reach, up to a close reach, and back to a broad reach. Trim the sails properly as you change course. Do not shove the tiller or wheel too hard. Develop a feel for how much pressure is needed to make a gradual turn, and how to avoid swinging past the new course.

Slalom. Weave among some buoys so you have to tack and jibe.

Stopping and Starting. Sailing on a

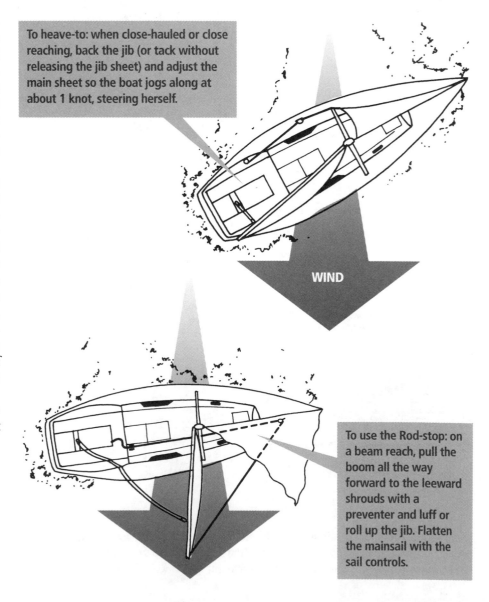

To heave-to: when close-hauled or close reaching, back the jib (or tack without releasing the jib sheet) and adjust the main sheet so the boat jogs along at about 1 knot, steering herself.

WIND

To use the Rod-stop: on a beam reach, pull the boom all the way forward to the leeward shrouds with a preventer and luff or roll up the jib. Flatten the mainsail with the sail controls.

beam reach, close reach, or beat, stop the boat completely by heading into the wind or letting the sails out all the way. When the boat is stopped (as a gauge, use a landmark or spit in the water), experiment with different ways to get going again. (Hint: trim the jib first, but not too far.)

Balance the Jib Upwind. Head into the wind so the jib is luffing directly over the centerline. Keep the jib luffing there until the boat almost stops, then back the jib (trim it to one side) and allow it to fill so the wind pushes the bow off to the other side.

Balance the Jib Downwind. Sail on a run, with the wind astern, keeping the jib luffing directly over the centerline. The challenge is to determine when the boat is running exactly downwind or sailing by the lee. Keep your head down in case the boat jibes. Feel the wind on the back of your head and neck.

Feathering and Forereaching. This drill develops the ability to slow and speed up the boat. Sail on a beat (close-hauled). Feather the boat into the wind by gently heading up a few degrees until the sails luff a little. Notice how the boat slows, heels less, and (in waves) stops rolling. Head off a couple of degrees and observe how she speeds up. Feathering is to sailing what edging the skis is to skiing — a small but effective check on speed. Head up a few degrees beyond feathering to a forereach (head reach), with the sails luffing about half way while the boat keeps moving. Note how different the boat feels when the sails luff and she slows. Experiment with different angles and sail trim. The goal is to keep the boat moving just fast enough so you have steerageway.

Estimate Your Speed and Distance Run. Develop a feel for how fast your boat is going and her distance run (how far she sails). You will be surprised at how much water you cover even at moderate speeds, and how quickly other objects disappear astern. Other boats and low land fall over the horizon astern at 4–5 miles, and a person in the water may be invisible in waves at only 100 feet. A helpful rule of thumb is that a boat covers approximately 33 yards a minute for every knot of speed. This means that even at a slow speed an object in the water may be out of sight from your boat within one minute.

Rules of the Road

The mariner's Navigation Rules, usually called the rules of the road, guide vessels when collisions threaten. We will examine them in much more detail in chapter 8. Here we will summarize them.

The basic rule: vessels that are more maneuverable must change course to avoid boats that are less maneuverable. Ships in a narrow channel are less maneuverable than a sailing boat, so she must give way to them. (Under the rules, the vessel that must alter course is the give-way vessel; the other is the stand-on vessel.) Alter course as early and as abruptly as possible so the other boat understands your intentions. Once you have changed to a new course, stay on it until the other boat is well clear.

When a sailboat is near another sailboat, the one on port tack must give way to the one on starboard tack. If they are on the same tack, the one to windward of (upwind of) the other is the boat that must give way.

When a boat under sail is near a boat under power, the boat under power usually must give way. A sailboat under sail and with her engine in gear is considered to be under power. The main exception is if the channel is narrow and the powerboat is unmaneuverable.

When one boat is overtaking another from astern, no matter what type either boat is, the overtaking boat must give way.

When boats under power are meeting bow to bow, they should turn to starboard so they pass port side to port side.

Proceed sensibly and defensively. Even if the rules allow you the right of way (the right to continue on your course), do not force it on other vessels.

Boat Speed and Distance Run

Boat Speed	Comment	Distance Run
1 knot	bare steerageway in small boats	100 yds./3 min.
3 knots	bare steerageway in large boats	300 yds./3 min., 1 mi./20 min.
5 knots	bow wave	500 yds./3 min., 1 mi./12 min.
7 knots	large bow wave; high speed (except in multihulls)	700 yds./3 min., 1 mi./9 min.
9 knots	very high speed, often barely in control	900 yds./3 min., 1 mi./7 min.

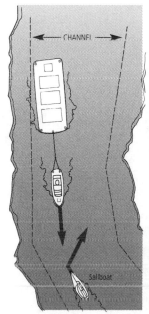

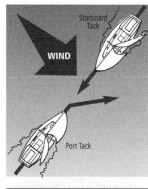

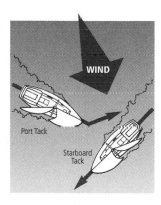

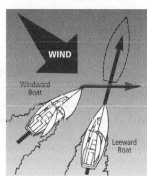

Under the Navigation Rules (rules of the road), a sailboat must avoid a large, unmaneuverable powerboat (left), a sailboat on port tack must avoid one on starboard tack (two above), and a sailboat to windward must avoid one to leeward (below).

Coming Back In

Picking Up a Mooring. Picking up a mooring under power is relatively simple. From dead downwind of the buoy, head slowly toward the mooring. The wind will help slow you. Practice with a stopping drill will tell you how much distance you must run. A crew member goes forward and with hand signals tells the steerer where the buoy is as the boat approaches it, pointing at it and holding her hand up in the air to indicate "stop." The steerer puts the engine into neutral or slow reverse gear to hold the bow right over the mooring as the crew reaches down to retrieve the buoy, using a boat hook if necessary. When the buoy and pendant are on deck, the engine should be in neutral. When the line is cleated, the crew shouts, "Made!" (meaning "secure"), and the steerer may turn off the engine.

The worst thing that can happen during this maneuver is for the boat to run over the buoy and tangle it or the mooring line in her propeller. That's why the steerer must know the buoy's exact location as he approaches it, and why the boat should be moving as slowly as possible while retaining steerageway.

Picking up a mooring under sail is more complicated. It should be done under mainsail alone, unless the jib is small. Large overlapping genoa jibs can take charge of a boat extremely quickly, and may also obstruct the steerer's vision. A genoa should be doused and securely tied down or bagged before reaching the mooring area.

Before proceeding, overhaul the halyards and main sheet, shaking the kinks out of them so they'll run out easily through blocks and fairleads. The boat approaches the buoy from downwind, her sails luffing as her momentum carries her. This is called shooting into the wind, and the distance that a boat shoots, or carries her way, depends on her weight (heavier boats carry their way longer than light ones) and the conditions. A boat will shoot longer in flat water and a calm than in waves and a fresh wind. There is no formula here; practice helps. If you think you're going too fast, swing the helm back and forth several times. The resistance of the rudder will brake the momentum.

You may also stop the boat right at the buoy by backing the mainsail: push the main boom out until the wind catches on the wrong side; the boat will stop and begin to back down. This method of stopping is not safe in fresh winds or with large sails, as booms can be extremely dangerous weapons. The boat must be stopped and headed dead into the wind

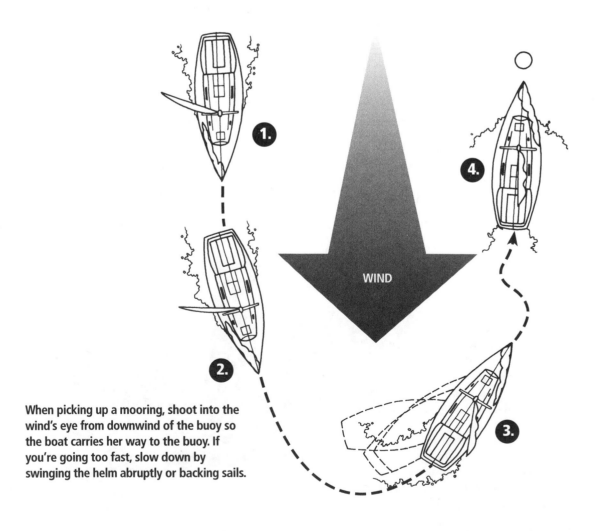

When picking up a mooring, shoot into the wind's eye from downwind of the buoy so the boat carries her way to the buoy. If you're going too fast, slow down by swinging the helm abruptly or backing sails.

WIND

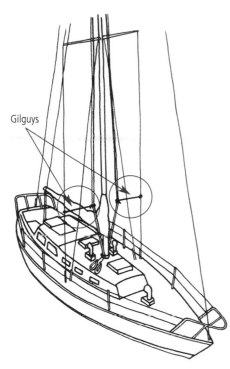

Gilguys

Tie off the halyards with gilguys to keep them from clanking against the mast.

when the buoy is brought on deck and the pendant is cleated. Otherwise she'll charge off on one tack or the other as the foredeck crew struggles to hold the mooring. If the foredeck crew is having trouble, cast off and try again.

As soon as the line is cleated and the crew has shouted "Made!," quickly lower the sails, forward sail first. The crew working the halyards should let them run out through their hands until the sail is lowered; otherwise, the halyard is likely to kink.

Neaten up by furling or bagging the sails, replacing sail covers, coiling sheets, and double-checking the mooring. Using light lines or lengths of shock cord led from the shrouds (called gilguys), tie the halyards as far away from the mast as possible so they don't slap and annoy neighbors, either ashore or in nearby boats. Secure the tiller or wheel so the rudder is centered under the hull, and turn off any electrical switches, fuel valves, and sea cocks (valves fitted in

pipes leading overboard). Lock up. Then you can go ashore.

Returning to the Launching Ramp. The major mistakes when sailing back to the launching ramp are forgetting to retract the centerboard and rudder (or outboard engine) when the water gets shallow, and then trying to stop the boat by sailing onto the beach. Damage can be avoided by dousing the sails relatively far offshore (or letting them luff in light winds), pulling up the appendages, and walking ashore, pulling the boat. While one crew member holds her in a couple of feet of water, another can be getting the car and trailer. Of course, there's no great risk in nudging the bow onto a sandy beach after you've inspected it for rocks. When the trailer has been backed down into the water, pull on the boat, secure the bow, and drive up the ramp. Hose off the trailer and boat if they've been exposed to salt water.

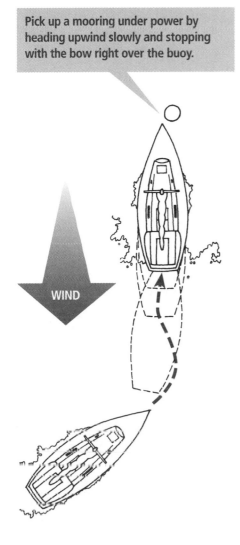

Pick up a mooring under power by heading upwind slowly and stopping with the bow right over the buoy.

WIND

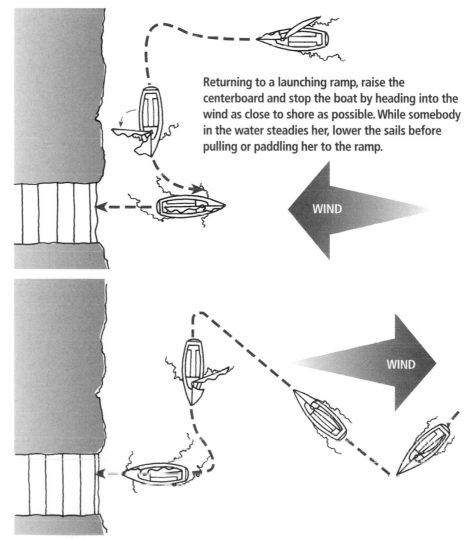

Returning to a launching ramp, raise the centerboard and stop the boat by heading into the wind as close to shore as possible. While somebody in the water steadies her, lower the sails before pulling or paddling her to the ramp.

WIND

WIND

Coming Back In

Docking. Docking is the departure from a float or pier played in reverse. Approach the docking area slowly, but with steerageway. Come in at as shallow an angle as possible, with the sides about parallel to the float. The best way to stop is to approach slowly and have spring lines ready to throw over cleats on the float to stop the boat. Remember that reverse gear is inefficient in most sailing auxiliaries, so don't rely on it to stop you on a dime. Neither should you anticipate that your crew or any bystanders on the float will be able to stop the boat by pushing on the shrouds and deck fittings. Do not underestimate the force of a moving boat. Don't put hands or feet between the boat and the float. When fending-off (pushing off), put a fender between the hull and the float.

Prior to approaching the float or pier, the fenders should be tied on and dropped over the side at the right level, and the bow, stern, and spring lines should be laid out ready to use on deck. The after spring line — the line that will stop the boat better than any of the other three — should already be cleated with several feet ready to hand to someone on the float or to drop over a cleat, bollard, or piling.

The best and simplest way to tie up is to use the after spring line and the stern line. If someone on the dock is willing to assist you, he may be inclined to take your bow line. But tell him that you want him to take your after spring and stern lines. As the boat snuggles up

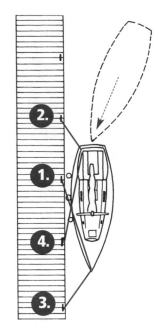

Docking, first secure the after spring line to stop her (1), then the stern line to restrain the stern (2), then the bow line (3) and forward spring (4).

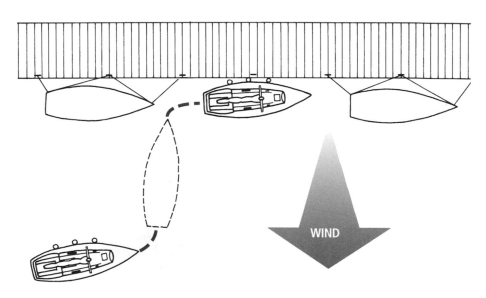

Approaching in an offshore wind, come in head to wind to slow her, then turn sharply.

WIND

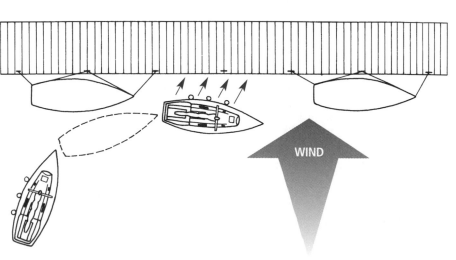

In an onshore wind, stop just to windward of the dock to allow the boat to be blown down to the float with the sails doused.

WIND

against the float, pass over these lines with instructions to secure the spring first in order to stop the boat. If your boat has cockpit winches, lead these lines to them so you can easily adjust tension. As the boat pulls against the line, her bow will swing in and her stern out, so rig the stern line to restrain the stern from swinging out. Next come the bow line and the forward spring. Each docking line should have a fair lead from its cleat on deck to the float — meaning that the line should run easily and not chafe (rub abrasively) against a sharp object. Adjust the springs until the boat lies with the centerline about parallel to the edge of the float (although on some boats one end may have to be pulled closer than the other to make it easier to step ashore). Then take tension on the bow and stern lines to keep the ends from swinging.

Sailing into a dock should not be tried with boats larger than about 30 feet unless you're absolutely confident of your ability to stop her where you want. This may be impossible if the approach is a run or a reach. Even under power you can use the wind to help your docking maneuver. A crosswind onto the float will push you into the dock with sails doused (lowered).

Entering a Slip. Returning to a marina slip is easier than leaving it because the return usually is bow-first. Except in a dinghy or other small boat, enter under power or by carrying your way (sustaining your momentum) after dousing the sails. Use the after spring line to stop her just as you would when docking.

Returning to a slip, use minimum steerageway and, if necessary, tie up to the end of the float before spinning around into the slip (A and D). Use appropriate docking lines to stop her and keep ends from swinging out. As when docking all boats larger than centerboarders and small keel boats, resist the temptation to stop her and fend off floats and other boats with your legs and arms. Let the docking lines do the work.

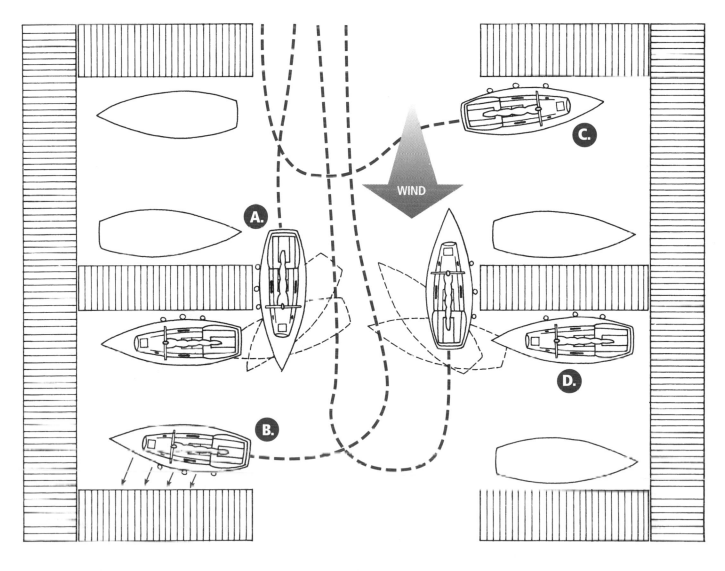

Maneuvering Under Power

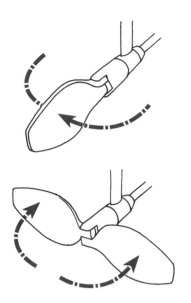

If your boat has an engine, you should be aware of the special handling characteristics that apply under power.

The Propeller. A propeller is sometimes called a screw because it seems literally to screw itself through the water, pulling the boat along with it. Yet its main force is forward thrust as its blades grab the water and redirect it aft. Depending on the weight of the boat and the horsepower of the engine, propellers vary in blade number, blade diameter, and pitch (blade angle). Pitch is measured in inches — the distance the propeller would travel forward during a single revolution. Outboards and other light, fast boats with engines that turn at high revolutions per minute tend to have small-diameter two- or three-bladed propellers with high pitch. On the other hand, low-RPM, heavy, slow boats like the typical sailing auxiliary usually have large-diameter, low-pitch propellers with two or three blades. In order to reduce resistance when the boat is under sail, many auxiliaries are equipped with special propellers that automatically fold up or that feather, edge first, when the engine is off.

Propellers work most efficiently when entirely submerged. Air bubbles

A propeller that folds when not in use reduces water resistance. Some propellers automatically feather for the same reason.

pulled down from the surface may cause water to detach from the blades. Called cavitation, this will decrease the propeller's thrust. Make sure that the stern is sitting low enough so the propeller is several inches under water.

Propeller Thrust. A clockwise-turning right-handed propeller slightly pushes (walks) the stern to starboard; a counterclockwise-turning left-handed prop pushes it to port. In reverse gear, this side force is to the opposite side and is usually more noticeable than in forward gear, which is why an auxiliary is hard to steer backward. You can always use walking to help pull the boat into the pier when docking. For example, if your boat has a right-handed propeller, give a quick burst with the throttle in reverse as you slide into the dock to push the stern to port. Practice helps.

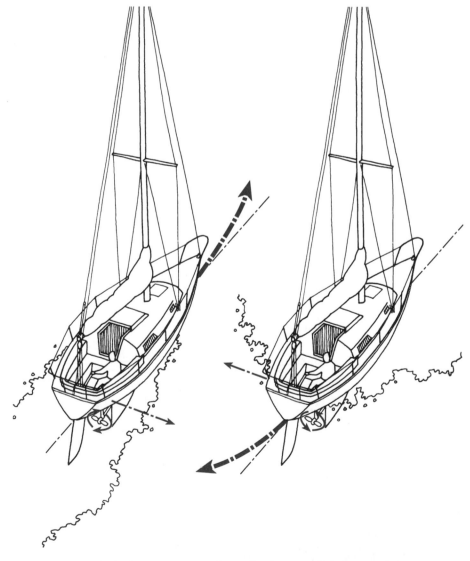

A right-handed, clockwise-turning propeller walks the stem slightly to starboard in forward gear (left) but walks it to port more noticeably in reverse (right).

Tips for Better Boat Handling

Once under way, you'll be facing plenty of challenges — including steering, trimming sails, finding your position, avoiding other boats, and coping with an ever-changing and sometimes challenging environment. All these problems are important and will be the subject of several chapters later in this book. But while you're dealing with them, keep in mind these seven basic guidelines for better boat handling:

Keep the boat moving. Steerageway is an absolute necessity. Know your boat well enough so you're certain when she has or doesn't have steerageway. When planning a maneuver, make sure you allow enough time and room for developing steerageway and for using it once you have it.

Be especially careful near land. Almost any boat of decent size can survive a storm in open water, but few boats can survive running into land. If you're unsure of your boat-handling capabilities or if the weather is dangerous, stay as far as possible from floats, piers, shallow water, and the land itself.

Take nothing for granted. Life aboard a boat is always changing, and you must constantly anticipate new wind and sea conditions, equipment breakdowns, crew errors, and the approach of other boats.

Develop standard operating procedures (SOPs) for handling sails, piloting, and other important actions. As skipper you don't have to be a tyrant, but you should be alert to everything that's going on near or on your boat, and also feel confident that your crew is doing their best to avoid trouble. While every sailor should concentrate on the job he is performing — whether it's steering or rigging docking lines or hoisting a sail — he should be sensitive to what's going on elsewhere on deck.

One hand for yourself, one for the ship. This old-time sailor's adage means that the seaman should always watch out for his own safety while he does his job. If unsure of your footing, walk on deck with a hand on the lifelines. When pulling a line that's under load, snub it on a cleat or winch. In rough weather, wear a safety harness to avoid falling overboard, or a life jacket so you won't drown if you do. Remember that your shipmates depend on you not only to perform certain tasks but also to be healthy and ready to pull your own weight.

Stay with the boat. If the boat swamps or seems to be sinking, be patient and hang on. Boats sink far less often than is generally believed. One good rule of thumb is: never abandon your boat until she is so far gone that you must step up into a life raft or rescuing craft.

Stay alert. A lot is going on at once. Many accidents occur when sailors stop paying attention because they are distracted, tired, or intoxicated.

Slow down for safety. Don't go so fast that you feel out of control. If the boat seems unsafe or is extremely uncomfortable, forereaching, feathering, luffing sails, or shortening sail (taking down the jib or reefing) should bring her back under control. Or you can always heave-to.

Relaxed but alert and secure, this young crew obviously is in command of its boat and aware of their surroundings.

CHAPTER 3 Sail Trim

A sailboat's engine is her sails and her throttle is her running rigging. In chapter 2 we provided an overview to get you and your boat under way. Now we'll look more closely at the skills and tools used in harnessing and making best use of the wind. A sailor needn't be a master of all of these techniques. You can sail quite contentedly without touching a Cunningham control, twisting a leech, or tacking downwind. But anybody desiring to retain control of the boat in windy conditions and get the best performance out of the sails in less demanding times should learn about these basics.

Sail-trimming must satisfy the goal of sailing the boat under control, in balance, and with speed. If the wind, waves, and point of sail never changed, meeting these aims would be simple. All you would do is cut sails out of metal to a scientifically predetermined shape, stick them onto the hull, and get going. These big airfoils would push the boat forward through the unchanging air and water with a predictable force. But the wind and waves are never steady, and a boat rarely stays on one point of sail for more than a few hours. As the conditions change, so does the optimum sail shape (and size too). A good crew is constantly aware of lulls and puffs, wind shifts, and changed headings — and they're always trying to keep the sails properly shaped to match the new conditions.

As the wind changes, the crew tries either to make the sails more powerful in order to harness more of the wind's force and make the boat perform better, or to make them less powerful in order to shrug off some of that force so she is more seaworthy.

Sail-trimming, therefore, demands two different skills. One is powering — making sails more full and powerful — in light to moderate winds. In these lightish winds, the sails may be baggy. The other is depowering — making sails more flat — in stronger winds. As the wind increases, its impact builds rapidly (the wind's force increases with the square of its velocity). Depowering usually is necessary in more than about 15 knots (apparent). As boats begin to heel, pitch, roll, and generally reach the edge of comfortable control, their sails are made less full or smaller in order to decrease the force of the wind.

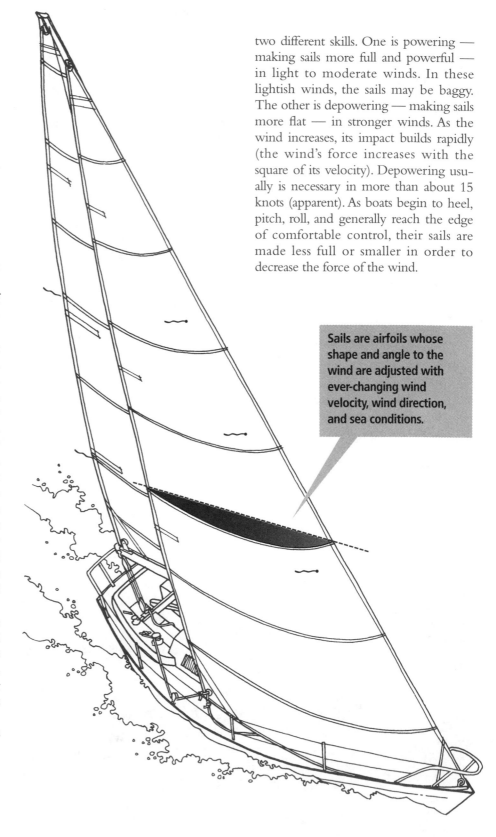

Sails are airfoils whose shape and angle to the wind are adjusted with ever-changing wind velocity, wind direction, and sea conditions.

Sail Controls

There are two interrelated parts of sail trim: the sail's shape and the sail's angle of attack to the apparent wind. Some sail controls affect only one, while others affect both.

The main sheet is the chief sail control for the mainsail (pronounced "main-sul" but sometimes called "the main"). The sheet pulls down on the boom, therefore affecting both shape and angle of attack more than the other controls for this sail: the outhaul, the Cunningham, and the boom vang (all of which we will discuss in a moment). Main sheet tension directly affects the

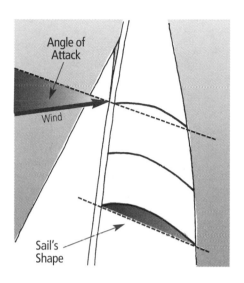

sail's angle of attack to the wind and also the shape of the after part of the sail. As the sheet is tightened and the boom is pulled down and in, the mainsail leech (back edge) becomes increasingly tight, or straight. If the sheet is trimmed too hard, the leech tightens so far that it cups to windward, which blocks the clean flow of wind across and off the sail. (In addition, the leech cord [leech line] in a mainsail that has one should not be too tight, for otherwise it will cause the leech to cup.) Besides constipating air flow, a too-tight leech creates excess weather helm. Ideally, the leech and the after part of the sail should be flat and curve off gradually to leeward between the clew and head.

The best indicator of leech tension (and mainsail performance in general) is the leech telltale on each of the top two mainsail battens. Telltales tell the story of the sail's trim. A leech telltale is a length of yarn or ribbon 6–10 inches long sewn into the leech near the batten pocket.

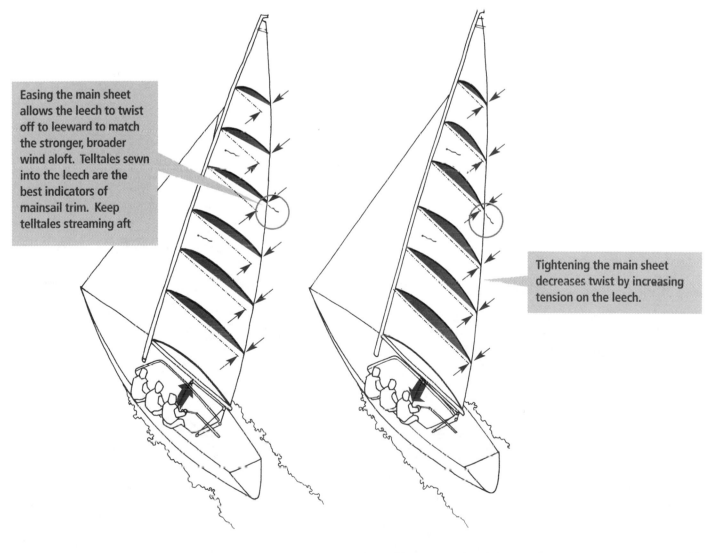

Easing the main sheet allows the leech to twist off to leeward to match the stronger, broader wind aloft. Telltales sewn into the leech are the best indicators of mainsail trim. Keep telltales streaming aft

Tightening the main sheet decreases twist by increasing tension on the leech.

Sail Controls

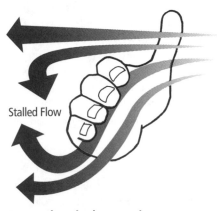

Stalled Flow

Too much main sheet tension can cause a cupped or tight leech, which blocks the clear flow of air across the sail. The leech should be flat.

(There also are jib telltales, placed on the jib's luff.) The telltale shows if wind is flowing across the sail on every point of sail except a run. When the telltale is streaming aft most of the time, the sail is trimmed right. If the telltale is stalled most of the time (hanging slack or making circles), the sail shape probably is off.

The leech should not rise in a straight line, like a mast. Rather, it should slightly twist to leeward, 5–10°. A properly curved or twisted sail matches the wind's changing direction and speed at different levels. Once free of the water's friction, the wind aloft generally blows harder than at the surface. Wind sheer, as this phenomenon is called, has been measured. C. A. Marchaj, in his advanced book on sailing theory, *Sail Performance*, writes that when the wind is blowing 5.4 knots about 6 feet above the water, it is almost 9 knots at 35 feet (the masthead of a 25-foot boat). Because the wind blows harder aloft, its angle of

attack there is broader. At boom level the boat may be close-hauled, but aloft the sail may almost be on a close reach. This is because on a moving sailboat, the closer the boat speed and the true wind speed are, the sharper is the angle of attack between wind and sails. Increase the wind speed without increasing boat speed, and the angle of attack broadens. This means that the sail must be trimmed closer at the boom than high up — its leech must twist off to leeward. (This is a general rule. Local weather conditions may create different patterns.)

Twist is put into or taken out of the main with the main sheet, which by pulling down on the boom affects the sail's leech. To twist off a sail, ease the sheet. To straighten it, trim the sheet. One reliable indicator of proper twist is the leech telltale. Another is the angle of the top batten, which should be about parallel to the boom when the boat is sailing close-hauled in all

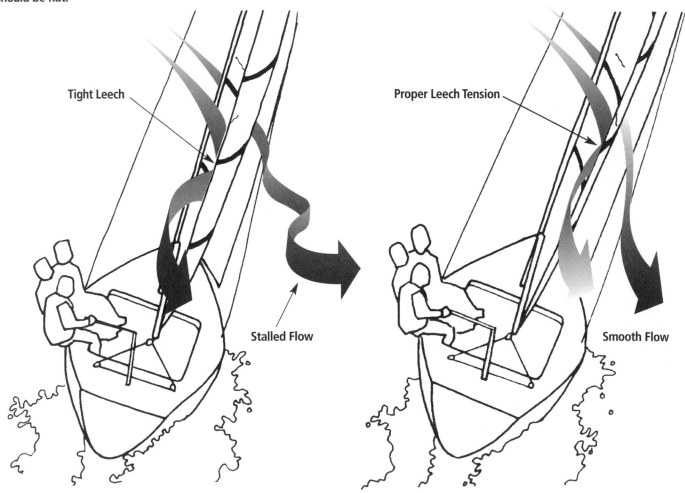

Tight Leech

Stalled Flow

Proper Leech Tension

Smooth Flow

but the lightest or freshest winds.

The jib sheet is the primary and, in many boats, only sail control for the jib (headsail, foresail). The jib sheet pulls the sail both aft to flatten it and down to control leech tension, or twist. Ease the sheet and the sail becomes deeper and rounder and the leech twists off. Tighten the sheet and the sail become flatter and the leech straightens. Pull too hard on the sheet and the sail becomes a flat, ineffective board with a cupped leech that backwinds (pushes wind into) the mainsail.

There must be some curvature in the jib to produce forward drive, and there must not be so much backwind that the entire forward portion of the main is aback (luffing). There is nothing wrong if the forward couple of feet of the mainsail is luffing slightly, since the air flow over that part of the mainsail is broken up by the mast, anyway. In fact, if there is no backwind, the mainsail prob-

ably is trimmed too tight. But a deep bubble extending a fourth of the distance aft into the main in moderate wind indicates that the jib is trimmed too flat and too far inboard. A helpful guide is the relationship between the jib's leech and the deepest part of the mainsail as it rises from the boom. The jib's twist should parallel, and almost nestle around, the mainsail's draft. This alignment helps the two sails meld together into a single effective airfoil.

Backwind and twist are reliable indicators of jib trim, but the most important is a set of telltales sewn in pairs (one on each side) into the jib's luff. (The mainsail's telltales are at the back of the boat, while the jib's are at the front.) The luff telltales should be spaced evenly along the luff's length. One should be in the middle, and the other two about halfway between it and the head and tack. Wool or acrylic yarn work well, as they do for the mainsail's

leech telltales. These jib telltales should be about 4 inches behind the luff — shorter distances for boats smaller than about 16 feet, longer distances for larger boats. They should be long enough to be seen clearly by the steerer. Bright red and green acrylic yarns are highly visible, distinctive, and represent the port side (red) and starboard side (green).

The jib sheet lead is the block on a track through which the sheet passes on the way to a cleat or winch. The mainsail's up-and-down shape is determined by trimming the main sheet so the leech telltale is streaming most of the time and by keeping the top batten parallel to the boom. But the jib uses the fore-and-aft position of the jib sheet lead as indicated by the luff telltales.

The jib sheet pulls both down and aft on the jib. When the lead is too far aft, the sail is pulled back too far and down too little. The sail is overly flat and twisted. When the lead is too far forward, the

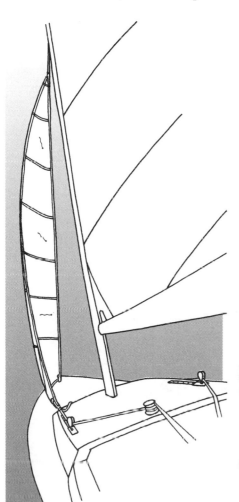

If the top jib telltale lifts first (left) the lead must be moved forward to tighten the leech and make the foot more full. If the bottom telltale lifts first (center) move the lead aft. When all telltales lift at the same time (right) the shape should be right.

Sail Controls

sail is pulled back too little and down too much, and the sail is too full and the leech is straight. To find the right position for the lead, get sailing on a close-hauled course. Slowly head up until the luff of the jib begins to luff (or bubble). The windward luff telltales should all lift at the same time and at the same angle — that is, the wind should be striking them all at exactly the same angle of attack. If the top windward telltale lifts before the bottom telltale, the angle of attack is wider up top than it is near the tack. Move the jib lead slightly forward and try again. If the bottom windward telltale lifts first, move the lead slightly aft. You'll soon find the right lead for the sail so that it works most efficiently from foot to head. Mark the lead on deck with a pen or a piece of tape, and duplicate the mark on the other side of the boat. Go through this routine for each jib you have on board. Since the sail's shape may change with the point of

sail and wind velocity, be prepared to move the lead as the conditions vary.

On some boats, the jib sheet lead may be moved inboard and outboard (sideways in and out) as well as fore and aft, either on athwartships tracks or by releading the sheet through another block (the Barber hauler), in order to change the jib's angle of attack to the wind. When the lead is far inboard, the jib's leech is close under the mainsail's luff and the air flowing aft from the jib may backwind the mainsail. In addition, trimming the jib sheet far inboard may cup the leech to windward and create unwanted lee helm. As the wind increases, the lead is let outboard and aft. While an inboard lead may allow a boat to point well (sail very close to the wind), and a forward one gives the sail a full shape, as the wind rises you want to depower the sail by moving the lead outboard and aft.

The mainsail traveler is used to adjust

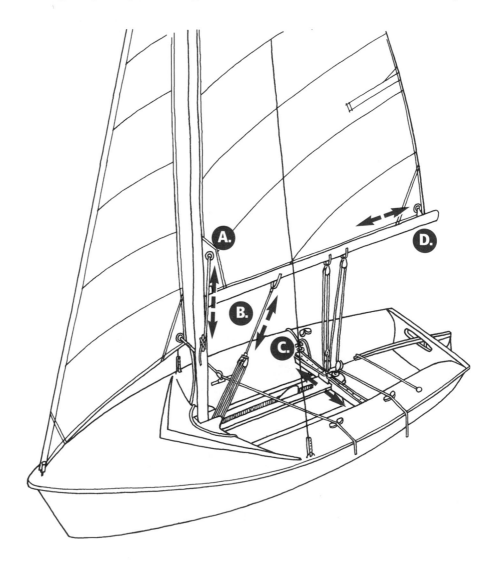

Like most boats, this dinghy has several sail controls besides the sheets: the Cunningham (A), boom vang (B), traveler (C), and outhaul (D).

the mainsail's angle of attack to the wind. This athwartships track sits under the boom. On it slides an adjustable car on roller bearings, and the main sheet runs through blocks on the car. The car can be pulled to windward of the centerline or let down to leeward — the first narrows the angle of attack of the sail, the second widens it. Narrowing the angle of attack improves pointing ability, increases side thrust, and causes weather helm; widening it increases forward thrust and decreases weather helm. The traveler is used primarily when sailing close-hauled to pull the boom up to the center of the boat in light wind and to let it down to leeward in strong wind. When beating in light to moderate conditions, the traveler usually is set so that the main boom is over the centerline (the imaginary line running from the center of the stern to the mast and bow). This may mean that the traveler car has to be pulled to windward. When the jib

lead and traveler car are at a narrow angle of attack in light winds, the sheets should be fairly slack to allow the leeches to twist off. As the wind builds, trim the sheets to control twist and move the jib lead and the traveler to leeward a little to reduce heeling force.

The boom vang controls the main boom's vertical rise and the mainsail's twist when the sheet exerts no downward pull on reaches and runs. In all but the lightest wind, the vang usually is set so the boom is parallel to the deck with 5–10° of twist up the leech. (The top batten and leech telltale are the best guides.) On small boats, the vang is a tackle running from the boom to the mast, but on larger boats it may be a tackle that holds the boom down integral with a spring-loaded rod that holds the boom up, replacing the main boom topping lift (a line running from the end of the boom to the top of the mast).

The outhaul pulls the mainsail aft

along the boom to flatten it, or lets it forward to increase the amount of draft, or fullness. The outhaul is effective only on the bottom third of the sail. This sail control is a tackle attached to the mainsail clew, which it pulls out to the end of the boom.

The Cunningham is a relatively refined sail control that stretches the mainsail's or jib's luff to change the fore-and-aft position of the point of deepest camber (draft or fullness). The word is capitalized because this simple but ingenious control was developed by Briggs Cunningham, a champion sailor from 1930 to 1970 (he was the winning skipper in the 1958 America's Cup). Sails are cut with a boltrope that, when stretched, pulls the attached cloth forward, thereby also pulling the point of deepest draft forward. To pull the draft farther forward as the wind increases, tighten the Cunningham. To ease the draft aft in lighter winds, let the Cunningham out. While not as important as the main sheet, the Cunningham does improve performance (for example, flattening the sail in fresh wind). And its use teaches some lessons about sail shape.

The leech line (or leech cord), found on well-made mainsails and jibs for boats larger than about 25 feet, is a light line running inside the leech from the clew to the head to control tension on the leech. When the leech flutters so violently that it chatters, the leech line is tensioned. When the leech cups, the line is eased.

(Left) The main sheet and traveler lines should be easy to adjust. They need tackles or winches. (Above) Tightening the Cunningham significantly alters sail shape.

An excellent boom vang for a larger boat is a spring-loaded rod that, when the sail is lowered, supports the boom.

Sail Materials and Design

Most sails, like clothes, are made by sewing together panels of cloth cut to patterns, curving the panels with tapered seams to produce a desired shape (called broadseaming), and laying out the panels in such a way that they resist stretch and other distortion. The panels of fabric are arranged so that the warp and fill threads woven at right angles to each other align as closely as possible with loads in the sail, rather than along the bias (at an angle across the panel). The greatest loads occur vertically along the leech, concentrating at the head and clew. The elaborate patterns in which the panels are arranged in radial cut sails demonstrate how far sailmakers go to reduce stretch so the sail holds its shape. Newer molded sails do not use panels, but apply fibers to a continuous membrane precisely along load paths in the sail.

The favored material for the large majority of mainsails and jibs is Dacron, a polyester to which special coatings (fillers) are applied to help control stretch. Spinnakers are made of nylon, which is lighter in weight. The fabrics come in a wide variety of weights. Since heavier cloth stretches less than light cloth, the higher the loads, the heavier the cloth. A dinghy like the Laser uses a mainsail made of 4-ounce cloth, while a 30-foot cruiser-racer may have a 6-ounce mainsail, a 3-ounce genoa jib, and a 5-ounce smaller jib. Spinnaker cloth weighs between ½ ounce and 2 ounces.

We have been speaking of sails made for the average cruising and daysailing boat. High-performance racing boats, on the other hand, use sails made of extremely low-stretch fibers such as Kevlar and carbon, which are shaped by sailmakers not by sewing panels of cloth together but, instead, by a process of molding. Among these high-tech sails are the elegant brown or black foils rising high above America's Cup boats. Much less stretchy for their weight than Dacron, these racing sails are also much lighter; but they are far more expensive

Most sails feature simple crosscut construction, which assembles panels of fabric horizontally.

Radial construction more accurately aligns woven fibers with loads in the sail, allowing lower stretch and lighter weight.

In molded sails, the fibers are not woven but are applied to a film along load paths.

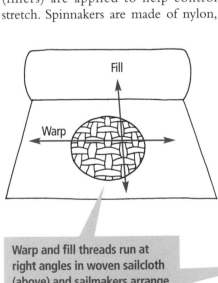

Warp and fill threads run at right angles in woven sailcloth (above) and sailmakers arrange the panels to best align threads with loads in the sail.

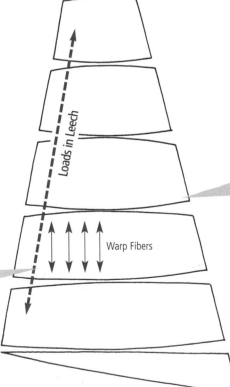

Fill

Warp

Loads in Leech

Warp Fibers

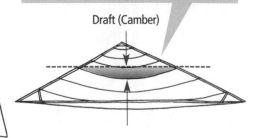

Draft is built into a sail by curving the edges of individual panels (left) in a process called broadseaming. When the panels are sewn together, shape is then induced into the sail. If you hold the edges tight (below) the bagginess that shows is the sail's camber or draft.

Draft (Camber)

and, because their fibers are brittle, tear more easily and may lose their shape earlier than a Dacron sail.

Careful handling is required for modern sails if they are to hold their integrity and their shape. Do not allow them to flog (luff violently) for even short periods of time. Avoid using light sails in strong winds. Keep them out of the sun under sail covers or in bags when they are not set, since ultraviolet rays weaken synthetic fibers. Guard against chafe (rubbing) by other objects. And fold them before putting them away.

Sailmaking is part art and part science, for while they use high-tech materials like Kevlar and cut it with computers, sailmakers must rely on traditional handworking skills to assemble the sail. Strong stainless-steel, bronze, or aluminum eyes are inserted in the clew, head, and tack, and Dacron boltropes that run along a mainsail's foot and luff and a jib's luff must be carefully sewn to the cloth.

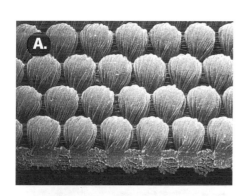

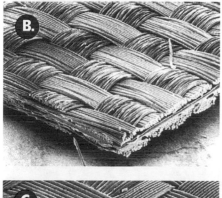

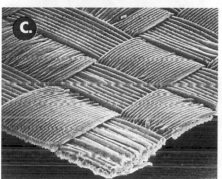

(Left) The most common sail fabrics are woven polyesters (A), known for their durability and low cost. Laminates combining Mylar film and woven fabrics (B) deliver less stretch and lighter weight. Nylon and lower stretch polyester spinnaker fabrics (C) feature an extremely close, flat weave to reduce porosity.

(Above) Low-stretch Mylar is used for sail panel templates as well as in laminated sail fabrics.

(Below) A sail's corners (the tack, clew, head, and reefing cringles) take heavy loads and must be reinforced with extra layers of sailcloth and/or nylon webbing.

Sail Types

Daysailer sails are simple: a mainsail, a jib, and perhaps a spinnaker. The larger sail inventory on bigger boats provides plenty of options for changing weather, with anywhere from 3 to 20 sails.

A mainsail is found on every boat. The chief option is a choice between traditional short battens or full-length battens that run from the mast all the way to the leech. The former are simpler and less expensive. The latter make the sail more powerful because they project the leech farther aft in a large roach (convex curve) and because tension on them may be adjusted to make the sail full. With full-length battens, the sail luffs less, which means that its life may be longer. On the other side, full-length battens are expensive and require special fittings along the luff. If they are under tension, hoisting and lowering the sail may be difficult unless the luff goes up and down on special slides with ball bearings.

The cruising cutter rig is flexible, with its choice of small jibs set in combination or alone. The dashed lines indicate reefs. The small sail abaft the mast is the storm trysail.

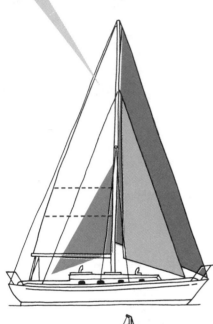

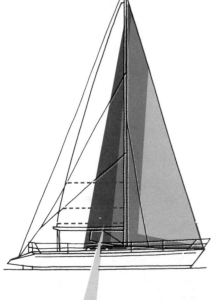

Sloops set one jib at a time. There is plenty of choice, with bigger jibs for light wind and smaller ones for heavy wind.

Full batten mainsails require special cars where the batten pockets meet the mast. The cars handle compression loads while allowing the battens to pivot from side to side.

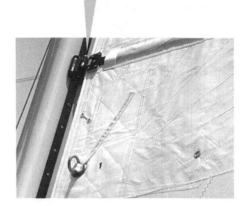

A mainsail with full-length battens can have a larger roach and therefore more sail area. By preventing flogging, these battens prolong the sail's life.

Cruising boats often carry two mainsails — the usual one and the tiny storm trysail, which is set in very strong wind, trimmed to the deck instead of to the boom. Storm trysails belong on all boats heading out of sight of land for longer than a day or two.

Jibs come in a number of types and sizes. Large, overlapping genoa jibs suitable for light and moderate winds of less than 15 knots are too big for stronger winds, when they develop more side force than forward force. So as the wind increases, the crew changes down to smaller jibs. These jibs are numbered, with the number 1 being the largest, the number 2 being the next largest, and so on. On a typical masthead-rigged cruiser-racer, the number 1 is trimmed about halfway back along the deck, the number 2 is trimmed a couple of feet forward of that, the number 3 (or working jib) usually comes no farther aft than the mast and is set in fresh wind. There

should be a tiny storm jib for strong wind. Ocean racing yachts may carry two big number 1 genoas of different sail cloth weight, the lighter, fuller sail being used in light winds and the heavier, flatter one in moderate winds. On racing boats, skilled crews can change sails very quickly using twin-grooved headstays and two halyards, so a large sail inventory can usually be exploited to match the weather conditions.

The normal cruising boat may carry only two or three jibs. Among single-masted boats there are two rigs, the sloop and the cutter. In the more popular sloop rig, there is a single large genoa jib that may correspond to the racing boat's number 2 (the number 1 being too big for small crews). This jib may be carried on a roller-furling device. The other jibs might be the number 3 plus a small number 4, good in fresh wind. In the cutter rig, a cruiser will set not one big jib but two small ones. One (called the

jib or jib topsail) is set from the headstay. The other, called the forestaysail, is set from the forestay running from partway up the mast to the middle of the foredeck. While usually less aerodynamically efficient in tandem than a big genoa jib is alone, these two sails are more seamanlike for small cruising crews, since they are easier to trim, set, and douse (lower). When the wind comes up, lower one of these sails and continue on with the other. The cutter rig is also called the double-headsail rig.

Besides size, jibs also differ in profile shape. Racing sails are usually cut (made) so their bottom edges, or feet, hug the deck to keep wind from escaping. While efficient aerodynamically, these deck-sweeping jibs cut off almost all visibility to leeward. In crowded waters a lookout must be posted in the bow to warn the steerer of approaching obstructions, such as other boats. This obviously is impractical for shorthanded cruising crews, and cruising sails are cut with a high clew so there is a large area of visibility between the foot and the deck. The problem is solved on dinghies and daysailers by inserting clear plastic windows in the mainsail and jib.

Ketches and yawls may carry a large inventory of these sails as well as mizzen staysails that are set from the mizzenmast when sailing downwind.

(Top) Because easy handling, good visibility, and moderate cost are high priorities with cruising boats, jibs are relatively small and high cut. Most are made of woven polyester (Dacron). A self-tacking jib on a boom allows changing tacks without handling sheets. (Left) Many racers, with their larger crews and budgets, carry big genoa jibs and other sails made of Kevlar and other low-stretch fabrics. Racing jibs tend to be low cut and are often called "deck sweepers." They restrict visibility to leeward.

Sail Shape

Mainsail Shape. The shape of a sail is indicated by draft (or camber). Draft is the sail's relative fullness and also the position of the point of deepest draft. Both are initially built in by the sailmaker, but the crew has considerable power to affect them using battens and sail controls.

The location of draft is an important but often overlooked concern. It may be changed temporarily by adjusting sail controls. Sailmakers usually put the point of deepest draft almost halfway back in the sail, about 45 percent of the distance between the luff and the leech. As the wind rises and the cloth stretches, that point will move farther aft in the sail, cupping the leech and making the boat slow and hard to handle unless you make adjustments. You can estimate draft position while sailing close-hauled by looking up from under the foot of the sail, adjusting the Cunningham control, and watching to see when the sail luffs. As you tighten the control and pull the draft forward, the first luffing in the sail will be forward, and as you ease it and the draft slides back, the sail will first luff toward its middle.

Moving the draft forward to about 40 percent or even less is a good idea in some situations. There, the sail is more forgiving — meaning that there is a wider room for error when steering close-hauled and when trimming sails. When the draft is far aft, the line between full and not-full is very narrow and highly critical. For this reason, draft forward is a good position when cruising and when racing in rough seas (when it's hard to steer a steady course).

The mainsail luff should not be smooth. It should carry slight horizontal pucker marks or wrinkles. If the luff has deep tension (vertical) wrinkles and the sail is almost flat over its after two-thirds, then the Cunningham is too tight. But if the luff is broken by many shallow wrinkles, if the forward half of the sail is flat, if the point of deepest draft is more than halfway back, and if the leech is cupped, the Cunningham is too loose and should be tightened. (Extreme aft draft may also indicate that the sail is blown out, meaning that it has been permanently stretched beyond its designed shape. Blown-out sails perform poorly, and for that reason sailing isn't much fun with them. This is the time to buy a new sail.)

The amount of draft is placed in the sail at its construction by tapering the panels' seams. Sailmakers refer to draft in

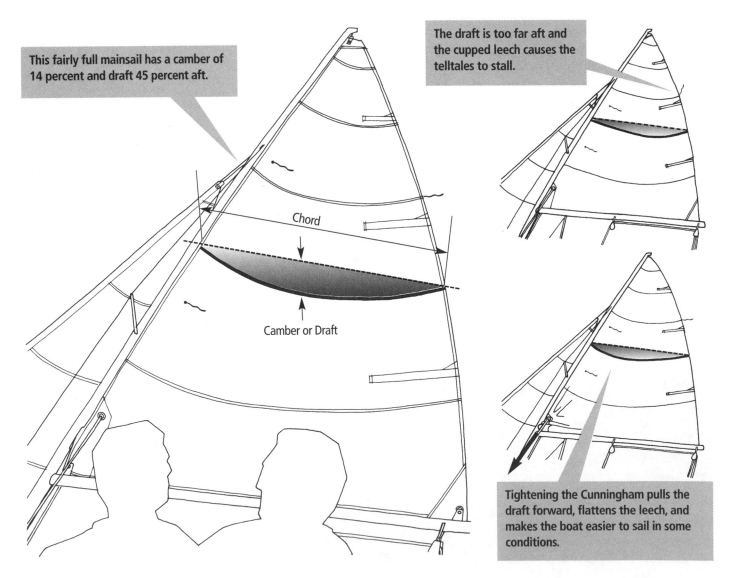

This fairly full mainsail has a camber of 14 percent and draft 45 percent aft.

Chord

Camber or Draft

The draft is too far aft and the cupped leech causes the telltales to stall.

Tightening the Cunningham pulls the draft forward, flattens the leech, and makes the boat easier to sail in some conditions.

terms of camber, a ratio that converts to a percentage. The ratio is between the sail's depth and the sail's chord length — the distance from the luff to the leech. If the depth is 1 foot and the chord is 10 feet long, the camber is 1:10, or 10 percent, a flat sail. Camber can be measured by taking a photograph of the sail from the foot looking up and then drawing chord

On a reach, with a trapeze moving the crew's center of gravity to windward, this catamaran can carry full sails for maximum power.

and depth lines on the print, or it may be estimated when the sails are hoisted by using a ruler and a tape measure.

Camber can be increased in several ways: easing the sheet, easing the outhaul, easing the halyard, and increasing tension of full-length battens (if the boat has them). As camber increases, the sail becomes more powerful. That would seem like a good thing. But while more draft theoretically increases power, it also may cause the wind flow to become detached from the sail, thereby turning off the boat's fuel pump. Tom Whidden, of North Sails, describes this paradox in his excellent *The Art and Science of Sails*: "Sail trim is a balancing act, however, and too much camber also can present problems, as the flow has trouble staying attached to a deeply curved section. With too much camber, the likelihood is that it will separate — the nice even curve above becomes an abrupt hairpin — and the flow will depart prematurely from the sail. Too much camber can decrease lift and increase drag."

So it is a mistake to make a sail too full. Camber of about 15 percent in mainsails and 18 percent in jibs is about as a full as a sail should get. Modern lightweight, easily driven hulls usually sail with flatter sails than their heavier ancestors.

Sailing close-hauled, flatten the sails, but not so far that there is no forward drive. Camber varies from boat to boat and with the conditions.

Sail Shape

Mast Bend. Although mast bend usually is regarded as a refinement for racing boats, you should understand it — if only to know how to remove bend from the mast, since a whippy mast may break. And, like the Cunningham, it also involves some helpful lessons about how sails and rigs function.

When the sailmaker constructs a mainsail, he anticipates the amount that the mast will be bent by building in luff curve, a convex curve of extra cloth. When the mast is bent, with the top coming aft and the middle bending forward, this extra cloth is pulled tighter and the sail is flattened. On dinghies and small boats, the mast is bent simply by trimming the main sheet. As the boom comes down, two things happen: the leech tightens, pulling the top of the mast back, and the gooseneck is thrust forward, bowing the bottom of the mast forward. The inherent stiffness of the mast and standing rigging keep mast bend within safe limits. Mast bend is most problematical in rough seas, when a bent mast may pump (flex) fore and aft several inches as the boat pitches, and finally snap when the boat lurches off a wave. In larger boats, mast bend is effected almost exclusively by shortening the backstay — the wire stay that runs from the masthead (top of the mast) to the stern — with turnbuckles, hydraulic ram, or block and tackle. The standing rigging will limit the amount of bend to keep the mast from breaking.

The sailmaker must know if your boat is equipped with mast-bending devices and if you plan to use them. Otherwise he'll probably assume that the mast won't be bent and will build in very little luff curve. You should bend the mast only as far as the amount of luff curve permits, for otherwise you'll simply suck all the draft out of the sail and distort it.

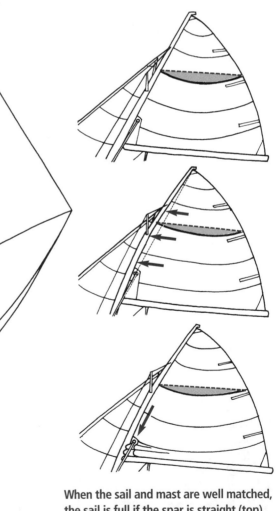

Leech tension and the boom's forward thrust bend the mast and flatten the sail on the stayless Laser.

Masts with standing rigging are bent by shortening the backstay.

When the sail and mast are well matched, the sail is full if the spar is straight (top) and gradually flattened as it is bent. Mast bend throws the draft aft (middle), so tighten the Cunningham to pull the draft forward (bottom).

Here are some points about mast bend:

First, mast bend throws the point of deepest draft aft in the sail. So as the mast is bent, the Cunningham should be tightened.

Second, mast bend is limited by the tension on lower shrouds aft of and forward of the mast. Running from the deck to the mast at the spreaders, they provide fore-and-aft support for the lower part of the mast. The after lowers are attached at the deck's rail slightly aft of the upper shrouds. The forward lowers are just forward (on many modern boats, the forward lowers are replaced by

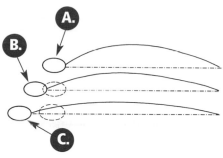

This cross-sectional view shows how mast bend extends the mainsail's luff and flattens the sail from a camber of 16 percent (A) to one of 13 percent (B). Overbending the mast beyond the extent of the luff curve removes most of the draft (C).

a single baby stay from the mast to the foredeck).

Third, some boats also carry running backstays to control bend. Connected at the mast high up (sometimes at two points) and running to the deck far aft, they are tensioned only on the windward side to pull the mast back. Tighten the runner to straighten the mast and keep it from pumping.

Fourth, mast bend is also affected by the position of the mast in the partners, the hole in the deck through which the mast passes on the way to its step in the bilge. To increase mast bend, push the mast forward in the partners until the lower part of the mast is bent forward, and hold the mast in place with mast blocks (wedges of hard wood or rubber) inserted in the after part of the hole. To decrease bend, remove the blocks, push the mast aft in the partners until the lower mast is straight, and insert the blocks in the forward part of the hole. (See chapter 17 for more on mast bend.)

All masts should be rigged with great care. The spreaders must be especially strong and securely fastened to the mast. The shrouds should be tightened in such a way that the mast is perfectly straight athwartships, with no side bend, when the boat is close-hauled in moderate winds; otherwise the aft bend in the mast may throw the spar severely out of column and break it. All shrouds, headstays, and backstays should have high safety factors of more than twice the anticipated maximum load, and be equipped with sufficiently large turnbuckles and eyes. Inspect frequently for bent turnbuckles, bent clevis pins, broken cotter pins, corrosion, and other problems. Bent fittings must be replaced immediately. If a turnbuckle is bent, it may be because there is no toggle at its base to allow the turnbuckle to adjust itself automatically to the angle of pull. Carry plenty of spare cotter and clevis pins that will fit snugly. Always use a pin of the right size; a pin that's too small is probably too weak for the job.

Maximum Bend

This mast is bent by increasing tension on the backstay, which pulls the top of the mast aft while increasing compression on the mast. Sighting up the mast from the gooseneck is the best way to observe the amount of bend.

Sail Shape

Jib Shape. The jib's draft can be slightly deeper than a mainsail's. The draft position is the same, about 45 percent of the way back from the luff. As with the mainsail, moving the draft forward by tensioning the halyard or Cunningham makes the sail more forgiving, providing a wide range in which it is full. In cross section, a good jib looks something like a fat airplane wing, with a round area forward and a flat surface tapering off aft. It's important that the

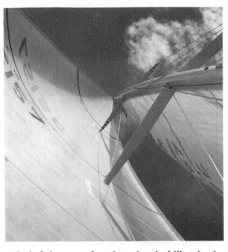

A helpful gauge for close-hauled jib trim is the sail's distance off the spreader. Don't let a spreader poke a hole in the sail.

leech not be tight or cupped, not only for the sake of airflow along the surface of the jib but because the jib greatly affects flow along the mainsail. A tight jib leech slows the boat dramatically.

Short battens in the smaller jibs help keep the long leech from flopping about, but battens are impractical on overlapping genoa jibs since they would break during tacks and jibes. Genoa leeches, then, are prone to cupping and noisy chattering, especially as the wind freshens. Usually, these annoyances (which can absorb some of the sail's driving force) can be controlled by adjusting the leech line.

Sailmakers build a luff curve into jibs as well as into mainsails, but it's a nega-

(Above) Horizontal black stripes sewn on the sail help the crew gauge camber and draft location. (Right) This overhead view shows camber, draft location, twist, mast bend, and the inevitable headstay sag. The mast is very straight as its bend is controlled by a running backstay tensioned against the forestay.

tive, concave curve since freestanding headstay sags off. If you can straighten the headstay, however, you can flatten the jib and generally improve pointing ability. The headstay can be straightened by shortening the backstay or the windward running backstay (if your boat has one). When you order new sails, be sure the sailmakers knows how straight you can make the headstay so they can shape the jib's negative luff curve to match.

Since a jib automatically becomes fuller as the sheet is eased, letting out the sheet is almost all you have to do to shape it properly for a reach or run. But also move the jib lead forward, so the three luff telltales continue to mimic one another as we described earlier. The jib lead could also be moved outboard, to the rail.

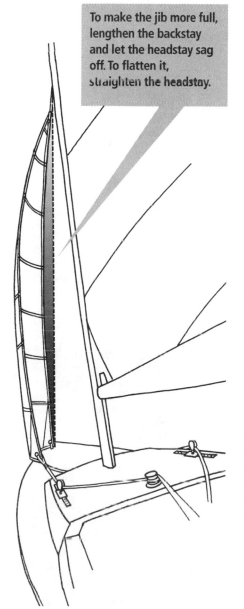

To make the jib more full, lengthen the backstay and let the headstay sag off. To flatten it, straighten the headstay.

Determining Wind Direction

You can't trim sails properly if you don't know which way the wind is blowing. Of course, you can feel it on your neck or face, but a visual reference point is a great help too. So there should be some wind indicators on board.

We've already described one set of wind indicators — the yarn telltales taped or sewn to the luff of the jib and the leech of the mainsail. If telltales are stalled or sagging, then the sail is not trimmed correctly. Experiment with sheet tension until they begin to stream. Jib telltales are located on both sides. You want them both to stream, with the windward one lifting a little bit. Some sailors put telltales on the luff of the mainsail, but because the mast greatly disturbs the air flow over the front 10 percent of the main, these don't help very much.

Telltales in the rigging indicate apparent wind direction. Tie 6-inch lengths of yarn or audio tape to the shrouds at a place where the steerer can easily see them while also looking at the jib, and a 10-inch telltale to the backstay to show apparent wind while running.

A masthead fly is a balanced wind arrow at the top of the mast above the air flow off the sails. Often flies are connected to electronic instruments that provide a readout on a dial in the cockpit, or to small computers that will figure the true wind direction and optimum angles of attack. Unfortunately the mass of antennas and other gear that sits at the masthead of many cruiser-racers often gets in the way of a masthead fly. Some skippers get around this problem by securing the masthead fly to the headboard at the top of the mainsail so it sticks up above and is clear of the other equipment when the sail is hoisted.

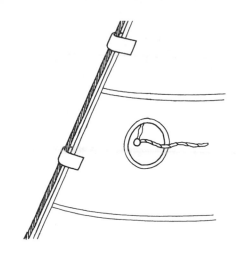

A window in the jib luff makes both windward and leeward telltales visible. Use different colored yarns. The leeward telltale should stream aft and the windward one should stream and occasionally lift. Here, the jib is trimmed too tight. The sheet should be eased until the leeward telltale streams aft.

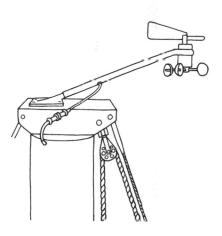

A masthead fly is a wind direction arrow that may be connected to an electronic system that reports wind direction and speed to the crew.

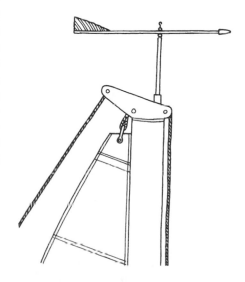

Sail Trim in Light to Moderate Conditions

In powering conditions, when the apparent wind is lighter than about 15 knots, here's what you should do to trim your sails for good speed and control. The wind speeds following are apparent.

Drifting Conditions (0–4 Knots). The biggest problem in really light winds is developing steerageway, so don't trim the sails too tight when sailing close-hauled. If possible, heel the boat by sitting to leeward in order to allow the sails to flop into shape and induce weather helm. Trim the jib fairly far outboard and carry the boom slightly to leeward of the centerline in order to maximize any forward force. The sails should not be too full when sailing close-hauled. By flattening the sail, you'll make it easier for the wind to stay attached to the cloth. Move around in the boat gently, and avoid making jerky motions with the tiller or steering wheel. In puffs, be careful not to over-trim the jib. It will pull the bow off. Above all, don't be greedy about pointing too close to the wind. Sail for speed. Runs and broad reaches are very slow in these conditions and slightly above, so increase the apparent wind by heading up to a beam reach

Light Air (5–8 Knots). Now that there's enough wind to provide steerageway, pull the traveler up until the boom is about over the centerline. But if the water is rough you may have to sacrifice pointing ability to keep her moving by carrying the sails farther outboard. The outhaul should be fairly loose, with slight wrinkles along the foot, and the Cunninghams should not be tensioned, since there's not enough wind to blow the draft aft. Off the wind, let the sails bag and do not over-tighten the boom vang.

Moderate Air (9–15 Knots). This is when sheets begin to pull and most boats spring to life. Upwind, sails are carried fairly flat with taut outhaul tension and the sheets trimmed a bit short of all the way. The jib lead and main boom should be slightly to leeward of where they were in light air, and eased down gradually as the wind increases or the waves become larger. As the wind pushes the draft aft in the sails, tighten the Cunninghams. Watch the angle of heel and be sensitive to the helm. Downwind, the vang should be snug to keep the boom about horizontal to the deck.

Pinching and Feathering. When sailing close-hauled, some helmsmen like to think that they can sail right up into

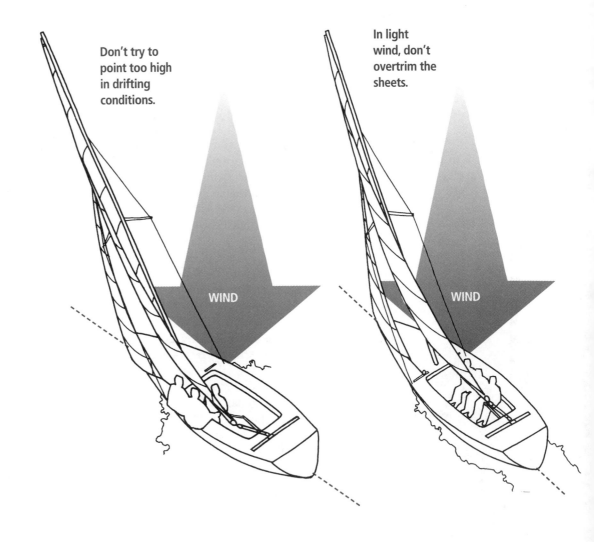

Don't try to point too high in drifting conditions.

In light wind, don't overtrim the sheets.

WIND

WIND

the wind's eye. Sailing with the jib "light," with the jib's windward telltale pointing straight up to the sky, is called pinching or feathering. You might be able to get away with pinching in smooth water and moderate wind, but as soon as the wind dies or the waves build, boat speed will plummet, and because the water flow is slowed, the appendages won't resist the sails' side forces as well as they should and the boat will make more leeway.

But there is one situation in which pinching can be helpful. Use it to sail the boat flat when beating or reaching in gusty winds. You may be overpowered so suddenly that you don't have time to ease a sheet or the traveler. When that happens, make the sails less efficient by quickly heading up 2–5° just as you feel the gust on your face. Don't allow the boat to heel much further, and keep the helm angle constant. This quick pinch will shrug off the gust. Once the first blast has passed, head off again.

HANDS ON: **Close-Hauled Trim**

Trimming sails on a reach or run is pretty simple. Just ease the sheets until the sail begins to luff and then trim them back a bit, keeping an eye on the telltales. Sail trim when close-hauled is a bit more tricky.

When the boat is flat or barely heeling, in light wind, the common mistake is to trim sails too tight and flat and try to sail too close to the wind. The boat just sits there. "When in doubt, let it out."

When the boat heels moderately, in medium wind, the usual mistake is to not trim the sheets far enough and so to leave the sails too full and baggy. The boat can't point well and she sails too far off the wind ("reaching around the course," sailors say). Trim the main sheet until the leech is fairly straight, with only some twist and with the leech telltale streaming about half the time. Tighten the overhaul and Cunningham.

When the boat is heeling far over, in strong, gusty wind, the common error is to trim the sails too tight and too close inboard. The boat wallows on her side. Twist the sails off more than usual, ease the sheets slightly to spill wind on the luff of the sails, and move the traveler and jib lead to leeward. In strong gusts, you'll sail mostly on the leeches of the sails.

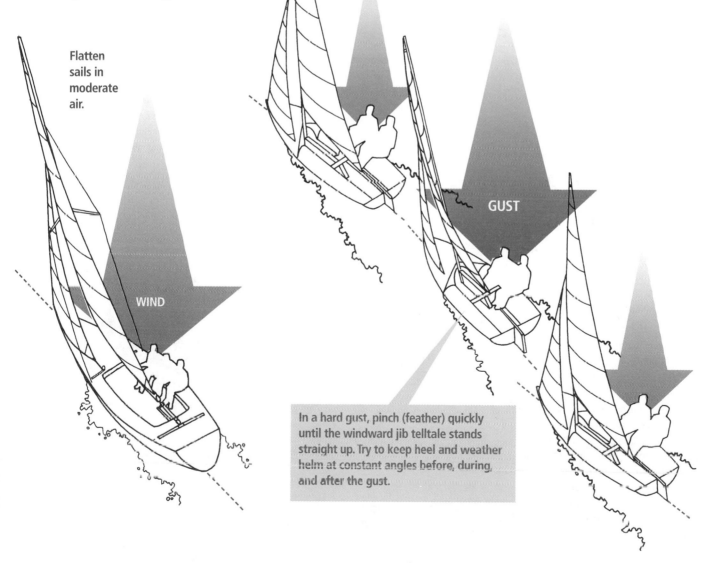

Flatten sails in moderate air.

WIND

GUST

In a hard gust, pinch (feather) quickly until the windward jib telltale stands straight up. Try to keep heel and weather helm at constant angles before, during, and after the gust.

Depowering in Fresh and Strong Winds

No matter how good the sails look, no boat sails well when she's at extreme angles of heel. When a dinghy heels more than 15°, a beamy keel boat heels more than 20°, or a narrow keel boat heels more than 25°, she slows down, develops severe weather helm, and wallows sluggishly and perhaps even dangerously, vulnerable to a strong gust. She must be brought back upright by depowering the sails — flattening them and trimming them farther from the centerline. A good measure here is the combination of angle of heel and boat speed. Try to keep them constant no matter how the sails and telltales look.

In wind between 20 and 30 knots (or any gusty wind), don't worry if you're spilling wind but are sailing under control. Even though a luffing mainsail may seem to be wasted, the boat is sailing more efficiently because she's sailing almost upright ("on her bottom"). In strong gusts you may find yourself sailing with the forward half of the jib and mainsail luffing but the back half full. It may look odd, but it works.

The main sheet works quickest. When a gust hits and the boat begins to heel over, feather up with a quick pinch (as we described on the previous pages) and quickly ease the sheet a few inches to twist the sail further. When the upper part of the mainsail twists off, wind is spilled aloft, where its leverage on the hull is greatest. This works both on the wind and off the wind. Either the steerer or a crew member can ease the sheet when they first feel the gust. Don't wait until the boat is knocked over on her side and the helm has to be fought.

The main sheet traveler should be carried down to leeward of the centerline when sailing close-hauled in fresh winds. Just how far is determined by the helm, for the two have a direct relationship. Drop the traveler car down until there is about 3° of weather helm (a noticeable but moderate tug). When the helm becomes neutral in a lull, pull the car back up to windward. If weather helm increases uncomfortably, drop the car farther. On many boats, the steerer can adjust the traveler herself, but sometimes another crew member will have to do it. When sailing off the wind, on a reach or a run, pull the traveler car up to the centerline in order to eliminate downward pull on the boom by the main sheet, and ease the boom vang to twist off the sail and spill wind aloft in gusts to keep the boat from heeling too far.

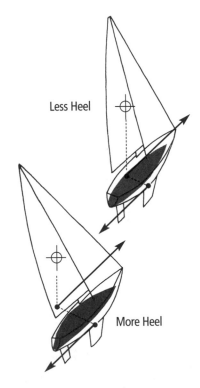

Less Heel

More Heel

As the boat heels, the underbody (shaded) becomes asymmetrical and the sail plan's center of effort (cross hairs) moves to leeward and aft of the hull's center of lateral resistance (lower dot). The boat tries to twist to windward. The helm resists this but at a loss of speed and comfort. Therefore, to decrease weather helm, depower the sails to decrease the heel and side force.

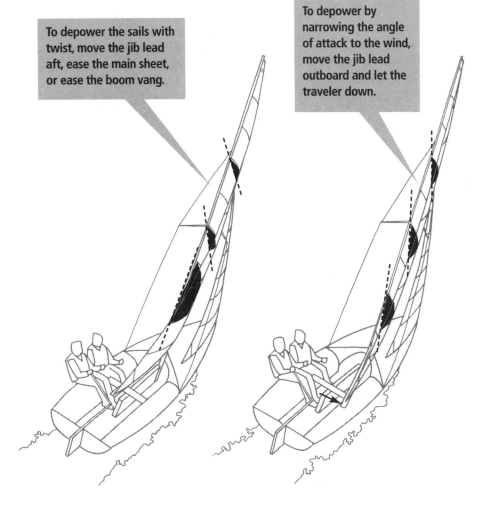

To depower the sails with twist, move the jib lead aft, ease the main sheet, or ease the boom vang.

To depower by narrowing the angle of attack to the wind, move the jib lead outboard and let the traveler down.

The jib sheet may also be eased quickly to spill air from the jib.

The jib sheet lead should be moved aft to increase the amount of twist in the upper part of the sail, spilling wind up high. When the lead is moved aft, the upper of the three jib luff telltales will flutter before the lower two do. The lead may also be moved outboard to decrease side force.

The boom vang is used to depower the mainsail when sailing off the wind. With the traveler car centered, the main sheet does not pull down on the boom, so the boom's rise and fall — and with it the mainsail's twist — can be adjusted by easing and tightening the vang. This works better on a reach than it does on a run, when letting the boom rise will allow the mainsail to plaster itself all over the leeward shrouds and spreaders. The resulting chafe may cause the sail to rip. Therefore, when running in fresh or strong winds, overtrim the main sheet so

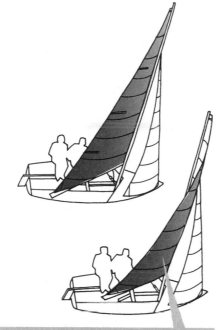

On a reach, depower instantly in puffs. Pinch and twist off the sails by easing the sheets and boom vang.

the boom is well in from the leeward shrouds, or tie in a reef to decrease the sail area.

The outhaul flattens the bottom part of the mainsail when it's tightened. Since flat sails create less sideways heeling force than full sails, pull the outhaul out as tight as you can in fresh and strong winds.

The Cunningham control pulls the draft forward and flattens the leech. Since a cupped leech on either the mainsail or the jib creates bad weather helm, the Cunningham should be pulled down hard in fresh and strong winds.

Mast bend flattens a mainsail. As you bend the mast aft, the headstay usually is straightened, which flattens the jib. At the same time it also increases a mast's chances of breaking. In fresh winds and relatively smooth waves, you can bend the mast far to flatten the mainsail, but as the seas build, you should not bend it too much. In a cruising boat, you will have reefed by this time anyway, effectively flattening the mainsail without mast bend.

Changing Down. In chapter 15 we'll look at reefing and sail changing in rough conditions. Here, in the context of fresh winds, we can say that a very effective way to depower a cruising boat or a cruiser-racer is to change to a smaller jib. When changing down, be sure to secure the old jib carefully. You can tie it on deck with sail ties (6-foot strips of synthetic fabric). Better yet, take the old sail below before a wave washes it overboard.

When daysailing or cruising, most boats can be depowered simply by lowering a sail. A sloop can sail under mainsail alone. When beating, let the traveler car all the way to leeward in order to decrease weather helm. A sloop may also be sailed under jib alone in smooth water. But in rough seas, without the fore-and-aft support provided by a mainsail, the mast may whip around and break. A ketch or a yawl can be sailed comfortably under "jib and jigger" — with the mizzen and the jib set and the mainsail furled — but with the same warning about the mainmast in rough weather.

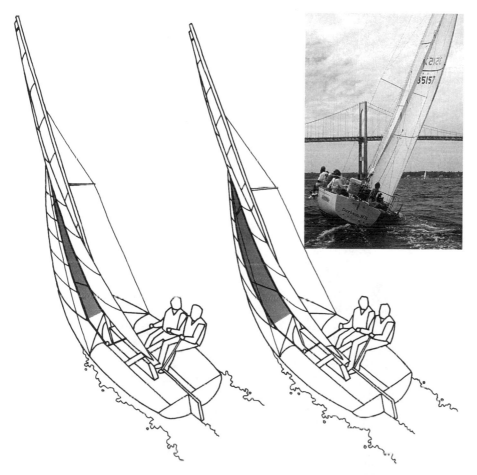

Trim both sails alike. Overtrimming the jib (left) throws the boat out of balance and creates lee helm. A proper gap between the jib and the mainsail (sometimes called "the slot") keeps the sails separated to permit efficient wind flow from the jib aft (right).

How Boats Balance

Helm is a function of balance. An unbalanced boat wants to turn one way or the other off her course, and the helm must be adjusted to compensate. This may be because she is heeled, since a heeled hull automatically tries to turn toward the side opposite to the one in which she tilts. Balance works more or less like a seesaw, with forces at either end (the mainsail and jib) applying pressure to either side of a fulcrum, which is the center of effort (CE) of the sail plan in tandem with the center of lateral resistance (CLR) of the hull.

There are two "areas" that a yacht designer includes on his drawings and tries to balance against each other. One is the sail area spread around the mast or masts. The effective center or balance point of this area is the CE. The other area is the lateral area of the underbody (the hull under water), and its center is called the CLR. The designer calculates the CE geometrically by drawing lines from each corner of each sail to the middle of the opposite edge. Where those lines cross is the CE for the sail. He then marks the CE for the entire sail plan by finding the balance point along the line between centers of effort for all the sails. The CLR is the balance point for the underbody, and it is almost under the CE. The relationship between these two centers determines how the boat will balance, assuming she floats the way the designer intended. Ideally the CE

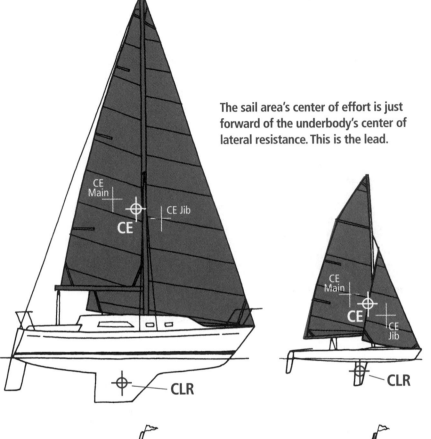

The sail area's center of effort is just forward of the underbody's center of lateral resistance. This is the lead.

An advantage of the yawl or ketch rig is that the boat can be balanced under a variety of sail combinations using the jib, mainsail, and mizzen: under full sail in light air (left), under main and jib in fresh air (center), or under "jib and jigger" in heavy air (right).

should be just aft of the CLR in order to create the desired 3° of weather helm that makes the rudder work most effectively — that is, the pressure of the sails on the after end of the boat makes the bow swing to windward around the fulcrum of her CLR. But because of certain inefficiencies in the sails (for instance, turbulence caused by the mast), and because when the boat heels she automatically develops weather helm, the designer arranges the two areas on paper so the CE is "led" slightly forward of the CLR. As the boat heels, the effective CE moves aft.

Correcting Imbalance. What if the boat doesn't float the way her designer intended? How do you bring her back into balance? One common problem is that the boat is too heavy in the bow and floats bow-down. This moves the CLR forward, and thus increases weather helm, since the CE's "lead" forward of the CLR has been eliminated. A solution to this problem is to move weight aft so the boat floats on her lines as the designer intended. You can move anchors or some other heavy weight back from the bow to the stern or lockers under the cockpit, or you can relocate any lead pigs that the builder put as ballast in her bilge. By bringing the CLR aft, you are effectively decreasing weather helm.

Sometimes, however, the CLR is too far aft and the boat has lee helm even when she's heeled. To induce weather helm, rake (tilt) the mast aft by lengthening the headstay. Alternatively, move the whole mast aft a few inches by sliding it back and adjusting the rigging. Moving the CE aft like this narrows the "lead" between it and the CLR, effectively increasing weather helm, and takes a little effort.

Previously we saw how you can cut back on weather helm by decreasing the amount of heel through depowering the sails. Here are some other ways:

Since a boat can usually heel an equal amount under a number of possible sail combinations, you might be able to increase weather helm by increasing the sail area aft and decreasing it forward, and decrease weather helm by decreasing the sail area aft and increasing it forward. The mainsail can be reefed or unreefed, different size jibs may be set, or the mizzen (on a yawl or ketch) can be set or doused. The important requirement is to keep in your mind's eye a clear picture of the location of the CLR of the underbody and that of the CE of each combination of sails you set.

A centerboard may be raised or lowered to change the helm. Raising the centerboard moves the CLR aft, which decreases weather helm. In dinghies, raising the centerboard or daggerboard has another effect that decreases weather helm. As the board is retracted, the amount of exposed lateral area is decreased — which means that the boat skids sideways. Therefore the sideways force of the wind on the sail is translated less into heeling and more into leeway. So while she slides more to leeward, she heels less and has less weather helm.

The Sailboard Example. A good example of balance in action is the sailboard. It does not have a rudder so it is steered by moving the CE by raking the mast, pivoted at the deck, forward and aft. Forward rake creates leeward helm and heads her off to jibe. Aft rake creates weather helm and heads her up to tack. When a boardsailor tacks, he makes the following motions:

1. He rakes the mast way aft until the sail's clew almost touches the water. The boat heads up into the wind's eye.

2. Then he walks around the front of the mast, grabs the wishbone boom on the other side, and rakes the mast way forward. The sail's CE pulls the bow downwind as the boat pivots around her CLR.

3. Finally, when the boat is at an angle of about 45° to the wind, he pulls the mast erect and sails off on the new tack. The boardsailor now moves the rig back and forth a few inches to make incremental course changes, just as a steerer would do with the helm in a boat with a rudder.

While a normal boat appears to handle more simply, the only difference between her and a sailboard is that her rudder does the compensating to bring the boat back onto a steady heading, not the rig.

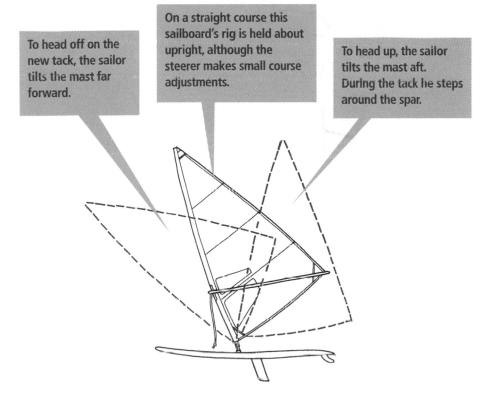

To head off on the new tack, the sailor tilts the mast far forward.

On a straight course this sailboard's rig is held about upright, although the steerer makes small course adjustments.

To head up, the sailor tilts the mast aft. During the tack he steps around the spar.

Rudderless sailboards are steered by shifting the center of effort fore and aft over the center of lateral resistance.

Boat-Handling Drills

Boat-handling techniques and the principles of balance may be learned during some exercises with and without rudders. Here are some drills to add to the ones in chapter 2. Try them out in open water, well away from other boats and obstructions.

Finding neutral helm. Sail on beating, reaching, and running courses, adjusting the sail controls and angle of heel until the helm is absolutely neutral with no weather or lee helm. Then make adjustments until you have the right amount of weather helm. Concentrate on making small adjustments to the Cunningham and traveler.

The standing start. Come to a dead stop, head-to-wind, and let the sheets all the way out. Before the boat gathers sternway (starts to sail backward), get under way, first under mainsail alone and then under jib alone. Finally, remove the rudder or lash the helm amidships with the rudder centered and try to get under way without steering.

Weaving without a rudder. Once you've developed steerageway, alter course in a serpentine pattern, first with the helm alone and then also easing and trimming sheets as you change course. Notice how much easier it is when the sails help the helm. Finally, remove the rudder (or lash the helm) and steer solely by trimming the mainsail and easing the jib (to head up) and easing the mainsail and trimming the jib (to head off). In a dinghy or other small boat, try steering by shifting crew weight to create heel: heel to leeward causes her to head up; heel to windward causes her to head off.

Steering backward. From a dead stop, gather sternway and steer backward using the rudder and backed sails. Then steer backward using the sails and heel alone. (Don't try this drill in a fresh wind, when the rudder may swing over and break.)

Shooting a mooring. Under a variety

A good way to learn how your boat balances is to sail a weaving course steering by trimming and easing sails rather than with the helm. Trim the jib to head off and the mainsail to head up. Small boats can be steered by shifting weight and changing heel angles. You can do this drill either alone or in a line of boats playing follow-the-leader.

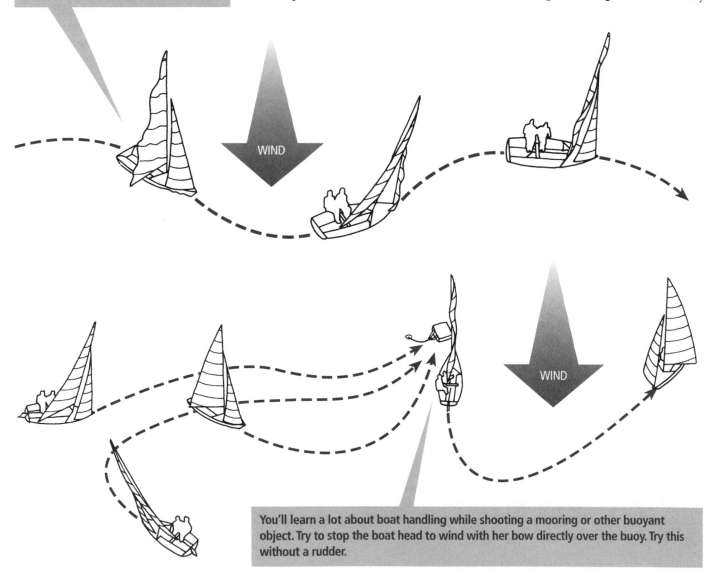

You'll learn a lot about boat handling while shooting a mooring or other buoyant object. Try to stop the boat head to wind with her bow directly over the buoy. Try this without a rudder.

of sail combinations, with and without a rudder, practice shooting (heading at and picking up) an upwind mooring or some other buoyant object, like a cushion. Try to slow down using sharp alterations in the helm or by backing the sails.

Shortening sail. Take down, luff, or reef sails to see how each sail affects balance and speed.

Heaving-to without a rudder. You can balance the windward-turning force of the mainsail against the leeward-turning force of the jib to slow your boat down to a near-stop and let her lie comfortably, even in rough seas. This tactic is called heaving-to. We described two ways to heave-to in chapter 2, but here is a review of the traditional method, which offers excellent lessons about how sail trim affects balance.

With the boat on a close reach, back the jib (trim it to windward) so the clew is near the windward shrouds, and trim the mainsail so it is mostly full. (Alternatively, tack the boat without releasing the windward sheet.) Adjust the main sheet or traveler until she jogs slowly. Try this with and without the rudder. The two sails work against each other as the boat sails a series of gradual swoops.

How to Measure Weather Helm

We have said that there should be about 3° of weather helm when sailing close-hauled to improve the leeway-resisting characteristics of the rudder and to make the steerer's job a little easier by providing a slight tug as a frame of reference. Anything much more than 3° will create a braking action. Anything less may cause the boat to wander all over the ocean or lake without any "feel" to alert the steerer. You can calculate exactly how far the tiller or wheel has to be pushed to have 3° of helm, and then mark it for easy reference while you're sailing.

The boat must be out of the water so the rudder and helm angles can be measured at the same time. With one crew member standing under the rudder, center it exactly so it aims fore and aft. Adjust the tiller so it lies exactly over the boat's centerline. If the boat has a steering wheel, adjust it so that a spoke is standing straight up with the rudder centered. That spoke is called the king spoke. Wrap a length of light line around the king spoke so it can be identified by feel. Next, turn the helm until the rudder is angled 3° to one side. A large protractor held under the rudder will help here. Mark the tiller position or the wheel with fingernail polish or tape. Repeat this process on the other side. You now have 3° reference points for both tacks.

This is about the right weather helm. You shouldn't have to fight the tiller or wheel to keep the boat on course.

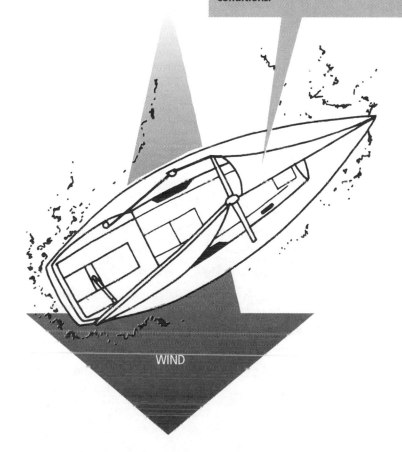

To heave-to, back the jib and then adjust the main sheet and traveler until the boat balances. Best known as a heavy-weather tactic, it steadies the boat and rests the crew in all conditions.

WIND

Upwind Sailing Techniques

The main requirement for successful upwind sailing is concentration: the steerer must focus her eyes on the behavior of the jib's telltales (always keeping the windward telltales streaming aft or barely lifting and the leeward ones streaming aft) while tuning her other senses to the pressure of the helm and the angle of heel. Try to keep the boat at a constant heel angle of less than about 20° — a steady moderate tug. Feather the boat in puffs to control heel and weather helm, or ease the traveler car down.

The steerer tries to point, or keep the angle of attack between wind and sails narrow enough to make distance to windward without sacrificing too much speed. When two boats are sailing upwind at the same speed, the one that can sail 1° higher will gain almost 200 feet to windward after a mile of sailing. This does not mean shoving the bow into the wind, for there must be a balance between pointing and speed. Footing (sailing at a slightly lower angle of attack) speeds the boat up slightly, perhaps enough to make up for the distance lost to windward. Footing usually works best in choppy waters, when the boat needs a little more speed to drive through waves.

Pointing ability varies from boat to boat. Very fast boats not limited by hull speed, like catamarans and planing dinghies, usually sail at wide angles of attack, as do relatively slow boats like heavy cruisers. Narrow keel boats gener-

ally sail best when they point high. If your boat is equipped with a speedometer, find the closest angle of attack that produces the best trade-off between speed and pointing. There are electronic instruments that calculate and display this trade-off, which is indicated as VMG, or velocity made good to windward (alternatively, to leeward when running).

In smooth water, many keel boats should be sailed in a series of long scallops: at first, head off slightly (with the jib's windward telltales streaming aft) to foot and gain speed, then head up a couple of degrees (with the windward telltales lifting) to use that momentum to climb to windward a little. When the momentum is expended, foot off again. Each scallop may last two or three minutes. The steerer will have the sensation of playing a game against the wind and sea.

In waves, all boats should be steered around breakers or especially large lumps

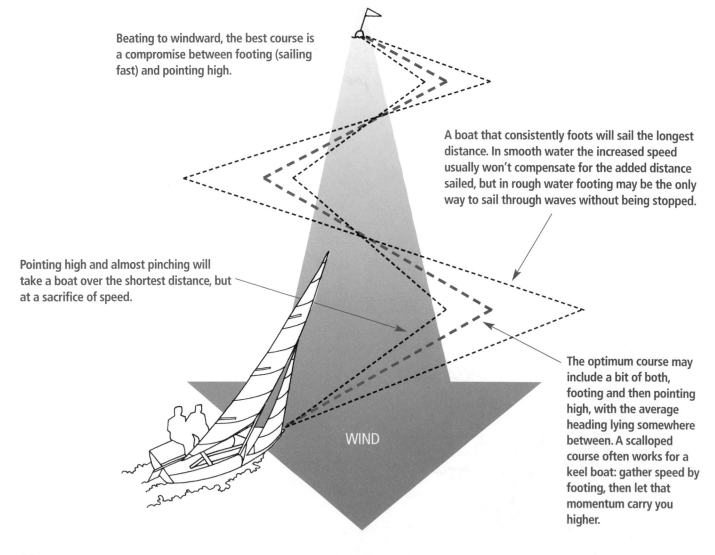

Beating to windward, the best course is a compromise between footing (sailing fast) and pointing high.

A boat that consistently foots will sail the longest distance. In smooth water the increased speed usually won't compensate for the added distance sailed, but in rough water footing may be the only way to sail through waves without being stopped.

Pointing high and almost pinching will take a boat over the shortest distance, but at a sacrifice of speed.

The optimum course may include a bit of both, footing and then pointing high, with the average heading lying somewhere between. A scalloped course often works for a keel boat: gather speed by footing, then let that momentum carry you higher.

WIND

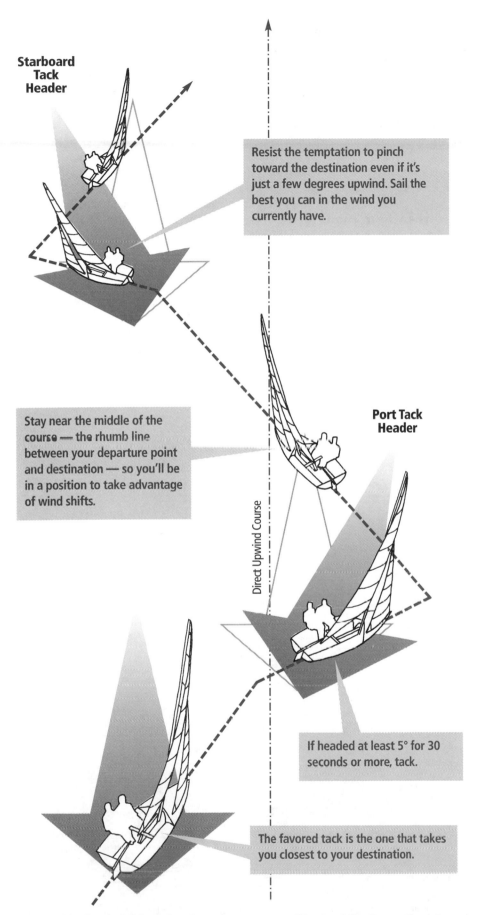

Starboard Tack Header

Resist the temptation to pinch toward the destination even if it's just a few degrees upwind. Sail the best you can in the wind you currently have.

Stay near the middle of the course — the rhumb line between your departure point and destination — so you'll be in a position to take advantage of wind shifts.

Direct Upwind Course

Port Tack Header

If headed at least 5° for 30 seconds or more, tack.

The favored tack is the one that takes you closest to your destination.

The wind is always shifting, often in a regular pattern of 5–10° shifts, first to the right and then to the left. If you can take advantage of them by tacking in headers, you'll reach your destination sooner.

whenever possible. You'll be able to point a little higher when sailing up the crest of a wave, since the decrease in boat speed effectively pulls the apparent wind aft. But when you accelerate down into the trough, there will be a header because the wind is pulled back forward. When tacking in rough weather, wait for a flat spot. Because big waves tend to come in groups of three, you usually can tack just after confronting a trio of waves.

Tacking on Headers. You'll sail a shorter, faster course if you sail on the tack that aims you closest to your destination. This is easy when the wind is off to one side: sail one long leg and, if necessary, tack and sail a short leg when you're near the destination. The rule is to sail the longest leg first. That way you're always sailing toward the mark and protecting against big wind shifts.

But if the upwind destination is into the wind's eye and neither tack seems to be favored, take advantage of the fact that the wind is always shifting a few degrees, often in a regular pattern from one side to the other. First, sail on the tack that takes you into the smoothest water, the most favorable current, or the fewest obstructions. The chances are that the wind will shift and head you, forcing you to head off a few degrees. When you are headed, tack. The new tack will now take you closer to your destination. When you're headed again, tack again. Tack only on substantial shifts of 5° of more, and don't change course until you've sailed into the header for 30 seconds, or the tack will take you right out of it. By tacking in headers, you will sail on the lifted, favored tack — the course that heads you closest to the destination. Keep an eye on the compass to track the pattern of wind shifts.

Some headers may be so large that most or all of the jib luffs. If that happens, tack immediately without heading off (assuming that the crew is ready). Otherwise, if you simply head off, you'll lose too much distance to leeward.

Downwind Sailing Techniques

Since a boat generally sails on a compass course or toward a buoy or landmark when on a reach or run, downwind sailing seems less difficult than upwind sailing. Once the sails are trimmed right for the apparent wind, with the jib luff telltales just lifting and the mainsail's leech telltale streaming, the steerer simply aims. But to get optimum performance while sailing downwind in a typical shifty wind can be as challenging as sailing close-hauled.

Freshen Your Wind. In light to moderate wind, a run or very broad reach will be very slow because the wind just pushes the sails. The aerodynamic shape of the sails is not brought into play to enhance the wind's force. Instead of allowing them to sit there, make them work by the technique that Midwestern sailors call "freshening your wind" and racing crews call "heating it

up": head up to a reach, trimming sails, in order to get the wind flowing across the sails from luff to leech. The lighter the wind, the more you must head up, but don't go above a beam reach. The boat accelerates. After a few minutes, slowly head off, keeping the apparent wind just abaft the beam. Notice how the faster you sail, the greater the difference between the true wind (which is aft) and the apparent wind (which is on the beam). When the boat slows and the apparent wind dies and hauls aft, head up again. This series of swoops will cover more distance than a straight-line broad-reaching or running course, but it will be faster.

Meanwhile, if you feel a puff of wind, you probably can sail a slightly lower course. "Head up in the lulls and off in the puffs" is a good rule of thumb for light-air running and reaching.

If there are waves, try to get surfing by turning the transom square to the crest

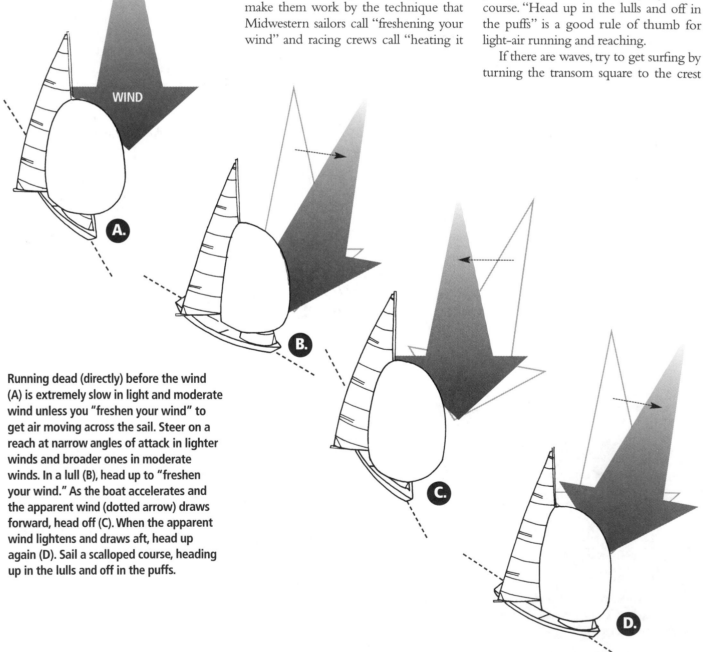

WIND

Running dead (directly) before the wind (A) is extremely slow in light and moderate wind unless you "freshen your wind" to get air moving across the sail. Steer on a reach at narrow angles of attack in lighter winds and broader ones in moderate winds. In a lull (B), head up to "freshen your wind." As the boat accelerates and the apparent wind (dotted arrow) draws forward, head off (C). When the apparent wind lightens and draws aft, head up again (D). Sail a scalloped course, heading up in the lulls and off in the puffs.

and then riding down the face. Centerboarders and some light keel boats will get planing with the assistance of waves; the crew can also help sometimes by giving two or three hard tugs on the sheets (this is called pumping the sheets). The apparent wind will quickly move forward as a boat accelerates on a surf or a plane, so be prepared either to head off or trim sheets.

Many boats roll badly on windy dead runs because there is no force pushing one side of the hull down. When this happens, head up to a broad reach and trim the mainsail to increase lateral pressure and steady the boat.

In a centerboarder, retract the board about one-third on a close reach, about one-half on a beam reach, about two-thirds on a broad reach, and almost all the way on a run — leaving just enough to provide some directional stability. In strong winds, retracting the board even more will decrease heeling on reaches, but leaving it down slightly more will increase directional stability on a run.

Jibing on Lifts. When running square before the wind or broad reaching in light and moderate wind, use a version of the principle of tacking on headers: sail on the jibe that takes you closest to your destination, and if the wind lifts you at least 5°, jibe. The new course should be the one closest to your destination. By sailing the shortest course, you will reach your destination quicker. But to get to a destination directly downwind in light air, instead of sailing straight for your goal on a slow dead run, take a series of faster legs on a near-beam reach, jibing periodically. Because this course looks like a beat to windward, the tactic is called tacking downwind. In moderate to fresh winds, however, tacking downwind may take longer than sailing right toward your destination.

When jibing in moderate winds and above, wait for a wave and then jibe as you surf down its face. With your increased speed, the apparent wind will decrease and the main boom will swing across with less force. Remember to head off slightly as the boom comes across in order to absorb the blow.

Running Wing-and-Wing. The jib isn't much use in its normal position on a run or a broad reach because it's blanketed by the mainsail. But you can catch the wind with it by setting it wing-and-wing. Pull it to windward and let it billow out, either by holding the sheet with your hand or, more permanently, by supporting it with a spinnaker pole rigged out from the mast. Lead the jib sheet through the end of the pole and, with the topping lift, adjust the pole height so the jib's leech is almost straight. The sheet must be led outside the shrouds to a block fairly far aft. If you plan to sail wing-and-wing for a while, or if you anticipate a jibe, rig a guy directly to the pole, which can flop around dangerously without its own control. This guy is a line secured to the pole itself and led aft. It provides independent control so the sail and pole are handled separately.

Many long-distance cruising boats carry jibs on both sides with the mainsail doused. The equal pull of the two jibs tends to keep the boat from rolling very badly, and there is very little chafe.

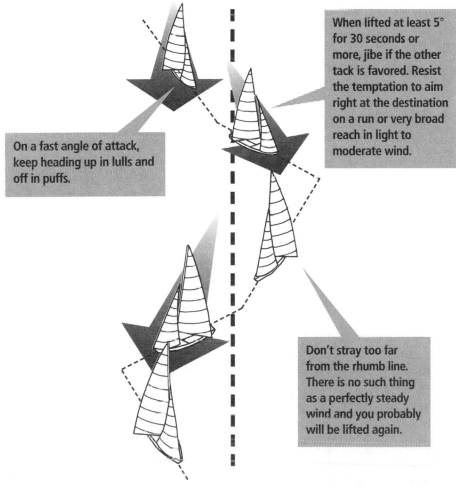

On a fast angle of attack, keep heading up in lulls and off in puffs.

When lifted at least 5° for 30 seconds or more, jibe if the other tack is favored. Resist the temptation to aim right at the destination on a run or very broad reach in light to moderate wind.

Don't stray too far from the rhumb line. There is no such thing as a perfectly steady wind and you probably will be lifted again.

Off the wind, jibing on lifts (tacking downwind) is as effective as tacking on headers upwind. Again, the idea is to sail as fast as possible on the course that takes you closest to the destination.

The Spinnaker

The spinnaker is a big, full, light-weight sail set when sailing downwind to increase sail area and speed. It is sometimes called the kite because it flies high and away from the boat. Sometimes it's called the chute, an abbreviation of parachute, which suggests its bulbous shape. While developed for racing, the spinnaker can be extremely useful aboard cruising boats and daysailers, especially in light air. There are two types: the traditional symmetrical spinnaker set from a spinnaker pole, and the asymmetrical spinnaker set from the bow or a bowsprit. Both are made of nylon cloth, which is much lighter and more resistant to rips than Dacron.

The Symmetrical Spinnaker. Here, the two leeches are the same length and the sail can be set with either side to windward. It is hoisted by a halyard led through a block just above the jib halyard, so the spinnaker is clear of the headstay. When the sail is set, each clew has a line led through a block aft on the deck; one clew (called the tack) is supported by a spar called the spinnaker pole that thrusts the sail out to windard and stabilizes the sail. A symmetrical spinnaker can be carried without a pole, but not with as much control.

The pole is attached to the mast, held up by the topping lift, and kept from rising by the foreguy (pole downhaul). The line led to the tack and pole is the afterguy (a guy is a line that controls the position of a spar). The other line, led to the other clew, is the spinnaker sheet. All these lines are secured to the sail and the pole with snap shackles or (on small boats) knots. On larger boats, two lines are led to each clew — one to serve as the afterguy when that clew is near the pole, the other to serve as the sheet when the pole is on the other side. This twin-sheet system permits optimum control of the spinnaker as the pole is freed from it during a jibe.

Preparing the Spinnaker. Before setting, the spinnaker is prepared. First the crew locates the head and then, with their hands, runs down the two leeches to make sure they aren't tangled. The middle of the sail is then stuffed into a

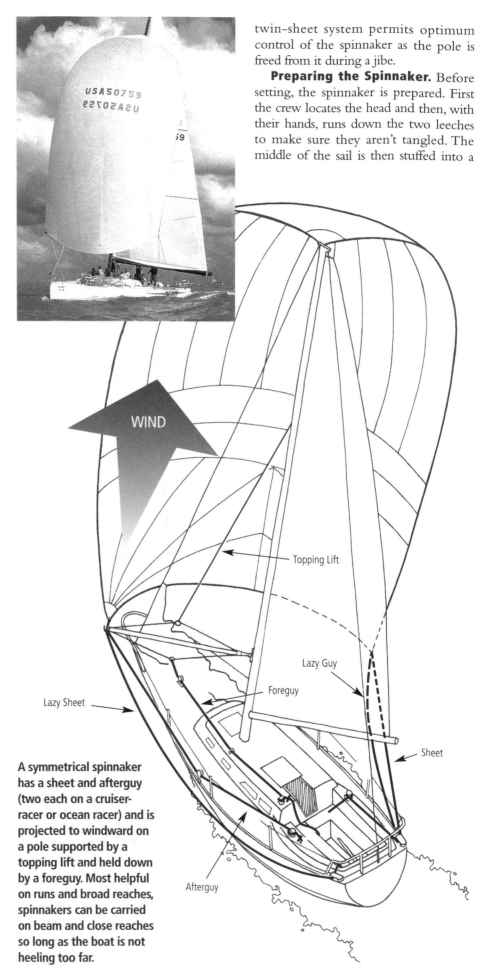

A symmetrical spinnaker has a sheet and afterguy (two each on a cruiser-racer or ocean racer) and is projected to windward on a pole supported by a topping lift and held down by a foreguy. Most helpful on runs and broad reaches, spinnakers can be carried on beam and close reaches so long as the boat is not heeling too far.

WIND

Topping Lift

Lazy Guy

Foreguy

Lazy Sheet

Sheet

Afterguy

container (a sail bag or plastic bucket) and the head and two clews are left dangling, exposed. To keep it from filling prematurely, the spinnaker may be stopped, or bunched every few feet by rubber bands or light twine. Before setting the spinnaker, the container is secured to the leeward side along the lifelines or near the leeward shrouds. Except in very small boats, spinnakers must be pulled up behind the mainsail and jib, where the blanket zone keeps them from filling prematurely. Because a spinnaker is so large, it must be hoisted all the way before it is permitted to fill with wind. The container should be held or tied down to keep it from lifting while the halyard is pulled up.

Then the spinnaker pole is set up. This is a heavy spar that must be handled carefully. Hook it to the mast with the outboard end "cup-up," so the afterguy is inserted from the top down. This arrangement allows the guy to lift itself

Hoist the spinnaker behind the jib. Lead the afterguy through the pole end and pull the tack to the headstay. Keep tension on the foreguy.

out of the pole during a jibe. Insert the afterguy and attach the topping lift and foreguy. Lift the pole to windward of the headstay until it is perpendicular to the mast at an appropriate height and resting against the headstay. On small boats the height is determined by the fixed fitting on the inboard end. But on larger boats the inboard end slides up and down on the mast, and predicting how high the pole should be may be difficult. Only experience will tell.

Pull the afterguy and sheet to the spinnaker's clews and snap them on. Snap the halyard into the sail's head. Check all lines for snarls — for example, the halyard may be hooked behind a spreader or a sheet may be under a lifeline.

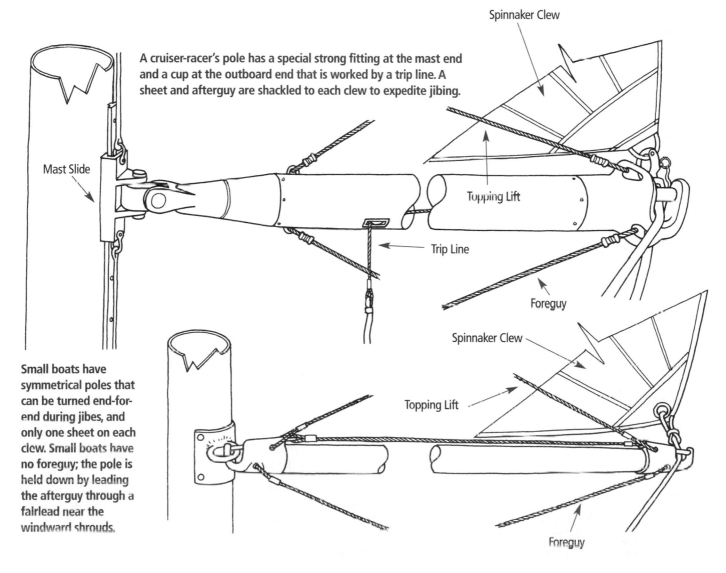

A cruiser-racer's pole has a special strong fitting at the mast end and a cup at the outboard end that is worked by a trip line. A sheet and afterguy are shackled to each clew to expedite jibing.

Mast Slide

Spinnaker Clew

Topping Lift

Trip Line

Foreguy

Spinnaker Clew

Topping Lift

Foreguy

Small boats have symmetrical poles that can be turned end-for-end during jibes, and only one sheet on each clew. Small boats have no foreguy; the pole is held down by leading the afterguy through a fairlead near the windward shrouds.

The Spinnaker

Setting the Spinnaker. Except during races, set the spinnaker on a broad reach. A beam reach imposes large strains, and on a run the spinnaker may be hard to fill and so may twist. Start out in light wind. The crew should first talk through the set by assigning and taking responsibilities. The heaviest loads are on the spinnaker halyard and afterguy. The steerer should be left free to concentrate on steering. If the helm is not tended carefully, the boat may broach (round up) in the middle of a spinnaker set and cause frightful problems as the big sail flies out of control.

The sail should always be hoisted behind and to leeward of the largest working sail, either the mainsail or a genoa jib, so it is blanketed until hoisted all the way. Once the steerer gives the command to hoist, the halyard is pulled smartly while the sheet is trimmed and the afterguy is pulled until the sail's tack is against the pole. Pulling on the clews spreads the leeches so they don't wrap around each other. There should be just enough strain on the sheet and guy to spread the leeches while the sail is hoisted — but not so much that the sail fills before it is two-blocked (hoisted all the way). The spinnaker pole must be against the headstay as sail is hoisted and the afterguy is pulled. Otherwise, hauling on the guy only pulls the spinnaker into the jib and prevents the leeches from spreading. The sail will twist and have to be lowered.

When the spinnaker halyard is two-blocked and cleated, the report "hoisted" is voiced. (As a guide, the halyard should be marked at the two-blocked position.) Then the crew squares the pole (trims the afterguy) until it is approximately perpendicular to the wind. As a guide, use telltales tied to the windward shrouds, the masthead fly, or the feel of the wind on the back of your neck and cheeks. The foreguy must be taut during

Trim the guy and sheet to spread the leeches as the sail is hoisted. When the spinnaker is two-blocked (hoisted all the way) and cleated, square the pole. Keep the jib well eased so it doesn't suck wind out of the spinnaker, and roll it up or lower it after the set.

HANDS ON: **Trimming the Spinnaker**

Trimming the spinnaker is a constant tension between playing (adjusting) the sheet and shifting the pole in order to keep the sail spread out and pulling forward, not to the side. As a rule of thumb, keep the pole at about a right angle to the apparent wind except on a run, when it should be pulled back just far enough so the spinnaker's center is about over the bow. (If the spinnaker is permitted to balloon to windward on a run or very broad reach, the boat will roll.)

Trim the sail by the appearance of the luff on the shoulder, or upper windward edge. Try to keep a small curl or twitch in the shoulder, which plays the same role in the spinnaker as telltales do on the luff of a jib. When the shoulder curls more than 1 foot, it is light (luffing) and the sheet should be trimmed. If it curls more, the pole is too far aft and should be let forward by easing the afterguy and tightening the foreguy. If it doesn't curl at all, the pole can be squared (pulled back) a little.

If the curl is below the shoulder, the outer end of the spinnaker pole is raised too high. If the curl is higher, the pole end is too low. A guide to pole location is the height of the clews, which should be at the same level. If possible, adjust the inboard end so the pole is parallel to the deck and perpendicular to the mast so it thrusts the spinnaker out as far as possible.

As you play the spinnaker, try to picture its chord — an imaginary straight line between the leeches and parallel to the foot — that should be pulling the boat forward. On a beam or close reach, let the pole forward until it's almost touching the headstay. If it leans against the stay, the pole may bend and break.

The spinnaker is so large that in a puff it may heel the boat over suddenly and make

With its clews level and the pole squared just right, this spinnaker is pulling hard.

her broach (swing suddenly into the wind), so a light weather helm gives the steerer control. The trimmer and the steerer must communicate with each other while the spinnaker is up. In moderate winds and above, the spinnaker controls the boat's progress and heading, and if the steerer senses that she is about to lose control, she must tell the trimmer to ease the sheet and let the sail luff. The problem may be that the boat is sailing on too close a reach and the spinnaker is pulling the boat over on her side. In that case, head off a few degrees.

In light winds, the sheet and guy may be cleated and the steerer can "steer the spinnaker full" by sailing by the sail's luff, much as she steers on a close-hauled course.

Ease the sheet until a curl appears. If the curl is more than 12 inches, trim the sheet a bit.

the set. If not, when the sail fills, the pole will sky (lift) and the spinnaker, pole, and perhaps the boat will go out of control. If the foreguy pulls hard, put it on a winch if one is free. The sheet is then played (trimmed and eased) as the trimmer looks at the sail's shoulder (the high corner of the luff).

On dinghies and other boats with small jibs, the jib may usually be left up when the spinnaker is carried, but overlapping jibs should be rolled up or doused and secured to the deck with sail ties. If you leave the jib set, undertrim it (trim it less than optimum), with the luff telltales standing straight up. Otherwise the sail may suck air out of the spinnaker and make it collapse. Some racing boats carry special downwind jibs called staysails under the spinnakers.

The Spinnaker

Spinnaker Problems. Sometimes the spinnaker goes up in a figure-8, with a twist in its middle because it was packed wrong or the leeches were not spread during the hoist. Pull down and back on the leeward leech and the twist may come out. Otherwise you will have to lower the spinnaker, untangle it, and haul it back up again. A twist may also result when the spinnaker sheet is let loose during the set.

Many control problems with the spinnaker are caused by letting the foreguy loose. The pole must be held down at all times.

On a run or broad reach in fresh wind, the spinnaker may oscillate wildly and cause the boat to roll. Steady it by choking it down: trim the sheet way forward through a block near the leeward shrouds, and lower and oversquare the pole (pull it aft a bit too far) as you trim the sheet to keep the sail from collapsing. The wide, flat, stable surface now presented by the sail should stop the rolling.

Jibing the Spinnaker. You must move the spinnaker pole from one side to the other as the boat jibes. You'll have to jibe the spinnaker as well as the mainsail when tacking downwind or making large course alterations, like rounding a buoy. The procedure is different on small and big boats.

On small boats like dinghies and daysailers, the spinnaker pole is double-ended: both ends have the same fittings. The topping lift and foreguy are led to the middle of the pole, allowing it to be jibed end-for-end. Unhook the inboard end from the mast and hook it on the sheet to leeward, which is now the new guy. Then unhook the other end from the old guy and secure it to the mast. This may be done before, while, or after the mainsail is jibed. During the spinnaker jibe, another crew member plays the sheets to keep the sail pulling and

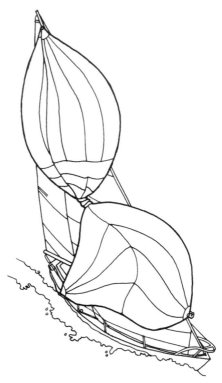

A figure-8 twist will result if the leeches are twisted while the spinnaker is being packed or if the clews are not spread during the hoist.

To jibe the spinnaker on a small boat like this Lightning, unclip the pole from the mast and the afterguy, then clip it to the old sheet and the mast. Keep the sail full and balanced over the boat's bow. If it collapses, it may wrap around the headstay.

the skipper steers slowly through the jibe, keeping the spinnaker balanced over the bow like a seal juggling a ball on its nose.

The jibe is more complicated on larger boats. The strains of big spinnakers are so great that the poles must be secured to the mast with special fittings that do not accept the afterguy. So the same end of the pole must be outboard on both tacks. That means the pole changes sides by dipping through the foretriangle, having its outboard end dropped and swung through to the other side. To accomplish this jibe, there must be two sheets on each clew. Between jibes, only one sheet is under strain; the other is lazy (unused) until the jibe. These are the steps of a twin-sheet, dip-pole jibe:

One crew member takes the lazy (slack and unused) afterguy on the leeward side forward to the bow. The outboard end of the spinnaker pole is opened by pulling a trigger (with a line led through the pole), allowing the old guy to float up and out (this is why the pole is arranged cup-up). A crew member eases the topping lift to lower the pole to the foredeck crew. When the outboard end reaches the foredeck crew, he clips the new afterguy (the old lazy guy) into the fitting. As the pole swings to the new windward side and is raised with the topping lift, a crew member aft trims the new guy. When the pole fitting comes up snug against the sail's clew, the old sheet is released. Large, well-trained racing crews can carry this maneuver off very quickly. But as long as the spinnaker is restrained from lifting high, a dip-pole jibe can be accomplished slowly and step-by-step by a small cruising crew.

The dip-pole jibe can be performed without twin guys, but only in light wind. After the pole is dropped from the old guy, a crew member pulls the new guy (under strain) down to the foredeck where it is wrestled into the pole fitting.

Except in light wind and small boats, one crew member should be assigned to trim and ease the main sheet through the jibe. If you're shorthanded, trim the mainsail amidships before the jibe, leave it there until the jibe is finished, and then pay out the sheet. The main boom must be kept from swinging across out of control, since it can injure sailors and damage gear. As the boom begins to come across, the steerer or main sheet trimmer announces loudly, "boom coming across!" Don't head up drastically on the new course until the crew is ready to trim both the mainsail and the spinnaker, otherwise the boat may be knocked right over on her side and broach out of control.

In heavy weather, larger boats may be jibed with two spinnaker poles, running out a new pole on the new side and clipping it up to the lazy guy before the jibe, and then removing the old pole.

On a large boat with a twin-guy system, the pole is dipped during the jibe after being unclipped from the afterguy. The crew at the bow is clipping the pole to the lazy guy on the new side and the crew at the mast will raise the topping lift. Usually the mainsail is trimmed amidships or carefully guided across, but here it is allowed to swing across freely since the wind is light.

The Spinnaker

Dousing the Spinnaker. Plan the spinnaker douse as carefully as you did the hoist, with a crew member assigned to each task. The sail usually is pulled down behind the largest working sail so it is blanketed and in control. The halyard must be carefully overhauled before it is let go to guarantee that there are no snags.

On a small boat, raise the jib (if necessary) and trim it properly for the course. One crew member then moves to leeward and grabs the sheet as another frees the afterguy, which runs out through the pole fitting. The sheet and leech are pulled in behind the mainsail, and as the halyard is eased quickly but under control, the spinnaker is pulled into the cockpit. The pole is removed and the lines and spinnaker are neatened up. Alternatively, in a small boat the spinnaker may be doused to windward. After trimming the jib, remove and stow the pole. Then release the sheet so the sail flags out ahead, pull back on the afterguy, and lower the halyard as the sail is pulled down. An advantage of this system is that nobody has to go to leeward, so heel can be controlled.

On larger boats, unroll or hoist and trim the jib and then lower the pole until the outboard end can be reached from deck. The foredeck crew trips (opens) the afterguy's shackle, and as the spinnaker blows behind the jib, one or more crew members gather the leeward leech behind the mainsail or jib. They can let the freed windward leech fly to leeward because, without a sheet, it won't fill. Only when they have complete control over the sail is the halyard eased and the spinnaker brought down on deck. Don't try to douse the spinnaker if it's filled aloft. Once the sail is below, lower and stow the spinnaker pole on deck.

When the afterguy is tripped, the pole will snap back violently as the guy rebounds from stretch. The foredeck crew must be to leeward of the pole. A big boat's spinnaker can be doused like a small boat's by letting the afterguy run out through the pole end, but the considerable friction of sheet against pole may allow the sail to fill far out to leeward of the jib's blanketing zone. In case you douse this way, be sure not to tie knots in the ends of the spinnaker sheets and guys.

Setting and Dousing Systems. Systems for setting and dousing a spinnaker involve a fabric sleeve or sock pulled around the sail. It holds the spinnaker while it is being raised. Once the sail is hoisted, a line is pulled to retract the sock and open up the sail. The sheets are trimmed to open the spinnaker and allow it to fill with wind. When dousing the sail, the sock is pulled down as the sheets are eased. The sock and sail are lowered on deck. These systems have tremendous value, especially for shorthanded crews who are unable to handle the various chores of a normal set and douse.

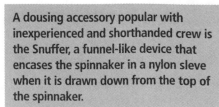

A dousing accessory popular with inexperienced and shorthanded crew is the Snuffer, a funnel-like device that encases the spinnaker in a nylon sleve when it is drawn down from the top of the spinnaker.

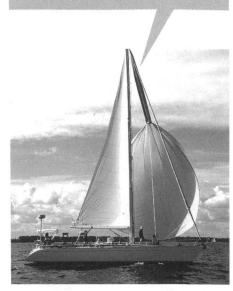

Dousing the spinnaker behind the mainsail or jib keeps it from filling (left and left below). Don't worry if it gets a little wet, but avoid catching a clew in the water. (Below) If you can't douse the spinnaker immediately, just let the afterguy out all the way (this is why you don't tie knots in the ends of spinnaker guys and sheets) and allow the sail to flag to leeward. When the crew is ready, head off to a run, pull the spinnaker in behind the mainsail, and lower it.

The Asymmetrical Spinnaker

Asymmetrical spinnakers (asymmetrics) also are lightweight and billowing, but they do not require spinnaker poles. They look and are set somewhat like a very full, broad genoa jib, although they are not set on the headstay. The luff is longer than the leech (it is this asymmetry that gives this spinnaker its name). Instead of being set on a pole thrust out to windward, an asymmetric is tacked down to or near the bow or a retractable pole (sprit) that extends straight out from the bow.

Asymmetrics are primarily reaching sails because they cannot project out to windward as well as a symmetrical spinnaker set on a spinnaker pole (some asymmetrics are designed to work effectively at deeper wind angles). The upside is that they don't require a heavy spinnaker pole with its potential danger and elaborate gear.

To jibe an asymmetric, head off, let one sheet go, allow the sail to fly forward of the bow, and pull on the other sheet.

There are two types of asymmetrics. The cruising spinnaker is tacked to the bow or to a short pendant. This pendant can be adjusted, like a Cunningham, to move the draft in the sail — forward on a close reach in order to flatten the sail's leech, aft on a broad reach to make the sail more like a parachute. (The cruising spinnaker need not be asymmetrical. A normal spinnaker may be set without a spinnaker pole by tacking it down to the bow.)

The cruising spinnaker is relatively small and tame compared with the racing asymmetric that is tacked to the end of a sprit sticking forward from the bow. This sprit allows a longer foot and also projects the sail well away from the other sails. Modern sport boats, America's Cup contenders, and offshore racers carry very large asymmetrics.

Many modern cruiser-racers fly asymmetrics from retractable sprits that extend from the bow (below). This design is optimized for reaching, with a relatively flat shape and a high clew.

(Above) Cruisers often fly asymmetric "Gennakers" with the clew attached to the headstay. These sails feature a small, easily managed profile that is forgiving to fly over a wide range of wind angles.

Sail Care and Repair

Tape over sail rips using a large overlap (top); sew rips and broken seams with a loose over-and-under stitch (above).

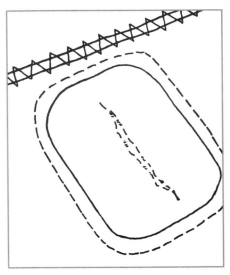

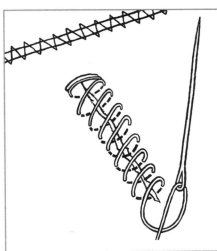

Sailcloth becomes more stretchy when it's heavily creased or wrinkled. Don't let sails luff too long. (An advantage of full-length battens is that they extend the life of a sail because they prevent extreme luffing.) Carefully flake, furl, fold, or roll sails after each use. To flake a mainsail on the boom, make neat 2- to 3-foot folds parallel to the battens and secure the sail with sail ties. Mains and jibs may also be folded after stretching the foot out on the foredeck, pier, or grass. The very stiff sails used on small racing boats should be rolled up. Sails made of soft cloth may be folded along the foot and placed in sail bags, while those made of stiff cloth are laid in long, sausage-shaped pouches without further folding.

Two main causes of sail damage are the sun's ultraviolet rays and chafe. To protect against the former, which eventually will destroy stitching, always cover or bag the sails when they're not hoisted. Chafe is most likely where the sail bears against the standing rigging. When the mainsail is eased all the way out on a run and the boom vang is not tight, its belly rubs against the leeward spreader and shrouds. Genoa jibs are likely to rip if they are trimmed against the leeward spreaders or lifelines. Reinforcing patches must be sewn or taped on the sails at the point of normal chafe. Nylon, which is stronger and stretchier than Dacron, chafes through very rarely, but a nylon spinnaker can be ripped by a fitting.

Keeping battens parallel to creases, fold mainsails and jibs in large flakes and stow them in long sausage-shaped bags.

Battens can break when sails luff violently in heavy weather, and their sharp ends may cut through the sail. This is another reason to keep luffing down to a minimum. Carry a spare set of battens.

Small rips and punctures in sails can be repaired quickly with special sticky-backed tape available from sailmakers and marine supply stores. Duct tape works as a temporary patch. Dry the sail, then stretch it over a flat surface and press the tape down hard. Use enough tape to extend several inches beyond the rip. A hot knife may be used to seal the edges. (Battery-powered hot knives also cut line, sealing the ends.) Eventually a rip must be sewn up. Carry a sailmaker's sewing kit consisting of special needles and twine, and a palm — a small glove with a hard center used to shove needles through cloth. A simple over-and-under stitch works best, six stitches per inch and taken loosely, since the sail will stretch around your seam once it fills.

If you sail on salt water, give your sails a thorough hosing off with fresh water every now and then. While they won't damage the sail's integrity, salt crystals absorb moisture, which increases the sail's weight and may lead to mildew.

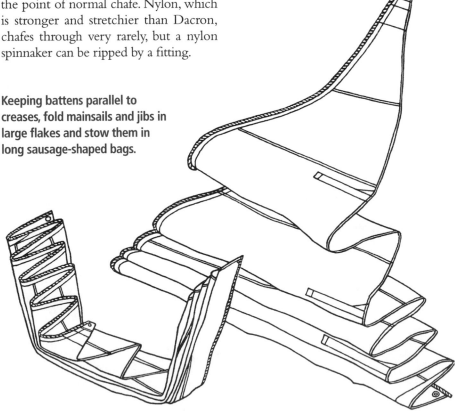

A sailmaker can easily sew a patch on a sail where it chafes against rigging or fittings. The jib above has spreader patches where the leech can rub against the spreader.

Never wash your sails in automatic clothes washers, dry them in dryers, or iron them. The tumbling and heat will take the life out of them. Sailmakers can clean sails properly after the end of the season and at the same time check them for damage.

No matter how carefully you look after your sails, they eventually will blow out (lose their shape). If the draft shifts aft permanently and cannot be repositioned by the Cunningham, or if the leech flaps around no matter how hard you pull the leech line, the sail should be replaced by a new one if you care about good performance.

Sail Care Under Way. "It is possible to do serious, irreversible damage to sails in a few bad minutes," says Bill Bergantz of North Sails. One common mistake is not looking at a sail while you trim or hoist it. You may pull it into the leeward spreader or the halyard sheave. Another is to hoist a sail when it's full, which will strain the luff and leech. Hoist sails when close hauled or close reaching, and with the sheets eased. And a third mistake is to hoist a sail without carefully checking that it's fouled. If a batten or the leech line fouls on a cleat, for example, you could rip the leech.

When making adjustments under way, anticipate that loads will be high, even in light air. The low-stretch materials used in today's sail fabrics, sheets, and halyards have little flexibility. When something busts, it busts with a bang. When tightening a halyard, ease the load by luffing the sail a little or pinching to spill wind. Otherwise, you could break the halyard (or pull one of your muscles). When putting the boat away at the end of the day, take the load off the sails by easing the mainsail's outhaul and the roller-furling jib's halyard a couple of inches.

If the sail has battens, never set it without them or the sail will quickly lose its shape. Roller-furled sails may be set partially rolled, or reefed, but not in a heavy blow or for an extended time if the cloth is lightweight and the corners are not properly reinforced. This is the time to set a smaller jib or work your way through the squall under mainsail alone.

When you take the sails off the boat at the end of the season and put them back on at commissioning (getting-ready) time, take some time to stretch them out on a clean lawn or floor and examine them for chafe, loose stitching and other wear. An especially vulnerable spot is along near the leech of an overlapping jib that has been trimmed too far and the spreader's tip has stretched it. Mark that place and take it to your sailmaker for a reinforcing patch called a spreader patch. Have the sailmaker resew worn or loose stitches and reinforce any loose corners or reef cringles, which take the largest load.

Finally, keep your eyes peeled for open cotter pins sticking out of turnbuckles or blocks and for meathooks in wire halyards. If something can snag a sail, it will snag a sail.

CHAPTER 4 # Weather

"Weather" means something more to sailors than it does to most landlubbers. It's not simply the day's local temperature, visibility, and precipitation, but a process. In the Northern Hemisphere, packets of warm and cool air flow from west to east, driven by huge whirlpools of wind located over the centers of the oceans and pulled along by the earth's spin. Weather can be predicted quite accurately not only by meteorologists but also by lay people who are alert to the sky and the environment. The most important telltales of coming weather are the current wind direction, cloud condition, and barometer reading, each of which, if properly "read," predicts weather changes over the next few hours. Other helpful factors are the previous day's conditions (weather is a system, not an isolated event), local geography (which can funnel air packets and change wind direction), the season (weather follows seasonal cycles), the time of day (winds generally shift as the land heats up in the afternoon), and weather hundreds of miles to the west (for weather generally moves from west to east).

A note on terminology: a wind is

As it does in many sailing areas, the afternoon sea breeze dominates San Francisco Bay's summer weather pattern. By mid-afternoon the wind pouring from the Pacific through the Golden Gate into the bay (opposite) reaches force 6 (22–27 knots) and the sky is clear. A fog bank or wall of fog (below) heralds the late afternoon cooling of the land and the death of the sea breeze.

The Daily Weather Cycle

named according to the direction from which it comes. Therefore, a "westerly wind" or "westerly" is a wind blowing from the west, while a boat on a "westerly heading" steers toward the west, perhaps into the teeth of a westerly.

Before looking at storms and large-scale weather, let's see how local conditions can affect wind and visibility. Our example is a typical summer day in San Francisco, California. The forces that affect weather over that bayfront city apply almost everywhere a harbor fronts on an ocean or a large lake. In other places, the rising afternoon sea breeze

wind blows from the east or south. But in few places does it blow as regularly and as hard as it does in San Francisco Bay, where almost every hot summer afternoon is swept by a cool southwest wind whistling through the Golden Gate at 20 or more knots. This afternoon southwesterly is only the most lively in San Francisco Bay's daily summer drama.

At dawn the bay is foggy, overcast, and calm. What little wind there is comes from the south southwest (200°). By late morning the sky has begun to clear and the breeze begins to pick up a bit as it veers (shifts clockwise) toward southwest (225°). By 2 PM the sky is blue and the wind is whipping up steep, short waves. By 4 PM it may be blowing at strong as 30 knots. Two hours later, the sun is dropping beyond the Golden Gate in a haze of fog rolling in from the Pacific, and the wind is fading. At chilly sunset, all that remains of the afternoon wind is a jumble of leftover waves. As the wind dies, it backs (shifts counterclockwise)

(Left) Fronting on the Pacific, San Francisco Bay is a good example of a sailing area whose winds are governed by the daily cycle of changing land, sea, and air temperatures.

into the south southwest. It has followed the sun all day by veering. Now that the sun has set, it returns to its night direction. By midnight there is only a light wind carrying the haunting toot of fog horns across the bay.

The daily summer weather cycle over San Francisco Bay illustrates general principles. First, the westerly component to the wind is largely due to massive geographical and atmospheric conditions. Sitting about 900 miles out in the Pacific is a mountain of moist, cool, high-pressure air. The Pacific high is one of a series of big high-pressure systems lying in a belt north of the equator (another belt lies south of the equator).

Second, this air is relatively stable and dense because it sits above a huge expanse of water. The sea's temperature, unlike that of land, usually changes little during a season. When it does change, the effects can be great and widespread. The astonishing amount of havoc wrecked across America during 1997–98 by the return of the Pacific's warm El Niño current illustrates just how reliably steady the ocean temperature is the rest of the time.

Third, this cool, wet air blows from the west over warm, unstable land. It is the dance between the land's temperature and the sea's that causes San Francisco Bay's summer weather pattern. "Air, moisture, and heat — these are the basic ingredients of earth's weather," writes Admiral William J. Kotsch in his *Weather for the Mariner.* A volume of cool, wet maritime air is more dense and weighs more than an equal volume of warm, dry land air, which is why sea air has a higher atmospheric pressure than land air. A barometer in the middle of the Pacific high (or Atlantic high) may read 30.5 inches (1034 millibars), while one toward the edge of the high, nearer land, may read as low as 30.0 inches (1016 millibars). On weather maps, areas with these pressure levels are bounded by lines, much the same way that mountain elevations are shown on contour maps. These lines of equal atmospheric pressure are isobars. The pattern of the isobars determines how the wind blows.

San Francisco Bay

Pacific Ocean

The Prevailing Southwest Wind

Like water flowing down a hill, air rushes from the peaks of the high-pressure "mountains" to the low-pressure "valleys." This rushing air is wind, and the greater the difference between atmospheric pressures, the steeper the slope and the harder the wind blows. The wind's path is not straight, but curved by the earth's spin. This curving tendency, the coriolis force or effect, twists all moving forces (including the wind and water in flushed toilets) to the right in the Northern Hemisphere and to the left in the Southern. It is greatest at the ends of

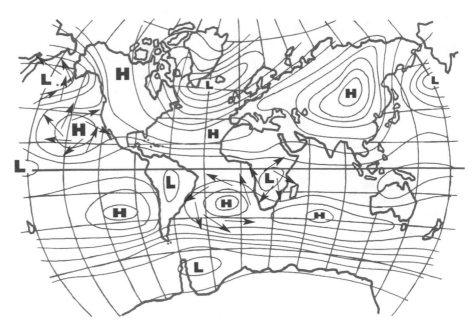

Air flows down the slopes between high-pressure "mountains" and low-pressure "valleys" in swirling patterns. In the Northern Hemisphere, air circulates clockwise and outward from a high and counterclockwise and inward to a low. South of the equator these directions are reversed.

If the earth were stationary, cold dense air would flow directly from the poles to the great low-pressure "valley" at the equator . . .

. . . but the coriolis effect of the spinning earth redirects flow to the right in the Northern Hemisphere and creates vortexes of moving air.

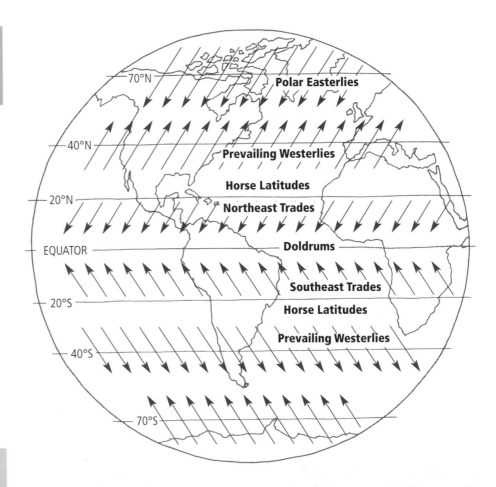

The vortexes of air are distributed in belts. The flow between belts of highs and lows is remarkably predictable. Between the belts of prevailing (or trade) winds lie belts of calm called doldrums. The patterns change seasonally with the earth's tilt relative to the sun.

the earth: about 15° at the poles, about 9° at New York and San Francisco, and about 6° at Miami. At the equator, the force is nonexistent. A high, then, behaves like a great pinwheel, throwing wind out to the right as it rotates clockwise. South of the high, the prevailing (normal) wind will blow from the north and east. North of the high, the wind will prevail from the south and west.

The belt of highs girds the globe at approximately 30° north latitude, which passes through northern Florida. Sometimes the highs are farther north, sometimes they're farther south. But usually, most of North America lies above the belt of highs and so the prevailing wind is a southwesterly or westerly.

Low-pressure air packets, or lows, work opposite to highs. Where highs spin air outward in a clockwise direction, lows pull in air in a counter-clockwise direction in the Northern Hemisphere as wind follows its curved downhill course across the isobars. When they're tangent, winds around a high and a low spin much like two interlocking gears, either greatly accelerating the wind or causing a calm.

Geography and Wind. When the Pacific high's prevailing winds finally reach San Francisco, they are westerlies, but the land deflects them into the south

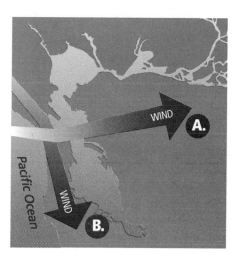

southwest. Early in the morning, before the sun has been up sufficiently long to warm the land, this wind brings cold, damp air off the ocean into the bay and city. Across the bay in Marin County, where there is a larger land mass than on the San Francisco peninsula, the land and air heat more quickly than in the city and the sky is relatively clear. But over in the city, people make their way to work in a clammy, gray morning. Ten miles out to sea at the barren Farralone Islands there may be a fresh westerly blowing at 20 knots.

When wind blows onto a shore like the San Francisco peninsula at an acute angle (A), it is deflected so it hits land at a right angle. If it blows at a shallow angle (B), it ends up parallel to the shoreline.

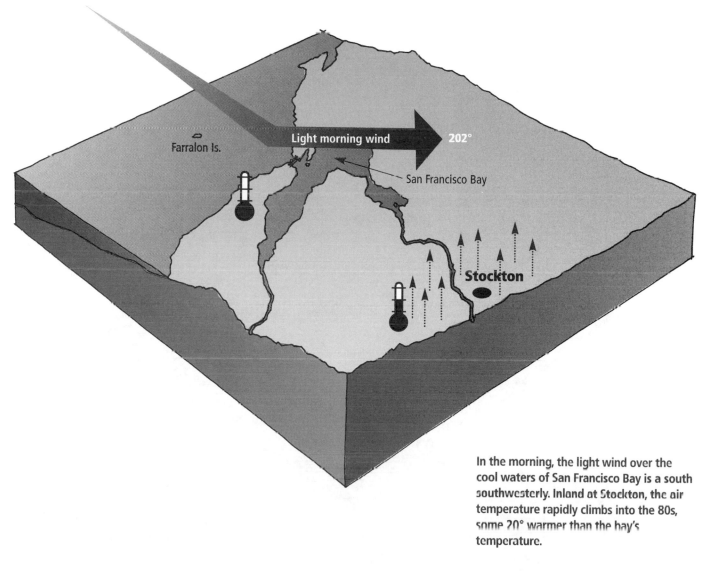

In the morning, the light wind over the cool waters of San Francisco Bay is a south southwesterly. Inland at Stockton, the air temperature rapidly climbs into the 80s, some 20° warmer than the bay's temperature.

The Thermal Effect

Meanwhile, the star of the San Francisco weather drama is just getting out of bed. Some 50 miles inland from the bay, the dry semidesert of the San Joaquin River Valley is beginning to heat up under the morning sun. The night before, the temperature at Stockton, the major city in the valley, may have dropped into the 60s as the great expanse of arid land cooled under a cloudless sky. Now Stockton's temperature is quickly climbing. By noon it's in the 80s, much higher than the temperature over San Francisco Bay. The hot, dry air expands and rises like a thermal mushroom cloud to create a local low-pressure system that pulls in the cooler air over the bay and Pacific.

"The wind doesn't blow here," San Francisco sailors say. "The valley sucks." The valley inhales air like an enormous vacuum cleaner. Tumbling down the intake hose that is the steep gradient between the two pressure systems come the cool, dense air particles of the Pacific high. As the temperature rises at Stockton, the suction builds. The wind increases on the bay until it rushes through the Golden Gate at over 20 and even 30 knots. As the wind builds, it veers into the southwest, since the powerful intake has tempered the land's effect. The wind blows away the fog, the sun gradually breaks through, and by mid-afternoon the bay is a glory of sparkling whitecaps.

In late afternoon the San Joaquin Valley starts to cool and the air over it settles. With its mainspring winding down, the great San Francisco Bay wind machine begins to slow. The wind dies as the air cools, and by sunset the breeze is less than 12 knots and gradually backing into the south southwest as the fog rolls back into the bay from the Pacific. By midnight the city is damp and still.

Especially dramatic on San Francisco Bay, this diurnal three-act play is acted

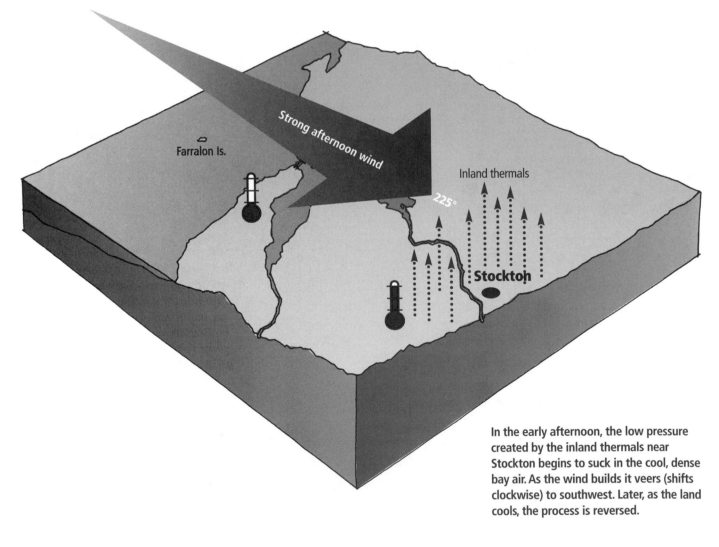

Farralon Is.

Strong afternoon wind

Inland thermals

225°

Stockton

In the early afternoon, the low pressure created by the inland thermals near Stockton begins to suck in the cool, dense bay air. As the wind builds it veers (shifts clockwise) to southwest. Later, as the land cools, the process is reversed.

out wherever warm land fronts on a large body of water. When hot, dry air rises over land, cooler, damp air is sucked in under it. This action produces the sea breeze or lake breeze — an onshore wind created by the temperature and pressure differentials between water and land. The larger the difference (up to a point), the stronger the wind. In some areas, the process is reversed at night: as the land cools more rapidly than the more stable water, the bay or lake sucks air out as a light offshore land breeze.

Often these sea breezes are called "thermals," but in fact a thermal is the rising column of warm air that sucks in cool air. The invisible cloud of hot air rising over California's San Joaquin River Valley is a thermal, not the wind that it pulls in. If the land mass fronts on a water mass to the east, the temperature difference will cause easterly winds; to the south, southerlies; to the north, northerlies. The strongest sea breezes often are the ones where the water is to the west of the land, because the wind is bolstered by the prevailing westerlies.

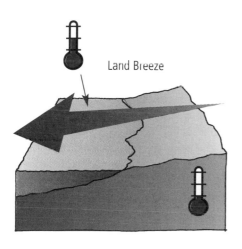
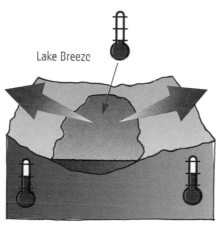

Land temperature is more unstable than the temperature of large bodies of water, so when the land cools at night an offshore land breeze may develop (left), to be replaced by the daytime onshore sea or lake breeze (right). The land breeze usually is less strong.

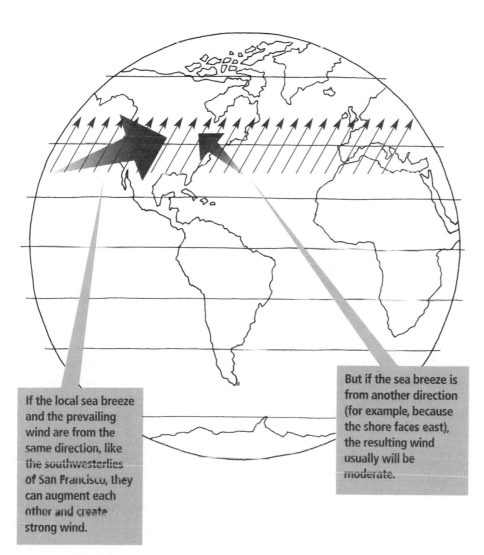

If the local sea breeze and the prevailing wind are from the same direction, like the southwesterlies of San Francisco, they can augment each other and create strong wind.

But if the sea breeze is from another direction (for example, because the shore faces east), the resulting wind usually will be moderate.

Trade Winds

Highs and Lows

Old-time seamen called the offshore prevailing winds "trade winds" (or "the trades") for the way they predictably carried waterborne commerce from port to port. Blowing in great highways from pressure system to pressure system, the trades were mapped and exploited as thoroughly (and as secretly) as a navy today traces undersea canyons for its submarines. The North Atlantic's strong northeast trades begin to blow hard so regularly in late December that in the Caribbean they are called the "Christmas winds." Yet the trades are not perfectly reliable. Between them lie narrow belts of calm, called the doldrums, that may expand and wander from their usual position. Sometimes the trades are tardy or weak, and sometimes the environment plays tricks.

The prevailing (trade) wind patterns change seasonally as the land, sea, and air temperatures are affected by alterations in the earth's tilt and, therefore, the angle at which the sun's rays strike.

The passage of pressure systems also changes the seasonal pattern, onshore as well as offshore. A low-pressure cell may march across the North American continent in four or five days, pick up speed over the Atlantic, and three or four days later cut across England and continental Europe. These are pockets of hot or cold, dry or wet air usually riding on the prevailing winds of the stationary pressure systems. They are like eddies and whirlpools formed at shallow points or edges of streams. Sometimes the vortex is weak and carries for only a while. Sometimes it is powerful and charges off on its own long course. Likewise, a low-pressure weather system may build up and die with no more consequence than a rain shower or two, or it may become a destructive tornado or hurricane, with a swirling column of tightly packed air ranging across land or water on an erratic path.

Pressure systems are created by differences in air temperature and humidity — and therefore in air pressure. If the differences are large, an immense amount of energy is released. Geography plays an important part. If the earth were smooth, with no valleys or mountains, and if the globe did not go through its seasonal cycle of tilts, there probably would be no differences in air temperature or pressure, and no storms. But neither is the case. Only rarely is the atmosphere stable. Air masses of varying intensity, temperature, and humidity bounce across the continents and seas, sometimes spawning other systems and often energized by changing temperatures in the ground and the sea below them.

These air masses are named for their origins: maritime (air coming from the sea), continental (from large land masses), polar (from the polar regions), and tropical (from the equator). Continental

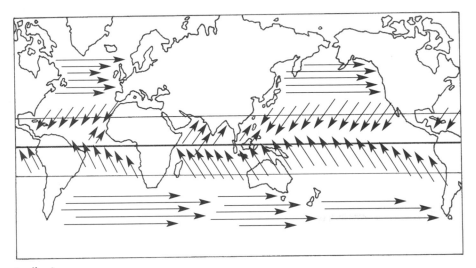

April – June

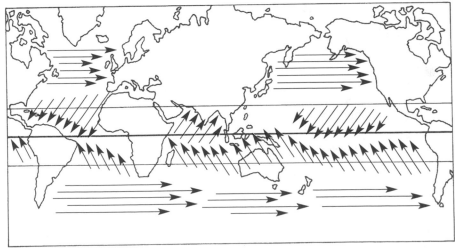

July – September

polar air sweeping down from Canada is cold and dry; continental tropical air coming up from Mexico is hot and dry. Maritime polar air moving south from Alaska or Greenland is cold and wet; maritime tropical air from the Caribbean is warm and wet. (Another air mass, Arctic, has extremely cold air but has little effect on summer weather.)

Air masses are known by their geographical origin: maritime (wet air), continental (dry), polar (cold), and tropical (hot). They can combine in different ways.

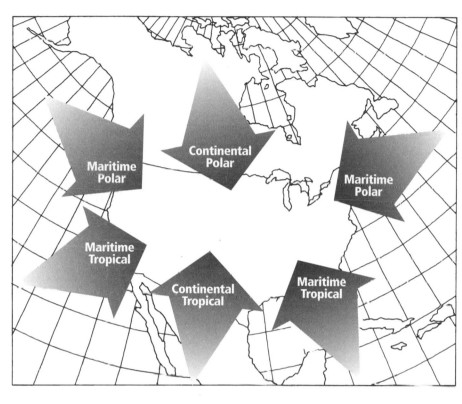

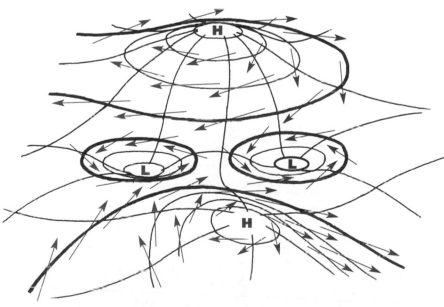

The coriolis effect, changes in air pressure and temperature, and other factors create chains of low- and high-pressure systems that can interlock like gears. If they turn in the same direction, the wind is stronger; if in opposite directions, there may be a calm.

Fronts

When one air packet confronts a different one, there is a front line between them and the front is called by the type of air that follows it. For example, a mass of continental polar air lumbering over the Canadian border on the jet stream — the west wind in the upper atmosphere — brings cold, dry, high-pressure air to the midwestern United States. If it collides with a packet of maritime tropical air that has wandered north from the Gulf of Mexico, bringing hot, damp air in a low-pressure system, sparks will fly. That is literally true, since one outlet of the energy created by the two masses is lightning. Another outlet is wind; a third is rain. The weather is most unstable and dangerous along the front line where the two masses meet. If it's a cold front, with continental polar air following maritime tropical air, the temperature will drop quickly and the damp clouds of the maritime tropical air will be blown away by gusty, cool northwest winds rushing down the steep gradient of the "mountain" of cold high-pressure air toward the "valley" of warm low-pressure air.

We all recognize a summer cold front. One day may be hot and humid under a suffocating layer of clouds. Black clouds slowly appear among the gray ones, thin currents of cool air pierce the thick blanket of humidity, and the atmosphere seems charged with the violent change. The western sky darkens, the wind races, lightning flashes, and rain whips horizontally. In the middle of the night you awaken in a chill and dig a blanket out of the closet. Hours later the sun rises on a clear, blue, cool day swept dry by a fresh northwest wind, "the clearing northwester." Inland and on the East Coast, the clearing wind is gusty and shifting because it arrives after a long journey across a continent of irregular land shapes and an atmosphere of warm and cold valleys and mountains.

Although they're drawn as lines on weather maps, fronts are thick zones of

Fronts

transition between 5 and 60 miles wide in which are mixed the characteristics of both air masses. On either side of the front the weather is relatively stable from hour to hour, but within it the weather is dynamic and sometimes dramatic.

There are four major types of front:

Cold front. Colder (usually polar) air replaces warmer (usually tropical) air.

Warm front. Warmer air replaces colder air.

Occluded front. A cold front overtakes a stationary or slow-moving warm front and pushes the warmer, less dense air aloft.

Stationary front. The front does not move, and air is not replaced or displaced.

The Cold Front. The cold front often is the most dangerous. As continental polar air passes over warmer land, it is heated and becomes unstable. This means that its component air masses never really settle down. A cold front's calling card

usually is a mass of dense towering cumulus clouds indicating vertical instability. Other signs are thunder squalls, lightning storms, and gusty winds. Cold fronts can move very fast, about 600 miles a day in winter, somewhat slower in summer, so they often take people by surprise.

As a cold front passes, the wind veers (shifts clockwise). If you stand with your back to the wind it will shift to your left as the front passes — more likely than not settling down around northwest and becoming extremely gusty.

Another herald of the front is a rapid drop in the barometer. As the front swings through, however, the cold, dense air of the new system brings the barometer up again. The steeper and more prolonged the drop in the barometer, the more intense the frontal storm and the stronger the wind.

A cross-section drawing of a cold front shows the new, heavier air forcing

A cold front is a fast-moving wedge of dense cool air prying up the warm air it meets in a tower of cumulus clouds, followed by squalls and strong wind.

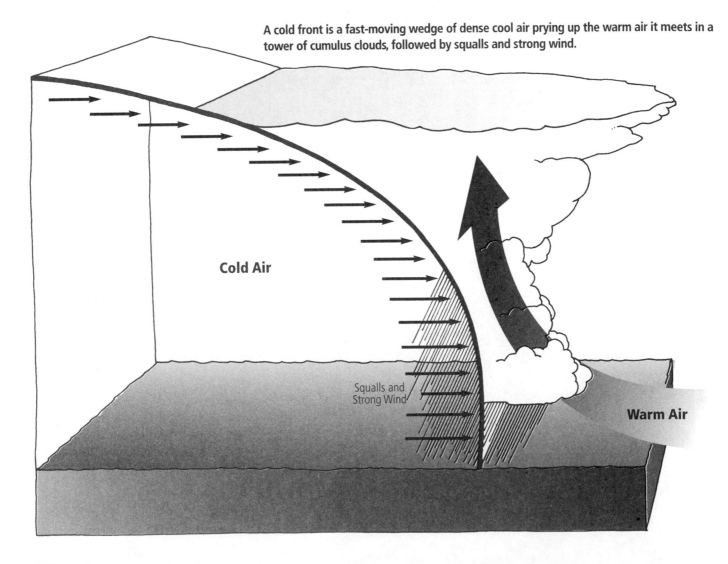

Cold Air

Squalls and
Strong Wind

Warm Air

its way under the old, lighter air like a wedge. A cold front's passage usually is sharp and may be violent, as when a lever pries up a boulder.

The Warm Front. A warm front is less dramatic because often it originates over water, whose temperature and humidity are more stable than land. The advancing warm, moist air slides over the cooler air ahead in a blanket of filmy high cirrus clouds. Warm fronts move about half the speed of cold fronts, at about 360 miles a day during winter and less than 180 miles a day in summer. The cold air slowly retreats to the east and the clouds gradually lower and thicken. Rain falls and continues unabated. The barometer falls, too: again, the steeper and quicker the drop, the stronger the wind. If there is a confused mix of air in the front, there may be local instability, with thunderstorms and rapidly building winds. Once the front finally passes, the rain stops or becomes a drizzle, the wind

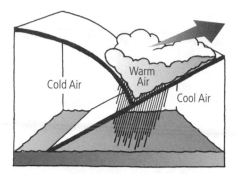

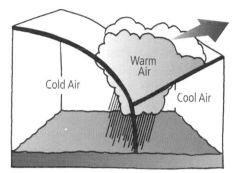

An occluded front can occur in several ways when cold air heaves up large packets of warm air.

veers, and the barometer steadies.

The Occluded Front. In an occluded front, faster-moving cold air shoves warm air ahead of it up and into the atmosphere, not simply wedging under it as the cold front does. The warm air rises in high cumulus clouds. If the temperature and humidity differences between the two systems are not great, an occluded front may lead to stable weather. But stormy, unpredictable weather results if the air packets are radically different.

The Stationary Front. A fourth type of front is the stationary front, in which two different air masses lie on either side of a distinct frontal line with no interaction — much like the ingredients of an oil-and-vinegar salad dressing. Usually this happens because neither air mass is particularly well defined. A change in their characteristics, or the arrival of another air mass, may transform this neutral front into either a warm or a cold front.

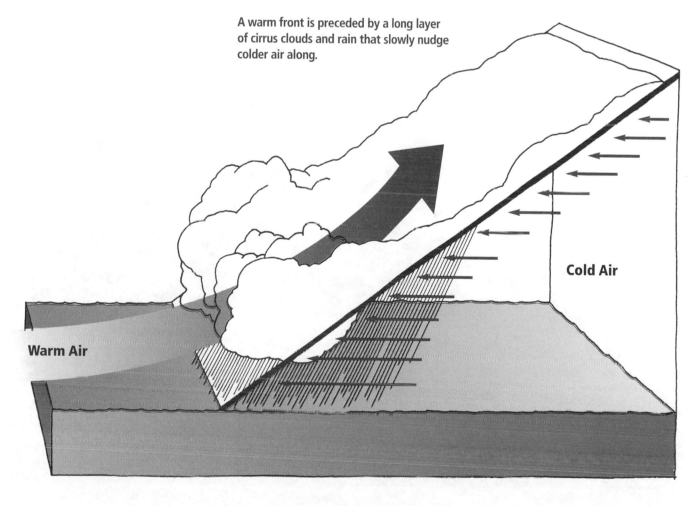

A warm front is preceded by a long layer of cirrus clouds and rain that slowly nudge colder air along.

Cold Air

Warm Air

Low-Pressure Systems

More dangerous than fronts are depressions, the tight, volatile, comma-shaped low-pressure systems often formed by waves of unstable air at the front edge of cold fronts. Sometimes the instability is caused by sharp local contrasts in air or water temperature. In many parts of North America, some of the year's most damaging storms occur around the volatile times of the spring and autumn equinoxes, when equal amounts of day and night produce widely flunctuating temperatures. The depressions that have helped give Cape Hatteras, North Carolina, the gloomy nickname "the graveyard of ships" are so destructive because the cape is a dangerous intersection where cold, dry air swinging down from the north crashes into warm, damp air flowing up from the south above the 80° waters of the Gulf Stream, passing just offshore.

Depressions, because their air pressure is low, suck in air in a spiral. As the upper-air spiral moves along, it pulls the bottom of the vortex along with it. A tornado is an extremely small, localized depression, as is a waterspout. In each case warm air is sucked into the column at its base and feeds it. A hurricane or typhoon is the most powerful kind of depression, formed over energy-rich hot tropical waters when a small, deep depression is charged by strong winds blowing far above the earth's surface.

As it pinwheels across Cuba and the Yucatan Peninsula of Mexico, Hurricane Allen displays the tight comma shape of a classic depression. It sucks in clouds from as far away as Puerto Rico. Another depression has formed in the Pacific off the west coast of Mexico.

A Classic Storm

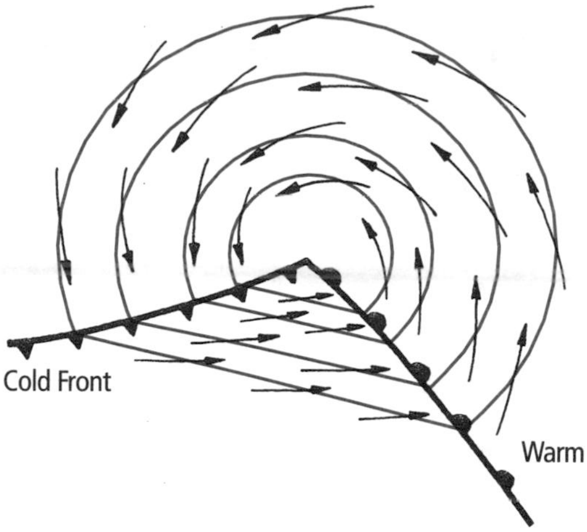

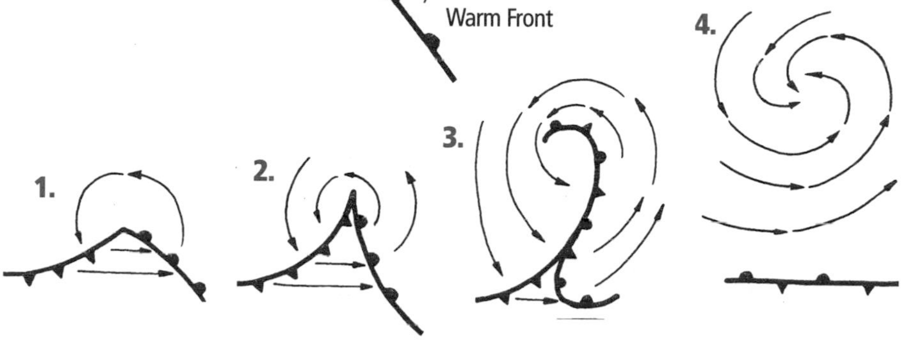

Depressions may be caused when air packets near cold fronts spin off on their own, fed by warm air sucked in at their base.

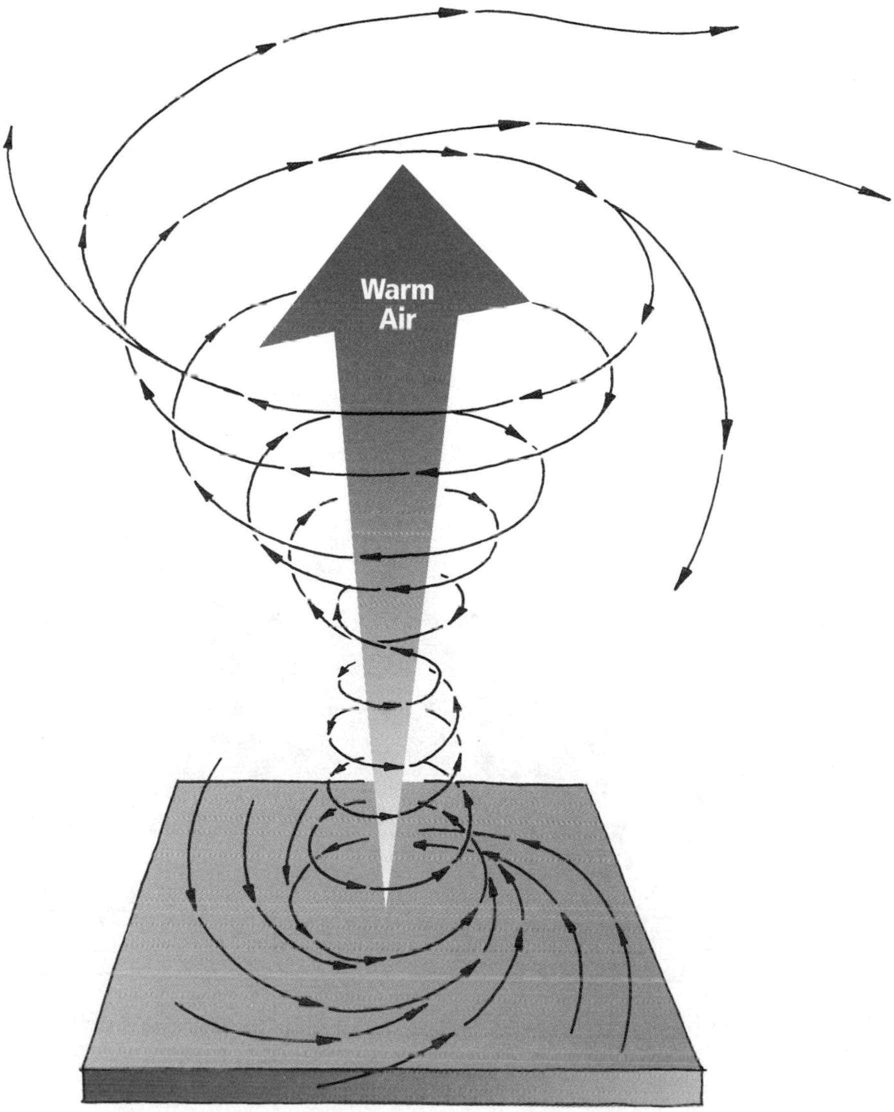

Cold Front

Warm Front

4.

3.

1.

2.

Warm Air

Perhaps the most famous storm in the history of pleasure sailing, the Fastnet Race storm of August 13–14, 1979, battered 303 ocean racing yachts and their 2,500 sailors. By the end of the day 15 sailors were killed, 24 boats were abandoned, and five boats were sunk.

Although this damage was done off the English and Irish coasts, the storm was an international event. It started life six days earlier and 6,000 miles to the west in the prairies on the border between the United States and Canada. This is a historic birthplace of destructive tornadoes because cold continental polar air mates with hot thermals rising from millions of acres of farmland. The depression was small, but it had an unseasonal force. It dropped almost 2 inches of rain on Minneapolis, Minnesota, on August 9, then sped east across Lake Michigan, upstate New York, and New England. Its greatest effects were to the south, where the gusty westerlies spinning counterclockwise around the depression's center blew the roof off a toll booth on the New Jersey Turnpike, tore a limb off a tree in New York's Central Park, killing a passerby, and capsized boats and caused many others to drag their anchors all along the coast of southern New England. One sailor who was safely ashore in Newport, Rhode Island, mistook the black, savage low for a hurricane.

The depression bolted into the Atlantic on August 11 and charged off toward Europe at a high speed of 50 knots. It was so compact that it was missed by many weather forecasters on both continents. A day later it was east of Newfoundland.

The dynamic chemistry of cold and hot ingredients that had blasted the depression east from the American plains was now made more explosive by two factors. One was a massive low-pressure system far to the north, moving slowly from Greenland to Iceland. Its own

A Classic Storm

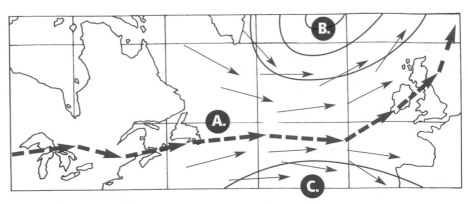

The 1979 Fastnet Race storm started in the American prairies, was re-energized by a patch of unusually warm water (A), and then rode across the Atlantic on a highway of westerly winds circulating around the low to the north (B) and the high to the south (C).

counterclockwise circulation pushed cold air south and into the path of the depression. The other was a large patch of exceptionally warm air created by water that had been heated to 5° above normal by a storm that had passed this way two days earlier. The new mix of cold and warm air reinvigorated the depression, which otherwise might have fallen apart in mid-Atlantic. The barometric pressure plummeted in a pattern that is called a "bomb": a depression in which the barometer drops at a rate of 1 millibar an hour for 24 hours, or about

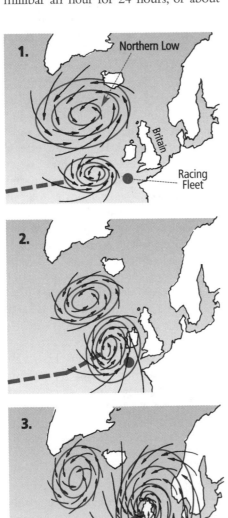

Overtaking the northern low, the storm changed course to northeast and swept up and across Britain and a fleet of 303 racing boats. The storm formed the typical comma that covered most of Britain.

three-quarters of an inch a day. The faster the drop, the stronger the wind.

As it was being energized, the depression slipped into an eastbound superhighway created by the big low to the north and the huge mid-Atlantic high-pressure system to the south, both of which created westerlies. These winds would have pushed the storm into the Bay of Biscay, off France's west coast, but on the morning of August 13 the big low to the north stopped near Iceland. Overtaking it at about noon on the 13th, the depression moved into the area where the wind blew from the southwest and therefore was redirected straight for Ireland. That night, its 50–70 knot winds blew across the Western Approaches, the 170-mile-wide body of water between the southwest corners of England and Ireland. And halfway across the Western Approaches at that very moment were the 303 boats in the Fastnet Race. For more than half a day we (the author was in the race) were battered by hurricane-strength winds and tremendous breaking waves.

A gale or other storm in the ocean can be as full of gusts, holes, and shifts as a light breeze inland. The Fastnet storm was more irregular than most, with rapid shifts in wind direction, sudden gusts, the occasional lull, and sets of waves of extraordinary height and power. Alan Watts, an English meteorologist, has explained the storm's cruel variability as originating in pools or cells of extreme low barometric pressure that blew along what he called "corridors of extremely strong winds" that generated huge waves. Each of these local gales had its own direction, as did the waves it kicked up. When waves from different corridors crossed each other, massive rogue waves resulted. Such a storm is not unusual during the winter. But this storm's deep low pressure, its extreme volatility, and its huge waves were rare summer occurrences even in England's typically rough weather.

Many of these terrible conditions also occurred in December 1998 off Australia in the Sydney-Hobart Race, in which six sailors died.

Squalls

A thunder squall may be the herald of an approaching cold front (sometimes traveling along a front line with other squalls) or it may be an extremely local storm caused when hot air rises over a baking summer landscape and becomes unstable when it encounters cool air aloft. Rain forms and creates electrical charges and lightning. Some cool air may drop back to the ground and the rapid rise and fall of air may heighten the storm. Winds may build to strengths of 60 knots or more, from any direction.

Not always caused by long- or even moderate-term patterns, squalls are unpredictable, and thus may be even more dangerous than the cold fronts or major depressions that forecasters announce a day or more in advance. Thunder squalls are usually preceded by extremely hot, humid weather, and are announced by swift moving black (or sometimes green-black) cumulus clouds. The distance to a squall may be determined by timing the difference in seconds between a lightning flash and its thunderclap, and dividing that time by 5. If the time difference is 25 seconds, the storm is 5 miles away. Since a squall may move faster than 20 knots, quickly take precautions for shortening sail. Avoid sailing under these clouds, which may produce violent downdrafts of wind and lightning, or a flat calm.

The towering dark cumulus clouds of this approaching squall should encourage any skipper to head to harbor and shorten sail.

Fog

Like pressure systems and wind, fog is caused by differences in air temperature. Every parcel of air has a temperature, called the dew point, at which the air becomes saturated with water. If the parcel already has a humidity of 100 percent and is entirely saturated with water, it is at its dew point. The lower the humidity, the more the air must be cooled to reach the dew point. The higher the humidity, the less the air must be cooled to reach its dew point.

The term dew point is derived from the moisture that forms on clear, cool summer nights, when the land chills low-lying humid air to the point where it can no longer hold its moisture and so deposits dew. Dew will not form if the temperature does not drop sufficiently (for instance, because an overnight cloud cover insulates the land and prevents warm air from escaping).

Fog forms because local conditions cool the air below the dew point. For example, a warm onshore wind may blow across an upwelling of cooler water and be chilled to its dew point. Or an area that is fog-free on clear days becomes choked with the stuff on an overcast day, heralding the arrival of a warm front, simply because the sun isn't available to keep the air temperature above its dew point. In both cases the absolute amount of moisture in the air remains constant, whether or not there is fog.

When the air reaches its dew point, it becomes completely saturated with moisture, much like a sponge that has been left in a dish of water. Cooling the air further compresses it and, like the sponge when it is squeezed, moisture is released.

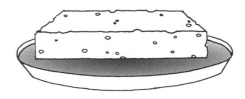

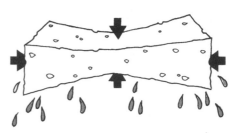

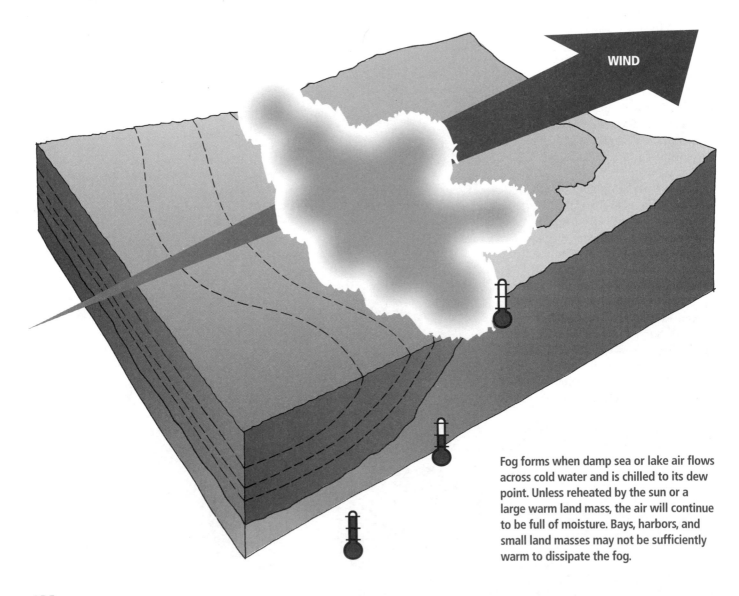

Fog forms when damp sea or lake air flows across cold water and is chilled to its dew point. Unless reheated by the sun or a large warm land mass, the air will continue to be full of moisture. Bays, harbors, and small land masses may not be sufficiently warm to dissipate the fog.

How to Predict Fog. To predict fog, you should first know the dew point — the air temperature at which fog will form. To help, there are two devices. The hygrometer compares the temperature shown on a dry, normal thermometer with that shown on a thermometer whose bulb is wrapped in a wet cloth. As water evaporates from the cloth, heat is drawn from the wet bulb. Water ceases to evaporate when the cloth's saturation is equivalent to the air humidity. When the wet-bulb temperature stabilizes, subtract it from the dry-bulb temperature, then enter the difference into Table 4-1.

A more portable instrument for predicting fog is the sling psychrometer, which measures relative humidity and dew point more quickly than the hygrometer. This also has two thermometers, one wet and one dry. To speed up water evaporation, the instrument is twirled (slung) around in the air on the end of a rope. When the wet-bulb temperature ceases to drop, take the difference between it and the dry-bulb temperature and enter it into the table. (If the temperatures are the same, the air is completely saturated with water. The dew point has been reached, and you should be surrounded by fog.)

In fog, distances to other boats and hazards to navigation are extremely difficult to gauge, so proceed slowly and keep careful track of your position.

Table 4-1: Predicting Fog

Dry-Bulb minus Wet-Bulb	Air Temperature (Dry-Bulb Thermometer)												
	35	40	45	50	55	60	65	70	75	80	85	90	95
1	2	2	2	2	2	2	2	1	1	1	1	1	1
2	5	5	4	4	4	3	3	3	3	3	3	3	2
3	7	7	7	6	5	5	5	4	4	4	4	4	4
4	10	10	9	8	7	7	6	6	6	6	5	5	5
5	4	12	11	10	10	9	8	8	7	7	7	7	6
6	18	15	14	13	12	11	10	9	9	8	8	8	8
7	22	19	17	16	14	13	12	11	11	10	10	9	9
8	28	22	20	18	17	15	14	13	12	12	11	11	10
9	35	27	23	21	19	17	16	15	14	13	13	12	12
10	—	33	27	24	22	20	18	17	16	15	14	14	13
11	—	40	32	28	25	22	20	19	18	17	16	15	15
12	—	—	38	32	28	25	23	21	20	18	17	17	16
13	—	—	45	37	31	28	25	23	21	20	19	18	17
14	—	—	—	42	35	31	28	26	24	22	21	20	19
15	—	—	—	50	40	35	31	28	26	24	23	21	21

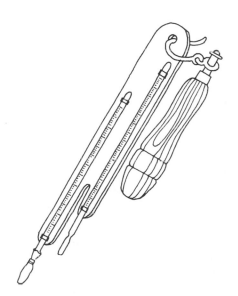

Using a sling psychrometer (above) and Table 4-1 (right), you can determine the dew point and thus predict the likelihood of fog.

Using this table, dry-bulb and wet-bulb thermometer hygrometer readings can be converted into a dew point, at which fog will occur. First subtract the wet-bulb temperature from the dry-bulb temperature and locate the difference in the left-hand column. Then read across to the column under the temperature nearest to the dry bulb's. Subtract the number at the intersection of the line and the column from the existing dry-bulb temperature to find the dew point. For example, if the dry-bulb temperature is 76° and the wet-bulb temperature is 66°, the difference is 10. Reading across to the column under 75°, we come to 16°. The dew point therefore is 60°. If the air temperature drops to 60°, there will be fog.

Fog

Fog Types. Six types of fog are commonly found at sea, along coasts, or in lakes and rivers. Some are dense fog banks, others local wisps.

Advection fog occurs day or night when warm air flows over colder water or land. This is the typical heavy moving bank of coastal fog. The warm air is cooled to its dew point, and fog results. Advection fogs usually do not occur over land in winds over 15 knots. Because of land's normally irregular texture, fresh winds cause vertical mixing of air, which is too unstable for even cooling. Instead of fog, stratus or stratocumulus clouds may form. But over water, which is much smoother than land, advection fog can form in strong winds. Southerly winds blowing over cold water near shore can cause thick advection fogs.

Frontal fog occurs ahead of warm and occluded fronts. Rain falls from the upper, warmer air into the cooler air of the retreating air mass, increasing the water content of the air. With the higher humidity, the air temperature must drop very little to reach its dew point (the greater the water content, the higher the dew point). Likewise, dense frontal fog may occur behind cold fronts as rain falls from the warm air aloft into the cooler air of the advancing system.

Inversion fog, often a fog bank, is caused by warm air blowing over upwellings of cold water, as happens off the entrance to San Francisco Bay or on lakes undergoing seasonal thermal turnovers in the spring and fall.

Radiation fog occurs over land on calm nights, when air at peak humidity near sunset is brought rapidly to its dew point by the cooling land. (Since water cools more slowly than land, radiation fogs are not seen offshore.) A very light wind helps form a dense radiation fog by mixing cool lower-air particles with warm upper-air ones, but a wind stronger than about 12 knots creates too much turbulence. But in a flat calm, the cool lower-air particles remain near ground, so the fog may be wispy and only a few feet thick. (This ground fog is favored by makers of horror movies.) A clear night is required for a radiation fog (as well as for dew), since insulating cloud cover keeps the earth and the air above it from cooling to the dew point.

Sea fog, as the name indicates, occurs at sea when warm air and cold water meet. There are often thick banks of sea fog in the Atlantic where the warm Gulf Stream flows near the cold Labrador Current.

Steam fog (sometimes called tulle fog) is often seen over rivers and small lakes. It is formed early in the morning by cool air sinking down hills and valleys onto warm waters. The mix of the cool new air and the warm air over the water produces low-rising columns of mist. (In polar regions, very cold air blowing over warmer water causes a similar type of variable fog called Arctic sea smoke.)

Fog generally is more likely over cold water than warm. It often involves a warm south wind. The foggiest sections of the United States' major boating areas are as follows (with their peak seasons): *northern Pacific Coast,* from Santa Barbara to the Canadian border (July–October); *northern Great Lakes,* Lake Superior and northern Lake Michigan (May–September); and *north Atlantic Coast,* especially northern New England (June– August; Maine may be fogged in as much as one-half of July).

Other regions that have some fog are: *mid Atlantic Coast* (December–May); *southern Great Lakes* (March–September); *southern California* and *south Atlantic Coast* (September–February; because the Pacific Ocean is colder than the Atlantic, southern California may experience three times the fog of the south Atlantic states on the same latitude). Along the *Gulf of Mexico,* fog is extremely rare.

Advection fog (the typical coastal fog) is caused by warm, damp air blowing over a colder surface in light or moderate wind.

Frontal fog precedes warm or occluded fronts as warm rain falls into the retreating cool air.

Inversion fog results when warm air blows over upwellings of cold water, either near or far from land.

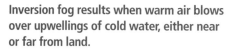

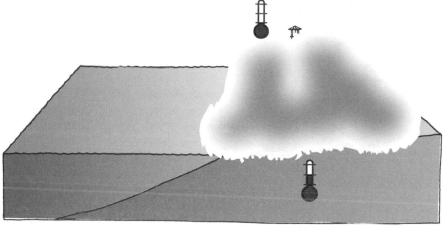

Radiation fog occurs on land when the air is rapidly cooled at sunset. A light wind increases its likelihood.

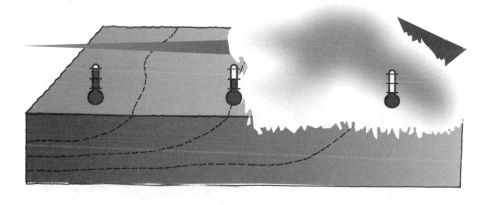

Sea fog appears when cold water currents confront warm, moist air out in the ocean.

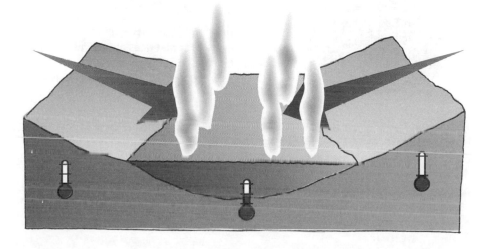

Steam fog occurs in the morning when cold air sinks and cools the air over a river or lake to its dew point.

Weather Forecasting

Weather changes are forecast with the aid of a variety of indicators, including the barometer, clouds, and wind direction, as well as radio and printed reports of experts. Experienced mariners use them all — keeping one weather eye on the barometer and the other on the sky above them and to the west.

Barometric Pressure. The simplest of these aids is the standard aneroid barometer, which indicates air pressure in both inches and millibars of mercury, and which has an adjustable hand to be used as a reference point against which changes are measured. When reading a barometer, first gently tap its face with a finger to help the indicator move to its correct position. On many barometers the words "fair," "changing," "rainy," and "stormy" indicate pressure readings that might cause those conditions, but these labels usually are not helpful when predicting changes.

What counts is not any one reading but the trend of readings. Keep track of changes during the day, regularly entering barometer readings in the log book. If the barometer rises or falls quickly, prepare for strong winds and possible storms, and if possible head for harbor. A special type of barometer called a barograph traces atmospheric pressure historically from hour to hour on a paper tape, providing a graphic display of barometric trends.

As a rule of thumb, a rise or fall of about 1 millibar (0.03 inches) every 3 hours or less indicates that the weather is about to change substantially. If the rate is 1 millibar every hour, a dangerous "bomb" condition threatens.

Often, barometric levels and trends

31.00 in.

30.00 in.

29.00 in.

Air pressure

The mercury barometer is the most accurate indicator of atmospheric pressure. Mercury in a glass tube open at one end rises when the atmospheric pressure increases and drops when it decreases. The tube is graduated in inches or millibars for easy comparison.

and wind direction together indicate changes in weather. Table 4-2 summarizes some predictions, starting with high pressure. In general, the lower the barometer level, the worse the weather; and the faster it falls, the stronger the wind. The atmospheric pressure at the center of the 1979 Fastnet Race storm was less than 28.8 inches (980 millibars), the third-lowest barometric reading in an English August since 1900. Equally significant was the very narrow interval between the isobars clustered around the center of the depression, over which the wind poured like water at Niagara Falls.

In addition, deep depressions typically drag along on their southern side a long, narrow occlusion situated between a warm front and a cold front. This proximity of warm and cold air provides more energy. The air temperature and humidity change rapidly before, during, and after the passage of intense depressions. Variations are more gradual around a shallow, slow-moving front. In Table 4-2, notice the quick, sudden changes whenever the barometer falls or rises rapidly as the different air masses race through on each other's heels.

A barograph tape of a depression like

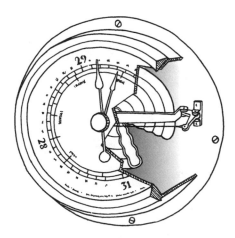

An aneroid barometer should be aboard every boat that goes out overnight. Changes in atmospheric pressure are read on a dial graduated in inches or millibars.

Table 4-2: Weather Forecasts Based on Barometric Pressure and Wind Direction

Pressure in Inches (Millibars)	Wind Direction	Forecast
30.2 (1023) and higher. Steady	SW-NW	Continued fair with little temperature change.
30.2 (1023) and higher. Falling slowly	SW-NW	Fair for 2 days with slowly rising temperature.
30.1 (1019) and higher. Falling slowly	NE-E	In summer in light winds, rain within 3 days. In winter, rain within 24 hours. Weak warm front approaching.
30.1 (1019) and higher. Falling rapidly	NE-E	In summer, rain within 12–24 hours. In winter, increasing rain or snow within 12 hours. Deep warm front approaching.
30.1–30.2 (1019–1023). Steady	SW-NW	Fair for 1 or 2 days with little temperature change.
30.1–30.2 (1019–1023). Rising rapidly	SW-NW	Fair; but rain within 2 days. Cold front approaching.
30.1–30.2 (1019–1023). Falling slowly	SE-S	Rain within 24 hours. Weak warm front approaching.
	NE-SE	Wind and rain increasing within 12–18 hours.
30.1–30.2 (1019–1023). Falling rapidly	SE-S	Wind and rain increasing within 12–18 hours.
	NE-SE	Wind and rain increasing within 12 hours.
30.0 (1016) and lower. Falling slowly	NE-SE	Rain for 1–3 days and perhaps longer. Weak warm front.
30.0 (1016) and lower. Falling rapidly	NE-SE	Rain and strong winds within a few hours, then clearing within 36 hours and lower temperatures in winter. Deep cold front.
30.0 (1016) and lower. Rising slowly	S-SW	Clearing within a few hours and then fair for several days. Weak cold front passes.
29.8 (1009) and lower. Falling rapidly	N-E	Severe storm and heavy rain within a few hours. In winter, snow followed by a cold wave. The typical "Nor' Easter" caused by a deep depression.
	E-S	Severe storm within a few hours, then clearing within 24 hours with lower temperatures in winter.
29.8 (1009) and lower. Rising rapidly	Veering to W or NW	Storm ending followed by clearing and lower temperatures. Passage of cold front or depression. Expect high winds with clearing, gusty and shifting if they come from over land or steady if they come from over sea.

the Fastnet storm shows readings in a sharp V shape — a steep drop, a momentary pause at a deep low, and a rapid rise. The passage of a less dramatic depression or a weak front is marked by a long, shallow slide in pressure, shown on a barograph as a wide bowl.

Official Forecasts. Weather forecasts are available from the United States National Weather Service, which continuously broadcasts weather forecasts that are much more detailed than the ones available over commercial radio and television. They may be received by onboard radiotelephones and usually may be accessed by pushing a special button. Some special radios receive only weather frequencies. Since these broadcasts have a range of approximately 40 miles, the reports cover limited areas; the 80-mile-diameter circles of coverage overlap, and adjoining broadcasts are made on different frequencies so that sailors may learn about weather beyond their local area.

The language used by the announcers is relatively non-technical. Three terms indicate increasing danger: "advisory," "watch," and "warning." A *weather (storm) advisory* identifies the existence of hazardous weather. A *weather (storm) watch* is an alert to a possible threat locally. A *weather (storm) warning* is an alert to an expected threat locally.

More detailed, technical weather information is sent out across the high seas over single-sideband (SSB) frequencies, which have a range of hundreds of miles and require special SSB radiotelephones. Most boats heading out into the ocean carry these radios. Many of these reports and forecasts provide enough information to allow the listener to sketch a weather map. SSB broadcasts also provide raw data for onboard weather facsimile machines that draw detailed weather maps.

The National Weather Service publishes Marine Weather Service charts that include lists of weather broadcasts. These charts are available from: National Ocean Service, Distribution Branch, Riverdale, MD; (301) 436-6990.

Weather Forecasting

Some shore-side facilities may display visual weather warnings, such as a single red flag (small craft should stay off the water), two red flags (gale warning), a red flag enclosing a black square (storm warning), and two red flags enclosing black squares (hurricane warning). Lights used for the same warnings at night are, respectively, red light over white light, white light over red light, red light over red light, and red light over white light over red light. While Coast Guard stations no longer display these signals, you may find them flying at yacht clubs, marinas, and other facilities.

Forecasting Services. Studying the daily synoptic (overview) weather map in your local newspaper or on television is an excellent way to keep track of weather trends. These maps are derived from extremely detailed maps sent out by the National Weather Service and commercial weather forecasting services. No matter how thorough it is, a weather map is not very helpful when studied in isolation — yesterday's weather map will tell you little about tomorrow's weather unless you know trends.

Many commercial airports provide information about wind direction and strength, either over the telephone or in broadcasts. There also are a number of commercial weather services that, for a fee, provide forecasts and maps to mariners, including pleasure sailors.

Forecasting with Clouds. "Weather forecasts must not be relied upon 100 percent," writes Peter Blake, the great New Zealand seaman; "it is important to 'look out the window' and make one's own assessment of the situation." Enough information is available in the immediate environment — in the clouds and wind — to help you make your own reliable short-term weather predictions.

Created by differences in temperature and humidity, clouds foretell weather changes for the next half day or so. Their Latin names describe their appearances, which in turn indicate the kind of weather below and to the west of them. *Cirrus* means "curl" or "tendril"; *stratus* means "blanket"; *cumulus* is a "heap" or a "swelling"; *alto* is derived from the Latin

A weather facsimile machine (weather fax) draws synoptic maps from data sent over single-sideband radio.

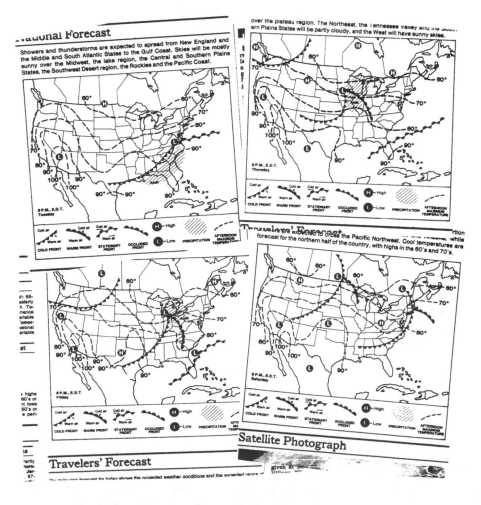

(Above) A newspaper synoptic weather map will help you predict weather changes. (Left) The night and day visual signals for bad weather, from top to bottom: small craft warning, gale warning, storm warning, and hurricane warning.

altus, or "high"; and *nimbus* means "violent rain." The important cloud types, described below from the highest to the lowest, use one or more of these words and characteristics.

Cirrus clouds are the highest and the least substantial. Composed of ice crystals, cirrus clouds lie at altitudes of about 45,000 feet. Wispy and lying at oblique angles, these clouds may herald the approach of a warm front.

Cirrostratus clouds (wispy clouds lying in sheets) may form a ceiling slightly lower than cirrus clouds as a warm front nears and layers of cold air mix with upper warm air. Cirrostratus may drape the entire sky in a gray haze and cause a halo around the sun or moon — a traditional indication of a nearing storm.

Cirrocumulus clouds (barely defined puffy balls), like cirrostratus, lie at altitudes of 16,500–40,000 feet, usually in large clumps. From below, these clouds may look like fish scales. The saying "Mackerel sky, mackerel sky / Not long wet, not long dry" describes them and the changeable weather that follows.

Altostratus clouds are sheets 6,000–23,000 feet up. Thicker, darker, and more claustrophobic than the higher cirrostratus clouds, they promise rain soon.

Altocumulus clouds (grayish white rolls) look like cirrocumulus but are darker and sometimes appear in layers. If the wind is steady between northeast and south, these clouds promise rain soon.

Stratocumulus clouds are dark, large puffy balls occurring in compressed layers and foretelling bad weather.

Cumulus clouds are less dangerous than cumulonimbus thunderheads. They're puffy white cotton balls at about 6,000 feet, and promise fair weather. Cumulus clouds may darken and be transformed into stratocumulus or cumulonimbus clouds. Cumulus clouds over land during the day indicate thermals and promise a good sea breeze.

Cumulonimbus clouds are dark, tightly packed balls that may churn and tower as thunderheads at about 6,000 feet. If a cumulonimbus is broader above than below, it's called an "anvil head." This shape is due to violent updrafts through a wide range of temperatures. As the updraft hits cold air, it condenses as a cloud. Winds are strong around these threatening clouds.

Cirrus

Altostratus

Altocumulus

Cumulus

Cumulonimbus

Weather Forecasting

These cumulus clouds at sunset indicate a probability of fair weather into the next day.

Nimbostratus clouds are the rain-laden, heavy, low-lying, dark-gray blankets that come with warm fronts and wet northeasters. Their soggy bases may lie just above the earth's surface and be indistinguishable from heavy fog.

Stratus clouds combine in a dense, gray overcast that promises light to heavy rain.

WEATHER SIGNS AND SAYINGS

Watchers of weather have traditionally found patterns that help them predict changes. Almost 2,400 years ago, the Greek scientist and philosopher Theophrastus, a student of Aristotle's, wrote an essay, "Concerning Weather Signs," in which he laid down hundreds of rules. Some seem bizarre today, for instance: "When sheep begin to breed late, it is a sign which fulfills itself in fair weather. So it is when an ox lies on his left side and also when a dog does the same." Yet many of his observations make perfect sense: "When birds flee from the sea" it is an indication of an approaching storm — and why not, since many storms originate at sea.

Since the time of Theophrastus, mariners have used easily remembered rules for predicting weather. One of these is:

Trace the sky the painter's brush,
The winds around you soon will rush.

Striking contrasts of color and shape usually indicate worsening weather, which is a product of contrasts of temperature and humidity. Bad weather is dramatic.

Clouds are often given colloquial names. High cirrus clouds are called "chicken scratches" after their fine lines and "mare's tails" for their filmy quality. Since they often precede a storm by a day or two,

Mare's tails, mare's tails
Make lofty ships carry low sails.

The changeable, puffy weather under fish-scaly cirrocumulus clouds inspired the saying, "*Mackerel scales, furl your sails.*" And then there is this list:

North winds send hail,
South winds bring rain;
East winds we bewail,
West winds blow amain;
Northeast is too cold,
Southeast not too warm;
Northwest is too bold,
Southwest blows no harm.

This is an accurate catalog of the winds of America's Atlantic coast, where the prevailing southwest wind is a fair-weather reliable.

Here are some more helpful sayings concerning wind and weather:

"In by day, out by night" describes the sequence of daytime onshore sea or lake breezes (as the land heats above the temperature of the water) followed by nighttime offshore land breezes (as the land cools below the water's temperature).

HANDS ON: How to Read Clouds

"The face of the sky is our constant, dependable barometer," observes Louis D. Rubin, Sr., in his valuable *The Weather Wizard's Cloud Book*. "Its many 'expressions' tell us what the weather is going to be, when it will change, and to what degree." Here are some hints for predicting weather by reading clouds:

1. Isolated, wispy, white, or very high clouds are indications of fine weather.

2. Crowded, dense, dark, and towering clouds indicate changing or worsening weather.

3. The sharper the edge of a thundercloud and the darker its color, the more violence it may contain. Don't sail below or near it.

4. The weather will change if cloud color, shape, and size change.

5. As puffy cumulus clouds darken and enlarge and become dark cumulonimbus clouds, expect squalls within 2 hours.

A westerly or southwesterly sea or lake breeze is often said to "follow the sun," meaning that it veers (shifts clockwise, in a westerly direction) during the afternoon as the land heats up and the thermal effect increases. A southwest wind becomes a west southwest wind and may end up in the west.

There are many sayings about squalls and storms. An erect cloud is a sign of storm, reported Theophrastus about cumulonimbus thunderheads. He also observed the effects of early changes in barometric pressure and humidity in nature: "When in fine weather bees do not fly long distances, but fly about where they are, it indicates that there will be a storm."

Here are others:

The sharper the blast,
The sooner it's past.

and

When the wind before the rain,
Let your topsails draw again;
When the rain before the wind,
Topsail sheets and halyards mind.

These two sayings reflect the fact that a small, relatively shallow front passes quickly, with rain only on the backside. Larger, deeper fronts and intense depressions are surrounded by bad weather whose precipitation may precede the strongest wind. Square-rigger crews would be wary about setting large topsails if they thought the wind would rise.

Rain long foretold, long last;
Short notice, soon will pass.

Warm fronts move slowly, preceded by several hundred miles of gradually lowering cirrus clouds and a day or more of rain. Faster moving cold fronts, on the other hand, pass through quickly and dramatically. After a sudden storm, the weather clears rapidly.

When the dew is on the grass
Rain will never come to pass.
When grass is dry at morning light
Look for rain before the night.

Dew forms only if the air is cooled to its dew point. At night this happens in clear weather, which allows the day's heat to escape into the atmosphere. Because cloud cover insulates the earth, if the grass is dry on a rainless summer morning, there were clouds at night. A clear night cools the air and also the water temperature. The following clear day raises the land temperature and creates thermals. A heavy dew at dawn, therefore, promises a fresh sea breeze that afternoon.

Red sky in morning,
Sailor take warning.
Red sky at night,
Sailor delight.

This is probably the most famous of all weather sayings. St. Matthew tells us that when the Pharisees asked Jesus for a sign from heaven, they were told, "When it is evening ye say, it will be fair weather, for the sky is red. And in the morning it will be foul weather today for the sky is red and lowering." A sharply defined red sunset or dawn is caused by the sun's rays shining through a cloud of dust particles in the air in clear, dry weather. Since in the evening the clear red sunset is to the west of the observer, good weather is on the way. But the red sun of dawn is weather that has already passed to the east. Given the two- to four-day cycle of most weather, the odds are that wet weather is overhead or imminent.

Humidity washes the air of dust particles and thus improves visibility, as the saying "The farther the sight, the nearer the rain" suggests. And since low, dense, rainy stratus and nimbostratus clouds keep sounds as well as heat from escaping into the atmosphere,

Sound traveling far and wide
A stormy day will betide.

Many of these and other weather indications are neatly summarized in a single six-line poem:

When the glass falls low,
Prepare for a blow.
When it rises high,
Let all your kites fly.
The hollow winds begin to blow,
The clouds look black, the glass is low.

Weather and air pressure are inextricably related. The "glass" (barometer) when low foretells ominous winds and black clouds, and when high anticipates fair weather for flying every sail.

HANDS ON: How to Read the Wind

Current wind direction is an excellent aid in forecasting weather changes, both short- and long-term. There are two rules of thumb that ask you to stand with the wind at your back (this wind is the one created by the prevailing pressure system, not the sea breeze or other local wind). The rules apply in the Northern Hemisphere. South of the equator, face the wind.

Buys-Ballot's Law says that when the wind is on your back, low pressure is to your left and high pressure to your right.

The crossed-winds rule, developed by the English meteorologist and sailor Alan Watts, is ingenious. With your back to the wind, look aloft for indications of wind direction at high altitude. If the flow of cirrus clouds or the flight path of birds is from your left, the wind is from your left and the weather probably will deteriorate in the next few hours. (The wind is veering, so a depression approaches.) If the wind aloft is blowing from your right, the weather probably will improve. (The wind is backing, so a high is approaching or a low is clearing out.) If the wind above you is from the same direction or from the opposite direction as the surface wind, the weather probably will not change.

The principles behind the crossed-winds rule are three. First, wind aloft is parallel to isobars of constant barometric pressure. Second, when isobars cross each other, different types of air are mixing and the weather will change. And third, as Watts explains in his book *The Weather Handbook*, "The wind veers with height when a warmer air mass is on the way and backs when a colder one is coming."

Waves and Tides

Strictly speaking, waves are not weather, but they are caused by weather and may be as dangerous as the 60-knot winds of a strong gale. Their force should never be underestimated. Since salt water weighs 64 pounds per cubic foot and fresh water 62.2 pounds per cubic foot, a large breaking wave can hurl tons of water at a velocity as high as 30 knots.

Tides. Almost all waves are driven by wind. The most important exception is the tide, that great wave of water that flows around the world, generally on a semidiurnal (twice-daily) schedule.

(Diurnal, or once-daily, tides may be found in deep, shallow bays or where the tidal range is small.) Tides are caused mainly by the gravitational forces of the sun and moon, with the moon having the greatest effect because it is closest. Tide levels and changes can be predicted with reasonable accuracy based on the positions of the sun and moon and the known effects of land masses.

A very broad area of high water flows around the world following the moon, and a similar mound of water moves along on the other side of the earth. Since the moon's "day" as it rotates around the earth is 24.8 hours long, tides normally cycle at an interval of about 12.4 hours, with semidiurnal changes every 6.2 hours — or every 6 hours, 12 minutes. Tide levels change from day to day for several reasons. One is that the sun, which also exerts a gravitational force, has a 24-hour "day" and the relative positions of the two heavenly bodies

change. When the sun and moon are either in the same direction (new moon) or in opposite directions (full moon), the highest and lowest tides occur because the two celestial bodies' gravitational pulls are augmenting each other. These large tidal ranges are about 20 percent higher and lower than average. They are called spring tides, and have nothing to do with the seasons. When the sun and moon lie at a right angle to each other, relatively low tidal ranges called neap tides occur.

If the moon is passing substantially north or south of the equator, then one of the semidiurnal tides in a given location will be about 10 percent higher than the other. And if the moon is at its perigee — when it is closest to the earth — its pull will be greater and the tides will be even higher. For example, the average rise and fall of the tide at Boston, MA, is 9.5 feet, which means that the mean (average) level at high tide

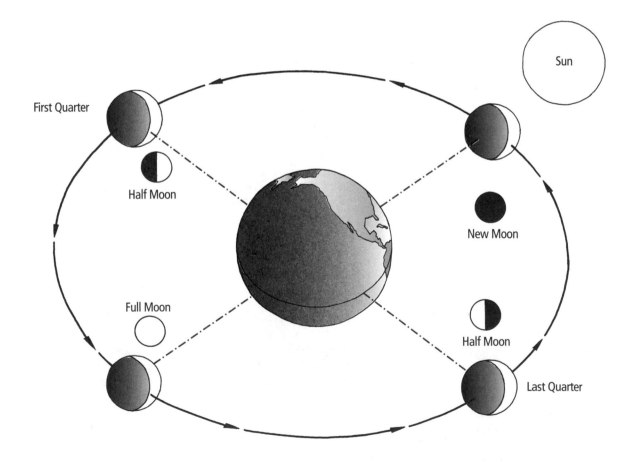

The main cause of tides is the gravitational pull of the moon, although the more distant sun also has some effect. Tide times and levels are predicted using the astronomical positions of these bodies as well as the known effects of land formations and ocean size and shape. The tides are highest at full and new moons (spring tide), when the bodies are aligned, and lowest at first and third quarters (neap tide).

is 9.5 feet above the mean level at low tide. When the moon is full, the spring tide is 11.2 feet. Ten days later, when the moon is in its third quarter, the neap tide level is 7.6 feet. On another day, the new moon and the perigee may coincide and the spring tide range will then be 12 feet, or 26 percent higher than normal.

The moon's gravitational pull is the greatest force acting on the wave called the tide, but there are others. High atmospheric pressure tends to hold water levels down and low pressure allows them to rise. A strong onshore wind blowing into a bay or an enclosed body of water like Long Island Sound may alter tide changes or increase the level of high tide. If the wind is caused by a hurricane or a depression, the high winds and low pressure of the storm may cause flooding, especially at spring tide. Similarly, strong offshore winds blowing out of bays may cause low, delayed tides.

Tidal Current. Tide and tidal current are two different things, although one causes the other. For instance, the tidal current runs fastest halfway through the rise or fall because in the typical semidiurnal tide, one-half the rise or fall occurs during the middle two hours of the tide.

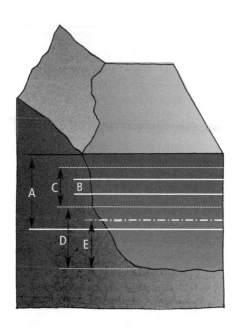

Spring tide (A) is the depth and range between high and low tides when the moon is full and new. Neap tide (B) is the depth and range at the moon's first and third quarters. Mean tide (C) is the average depth and range. Mean low water (D) is the average low-tide level excluding spring and neap tides. (E) Mean lower low water is the average of the lower of low tide levels.

The gravitational pull of the moon tugs on a point on the earth (and a point exactly opposite it on the other side of the globe). The point is constantly changing. The tidal current flows strongest in constricted channels, such as narrow entrances to bays or sounds where large quantities of water flood and ebb in a tumult in the roughly 6 hours, 12 minutes allowed to each tide in a semidiurnal system.

Waves and Tides. Published current charts show direction and velocity of tidal currents. Since tidal currents can flow nearly as fast as a typical sailboat can sail (4-knot currents are common in some narrow channels), knowing the time and characteristics of a tide and its currents is vital. The saying "still waters run deep" is wrong. Current runs fastest in deep water that has gouged out the bottom. Where currents clash, there may be tide races or rips (patches of swirling, choppy water). And where tidal currents meet the wind, the waves may be especially steep. When a current as slow as 1 knot runs against wind-driven waves, the waves may double in size. We will say more about tides and currents, and how to navigate in them, in chapter 12.

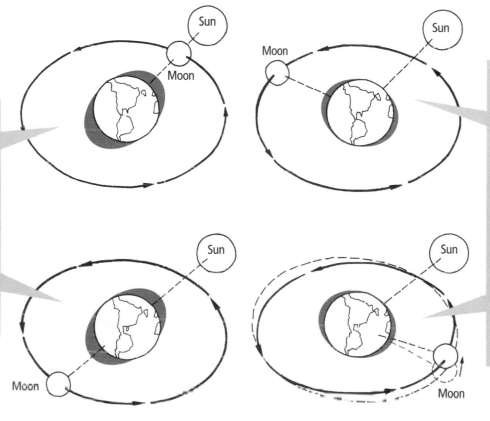

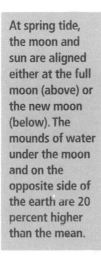

At spring tide, the moon and sun are aligned either at the full moon (above) or the new moon (below). The mounds of water under the moon and on the opposite side of the earth are 20 percent higher than the mean.

At neap tide, the moon and sun are at a right angle and their gravitational pulls conflict, so the mounds are 20 percent lower than the mean. (Below) If the moon swings far above or below the equator or is at its perigee, tide ranges will be larger.

Waves and Tides

Wave Shape. Wind-driven waves have a natural rhythm, like the pulsing of a long rope whose ends are held by two people who swing them up and down steadily. The greater the arc through which they swing their ends, the longer are the waves up and down the rope. These waves are called "sine waves," since they look like the fair, symmetrical arcs of sine curves. While the rope seems to be moving, its fibers actually are stationary on the horizontal plane as the waves snake through it from one end to the other.

If one of the rope-holders changes the rhythm, the fair sine waves are broken up into a jumble of irregular waves, but after a while a new pattern takes over and either larger or smaller sine waves are formed. This is what happens when a new wind increases over calm water. The wind causes ripples, which gradually build into wavelets, which become waves. At first there are thousands of ripples, then hundreds of wavelets, then tens of regular waves. The larger the waves, the fewer there are of them. And the longer the wind blows, the larger the waves. If the wind were to shift suddenly, an entirely new group of ripples, wavelets, and waves would come in from the new angle, breaking up the regular pattern of the original waves. The water would be confused by clashing sets of waves until, after a while, the first set would die down and a new regular pattern would take over. Just as with the swinging rope's fibers, the actual mole-cules in the water do not travel with the waves (although they are subject to local stresses and tensions and may move slightly).

Wave Size. Waves are measured in length (the distance from crest to crest), height (the distance from trough to crest), and period (the time interval between crests). Size is determined by several factors. One is wind strength. The harder the wind blows, the bigger the waves will be. In addition, the longer and steadier the wind blows, the longer and larger the waves. When the wind first comes up on the ocean, the waves are short and square (and dangerous, too, if it's blowing a gale). But after several hours the waves lengthen to the sine-wave shape in a steady, prevailing swell running with the prevailing wind.

Another factor affecting wave size and shape is the depth of water. In shallow water, a new fresh wind can kick up steep, breaking waves very quickly, in a

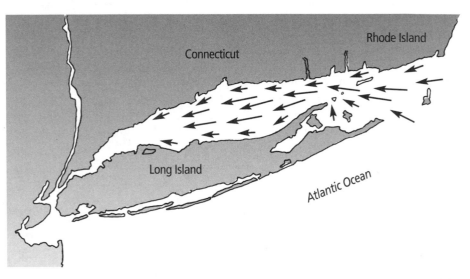

As the current vectors (force arrows) on this chart of Long Island Sound show, tidal current flows fastest in the deep, narrow waters (long vectors) in the center and in its entrances and slowest in shallow water near shore (short vectors).

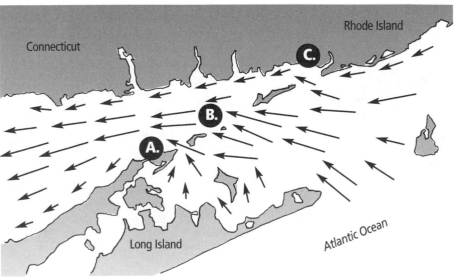

Tidal current flows fastest of all in constricted, deep channels between large bodies of water. Here, the flood (incoming) current enters Long Island Sound at almost 5 knots in the deep channels at A and B, but at only 2 knots in shallow channel C.

few minutes. (As the wind dies, the waves flatten just as quickly.) But in deep water, except in a gale, the waves grow more slowly. When ocean swells approach a shoal (shallow water) or an island, they become steeper and eventually break. In 20 knots of wind, a bay or lake with less than about 20 feet of water will be broken by many more, smaller waves than the ocean or a deep lake. These lake waves are square in shape and can be violent.

The most dangerous wave is a breaking wave. This is not the whitecap — a relatively small wave with a small curl of white water at its top. A breaker is a wave that falls apart. Its base cannot support its top, which either falls off or is blown down in a loose, dangerous pile of hundreds or thousands of pounds of foaming water. Breakers have destroyed lighthouses, torn masts and people out of boats, and turned 40-footers upside-down with the ease of a child capsizing a toy boat in the bathtub. In a rapidly building gale, the wind increases very quickly and the wave base may not be as big or sturdy as it should, and breakers may form prematurely. In less extreme conditions, a contrary tidal current or waves from different directions may create breakers. And if large waves created in deep water cross a shoal, they will become dangerous breakers.

Every body of water is vulnerable to the so-called rogue wave. An oceanographer has estimated that one out of 20 offshore waves is a rogue. This may be a thundering breaker that appears out of nowhere on a relatively quiet night, or a sequence of two or three big rollers twice the size of every other wave in the neighborhood. Rogue waves may be caused by the collision of two or more waves from distant weather patterns — the remnants of gales thousands of miles apart that meet somewhere in mid-ocean, join forces, redoubled in strength, and roll on in a new direction. Most of these end their lives relatively harmlessly on a barren coastline. Some, unfortunately, sweep an unlucky boat or two before them.

For sailors concerned about safety and comfort, it's not enough to know the wind speed. A 15-knot northwesterly blowing over waters churned up by the previous three days' northeasterly will create an extremely confused seaway. Fortunately, the northeast waves probably will die within a few hours, but until then the boat's motion will be hellish. An offshore wind will create waves much smaller than those churned up by an onshore wind of the same strength.

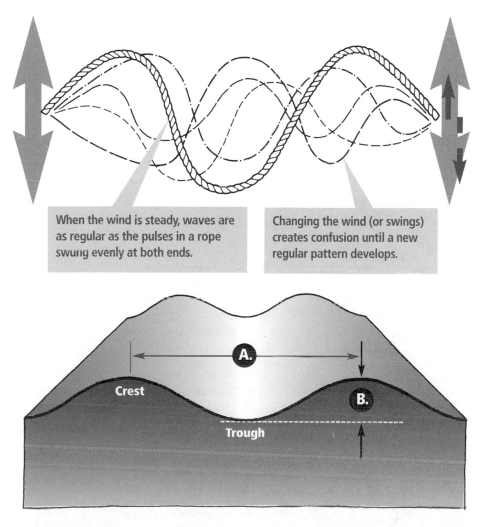

When the wind is steady, waves are as regular as the pulses in a rope swung evenly at both ends.

Changing the wind (or swings) creates confusion until a new regular pattern develops.

A wave's length (A) is the distance from crest to crest, its period is the time between two crests, and its height (B) is the distance from trough to crest.

How Hard Is It Really Blowing?

Most people describe sailing conditions using only an estimate of wind strength. But the fact is that wind strength alone is not the sole relevant indicator of weather. As we have seen, waves also affect a boat. In bad weather they may be the main factor.

The combined effect of waves and wind is so important that mariners usually refer to sea conditions by a number that reflects both wind strength and wave height and shape. They take this number from the Beaufort Scale of wind force. Developed in 1805 by Admiral Sir Francis Beaufort of the British Royal Navy, the scale divides wind and sea conditions into 12 "forces," ranging from calm to hurricane. It describes typical conditions offshore in large bodies of water. For restricted, protected waters such as rivers, small lakes, and bays, the Beaufort Scale may be modified by reading sea conditions one force higher and ignoring wave height. For instance, at sea whitecaps form in force 4 winds, but in protected waters they may not appear until the wind is blowing about 18 knots, or force 5.

Note that the wind speed is in knots. Since 1 knot equals 1.15 statute miles per hour, multiply these figures by 1.15 to convert to MPH. To convert back to knots, multiply by 0.87. Be conservative: it's easy to overestimate wind strength and wave height.

The Beaufort Scale appears in Table 4-3.

The Beaufort Scale and Boat Handling. Like green "beginner and novice," blue "intermediate," and black-diamond "expert" signs on ski trails, the forces on the Beaufort Scale indicate the difficulty of sailing conditions. Sailors

Table 4-3: The Beaufort Scale of Wind Forces

Force	Wind Speed (Knots)	Wind Description	Sea Conditions	Probable Wave Height
0	0	Calm	Smooth, like a mirror.	0
1	1–3	Light air	Small ripples, like fish scales.	$\frac{1}{4}$–$\frac{1}{2}$ foot
2	4–6	Light breeze	Short, small pronounced wavelets with no crests.	$\frac{1}{4}$–$\frac{1}{2}$ foot
3	7–10	Gentle breeze	Large wavelets with some crests.	2 feet
4	11–16	Moderate breeze	Increasingly longer small waves, some with whitecaps (foam crests).	4 feet
5	17–21	Fresh breeze	Moderate lengthening waves, with many whitecaps and some spray.	6 feet
6	22–27	Strong breeze	Large waves, extensive whitecaps, some spray.	10 feet
7	28–33	Near gale	Heaps of waves, with some breakers whose foam is blown downwind in streaks.	14 feet
8	34–40	Gale	Moderately high waves of increasing length, and edges of crests breaking into spindrift (heavy spray). Foam is blown downwind in well-marked streaks.	18 feet
9	41–47	Strong gale	High waves with dense foam streaks and some crests rolling over. Spray reduces visibility.	23 feet
10	48–55	Storm	Very high waves with long, overhanging crests. The sea looks white, visibility is greatly reduced, and waves tumble with force.	29 feet
11	56–63	Violent storm	Exceptionally high waves that may obscure medium-size ships. All wave edges are blown into froth, and the sea is covered with patches of foam.	37 feet
12	64–71	Hurricane	The air is filled with foam and spray, and the sea is completely white.	45 feet

should be careful not to be caught in wind and sea conditions far beyond the limits of their experience, knowledge, and physical ability. This does not mean that new, challenging conditions should be avoided out of timidity, because skills improve with experience.

Forces 0–3 (0–10 knots of wind and smooth sea) are light conditions and should be safe for all sailors, assuming that the body of water is not too crowded, the boat is properly equipped, and there are a sufficient number of crew members.

Force 4 (11–16 knots and moderate sea) is a moderate condition that will challenge beginning and novice sailors, particularly if they're sailing small, capsizable boats.

Force 5 (17–21 knots and white-capped waves) is a fresh condition in which beginners and novices may lose control of their boats and generally feel overwhelmed.

Force 6 (22–27 knots and large waves) is strong — heavy weather for a beginner or novice. Very experienced sailors feel challenged and sometimes overpowered in a strong wind. Many sailboat races are called off if the strength reaches 25 knots.

Forces 7–9 (28–47 knots and foaming seas) are gale conditions. In the lower range, large cruising boats that are well handled can make progress to windward, but when the wind gusts up into the 40s, most boats must heave-to or run with it. Small boats should not leave shore.

Forces 10–12 (48–71 knots and breaking seas) are storms where survival may be at stake, even on strong, well-handled vessels.

Most people overestimate both wind strength and wave size, so to provide some standards of measurement here are some boats in forces 2–9. Since waves tend to be flattened by photos, the seas are larger and steeper than they appear.

FORCE 2: A dinghy (left) barely makes way in small ripples, her crew to leeward to induce weather helm with heel.

FORCE 4: A sloop on a close reach in a moderate wind and short waves almost makes hull speed.

FORCE 5: A cruising cutter makes knots on an ideal reach as whitecaps just begin to appear.

FORCE 6: A cruiser-racer pounds into a strong wind and steep waves.

FORCE 9: A dismasted ocean racer is taken under tow in a gale's breaking waves.

Sail-Handling Gear and Knots

If sails are a sailboat's muscle, rope (called "line" when used in a boat) is her sinew, and her joints are her blocks, shackles, and winches. In this chapter we'll look at them and at other uses of rope and line, as well as at the knots and splices used to secure them.

LINE AND ROPE

In boating language, "line" is distinct from "rope." **Rope** is the stuff produced by manufacturers and delivered to chandleries (marine hardware stores) on large drums. A **line** is a length cut from that rope for a specific purpose on a boat. A sheet is a line, and so are a halyard, a docking line, an anchor rode, and the length of rope sewn into the edge of a sail to strengthen it called a "boltrope." A 500-foot length of ½-inch-diameter nylon rope can be cut into several lines — say, six 20-foot docking lines and two 190-foot anchor lines (rodes). Almost all rope today is constructed of synthetic polyester fibers, which unlike the natural fibers manila and cotton are strong and resist rot. These synthetics include Dacron, nylon, polypropylene, and the recent generations of specialized, very low-stretch materials. Each type has its own characteristics that are used to match the demands of the job. Some are available in a variety of colors, for quick identification and specific tasks.

Laid Rope and Braid. Rope is constructed in two ways: it is laid in twisted strands, or it is braided. The more traditional type is laid construction. Yarns are twisted into strands. Three strands are then twisted around each other, usually in a clockwise direction.

Braided rope stretches less and often

On this well-rigged cruiser, the jib sheets will be led through the adjustable blocks on the tracks on deck, back to cockpit winches. Most halyard winches are on deck because crews are most steady when kneeling or sitting. Dorade vents (white cowls) let air below. The jack stay (aft of the forward hatch) supports the lower section of the mast. High double lifelines surround the deck, whose textured surface provides excellent traction.

is easier to handle than laid rope. In braid, the fibers are interwoven along the length of the rope with clockwise and counterclockwise torques balancing each other out. From a near distance, the fibers in braided rope seem to be running in the same direction (although they actually vary by a few degrees), whereas the fibers in laid line run distinctly on the bias. Braid usually has two parts: a hard, low-stretch core, and around the core a soft cover that is easier to handle. Some braids have two braided cores. Because of its relatively complex construction, braided rope is more expensive than laid rope of the same size. Since Dacron braid is usually less stretchy and easier on the hands than Dacron laid line, the extra cost is often worthwhile. In nylon, braid and laid line may be comparable in strength, but, again, braid is not as rough on hands.

Both types are apt to develop kinks unless handled carefully. A kink (also called a hockle) in a line can be an annoyance or even a danger if it won't allow you to let out anchor rode or ease a sheet or halyard at a crucial moment. Before using a line, overhaul and fake it — place an end on deck and then lay the line out in long, loose loops with the same arm motion you would use when watering grass. As the line passes through your hands, work out any kinks that you feel. Alternatively, holding one end of the line, shake it for a few seconds and kinks will work themselves toward the far end. If the line is badly kinked, towing it astern for a few minutes will untwist it.

Rope Material. The various synthetic materials — nylon, Dacron, low-stretch, and polypropylene — used in rope have unique strength and stretch characteristics that can be exploited for particular jobs.

Nylon is one of the strongest and stretchiest fibers. It is best used when stretch is desired in order to absorb sudden jerks and loads. When the boat moves back and forth at anchor or when she is docked, the anchor may be tripped (pulled out of the bottom) or cleats may break unless the anchor rode or docking lines stretch and take some of the shock load instead of transmitting it to the boat. Stranded nylon can stretch up to over 30 percent its length at one-half its breaking strength and then rebound

Laid rope is made up of synthetic fibers, yarns, and strands twisted tightly around each other.

Braided rope, more common today than laid rope, has a strong, hard core inside a soft cover.

Line and Rope

without permanent damage to its fibers. Nylon braid stretches less than laid nylon, about 15 percent its length at half its breaking strength. Nylon fibers are rough and can irritate hands, so a crew member with soft hands may want to wear gloves when handling the anchor rode.

Dacron, which stretches about 10 percent at half its breaking strength in both laid and braid form, is used in sheets on cruising and racing boats, and often in halyards, too, instead of wire rope. (Dacron is capitalized because it's a trademark.) Low-stretch means a line needn't be adjusted when the wind increases.

The relatively new **low-stretch synthetic fibers,** including Kevlar, Spectra, and other brand-named exotic materials, stretch much less and are extremely strong. (Kevlar was originally developed to reinforce automobile tires and also is used in bulletproof vests.) They stretch less than 5 percent when loads are one-half breaking strength, and so are often used in halyards and sheets. These lines are more expensive than Dacron and,

because they are stiff, they usually are hard to handle and can abrade quickly, even when protected by Dacron covers. Since these fibers have almost no give, they may fracture when making sharp bends, for example, in knots and in blocks. The point of greatest wear should be shifted every few months by cutting off the line's end. Special equipment usually is needed for attaching shackles. These ropes are often found in racers and well-equipped cruising boats.

None of the rope discussed so far can float. Buoyancy sometimes is desired in a line — for example, in the painter of a dinghy towed astern. If the line does not float, it may tangle in the propeller or rudder. The Gordian Knot is child's play compared with a dozen wraps of Dacron line around a seized-up propeller shaft. The only solution to the problem is to dive overboard and slice away at the tangle with a sharp knife or hacksaw. Prevention is provided by

polypropylene line, which floats and comes in a variety of highly visible bright colors. It has significant drawbacks. It is strong enough only for light duties, like towing a small boat. Its surface is so slippery and hard that it cuts hands, slips on cleats, won't hold knots, and abrades easily when a line rubs up against a fitting. And polypropylene is unusually sensitive to ultraviolet rays. The sun's rays weaken all synthetic lines somewhat through prolonged exposure, but they destroy polypropylene.

Selecting a Line. Lines should be chosen for how their inherent characteristics fit the job. For any line, as a rule of thumb, the breaking strength (which the manufacturer provides in its literature) should be at least twice the anticipated load. In chapter 14 we'll talk about selecting the right size nylon for an anchor rode. With sheets, the loads vary with the sail's size and the wind velocity. The wind's power increases with the

Each type of rope has characteristics that suit it for specific jobs: strong, stretchy nylon for anchor rodes and docking lines; buoyant polypropylene for painters; low-stretch Dacron or Kevlar for sheets and halyards. Whichever line you use, make it large enough to handle comfortably — at least ⅜-inch diameter for most jobs on boats larger than 20 feet.

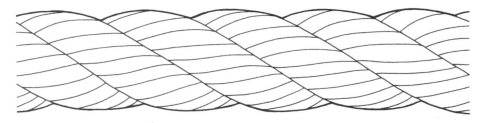

Laid construction is usually found in nylon anchor rodes.

Braided Dacron is used in sheets and halyards.

Braided nylon, like laid nylon, is good for anchor rodes and docking lines.

Buoyant polypropylene rope serves best in painters.

cube of the increase in its speed, meaning that the power of a 20-knot wind is eight times that of a 10-knot wind. And as the wind force increases dramatically, so do the forces of the waves that the wind kicks up. The loads in 20 knots of wind, therefore, are very high, and they demand strong equipment.

So it's a mistake to have sheets and halyards that are too small. Small Dacron line — 3/16 inch diameter, for example — may be appropriate on small boats, but it stretches earlier and more than larger line, and it's also much harder to handle. Another advantage of large line is that it requires fewer turns on a winch. A line of 3/8 inch diameter is about the smallest for comfortable handling, and 1/2 inch is better yet. (Whatever line you use, if you have not built up sailing calluses on your hands, wear leather sailing gloves to improve your grip.)

Coiling. A coil is a set of compact loops made in the line so it can be

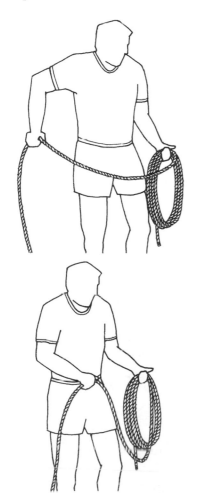

When coiling laid rope, twist your wrist a quarter turn clockwise with each loop to compensate for torque and remove kinks.

stowed or set aside when it is not in use. When coiling, make clockwise loops about 2 feet long with the right hand, laying each loop in the open palm of the left hand. When coiling laid line, you must make a quarter turn to the right with each new loop. If the loops are made counterclockwise or without the quarter turn, the line will kink badly when you try to use it — so badly, in fact, that the line will not render through blocks or even straighten itself out.

Braid is easier to coil than laid line. Since no torque is woven into the line, there is none to be removed by making the quarter turn — in fact, the turn causes kinking. A proper coil of braid will hang in 8s.

When you have almost finished a coil, with about 2 feet of line remaining, wrap half of it around the middle of the loops two or three times, forming a figure-8. Then push the bight (middle) of the remainder through the top hole in the 8, pull the bight over the top, and slide it to the middle again. Tighten it and hang the coil up with the remaining bit of line. When coiling the tail (leftover part) of a cleated line, go through the same steps, starting the coil near the cleat, but don't finish it off with the figure-8, which would delay uncleating and easing the line. Instead, reach through the coil and grab a few inches of line near the cleat. Pull out this bight and twist it to form a loop. Hang the loop over the cleat and the coil will be secure.

Heavy or extremely long lines, such as anchor rodes, should be coiled in loops lying on the deck since they are too awkward to hold in one hand. To coil a line on deck, stand over a clear area and pay out the line in 3-foot clockwise loops, making sure to twist a laid line a quarter-turn clockwise with each loop. To finish off the coil, tie a few short lengths of light line around it at equal intervals using a bow knot so it can be undone quickly. Alternatively, you can tape the coil in four corners. You will need a knife to cut the tape when you want to use the line, but until then the coil won't undo itself.

A **Flemish coil** is a traditional, decorative way to coil line. The line is laid out flat on deck in a tight spiral, with an end in the middle and a series of concentric circles. A Flemish coil may cause a line to kink.

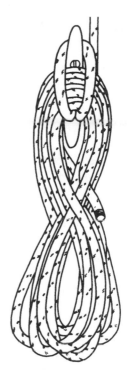

The right way to neaten up a line in use, this coil can be quickly undone. Braided line should hang in loose figure-8s.

A more permanent coil is made before stowing an unused line, for example, a halyard for a roller-furling jib. But do not use this coil for lines that may be cast off quickly, like a main halyard or a sheet.

Line

Splicing. A splice is an interweaving of strands that either joins two lines of the same diameter or forms an eye or a stopper in the end of a line. The strength of a splice depends on the friction between the interwoven strands of the line. The strands are tucked under one another in a set pattern, with three to six sets of tucks being the norm. A good splice weakens a line by 10–15 percent, while a knot may weaken it by far more.

To make an eye splice in laid line so a shackle or block can be secured to the line, unravel the three strands about 6 inches, then form the eye (loop). Lay the unraveled end over the standing part (main portion) of the line with the strands lying naturally. Tuck the center strand under a strand on the standing part, then tuck the left-hand strand under the next strand up. Now take the right-hand strand partway around the standing part to the right and tuck it under the remaining strand. Pull on the three strand ends to smooth out the tucks and then take three to six more tucks (over one strand and under the next one) in a center-left-right sequence, smoothing out the splice as you go along. When finished, rub the splice hard between your two palms to seat the strands more deeply, then cut off the ends of the strands. Since an eye splice is permanent, it should be made in lines that you don't intend to knot — for example, in the end of an anchor rode where the eye will be shackled to the anchor, or in the ends of docking lines. Where the eye will chafe against a metal

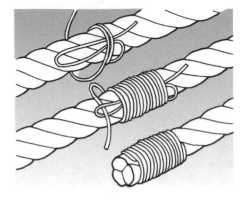

Whip a laid line's end by wrapping twine around it (above) or passing a needle and twine through it and making wraps.

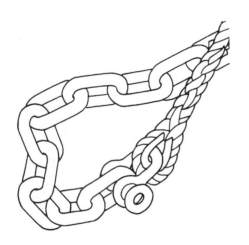

Because it's permanent and weakens line less than a knot, an eye splice is often used at the end of anchor rodes or docking lines.

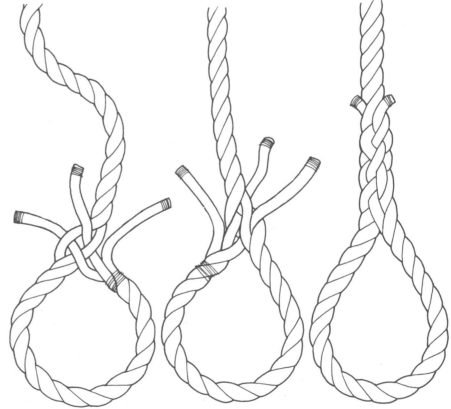

To make an eye splice in a laid line, unravel the strands and take tucks, over one strand and under one, in a center-left-right sequence. Take several tucks, pulling them tight as you go.

fitting like a shackle, put a metal or plastic loop called a thimble inside the eye.

Most braided line can be spliced into eyes according to the manufacturer's instructions by removing the core from the end and doubling it back into the cover. A loop can also be tied easily using a bowline (every year, cut off the bowline and tie another one in order to relocate the point of greatest abrasion).

Whipping. A line may unravel unless it is whipped, or secured at its end with tight loops of light waxed line called sailmaker's twine. In the simplest whipping, loop the twine around the end several times and tie the ends with a square knot. A more permanent whipping is made with a strong sewing needle and sailmaker's twine. To start the whipping, pass the needle through the line and pull the twine until the knot at its end stops against the line. Then make several tight wraps before finishing the whipping off with two or three more

passes through the line. The whipping's length should equal the line's diameter. The whipping will be neater if you do it before cutting the line.

The end of a braided line will unravel very quickly unless it is either whipped or sealed by burning with a match, a blowtorch, or a hot knife blade.

Heaving a Line. You may sometimes have to pass a line from your boat to a pier or another boat over a long distance. Ideally you would have a heaving line aboard. A traditional heaving line is a long, skinny line at the end of which is a piece of ropework called a monkey's fist, to add weight for throwing. The monkey's fist is whirled and thrown across, and the other crew hauls in the heaving line and the heavier tow line or docking line tied to it. Modern heaving lines are stowed in small bags. The end is pulled out and held in the thrower's spare hand while the bag is thrown. The weight of the line coiled in

the bag provides momentum for a throw as long as 30 feet.

If you don't have a proper heaving line, here's how you can get your line across. First, fake the line on deck and pull off enough to cover the distance, plus 6 feet. Coil this amount carefully and divide the coils between both hands. Take three coils in your throwing hand. Move as far as you can from obstructions, such as the mast and rigging. Open your nonthrowing hand so the line will pull off smoothly, then heave the line with a sweep of your other hand, ending with a flick of the wrist (like throwing a Frisbee underhanded). Aim just upwind of your target. As the coils fly out from your throwing hand, extend your other arm so the remaining line trails out smoothly behind.

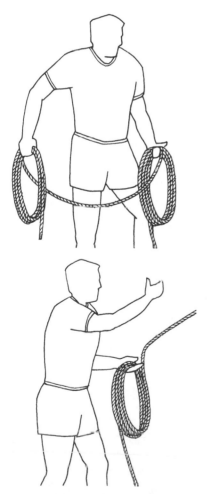

Heaving a line, throw three coils while letting the rest run off the other hand. Aim upwind of your target.

HANDS ON: **A Rescue**

1. Stop the boat entirely (otherwise you will tow the swimmer under) and, if possible, upwind of the swimmer.

2. Tie a large loop in the end of the line using a bowline knot.

3. Heave the bowline to the swimmer, then cleat your end.

4. Don't pull on the line until the swimmer has looped the line around her or his chest under the armpits. If the person is unconscious or needs assistance, someone will have to swim out from the boat. (This person must be wearing a life jacket and be connected to the boat with a separate line.)

5. Pull gently, keeping the victim's face free of the water as you haul him or her to you.

Wire Rope

Wire rope is steel stranded wire. Flexible 7 x 19 wire rope is used in halyards and other hoists in racing boats and many cruisers larger than 25 feet, while stiff 1 x 19 wire is used in stays. The first number represents the number of strands in the wire, and the second number indicates the number of individual wires in each strand. Size for size, 7 x 19 wire rope is about 25 percent stronger than nylon rope and 35 percent stronger than Dacron rope. However, it usually is no stronger and no less stretchy than exotic low-stretch fibers like Kevlar. Since wire rope is hard to handle, can be dangerous when it flies about, and requires a complicated splice or swaging in order to attach a shackle or a rope tail (the end handled by the crew), many boats up to 60 feet are rigged with low-stretch or Dacron rope halyards.

Wire rope's strands can break and stick out. These breaks are called "meat

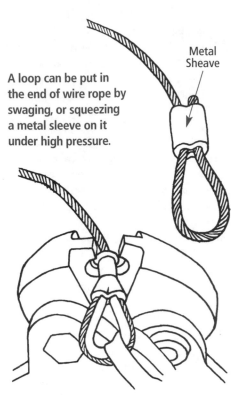

A loop can be put in the end of wire rope by swaging, or squeezing a metal sleeve on it under high pressure.

Metal Sheave

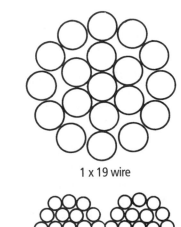

1 x 19 wire

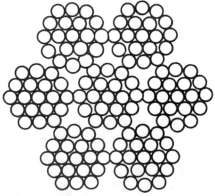

7 x 19 wire

Flexible 7 x 19 wire rope (bottom) is often used in halyards. Less flexible 1 x 19 (top) wire is used in stays. The first number is the number of strands and the second is the number of wires in each strand. Wire can be spliced by professional riggers.

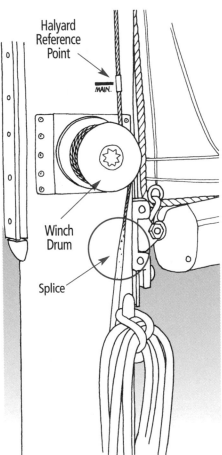

Halyard Reference Point

Winch Drum

Splice

With the sail hoisted, the splice between the wire halyard and the rope tail should lie between the winch and cleat when at least six turns of wire are on the winch drum. Mark the halyard over a reference point on the mast.

hooks" because the sharp wires can snag hands or clothing as efficiently as a butcher's hook. You must be extremely vigilant about keeping wire rope free of meat hooks, which, besides damaging sailors, can rip sails. Tape a meat hook, or snap it off with wire cutters. Best yet, rub the meat hook with a round steel object like a marlin spike (the spike in a sailor's knife) or a screwdriver's shaft. This will break off the wire at its base.

Because it is so much smaller than synthetic rope, wire rope requires special sheaves in blocks, with deep, narrow grooves that capture the halyard and keep it from jumping out and jamming. This accident is called jumping the sheave.

The weakest part of a wire halyard is the wire-to-rope splice, which can reduce the haylard's strength by more than 10 percent. The splice itself should carry as small a load as possible. Do not position the splice above the halyard winch, where it will take all the load. The splice should always be below the winch (between it and the cleat) and there should be at least six turns of wire on the winch drum. This may be difficult or even impossible when the sail is reefed, and for that reason many boats have rope main halyards so there is no splice. Some older boats may be equipped with an all-wire halyard leading to a special winch called a reel halyard winch, which works like a fishing reel. While this arrangement eliminates the problem of the wire-to-rope splice, a reel halyard winch, when a winch handle is installed, is extremely dangerous unless handled with great caution.

Meat hooks (broken wire strands) rip hands and sails. Clip them off with wire cutters.

Line Maintenance

While synthetic rope (like a synthetic sail) does not rot, it can mildew and become stained. Rinse lines regularly in fresh water and allow them to air dry thoroughly before you store them below. When you're not sailing, keep sheets out of the sun just as you would sails, since ultraviolet rays severely damage synthetic fibers.

Chafe (abrasion) can happen to any line within a few minutes once it comes in contact with another object — for example, when halyards wrap around each other, or when a sheet rubs against a life line. The best way to deal with chafe is to avoid it in the first place by leading a line away from other objects through fairleads (eyes) or blocks. Redirection at a low angle adds slight friction, but if you change the line angle by more than 60°, the load will be much larger. Therefore, turning blocks (called foot blocks when used for jib sheets) must be installed carefully and through-bolted.

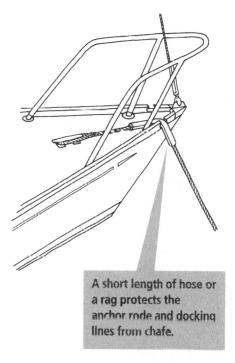

A short length of hose or a rag protects the anchor rode and docking lines from chafe.

When chafe is unavoidable, try to minimize and spread it. You can wrap tape (such as duct tape), heavy cloth, a piece of leather, or a split piece of garden hose around the line. Or you can adjust the line every hour so the chafe is not concentrated on one spot.

If one end of a line is badly worn, simply end-for-end it to put the abraded part where the load is least. Better yet, cut the worn section off. This is a good reason to cut new halyards, sheets, and docking lines much longer than you would at first think necessary. As a rule of thumb, the jib sheets should be at least twice the boat's length, and the main sheet and halyards should be long enough to do their jobs easily, plus at least 10 feet. A well-equipped boat carries a spare main halyard, a spare jib halyard, and spare main and jib sheets.

Sails also chafe. A good sailmaker anticipates chafe by wrapping the tack, head, and clew with leather patches that can be readily replaced. Likewise, jib halyard shackles that abrade in the narrow notch between the headstay and the mast should also be protected with leather.

Halyard and Sheet Marks. One common cause of chafe is hauling a halyard too high so the shackle or the head of the sail jams in the halyard sheave; another is trimming a sheet too far in so the sail rubs against the standing rigging. The best way to prevent these mishaps is to mark the halyards and sheets at a clearly visible spot so the hauler or trimmer knows when to stop pulling. Sometimes you may have to mark the deck or mast under the line to provide a reference point. You may also mark the sheets to indicate proper trim for certain wind strengths. Use indelible pens on synthetic rope. Wire rope can be marked with plastic tape or by weaving a piece of light wire between the strands. Mark the main halyard to show proper heights for the reefs; this will save time and guesswork when reefing.

Knots

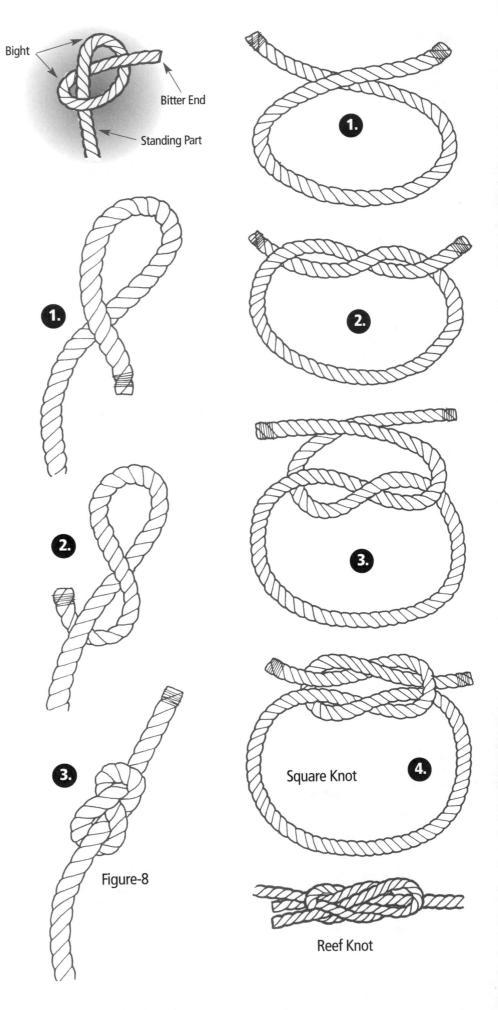

Bight

Bitter End

Standing Part

Figure-8

Square Knot

Reef Knot

While a knot, technically speaking, is an alteration in one line not affecting other objects, the word "knot" has come to also include the definitions of "hitch" (which secures a line to a fitting) and "bend" (which secures one line to another). No matter what you call it, a knot, bend, or hitch holds because of the friction created by turns in the line. There is a tradeoff between security and facility: the knots that are most secure, even when shaking about violently, are the ones that are most difficult to untie and may even have to be cut. Of the thousands of knots that have been invented over the centuries, the ones described here are most often used on pleasure boats.

First, some terminology: **the bitter end** of a line is its very end, the **standing part** is the main section, **the bight** is the U-shaped portion of the standing part, and **the loop** is a small circle in the standing part.

The Essential Knots. The **figure-8** is tied in the ends of lines to stop them from running out through blocks. Because it's easier to untie than the simple overhand knot, the figure-8 can be used in the ends of lines that will have to be rerigged frequently (jib sheets, for example). But for the same reason, the figure-8 should not be used in the end of a line that is rarely rerigged or that will shake or vibrate. The overhand knot, which cinches so tightly that it may have to be cut off, is best for these lines, which include halyards. Tie the figure-8 or overhand at least 4 inches from the bitter end so it has room to slip. Do not tie these knots in the ends of spinnaker sheets. If you lose control of the spinnaker, you will want to let the sheets run.

The **square knot** ties two lines of the same diameter together. It's nothing more than two overhand knots. The first is tied "right over left" by passing the right-hand bitter end over and under the left-hand standing part. Next, go "left over right" by passing the new left-hand

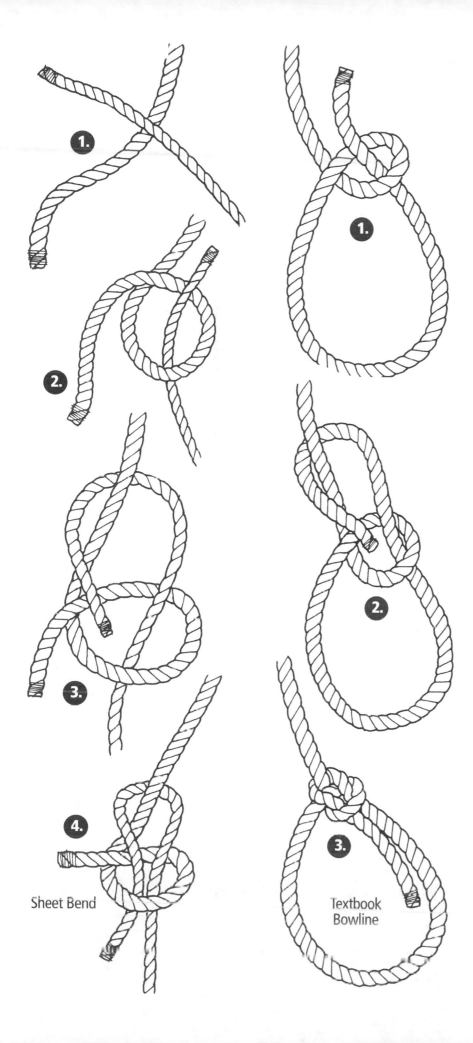

Sheet Bend

Textbook Bowline

bitter end over and under the new right-hand standing part. If you've done it wrong you have a granny knot, which will come undone very quickly. The square knot is easy to untie except when it's wet under heavy strain. Because the turns are abrupt, it's 50 percent weaker than the lines themselves, so is not a knot to stake your life or rig on. A version of the square knot is the **reef knot,** used to tie a reef point around the middle of a reefed sail so it is secured to the boom, and for other purposes when quick release is desired. Here, the "left over right" is not completed but left with a bow, which allows the knot to be untied by simply pulling the bow out.

The **sheet bend** is used in place of the square knot to tie together lines of the same or different diameters. Form a loop with the end of the larger line, with the bitter end lying on top of the standing part. Pass the smaller line's bitter end up through the loop, around the standing part, and back through the loop. Be sure to slide the smaller line down hard onto the loop. The sheet bend usually is easily untied.

The **bowline** is the most easily untied, reliable knot for making loops — for example, to tie jib sheets to the clew or to make an eye at the end of a docking line. The bowline rarely jams even when it's wet. It is about 40 percent weaker than the line and 30 percent weaker than an eye splice.

There are several ways to tie it. To tie the **textbook bowline:** Form a small loop in the standing part (the line to the bitter end should be twice the length of the loop you want to make). Pass the bitter end up through the small loop, around the standing part, and back through the small loop, leaving about 3 inches of tail. Cinch the knot tightly. Generations of sailors have learned how to tie the bowline by remembering, "The rabbit goes up through the hole, around the tree, and back down into the hole." To make the bowline more secure, for example when using slippery line, push the bitter end into the middle of the knot so the end is squeezed as the knot tightens.

Knots

The **quick bowline:** Lay the bitter end over the standing part and then twist the standing part up and away from you, forming a loop with the bitter end sticking up through it. Pass the bitter end around the standing part above the loop and pull it back through the loop.

The **tied-in-place bowline:** Pass the bitter end through the object to be secured (for example, the jib clew). In the standing part, form a slip knot so that the standing part is the section that "slips." Pass the bitter end through the slip knot about 6 inches. Tighten the slip knot and, with your hands, "capsize" it by rolling it

over. (Since this handy system was first seen in use by a garbageman loading his truck, it's also called "the garbageman's bowline.")

The **buntline hitch** also makes a loop, but one that is more compact and less likely to open than the bowline, which can shake loose. To tie the buntline hitch,

pass the bitter end through the object and then tie a hitch, or loop, around the standing part. Then tie a second hitch, but this time leave the bitter end on the side toward the object, wedged between the two hitches. As a strain is taken, the buntline hitch slides down the standing part, automatically squeezing the bitter

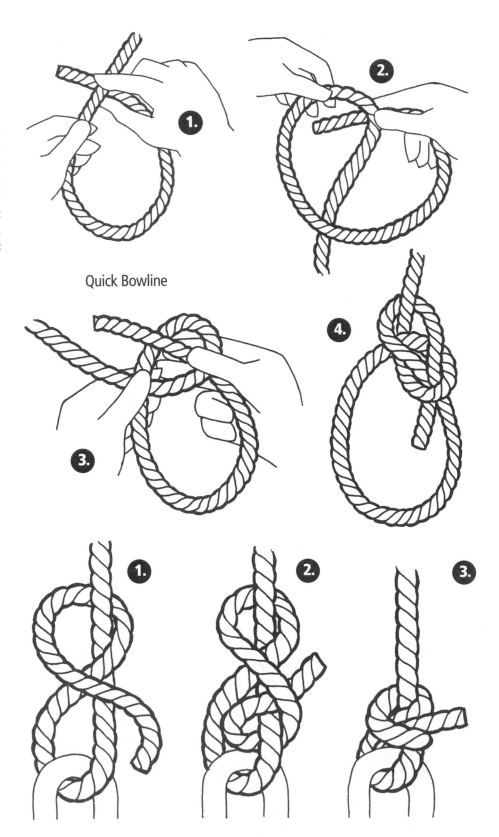

Quick Bowline

Buntline Hitch

end. The buntline cinches itself so tightly that, after time, it usually cannot be opened and so must be cut off. Therefore it is the best knot for permanent or semipermanent use — for instance, tying a rope halyard to a shackle.

The clove hitch, two loops side by side, is used to make a docking line fast to a bollard (a post on a pier), or to tie a fender to a lifeline. It can be tied two ways. One is to loop the bitter end around the object twice, tucking it under itself. The other way is to "throw a clove hitch" by forming the loops first and then dropping them over the bollard or post. While simple to tie and untie, the clove hitch can loosen itself. Secure it with a half hitch tied around the standing part and pulled down hard against the object.

The **double half-hitch** is two half-hitches (or a clove hitch) tied around the standing part to form a loop that can be adjusted by sliding the double half-hitch up and down. Unlike the buntline hitch, the double half-hitch does not hold the bitter end captive, so this knot is less secure but easy to untie. It's a quickly tied knot for low-load, temporary chores. The bowline is more secure, the buntline hitch far more secure. To increase its security, take a round turn (a full turn) around the object to absorb some of the strain.

The **fisherman's bend** (also anchor bend) is often used to tie a rode to an anchor. Pass the bitter end through the fitting twice, then tie a hitch with the bitter end passing under the two loops. Finish it off with a double half-hitch around the standing part. With laid line, tuck the bitter end under a strand in the standing part to prevent an accidental untying.

The **rolling hitch** grips a spar or other line. It is especially useful to take the strain off another line, such as a jib sheet, while the end of that line is untied or repositioned. To tie it, make three loops with the bitter end around the object, overlapping the first and second turns. To jam the rolling hitch, pull the line in the direction of the overlapped turn; to slide it, pull the line the other way.

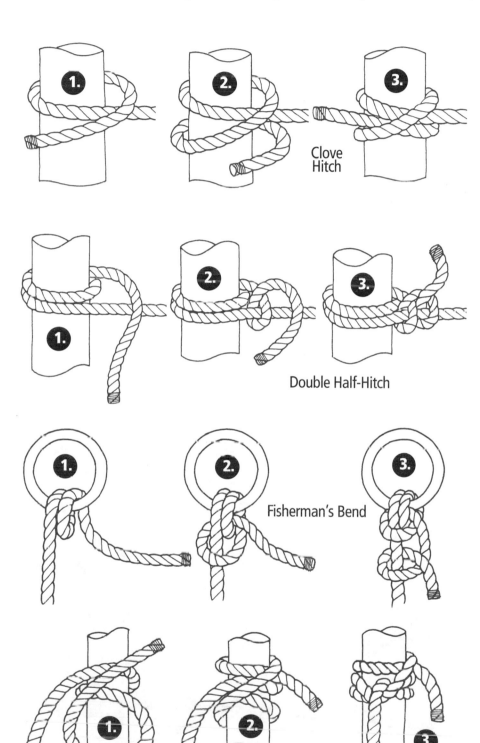

Clove Hitch

Double Half-Hitch

Fisherman's Bend

Rolling Hitch

The Preventer, Vang, and Topping Lift

Various lines are used to control the main boom.

In a boat longer than about 25 feet, the **preventer** is a line rigged from the boom to the deck that prevents the boom from swinging across the boat and hitting crew members. The history of sailors who have been killed or knocked overboard by out-of-control booms is a long and grim one. The force of a swinging boom is very considerable, even in light winds when the boat is rolling in waves. Therefore, preventers must be rigged permanently using sturdy fittings and ⅜-inch or larger Dacron or nylon line. Many skippers prefer to use nylon line because its stretch will absorb shock loadings that might break the boom. Since at least moderate tension must be kept on the preventer at all times, it must be easy to adjust when the main sheet is eased or trimmed. It should be led to a winch or cleat in the cockpit near the main sheet's cleat. Port and starboard preventers should be permanently rigged so that when the boat changes tacks, as one preventer is eased the other can be quickly trimmed.

There are two types of preventer. The **combination preventer-vang,** which holds the boom out and also down, is the most common type. A line is shackled or tied to the boom about 5 feet behind the mast, and then led through a sturdy block on the rail near the shrouds and aft to the cockpit. The **offshore preventer** does not provide any downward pull. It is led from the end of the boom to a block on the bow and then aft to the cockpit. It allows the boom to rise if the boat is rolled over so far that the boom drags in the water in a large ocean swell.

The **topping lift** is a line or plastic-coated wire leading from the top of the mast to the end of the boom to hold the boom up when the sail is not set. There is a tackle that makes adjustment easy. The lift will damage the sail and battens if it is allowed to fly around. Instead of pulling the topping lift taut (which will put excess load on it), rig a length of shock cord (bungee cord) from the line to the boom to absorb slack.

The **boom vang** is a tackle or rod that holds the boom down or at a desired level to keep the sail from twisting off and spilling wind. A vang made of a rod has the added advantage of holding the boom up as well, which permits dispensing with the topping lift.

(Right) A tackle type boom vang only prevents the boom from rising. (Below) A rod type boom vang both holds the boom down and holds it up. This is an important safety feature in boats larger than about 30 feet. (Left) A preventer holds the boom out so it doesn't swing across the boat and hit heads. A simple preventer is a line led from the boom to the deck near the shrouds, and then aft to the cockpit.

Cleats

Except in small sailing dinghies, which are at risk of capsize, most lines are cleated when they aren't being eased or trimmed. Sometimes the line is not completely cleated but, instead, it's snubbed with only one turn around the cleat to take the load. The most reliable cleat is the metal or wooden horn cleat, a short bar supported by legs an inch or two above the deck or spar. The cleat should be fastened with long screws or bolts. The cleat bar should be angled 15° to the side so the line won't jam on itself. Avoid cleats made of lightweight material and those with a rough finish that will abrade the line.

Cleats must not be too small, for otherwise the line will either not fit under the horns or will jam under them. Cleats for anchor rodes and docking lines especially must be large and sturdy and carefully bolted to the deck through backup plates. Regularly

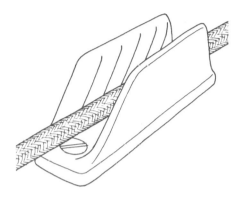

A plastic or aluminum Clamcleat must fit its line.

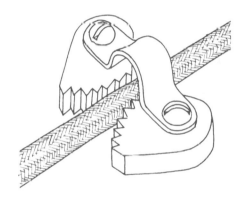

Cam cleats release lines quickly but their moving parts may break.

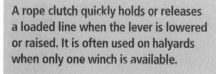

A rope clutch quickly holds or releases a loaded line when the lever is lowered or raised. It is often used on halyards when only one winch is available.

check your cleats for bending and corrosion.

Using the Horn Cleat. To cleat a line, first pass it around and under the back horn, then around and under the forward horn. This full turn usually creates enough resistance to snub the line against heavy strains, so long as a light pull is kept on the tail. To secure the line completely, cross it over the cleat and pass it around the back horn in the opposite direction from the way you originally led it. Cross it back again and under the front horn and finish off by looping it in a half-hitch. You've done it correctly if the bitter end lies parallel to the first cross-over loop you made.

The half-hitch locks the line so it won't fall off the cleat. With thin line that is too small for the cleat, that may not be a threat, and the half-hitch may jam. But if the line and the cleat are correctly mated, the cleating system that we've just described — one round turn, two cross-overs, and a half-hitch — is secure and handy to use.

Once the line is cleated, you can coil it. Some well-thought-out boats are equipped with small sacks for the tails of sheets and halyards. On other boats, small lengths of line or shock cord (bungee cord) are used to secure coils of line so they don't get loose and drag overboard. More than one person has compared a sailboat with an unruly spaghetti factory; try to keep all that pasta in the pot. Color-coding may ease some of the confusion.

Quick-Action Cleats. Besides the traditional horn cleat, there are several types of quick-action cleats in which the line is gripped by teeth. The **cam cleat** has two moving jaws that spring tight on a line dropped between them. A **rope clutch** grips a line passing through it when a lever is engaged and lets it go instantly when the lever is disengaged. The aluminum or plastic **Clamcleat** grabs line dropped between the teeth in its channel. While all three types grip line quickly, the rope clutch works faster than the other quick-action cleats when letting go a heavily loaded line, since all you have to do is raise the lever. To let go a loaded line in a cam cleat or Clamcleat, the crew usually must trim the line a few inches while lifting it out. In all these cleats, any moving parts should be cleaned and the teeth should be sharpened regularly.

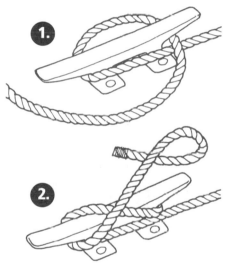

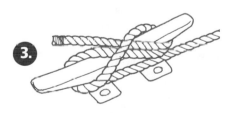

To cleat a line, start by snubbing it with a full turn (top) and finish with a half-hitch.

Blocks, Tackles, and Shackles

catalogs specify safe load limits, including safety factors. By matching these specifications to the anticipated loads and the line's size and breaking strength (also supplied in catalogs), you'll be able to make a safe choice.

Blocks should be inspected regularly for loose fittings, bent sheaves, and miss-

ing bearings; they also should be rinsed out with fresh water and lubricated.

Tackles. Tackles are systems of blocks and lines that increase pulling power. A tackle's power, called the mechanical advantage, can be calculated by counting its parts — the number of short lengths of line in the tackle. In a four-part tackle,

Blocks. A block is a nautical pulley. It consists of a sheave suspended between cheeks (sides) either on a pin or on two ball-bearing or needle-bearing races. The block is attached to the deck, a spar, or other fittings with a shackle (which we'll say more about later). The larger the block, the higher the load it can take. Blocks must be matched with the lines that are rove (passed) through them. There are several types of blocks:

A **single block** has a single sheave, a **double block** two sheaves, side by side, and a **triple block** three sheaves. In a **sister block,** two sheaves are arranged end to end.

A **becket block** may have one, two, or three sheaves plus a stationary eye to which a line is dead-ended (tied at its end).

A **snatch block** has a side gate that opens and closes so a line may be inserted at its standing part rather than threading the bitter end.

A **halyard sheave** is a sheave inserted high up a mast to carry a halyard.

Turning blocks redirect lines away from chafe or to provide a more effective angle to a winch or cleat. Foot blocks, used on jib sheets, and small cheek blocks are types of turning blocks.

A **ratchet block** has an internal mechanism that prevents the sheave from turning in one direction, thereby snubbing the line, or taking some of the load off it. Ratchet blocks usually are found on boats smaller than about 30 feet.

Blocks come in many different sizes to meet most sail-handling needs, and are made of plastic, metal, or wood. When buying a new block, be sure you know how it will be used. Wire rope requires special grooved sheaves which, because wire is brittle, must be larger in diameter than sheaves for synthetic rope. Some jobs impose especially heavy loads and therefore require especially large blocks — foot blocks come under sharper, more intense strains than jib sheet leads, for example. Manufacturers'

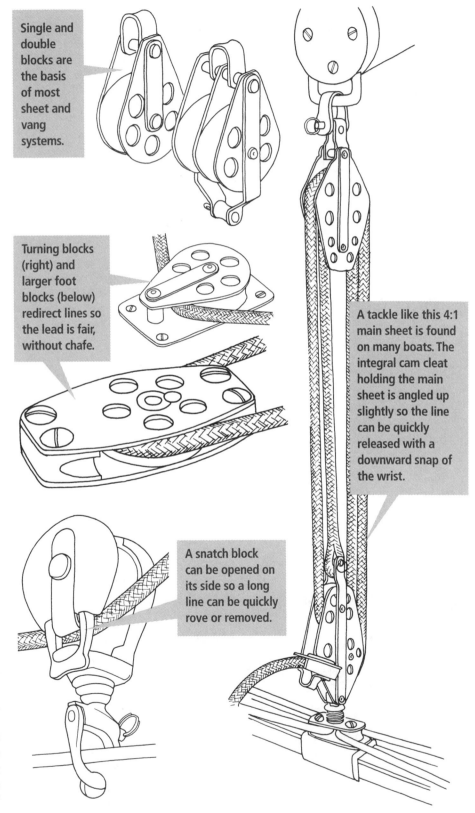

Single and double blocks are the basis of most sheet and vang systems.

Turning blocks (right) and larger foot blocks (below) redirect lines so the lead is fair, without chafe.

A tackle like this 4:1 main sheet is found on many boats. The integral cam cleat holding the main sheet is angled up slightly so the line can be quickly released with a downward snap of the wrist.

A snatch block can be opened on its side so a long line can be quickly rove or removed.

a double block and a double block with a becket divide the line into four sections to make a mechanical advantage of 4:1 (though the effective power ratio is a little less due to friction). What this means is that you can haul almost a 100-pound load by exerting 25 pounds of pull on the line. You must pull four times as much line, however. "Tackle" is traditionally pronounced "tay-kel."

Shackles. Shackles — U-shaped fittings in which the gap is closed by pins (clevis pins) or arms secured usually by clevis pins — hold things together. They link halyards to sails, spinnaker sheets to clews, main sheet blocks to the boom. When a shackle or its clevis pin is bent or dented, it usually cannot be repaired without losing some of its strength. Boats should carry spare shackles and pins for every function on board. Manufacturers specify safe working loads and a safety factor of two is common, meaning that the shackle should be designed to take twice the expected load.

The most widely used shackles are these:

Screw shackles are closed by a threaded clevis pin. Though slow to open and shut, a screw shackle is the most secure shackle available. It's usually used on the main halyard and the anchor, and to secure blocks permanently to fittings. To doubly secure a screw shackle, wire, lash, or tape its pin after it's been screwed in tightly. A version of the screw shackle, the twist shackle, used on small boats, is closed by pushing a pin through a hole and twisting it. Some pins are captive, meaning that they cannot fall out of the shackle, even when disengaged. Non-captive pins should be secured to the shackle by a short lanyard, or length of light line.

Snap shackles open and close around a manually operated, spring-loaded pin or latch. Because they work quickly, they are used on jib and spinnaker halyards and spinnaker sheets. Most snap shackles include swivels to keep the line from twisting. While these swivels decrease the fittings' strength, the main weakness in a snap shackle is the spring that holds the pin shut and the shackle closed. For added security, snap shackles may be wrapped in tape. The pins should be inspected periodically for wear and corrosion. Lanyards (tails of light line) may

be tied to the pins for use as trip lines, but they should be no longer than 2 inches. Any longer and they are liable to catch in rigging and open the shackles while a sail is being hoisted.

Cotter pin–type shackles are used in permanent connections between fittings. Their clevis pins are held in place

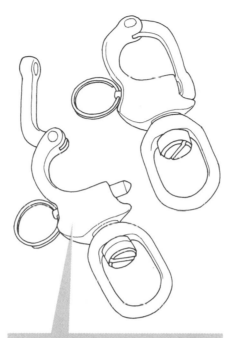

A snap shackle is used when a sheet or halyard is frequently removed. For added security, wrap tape around the pin when it is closed.

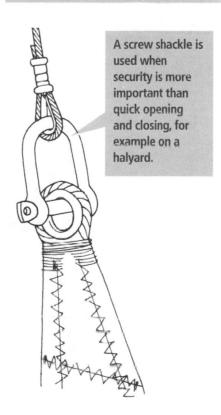

A screw shackle is used when security is more important than quick opening and closing, for example on a halyard.

by a straight or circular metal pin.

Snap hooks are smaller than snap shackles, but also are spring-loaded. When used to hook jibs onto the headstay, they are called hanks.

Brummel Hooks (sometimes called sister hooks) are lightweight aluminum shackles used in pairs. When the slot of one hook engages the slot on the other, they are secured. Since there are no moving parts, the only problem to look out for is corrosion. These shackles are not strong enough for use except in small boats, where they often are used on spinnakers.

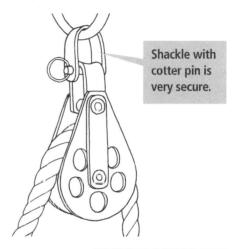

Shackle with cotter pin is very secure.

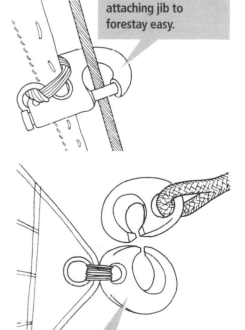

Snap hooks, often used on jib luffs, make attaching jib to forestay easy.

Brummel hooks are very light, making them ideal for attaching sheets and guys to spinnakers on small boats.

157

Winches

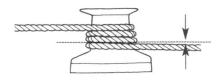

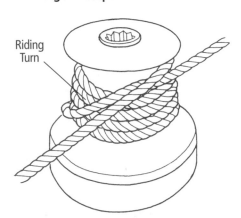

(Above) Leading the line up to the winch at a slight angle will prevent riding turns. (Below) Unwind a riding turn by pulling the sheet out counterclockwise or taking the load off with another line and loosening the wraps.

Riding Turn

A winch is a mechanical aid that increases a sailor's pull on a sheet, halyard, or other loaded line. It consists of a revolving drum mounted on a secure base. The drum rotates clockwise when it is turned by a metal arm, called a winch handle, inserted in its top. (Some winches are turned by electric motors.) The handle usually works through gears that increase the mechanical advantage already provided by its own lever effect. The simplest winches have only one gear; more complicated ones have as many as four gears that are changed by turning the winch handle the other

way or by activating switches.

The sheet or halyard led to the winch should come up to it at a slight angle (or the winch should be cocked slightly); otherwise, if the sheet is led down or at a right angle to the drum, the turns of the line on the drum will overlap each other and jam. Called a riding turn, this jam-up can be removed in light air by heaving back on the sheet; in fresh air you may have to take the strain off the sheet with another line, using a rolling hitch, and unwrapping it.

How to Use a Winch. To operate a winch, wrap the sheet or halyard clockwise around the drum. If you're just taking in slack — say, when tacking — use only one turn, but increase the number of turns as the load builds. With large-diameter line, which creates excellent friction on the drum, you'll need fewer turns than with skinny line. Four turns should be all you need when using synthetic line,

On this typical 38-foot cruiser-racer, most winches are of the self-tailing type, which permit a crew to haul a sheet or halyard singlehanded. Although a line can be cleated in a self-tailer, the owner has wisely installed horn cleats as backups. The traveler (below the wooden companionway slat) runs across the cockpit and is cleated on each side so it can be quickly adjusted. An inclinometer (just below the traveler) indicates if the boat is heeling too far and the traveler should be let down. Speed indicators are on the bulkhead to the right of the slat.

but six or more turns with wire rope.

To trim the line, insert the winch handle in the top of the winch and turn it with one hand while tailing (pulling on the tail of the line behind the winch) with the other. Use more powerful gears if you need them, or turn the handle with both hands while somebody else tails. The best position for grinding the winch handle with both hands is to stoop or lean over it, facing down, so you get your arms, shoulders, and back into the job. When trimming a short amount of line, sit or stoop facing the sail or other object that you're adjusting and pull the handle toward you. Always remove handles when they're not in use, since they can snag sheets or legs.

To ease the line, hold the tail with one hand and push the palm of the other hand against the turns on the drum. Then ease out the tail and your braking hand simultaneously, letting out about 2 inches at a time. To cast off a line

when tacking or lowering a halyard, pull it up and off the drum and let it run out through your hands. Be careful not to let fingers, long hair, or clothing catch in turns around a winch. It can be awkward and painful.

When you're using a winch and there isn't a free cleat, secure the line to the winch with the towboat hitch (also tugboatman's hitch). Make a bight in the tail and pass it under the standing part between the winch and the tail and over the drum. Then snug it tight enough to secure it, but not so tight that you can't get it off quickly.

Special Winch Gear. Some winch handles have locks that secure them when they are inserted. These lock-in handles should always be used when working a vertically mounted winch on a mast, for otherwise the handle will slip out and go overboard — or worse, injure a crew member.

Many winches are equipped with

integral cleats, called self-tailers, that hold the line as it is trimmed. This allows a single person to trim a sail alone. Self-tailing winches are more expensive than regular winches but are well worth the added cost, particularly for shorthanded sailing with small crews.

A coffee grinder is an extremely powerful deck-mounted winch consisting of a large drum and one or two sets of vertical handles at which two or four grinders can work. These elaborate winches are standard equipment on big ocean racers and America's Cup yachts.

A windlass is a type of winch, usually powered by electricity, placed on the bow and used to handle anchor rodes. Most windlasses have a drum for rope rodes as well as a wildcat — or notched drum — for chain rodes. The links and the notches in the wildcat must match up, otherwise the chain will not hold. Windlasses should be inspected, greased, and cleaned out more frequently than winches since their location on the foredeck is wetter than a winch's position back in the cockpit. Mud and weed that come up with the anchor chain will foul the windlass unless they're scrubbed off.

A self-tailing winch automatically secures a line as it is trimmed, allowing the grinder to wind without tailing.

The towboat hitch secures a sheet when a cleat isn't free. Just loop a bight of the tail under the strained part and over the winch.

Have at lest three turns on the winch when pulling in a loaded sheet or halyard.

Release a sheet or halyard by pulling the wraps up and off the drum.

CHAPTER 6 The Sailor's Health

Seamanship in its broadest sense means to sail safely and enjoyably in any kind of weather and situation. Pleasure usually correlates with safety. While a degree of risk is inherent in sailing — in fact, for many sailors the challenge is one of the pastime's main appeals — foremost among the seaman's arts is the skill to manage and minimize risk by anticipating danger. Forehandedness, as the navy calls this art, is crucial.

A good seaman, therefore, not only has mastered the principles and techniques of boat handling and piloting but also is looking ahead one or two steps to possible problems. In this and the next two chapters, we will look at the arts and rules of boating safety — including crew organization, proper clothing, preventing and dealing with health problems (including seasickness, hypothermia, and injury), crew-overboard rescue, life jackets, and avoiding collision.

All these are important considerations for anybody who wants to follow the sailor's life.

When well-led, assigned to specific tasks, and properly outfitted, a good crew of a good boat is cheerful and fully prepared.

Roles on Board

The Skipper. Somebody has to be in charge. The crew may vote on where to sail to, what to eat for dinner, or when to get under way in the morning, but there must be a commander. The very best skippers are men or women able to steer, manage the engine and sails, anchor, pilot, and do all the big and little chores that are required to get the boat and her crew safely through the day. They also are well organized. Good skippers don't forget to buy lunch. They don't leave the charts in the car.

The skipper should also be a leader, skilled at delegating authority, willing to teach, and (most of all) able to take charge decisively. A test in any job, this is especially challenging on a pleasure boat, which, unlike an army platoon or a division of a corporation, is a purely voluntary organization. People go sailing for fun, and many will get off the boat if they're not having any. Captain William Bligh of the *Bounty* may have been an excellent seaman and an extraordinary leader in emergencies, but the mere mention of his last name evokes images of a petty, cruel autocrat more interested in his ship than in his men. A skipper must indeed care for his vessel, but she or he should also command with the attitude of being first among equals rather than God Almighty.

As tactfully as possible, the skipper should from the beginning of the day's sail or the week's cruise establish a clear routine. The skipper's first job is to be sure that the crew knows how to use vital equipment, certainly the toilet and possibly also the engine, the radiotelephone, the bilge pumps, and the stove. Here he may have less trouble instructing landlubbers than changing the habits of experienced sailors familiar with other systems on different boats. Next the skipper should point out the location of safety equipment such as fire extinguishers, life jackets, and safety harnesses. Then he should lead a calm discussion about emergency procedures, including rescues and firefighting.

Next comes the delegation of authority, which can be difficult. For trips longer than a day, the skipper should appoint a second-in-command. This should be somebody whom the skipper trusts both as a sailor and as a leader. On many boats, these two people — the owner and his mate — do all the work. All seamen are proud of their skills, but a ship with only a couple of performers is an unhappy one. The reasons for this star system are understandable. When new crewmembers come aboard, at first they are as awkward as they are hopeful. The skipper should respect their eagerness; he should encourage and include them by giving them jobs to do. Obviously the job should not be a vital one, like steering through a crowded anchorage in a 30-knot wind. But casting off the mooring or dock lines, hoisting and dousing sails, trimming sheets, and dropping anchor are chores that in normal weather are simple and easily learned. Anybody doing them, whether a six-year-old child or a 60-year-old grandmother, will be satisfied that she is making a contribution. Later on, in open water, allow everybody a chance to steer.

There are a few jobs that are always challenging and sometimes tricky and a bit dangerous. One is steering up a crowded channel. Another is anchoring. Clear command is important at such times. A novice may bristle when relieved at the helm or windlass at such a moment unless the crew member sees the situation from the captain's point of view.

There are right and wrong ways to accomplish just about every important task on a boat, but often there are several correct ways among which each skipper has a personal favorite. He should tactfully but firmly make clear how and why he wants jobs done his way, demonstrating both correct and incorrect techniques. Among the key tasks where a mistake could lead to disaster are cleating a halyard incorrectly, taking a bearing carelessly, and going on deck in rough weather without a safety harness. Somebody on board might be used to different equipment. If so, the skipper should explain why she prefers her procedures — but be open to suggestions for better ways.

A skipper should not emulate Captains Bligh or Queeg. But he or she should be decisive and also aware of the limitations of the crew, the boat, and him- or herself.

Roles on Board

Beginners must start somewhere, so when the situation allows, let inexperienced sailors take a trick at the helm.

The Crew. Each crew member on a boat has a responsibility to him- or herself and everybody else aboard, beginning by frankly admitting any physical or other limitation on his ability to perform that responsibility. Don't give a misleading or false answer exaggerating your abilities. If you have a tendency to get seasick, bring your own pills and take them before you get under way. Try to help out, but don't get in the way during maneuvers. If you don't know how to do a chore that you have volunteered for or that has been assigned to you, ask — nobody will think less of you for wanting to do a job right, but the wrath of Poseidon will descend on you if your claims of competence prove to be false. Many skippers get excited when they're tense. Try not to take their comments personally. At first you may be annoyed by a skipper's seemingly militaristic procedures, such as asking you to repeat orders after they're given or to coil lines in a specific way. You can respond by simply ignoring them, but such passive-aggressive behavior eventually will lead to worse problems. Better yet, take the edge off your frustration by asking (at the appropriate moment), "Why do you do it this way, Skipper?" A true Bligh will answer such a reasonable question with a cold, withering stare, convincing you that perhaps you might enjoy yourself more on somebody else's boat. But a skipper with a sense of fair play will answer politely and thoroughly.

The old adage, "One hand for yourself, one for the ship," means to take care of yourself while you take care of the vessel. This is literally true in rough weather, when you must hold on with one hand while doing even the most menial jobs, but the saying's deepest meaning is that you should always be alert to what is going on, both on deck and below. Don't assume that the skipper is keeping a perfect lookout, or is on top of every maintenance job. On cruises and long daysails, your "one hand for the ship" might be a small donation to the boat's provisions, even if it's only a bag of fruit or a six-pack of drinks.

On long sails, people can easily get on each other's nerves, just as they would in a crowded automobile on a long drive. Try to understand and minimize your own eccentricities just as you attempt to tolerate your crewmate's. Whistling, constant talking, and repeated humming of the same song are among the otherwise petty annoyances that have led to discord, but the worst flaw of all is sloppy seamanship. Do your job right and you'll be respected.

Sailing with Children. Children can be very enjoyable company on boats — for some people. So warn your guests ahead of time that your or somebody else's kids might be joining the cruise. The age of the child plays an important role in her accommodation to boating. Very young children get along well just about everywhere as long as they're in good health. A young child's playfulness and eagerness to learn can be a joy on board if the parents and other crew are willing to tolerate the constant anxiety about her falling overboard. In the later years a child usually is old enough to learn a few basic safety rules — among them, "always do what the skipper says"— and may be helpful with small tasks that tolerate a short attention span. Most important when sailing with children, make sure they know by the tone of your voice when they must follow orders. The world of children is so benign that they are not attuned to the kind of quick-rising dangers that can occur on the water. But even when they are as old as 11 or 12, children should not be treated as regular working crew members. They may enjoy steering, trimming sails, or helping with the navigation (a wonderful job for a kid with an interest in computers). But they still are children.

Clothing

In chapter 2 we introduced the clothing that sailors should take aboard. Here we will go into greater detail.

Wet, cold sailors inevitably make careless errors, endangering themselves, shipmates, and the vessel. Be realistic, not hopeful, about your resistance to cold. Go aboard overprepared. You should take at least a waterproof jacket, a fleece pullover or wool sweater, and a long-sleeve shirt and baseball cap to keep the sun off your arms and face. Carry this gear and anything else that you take aboard in a small duffel bag that on boats is called a sea bag. (Never go aboard with a rigid suitcase, which scratches the boat and is bulky to stow.) Good sea bags have waterproof pouches for wet clothing. Otherwise, take along a plastic garbage bag for your damp laundry.

Shoes. Going barefoot may seem salty, but except on very small boats, the inevitable torn toenails, broken toes, scrapes, and tumbles on wet decks are a great price to pay for that transitory self-image. Some general-purpose sneakers (with white soles so they don't mark up the deck) may provide good footing, but if you plan to do a lot of sailing, buy boating shoes called "deck shoes" or "Topsiders" (the trademark of one of the first boating shoes). The slitted soles in deck shoes will hold even on wet decks. They also will pick up dirt and oil, so many experienced sailors make a practice of wearing them only when they're on board.

For sailing in cold spray and rain, nothing beats rubber sea boots, knee-high for ocean sailing and calf-high for calmer waters. Since the fit varies widely from manufacturer to manufacturer, try different styles before you make your choice.

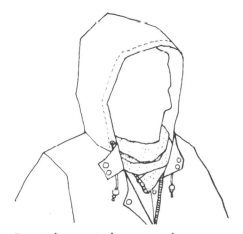

Expect the worst when you pack your sea bag. Include a towel to keep water from dripping down your neck.

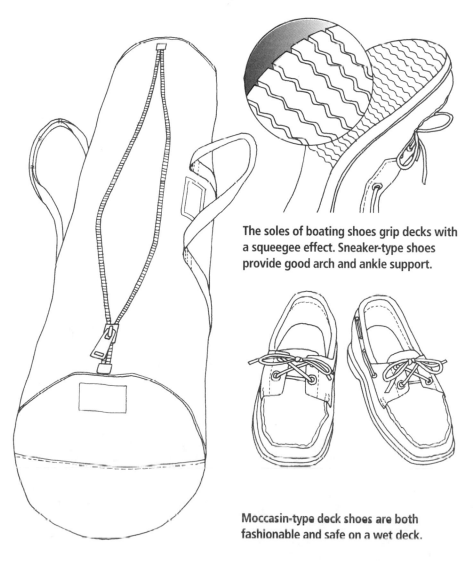

The soles of boating shoes grip decks with a squeegee effect. Sneaker-type shoes provide good arch and ankle support.

Sea boots prevent the cold and discomfort of soggy socks.

Moccasin-type deck shoes are both fashionable and safe on a wet deck.

Foul-Weather Gear

Since water conducts heat 25 times faster than air, a wet body is probably a cold body. Keeping dry is the key to staying comfortable and effective. Here are some tips for selecting the waterproof outermost layer — the jacket and trousers widely called foul-weather gear but also known as slickers, wet gear, oilskins, oilies, and foulies. There are two styles of foul-weather gear: the two-piece suit with separate jacket and trousers, and the one-piece jumpsuit.

The most versatile is the traditional two-piece suit. The jacket may be worn alone in light or moderate spray or rain, and, as conditions degrade, with the trousers. The design of each unit is important. It should provide double protection over the body's trunk, which must remain warm in order to hold off hypothermia (extreme chilling of the body). So the jacket should drop at least to the waist and, better yet, well below it. (For sailing in very heavy weather or in the tropics, the jacket may be a knee-length smock.) Trousers should extend well above the waist in a chest-high bib held up by stretchy suspenders. Trousers that come only to the waist are inexpensive, and also ineffective when you really need good protection. A one-piece jumpsuit is fine in cool, damp weather when you will always want to wear pants and a jacket at the same time. The rest of the time the jumpsuit may be confining and sweaty.

A good outfit has heavily reinforced seams covered with sturdy tape, as well as at least two layers of fabric at the seat and knees. There should not be any seams on such vulnerable spots as the seat and shoulders, where they may leak. The zippers must be large and easy to use, without snagging fabric. The jacket zipper should open from the bottom as well as the top to allow ventilation. A nylon liner provides an air baffle that

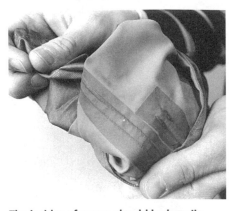

The insides of seams should be heavily taped so there is less chance of leaks.

The two-piece foul-weather gear suit is more versatile than other outfits. The trousers should have sturdy stretchy suspenders and be chest-high. Note the large flap to go across the neck, the reinforcements at the knees, and the number of pockets for stowing personal gear and warming hands.

cuts uncomfortable condensation on the inside. Some jackets have insulation for cold-weather sailing. Well-designed elastic cuffs and a tight fit around the neck keep out water. Small drips through openings are inevitable, but you can stop some of them by wearing a small towel around your neck under the jacket. The trousers should have strong suspenders and snaps. Both top and bottom should have sturdy pockets for a knife and other items. A good hood has a short bill to keep water off the eyes and should be capable of being rolled up out of the way. Buy only red, orange, or yellow jackets so you'll be visible if you accidentally fall into the water. White, green, and blue make a person in the water invisible to would-be rescuers.

A foul-weather suit is made of one of three families of fabric. All are good at keeping water out, but some are better than others at minimizing humidity on the inside. Without good ventilation, perspiration and other moisture soaks the body from the inside out, leaving the body as wet and cold as it would be with leaky foul-weather gear.

If the fabric is slick on the outside, it is **PVC (polyvinyl chloride)** — heavy, sturdy, and relatively inexpensive. PVC gear is waterproof in part because there are no sewn seams to leave holes. The fabric is joined at seams by heat welding. But PVC is confining and hot. You may be able to ventilate by opening up the cuffs, neck, and front of the foul-weather jacket. Because it's easy to clean, PVC is often used by fishermen and other commercial mariners.

If the fabric is slick on the inside and textured on the outside, it may be **urethane,** lighter and somewhat more expensive than PVC and used in most foul weather gear for normal use. Or it may be sturdier, even pricier **neoprene,** which goes into many suits for offshore use. Both are less confining than PVC.

Then there are the "breathable" **microcellular fabrics,** the best known of which is Gore-Tex. More expensive than the others, foul-weather gear made of these fabrics is lightweight and has the special feature of allowing air to escape through the fabric so moisture does not build up inside the jacket and trousers.

When buying foul-weather gear, be sure to try it on over all the clothing you may wear in cool weather, such as a heavy fleece jacket or a warmup jacket worn for insulation. Touch your toes and grind an imaginary winch to see if you have the right size.

Warm Clothing. It's often cooler on a boat than on land. Except in deep winter, water is colder than land, which means that the air immediately above the water, at deck level, is colder than the air ashore. In addition, there is the windchill factor: the wind cuts the air temperature (as felt by a human) by a little less than 1 degree for every 1 knot of apparent wind. This is why a run before the wind feels much warmer than a beat into it, when the apparent wind is much higher. So you have to take clothing that will insulate and block the wind. Foul-weather gear does the second job. But there are several options for clothing to wear under it.

Among insulators, wool used to be the best material for cold-weather clothing because, unlike cotton, it has long fibers that hold heat and it insulates when wet. At least as effective as wool (and lighter in weight) is the modern synthetic material known as fleece or bunting (short fibers) and pile (long fibers). These synthetics trap air, provide excellent insulation when wet, dry quickly, and wick perspiration off your skin to leave your body dry (and dry means warm). Fleece and pile go in shirts, pullovers, gloves, socks, pants, and hats. Other synthetics, including polypropylene, are used in socks and long underwear. (Silk also serves well in underwear and socks because of its insulating and wicking abilities.)

A high priority in cool and wet weather is covering the head, which serves like a chimney to vent away warmth. Take along and wear a wool or fleece hat or watch cap.

(Left) A one-piece jumpsuit is desirable when the weather is almost always cold and wet. Some suits have built-in safety harnesses. (Above) Cuffs should be sealed with elastic and Velcro straps.

Foul-Weather Gear

Dry and Wet Suits. Board sailors, dinghy sailors, and others who expect to get wet while boating often wear dry or wet suits in place of foul-weather gear. A dry suit is a one-piece waterproof jumpsuit made of lightweight material with strong waterproof seals at the neck and cuffs. Access is through a flap on the back. Most dry suits are worn by dinghy racers and sailboard sailors, although they often have been used offshore in demanding weather. Where dry suits keep wearers dry and warm, wet suits keep them damp and warm. A wet suit is a synthetic, tight pullover that traps water between its surface and the wearer's skin. The body quickly heats the water layer to form a thin warm insulator. Wet suits come in different thicknesses for a variety of water temperatures and in several styles, some for the whole body and others for the top or bottom only. Although they provide buoyancy, wet suits must not be used in place of life jackets because they will not always float a swimmer head up. Both wet and dry suits are difficult to put on and take off quickly.

Survival Suits. Developed originally for military use in extreme climates, survival suits (also called immersion suits) are exactly what the name suggests. They'll float swimmers while protecting them from cold and wet for long lengths of time. However, survival suits are too bulky to wear while trying to sail a boat actively. Boats heading far offshore in cold weather should be equipped with at least one survival suit in case of emergency.

Keeping Warm and Dry. Layering is the best approach for dressing for sailing.

Most sailing is a mix of energetic activity and patient waiting. You may exert yourself strenuously for a few minutes while tacking or changing sails, then sit quietly for an hour. In warm weather, swim suits, shorts, and T-shirts (with high collars to protect the neck from sun) may be all the clothing you need for both periods. But be alert to the rosy hues on thighs, upper arms, ankles, and necks that indicate a fast-developing sunburn.

As the day advances and the wind rises, add more clothes. Think in terms of layers. Experienced sailors carry several light- or medium-weight fleece, pile, or silk layers — from long underwear through pullovers and pants — that they add as the air cools until they are wearing three or four layers under their foul-weather gear. Fully suited up, they may have nothing made of a natural material except a handkerchief. This layering system using modern synthetics provides flexibility for all conditions.

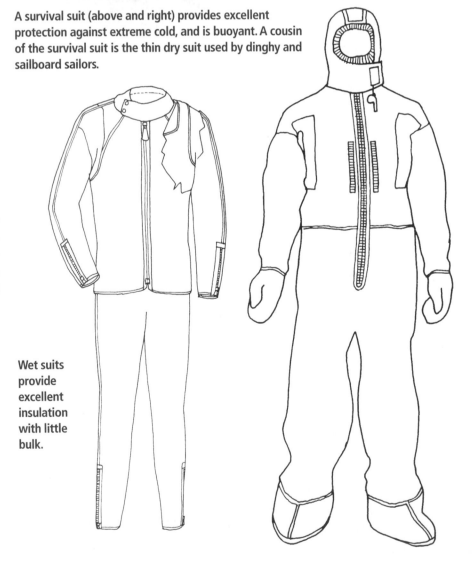

A survival suit (above and right) provides excellent protection against extreme cold, and is buoyant. A cousin of the survival suit is the thin dry suit used by dinghy and sailboard sailors.

Wet suits provide excellent insulation with little bulk.

Medical Problems

The most common health problems on a boat are hypothermia (low body temperature), dehydration, seasickness, and sunburn. Here we will look at their prevention and treatment.

Hypothermia. Risky cooling of the body occurs on and near boats far more often than most sailors wish to admit. Because air and water temperature are almost always colder than the body, any sailor can become hypothermic anywhere if she is wet enough for a long enough period of time. The symptoms include shivering or, worse, a body so

Symptoms of Hypothermia

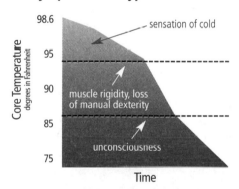

(Above) **Effects of increasing hypothermia.**

cold that it cannot shiver. Another symptom is poor thinking and loss of agility. If you are hypothermic, not only will you feel chilled but your flexibility, strength, endurance, and mental acuity will decline rapidly. You'll make careless mistakes like cleating a line incorrectly and forgetting the rules of the road. Your hypothermic brain may become so stupid that you don't know how stupid it is.

This thickheadedness is functional. It shows that the body is taking care of itself. As its temperature drops from 98.6°, the body preserves the vital organs in the trunk by cutting off blood circulation to the extremities — first the fingers and toes, then the hands and feet, then (as temperature drops into the low 90s) the head. This is why in cold weather or water we first feel numbness in the end of our limbs, and also why as we become colder we become mentally vague, clumsy, and even incompetent. An alert shipmate will notice this condition and question the victim. If she vaguely responds, through chattering teeth, that she is "all right," consider that one more reason to escort her below and treat her as described below.

Shivering is a healthy sign, for it means the body is trying to warm itself. But when the body's temperature drops to about 93°, the muscles become rigid

(Below) **Bring a hypothermic crew member's temperature back up by placing her or him in a sleeping bag with warm towels. Do not use stimulants.**

and mental disorientation intensifies. At lower temperatures, a body may go into a deathlike hibernation. If you're a rescuer, never give up on a cold body. The rule is, "No one should be considered cold and dead until he's warm and dead."

Treating Hypothermia. Once hypothermia is diagnosed by observing a shipmate's mental vagueness or shivering, get her out of the elements and allow her to get warm *gradually,* keeping a close eye on her recovery. If she is seriously hypothermic, you must do the work of providing heat for her. Unfortunately, the common wisdom for treating hypothermia that has been handed down by our grandparents is wrong. A cup of hot coffee, a glass of brandy, a few jumping jacks, or a vigorous massage may well kill the patient, not cure her. Rapid warming, caffeine, liquor, and exercise will quickly start frigid blood flowing from the extremities into the central organs and perhaps stop the heart.

Warm the body gradually — that is the lesson of recent studies and considerable experience. If she is mildly chilled and conscious, give the victim a warm (not hot) non-caffeine, non-alcoholic drink and help her change into warm, dry clothes. Lay her down in blankets or a sleeping bag, and apply warmth. Another person's warm body, warmed blankets, or warm water bottles work well, as do damp, warm towels on the groin, chest, neck, head, and sides. Reapply the warming object as often and as long as necessary, keeping the patient still and periodically checking her pulse rate (which should increase gradually). After a while the patient should once again be able to generate her own body heat inside a sleeping bag or under blankets. Once she is conscious, she may be given warm, sugary drinks.

Dehydration. Many onboard health problems begin with or are accelerated by dehydration, which can promote seasickness, constipation, headache, and exhaustion. A good rule (ashore as well as afloat) is to drink enough water so that your urine is clear by 11 AM and remains clear throughout the day, except immediately after meals. Drink liquids at a rate of at least a large glass every hour. Fresh water is the best hydrator. Coffee, beer, and other stimulants do not do the

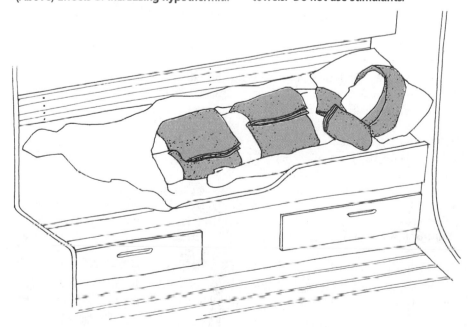

Medical Problems

job, and salt water should never be used since it may harm internal organs. (In extreme survival conditions sea water may be used when mixed with fresh water or food, but only with risk.) On well-prepared boats, jugs of water are carried in the cockpit, sports drinks and juices are on hand, and stimulants are rationed until the anchor is down.

Seasickness. Seasickness is more likely to afflict a sailor in normal weather and conditions than hypothermia. Extreme seasickness can be just as dangerous. A fairly mild case can be incapacitating, and even a slight dose can ruin an afternoon's pleasure. Some people are more prone to motion sickness than others. Since bad experiences in cars or airplanes probably have made this known early in their lives, they should come aboard well prepared with medication. Over the counter anti-seasickness pills may work, but they may have unpleasant side effects that include drowsiness, dry mouth, and psychological disorientation. Many sailors swear by the prescription drug Scopolamine, which is released into the body through a patch worn behind the ear (and which has a few side effects for many people).

For some lucky ones, seasickness comes and passes quickly (if messily). But most sufferers endure its miseries for hours at the very least, although their systems may quiet down in calm water or after a day or so at sea. The extreme results of seasickness include dehydration and exhaustion. Not much can be done for a victim at this stage other than providing fluids, rest, and encouragement.

Even if invulnerable to manifest seasickness, every sailor has felt queasy at one time or another, so take precautions. Before going aboard, watch your diet: a greasy dinner the night before or too much alcohol (even any alcohol) may make it hard to adjust to the boat's motion. Take your seasickness medication at least an hour before going aboard.

Many sailors prone to seasickness use medication in a Scopolamine patch, which slowly releases the medication into the body.

Early in a cruise, before your metabolism has settled into its new routine on a platform that is constantly in motion, you may begin to feel queasy. A slight headache and constipation often accompany the feeling of unease. If the constipation is allowed to continue, your system may never calm down. A diet that includes fresh fruit and vegetables and, and if necessary, a gentle laxative will eventually return your bowels to their normal schedule.

If you feel uncomfortable, quickly go on deck, focus your eyes on the horizon, and get busy. Fresh air, a steady visual reference point, and distraction should help. So might a drink of Coca-Cola Classic (and no other soft drink, for some reason). Don't feel ashamed if you get actively sick. Most sailors, including some of renown, have suffered the agony. Make the best of the situation with the least bother, leaving the mess in the ocean. The smell of one person's vomit in a cabin will sicken everybody there. Hold off dehydration and weakness by sipping liquids and nibbling on unsalted crackers.

Sunburn. Sunburn used to be considered sexy. Now it's proven to be stupid. Besides hypothermia, dehydration, and seasickness, sunburn is the fourth typical health worry, and for the long term it may be the greatest danger of them all.

Even at very low levels of ultraviolet (UV) radiation — in the early morning and late afternoon — a dangerous sunburn appears in only 30 minutes on a person with highly sensitive skin (skin that is normally white where not exposed to the sun) and in two hours on a person with insensitive skin (skin that is normally dark brown or black). At peak UV — in hazy or direct sunlight between mid-morning and mid-afternoon — sensitive skin burns in four minutes, insensitive skin in 15 minutes. Daily UV levels ranging from a low of 0 to a high of 15 are often provided in weather forecasts.

Prolonged exposure to sun can lead to skin cancer. Children who are badly burned are twice as likely to develop melanomas as adults than children whose skin is protected. Water only increases the sun's power through reflection, and a misty haze or even fog may further intensify its capacity to burn. The best sun protection is a cover-up: a long-sleeve shirt, long trousers, and a wide-brimmed hat or cap with a long, wide bill to shade the face. (To cut glare, the bottom of the bill or brim should be dark.) Once you have the right clothing, repeatedly apply sun lotion with a Sun Protection Factor (SPF) in the 15–30 range, plus special coverage (zinc oxide, for example) for noses, lips, and ears.

Eye Strain. The sun's glare can cause painful eye strain and headaches that might cause bad judgment. Worse, the sun may permanently damage your eyes as badly as it can your skin. Sunglasses with polarized lenses should be worn, along with a baseball cap or other wide-brimmed hat whenever your eyes feel even a little strain. Hazy sunshine can be more glaring and dangerous than direct light. Glasses should be secured around your head with a length of string or elastic; in any case, carry an extra pair of sunglasses. In heavy spray, some sailors wear goggles to protect their eyes.

Rope Burns. The calluses on a sailor's hands take a long time to build up. Until they appear, protect your palms and fingers from rope burn and cuts with leather gloves available at chandleries. The tips of the fingers on these gloves are cut off to aid manipulation of shackles, tools, and other objects. Even if your hands are well callused, you'll probably have to wear gloves when working with lines smaller than ⁵⁄₁₆-inch diameter.

First Aid

If someone is injured, unconscious, or disturbingly ill, call for medical assistance over the telephone (911) or radiotelephone (channel 16). See chapter 16 for distress calling procedure. Until help comes, a CPR course and a Red Cross first-aid manual are your best guides. Here we will overview what to look for and the basic treatment. In every case, be sure to give the victim verbal assurances that the treatment will succeed.

Check for circulation by taking the pulse every minute.

Check for breathing and responsiveness. If necessary, clear the airway by removing objects such as vomit, chewing gum, seaweed, or dentures from the mouth and air passages. If there is a pulse but no breathing, administer CPR or artificial respiration. The victim will require oxygen through either an oxygen tank or mouth-to-mouth breathing after his tongue is moved to the side.

If the victim is choking, have him try to cough up the matter. Or use the Heimlich Technique: stand behind the victim with both of your arms around him just above the belt line. Allow his head, arms, and upper torso to hang forward. Grasp your right wrist with your left hand and pull up quickly into his abdomen. Or put the victim on his back and give five abdominal thrusts.

If there is a wound, stop the bleeding by applying direct pressure with a bandage or sterile cloth to protect the wound from contamination. A tourniquet should be used only in cases of life-threatening arm and leg bleeding that cannot be controlled otherwise. Treat for shock. Symptoms may include glassy eyes, rapid or slow breathing and pulse, cold skin, and vomiting. Keep the patient lying down with feet slightly elevated, maintain a moderate body temperature (out of the cold and heat), give him small amounts of water, and get medical assistance as soon as possible.

Burns. The most common injury onboard sailboats is a burn.

A first degree burn is red, with mild swelling and some pain to the victim. This kind of burn may be a bad sunburn or the result of an accident at the cooking stove. Relieve the pain with cloths soaked with ice water or with cold running water over the affected area. A dry, sterile dressing may then be applied to protect the burned skin.

A second degree burn may cause blisters. Cold running water (but not ice water) or cold cloths will help to relieve pain. Then blot the wound dry with a sterile or clean cloth and apply another sterile or clean cloth as a protective dressing. Do not break the blisters or remove shreds of skin tissue. Also, do not apply home medications — only a doctor should apply medicine. Treat the victim for shock, as described in the next section.

A third degree burn is a very deep burn with a complete loss of all layers of skin. Cover the burn with a sterile or clean cloth and treat for shock. Elevate the affected parts of the body. Obtain medical attention as quickly as possible.

Do not remove charred clothing from the wound or apply ice water or home medications to the burn.

Heat- and Sun-Related Injuries. Heat exhaustion may cause fainting, pounding of the heart, nausea, vomiting, headaches, or restlessness. Another symptom is sweating. To treat for heat exhaustion, move the victim to a cool place, lay him down, and treat for shock.

Heat cramps are caused by depletion of salt from body fluids through excessive sweating. They may be recognized by severe pain and be treated by drinking cool fresh water with ½ teaspoon of salt per glass.

Heatstroke is characterized by an extremely high body temperature and no sweating. Heatstroke can prove fatal and the body temperature must be lowered immediately. Place the victim in a cool spot, remove his clothing, lay him down with head and shoulders slightly elevated, and pour cold water over his body. Rub him with ice and place ice in his armpits. Give him cool (not iced) drinks, but do not give him stimulants such as tea, coffee, or liquor.

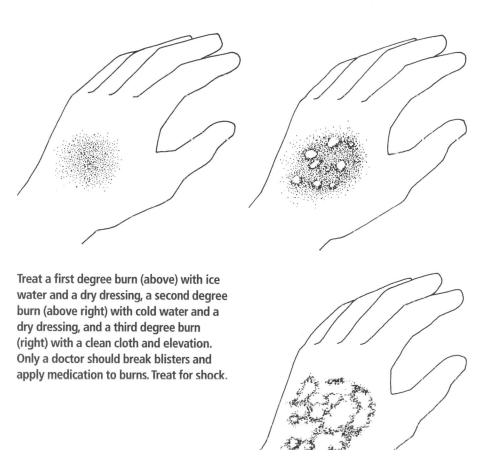

Treat a first degree burn (above) with ice water and a dry dressing, a second degree burn (above right) with cold water and a dry dressing, and a third degree burn (right) with a clean cloth and elevation. Only a doctor should break blisters and apply medication to burns. Treat for shock.

First Aid

Other Injuries. Fish bites and stings should first be treated by stopping any bleeding. To treat for the sting of a jelly-fish, Portuguese man-of-war, or similar stinging fish, remove the tentacles and wash the affected skin with alcohol. Apply ammonia or calamine lotion, or provide a hot-water soak. Application of meat tenderizer (monosodium gluta-mate) will help relieve pain. The victim may go into shock and require CPR.

Broken bones may be recognized by pain, swelling, discoloration, and a deformity of the injured part. If a fracture is suspected — and assume that an injury is a fracture unless proven otherwise — protect and immobilize the victim and splint the injury. "Splint them where they lay" is the rule. Inflatable splints and splints made by wrapping flexible foam around the injury are easy to use and compact enough to be stored in a boat. The splint should be long enough to immobilize the joints above and below the injury, snug but not so tight as to cut off circulation. Leave the victim's toes or fingertips exposed to check for adequate circulation. Treat the victim for shock.

A heart attack may be recognized by shortness of breath, chest pains, blue lips and fingertips, chronic cough, and swollen ankles. Be prepared to administer CPR.

Begin artificial respiration by clearing the throat (1). Then lift the neck (2) and, closing the victim's nose, breath into his mouth (3). Breathe once every 5 seconds for 12 cycles, rechecking the pulse every minute.

CPR includes pumping on the chest and artificial respiration. Alternate pumping 15 times (being careful not to break ribs) and two deep breaths for four cycles. Check for a pulse. Call for medical assistance. To try to restart the heart, continuously massage the victim's lower breastbone with the heel of one hand (right).

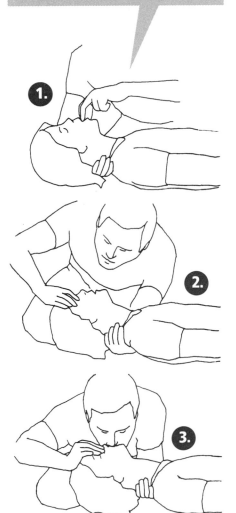

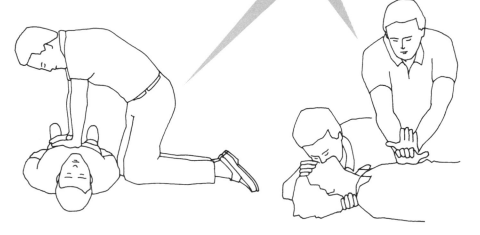

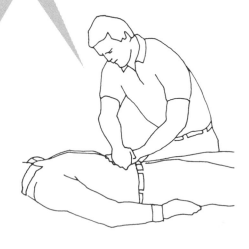

A choking victim should be treated with the Heimlich Technique by pulling in on (left) or pushing onto (right) his abdomen. Either may dislodge the obstruction.

A stroke may cause unconsciousness and paralysis of the limbs, or it may cause only a bad headache and dizziness. Treat for shock and get to a doctor.

Poisoning should be treated, first, by having the victim drink milk or water in order to dilute the poison, and second, by inducing vomiting (although instructions on the material's container may specify other treatment). Find a doctor as soon as possible.

The First-Aid Kit. Every boat needs a first-aid kit. It should include at least the basic materials that you have on your home's emergency shelf, and then be customized around the special needs of your crew. Excellent first-aid kits assembled by doctors for boaters are available from chandleries and boating equipment catalogs. For specific guidance in addressing your and your crew's unique medical situation, consult your doctor or the American Red Cross. There at least should be bandages of different sizes,

gauze, tape, sterile cloths, scissors, splints, laxatives, a thermometer, and over-the-counter pain medication. No less important are seasickness medications, plenty of sun lotions with high Sun Protecting Factors, a pain relief cream (such as Ben-Gay) for sore muscles, aloe cream lotion and talcum powder for sunburn and damp skin, a small knife

and tweezers for removing fish hooks, and meat tenderizer for fish stings. The longer the voyage, the more dependent you will be on your own medical supplies. Transoceanic cruisers routinely stock morphine or other painkillers on a doctor's prescription, and many cruisers have a doctor or medical technician in their crew.

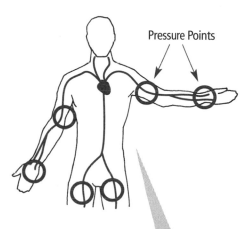

Pressure Points

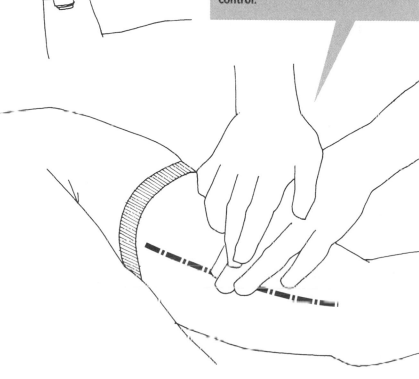

When treating a bleeding wound, first apply a pressure bandage directly (left) and keep it elevated above the heart. If the bleeding continues, locate a pressure point over one of the arteries (above) and apply pressure there (below). Don't remove bloody clothing or bandages. Keep adding more layers of cloth until the bleeding is under control.

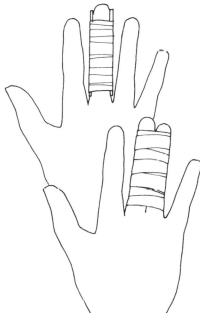

Broken bones (above and below) should be treated with splints before moving the victim. Treat the victim for shock.

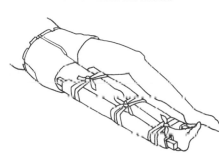

CHAPTER 7 Personal Safety

While the fatality rate in boating is small, the risk remains. Most boating fatalities are drownings after boaters fall overboard, according to the United States Coast Guard (USCG).

This chapter is about reasonable safety concerns that affect the well-being of individual sailors. Here we will describe skills and safety gear that save lives. Think of them the way you would a major medical insurance policy or an automobile seat belt. You may never use them, but knowing they are on call provides a sense of security that allows you to take the prudent risks that are a necessary part of good seamanship.

Stay with the Boat. If there is one essential, uncontrovertible rule of thumb in emergency situations, it is "stay with the boat." This rule applies whether the boat is a leaking ocean cruiser, a capsized dinghy, or a life raft. Do not try to swim more than a very short distance for help. If safety records prove anything, it is that even expert swimmers in calm water will very quickly tire and drown when attempting to swim without life jackets.

Experiments have proven this point.

In tests at the United States Naval Academy at Annapolis, midshipmen wearing foul-weather gear and sea boots were asked to swim in an indoor swimming pool. Despite their excellent physical condition, these young women and men were able to swim no farther than 50 yards without becoming exhausted.

Small Boats and Dinghies. The art of keeping small, unballasted boats upright and their crews out of the water can be summarized in two rules. First, keep your weight concentrated on the

Sailing in small, and even big boats can often be exciting. The skipper's responsibility is to make sure that it's exciting and also safe.

windward side or (if wind is not a factor) in the center. Second, keep your weight as low as possible so the boat does not roll about. Don't stand up. In boats like these, each crew member should be wearing a life jacket of the right size so if your boat does capsize you will have buoyancy assistance. If the boat capsizes, don't panic. Almost all boats smaller than 20 feet float when capsized and can be righted after they go over on their side. Smaller boats may be righted even after they have turned turtle (been turned upside down), though with great effort.

If there are two or more crew, cast off the sheets, swim the bow of the capsized boat into the wind, and right her by pulling down on the centerboard and the elevated rail. Righting a small catamaran is more of a challenge. Many catamarans are rigged with righting lines. Once the boat is upright and stable, climb back into the cockpit on the windward side (or with a crew member on either side) to keep the hull from flipping over again. Retrieve any equipment that has floated away.

If the boat is self-rescuing, meaning that the water drains out automatically when she is under way, open the self-bailers (sluices in the bilge) and sail as fast as possible on a reach until suction through the bailers pulls the water out. If the boat is not self-rescuing, bail her out with buckets (you may have to lower the sails to stabilize her).

If the boat cannot be righted, hang on to the hull and attract the attention of a nearby boat by waving your arms. Don't panic — but do stay with the floating boat.

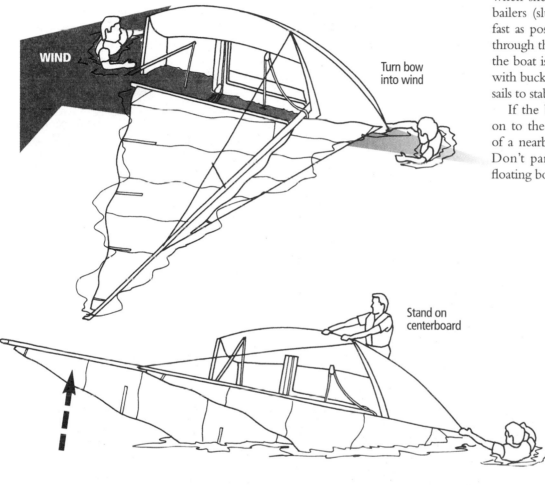

WIND

Turn bow into wind

Stand on centerboard

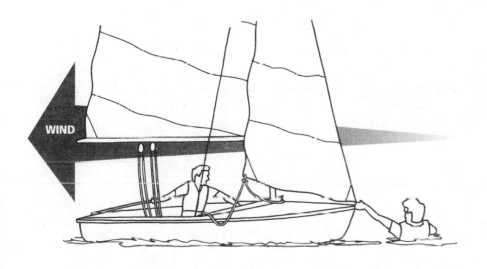

WIND

The most common method for righting a capsized dinghy: cast off sheets, turn the bow into the wind, then stand on the centerboard, pulling on the rail until the boat swings upright. The crew at the bow climbs back aboard. Small catamarans may be righted much the same way but using lines over the high side.

Life Jackets

The primary personal safety item is the object known variously as the life jacket, the life vest, flotation, buoyancy, and (officially) the personal flotation device, or PFD. We will use these terms interchangeably.

The importance of a life jacket in preventing drowning (and the exhaustion and hypothermia that lead to it) is common knowledge. Research supports that insight. According to the National Transportation Safety Association, in 60° water a life jacket will double the survival time of a swimmer before hypothermia sets in, from three hours without flotation to more than six hours with it. The key factor is the buoyancy that the device adds. Most human bodies require about 8 pounds of buoyancy in order to float with the head barely above salt water. Even in perfectly smooth water, the swimmer will tire and soon drown. The problem is to keep the face and mouth clear.

Obviously, then, buoyancy is needed to float swimmers safely without any effort on their part. This is the job of the life jacket, which provides between 11 and 35 pounds of additional buoyancy (depending on type) in order to float the swimmer's head above the water. Additional buoyancy of 15 pounds for adults and 11 pounds for children usually will float the head clear of flat water without treading water, depending on body type — but it may not automatically float the swimmer face-up (a serious concern if the swimmer is unconscious, hypothermic, or otherwise helpless). Additional buoyancy of 22 pounds may well float any person with the face up and well clear of the water in waves. Additional buoyancy of 35 pounds is the best solution. PFD performance also depends on the device's design.

The best life jackets are made of tough fabric. Some have internal, fixed

The Type I Offshore Life Jacket provides at least 22 pounds of fixed buoyancy. It should float most wearers high with their faces safely clear of the water.

Less effective is the Type II Near-Shore Life Vest, with 15.5 pounds of fixed buoyancy. Wearers may float face-down.

Also with 15.5 pounds of fixed buoyancy, the Type III Flotation Aid is more comfortable.

The steerer here is wearing an uninflated inflatable PFD with a safety harness. The crew wears a Type III vest.

flotation material; others are inflated. Good jackets carry reflective tape so they can be spotted by flashlights at night. Life jackets must be stowed where they are dry and clear of sharp edges that might cause tears, and must be readily accessible to the crew. The best-organized boats have occasional drills to see that everyone can get into a life jacket quickly.

Life Jacket Regulations. In the United States, most life jackets conform to federal government requirements imposed and regulated by the Coast Guard. These approved devices (known as Type I, II, III, IV, and V PFDs) are the ones referred to in the basic USCG rules. They come in two general designs: wearable Types I–III and V and throwable Type IV (meant to be heaved and to support the swimmer while being held). According to the rules, wearable PFDs must be "readily available" while throwable ones must be "immediately available." As a guide, wearable life jackets may be stowed in a handy locker, while throwable devices, like a cushion, must be in the cockpit.

Boats 16 feet long and shorter: there must be one approved wearable life jacket chosen from Types I–III and V (described below) on board for each person. Each must be the right size for the designated person, and they all must be readily available.

Boats longer than 16 feet: one USCG-approved Types I–III or V wearable jacket for each person on board, plus one throwable Type IV device in the boat.

There are a few exceptions to these federal rules. A few small, highly buoyant specialized craft, such as sailboards, canoes, rowing shells, and kayaks may be exempt. However, some states do not recognize these exceptions.

It is important to note that these are minimum requirements. The law requires only that most approved wearable life jackets need only be carried on board and readily available to the crew (the exception is the Type V hybrid, which must be worn if used to satisfy the law). You may choose to wear a non-approved life jacket so long as there is an approved one on board and readily available.

Life Jacket Types. The Coast Guard approves devices of five distinct types distinguished by size, amount of buoyancy, design, and whether the buoyancy is **fixed** (using foam) or **inflated** (provided by filling an airtight chamber with air) The approval label on the device indicates its type and the weight it was designed to float. Some jackets have crotch straps to keep the jacket in place. Never cut off a crotch strap. It may be awkward, but it keeps the life jacket on.

These federal regulations provide considerable freedom of choice because the Coast Guard wants to get life jackets onto as many people as possible. For example, the rules allow both fixed buoyancy and inflatable devices, the second having far more flotation than some of the former but at the price of added cost. Do not interpret this flexibility as a command to purchase the least expensive, least effective PFD available, which is the Type II with 15.5 pounds of buoyancy and non-optimum characteristics. If you or your family go into the water, cost suddenly becomes an unimportant concern. You will want to be wearing

The most comfortable and buoyant life jacket is the Type III Inflatable Vest, with as much as 35 pounds of buoyancy after inflation. Here is one supporting a person's face clear of the water.

Life Jackets

the life jacket that provides the greatest, most effective buoyancy, which means either a Type I Offshore Life Jacket (at least 22 pounds of buoyancy), a Type III Inflatable Vest (22–35 pounds), or a Type V Inflatable Vest with Harness (22–25 pounds).

The Type I Offshore Life Jacket has at least 22 pounds of fixed buoyancy in adult sizes (11 in child sizes) and is intended to turn an unconscious per-son's face clear of the water. Among non-inflatable PFDs with fixed buoyan-cy, this is the best one to put aboard a boat that may sail well away from possi-ble rescuers or in cool or cold water which can quickly cause hypothermia and unconsciousness. Its bulk (which has given it the nickname "Mae West" in honor of that buxom movie star of old) can make this an awkward life jacket to wear on deck or below. For this reason, many sailors choose to use inflatable life jackets with 22 or more pounds of buoyancy, described below.

The Type II Near-Shore Life Vest pro-vides at least 15.5 pounds of fixed buoyancy (11 for children), is less bulky than the Type I, and is inexpensive and easy to stow. But the wearer may well float face-down, and the jacket is uncomfortable to wear out of the water.

The inflatable life jacket is increasingly popular on all types of boats, and for very good reason. Extremely compact when uninflated, it can be comfortably worn during active sailing. Many have integral safety harnesses. An inflatable inflates to a PFD with 22–35 pounds of buoyancy that holds the face well clear of the water. It may be triggered manually by the wearer or inflated by blowing into a tube. Some inflatables are triggered automatically when they go into the water. Automatic systems must be inspected and replaced regularly.

It is not a life jacket of choice.

The Type III Flotation Aid also has at least 15.5 pounds of fixed buoyancy (11 for children) and has a compact, comfortable design. Yet it also may well float an unconscious person face-down. Among fixed-buoyancy PFDs, it is a good choice for such activities as waterskiing and dinghy sailing where rescue is close.

The Type III Inflatable Vest has 23–35 pounds of inflated buoyancy. It is inflated by filling a chamber with air from a carbon dioxide (CO_2) cartridge triggered manually when the wearer pulls a ripcord. It may also be inflated by mouth. Before inflation, it is the most compact of all types, with the look and feel of a sturdy pair of suspenders. Therefore, it is more likely to be worn all the time than bulky fixed-buoyancy life jackets. When inflated, it provides tremendous buoyancy that keeps the face high and clear of the water. Somewhat more expensive than fixed-buoyancy PFDs, it is the best device for all situations.

The Type III Float Coat is a parka with at least 15.5 pounds of fixed buoyancy. This combination of warm outer garment and life jacket appeals to sailors in cold regions, but the buoyancy is small.

The Type IV Throwable Device has at least 16.5 pounds of fixed buoyancy for floating a person leaning on it. Examples are seat cushions and life rings. Cushions are designed to be leaned on; they must never be worn on the back because they will force the wearer's head into the water. Horseshoe-shaped life rings usually are stowed on the decks or lifelines of larger boats. Cushions and life rings may become waterlogged by rain, so they should be stowed below when the boat is not in use, and replaced regularly.

Type V Special Use Devices include inflatable life jackets with integral safety harnesses (an excellent device for a sailor heading offshore), jackets for whitewater canoeing, and hybrid life jackets, which have enough fixed buoyancy to float most swimmers with their heads barely above water plus an inflation system to provide more buoyancy. (Unlike life jackets in Types I–III, hybrids must be worn in order to satisfy government regulations.)

Inflatable Devices Inflatable life vests are available with two types of inflation systems. One is a CO_2 cartridge that is triggered manually, with a back-up system that allows the swimmer to inflate by mouth. The other is a water-activated automatic inflation system that is triggered when a water-soluble pellet crumbles when soaked, allowing inflation. (It also has an oral inflation system.) The automatic system allows inflation even when the wearer is unconscious — for example, after being hit on the head by the boom. Occasionally, if left unprotected by a covering flap, an automatic system may be activated by prolonged exposure to very heavy spray or rain. Automatic inflation systems are not USCG-approved as of 1999.

Another type of good, though non-approved, inflatable is a small life ring that before inflation is carried in a compact pouch worn on the belt. When the wearer goes into the water, she or he inflates it by pulling a ripcord and then pulls the ring around the body. A third type is an inflatable warmup jacket with 20–35 pounds of buoyancy.

All inflatables must be maintained carefully. They should be regularly inflated orally and tested for leaks. A backup supply of CO_2 cartridges should be on hand.

Personal Lights. If you go into the water at night or during the day in waves, the odds are that the crew on deck will not see you unless you can show a bright light. The best light is a small strobe, like the lights on airplanes, that flashes an intense white light. Some strobes switch on automatically when they are in the water, while others must be manually switched on. The light can be attached to clothing or carried in a pocket. The flash of a strobe light is so bright that it usually can be seen underwater even when inside the pocket of a foul-weather jacket.

An alternative to a personal strobe light is a set of pocket-sized flares that can be fired off in the water to attract the boat. Another is an ordinary bright flashlight. (Crewmembers on deck should already have their own individual small flashlights when sailing at night in order to see sails and gear.)

Some offshore sailors carry personal emergency position-indicating radio beacons (EPIRBs). These small radios send out a signal that can be picked up by an overhead airplane or satellite, or by a special receiver on the boat.

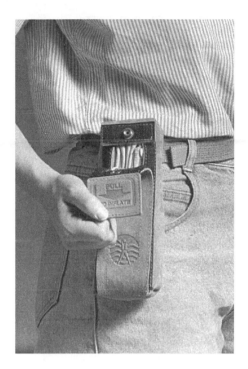

(Above) A belt-mounted inflatable PFD is extremely compact.

Every sailor at night should a personal rescue light to signal if she falls overboard. This model also has a flashlight.

Staying on Board

The best way to avoid drowning is not to fall overboard in the first place. Remember the traditional mariner's rule, "One hand for yourself, one hand for the ship." While this advisory obviously applies in rough weather, it must be observed in other conditions, too. In a calm, the wake of a passing powerboat may roll a boat extremely violently. No matter what the conditions, experienced seamen rarely place themselves where they cannot reach a handhold.

Footing. Keep your center of gravity low and use handholds. Experienced sailors are the women and men who unabashedly hold on tight to lifelines and grabrails, slide along on their butts, and wear safety harnesses. Shuffle along in a boxer's crouch with your legs far apart. Face the direction in which you are moving, with your body weight centered over a spot halfway between your feet, and keep a grasp on lifelines, grab rails, and other handholds. Always go forward and aft on the windward side, where you are visible to shipmates and where, if you fall, you're more likely to land on the boat than in the water.

Handholds include grabrails, wire lifelines, the stanchions supporting lifelines, and the bow and stern pulpits. Tests at the Naval Academy have shown that the least reliable is the after pulpit (pushpit, stern rail), whose design is inherently weak. Nobody should lean or sit on it. Regularly check lifelines for corrosion and loose fittings. When a stanchion fails, it's often at the base

Most offshore cruising and racing boats have grabrails along the cabin top and on the overhead down below to aid crew movement.

When a boat is pitching or rolling, experienced sailors learn to move with their center of gravity low, using lifelines as guides. If they still feel unsteady, they crawl. Wear and clip on a safety harness.

HANDS ON: **If You Fall Overboard**

Even a swimmer wearing a high-buoyancy life jacket is at risk in the water. Since water conducts heat away from the body 25 times faster than air, hypothermia (which can lead quickly to drowning) is a major threat. The swimmer must conserve energy by avoiding all unnecessary exercise. Yet some body movements will be required. Here are some tips.

Do not swim unless certain rescue is very close nearby, within a few yards.

Use the "HELP" position. Get into the fetal "heat escape lessening posture" (HELP position) in order to conserve heat and energy. In this position, you cover the groin and armpits, from which heat escapes the most quickly. If you are with others, huddle together to conserve heat.

Good fit. Get your life jacket to fit as snugly as possible using the crotch and waist straps.

Get rid of objects with negative buoyancy except a flashlight (which may attract rescue) or a knife (which you may need to cut away obstructions).

Do not pull off clothing. You may shake off shoes or boots, which have negative buoyancy and may hinder movements, but clothing provides insulation and shedding it expends energy. Putting on a hood or hat will lower heat loss through the head and also improve your chances of being spotted in the water. Trap or breathe air under the foul-weather jacket to provide some buoyancy.

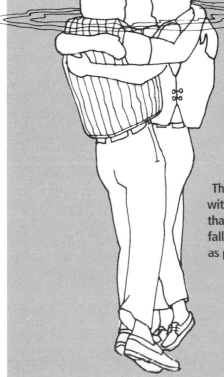

The HELP (fetal) position and huddling with other swimmers are two postures that minimize loss of body heat if you fall into the water. Exert yourself as little as possible while you await rescue.

because the setscrew is loose or the base is crimped by the socket on deck. The wooden or metal grabrails should be through-bolted. Additional security can be provided by rigging loops of webbing or line as grablines around cleats, winches, and other strong fittings.

On the foredeck, while working with jibs or the anchor, sit down and keep your feet braced against cleats or the toerail around the deck. When sitting in the cockpit, lean against the windward (uphill) back rest and brace your feet against the leeward (downhill) seat. A dangerous location is the companionway or hatch, where you may be caught off balance while leaving or coming on deck. In rough weather, the best way to negotiate these openings is to get down on your knees or belly and snake along, with your safety harness hooked on at all times.

Safety Harnesses

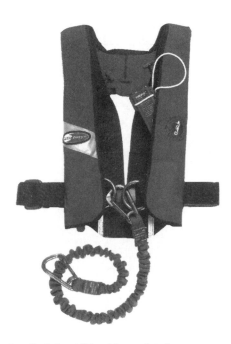

A sailor's best friend is a safety harness with a stainless steel hook at the end of a 6-foot tether. The webbing, stitching, and metal gear must be extremely sturdy. Many modern harnesses (like this one) are integral with inflatable life jackets, have elastic tethers to absorb shock loadings, and have hooks or shackles at the tether's body end so a person in the water can unhook herself from a moving boat and avoid being pulled under. Having two tethers makes it easier to be always hooked on as you move around the deck. At night, carry a personal strobe light to attract attention if you go in the water.

On cruising boats and cruiser-racers, the most important piece of personal safety besides the life jacket is a safety harness hooked to a sturdy attachment. The best of both types of safety equipment is a combination inflatable life jacket/safety harness.

The harness will brace you when you need to stand, keep you on board if you're knocked off your feet, and serve as a "third hand" to hold on with when your own two hands are busy — for example, when anchoring or steering. There should be one harness for each crew member so everybody can be on deck and hooked on to the boat at the same time. Good safety harnesses are built to the standards of the Offshore Racing Council (ORC): the harness must have a breaking strength of 3,300 pounds, the tether 4,950 pounds, and they are made of 1½-inch heavy webbing with sturdy multiple-stitched seams. The tether should be no longer than 6 feet and have shackles at both ends so you can detach if you are thrown overboard and dragged through the water. The design should be simple enough to allow the harness to be easily put on without assistance in the dark and in rough conditions. Otherwise, people will have excuses for not wearing harnesses.

Good harnesses come in several versions. Some are adjustable to allow a close fit no matter how many layers of clothes are being worn. Another option is a second tether that allows the wearer to move from attachment point to attachment point while always staying

HANDS ON: Safety Harness Use

Every sailor who has experienced a gale or two knows the violent power of waves and the wild rolling of a boat. At those times you will be thankful for the "third hand" provided by a safety harness hooked to a strong attachment point.

Hook on whenever you begin to feel unstable. Nobody should have to apologize for using a harness even in calm weather. A good rule of thumb for a crew is to require everybody to wear harnesses when the most unsteady person in the boat feels insecure.

Hook on whenever you are on your own. This includes when sailing single-handed and when a shipmate cannot see or help you (for example, at night or when working on the foredeck).

Hook on when steering in rough weather. Steering is a two-handed job, leaving you no hands for holding on. Let the harness do that job. The harness should be hooked to the windward (uphill) side in such a way that you can lean against it when at a comfortable steering posture.

Put on the harness before going on deck. A rolling, pitching deck is no place to put on gear. The most dangerous place to be without a harness on often is the companionway, since you need two hands to crawl out of the cabin into the cockpit.

Hook on only to through-bolted fittings and strong lines or wires between them.

Always hook on to the windward (uphill) side. If you fall the length of the tether, you will fetch up on deck with relatively little force. But if you are hooked on to the center of the boat, you may fall from the windward side all the way across the boat, or twice the length of the tether, until you smash heavily onto the leeward side. This type of fall may cause injury. If hooked on to the leeward (downhill) side, you probably will be thrown overboard and towed through the water until you can trip the shackle on the tether.

Keep the tether as short as possible. Short tethers mean short falls — which mean less risk of physical injury.

Don't depend entirely on the harness. The harness is not a guarantee, but only an insurance policy to help keep you on board should you fall.

Take care of your harness. Stow it and its gear in dry places, and frequently wash it in fresh water and inspect it for wear.

hooked on. Some foul-weather jackets and parkas have built-in safety harnesses. While this option is a good investment for a sailor who frequents wet, cold, windy areas, it is not a good idea for people who will often need the harness in warm weather and who may not want to wear foul-weather gear (for instance, when on a rolling run in rough weather and warm sunshine).

Jacklines and Other Attachments. A safety harness is only as strong as its attachment points. Good points that a tether may be hooked to or wrapped around include through-bolted objects (like padeyes, cleats, and winches) as well as stays and the mast. Stainless steel eyes on the base of stanchions and pulpits usually can be relied on. Unreliable and even dangerous attachments include sheets, the grab rail over the cockpit compass, cockpit dodgers, pulpits and stanchions (which may bend), and lifelines (which may break).

The best attachment is one that allows a crewmember to move about the boat without unhooking. This is a jackline (jackstay, jackwire) — several feet of strong webbing, wire, or rope secured at either end to a sturdy fitting like a padeye or cleat.

The primary jacklines run between the bow and stern on the side decks. They should lead as far aft as possible so the crew in the cockpit can hook on before climbing on deck, and as far forward as possible so the crew doesn't have to unhook while going forward to work with the jibs or anchor. While every boat's deck arrangement will determine how the jackline will be laid out, a few general rules of thumb apply. First, run the line in such a way that anybody who uses it is not obstructed or entangled by jib sheets and the shrouds. Second, leave enough slack in the jackline so you can work on the leeward side while hooked on to the windward line. If you don't have to unhook to go from one side of the boat to the other that's one less chance of being caught unprotected. Third, make the line or wire strong.

Webbing is best for jacklines because it is strong, resists chafe, and stretches to absorb sharp loads before they are transmitted to the harness. However, it can be weakened by prolonged exposure to the sun. Rope may be confused with jib sheets and other lines on deck. Wire, while easy to spot, has no stretch, acts like a ball bearing underfoot, and may corrode out of sight under its plastic cover. If you use wire, put eyes in the ends about 1 foot short of each attachment point and secure them with some passes of medium-size nylon line to act as a shock absorber and allow for adjustment.

Through-bolted padeyes, grab straps, or jacklines inside the cockpit allow people to hook on as they come up and go down the main companionway. In heavy weather, some sailors like to stay hooked on to a deck fitting when they go below, and then unsnap the tether from the harness so the tether hangs through the companionway. They wear the harnesses when below, even while sleeping. If they must go on deck quickly, all they have to do is reattach the tether and climb up through the companionway.

Jacklines running along the deck, cabin top, or cockpit provide a place to attach a safety harness tether while allowing fore and aft movement. Always snap onto the windward jackline, avoid snapping onto lifelines or stays, and keep the tether as short as possible. Best yet, hook onto a padeye or other fixed object when not moving around the boat.

Crew-Overboard Rescue

Much thought has gone into solving the frightening problem historically known as "man overboard" (MOB) but, since women fall overboard also, more accurately called "crew overboard" (COB). Thanks to the energetic efforts of sailors and researchers during the 1980s and 1990s, we have simple, more efficient equipment and doctrines that will help save many sailors' lives. In every rescue of a swimmer in the water (COB) there are six steps:

1. Avoid panic. Clearly and calmly stated commands by a decisive captain are far better than a highly charged, emotional group process. Keep focused on the task at hand. Meanwhile, encourage the COB. People who have survived falling overboard report that the sight of the boat sailing away from them brought on instant despair. Shouting assurances that the crew is returning will forestall panic at both ends.

2. Keep the COB in sight. Once the COB is out of sight, the odds of finding and recovering her plummet. It does not take long to lose sight of a person. A human head in the water is about the size, shape, and color of a half-submerged coconut, making an extremely small target even in calm weather and broad daylight. And a boat is moving at a rate of 100 feet a minute even at only 1 knot. Do not sail more than 1 minute away from the COB. Assign a crew member in the cockpit to look and point at the victim; stress that he is not to take his eyes off her for a second, no matter what else is going on. The navigator should fix the boat's position at the time of the accident. Many GPS navigation instruments have emergency buttons that, when pushed, record and store the boat's position. At night, throw buoyant flashlights or strobe lights into the water. On many boats, crews on deck at night are required to carry small strobe lights.

3. Get buoyancy to the COB if she does not already have a life jacket. This is a race against time and cold water. Immediately throw cockpit and seat cushions and life rings.

4. Make physical contact with the COB either with a line or by stopping the boat alongside. As we saw earlier, even extremely fit people tire quickly in the water, so you cannot count on the COB's swimming back to the boat. A valuable skill at this stage is the ability to accurately heave (throw) a sturdy line a distance of 20 feet or farther. We described heaving a line in chapter 5. The line should have a large loop in the end tied with a bowline. The victim will place the loop under her shoulders so she can be pulled back to the boat. Don't throw the heaving line until you are stopped dead in the water. You won't be able to make the rescue if you have to tow the swimmer. There also are excellent lightweight heaving lines that can be thrown accurately over a long distance. One of these should be in the cockpit.

5. Stop the boat. You must be able to come to a halt or a near-halt (a speed of less than 1 knot) within 20 feet of the COB. One way is to sail closehauled alongside with the sails luffing. Another is to lie stationary directly upwind of the COB. From there you can heave a line to the COB. You may also heave-to, using the traditional and Rod-stop techniques described in chapter 2 to

When someone goes into the water, his head is almost invisible. This picture was taken with waves smaller than two feet. The swimmer is near the small powerboat less than 50 yards away. If someone goes in the water, assign a reliable person to serve as a full-time spotter. Shout encouragement to the swimmer as you return to pick him up.

slow the boat so she can sail herself. All these skills should be practiced by throwing cushions in the water and attempting recovery.

6. Get the COB back on board. This may be the most difficult step. A soaking wet COB is far heavier than her normal weight and may be too exhausted to help herself. The topsides are high, lifelines are obstructions, and the boat is rolling.

By breaking a rescue down to these steps, you will turn what at first seems a wildly unmanageable problem into a series of relatively simple ones that can be solved with a small number of skills and items of equipment. And each of these steps can be discussed and practiced by the crew.

HANDS ON: **COB-Rescue Methods**

Several techniques for rescue have proved to be successful when properly applied by crews that have practiced them.

Under Power. One that many people think of first — but that can create more problems — is a rescue attempted under power: turn on the engine, douse the sails, and return to the victim. The turning propeller may well snag lines and injure the swimmer (a number of rescues attempted under power have had tragic results). If you do return under power, be especially careful to take the engine out of gear when near the swimmer and when lines are in the water.

One technique is to power to a position about 20 feet upwind of the COB with the boat lying across the wind. Use the engine to hold this position so the boat smooths the water. Throw a line downwind to the victim or allow a Lifesling device or a life ring on the end of a line to drift down to him. Take the engine out of gear once the victim has the line securely and pull him to the boat.

Under Sail. We favor rescues under sail in maneuverable boats except in winds so light or so heavy that the boat cannot sail. Two good methods for making rescues under sail are the quick stop and the reach-and-reach. Try them out, choose the one that works best for you, and practice it.

The quick-stop rescue technique works superbly when the boat is sailing fast enough to be maneuverable. But it may not work on heavy, relatively unmaneuverable boats or even on lively boats at speeds less than 2 knots. As soon as the person falls overboard, throw a seat cushion (or other flotation) to the victim and shove the helm hard down. The boat will head into the wind and tack. Assign a crewmember as a spotter to watch the victim. Shout encouragement. As the boat tacks, *do not let go the jib sheet.* Keep it trimmed on the old windward side to allow the jib to back. Also trim the main sheet. The backed jib will pull the boat off on the new tack and the flat sails will slow her. Don't worry about neatness or whether the sail will rip or the mast will

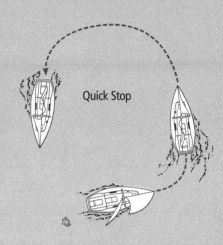

Quick Stop

stay in. Modern sails and rigs can take enormous loads. Once beyond the COB, push the helm over in order to circle around her. Keep circling slowly until a crew member is ready to throw a line to the victim. Head into the wind near the victim, drop the sails, and throw the line. Retrieve the victim using one of the techniques described later.

A boat can do a quick stop even under spinnaker. Head up until the bow is almost in the wind's eye. Ease the spinnaker pole forward to the headstay and tighten the foreguy (spinnaker pole downhaul). Then let go the spinnaker halyard without checking it as the crew retrieves the sail under the main boom with the sheet. The spinnaker will get wet, but it will come down quickly. (The halyard should be coiled, and there should be a knife handy in case you have to cut it.) When running wing-and-wing with a jib poled out, you won't be able to do a quick stop unless the jib sheet can be eased out through the end of the spinnaker pole.

The reach-and-reach stop is a good technique for slow, unmaneuverable, heavy-displacement cruisers and for any boat in very light or very heavy weather. Also known as the figure-8 or six-second stop, it keeps the boat near the victim and requires only one easily controlled tack at a time when a jibe would be slow or dangerous or both.

When the person falls overboard, throw buoyancy, assign a spotter, and shout encouragement. Quickly alter course to a beam reach and slowly count to six as you sail away from the victim, gathering speed. At "six," tack and turn back; a jibe is slow and potentially risky and will carry the boat downwind. Don't tack too quickly or the boat may be stopped.

On the new tack, head off to a broad reach and steer for a spot about two of your boat's lengths downwind of the victim. When nearly downwind of her, head up into the wind, luffing the sails, and stop the boat near her. Throw a line but don't tension it until the boat is almost stopped. Pull the victim to the boat and retrieve her to the deck.

In light wind or an especially heavy boat, six seconds may not be long enough to sail on the beam reach in order to gather speed for the tack. But in no case should you sail away from the victim for longer than a minute.

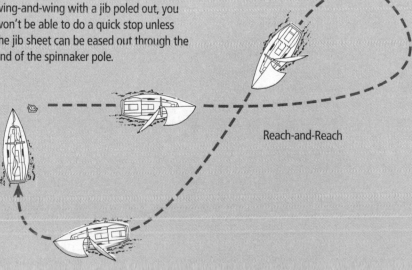

Reach-and-Reach

Crew-Overboard Rescue

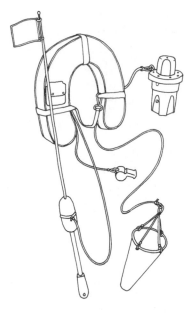

Getting Buoyancy to the COB. The quickest way to get flotation to the victim often is to throw a cockpit cushion, which is fairly heavy and compact. This is a good reason why cockpit cushions should be of high-visibility colors like red and orange, and why they should not be allowed to become waterlogged. Throw cushions or life rings slightly upwind of the COB so they will not be blown away.

A life ring may be tied to a tall, buoyant bamboo or plastic pole (called a crew-overboard pole or man-over-board pole) visible from a distance. Tied to this gear should be a drogue to resist downwind drift, a bright strobe light whose flashes are visible even in daylight, and dye marker to attract aircraft and big ships. Stowing a pole so it is both secure and easy to deploy can be a problem. On many boats, the pole is tied to the permanent backstay or lifelines using light cordage that can be broken by hand or cut with a pocket knife. A few practice exercises in a variety of conditions will tell you how and where the pole should be stowed.

A more compact version of the COB pole and ring is a patented device called the Man Overboard Module (MOM), manufactured by the Survival Technologies Group. When triggered by a crew member, it drops overboard from a container on the stern pulpit and automatically inflates into a life ring and high-visibility pylon. Options include a strobe light, an emergency pack, and a one-person life raft. A more compact inflatable rescue device is a throwable canister that opens when it hits the water and expels a life ring. This device (also made by Survival Technologies) would be good to have within reach of the steerer in case somebody goes over the side. Inflatables must be maintained with care, and backup CO_2 cartridges should be carried.

In traditional rescue systems, rigid poles are attached to life rings, strobe lights, and whistles to help crew locate the COB. These systems are often awkward and slow to use.

Retrieving the COB. Getting an exhausted person weighed down by wet clothes up and over the high topsides of a modern sailboat can be very difficult. Many rescues have reached this stage only to fail, with tragic results. Rescue systems break down into two categories, active and passive.

In an **active recovery,** the swimmer is able to assist in the rescue, usually by climbing up a swimming ladder temporarily hung on the topsides or permanently mounted on the transom. The first may be easier to grab because it's hung near the middle of the boat, where the deck is lowest and the hull is most steady, but the ladder may be wobbly and its mountings weak. A transom-hung ladder may have a stronger installation, but since the stern can pitch wildly in waves it may be hard to grab and may also lure the swimmer under the stern.

If there is no swimming ladder, you

Getting a helpless, exhausted, and soaking wet COB back aboard is difficult for several strong people and may be impossible for one or two. A tired victim probably won't even be able to use a ladder.

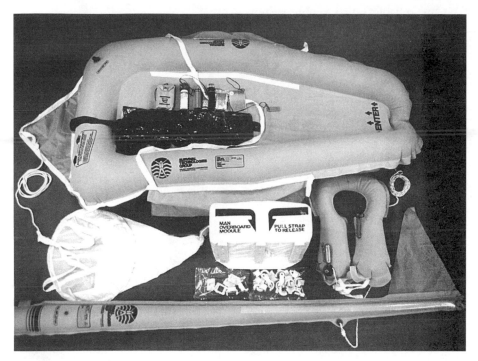

Inflatable rescue devices include the Man Overboard Module (MOM), which automatically inflates into a life ring, pylon, or small life raft.

can improvise one by draping a line over the side, securing it at one end and leading it through a block to a winch 10–20 feet away. Now you can use the elevator method of recovery. The COB, hanging onto the rail, steps on the line with both feet. The line is pulled at the winch. As the line tightens, it lifts the person. The farther apart the ends of the line are, the easier it will be to lift the person.

Passive recovery methods are necessary if the COB is exhausted, hypothermic, or injured. After even a few minutes in cold water, swimmers may not have the strength and agility needed to pull themselves up a few feet. One passive rescue system is to have several people grab the COB by the arms and belt and haul him on deck. Alternatively, they can loop a length of heavy line under his arms and lift. But while this may work with a large team of strong and agile rescuers or with a victim who is a child, two or three average-size people cannot haul in an adult swimmer whose weight may have been doubled by waterlogged clothes.

The Unconscious COB. The worst situation is when the COB is separated from the boat and unconscious or otherwise helpless. Here you must put another person into the water. The rescuer must wear a life jacket, be attached to the boat with a retrieving line, and carry flotation (if needed) and a second line for the COB. Each of these lines must be handled by a crewmember on deck. Once the rescuer swims to the COB, the life jacket and second line are attached and the COB is pulled to the boat, where you will use passive recovery methods.

In the elevator method of recovery, the COB steps on a line that is tightened, lifting him to the rail.

The Lifesling System

One reliable COB rescue system combines buoyancy for the swimmer, attachment to the boat, and a hoisting sling for passive recovery. Developed by the Sailing Foundation in Seattle, Washington, this is the patented Lifesling (sometimes called "Seattle sling"). It was designed specifically to solve the problems faced by one person of limited strength who must singlehandedly recover a COB.

The equipment is a buoyant yoke that looks like a life ring but is larger and more flexible. It's tied with a large bowline to the end of a long length of buoyant polypropylene line whose other end is tied to a strong fitting on the boat's stern (for example, a docking cleat). The yoke and line are stored ready for use in a protective pouch hung inside the after pulpit.

Recovery with the device begins with the quick-stop maneuver described above. As the boat circles, the yoke is

The Lifesling system is deployed as the boat does a quick stop. The boat sails around the COB until he reaches the line or yoke. The sails are lowered. The COB pulls on the yoke and is pulled to the boat. The Lifesling may also be thrown to the COB or allowed to drift down to him from upwind.

towed astern until the COB grabs it and gets into it. The crew then stops the boat and lowers sails. With the boat dead in the water, the crew pulls the swimmer to the boat's side and hauls the bowline securing the polypropylene line over a winch or cleat so the swimmer's head is clear of the water. The crew shackles a halyard to the bowline and winches the person out of the water and on deck. A tackle may be rigged to reduce the strain at the winch. With a helpless COB, the Lifesling may be swum out to the COB.

COB Drills. It should be clear by now that crew overboard rescues won't happen if crews don't know how to do them. Start out practicing on a calm day with a cushion as your "COB," sailing up to it until you can stop the boat right alongside. When you feel confident, practice with a crew member wearing a life jacket or wet suit as a friend in another boat stands by.

Pay special attention to mastering the sailing skills and sail-handling requirements. It's a good idea to write out a standard operating procedure (SOP) that takes into account your boat's and crew's unique characteristics, weaknesses, and strengths. When out for a sail, occasionally heave a cushion over for more practice. Since there's no way to predict who's going to fall overboard, make sure that everybody in your crew knows how to steer the boat back to the COB and how to rig and use the rescue gear.

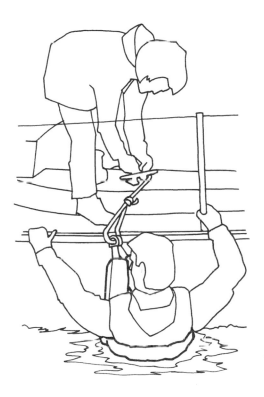

The crew cleats the Lifesling line to keep the COB's head clear of the water, then attaches a tackle led to a halyard (or the halyard itself) and winches the COB on deck.

CHAPTER 8 Rules of the Road

There is a risk of collision every time boats come near each other. Recognizing this, early seamen devised local rules of thumb to guide them out of each other's way. As the sea was internationalized, so were these rules, which came to be called the rules of the road or, more formally, the Navigation Rules. These rules (like those that apply to roads ashore) lay out specific requirements for ways in which boats maneuver near each other and signal each other. These rules apply to all craft — cruising sailboats, aircraft carriers, personal watercraft, sailboards, seaplanes, rowboats, tankers — and are enforced by the United States Coast Guard, state and local maritime police, and courts of law. The rules are summarized below. The complete rules are contained in the well-illustrated Coast Guard booklet *Navigation Rules: International-Inland*, available at many marine stores and from Coast Guard district headquarters. Boats larger than 39 feet are required to carry a copy of the rules.

The Navigation Rules have two very similar parts. One, the Inland Navigational Rules, or Inland Rules, applies to lakes, rivers, and near-coastal waters inside a boundary that is a few miles offshore and is marked on charts.

The other is the International Regulations for Preventing Collisions at Sea — also known as the International Rules of the Road or COLREGS — which applies to outer coastal waters and the high seas.

The Inland Rules and COLREGS use the same numbering system and arrangement and are almost exactly the same, with the important exception being different requirements for alerting nearby vessels of your maneuvers using whistle, horn, and light signals.

The rules lay out specific rules for action as well as general guidelines. Caution and forehandedness are essential. For example, Rule 8 instructs us to slow down or stop if a situation is of doubtful safety, and Rule 2 makes it clear that the specific regulations are no substitute for good seamanship. Good seamen know their own and their vessels' capabilities, are alert to nearby vessels, carefully regulate their vessels' speed, keep a lookout in periods of restricted visibility, and are always looking ahead, anticipating trou-

ble. If you have any doubt about another vessel's intentions, call her on radiotelephone channels 6, 9, 13, or 16, or shine a light at her, or make the danger signal (five or more short horn blasts or light flashes) — or do all three.

Give-Way and Stand-On Vessels. Under the rules, when two or more boats are in a situation that might lead to a collision, at least one of them has to stay out of the way by altering course, speed, or both. A boat that must stay out of another vessel's way is called the **give-way vessel**. A boat that does not have to get out of the way is called the **stand-on vessel**. (These terms replace the old "burdened vessel" and "privileged vessel.")

Sometimes under the rules all the boats are give-way vessels (for example when powerboats are headed directly at each other). In that case, every boat involved must alter course. But most of the time there is at least one give-way vessel and at least one stand-on vessel. The give-way vessel must get out of the other vessel's way by altering course and/or speed. The stand-on vessel *must* continue on her course at her current rate of speed in order not to mislead the give-way vessel. Of course, if the give-way vessel does not get out of the way, then the stand-on vessel must alter course, change speed, or both.

The preferred course alteration is to starboard (the right). However, if a turn to starboard will take you into the path of the other vessel, you may turn to port (the left), or you may stop or back down. There are prescribed signals for announcing actions or intentions.

Size Ranges. The rules sometimes specify different requirements for different size boats. The demarcation is the overall length in meters: 7 meters (23.1 feet), 12 meters (39.6 feet), 20 meters (66 feet), and 50 meters (164 feet). To simplify, we'll use the next smallest whole foot of overall length: 23 feet, 39 feet, 66 feet, and 164 feet, respectively.

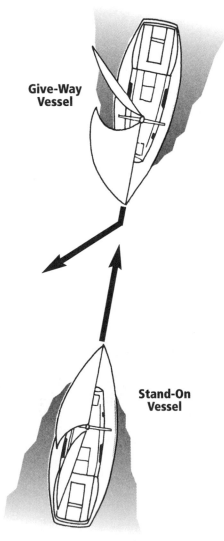

Give-Way Vessel

Stand-On Vessel

The give-way vessel, here on port tack, is the one required by the rules to alter course to avoid the stand-on vessel, here on starboard tack.

The Rules in Summary

More maneuverable vessels give way to less maneuverable ones — that is the broad reasoning behind the rules of the road. This is why a moving boat usually gives way to a stopped boat (like a fishing boat); why a moving powerboat gives way to a sailboat; and why in the tight quarters of a narrow channel all three give way to a big ship. *Note: when an auxiliary sailboat's engine is on and in gear, she is a powerboat under the rules of the road.*

A Moving Boat and a Boat Not Under Way. The moving boat gives way to the stopped boat. A vessel that is under way usually must stay out of the way of a stationary boat — for example, an anchored boat or a fishing boat.

In Narrow Channels and Traffic Separation Zones. Small boats give way to ships. Ships, ferryboats, tugs with barges, and other large vessels are the stand-on vessels in tight channels and in traffic separation zones (lanes for shipping shown on charts). Boats smaller than 66 feet, boats engaged in fishing, and sailboats must give way in order to allow the ship to continue on in deep water and on a direct course.

Sailboat and Powerboat. Power vessels usually give way to sailboats. Sailing boats are the stand-on vessels, with some exceptions: when overtaking another vessel, when near ships in narrow channels and traffic separation zones, when near stopped vessels, when near fishing boats with nets and lines out, and when near other vessels restricted in their ability to maneuver (such as tows, dredges, and ferries).

Sailboat and Sailboat. Port-tack boat gives way to starboard-tack boat.

When boats under sail with their engines off or out of gear are on different tacks, the port-tack boat gives way to the starboard-tack boat.

Windward boat gives way to leeward boat. When sailing boats are on the same tack, the windward boat (the boat upwind of the other) gives way to the leeward boat.

All Vessels. An overtaking vessel gives way to one ahead. The boat behind must stay out of the leading (lead) vessel's way.

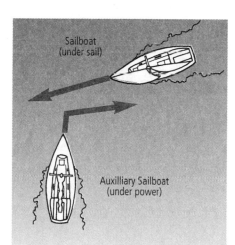

Sailboat
(under sail)

Auxilliary Sailboat
(under power)

HANDS ON:
Making Turns

The give-way vessel's course or speed alteration must not be subtle, impulsive, or otherwise depend on the supposed mind-reading skills of the other skipper. There must be no doubt about the give-way vessel's intentions. The alteration must be made in ample time, be substantial enough to be seen clearly by the other boat either visually or on radar (one big turn is favored over a series of small ones), and allow for a large margin of error. A small course change may be interpreted by the other skipper as a small steering error, confusing the stand-on vessel. Turn at least 20°. Better yet, either turn your side toward the other boat or aim astern of her. As the Pacific Northwest commercial pilot John W. Trimmer wrote in his eye-opening little book, *How to Avoid Huge Ships,* "Make one sensible and substantial change early to clear the ship. The key word here is *early.*"

(Left) An auxiliary sailboat under power is considered a powerboat and must give way to a sailboat.

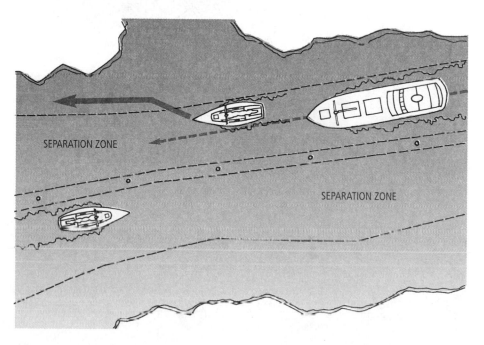

SEPARATION ZONE

SEPARATION ZONE

(Right) In a traffic separation zone or narrow channel, smaller vessels less than 66 feet (including those under sail) give way to ships and other large vessels.

The Rules in Summary

Sound and Light Signals. In many situations, the rules require one or more boats under power (including sailboats with their engines on and in gear) to signal their intentions or actions with prolonged (long) or short (one-second) blasts from a whistle or horn. At night, they must also make flashes of a white light in the same pattern. Boats under sail should not use these signals. On boats bigger than 66 feet, the horn must be audible at least 1 mile away (which means a built-in horn), and on 39- to 65-footers, ½ mile (a hand-held Freon horn should do the job). Smaller boats do not have to carry horn signals, but should.

When leaving dock, sound a long blast.

If you back down, sound three short blasts to announce that your engine is in reverse.

If a collision seems imminent, or if the other crew seems unresponsive to your signals and actions, make the danger signal of five or more short blasts.

When turning, use a sequence of short blasts. Turning to starboard, make one short blast (flash). Turning to port, make two short blasts (light flashes).

Intent-Agreement and Rudder Action. When turning (and in some other maneuvers), the timing of the signals is different in inland waters and international waters. (This difference is one of the few disagreements between the Inland Rules and COLREGS.)

In inland waters (lakes or near-coastal waters), under the Inland Rules, boats exchange signals before a turn is made, using the intent-agreement sequence: signal before making your turn to show your intention and do not turn until the other boat makes the same signal as a sign of agreement with your intention. If the other boat disagrees and her response differs, the signals cross. In that case, sound the danger signal and stop.

In international waters, where COLREGS applies, use the rudder action

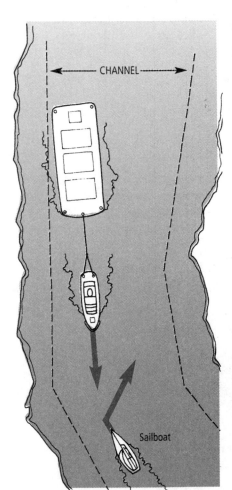

Sailboats must give way to ships and unmaneuverable power vessels in constricted channels.

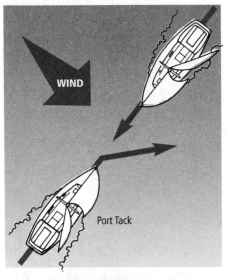

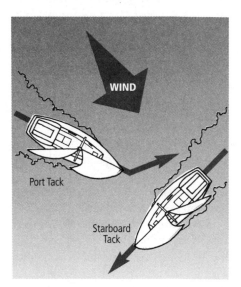

Sailboats on port tack must give way to ones on starboard tack either by altering course to one side (above left) or by passing astern (above).

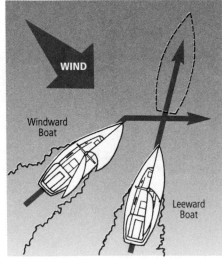

When sailboats are on the same tack, the windward boat is the give-way vessel and must avoid the leeward one.

sequence: make the horn (light) signal as you make the turn.

When a Boat Overtakes Another. The overtaking boat is the give-way vessel. A sailboat or powerboat coming up from astern on another boat must give way to the lead boat. This is the case even if the overtaking boat is under sail and the lead boat is under power.

Sound and light signals in inland waters. Under the Inland Rules, intent-agreement signals are made. The overtaking, give-way boat sounds one short blast (plus a light flash at night) if she intends to pass to starboard, or two short blasts if she intends to pass to port. If the leading, stand-on vessel agrees, she repeats the overtaking vessel's signal, one blast meaning "pass to starboard" and two blasts meaning "pass to port." If the leading vessel's response is a cross-signal (for example, one blast answering the overtaking boat's two blasts), the overtaking vessel should not attempt to pass

but should repeat her signal. If the leading vessel sounds the danger signal, the overtaking vessel should not attempt to pass until the leading vessel signals that passage is safe by sounding the correct agreement to the overtaking boat's original intent signal.

Sound and light signals in international open waters, away from narrow channels. Under COLREGS, an overtaking power vessel uses rudder action signals. She sounds one short blast (plus a light flash at night) when she alters course to starboard, or two short blasts (flashes) when altering course to port. If backing down and not passing, she makes three short blasts as she shifts into reverse gear. The leading vessel does not acknowledge these signals, but if she anticipates a collision, she sounds the danger signal (five or more short blasts).

Sound and light signals in international waters in a narrow channel. Under COLREGS, if the leading vessel must

alter course to make way for the overtaking vessel to pass, an overtaking power or sail vessel sounds two long blasts followed by one short blast to indicate that she plans to pass to starboard; or two long blasts followed by two short blasts to indicate that she plans to pass to port. The leading vessel must acknowledge this signal. If the leading vessel agrees with the overtaking vessel's intentions, she sounds one long, one short, and one long, which is the International Code signal for "Charlie" or "affirmative." She must then make way for the overtaking boat. But if the leading vessel disagrees with the overtaking boat's plan, she sounds the danger signal (five or more short blasts). The overtaking vessel must not attempt to pass until the leading vessel agrees.

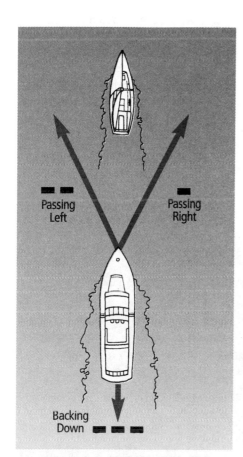

Overtaking boat keep clear. Under the Inland Rules, sound one short blast if you intend to pass to starboard and two it to port. Await the leading boat's agreement signal. Three short blasts signal backing away.

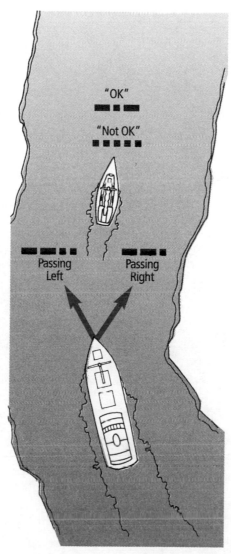

Different signals are used under COLREGS when passing in a narrow channel, but the leading boat must still agree or otherwise use the danger signal to show her non-agreement.

The Rules in Summary

When Powerboats Meet. Both boats must give way, preferably by turning to starboard. Vessels meet when they approach each other on reciprocal or nearly reciprocal courses, bow to bow or nearly so. Both vessels here are give-way vessels. Both must alter course, preferably to starboard so that they pass port side to port side (although the rules make a provision for starboard side to starboard side passage). "Show her your port side" is the rule of thumb.

Sound and light signals in inland waters. Under the Inland Rules, intent-agreement signals must be made if two powerboats are passing within ½ mile of each other. These signals are one short blast for course alteration to starboard, two short blasts for course alteration to port, or three short blasts for backing down. (At night also show light flashes.) When one vessel hears the other vessel's signal, she either sounds the same signal to indicate agreement or sounds the

danger signal (five or more short blasts) to indicate disagreement. If there is disagreement, both vessels slow or stop. If they agree, the vessels turn to starboard (or port) in order to make safe passage. If the signals cross — for example, if one boat sounds three blasts and the other sounds one blast — both boats should sound the danger signal and take appropriate precautionary action.

When meeting, if you have any doubts about the safety of a situation:

1. Assume that you are meeting the other vessel.

2. Sound one blast ½ mile from the other vessel.

3. Listen carefully for her response.

4. If there is agreement, turn to starboard well to the side of the other vessel.

5. If there is disagreement, sound the danger signal and stop.

Sound and light signals in international waters. Under COLREGS, if a port side to port side passage can be safely

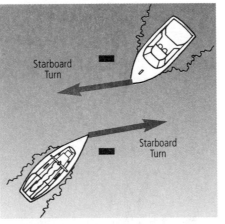

Powerboats meeting head-on sound a short blast (for a turn to starboard) or two short blasts (for a turn to port). Under the Inland Rules, the other boat must agree with the same signal before the turn is made. Under COLREGS, the signal indicates that the turn has started.

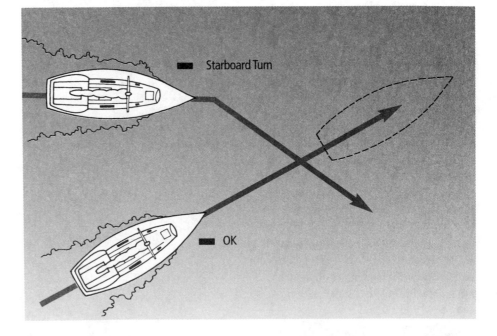

Crossing, the give-way powerboat is the one to port and sounds one short (turn to starboard), two shorts (turn to port), or three shorts (backing away). The stand-on powerboat must signal agreement under the Inland Rules.

made, no signals are required. But if a collision is possible, each vessel must make a rudder-action signal as she turns: one short blast for turning to starboard or two short blasts for turning to port. If a vessel is forced to back down, she makes the backing-down signal of three short blasts.

When Powerboats Cross. The boat to the left is the give-way vessel. Boats that converge without either meeting or overtaking are crossing. The one on the other boat's port side is the give-way vessel.

Sound and light signals in inland waters. Under the Inland Rules, intent-agreement signals are exchanged by vessels in a crossing situation. If the left-side, give-way vessel intends to turn to starboard and go astern of the right-side, stand-on vessel, she sounds one short blast. When the stand-on vessel indicates her agreement with one short blast, the give-way vessel makes her turn (usually slowing down as well). If the give-way vessel intends to turn to port, she makes two short blasts. (Thoughtless skippers sometimes make two or more blasts to announce that they are barging across the stand-on vessel's bow, regardless of the rules of the road.) It's always safer for the give-way vessel — the one to the port of the other vessel — to sound one short blast, and when the stand-on boat echoes it, to turn hard to starboard and pass well astern. If signals cross, the stand on vessel should make the danger signal and stop or slow down. Again, at night, light flashes are made simultaneously with sound signals.

Sound and light signals in international waters. Under COLREGS, the left-side, give-way vessel sounds one short blast as she turns to starboard (toward and astern of the stand-on vessel), two short blasts if she turns to port (but not into the stand-on vessel's projected course), or three short blasts if she backs down to allow the stand-on vessel to pass ahead. But if the give-way vessel intends to slow down or stop, she makes no signal. The right-side, stand-on vessel neither signals nor alters course unless a collision is imminent. If a collision threatens, the stand-on vessel sounds the danger signal (five or more short blasts) and takes appropriate action, usually by stopping, backing down, or turning to starboard, carefully making the appropriate signals.

In Restricted Visibility. The more restricted the visibility, the slower the speed. The Inland Rules and COLREGS both require that every vessel "at all times proceed at a safe speed so that she can take proper and effective action to avoid collision and be stopped within a distance appropriate to the prevailing circumstances and conditions." Each vessel is required to maintain a lookout for lights and sounds such as foghorns or the wash of other vessels — no matter what the visibility. Lookouts must be especially attentive to the bearings on approaching vessels. If the bearings do not change as the boats converge, there will be a collision. If the bearings do change, one boat will pass astern of the other.

In poor visibility, vessels are required to reduce speed to a minimum when their lookouts hear another vessel's fog signal from forward of the beam. This is an indication that the boats are approaching each other, and such an approach should be made at the lowest possible speed until all are certain that there is no danger of a collision. There are several required fog signals, each for a different situation. The signals must be made with bells or whistles by vessels 39 feet or longer. Smaller boats are not required to, but should, sound fog signals in periods of restricted visibility.

Sound Signals in Fog. Whistles and bells used as fog and other signals are in both COLREGS and the Inland Rules. Below is a summary.

On vessels that are under way, the following whistle or horn signals are made at intervals of 2 minutes or less:

Sailboats, vessels engaged in fishing, towing, or pushing, and vessels either not under command or restricted in their maneuverability: one long blast followed by two short blasts (long-short-short).

Powerboats making way through the water: one long blast (long).

Powerboats under way but stopped: two long blasts (long-long).

A vessel being towed: one long blast followed by three short blasts (long-short-short-short).

(Under COLREGS only) A powerboat whose room to maneuver is constrained by her deep draft: one long blast followed by two short blasts (long-short-short).

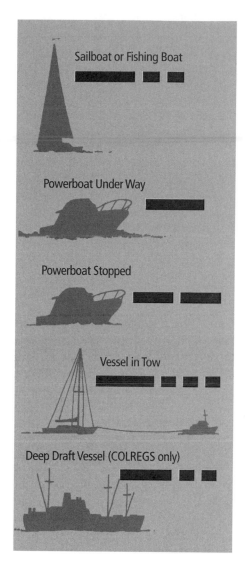

Special sound signals identify different types of boats in fog.

The Rules in Summary

On vessels that are not under way, these signals are made in periods of limited visibility:

Vessel at anchor: if shorter than 328 feet, a bell forward is rung rapidly for 5 seconds every minute; if longer, a bell forward and a gong aft are rung rapidly for 5 seconds every minute; in addition, an anchored vessel may sound her horn in a pattern of one short blast, one long blast, and one short blast (short-long-short) at intervals necessary to alert approaching vessels.

Vessel aground: if shorter than 328 feet, the vessel every minute sounds three distinct bell strokes, then rapidly sounds a bell forward for 5 seconds. If longer, that sequence is followed by the rapid sounding of a gong aft for 5 seconds. A vessel aground may also sound the whistle code signals "F" (short-short-long-short, meaning "I am disabled; communicate with me"), "U" (short-short-long, "You are running into danger"), or "V" (short-short-short-long, "I require assistance") at necessary intervals.

(Under the Inland Rules only) An anchored vessel engaged in fishing or restricted in her ability to maneuver: one long blast followed by two short blasts (long-short-short) at an interval of 2 minutes.

A vessel moored at the end of a pier: make any noise with a horn, bell, or gong.

Other Sound Signals. *A vessel about to round a bend* in a river or channel where the other side of the bend is obstructed must sound one long blast, to be acknowledged by any vessel approaching the bend on the other side.

The signal for requesting the opening of a drawbridge is one long blast followed by one short blast (long-short), to be echoed by the bridge tender within 30 seconds if the draw is to be opened immediately. If there is a delay, the response is five short blasts — the danger signal. If the skipper, for reasons of emergency, must pass immediately, she then makes the danger signal. When approaching an open bridge, the vessel should make the long-short signal. The bridge tender will not respond unless he plans to close the span before the vessel passes through. If the skipper requests an opening over the radiotelephone, she should not make a horn signal.

Special Circumstances. Both the Inland Rules and COLREGS allow for special circumstances — situations when for one reason or another the rules don't quite cover all possibilities. In those cases there is no stand-on vessel, and all boats involved are to consider themselves give-way vessels regardless of their original evaluation of the situation. There may, for example, be a third vessel that due to damage cannot comply with the rules or that has been thrust into the scene. Or a stand-on vessel in a crossing situation suddenly realizes that the give-way vessel to port is attempting to inch across her bow regardless of the signal she gave.

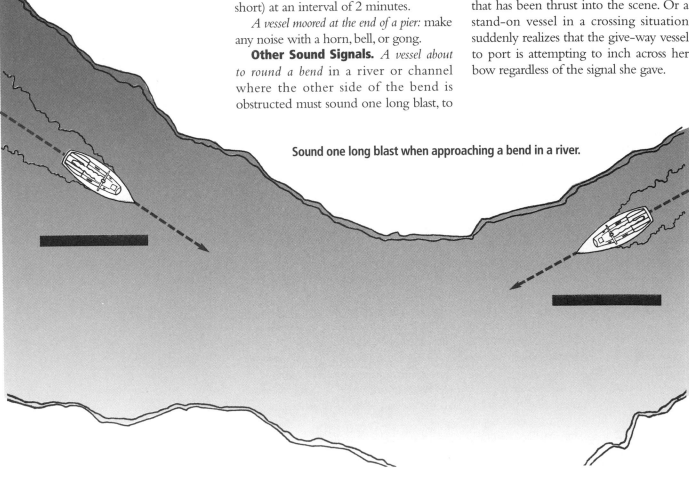

Sound one long blast when approaching a bend in a river.

Navigation Lights

All vessels that are under way or at anchor must show (or be prepared to show) at least one navigation light at night and in restricted visibility. Each type of vessel carries a specified combination of navigation lights (running lights) in order to make it easier for other boats to identify her. Here is a description of the lights that most boats must carry (and some day signals, called day shapes, as well):

Sidelights, red for the port side and green for the starboard side, are shown when the vessel is under way. They cover from dead ahead to 112.5° off to each side of the bow (or from 12 o'clock to almost 4 and 8 o'clock).

If you don't see another vessel's sidelights, you are astern and may be overtaking. If you see a red light, her port side is turned toward you. If you see her green light, her starboard side is turned to you. If you see both the red and green lights, she is headed directly at you. Sidelights may be placed on either side of the bow, in the shrouds, in a single lantern on the bow, or (in sailboats smaller than 66 feet) in a tricolor light at the top of the mast (see below).

The stern light is a white light showing aft from the stern through 67.5° on either side, or an arc of 135°. Like the sidelights, it is turned on only when the boat is under way.

The masthead (steaming, bow) light, which when lit indicates that the boat is under power, is a white light located not at the top of the mast, as the name suggests, but partway down. (On small power vessels it may be placed at the top of a short vertical spar). On most sailboats it's about a third of the way down from the actual masthead. Showing over the same arc as the sidelights, it is turned on only when the boat is under power.

The tricolor, a three-in-one light at the top of the mast, may take the place of the stern light and sidelights — but only on a boat smaller than 66 feet

There is a choice of three lights to carry at the top of a sailboat's mast. (1) The tricolor light combines the red and green side lights and the white stern light. It may be lit only when the boat is under sail. It is legal only on boats shorter than 66 feet. (2) A white all-around light, which is lit when the boat is at anchor. (3) A flashing all-around emergency strobe light, which may be lit only to signal distress.

The forward-facing masthead light (steaming or bow light) is lit only when the boat is under power.

Required on sailboats larger than 23 feet, the aft-facing white stern light alerts vessels astern of your presence.

The forward-facing red (port) and green (starboard) sidelights tell other vessels which side is turned to them or whether the boat is headed directly at them.

Navigation Lights

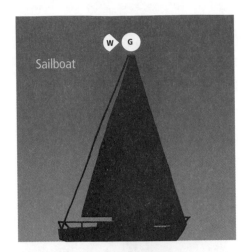

Sailboat

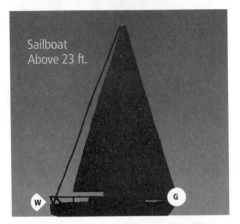

Sailboat
Above 23 ft.

when she is under sail. Because it is high up and uses only one bulb, it both provides the greatest range of visibility and saves electricity. When the engine is turned on and in gear, the tricolor is turned off and the normal sidelights and stern light are lit with the masthead light. The reason for this is that the sidelights and stern light are required by the rules to be lower than the masthead light in order to indicate clearly that the boat is under power. If the tricolor is on when the boat is under power, other vessels cannot accurately read her status

under the rules of the road.

An all-around light is any light shining through 360°. An all-around fixed (not flashing) white light hung in the rigging or at the top of the mast indicates that the boat is at anchor. A flashing strobe light at the top of the mast warns off nearby ships.

Navigation lights help mariners identify the type, size, and heading of vessels they see at night. This helps crews understand the situation and determine the course of action they should take. Here is a brief summary of the rules on navigation lights, which must be shown between sunset and dawn and at other times of restricted visibility. The complete rules are contained in the Coast Guard booklet *Navigation Rules: International-Inland.*

Under Sail. A boat longer than 23 feet that is under sail or being rowed must display red and green sidelights and a white stern light. A boat under sail

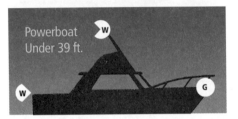

Powerboat
Under 39 ft.

To help crews identify other boats so they can make the correct maneuvers and avoid collision, each type of vessel carries a unique combination of navigation lights. Sailboats shorter than 66 feet under sail may carry sidelights and the stern light in a tricolor combination light at the top of the mast (top).

Vessel in Tow

Large Power Vessel

between 23 feet and 66 feet may show these lights in a tricolor combined light at the top of the mast.

A boat shorter than 23 feet that is under sail or being rowed should display sidelights and a stern light. But if these lights are not displayed, a boat in this category must carry a flashlight or lantern that can be quickly lit and displayed in time to prevent a collision.

Under Power. An auxiliary sailboat that is under power must observe the same rules that all powerboats observe except that during the day a sailboat under sail and being propelled by her engine must display a black cone point down (the Inland Rules do not require this of boats smaller than 39 feet). The basic rule for powerboats is that only the masthead (steaming) light, the sidelights, and the stern light must be lit, with the steaming light above the sidelights. An option for a power-driven boat shorter than 39 feet is a pattern of sidelights and

an all-around white light. If this optional pattern is displayed, the stern light and masthead light must not be lit.

A vessel longer than 164 feet must show a second masthead (steaming) light abaft of and higher than the forward one.

Under COLREGS only, a power-driven boat shorter than 23 feet that has a maximum speed of 7 knots or less may show an all-around light.

Large Vessels and Tows. Other types of lights are specified for larger power-boats and for fishing boats, tow boats and tows, and other vessels with limited maneuverability. In general:

A yellow aft-facing light indicates a tow. It is placed just above the stern light on a tug or other boat that is towing or pushing another. A flashing forward-facing yellow light is on the bow of a barge being pushed. Barges show sidelights and stern lights, each barge being considered a separate vessel. The day shape for a towed vessel is

a black diamond.

Two or more forward-facing white lights one above the other indicate that the vessel is towing or pushing one or more other vessels.

A red or green all-around (360°) light indicates a working or other boat with poor maneuverability. It can be found on a fishing boat, dive boat, or other work boat that is restricted in her ability to maneuver. Often these boats have nets or equipment to the side or astern. If there are no sidelights showing, the vessel is stopped. If there are sidelights, she is moving ahead slowly and with poor maneuverability.

Range lights (two forward-facing white lights on separate masts, one lower than the other) indicate a large vessel's course. The lower mast is the forward one. When the lights are one above the other, the vessel is headed at you.

Day shapes (black diamonds or ball-diamond-ball sequences) hung in the

Tug Pushing Ahead

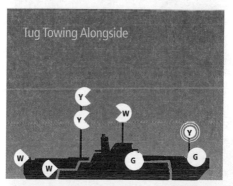

Tug Towing Alongside

By identifying a vessel's navigation lights, you can determine the direction in which she is headed and also the length of her tow if there are barges.

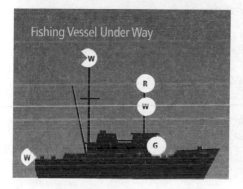

Fishing Vessel Under Way

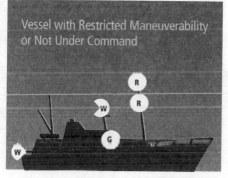

Vessel with Restricted Maneuverability or Not Under Command

Navigation Lights

rigging of a tug towing one or more barges indicate limited maneuverability.

Fishing Vessels. While fishing, if stopped they do not show sidelights and stern lights, but they do show them while under way. In both cases they show all-around red-over-white lights at the masthead, and if their gear extends more than 492 feet to one side, an all-around white light. Day shapes for fishing boats are two black cones with their points together or, for vessels shorter than 66 feet, a basket plus a black cone whose point aims toward outlying gear.

Trawlers dragging nets do not show sidelights and stern lights when they're stopped, but while moving they show sidelights. In either case they show a green-over-white all-around light. Trawlers show the same day shapes as fishing boats, but do not have indicators of outlying gear.

Vessels Not Under Command. In the circumstance that she cannot be steered or make way, a vessel shows two all-around red-over-red lights in a vertical line where they are best seen, and if she's underway, sidelights and a stern light. Her day shape is two black balls in a vertical line.

Pilot Vessels. Vessels that carry pilots out to arriving ships display sidelights, stern lights, and an all-around white-over-red light at the masthead when they are under way. At anchor they light the white-over-red light and the proper anchor lights; during the day they show one black ball for their day shape.

All Vessels at Anchor or Aground. When anchored, a boat smaller than 164 feet shows an all-around white light where it is best seen, unless she is anchored in a Coast Guard–approved special anchorage (see chapter 15), when she need not display an anchor light. The 360° light at the top of a sailboat's mast serves as an anchor light unless it is a strobe, which indicates distress; so does a lantern hung off the headstay. Large vessels show two anchor lights, one forward and one aft. The day shape for an anchored vessel is a ball. If aground, the vessel shows her anchor light or lights plus an all-around red-over-red light where it is best seen.

Other Lights. Law enforcement vessels usually show a flashing blue light. Moored barges carry two white lights. Partially submerged vessels or objects under tow in inland waters carry an all-around white light at each end if less than 82 feet wide, four all-around white lights if wider, and, if very large, all-around white lights no more than 328 feet apart. Submarines in the United States Navy carry normal navigation lights plus a flashing yellow light that flashes once per second for 3 seconds and then is off for 3 seconds.

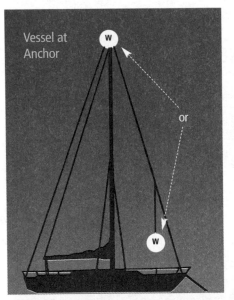

Vessel at Anchor

or

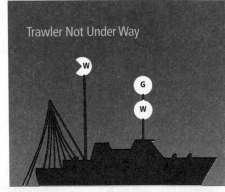

Trawler Not Under Way

Vessel Aground

Maneuvering in Collision Situations

If you are converging with another vessel, take compass or relative bearings on her every 30 seconds. If the bearings move forward, she'll cross ahead of you; if aft, she'll cross behind you. But if they don't change, you are certainly on a collision course. "Constant bearing, closing range" is the rule of thumb. You must take immediate action. Slow down or speed up and take more bearings. Better yet, turn radically toward her wake, let her pass ahead, then turn back on your original course. Whatever you do, you can't afford to wait until the last moment. Converging courses are especially hard to judge if the other boat is at a great distance and going much faster than you are. Large commercial vessels offer a particular challenge because while they seem to be moving slowly, they're actually going twice or three times your speed.

On a bow-to-bow reciprocal course with another vessel, alter course hard to starboard — at least 20°. "Show him your port side." The closer the boats are to each other, the greater the alteration should be. If the other boat confusedly alters course to her port, into your new path, you can steer hard to port for a starboard side to starboard side passing, you can stop and let her pass, or you can keep going to starboard. Watch her like a hawk. In this situation, taking bearings won't tell you much about the chances of evading collision.

When near a personal watercraft (PWC, Jet Ski), be especially defensive. The noise and quickness of the machine may well overwhelm whatever interest the operator has in observing the rules of the road. These little power vessels are notoriously prone to accidents. For example, in Florida in 1996, personal watercraft comprised 8 percent of registered boats but were involved in 37 percent of the state's boating accidents. Most PWC accidents involved collisions with other vessels, and almost half the drivers had less than 20 hours' experience in PWCs.

At low speeds or in high waves or strong winds, your boat has limited maneuverability and will be blown sideways downwind. Stay far upwind of other vessels.

Near Ships. The so-called "gross tonnage rule," an informal advisory, says that small boats should always stay out of the way of big boats, no matter what the Navigation Rules say. Not only are big vessels unmaneuverable, but they will

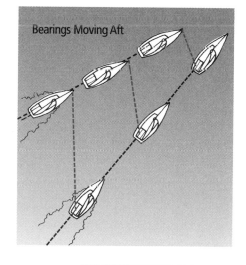

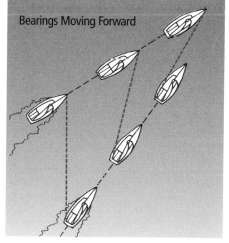

Bearings taken every 30 seconds on a boat on a converging course indicate whether a collision is imminent. If the bearings don't change, you will collide. If they move forward, the other boat will pass ahead. If they move aft, you'll pass ahead.

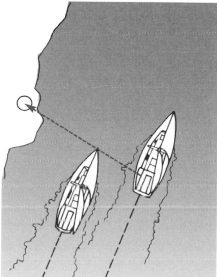

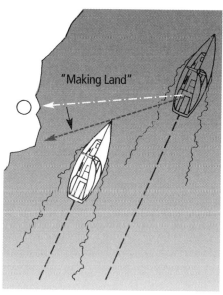

Convergence may also be gauged by judging the other boat's relationship to the land behind. If the land seems to be moving ahead of her, you're going faster. If it seems to be falling back, she's going faster. This is called "making and losing land." Otherwise, you will collide.

Maneuvering in Collision Situations

blanket your wind, and their large wake can pull a boat into their hulls, tow lines, or a barge. Never attempt to sail across a tow line; it's shallower than you think.

Exploit your range of visibility, or the distance to the horizon. Someone standing on the deck of an average cruiser-racer, with eyes 10 feet above the water, sees about 3½ nautical miles (4 statute miles) in clear weather. Of course, ships, with their high sides and bridges, will be visible many miles farther away, assuming clear weather. The range of visibility from the deck of our cruiser-racer to a barge with 50 feet of freeboard is about 11 miles. (We will describe range of visibility calculations in the next chapter.) Since barges move slowly, you'll have plenty of time to take evasive action.

Compare that with the sighting of a 20-knot tanker. The range to its bridge, 100 feet above the water, is about 15 miles. Since the tanker is making a mile

every 3 minutes, the two vessels will meet in no more than 45 minutes. If they are moving toward each other, a collision situation may develop in only half an hour. Once the two vessels are within a couple of miles of each other, the ship will be helpless to avoid collision, assuming she even sees your boat, which may not be visible to the crew way aft in the bridge. Even if they did see you, it takes 1–2 miles to stop the ship.

Therefore it is crucial to begin to track large ships as soon as you see them. Once you spot a tanker or freighter, assign a crew member with good eyesight and judgment to lookout duty. Nothing should distract this person from looking at and taking bearings on the ship until it's clearly ahead. While the ship may seem to be moving slowly, do not be fooled. A large vessel at high speed makes very little wake. The best indicator of its speed is how quickly the vessel grows larger and

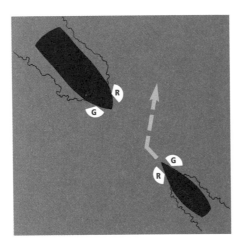 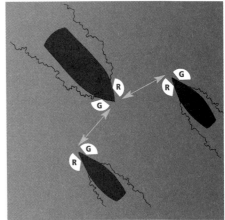

(Left) If you see both of the other boat's sidelights, you're on a bow-to-bow collision course. Turn sharply to starboard to "show her your red." (Right) You're safe if both boats' red or green lights are turned toward each other. When altering course, try to minimize all ambiguity even if you must slow down, stop, or circle around.

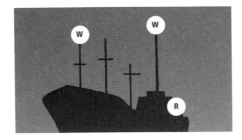 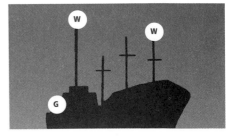

The relationship between the range lights on a ship indicates its heading. The farther apart the two lights are, the more parallel are the courses of your boat and the ship. When they are in line, one appearing slightly above the other, the other vessel is headed at you. If the higher light is to starboard (left), the ship is heading to your port; if to port (right), it is heading to your starboard.

higher as it races toward you.

Do not anticipate that the ship will alter course for you. Unless you're absolutely sure that you'll cross its bow at least 1 mile ahead, alter course so that the ship crosses *your* bow. Chances are that it's on autopilot, with the deck watch preoccupied with various chores. If the wind were to die or your engine to poop out, there would be nothing to stop the ship from running you down.

Night Sailing. At night, judging the other boat's position, course, speed, and intentions is especially difficult since you have only her navigation lights to go by. You may not be able to distinguish them from her cabin lights or flashlights, or high waves may obscure them.

You must identify the other vessel as soon as possible. If she shows range lights, she's a large power vessel moving faster than first appears. If you see a yellow light, there is a tow. A single masthead light indicates a boat under power — if it's high up, she's probably a sailing auxiliary, which means she's slow. If you don't see any masthead lights, that means only one thing: she's a sailboat under sail, and her maneuverability and crew's visibility probably are limited.

If the only sidelight you see is the red light, alter your course to starboard (if necessary) to "show her your red" and pass port side to port side. If you see the green light, make whatever adjustments are necessary to clear her at a safe distance, preferably port side to port side but, if necessary, starboard side to starboard side. If both sidelights are visible, she's heading directly at you on a collision course. Alter course hard to starboard until you see only her red light, sail on a little farther to be safe, then turn back to your original course. If you see a white light down low, it's probably a stern light and you're overtaking.

Since red and green have about 25 percent less visible range than white, you often see masthead lights, stern lights, and ranges well before the sidelights appear, especially on large ships. If you can't see the sidelights, study the range lights. If they're in line, she's heading at you; if the range light is to the right of the masthead light, she's heading to your port; if the range light is to the left, she's heading to your starboard. If neither light is visible, she's powering away from you. Since many collisions and near-collisions involve large power vessels and smaller boats, don't allow a pair of range lights to appear on the horizon without analyzing which way the ship under them is sailing.

Always keep a lookout, and don't assume that the other crew sees you. Make your boat as visible as possible. At night, show navigation lights in the

HANDS ON:
Talking to the Other Vessel

If you have doubts about a nearby vessel's intentions and you have a VHF/FM radiotelephone, do not hesitate to call the vessel on channel 6, 9, 13, or 16. In such fast-arising danger situations, a small hand-held radiotelephone in the cockpit within reach of the steerer is extremely valuable, since it allows the call to be made instantly. In crowded waters, especially at night, leave it or the main radiotelephone on and switched to channel 16 so you can hear another vessel's query.

When calling, identify the other vessel and yours by the type of your boat and your location relative to her, for example, "Freighter on course of 300°, this is the blue sailboat on your port bow. We intend to change course to starboard and pass you port side to port side. Please acknowledge." If her crew shows no awareness of you or the danger of the situation, make the danger signal (five or more short blasts of a whistle or horn and, at night, five or more short flashes of a white light) and quickly move away.

You may also attract another boat's attention with light or sound signals, including many blasts on a horn or whistle, a flashing strobe light, flares, or a searchlight. Do not aim the light at the other boat; it will blind and seriously annoy the crew.

proper combination. Someone who does see you will be able to predict your future position if you steer a steady course at a steady speed. In fog, use a radar reflector, but don't assume that you will appear on every ship's radar scope. The ship's long deck, islands, and larger boats may screen you, as may rain or rough waves. At close ranges, a ship's radar may not notice you because the vessel may be rolling.

If a collision seems likely and the other crew obviously doesn't know you're there, do everything you can to make your boat visible. Carry a bright hand-held light to shine on your sails or at the oncoming vessel's bridge. If that doesn't do any good, fire off flares or turn on a strobe light to attract the other crew's attention to your location.

CHAPTER 9 Navigation Aids

"The lonely sea" and its more confined sounds, lakes, bays, and harbors become much safer if you know where you are on them. Sailors use many navigation aids to help them to avoid running aground and to plot (chart) their position. These aids include buoys, lighthouses, and landmarks that guide boats to safe water and away from shoals, as well as published tools (charts, tide tables, and tidal current charts).

In the sweep of maritime history, these many, sophisticated aids are relatively recent. When the ancient Phoenicians first ventured across the Mediterranean Sea, they were guided by the stars. For centuries Polynesians navigated the Pacific Ocean with amazing accuracy over distances as great as 2,000 miles without the use of compasses or charts, using the stars and changes in wave shape and height as their guides. When the long swell generated by the trade wind in the open ocean begins to shorten and steepen, or when it sweeps along in a slightly altered direction, a native navigator knows that an island lies just over the horizon. A modern navigator, too, can read the water. When big, stable waves turn into many stubby breakers, the water is becoming shallower.

Navigation is the art and science of finding your current position and plan-

ning what course you will sail to reach your destination. It includes three disciplines: piloting, celestial navigation, and electronic navigation. Piloting is the foundation for the other two disciplines, so it receives much of the attention in this and subsequent chapters. Later, we'll introduce the tools and concepts of celestial and electronic navigation.

Alongshore piloting — proceeding safely within sight of land — is a crucial skill. When seafaring began in ancient times, sailors' ambitions were as modest as their ships were small. They rarely went out of sight of land, and at night they pulled their reed-and-cedar boats up on the beach or anchored in quiet coves. Their only piloting aids were familiar landmarks, the temperature and humidity differences between winds from varying directions, and poles for measuring water depth. Today our dependence on visible reference points and markers is just as great as it was 5,000 years ago, even though we have much more sophisticated ways to determine wind direction and water depth, and with the flick of a switch can find our position using space-age electronic devices.

Besides natural landmarks and water depth, the reference points used to find your position when sailing along shore include buoys, lighthouses, and radio transmissions, known collectively as aids to navigation. They are used in close conjunction with charts and the magnetic compass.

This lovely old lighthouse guided mariners through Chesapeake Bay's Hooper Strait before being moved to the Chesapeake Bay Maritime Museum at St. Michaels, Maryland.

Buoys

The most common aid to navigation is the buoy, channel marker or mark, whose ingenious combination of characteristics indicates safe water. More than 20,000 unlighted and lighted buoys are installed and maintained by the United States Coast Guard. With minor exceptions that we'll describe later on, all these buoys conform to the federal buoyage system, and the Region B Lateral Maritime Buoyage System of the International Association of Lighthouse Authorities (IALA). It's called the lateral system because the buoys mark the sides of channels passing safely around shoal water and other hazards, and Region B because the red buoys are kept on the starboard side when entering a harbor (in the Region A system, red buoys are kept on the port side). In Europe and other countries (and in some US inland waters), buoys are sometimes laid out according to the cardinal system, in which the buoy's shape and color indicate the cardinal (north, east, south, and west) compass direction to the hazard and, therfore, the safe channel around the hazard.

Under the federal lateral system, the buoys indicate the safe channel or, when there is a choice, the preferred one of two options. When a boat enters a harbor, this lane or area of safe water lies between green buoys on the port (left-hand) side and red ones on the starboard (right-hand side). In mariner's parlance, buoys are "left to starboard" or "left to port." To leave a buoy to starboard, keep it on your starboard, or right-hand, side as you pass it. To leave it to port, keep it on your port, or left-hand side. Another way to say this is, "Keep the buoy on your starboard hand" or "on your port hand."

In the lateral system, buoys are somewhat like the curb of a road, except that they don't mark every foot along a channel's edge. As you run down a channel, keep in mind imaginary lines extending between buoys on the side. Try to stay near the center of the channel unless going around a bend (where the water is often deepest toward the outside) or when encountering other boats (when the rules of the road prefer that you stay to starboard). Since they are anchored, buoys may shift position as the tide rises and falls, or may even drag, so don't assume that one is located exactly where the chart says it is.

Stay away from buoys, which are made of metal and are securely

Two cans numbered "1" and "13" are stationed where the river narrows.

Red flashers announce Island Creek and La Trappe Creek.

A nun "2" marks the safe entrance to Lecompte Bay.

Buoys mark the entrances to five creeks and bays and the Choptank River, which cuts into Maryland's eastern shore. Cans, nuns, and green and red lighted buoys line the main channel, which starts off the chart to the left and is the deeper water (water depths are indicated by the small numbers; shaded areas are shallow water).

Buoys

anchored. In a swift current, a buoy can be a half-submerged obstruction capable of holing any boat swept up on it. It is illegal to tie up to a buoy or to deface it in any way.

Buoy Characteristics. Buoys have distinctive colors, shapes, and other characteristics that help the sailor determine the location of the channel or the preferred one of two choices.

Color: "Red Right Returning." Most buoys are either red or green. "Red Right Returning" is the rule of thumb. This means that when your boat enters a body of water from a larger body of water (say, when returning to a harbor from a bay or sound), the safe passage is the one in which the red buoys are left to starboard (kept on the starboard hand) and the green buoys are left to port (kept on the port hand). Red buoys mark the starboard (right-hand) side on entering, and green buoys

mark the port (left-hand) side. On departing the smaller body of water, the rule is reversed: "Green Right Leaving."

Determining whether you are returning or leaving often is fairly easy, but if you have doubts, study the chart and ask yourself which body of water is most protected by land, is farthest from the sea (or lake), and provides the safest anchorage. The answer to each question will be the body of water that you're entering.

Where there is no channel, the Coast Guard arbitrarily lays out red buoys closer to the seashore. Therefore boats are "entering" as they proceed south along the Atlantic Coast, north and west along the Gulf Coast, and north along the Pacific Coast. Great Lakes buoys are laid out under the assumption that boats enter at lake outlets, so a boat heading west on Lakes Ontario and Erie, north on Lake Huron, west on Lake Superior, and south on Lake Michigan will leave red buoys to starboard. On the

Mississippi and Ohio Rivers, buoys are laid out assuming that boats enter at the river mouth, so a boat heading upstream leaves the red buoys to starboard.

Note: The Coast Guard may move buoys or change their light characteristics. Only an up-to-date chart (supplemented by information found in the Coast Guard's publication *Local Notice to Mariners*) will keep you abreast of any alterations.

Numbers. An official numbering policy helps indicate the direction of the harbor, since buoy numbers start at 1 (green buoy) and 2 (red buoy) at the entrance to a harbor and increase as you enter it. Green buoys carry odd numbers and red buoys carry even numbers. If you get lost, simply find two green or red buoys. The one with the highest number is toward the harbor. Numbers are painted or taped on with red or green reflectors. Many buoys carry radar reflectors to make them stand out espe-

Buoy numbers increase in Chesapeake Bay from its mouth at the south end toward the north (at the top of this chart). Red buoys are to the right, green to the left. Buoys to the side mark entrances to bays and rivers.

This range indicates a measured mile — exactly 1 mile laid out between ranges that mariners may use to calibrate their vessels' speedometers.

Thomas Point Shoal lighthouse has two lights. One, marked "Fl 5sec," is a white light that flashes every 5 seconds. If you see it, you're in the main channel. The other light, "RED SEC," is a steady red light. If you see that light, you are to the side of the main channel and should proceed with special caution.

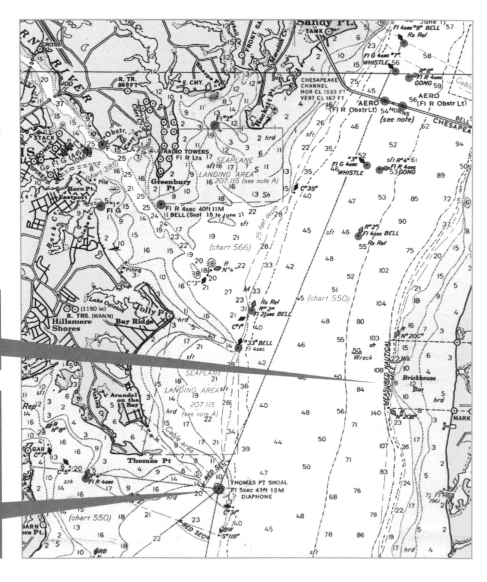

cially vividly on a boat's radar. If so, "Ra ref" is printed next to the chart symbol. Some buoys carry a Racon, a beacon that sends out a quick reply to a vessel's radar, thereby making the buoy larger and brighter on your radar scope.

Buoy Types. Here we will describe the types of buoys that serve as navigation aids (sometimes called marks or channel markers). This list is organized according to their distinctive individual appearance, which immediatly signals to the sailor how the buoy should be passed. As we will see, buoy lights and sounds also help in safe navigation.

Most buoys have one of four color schemes: red, green, red-and-green banded horizontally, or red and white striped vertically. A few other color schemes are used in highly specialized buoys, but the vast majority of buoys encountered on American waters (and also the large majority of daybeacons, used in shallow water) have these colors.

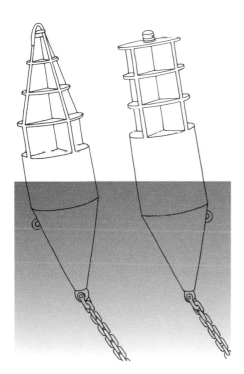

A nun is red and has a pointed top, a red reflector, and an even number. A can is green and has a flat top, a green reflector, and an odd number. On entering, leave nuns and other red buoys to starboard, cans and other green buoys to port. The buoy's skeleton may be visible, as shown here, or plated over.

Green buoys mark the port (left-hand) side of a channel when a vessel is entering a smaller body of water. Green buoys have odd numbers. There are two types. One is the flat-topped, unlighted can buoy, indicated on the chart by a green diamond, the label "G C," and the number. The other is the green buoy with a flashing green light and sometimes a sound signal. The light, in a tower-like framework called a pillar, flashes at night and in periods of daytime poor visibility. The lighted buoy is indicated on a chart by a green diamond with a purple circle (indicating a light) and the label "Fl G" with the interval between flashes in seconds, the buoy's number, and the type of sound, if any.

Red buoys mark the starboard (right-hand) side of a channel when you enter. They have even numbers. One type has a pointed top (like a nun's cowl) and is called a nun buoy. The chart symbol is a red diamond, "R N," and the number. A red buoy with a flashing red light and sometimes a sound signal also marks the starboard side of a channel on entering. The lighted buoy is indicated on a chart by a red diamond with a purple circle and the label "Fl R" with the interval between flashes in seconds, the buoy's number, and the type of sound.

Red and green horizontally banded buoys show the preferred channel. They are called *junction buoys* and *preferred channel buoys*. Where cans and nuns indicate only one safe channel, these buoys indicate the preferred of two or more courses (for example, either side of a rock). Junction buoys are shaped like cans or nuns, or they have the tower-like framework (pillar) of lighted buoys. If you see one of these buoys, consult the chart before you reach it, since the water around it may be broken by shoals and rocks. If the buoy is shaped like a can and the top band is green, you will be in the preferred channel if you leave this buoy to port when entering. You may leave it to starboard, but it's safer to leave it to port. Likewise, a nun-shaped junction buoy whose top band is red should be left to starboard on entering. Preferred channel buoys are not numbered but may carry letters. The chart symbol is a diamond with red and green bands (the top band indicating the preferred side), the letters "RG" or "GR," and the letter if it has one. Lighted pre-

ferred channel buoys carry green or red lights in patterns described later.

Red and white vertically striped buoys stripes indicate the middle of a channel. Either round or having the tower-like framework, they are called midchannel (fairway, safe water) buoys. They may be passed on either side. (But since the rules of the road prefer a boat to go down the starboard side of a channel, they should be left to port on entering.) These buoys are not numbered but may be lettered. Their chart symbol is a white diamond divided vertically by a line and "RW" plus the letter. Lighted midchannel buoys, the ones with a tower-like structure, carry white lights that repeatedly blink Morse code letter "A" (short-long-interval-short-long-interval, etc.). The chart symbol is "RW Mo (A)."

Black and red horizontally banded buoys with two black balls on a pole above a tower-like structure are isolated danger buoys. They may be lettered. They are anchored near isolated rocks and other hazards surrounded by navigable water. Lighted isolated danger buoys have white lights that show in pairs in the group-flashing (2) sequence: two flashes, interval, two flashes, interval, etc. On the chart, isolated danger buoys are indicated by a black- and red-banded diamond with two black balls on top and "BR."

Solid red or green buoys are wreck marks. They may have quick flashing lights, with no pause between.

Yellow buoys (often with flashing yellow lights) are special marks. They attract attention to pipes, traffic schemes, fishing grounds, and other items of note. They usually do not indicate a preferred side to pass on.

Buoys

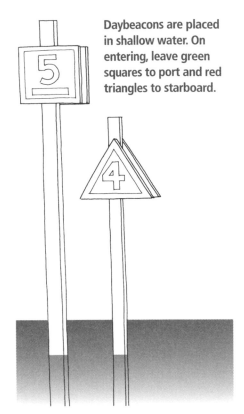

Daybeacons are placed in shallow water. On entering, leave green squares to port and red triangles to starboard.

Daybeacons. In shallow water, instead of buoys, channels are often marked by daybeacons — sticks pounded into the bottom and carrying signs called daymarks (dayboards). They use the same color and numbering schemes used with buoys. Daymarks may have flashing lights, called "minor lights." For descriptions of lights, see the buoy section above or the section below. Again we will introduce channel markers by their appearance.

A triangular red daymark with a reflective red border and an even number is the equivalent of a nun and is left to starboard on entering. On the chart, it is shown by a red triangle and "R." It may show a flashing red light.

A square green daymark with a reflective green border and an odd number is like a can and left to port. Its symbol is a green square and "G." A green daybeacon may show a green flashing light.

A square horizontally green-and-red banded daymark with the green band above the red band is a preferred channel marker or junction marker indicating that the preferred channel is to its right. You should leave this mark to port, but may leave it to starboard. On the chart, it is indicated by a white square and "GR." It may show a green flashing light.

A triangular banded daymark with a red reflective border and the red band above the green one indicates that the preferred channel is the one in which the daymark is left to starboard. Its symbol is a white triangle and "RG." It may carry a red flashing light.

An octagon with red and white vertical stripes is a midchannel (fairway, safe water) mark. A white square and "RW" mark it on the chart. It may carry a white light flashing Morse code "A" and labeled "RW Mo (A)."

Lighted Buoys and Daybeacons. At key turns in the channel, buoys and daybeacons usually carry flashing lights in a variety of colors and phase characteristics (patterns). Lighted buoys consist of a tower-like framework (pillar) that holds a light, batteries, and a solar panel to generate electricity. Most lights switch on automatically at dusk or in fog and other times of poor visibility; some lights may flash all the time. Lighted buoys are colored and numbered just like cans and nuns. A lighted buoy or beacon is indicated on a chart

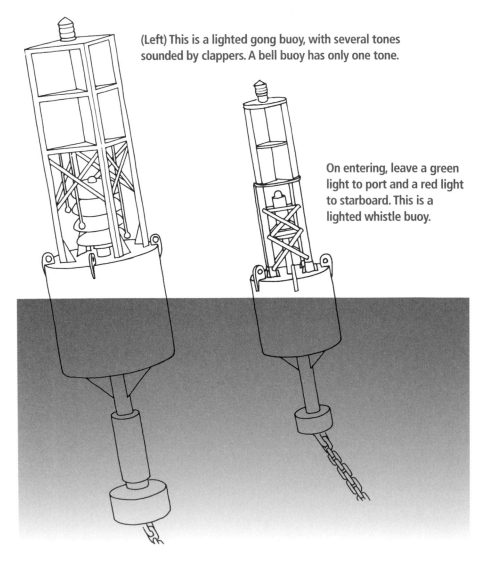

(Left) This is a lighted gong buoy, with several tones sounded by clappers. A bell buoy has only one tone.

On entering, leave a green light to port and a red light to starboard. This is a lighted whistle buoy.

HANDS ON: **Buoys and Phase Characteristics**

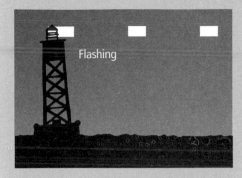

Flashing

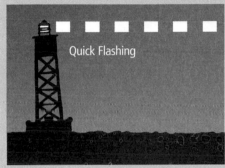

Quick Flashing

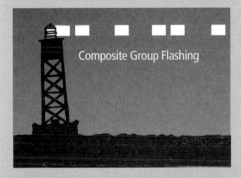

Composite Group Flashing

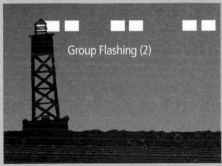

Group Flashing (2)

Morse Code "A"

The first step when trying to identify buoys is to be rigorously honest with yourself. You will regularly face the temptation of locating exactly the buoy you want to find. Natural human optimism can quickly turn a can into a nun, red into white, a 1 into a 7, and a 3-second flash into a 4-second flash. Hopeful misidentification may well run you aground. So be cautious. If you can't be certain about an identification and the waters are dangerous, don't proceed until you are dead sure.

Distinguishing colors from a distance may be a problem on a hazy day or when the sun is low on the horizon, so look carefully at the shape. At night, when both color and shape are indistinguishable, you can identify a buoy by shining a flashlight at it. The light will quickly pick up the red (for a nun) or green (for a can) reflector.

To identify the phase characteristic or rhythm of a light, you can use a stopwatch if there is a red light available to see the watch by. If you use a regular white flashlight you will quickly lose your night vision. Better, practice counting seconds, using "thousand" or "elephant." Start the count when the light goes off and end it when the light comes back on. Repeat the count until you're absolutely sure of it. To avoid double vision, don't stare at the buoy. Instead, keep your eyes moving so you see it out of the corner of your eye. Don't panic if a phase characteristic seems wrong or the light doesn't seem to be where it belongs. Land, another boat, or waves may be obscuring it. Slow down, rest your eyes, and then look again.

These are the phase characteristics most often seen on lighted buoys and daybeacons.

by a diamond connected to a purple circle, a letter indicating the kind of light, and the color. "Fl" alone indicates a white light. "Fl G 4s" is a green flashing light with a 4-second interval of darkness between flashes. (You may not see an "s" on an older chart.)

Green and red lights go on green and red markers, respectively, at the sides of channels. If you see a green light, treat it like a can; a red light, like a nun. The light's phase characteristic has no special meaning except to distinguish that light from others of the same color. On a chart, these lights are labeled as "Fl G" or "Fl R" with the time of the interval between flashes and the buoy's number.

White lights are used on midchannel (fairway) buoys. The chart label reads "Fl," with no color designation.

Phase Characteristics. The following phase characteristics are the ones usually encountered:

Flashing red or green, with a light flashing at regular intervals, is used on most red or green buoys. The chart symbol is a red or green diamond with a purple circle, "Fl R" and "Fl G," and the interval of darkness between flashes in seconds. "Fl G 4s" is a green light that flashes green every 4 seconds.

Quick-flashing red or green, a continuous series of flashes, one per second, is placed on red or green buoys at crucial parts of a channel, where special caution must be exerted. The chart symbol is "Qk Fl R" or "Qk Fl G."

Composite group flashing red or green has a repeated syncopation and is found on preferred channel (junction) buoys or marks. A chart label "R G Fl (2+1) R 6s" is a preferred channel marker with a 6-second sequence of red flashes: two quick flashes, then an interval, then a quick flash, then another interval. The sequence goes on repeating itself.

Morse code letter "A" white (short-long-interval-short-long-interval, etc.) is used on midchannel (fairway) buoys. The chart label is "RW Mo (A)" plus the buoy letter.

U.S. AIDS TO NAVIGATION SYSTEM
on navigable waters except Western Rivers

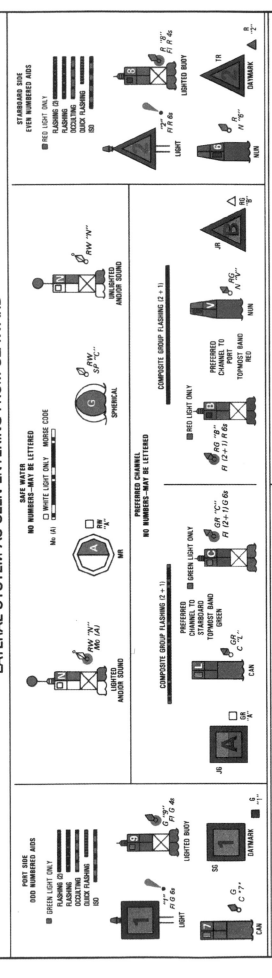

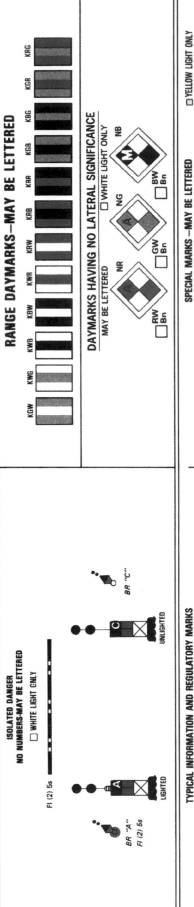

LATERAL SYSTEM AS SEEN ENTERING FROM SEAWARD

Aids to navigation marking the Intracoastal Waterway (ICW) display unique yellow symbols to distinguish them from aids marking other waters. Yellow triangles △ indicate aids should be passed by keeping them on the starboard (right) hand of the vessel. Yellow squares □ indicate aids should be passed by keeping them on the port (left) hand of the vessel. A yellow horizontal band provides no lateral information, but simply identifies aids as marking the ICW.

Plate 1

208

U.S. AIDS TO NAVIGATION SYSTEM
on the Western River System

AS SEEN ENTERING FROM SEAWARD

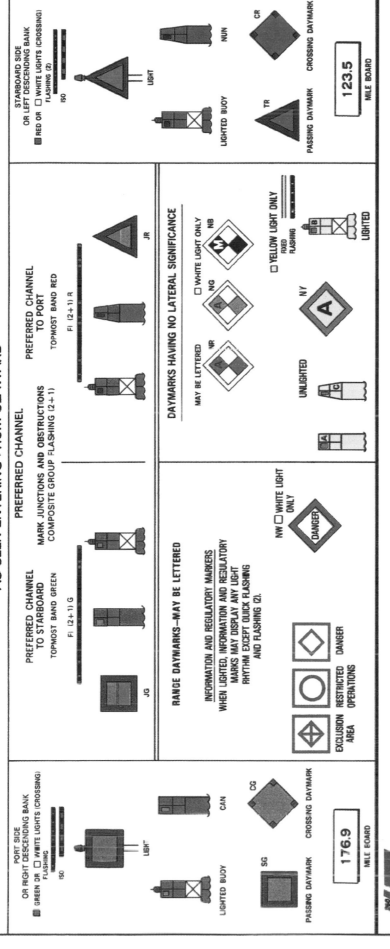

STARBOARD SIDE OR LEFT DESCENDING BANK
■ RED OR □ WHITE LIGHTS (CROSSING)
FLASHING (2)
ISO

LIGHT
NUN
LIGHTED BUOY
TR
CROSSING DAYMARK — CR
PASSING DAYMARK — TR

123.5
MILE BOARD

PREFERRED CHANNEL TO PORT
TOPMOST BAND RED
FI (2+1) R
JR

PREFERRED CHANNEL TO STARBOARD
TOPMOST BAND GREEN
FI (2+1) G
JG

MARK JUNCTIONS AND OBSTRUCTIONS
COMPOSITE GROUP FLASHING (2+1)

DAYMARKS HAVING NO LATERAL SIGNIFICANCE

MAY BE LETTERED
NR
NG
NB — □ WHITE LIGHT ONLY

NY — □ YELLOW LIGHT ONLY
FIXED
FLASHING
A

UNLIGHTED
LIGHTED

NW — □ WHITE LIGHT ONLY
DANGER

RANGE DAYMARKS—MAY BE LETTERED

INFORMATION AND REGULATORY MARKERS

WHEN LIGHTED, INFORMATION AND REGULATORY MARKS MAY DISPLAY ANY LIGHT RHYTHM EXCEPT QUICK FLASHING AND FLASHING (2).

◆ DANGER
○ RESTRICTED OPERATIONS
◈ EXCLUSION AREA

PORT SIDE OR RIGHT DESCENDING BANK
■ GREEN OR □ WHITE LIGHTS (CROSSING)
FLASHING
ISO

LIGHTED BUOY
SG
CAN
CG
PASSING DAYMARK — SG
CROSSING DAYMARK — CG

176.9
MILE BOARD

UNIFORM STATE WATERWAY MARKING SYSTEM

STATE WATERS AND DESIGNATED STATE WATERS FOR PRIVATE AIDS TO NAVIGATION

REGULATORY MARKERS

◈ SWIM AREA — BOAT EXCLUSION AREA

EXPLANATION MAY BE PLACED OUTSIDE THE CROSSED DIAMOND SHAPE, SUCH AS DAM, RAPIDS, SWIM AREA, ETC.

→ BULLET LINE / DIAGR PAPER — INFORMATION

FOR DISPLAYING INFORMATION SUCH AS DIRECTIONS, DISTANCES, LOCATIONS, ETC.

◆ ROCK — DANGER

THE NATURE OF DANGER MAY BE INDICATED INSIDE THE DIAMOND SHAPE, SUCH AS ROCK, WRECK, SHOAL, DAM, ETC.

○ SLOW / NO WAKE — CONTROLLED AREA

TYPE OF CONTROL IS INDICATED IN THE CIRCLE, SUCH AS SLOW, NO WAKE, ANCHORING, ETC.

5 — BUOY USED TO DISPLAY REGULATORY MARKERS
MAY SHOW WHITE LIGHT
MAY BE LETTERED

AIDS TO NAVIGATION

3 — MAY SHOW GREEN REFLECTOR OR LIGHT
4 — MAY SHOW RED REFLECTOR OR LIGHT

SOLID RED AND SOLID BLACK BUOYS
USUALLY FOUND IN PAIRS
PASS BETWEEN THESE BUOYS

PORT SIDE ←— LOOKING UPSTREAM —→ STARBOARD SIDE

LATERAL SYSTEM

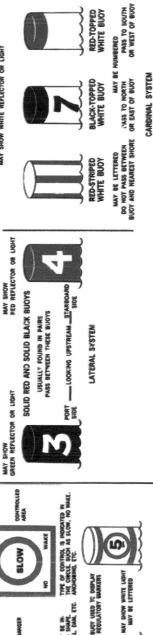

MAY SHOW WHITE REFLECTOR OR LIGHT

RED-STRIPED WHITE BUOY
MAY BE LETTERED
DO NOT PASS BETWEEN BUOY AND NEAREST SHORE

BLACK-TOPPED WHITE BUOY
MAY BE NUMBERED
PASS TO NORTH OR EAST OF BUOY

RED-TOPPED WHITE BUOY
PASS TO SOUTH OR WEST OF BUOY

CARDINAL SYSTEM

MOORING BUOY
WHITE WITH BLUE BAND
MAY SHOW WHITE REFLECTOR OR LIGHT

Plate 4

209

Buoys

Sound Buoys. The presence of some important buoys is emphasized by sound makers. There are four kinds of sound buoys, any of which may be lighted. In fog, although the sounds may be clear, you may have difficulty tracking them to their source as they reverberate through the damp air. But sound buoys will tell you generally where you are and warn you away from shoals and rocks.

Bells have a single bell against which four clappers swing, banging out the same tone as the buoy rolls with the waves. Some bells are run automatically by an internal mechanism.

Gongs have two, three, or four bells, each with its own clapper and unique tone.

Whistles create a moaning sigh as air is forced up through a pipe when the buoy rolls.

Horns are electrically powered so they work in smooth water. Their sound is more abrupt than the whistle's moan.

Other Buoyage Systems. Although "Red Right Returning" is the general rule, the Intracoastal Waterway, the Western Rivers — the Mississippi and its tributaries, the Red River, the upper Atchafalaya River, and other rivers so designated by the Coast Guard — and many state waters are subject to special buoyage systems and rules. These and other rivers and waterways make good use of markers called *ranges,* which are pairs of charted objects that when lined up precisely identify a channel or the

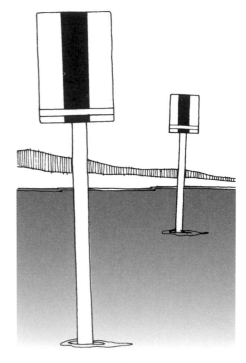

When daymarks are lined up in a range, the observer is in the channel.

Ranges — a pair of charted objects — sometimes are used to precisely indicate channels or mark other important locations, such as measured miles.

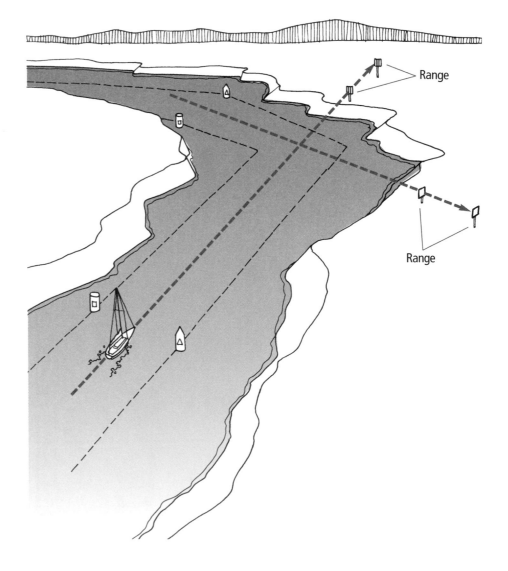

Range

Range

location of an object. Ranges are especially helpful when a crew aligns a boat in the center of a channel after making a sharp turn in a waterway. Ranges also mark the beginning and end of a measured mile, a stretch of shoreline exactly a mile long that mariners may use to calibrate speedometers.

On the Intracoastal Waterway (ICW, sometimes called the inland waterway) buoys and daymarks comply with the federal system. Sometimes there is a conflict with the local channel. In that case, the ICW is marked using buoys or daymarks with yellow triangles to indicate that they be left to starboard and with yellow square to indicate that they be left to port. The rule is triangles to starboard and squares to port when heading toward Florida and New Orleans, and squares to starboard and triangles to port when heading toward New York.

On Western Rivers, including the Mississippi, buoys and daymarks have slightly different color schemes from the ones in the federal system described above. Only lighted buoys are numbered, and the numbers indicate mileage upstream from a charted reference point.

The Uniform State Waterway Marking System. Outside of coastal waters and major tributaries, which lie in federal jurisdiction, the Uniform State Waterway Marking System applies. It is used on small lakes and rivers. "Red Right Returning," the foundation of the lateral system, applies in most USWMS waters, where you will find small green cans with odd numbers and small red cones with even numbers. But the USWMS also includes the cardinal system, which, instead of laying out buoys to mark the sides of channels, uses them to indicate the compass direction to an obstruction, and therefore to the safe channel.

In this system, numbers on buoys increase and letters proceed in alphabetical order going upstream. Green buoys use only green lights and red buoys red ones, either flashing or, to indicate caution, quick-flashing.

Other buoys in this system have three different color schemes:

A black-topped white buoy indicates that boats should pass to the north and east of its location. Its light (if it has one) is quick-flashing white. It may have a white reflector.

A red-topped white buoy warns boats to pass to the south and west of its position. It may also have a white quick-flashing light and a white reflector.

A red-and-white vertically striped buoy indicates that boats should not pass between it and the nearest shore.

White buoys with two orange bands display written warnings or speed limits.

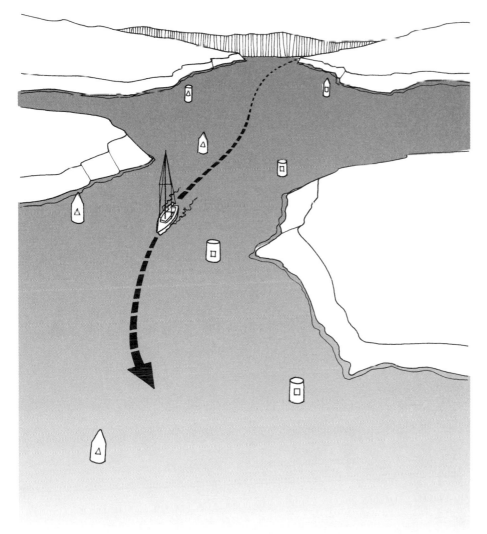

On the Intracoastal Waterway, red buoys carry yellow triangles and are left to starboard heading from New Jersey toward Texas, and green buoys carry yellow squares and are left to port.

Lighthouses

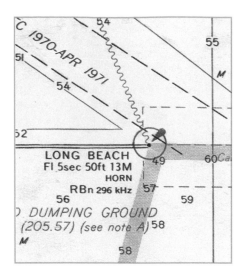

No land-based object is more symbolic of the sea and ships than the lighthouse, the tower of stone capped by a glass house with a bright light sweeping over the far horizon to embrace and comfort lost sailors. As the sea became commercialized after the 16th century, shipping companies and governments built lights on cliffs, points of land, rocks, and islets to warn ships away from reefs and the shore. Soon these led to extensive systems of lights that could lead merchantmen from harbor to harbor. When there was no land to support a light, it was placed on a lightship moored to great anchors far offshore. After World War II, lightships were replaced by towers constructed like offshore oil rigs. Many light towers were later replaced by large sea buoys.

Lighthouses ashore often have a distinctive appearance, with bright stripes, so they stand out from the land and buildings around them. Similarly, their lights have red, green, or white lights — sometimes two or all three colors in the same light — in a wider range of phase characteristics than are used with lighted buoys. This variety is essential due to the long range of visibility of lighthouses. Because many lights may be seen simultaneously from the deck of a boat, each must have its unique characteristics.

On charts, lighthouses are indicated in two ways. If the lighthouse is on shore, the symbol is a red exclamation mark emanating from a black dot; if offshore on a built-up underwater foundation, the symbol is a red exclamation mark emanating from a black dot within an irregular circle that looks like the outline of a daisy. This circle indicates rip-rap, or rocks and piles extending beyond the lighthouse's base.

Light Characteristics. As with buoys, lighthouses are identified using different light characteristics, which are clearly shown on charts. A government publication called the *Light List* provides

This lighthouse flashes a white light every 5 seconds and the light has a nominal range of 13 nautical miles. The lighthouse is 50 feet above mean high water, sounds a horn in fog, and has a radio beacon transmitting over a frequency of 296 kHz. (Below and opposite page) Some lighthouse light phase characteristics.

light characteristics as well as other data about lighthouses not given on the chart. The most important light characteristics and symbols for lighthouses are the following:

A flashing light repeats a flash at regular intervals. The period of light is shorter than the period of darkness except in a quick-flashing light. A white ("Fl"), red ("Fl R"), or green ("Fl G") light may be used. On a chart, the label "Fl 8sec" indicates a white light flashing every 8 seconds. Sometimes high-visibility strobes are used in flashing white lights.

In **an alternating light,** two or three colors alternate at regular intervals. "Alt Fl R & G 10sec" means that red and green flashes alternate every 10 seconds.

Fixed lights remain illuminated. Some lighthouses show one type of light over safe water and fixed red lights (red sectors) over shoal water and other areas that require special caution. "F" indicates

Flashing

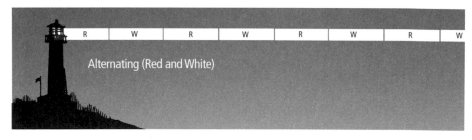
Alternating (Red and White)

Group Flashing

Composite Group Flashing

fixed white, "FG" fixed green, "FR" fixed red, and "RED SEC" a red sector.

Group flashing is the term for a light that flashes twice or more in regular intervals. "Gp Fl (2) 5sec" means that every 5 seconds there are two white flashes. In an alternating group flashing light, the lights alternate in color. "Alt Gp Fl R & G (2) 6sec" means that every 6 seconds there is a group of one red flash and one green flash.

Composite group flashing lights have distinctive syncopations. For example, "Gp Fl (1+2) 8sec" is a white light flashing in this phase sequence: flash, 8-second interval, two flashes, 8-second interval, flash, and so on.

Fixed and flashing lights have a fixed light interrupted regularly by a brighter light. "Alt FR FlG l4sec" is an alternating fixed-flashing light whose red fixed light is broken every 14 seconds by a green flash.

Fixed and group flashing lights have a fixed light interrupted regularly by groups of two or more flashing lights. These lights may be alternating — for instance, "Alt FG Gp Fl (2) 15sec" describes a fixed green light interrupted every 15 seconds by a group of two white lights.

An occulting light shows a flash that is longer than the period of darkness between flashes. White, green, or red lights are used singly or in alternating sequence. "Occ G 4sec" means a green light is off for 4 seconds. "Alt Occ W & R 7sec" means that white and red lights alternate every 7 seconds.

Group occulting lights are white and consist of groups of two or more occulting lights (lights that are illuminated longer than they are dark). The chart label is "Gp Occ."

Composite group occulting lights have several groups with different combinations of flashes. For instance, "C Gp Occ (1+3)" describes a composite group occulting light with a sequence of one flash and another of three flashes.

Isophase (equal interval) lights are off for the same length of time that they are on — for example, "Iso 4sec" is a white light that flashes on or off every 4 seconds.

Long-flashing lights have a flash that is 2 seconds or longer — for instance, "Lfl 3sec."

Morse code lights show a sequence of dots and dashes representing a letter in Morse code. A familiar one is "Mo(A)" — a white light in a repeated short-long sequence.

Quick lights flash every 1 second in one of several patterns. "Q" is a quick white light flashing 60 times a minute. "Q(3)" is a group quick light (not used in the United States) in which the quick flashes come in groups of three. And "IQ" is an interrupted quick light in which quick flashes are regularly interrupted by darkness.

Other Characteristics. A lighthouse may have a foghorn, identified on the chart by the word "HORN." The horn starts operating automatically in poor visibility. A type of horn called a

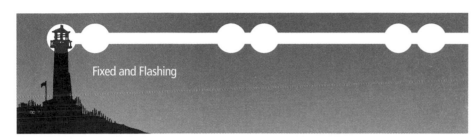

Fixed and Flashing

Fixed and Group Flashing

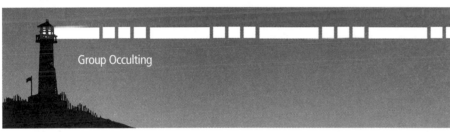

Group Occulting

Composite Group Occulting

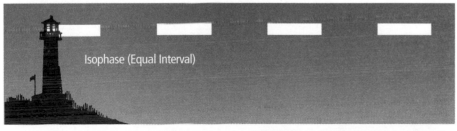

Isophase (Equal Interval)

Morse Code "A"

Lighthouses

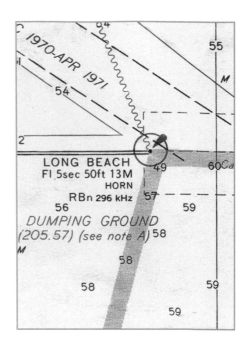

diaphragm horn has two or three pitches. The phase characteristic of the horn is not shown on the chart, but it is given in the *Light List* and some local pilot or tide books. Some lighthouses may also have bells, sirens, or dual-tone diaphones. Use extreme caution when piloting by these sounds, since they may be distorted or even masked by the fog, clouds, or the lighthouse itself.

Many lighthouses used to have radio beacons used in navigation with an onboard radio direction finder (RDF). With the decline of importance of RDF

in navigation, there are fewer beacons.

Range of Visibility. The range at which a light (or any other object) is visible is important. With a light, there are two ranges of visibility: the nominal range and the geographical range.

The nominal range of visibility is the mileage in the chart lighthouse label. "13M" indicates that a light is bright enough to be seen 13 nautical miles away.

The geographical range of visibility is the distance at which any object actually can be seen — the distance to its horizon. Geographical range ignores the light's brightness (its nominal range). It determines only how the curvature of the earth limits the range from the deck of your boat to the object. The taller you are (or any object is), the broader your horizon and so the greater your geographical range.

To start, find the light's height on the chart label. You can enter that into the

Using Table 9-1, the pilot determines that the geographical range of the 50-foot Long Beach light is 8.1 miles, well under its 13-mile nominal range.

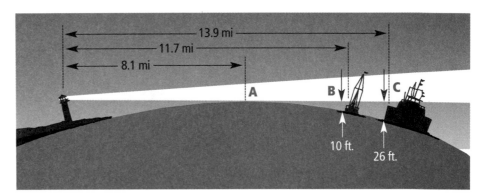

At water level (A) the light is visible up to only 8.1 miles away due to the earth's curvature. To determine geographical range from greater heights, use the table and add the ranges of the light and the observer. A sailor 10 feet up (B) can see the light from 11.7 miles; if the nominal range were equally great, somebody 26 feet up (C) could see the light from 13.9 miles.

Table 9-1: Geographical Ranges of Visibility in Nautical Miles
NOTE: To find range in statute miles, multiply range in nautical miles by 1.15.

Height (Feet)	Visibility (Nautical Miles)	Height (Feet)	Visibility (Nautical Miles)	Height (Feet)	Visibility (Nautical Miles)
6	2.8	55	8.5	110	12.0
10	3.6	60	8.9	120	12.6
15	4.4	65	9.2	130	13.1
20	5.1	70	9.6	140	13.6
26	5.8	75	9.9	150	14.1
30	6.3	80	10.3	160	14.5
36	6.9	85	10.6	170	14.9
40	7.2	90	10.9	180	15.4
46	7.8	95	11.2	190	15.8
50	8.1	100	11.5	200	16.2

table here, or you can use the following formula:

**Geographical range (nautical mi.) =
1.144 √ lighthouse height in ft.**

For statute (land) miles, the formula is the same but with 1.317 as the multiplier.

If the lighthouse height is 50 feet, its geographical range is 8.1 nautical miles. That is the distance from the light to its horizon. Someone on the deck of a boat would see the light before then because this person also has a range of visibility that increases with the height of his eye above the water. Typically, the height of eye of someone of normal size standing on the deck of a medium size sailboat is 10 feet, meaning a range of a little over 3.6 miles.

To calculate the range at which this person should see the 50-foot light, add the two geographical ranges of visibility to each other. The range of the 50-foot lighthouse is 8.1 miles and that of the sailor is 3.6. The total, 11.7 miles, is less than the light's nominal range of 13 miles. Someone standing on a freighter's deck 26 feet above the water will see this light at the limit of its nominal range in clear weather, but not a sailor on a sailboat.

The range of visibility can be an important piloting tool. Many boating areas have a string of lighthouses with overlapping coverage that you can use as stepping stones as you sail along the coast on a clear night. Precalculate the geographical range of visibility for each light and, using a drawing compass, draw them to scale on the chart. Once a new light appears over the horizon, you will have a close approximation not only of its distance but, since you can take a compass bearing to it, also of your position. Using ranges and bearings on another light, you can pinpoint your position even more reliably.

This technique is not limited to lighthouses. During the day, you may use it to estimate your distance from any charted object of a known height — for example, a radio tower and another boat's mast.

Changing Visibility. We have been assuming good visibility. Changing atmospheric conditions can play tricks with your exploitation of the range of visibility. A dense fog or heavy rain may cut off the light well short of its nominal range. A light overcast or thin fog may lengthen it by enhancing the light's loom, as may heavy cloud cover before the arrival of a warm front, when humidity rinses the dust out of the air and the clouds behave like a mirror to bounce the light several miles beyond its limit. A light may disappear due to a power failure or other accident. Lighthouses have backup electrical systems and lights, whose nominal range and characteristics may be shorter.

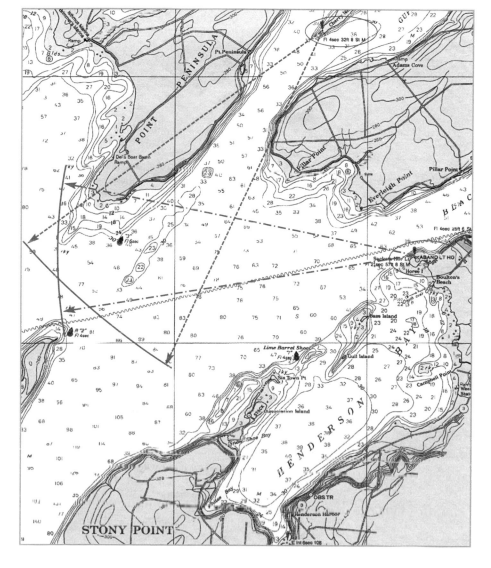

Geographical ranges of visibility to a lighthouse can be used in night navigation on clear nights. Before approaching land, calculate the ranges to several lights and draw arcs on the chart using a drawing compass set to those radiuses. If you see both lights, your are in a known area.

Charts

Charts are for seamen what topographical maps are for hunters, trail guides are for hikers, and road maps are for drivers — highly detailed, miniaturized, two-dimensional representations of the physical environment. A chart is an overhead view of the sea, a lake, or a river and its shores, emphasizing natural and artificial obstructions to safe sailing and anything that sailors can use to find their way. As the waters of the earth were explored they were mapped, and as they were sounded, dredged, channeled, and dotted with aids to navigation they were charted. The first charts contained enough crucial information to be state secrets. Eventually, enough was known about the New World, the East Indies, and other treasure grounds for each maritime nation to develop its own charts. Understandings soon developed about ways to recreate the three-dimensional global sphere on a two-dimensional piece of paper, and to locate places with cross references called latitude and longitude.

Hydrographic survey ships examined the seas and harbors of the world, and their reports, combined with data sent by merchant and naval vessels, became the authorities for sailing instructions and new charts. In the past, most of that work was done painstakingly by hand — for example, taking soundings by manually dropping a lead line (a weighted, graduated line) overboard and looking for rocks by dragging cables across the bottom. Today, much oceanographic research is conducted with electronic technology. Satellites, echo sounders, and sonar devices survey land and take soundings with unprecedented precision and thoroughness, often finding rocks, wrecks, and shoals that the old methods missed altogether. Meanwhile, paper charts are being replaced by microfiches and computerized charts.

Chart Projections. While reliance upon charts must be implicit, every pilot must also be aware that certain distortions are inevitable whenever the surface of a round object like the globe is projected onto a flat surface like a map sheet. If you've ever tried to flatten an orange peel, you know how difficult this problem is and how many ways there are to solve it. Although its effect on the average sailor covering short distances is minor, chart distortion influences how a navigator does her job.

The solution to the projection problem has taken a variety of forms, all of which have at least one thing in common: in each, a grid of imaginary lines called meridians of longitude (running up and down from the North Pole to the South Pole) and parallels of latitude (circling around the earth east to west) is assumed to exist so the navigator or pilot has a frame of reference. Each projection represents the globe and the grid in different, slightly distorted ways.

The simplest projection of the round globe upon flat paper was devised in 1568 by a Flemish geographer, Gerhard Kremer, better known by the Latin form of his name, Gerardus Mercator. On the **Mercator Projection,** the meridians of longitude run exactly parallel to each other up and down the chart sheet, and the parallels of latitude cross them at right angles. This is a major distortion, since on a globe meridians actually converge like seams between orange slices as they approach the poles. But by assuming that meridians are parallel, Mercator greatly simplified navigation and piloting. His rectilinear grid allowed short courses to be plotted not in complicated curved lines but in straight lines.

The distortion on a Mercator Projection map is greatest near the poles, less in the temperate zones, and nonexistent on the equator. This is because geographical "north" and "south" are not pinpoints, as on the globe, but general areas above and

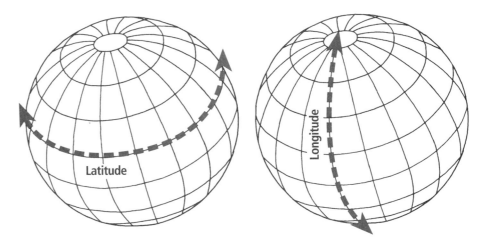

Meridians of longitude run north to south and parallels of latitude run east to west.

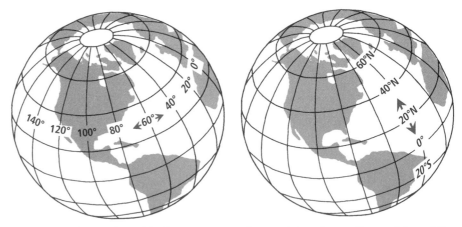

Longitude (left) is reckoned in degrees west and east of the prime or Greenwich meridian, or 0°. Latitude is in degrees north and south of the equator.

below the sheet. On this world shaped like a beer can, each degree between meridians represents exactly the same distance. But on a globe, 1° equals 60 miles at the equator and 0 miles at the poles. One result of this distortion is that extreme northern and southern areas are shown larger than reality. For example, Greenland shows up much bigger than South America, whereas South America is actually about eight times larger than Greenland. If you were sailing far north and far south, these misrepresentations might mislead you badly, but since most boating is done between about 40° north and 40° south, the distortion is unimportant to most sailors.

Another effect that has considerably more impact on the average pleasure sailor is that the parallels of latitude must also be distorted in order to keep them parallel and running at right angles to the meridians. Mercator did this by gradually narrowing the distance covered by 1° of latitude, working north and south from the equator. Like a degree of longitude, 1° of latitude equals 60 miles near the equator. Since a degree equals 60 minutes, the rule of thumb is "a mile a minute." Farther north or south, a Mercator chart's degree of latitude is smaller than a global degree of latitude. Most Mercator charts are designed so that the latitude increments on the sides follow the mile-a-minute rule. This allows the pilot to measure distances on the chart (for instance, the length of a course track from departure to destination) using the latitude exactly to the side of that track. The scale south or north will be slightly inaccurate. The bar scale printed on the chart is the average for the entire chart. As we'll see in later chapters, accurately measuring the distance is important in piloting.

The Mercator Projection is used on almost all the charts carried by saltwater sailors. Yet there is one type of sailing where its distortions can cause big errors. This is long-distance sailing toward the east or the west. You can sail the straight-line course between your departure and destination — but what looks like a straight line on the Mercator Projection chart is a long curved line in reality. A course plotted as a straight line on a globe would be about 12 percent shorter. This course is curved on a Mercator chart, and is called the "great circle."

To plot great circle courses, navigators use special charts drawn to the **Gnomonic Projection,** whose meridians of longitude and parallels of latitude are curved, and which better represents the earth's actual shape. While more complicated to use than the rectilinear grid on the Mercator Projection, the Gnomonic Projection is preferred for long-distance sailing.

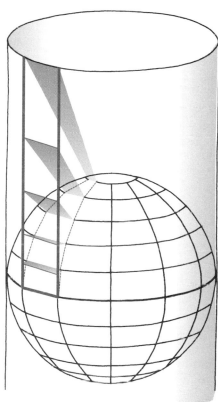

Transferring the grid from a globe to a sheet of paper inevitably leads to distortions. The Mercator Projection presents a world shaped like a beer can, with equidistant meridians of longitude and a varying latitude scale, and shows northern and southern land masses larger than they really are. It is used on most saltwater charts.

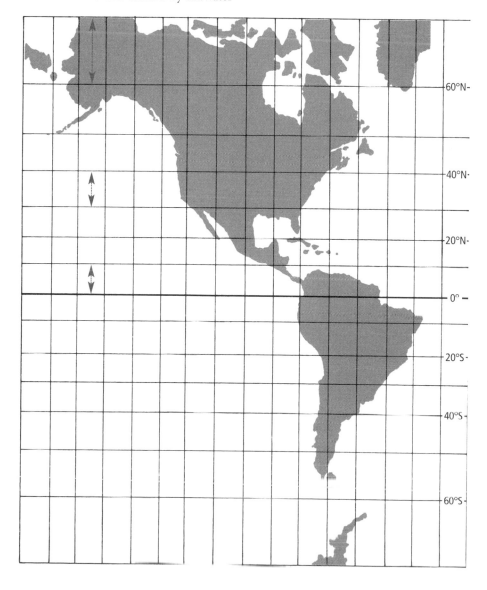

60°N-
40°N·
20°N·
0° —
20°S·
40°S·
60°S·

Charts

On most Great Lakes charts, the **Polyconic Projection** is used. Where the Mercator Projection shows the earth as a cylinder, the Polyconic Projection shows it as a series of cones whose points are above the poles. A steep, tall cone is tangent to the earth around the equator. Progressively shallower and lower cones are tangent and cover areas working toward each pole. There is less distortion with this projection because the meridians of longitude converge toward each other. The center meridian on the chart or map is vertical, meridi-

ans on either side lean toward it, and the parallels of latitude are concave. While more representative of shapes than the Mercator Projection, this grid is less simple. The distance covered by a minute or a degree of latitude is the same anywhere up and down the side scales of the chart, so measuring distance with these scales is more accurate than on the Mercator Projection. (Distances often are in statute miles — land miles — on Great Lakes charts.) But because the meridians converge toward the middle on a Polyconic chart, laying off a straight-line west-east or east-west course may be difficult, for it will cross each meridian at a slightly different angle — much the way a great circle course curves across the rectilinear grid of a Mercator chart. For example, the charted magnetic course from one end of Lake Superior to the other varies 4° over 300 miles, requiring a series of small course alterations.

Chart Scale. Different charts cover different size areas in varying detail. The amount of land and water and the degree of detail are indicated by the chart's scale shown in a ratio in its upper left-hand corner (under a label indicating the projection being used). Charts and maps are referred to as being "small scale" or "large scale." The larger the second number in the ratio, the smaller the scale and the more territory is covered.

Large scale=small area; small scale=large area. A map of the world may have a scale of 1:75,000,000, meaning that 1 inch represents 75 million inches (1 inch = 1,184 miles). That is an extremely small scale. A map of the United States, a smaller area, has a larger scale, for instance, 1:12,038,400 (1 inch = 190 miles). And the scale of a map of the Great Lakes may be 1:2,977,920 (1 inch = 47 miles), the largest scale of the three.

Types of Charts. The National Oceanic and Atmospheric Administra-

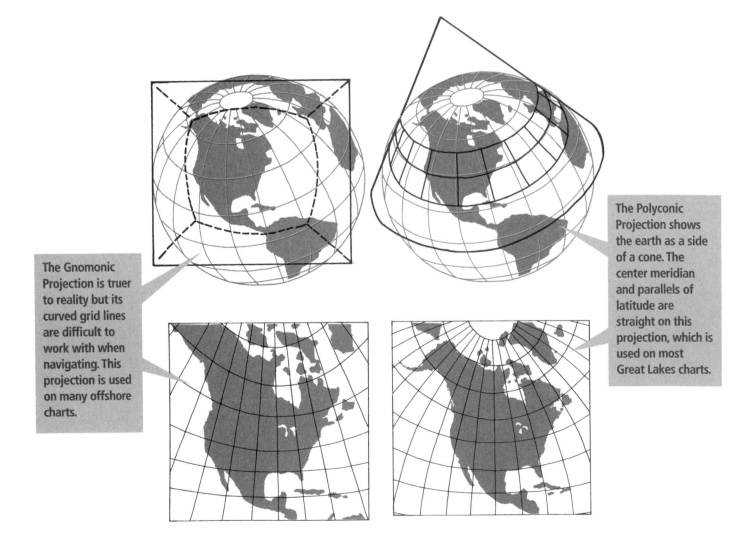

The Gnomonic Projection is truer to reality but its curved grid lines are difficult to work with when navigating. This projection is used on many offshore charts.

The Polyconic Projection shows the earth as a side of a cone. The center meridian and parallels of latitude are straight on this projection, which is used on most Great Lakes charts.

tion (NOAA), a branch of the United States Department of Commerce, through its National Ocean Service, publishes several types of charts as well as chart catalogs for American coastal, waterway, and lake areas. We start with the smallest scale (largest area) and move to the largest scale (smallest area).

The sailing chart is used when plotting positions and shows very little detail. A typical sailing chart is number 13003, "Cape Sable to Cape Hatteras." It covers America's middle and northern East Coast, from Cape Hatteras, North Carolina, to Nova Scotia. This chart is useless for navigating in Long Island Sound, Chesapeake Bay, or any other body of water along this coastline — but it will help a navigator on the open ocean. The largest scale on a sailing chart is 1:600,000 (1 inch = 10 miles).

The general chart covers a large subsection of a sailing chart. With scales ranging from 1:600,000 to 1:150,000

SALEM, MARBLEHEAD AND BEVERLY HARBORS

Mercator Projection
Scale 1:10,000 at Lat. 42°31'
North American Datum of 1983
(World Geodetic System 1984)

SOUNDINGS IN FEET
AT MEAN LOWER LOW WATER

The smallest area and the largest scale (1:50,000 and larger) are on a harbor chart, which also shows the greatest detail. Covering a larger area, a coast chart has a relatively large scale between 1:150,000 and 1:50,000.

The shortest east-west track is plotted as a straight line on a globe or Gnomonic Projection (below). But on a Mercator Projection it is an arc called the great circle, which is 12 percent shorter than the straight-line track.

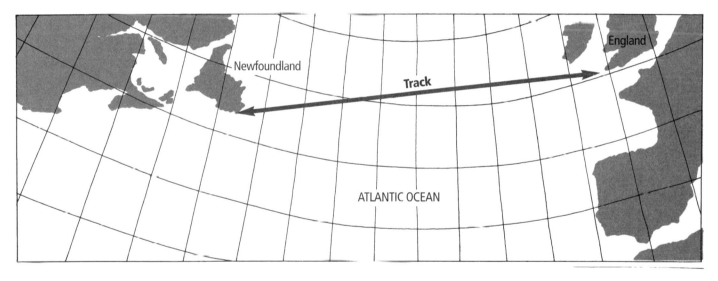

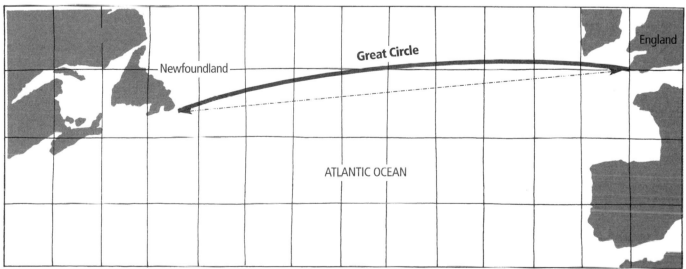

Charts

(1 inch = 10 miles to 1 inch = 2.4 miles), general charts can show the most important buoys and landmarks at the entrances to major bays, and so are helpful when making approaches from seaward. In sailing chart 13003, there are nine general charts, among them chart 12220 ("Cape May to Cape Hatteras"), covering the entrance to and land near Chesapeake Bay.

Coast charts cover the bodies of water within a general chart, showing reefs, shoals, channels, and other objects in detail. They are used in coastal navigation. Their scale varies from 1:150,000 to 1:50,000 (1 inch = 2.4 miles to 1 inch = 0.8 mile). In the area covered by sailing chart 13003 there are 31 coast charts, including two for Long Island Sound and five for Chesapeake Bay.

Harbor charts cover small waterways, harbors, and islands in great detail, with a scale of 1:50,000 (1 inch = 0.8 mile) or larger. They show how to get into the port once you have used the sailing, general, and coast charts to get to it. There are 135 harbor charts for the area covered by sailing chart 13003, including one each for Annapolis, Norfolk, and Newport, RI, and six for New York City.

Small-craft charts are booklets showing a series of harbor charts and

Chart catalogs, available from chart agents, show all available charts and provide a wealth of other valuable information. The catalogs must not be used for navigation, since they show no detail.

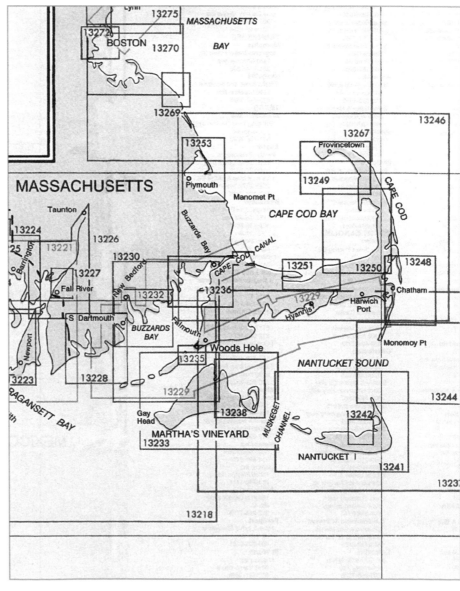

portions of coast charts that cover certain popular bodies of water.

Buying Charts. The National Ocean Service has an inventory of more than 1,000 charts covering 95,000 miles of coastline and 3.5 million square miles of lakes and ocean. To find out which charts you need, look at the National Ocean Service Nautical Chart Catalog that covers your area. Catalog 1 includes the Atlantic and Gulf coasts, Puerto Rico, and the Virgin Islands. Catalog 2 covers the Pacific coast plus Hawaii, Guam, and Samoa. Catalog 3 is for Alaska. And Catalog 4 lists all charts available for the Great Lakes and adjacent waterways. Catalogs are available at no cost from the hundreds of authorized chart agents, which include many chandleries (marine equipment stores and mail-order services). The catalogs list names and addresses of agents. Charts may also be ordered from the Distribution Division, National Ocean Service, Riverdale, MD, (301) 436-6990. In addition, commercial publishers and marine outlets sell waterproof charts, which are handy for use in cockpits.

Charts for Canadian, Arctic, and foreign waters and for many American lakes and rivers are available from a variety of agencies whose addresses are listed on National Ocean Service chart catalogs. Buy enough charts to cover your anticipated cruising area with some spillover into adjacent areas. You should carry aboard a harbor chart or a small-craft chart covering every harbor that you might enter. Also take along a harbor chart for one or two ports that have boatyards with marine railways, even if you don't plan on calling there. Some day a major emergency may force you in, most likely in difficult weather. And carry the coast charts covering the area and surrounding waters, plus relevant general charts. Sailing charts won't be of much help unless you're planning a long offshore passage.

Chart Books and Electronic Charts. Bound collections of reproductions of government charts covering popular boating areas are published by private organizations, sometimes on waterproof paper. The cost of these chart books may be considerably lower than that of buying all the charts separately. Charts also are reproduced on microfiches and CD-ROMs so they can be examined on electronic readers and computers. Computerized electronic charts can interface with GPS and other electronic navigation systems so the navigator has a complete picture of the boat's position on the instrument's display. Since these systems are dependent on the boat's electrical system, which is never 100 percent reliable, they must be backed up by an inventory of paper charts.

Revisions and New Editions. Whichever form they are in, your charts must be up to date. The National Ocean Service annually revises many charts to reflect changes in the characteristics of aids to navigation and alterations in channels or shorelines. The edition number and date of each chart are clearly printed on the bottom left hand corner of the chart sheet and on the cover of a small-craft chart. You may not need to buy each new edition of the harbor chart for your home port and other waters that you know well. The widely distributed government publication *Local Notice to Mariners* (described in a moment) notes changes that you can make on your charts. Emergencies such as drifting buoys and extinguished lights may be announced over National Weather Service VHF/FM (Very High Frequency) marine radio bands.

Always use the most recent edition when entering unfamiliar waters. Coast charts, showing relatively large areas, should be replaced by new editions as they are published and the old charts taken ashore. Since few coast charts are usually carried, the cost is minimal.

Stowing and Using Charts. Since chart sheets can be as large as 36 by 54 inches, stowing them and laying them out for use can be a problem in a small boat. They can be rolled up and secured in a dry locker, or folded and kept under bunk mattresses. Some boats have large chart tables that will hold a dozen or more folded charts. When folding, make sure the creases don't cross especially difficult channels or important aids to navigation.

Keep your charts dry and treat them gently. Although they're made of heavy paper, charts will crumble and mildew when damp. Use a soft lead pencil when plotting courses on the chart, and make only the marks that you need. Erase the marks later so they won't confuse you the next time you use the chart.

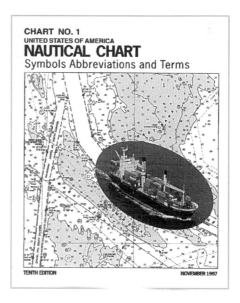

Chart 1 is a booklet showing and explaining all chart symbols.

Charts

What Charts Show. Using a large variety of symbols, labels, and colors, charts provide a tremendous amount of information about buoys, lights, water depths, shorelines, landmarks, islands, reefs, and hundreds of other natural and man-made hazards and landmarks. One National Ocean Service (NOS) pamphlet is dedicated solely to explaining chart symbols. This is Chart 1, titled *Nautical Chart Symbols, Abbreviations, and Terms,* available for a price much lower than its considerable value from the NOS and its authorized chart agents. Chart 1 shows and identifies more than 800 symbols and labels.

Here we'll look at some of the more important data, using as our example NOS chart 13218, Martha's Vineyard to Block Island, an area that includes Newport, RI, and some of the most popular and interesting boating waters in America. This is where the America's Cup races were held for more than half a century. Here, too, *Queen Elizabeth II,* the cruise ship, ran aground on a rock just south of Cuttyhunk Island.

There's no confusing this chart with any other, for it's clearly labeled in its upper left-hand corner:

UNITED STATES – EAST COAST
MASSACHUSETTS – RHODE ISLAND
MARTHA'S VINEYARD
TO BLOCK ISLAND

Immediately below the label, we see that this chart is a Mercator Projection. With a scale of 1:80,000 (1 inch = 1.3 miles), it is a coast chart. Heights and depths are based on a datum (reference plane) according to an international treaty. Soundings (water depths) are often in feet but on some NOS charts, they are in meters or (in very deep water) fathoms of 6 feet. "At Mean

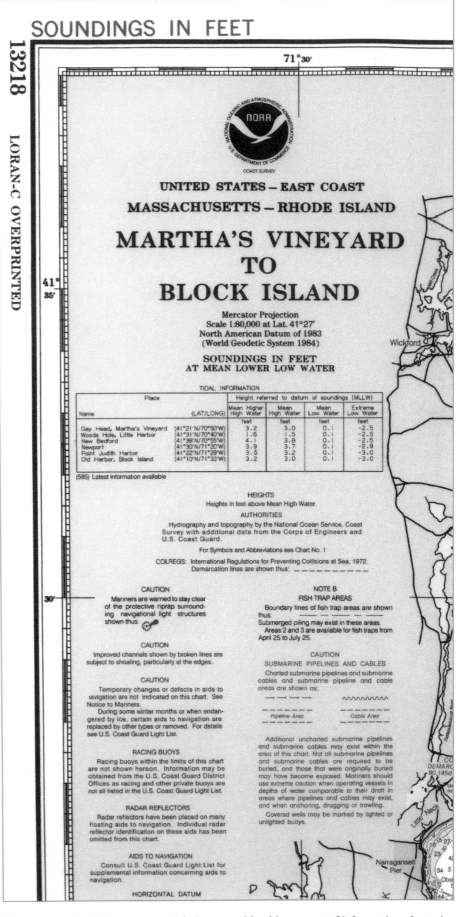

On every coast chart, one corner includes a considerable amount of information about the chart and the area it covers.

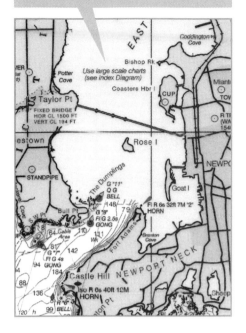

Lower Low Water" means that soundings show the water at its average lowest level relative to the datum. Next comes a table that summarizes water depths at six points on the chart. There follow a number of cautions and warnings about fish nets, buoys, and other possible obstructions or confusions. We then learn who is responsible for the chart. A note shows the symbol for the demarcation line between international and inland waters for determining applicability of the Rules of the Road. Below the label are two columns of information about hazards, storm warnings, aids to navigation, and calibration of radio beacons.

All this information does not always go in the upper left-hand corner, but it can be found somewhere on all coast charts and some harbor charts.

To the right of this section on the chart are a drawing showing when portions of this area were surveyed for the chart, a catalog of adjoining harbor and coast charts, lists of local weather forecasting and Loran-C electronic navigation systems, a distance scale (the average for this chart), and a reference to the previous edition of this chart when it was published under another number. Elsewhere, and repeated on the sheet, are the chart number and the date of the latest edition.

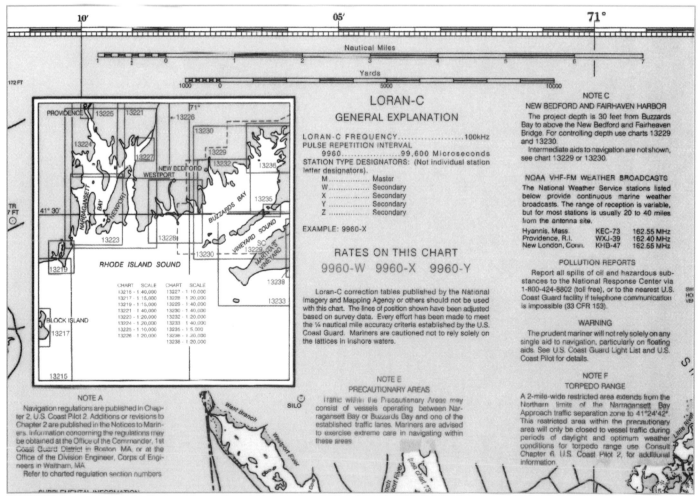

Charts include a chart catalog, a distance scale, information about weather transmissions and Loran-C electronic navigation, and clear warnings against becoming too dependent on individual aids to navigation.

Charts

Major landmarks visible from the water — including a flagpole, the north-westernmost of four spires, five radio towers, a stand-pipe, two towers, a cupola, and two bridges — are identified, as are roads, urban areas, piers, and railways.

The ink colors used on charts have been selected to provide the greatest contrast and visibility, particularly under the red lights usually used by navigators to preserve their night vision. Besides the red and green for buoys, the National Ocean Service uses six colors in several tints: gold for land, white for

Point Judith is surrounded by dangerous rocks that are awash (+) and rocks visible at low tide (*). Mud banks (behind dotted and scalloped lines) extend from shore. A partially submerged wreck (hull) lies approximately (PA) where shown. To its north lies an obstruction 3 feet down — the dotted circle indicates it's a hazard to navigation. A sewer pipe extends from shore. Only the lighthouse guards this dangerous point as an aid to navigation, but the pilot may take bearings on the gas or water tank on shore and the town (shaded area).

The buoys maintained by the US Navy for training have no navigational significance since they do not conform to the federal system. The wreck's depth of 85 feet has been determined by a sweep with a wire sounder (upturned bracket), and the long-ago date near the depth charge indicates that it's not a hazard. Since the garbage dumping ground is no longer used, you need not worry about barges being stationed over it.

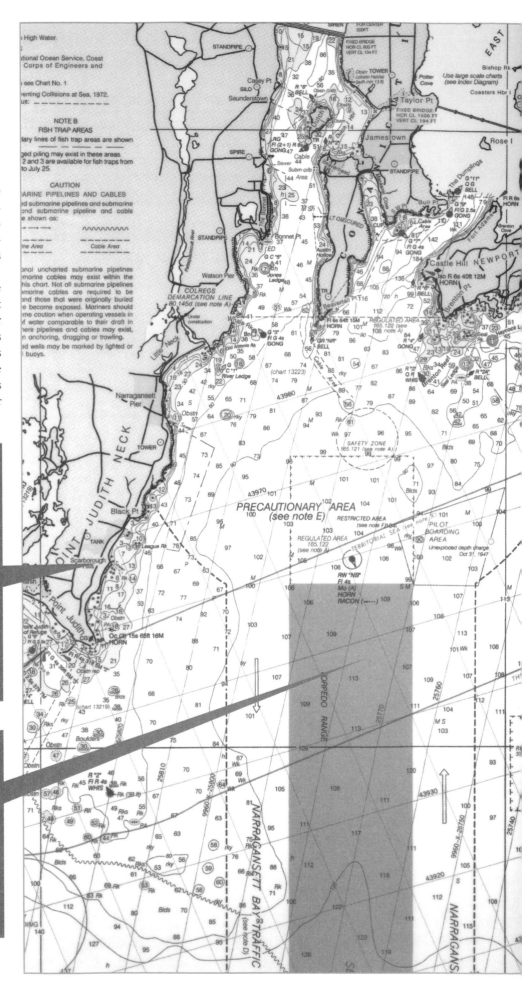

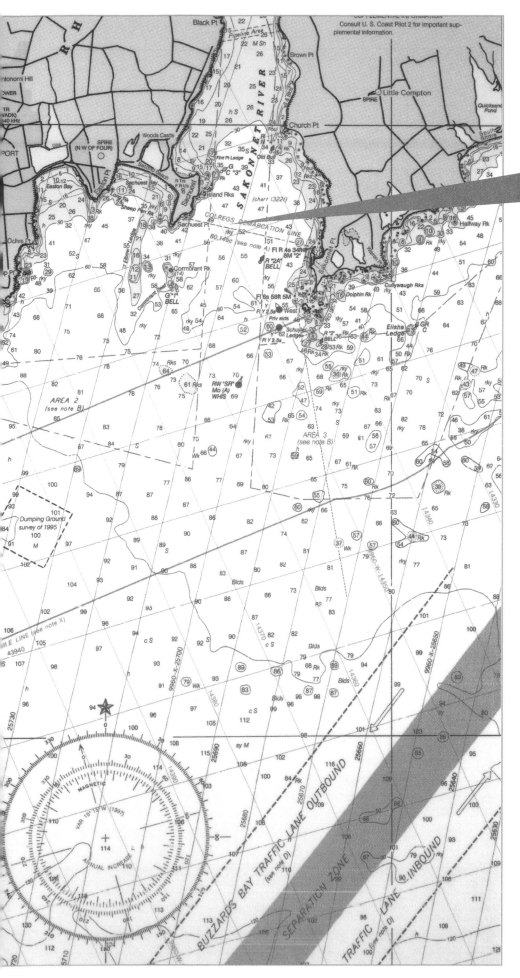

The entrance to the Sakonnet River is hazardous. Cormorant Rock surfaces at low tide (dots in broken line — shown green on a chart), and near it is a rock that is awash, or just under the surface (+ with dots). The most visible landmarks are the silo and radio towers (with fixed red lights) on Sachuest Point, the abandoned lighthouse off Sakonnet Point, and the flashing 4-second light in the 30-foot tower at the end of the Sakonnet Point breakwater (solid line east of bell R "2A"). The cove north of Sachuest Point is a good anchorage, since its bottom is sticky mud (stk); the rocky bottom (rky) of Sachuest Bay is harder for an anchor to grab. Bell R "2" off Sakonnet marks a shoal.

deep water, blue for shallow water or areas shown on other charts, green for land exposed at low tide and submerged at high tide, black for lettering, and purple for caution. Purple, which is especially bright under a red light, is used to indicate the lanes in traffic separation zones, government-regulated highways for ships entering and leaving Narragansett Bay and Buzzards Bay.

A dotted black circle around a presumed danger area shows where an unexploded depth charge has sat for many years. This cautionary advice should not deter any yachtsman from sailing in this area. Neither should the stark identifying label "Torpedo Range," which describes a navy training area. "Anchorage Areas" identifies three assigned general anchorages that are labeled on the chart and that conform to Coast Guard regulations. Notes printed on the chart and referring to labels on the chart ("Note A," "Note B," etc.) provide explanatory information. For example, Note A concerns an area where boats may not anchor around Noman's Land, the island under the western tip of Martha's Vineyard, where the military conducts target practice.

Charts

The black contour lines around the land indicate changes in depths. The contour interval is described on the chart, and some of the lines have numbers showing their depth. Contour intervals differ from chart to chart — the deeper the water, the larger the interval. Contour lines showing elevations of land on shore are drawn on harbor charts, whose large scale encourages such detail. Note how much attention is given to the type of bottom. This information assists in choosing an anchorage, since mud and sand bottoms are more secure than rocky ones.

The spider's web of lines and dashes on a chart is bewildering to new sailors. Here is a brief guide:

Black straight lines running across and up the sheet either parallel or at right angles are meridians of longitude and parallels of latitude.

Black curved lines, usually irregular and sometimes dashed, are underwater contour lines joining points of the same depth.

Fine blue, gray, yellow, and purple lines labeled with numbers are part of the Loran electronic navigation system.

Dotted purple lines define areas where caution should be exercised.

The gray line labeled "Territorial Sea (see Note X)" marks the junction between the American territorial sea and a contiguous zone — a distinction important in maritime law.

Finally, on portions of this chart are several circles that look like the faces of compasses. These are called compass roses, and they will play an important role in our discussion of the marine

You'll need a larger-scale chart to determine if Robinsons Hole is navigable by a deep boat. Because it and Quicks Hole are deep, narrow, and connect two bodies of water in an area where tidal range is large, expect currents to run fast.

A chart's compass rose shows true north and degrees (outer ring), magnetic north and degrees (inner ring), and the variation between the two.

Steep cliffs (vertical lines) run along the south shore of Noman's Land. The arc labeled "Lt Obscured" indicates that in that area the island blocks the Gay Head lighthouse's light. "Prohibited Area" indicates that nobody should anchor or sail in this area (the military conducts target practice on Noman's). The colorful names of some of the rocks ("Lone Rk," "Old Man") suggests that they have been hazards to navigation for many generations of mariners.

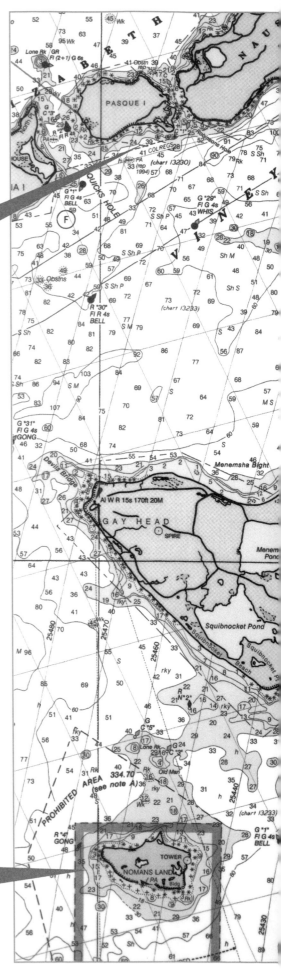

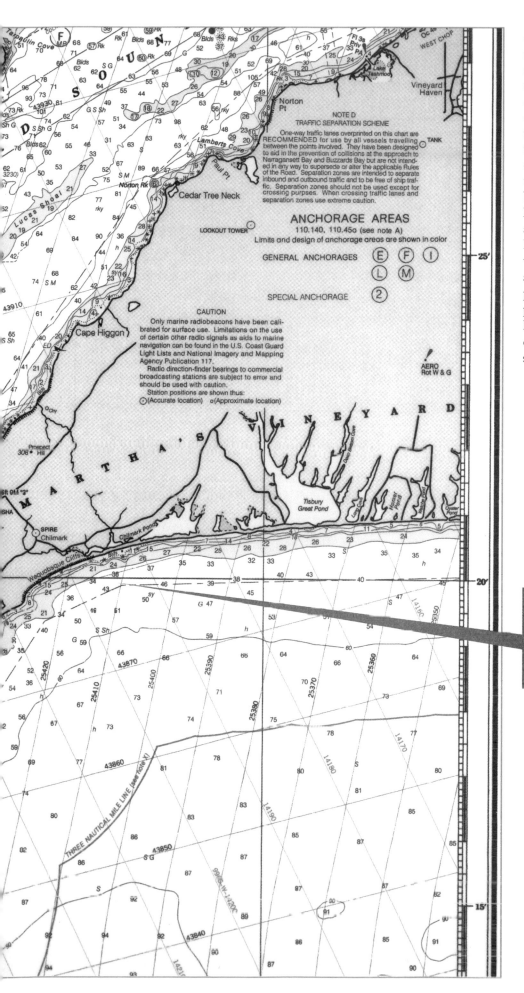

compass in the next chapter. Suffice it to say here that the outer of the two rings represents true, or geographical, directions, and the star indicates the direction of true (geographical) north, or the North Pole. The inner ring on the rose shows magnetic directions — the compass face as it is affected by the earth's magnetic field. The label inside the rose gives the difference in degrees between true and magnetic directions. By using the compass rose on the chart and the compass in her boat, the sailor has a constant reference point with which she can translate actual courses and bearings onto her miniaturized paper "sea," use them to calculate her position, and then convert them back to help her guide the boat safely. Without a compass, a compass rose, and a chart, the sailor in unfamiliar waters is lost.

Labeled fine lines are Loran-C time difference (TD) lines, heavy straight ones are meridians and parallels, and heavy irregular ones are depth contours.

Other Publications

Besides charts and chart catalogs, numerous government and privately published books cover every major sailing area. Most are available from chart agents.

Local Notice to Mariners is a weekly review of changes that affect navigation along waterways and shore fronts and in charts — for example, a shoal area caused by a recent storm or a change in a light's phase characteristics. Eventually this information will go onto a chart. While new editions of charts are published relatively infrequently, the US Coast Guard, other agencies, and nature herself are constantly at work, and *Local Notice to Mariners,* published by each Coast Guard district, reports on the effects of those labors. It is kept on file by chart agents, and subscriptions are available from local USCG district headquarters, whose addresses are listed in chart catalogs. This information also appears on USCG Internet sites.

The United States Coast Pilot is a series of nine books, published by the federal government and written for all mariners, that in considerable detail describes channels, anchorages, ports, weather, and hazards in almost all the waters covered by National Ocean Service charts. Each volume covers an area such as the Great Lakes, or Sandy Hook to Cape Henry. New editions are published annually or semi-annually.

Cruising guides are the commercial equivalent of the *Coast Pilot.* They are guidebooks to popular sailing areas like southern California, Chesapeake Bay, and the New England coast, and focus on a large number of navigational and housekeeping problems.

Tide tables and tidal current tables are essential aboard any boat in an area where there are tides. Tide tables list the times of predicted tide changes and high and low water for every day of the year and thousands of locations. Tidal current

A typical privately published tide table, in annual editions, provides times of changing tides and currents.

CURRENT TABLE
POLLOCK RIP CHANNEL, MASS.

Day of Month	Day of Week	MARCH				Day of Month	Day of Week	APRIL			
		CURRENT TURNS						CURRENT TURNS			
		NORTHEAST Flood Starts		SOUTHWEST Ebb Starts				NORTHEAST Flood Starts		SOUTHWEST Ebb Starts	
		a. m.	p. m.	a. m.	p. m.			a. m.	p. m.	a. m.	p. m.
1	W	7 21	7 49	1 33	2 06	1	S	9 04	9 49	3 12	3 58
2	T	8 18	8 52	2 29	3 08	2	S	10 15	11 01	4 20	5 06
3	F	9 22	10 01	3 30	4 15	3	M	11 25	. . . . .	5 27	6 09
4	S	10 30	11 11	4 35	5 22	4	T	12 06	12 30	6 31	7 07
5	S	11 38	. . . . .	5 41	6 26	5	W	1 05	1 27	7 28	8 01
6	M	12 18	12 42	6 43	7 25	6	T	1 58	2 20	8 21	8 48
7	T	1 19	1 41	7 41	8 19	7	F	2 45	3 07	9 10	9 33

Besides the relevant charts and tide tables, the *Coast Pilot* or a commercial cruising guide is essential to help you navigate along shore.

5. VINEYARD SOUND AND BUZZARDS BAY

Vineyard, is a prominent high bluff. It is marked by **Gay Head Light** (41°20.9′ N., 70°50.1′W.), 170 feet above the water, shown from a 51-foot red brick tower on top of the head. A lighted gong buoy is 1.6 miles northwestward of the light.

Devils Bridge is a reef making off 0.8 mile northwestward of Gay Head. The reef has a depth of 2 feet about 0.4 mile offshore and 17 feet at its end, which is marked by a buoy.

Nomans Land, about 5.5 miles southward of Gay Head, is a prominent, high, and rocky island. Except for a small section on its northwestern side, the shore consists of clay and gravel cliffs 10 to 18 feet high with boulders lining the shores. In the interior of the island are many hills, the highest over 100 feet high, with considerable marshy area between the hills. A **danger zone** surrounds Nomans Land. (See **204.5,** chapter 2, for limits and regulations.)

Several sunken rocks and ledges are in the pas-

on Juniper Point, a standpipe 2.2 mile of Nobska Point, a water tower and town, the cupola of the Woods Hole C ic Institution, and the buildings of t Marine Fisheries Service and the Marir Laboratory.

Channels.–Woods Hole Passage, a c tion through the northern part of V connects Vineyard Sound and Great Buzzards Bay, and consists of **The Stra** channel known as the **Branch** at the w The Strait, and **Broadway,** the southe to The Strait from Vineyard Sound. I the controlling depths were 8 feet midchannel) in The Strait, 11 feet in and 6 feet (12 feet at midchannel) ir The northerly entrance from Great The Strait is preferred over Broadv sharp turn, which is difficult in stro especially for low-powered vessels tables give the times, direction, and velocities of the current caused by tides (these are predictions; weather may affect tides and their currents). While these two tables are no longer published in book form by the National Ocean Service, they are available on CD-ROM. They cover the entire globe. Many local tide and tidal current tables are published privately.

Tidal current charts are graphic displays of predicted current direction and velocity. To make use of a chart, all you need to know is the time of day and the schedule of tide changes. The National Ocean Service publishes them in pamphlets, as do various commercial publishers.

The Light List, published by the US Coast Guard, is a roster of all the lighthouses and lighted buoys. It includes some information not usually given on charts — for example, the characteristics of seasonal buoys, lighthouse emergency

lights, and fog signals. There are six volumes in the series covering US coastal and inland waters, as well as the Pacific.

Pilot charts are unique maps of the oceans and seas that provide weather information for each month of the year. In graphical form, they describe the normal wind direction and strength, the frequency of gales and calms, the average water temperature, usual wave heights, and current direction and velocity. This information is essential to planning an offshore passage. Pilot charts are published by the government's Defense Mapping Agency.

Current charts are coordinated with times of tide change at reference stations. Arrows indicate the direction of the current, numbers show its strength. In areas like the one shown below, where the currents run hard, it's foolish to set a course without taking tidal current into account.

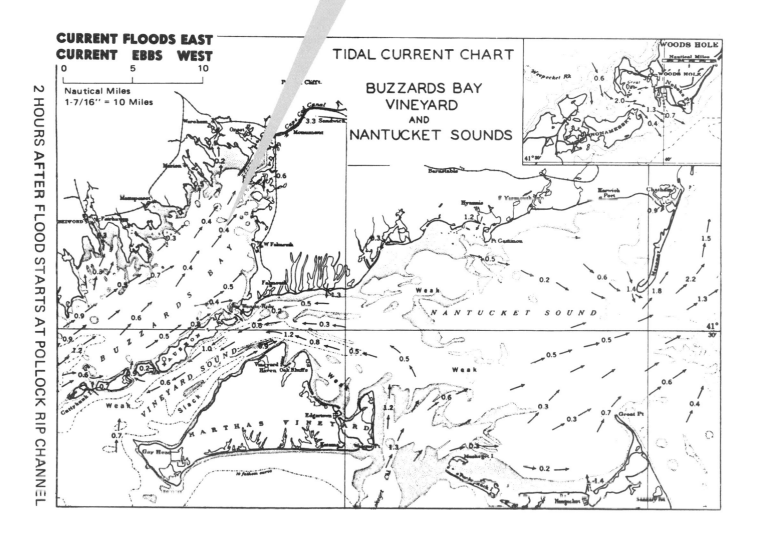

CHAPTER 10
The Magnetic Compass

In his definitive *Mariner's Dictionary,* Gershom Bradford defines dead reckoning as "the calculation necessary to ascertain the ship's whereabouts by using the courses steered and the distances run." The goal is to produce the **dead reckoning plot.** A series of dead reckoning positions marked on a chart during a passage, it's called "the DR plot" (or

The key piece of navigational equipment in any boat is the magnetic compass, which is essential for guiding the boat on a safe course as determined by the navigator. The compass also is the crucial tool for determining the boat's position in the absence of an electronic navigational device like GPS, the global positioning system, which uses signals from satellites in the sky.

Dead Reckoning. Even if the boat has GPS, positions displayed on the electronic device must be supplemented and checked using the compass and the traditional techniques of dead reckoning. A careful seaman never depends on a single system of navigation. So before discussing the compass itself, let's introduce the crucial navigational tool and concept of dead reckoning, which depends on the magnetic compass.

While dead reckoning certainly has nothing to do with death, there is some disagreement about what "dead" actually does mean. A few authorities believe it is an abbreviation of "deduced" because positions found by these skills are logically deduced from a set of facts. More likely, however, "dead" stands for "precise." When a boat sails directly before the wind, she is on "a dead run." When the wind blows over the bow, it is "dead ahead." In other words, a dead reckoning position is the most precise position for the boat that a navigator can come up with using the compass, the chart, and an estimate of the boat's speed.

Starting out at 10:00 AM, (A) this boat beats against a variable wind, tacking fraquently (B, C, D) to take advantage of shifts. Carefully noting the course and speed on the chart, the pilot keeps a dead reckoning plot of her progress by updating distance run on a given compass course. If the compass were wrong, this DR plot would be worthless.

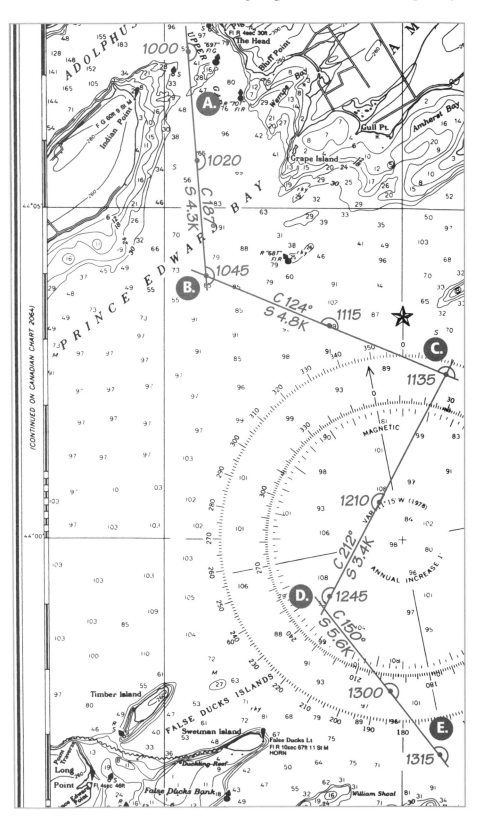

230

"DR") and is used in coastal piloting (navigation within sight of land and buoys and other aids to navigation), in celestial navigation (navigation far offshore using star and sun sights), and as a backup to electronic navigation. If you know what course you're steering, what the effect of tidal currents is, how long you've been underway, and how fast you're sailing, you can keep a DR plot and, with it, quite accurately chart your position over a period of time.

The compass is equally crucial when estimating and fixing your position using one or more cross-bearings taken on charted objects off the boat, like a lighthouse or a buoy. Bearings are compass directions. Where one crosses your course or another bearing, that is your estimated or fixed postion — which should be near your dead reckoning position.

No matter how you plot your boat's position, whether with GPS, dead reckoning, or cross-bearings, when you know it, you can then figure and steer the right course to your destination using the magnetic compass. The magnetic compass, then, is the *sine qua non* of navigation.

Magnetic North and the First Compass

For millennia before the development of the magnetic compass, seamen everywhere used natural phenomena as fixed references against which they measured their courses. The wind rose indicated wind direction for early Greek seamen, and Polynesians navigated by wave size and direction.

Ancient mariners realized that the firmament moved above their heads in repeatable patterns, and that certain constellations were reliable guides in certain seasons of the year. Seamen eventually came to depend on a star that never seemed to waver throughout the year: Polaris, the North Star. Actually the North Star is not exactly fixed, since it lies about 2° off to the side of the North Pole and so rotates around a small

radius. But few helmsmen can steer to within 2° of a course, even with modern instruments. So for many centuries courses were determined, sailed, and recorded in reference to this one almost fixed star over the top of the globe. As long as a mariner could see Polaris and knew what the angle of his course should be relative to it, he could find his way to his destination.

About 1,000 years ago, mariners began to measure their progress against another constant. This is the earth's magnetic field. A rock called lodestone, found in a region of Asia Minor, Magnesia, had long been known to attract metal. By the 11th century navigators were using it in the first magnetic compasses. A piece of lodestone or a sliver of iron that had been rubbed on it was placed on one end of a stick of wood in a pool of water. The stick then automatically oriented itself to the earth's magnetic field, rotating until the end supporting the rock or iron pointed approximately at the North Star, no matter where on the globe the compass was located.

This invention was revolutionary. With something on board that always points in the same direction regardless of the location, the boat's heading, the wind

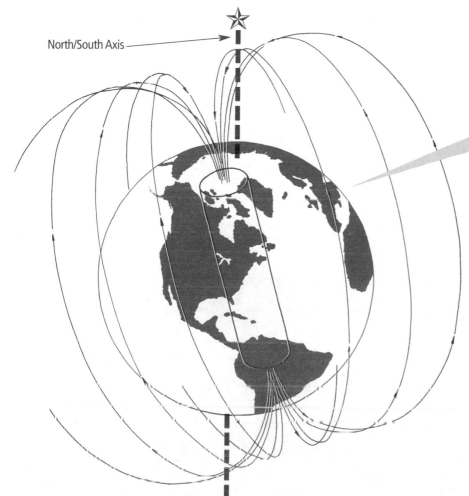

North/South Axis

The earth's magnetic field works as though a huge bar magnet lay at the core at a slight angle to the globe's north-south axis, with the bar's upper tip (magnetic north) slightly to the side of true north.

(Above) A primitive compass was a stick floating in a bowl of water and supporting a piece of magnetized material, which pointed at magnetic north.

Magnetic North and the First Compass

Magnetic North and True North

direction, the state of visibility, and other factors, a navigator has a fixed reference point. If you left, say, the north coast of Africa headed toward Sicily, and knew that Sicily was north of you, all you had to do was to keep the boat's bow pointed in the same direction as the needle. You would know that was north, even if clouds obscured Polaris, the sun, and the constellations, and even if you were unsure of the wind's direction. And if you knew that Italy was somewhere to the right of Sicily, you would aim to starboard of the needle.

Since the horizon forms a circle around a boat, the angles from the needle to these landmarks could be measured in fixed intervals, like slices in a pie, called compass point. The most important are the four cardinal points (north, east, south, and west) and the four intercardinal points (northeast, southeast, southwest, and northwest). The gaps between these eight points eventually were subdivided, making a total of 128. In time they were placed on a circular, floating compass card (or dial), which also contained the magne-

tized needle. Finally, the angles were broken down by degrees, of which there are 360 in a circle, and marked on the compass card.

The needle does not point exactly at geographical north. Rather, the needle is attracted to a locus of magnetism called magnetic north, which is slightly to the side of the North Pole. Just how far to the side varies with the earth's constantly changing magnetic field. Magnetic north is at approximately 74° north, 101° west, but it moves around slightly. Because the earth's magnetic field is constantly changing, the angle between the geographic North Pole and magnetic north, called variation, is in flux. The meridians of longitude on a Mercator Projection chart run straight up and down, parallel to the earth's axis between the two poles. But because of magnetic variation, the imaginary lines that aim toward magnetic north run at angles to the chart's edges.

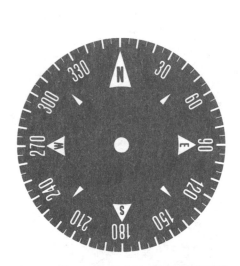

The compass card (dial) is divided into 360 degrees at regular, clearly marked intervals between the four cardinal points. The card shows only direction to and relative to magnetic north (right).

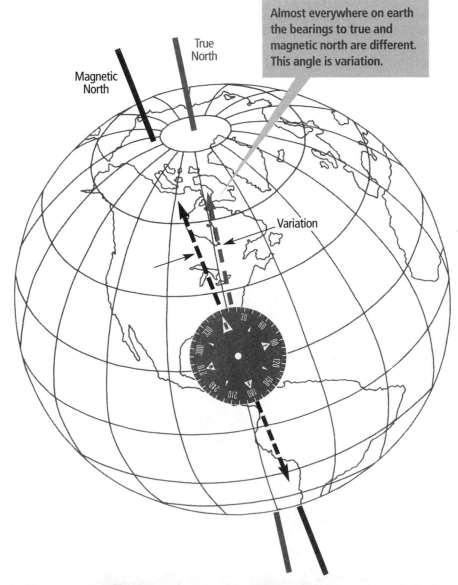

Magnetic North

True North

Almost everywhere on earth the bearings to true and magnetic north are different. This angle is variation.

Variation

Variation

Almost everywhere on the globe there is an angular difference between the bearing (direction) to true north and that to magnetic north. This angle is called variation. It is given in compass degrees east and west, and it changes as you move around the globe. In the United States, the coast-to-coast difference in variation is about 25°. The variation at San Francisco is about 17° east, meaning that, there, the bearing to magnetic north is about 17° east of the bearing to true north. At the same time, on the other side of America, at Annapolis, the variation is about 8° west.

Variation, again, is not fixed. In most areas variation changes by about 1 minute (1/60 of a degree) annually. This shift is indicated on charts on the printed compass rose, along with the variation in a recent year.

The chart's printed compass rose is a graphic representation of two truths. One — that there is one true direction against which all others are measured — has been imposed by geographers to help us understand our planet. The other — magnetism — has been imposed by our planet on geographers. The outer ring on the rose reflects the first truth. The star over 0° represents true north, the direction to the geographic North Pole. The 360 degrees in the compass circle are broken down into 1°, 5°, and 10° increments. A line drawn between 0° and 180° parallels all meridians, or lines of longitude, thanks to the distortion of the Mercator Projection and to geographers' decision that all meridians meet at the North and South Poles.

The inner ring reflects the second truth. It mimics the outer, true ring but is tilted the same angle as the local variation. This is the rose's magnetic ring. True north is not important on a boat unless you're steering by (aiming at) the North Star, or are using a small-scale chart that does not include magnetic roses because its coverage extends over many different variations. Some navigators plot courses and bearings on chart in true degrees after converting them from magnetic degrees, using a system that we'll describe later. But most prefer to use magnetic degrees in all calculations because those are what the boat's compass uses.

In fact, the only north that means anything on deck when steering or taking bearings is magnetic north, which brings us right back to the magnetic compass.

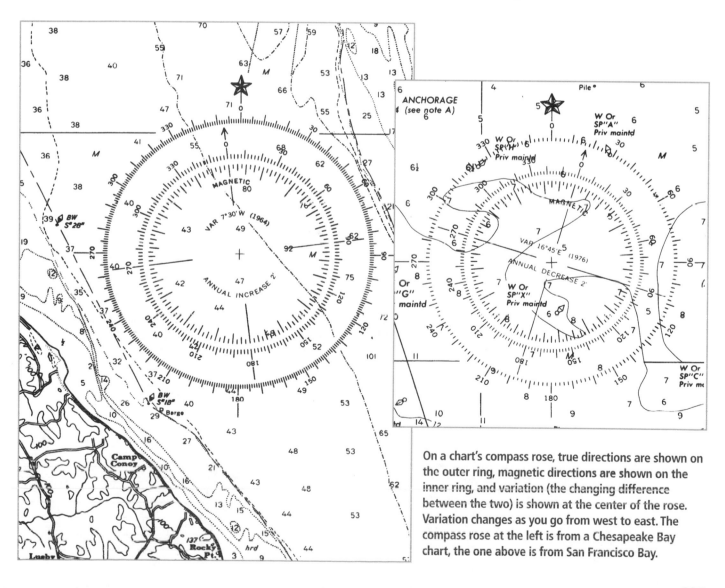

On a chart's compass rose, true directions are shown on the outer ring, magnetic directions are shown on the inner ring, and variation (the changing difference between the two) is shown at the center of the rose. Variation changes as you go from west to east. The compass rose at the left is from a Chesapeake Bay chart, the one above is from San Francisco Bay.

Parts of the Compass

The magnetic compass has changed considerably since the 11th century. Its heart is the aluminum compass card or dial, a circle around whose perimeter degrees are marked in even increments. The larger the card, the more detail is shown. Many pleasure boats use the relatively small 4-inch compass (the dimension is the apparent size of the compass card). Degrees usually are shown only in 5° increments, and labels are printed at 30° intervals (30°, 60°, etc.). Any more information would clutter the card and confuse the steerer (helmsman). The cardinal points are abbreviated: "N" for north, "E" for east, and so on. Intercardinal points — "NE," "SE," "SW," and "NW"— are sometimes shown at the 45° intervals of northeast, southeast, southwest, and northwest.

Before World War II, most compass cards were marked with the points of the compass. There are 32 "whole" points at 11¼° intervals, each of which contains a half-point and two quarter-points at intervals of 2¹³⁄₁₆°. Old-time sailors "boxed the compass" by memorizing all 128 of these points. "Northeast by east" (written "NE x E") meant as much to them as 56° does to us. "South by west one-half west" ("S x W½W") was how they indicated 197°. After World War II, the compass point system gradually gave way to the use of degrees, which was how the navy referred to compass directions. The half-points and quarter-points have little use today (though they're fun to learn). Still, the 32 "whole" compass points can come in handy. Since we have no trouble with the cardinal and intercardinal points (north, southwest, etc.), using the compass points in between should come easily, if we remember that a north northeast (NNE) wind is between northeast and north and that an east northeast (ENE) wind is between northeast and east.

At the center of the card or dial is a short vertical stick called the pivot post, which is used to help align the compass and to take bearings. On a ring around the card, but not touching it, are several other posts called lubber's lines. The number of lubber's lines depends on the compass, but there always are at least three of them, one at the forward side and two opposite each other at the left and right sides. The boat's heading or course is the number on the compass card under or next to the forward lubber's line, and bearings to objects dead abeam are shown by the side lubber's lines. The side lubber's lines may also be used as guides by helmsmen sitting either side of the compass.

On sailboat compasses there may be two other lubber's lines halfway between the side lines and the forward one. If the boat is headed due north, these intermediate lubber's lines will be over 45° (northeast) and 315° (northwest), and the side lubber's lines will be over 90° (east) and 270° (west). The intermediate lines are helpful when the steerer sits to the side of the compass, and when calculating wind direction, as most sailboats sail close-hauled at an angle of about 45° to the true wind.

So that the compass card stays level and can be read even when the boat is heeling or rolling, it is supported by gimbals. Picture a performing seal balancing a ball on its nose while it does flips and somersaults and you have an idea of the relationship between a pitching, rocking boat and her gimbaled

Anatomy of a Typical Marine Compass

Hemispherical Dome · Lubber's Line · Pivot Post · Compass Dial · Fluid Filled Chamber · Magnet · Jeweled Pivot · Gimbaled Supports · Expansion Chamber · Counter Weight compass. To dampen the motion of the gimbals, the compass dome is filled with a liquid — mineral oil or some other non-freezing solution. Rapid changes in temperature or air pressure will cause the liquid to expand or compress, leaving an air bubble under the dome that greatly obstructs visibility. For this reason good compasses have rubber expansion chambers in their base to compensate for changes in the liquid's density. An air bubble indicates that the compass is leaking oil and should be refilled through the plug on its bottom. (Do not fill the compass with water, which may cause rust.)

The hemispherical plastic dome protects the compass and magnifies the compass card. (The card on a 4-inch compass actually is half that diameter.) The dome should be kept out of the sun when not in use, otherwise it may yellow. When cleaning a compass dome, do not use an abrasive, such as sandpaper, cleaning powder, or a knife, which may scratch the surface irreparably.

The business part of a compass is out of sight. This is a set of tiny magnets glued under the compass card and surrounding the jeweled pivot that supports the center of the card. These magnets have a combined force that aligns the card with the earth's magnetic field,

In a typical 4-inch compass, degrees are shown in 5° increments, with heavier lines every 10° and labels at 30° intervals.

much the way the old sliver of lodestone did for the stick in the water. With the development of very lightweight metals, the weight of these magnets — and therefore the card — has been reduced considerably, thereby minimizing the friction between the card and the jeweled pivot. This is important for the mariner because the spin of a turning boat (transmitted through the pivot) has much less effect on the alignment of the card than previously. In older compasses the card would "lay" (drag or spin slightly) as the boat turned and continue to spin after she settled down on a new course. The newer, lighter, almost friction-free cards are more independent of the boat's motion. Jerks and swings are dampened by the oil under the dome and a counterweight under the pivot. There may also be adjustable compensating magnets in the compass's base or containing binnacle.

Fluxgate and Electronic Compasses. Other types of compasses have the added two advantages of offering digital readouts, which may be easier to use than compass cards, and of adaptability to GPS, radar, and other electronic instruments so that magnetic directions may be used in electronic navigation. One of these compasses is the fluxgate, another is the electronic compass. The fluxgate must be perfectly level to be accurate, and the electronic compass must be installed with special care. In some boats, these compasses are installed deep in the boat either on gimbals or remote from all metal, and then connected to readouts in the cockpit and navigator's station.

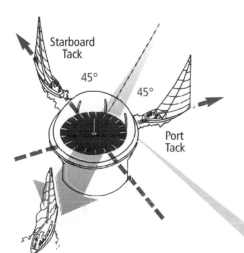

The forward lubber's line indicates the compass course.

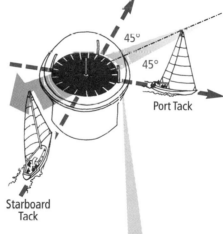

Side lubber's lines are used for beam sightings, as a reference when steering from the side of the compass, and (since most boats tack in 90° or less) to estimate the heading on an opposite tack when beating to windward, as shown.

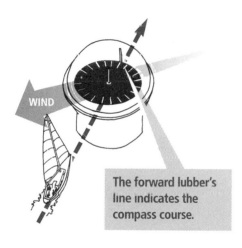

Intermediate lubber's lines are installed at 45° on sailboat compasses and are used to estimate tacking angles. If your boat is luffed directly into the wind, the intermediate lubber's lines will indicate the approximate courses on starboard and port tack.

Compass Types

Steering compasses are permanently mounted near the helm where steerers can easily see them. Most boats with steering wheels and many with tillers have a hemispherical, domed steering compass installed immediately forward of the helm in a base called a binnacle, which may be secured in a pedestal to which the steering wheel is attached. Binnacle compasses have hoods that protect them from sun and spray and red electric lights for illumination during night sailing, since white lights spoil night vision.

Otherwise, the steering compass is installed in a recess in the deck or the bulkhead that is the after side of the cabin. Deck compasses usually have low, flat domes, which, while they don't magnify the compass card as much as hemispherical domes do, offer little obstruction to feet and gear. Bulkhead compasses are hard to use when taking compass bearings.

Hand-bearing compasses are small, hand-held compasses with sighting lines or notches that allow the user to take accurate bearings (determine compass directions to objects) in order to fix the boat's position. While much smaller than steering compasses, they may be used for steering in an emergency.

Installation. Two important considerations when installing a compass are that it be square to the boat and visible to the steerer. The line between the pivot post in the center and the forward lubber's line must be exactly parallel with the boat's centerline, the imaginary line running fore and aft along the center of the deck and cockpit. Otherwise the course shown at the forward lubber's line will be different from the direction in which the bow is heading. The compass must also be installed forward of the steerer's normal station where it will not be screened by crew members, sails, or cushions. With a binnacle, the compass can be on the centerline. Otherwise, the compass must be set slightly to the side.

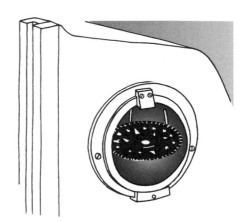

Boats without steering wheels often have their compasses recessed in the bulkhead on the aft side of the cabin. Taking accurate hearings over a bulkhead-mounted compass may be difficult because the whole card is not visible.

A quick, precise bearing can be taken with the compact hand-bearing compass.

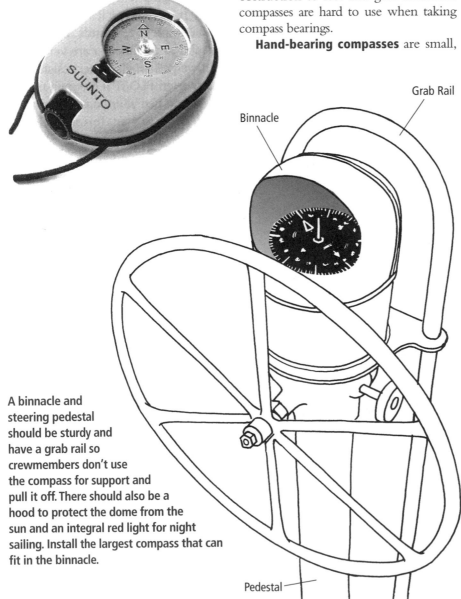

Binnacle

Grab Rail

A binnacle and steering pedestal should be sturdy and have a grab rail so crewmembers don't use the compass for support and pull it off. There should also be a hood to protect the dome from the sun and an integral red light for night sailing. Install the largest compass that can fit in the binnacle.

Pedestal

Compasses may be recessed in the deck to allow the steerer and crew to see them easily from either side. They should be placed so people don't trip over them.

Deviation

Once you've decided where to install the compass, identify and correct for deviation. This is error in the compass caused by nearby steel, magnetic, and electronic objects. Deviation may be caused by a steel object like an engine, fire extinguisher, or wrench, or by an electronic instrument with an amplifier (a magnet), such as a radar, radio, or loudspeaker. These objects must be installed at least 3 feet from the compass. Wires carrying electricity may also cause deviation unless they are twisted around each other.

Zeroing-In. The first step in correcting deviation in a new compass is to neutralize the effects of any binnacle compensators, which are small magnets in a binnacle adjusted with screws. Sometimes compasses are delivered with the compensators exerting some pull on the card magnets, throwing them off alignment. Zeroing-in identifies and corrects any misalignment. You will need a bronze, nonmagnetic screwdriver for this job and all other work around a magnetic compass.

1. Ashore, well away from any magnetic, iron, or steel object (including your wristwatch or belt buckle), screw the compass to a straight board with nonmagnetic (bronze or stainless-steel) screws. The edge of the board should exactly parallel the centerline of the compass (the imaginary line running from the pivot post to the forward lubber's line). Turn the board until the lubber's line is at north on the compass card. Slide a large book or another straight board against the compass board.

2. Holding the book in place with one hand, move the compass board away, rotate it 180°, and slide it back against the book. The lubber's line should be at south. If so, there is no error or the compensators were neutralized at the factory.

3. But if the lubber's line is not at south, there is an error. Make a mental note of it. For instance, if the lubber's line is at 172° (instead of south, or 180°), the error is 8° east. With a bronze screwdriver, adjust the compensators until you find the one that most greatly affects the card with the compass in north-south alignment. On most compasses, if there are two compensators they are labeled "north-south" and "east-west." With the lubber's line at the inaccurate south mark, remove one-half of the error. In this case, turn the "north-south" screw until the lubber's line is at 176°.

4. Realign the compass board and book, but this time with the lubber's line at south. Then reverse the board as above. If the lubber's line is exactly at north, the compass is zeroed-in on the north-south axis. If not, remove one-half of the error and reverse the board. Keep repeating these steps until there is no error at either north or south. If you can't eliminate all error, either the compass is defective or a magnetic object nearby is affecting the compass.

5. Repeat steps 1–4 for east-west alignment using the other screw.

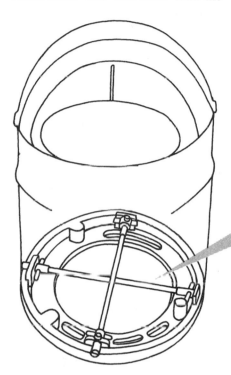

Magnetic compensators or adjusters are turned with screws to make compass corrections on the north-south and east-west axes. Use a bronze screwdriver.

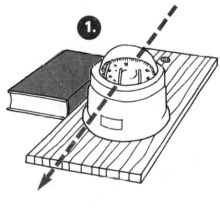

To zero-in a compass, screw it to a straight board and align the forward lubber's line with north (1). Using a book as a stationary reference, turn the board. If the lubber's line is not at south, take out half the error with the compensator (2). Repeat these steps until all error is removed, then turn the board and book on the east-west axis and repeat the process (3).

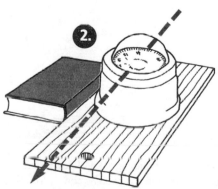

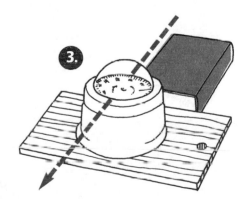

Deviation

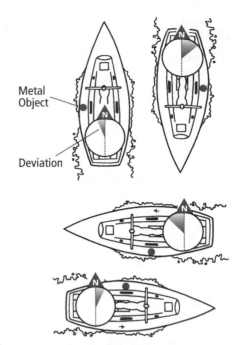

Metal Object

Deviation

A metal object set to one side of the compass may cause different amounts of deviation on different headings.

Swinging Ship. After the compass is zeroed-in, reinstall it in the boat. The next job is to find out if there is deviation, or compass error due to surrounding steel or electronic objects. The deviation should be eliminated or reduced by moving equipment or adjusting the compensators. And third, if the deviation is not entirely removed, it must be written down on a deviation card or table, which the navigator will refer to.

"Swinging ship" is the technique used to determine deviation. We recom-mend that you hire a professional com-pass adjustor to swing ship, adjust the compass, and fill out the deviation card. Names of compass adjustors are available in the telephone book and at local boat-yards and chandleries. But if you want to try to adjust your own compass, here's how you swing ship. The goal is to esti-mate the effect of the hull, engine, and fittings on the compass when the boat is on each of the four cardinal headings, north, east, south, and west. The reason for testing on all four headings is that a magnetic or steel object usually affects the compass differently on different headings (the exception is when the object is directly above or below the compass). You will need a bronze non-magnetic screwdriver.

1. Using a large-scale harbor chart, identify several ranges on shore. A range is a pair of fixed, charted objects that when lined up one behind another pro-vide clear, visible confirmation that you

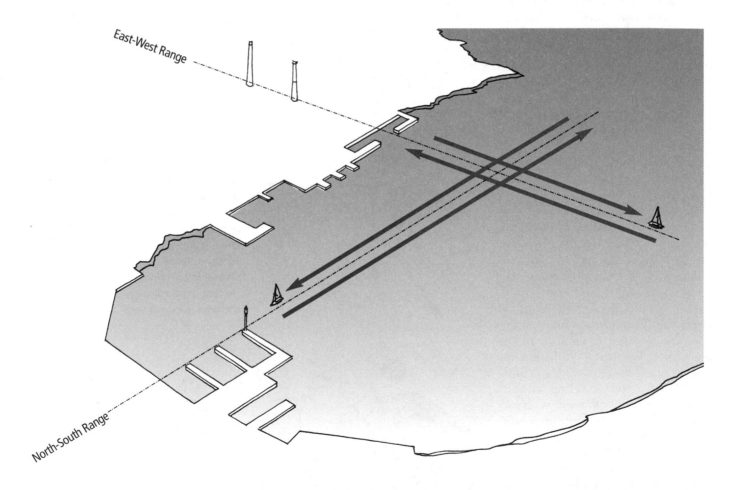

East-West Range

North-South Range

Swing ship by running up and down ranges on the east-west and north-south axes, comparing compass courses against the charted headings. Repeat the exercise under different conditions and with the engine and electronics on. If you have any doubts, hire a professional compass adjustor.

are on a given bearing. These should be shoreside landmarks in north-south and east-west alignments. One range might be a radio tower behind a flagpole, another a lighthouse in front of a water tower, a third the end of a pier ahead of a fuel tank. (Do not use buoys in a range since they move with the wind and tide.) At least one range should be suitable for testing easterly and westerly bearings, and another one should work for northerly and southerly bearings.

2. On the chart, draw lines through the ranges and calculate the two compass directions of each line, one from the water through the range, the other that first bearing's reciprocal (opposite) bearing, from the land to the water.

3. Get under way at a time when the tide is slack, the current is minimal, and the wind is light. A strong wind or current will push the boat off course while you're concentrating on being precise. Slowly proceed down the range lines under sail or power, first toward the ranges and then away from them. While the steerer keeps the boat accurately on the range lines, a crew member studies the compass and writes down any deviations from the calculated headings.

4. Using the bronze screwdriver on the compensators, try to remove the error one-half at a time for those headings closest to north, south, east, and west.

5. Make these runs with the engine and electronics (including running lights) both on and off to check for their effect, and at different angles of heel.

6. If deviation cannot be compensated, if it is considerably greater on one heading than on another, if it is greater than 3° for intercardinal headings (northeast, southeast, southwest, and northwest), or if you have any doubts about the effectiveness of your work, hire a professional compass adjustor.

If there is minor deviation, move any magnetic or steel objects near the compass. With all her gear, a sailboat creates her own magnetic field that will rarely be in alignment with the earth's. Sometimes one or more large metal objects — say, a stove or the engine — will create deviation on one heading that will be nonexistent on another. More often, deviation is caused by a steel tool or knife lying unnoticed near the compass. If the metal object cannot be moved, a commercial demagnetizer (available from electronic supply stores) can be used to neutralize it. Sometimes electric wires create a small, local magnetic field that causes compass deviation. If so, twist the positive and ground wires around each other to neutralize their effects.

Sun Azimuths. Instead of using ranges or known bearings to landmarks, professional compass adjusters frequently compare compass bearings with sun azimuths, or bearings to the sun. The celestial position of the sun and bearings to it from most points on the earth can be calculated from tables in the *Nautical Almanac,* an astronomical reference book used by celestial navigators. All the adjustor needs to know is the exact time and the boat's position. Azimuths are computed in true, rather than magnetic, degrees. To convert a true bearing to a magnetic bearing, subtract any easterly variation or add any westerly variation. The sun's magnetic bearing can be found by aiming the boat at it when it is low on the horizon and reading the degree mark directly under the pivot point's shadow. Since this is the opposite of the actual magnetic bearing, add 180° and compare the sum with the computed magnetic bearing.

Pelorus Bearings. A special sighting instrument called a pelorus can be useful when checking for deviation. It's like a hand-bearing compass except that the card is not magnetized and can be turned manually, and that an adjustable sighting arm is located around the perimeter. With the pelorus, a navigator or compass adjustor can take highly accurate relative bearings to objects.

First, turn the rose until the number under the forward lubber's line is the same as the boat's course. Then adjust the sighting arm to take a bearing on a charted object, read the bearing, and compare it with the bearing computed on the chart. The difference is the amount of deviation.

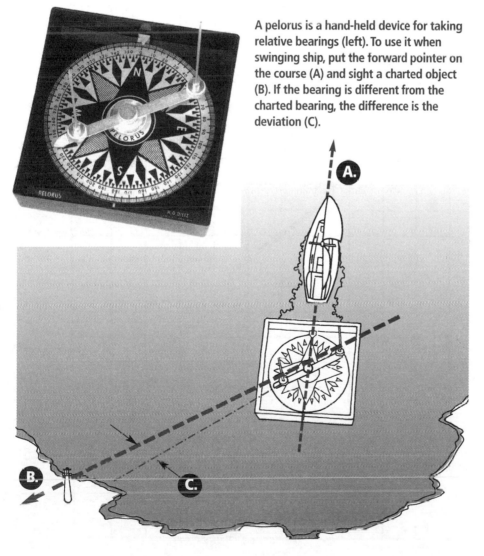

A pelorus is a hand-held device for taking relative bearings (left). To use it when swinging ship, put the forward pointer on the course (A) and sight a charted object (B). If the bearing is different from the charted bearing, the difference is the deviation (C).

Deviation

When to Swing Ship. You should check for deviation whenever your boat has been altered in a substantial way, including the installation of radar, new electronic devices, or a new engine. Magnetism is a curious phenomenon. For instance, a boat's own magnetic field may be altered simply by lying in an east-west plane during the winter. Or the compass may suddenly go out of compensation if the boat is struck by lightning. It's a good idea to establish a set of ranges in your home port and then check your compass against them once a year, after making sure the objects in the ranges haven't been altered or removed. If you have any questions or doubts, consult a professional compass adjustor.

Deviation Tables. If you or the compass adjustor cannot compensate the compass using the internal compensators, you must draw up a deviation table or card or install special magnets near the compass. The first step is often preferred. It's usually more satisfactory to know exactly what the old problem is rather than wrestle with a probable new chain of worries. A deviation table or card is a written record of deviation on different courses. The table should be posted near the navigator's station and any deviation will be added to or subtracted from calculated magnetic courses to produce accurate compass courses.

To use a deviation table *when converting magnetic to compass courses:*

1. Locate the desired magnetic course in the table — say, 45°.

2. In the table, determine the deviation for that course, interpolating if necessary.

3. If the deviation is westerly, add it to the magnetic course; if easterly, subtract. If the deviation is 2° west, the desired compass course is 47°.

Sometimes the navigator must convert compass courses to magnetic courses. For instance, on a course of 220° the steerer sees a buoy that bears 015°. The navigator wants to record the

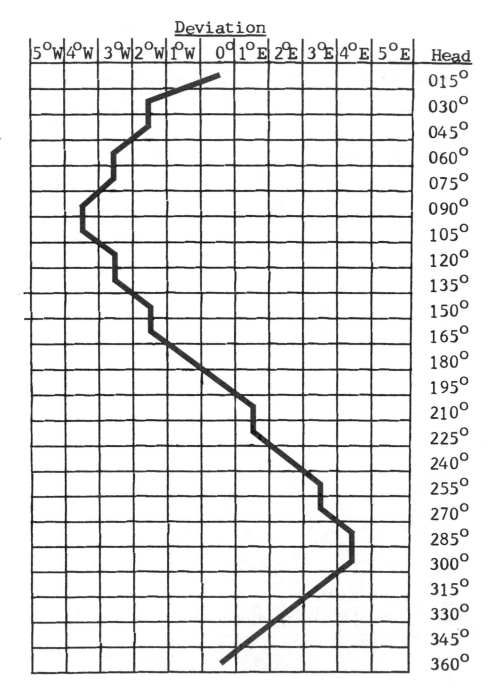

A deviation table or curve can be posted over the chart table to help the navigator determine courses and bearings.

bearing on the chart. The most important thing to remember here is that the amount and direction of deviation are determined by the course you're sailing, not by the bearing. So the deviation to be used in the calculation is 1° east, the one for a course of 220° (and not 1° west, the deviation for the bearing of 015°).

1. First, the navigator *converts compass degrees to magnetic degrees*. When going in this direction, the rule is add easterly error, subtract westerly error. Adding 1° to 220°, she arrives at a magnetic course of 221°.

2. She goes through the same steps to calculate the magnetic bearing to the buoy: 015° + 1° = 016°.

A deviation table or card may also be arranged either in a graph, with the course on one axis and the deviation on the other axis, or in nested compass cards. In the latter, a compass card or rose is cut out and placed inside another card. The outer one represents the cor-

rect magnetic compass, the inner one the boat's deviated compass. Lines between the two indicate the deviation as various courses.

Once you have a deviation card or graphic, keep the original and a backup photocopy on board. If the deviation is affected by heel angle or by electronic instruments in operation, make up separate deviation tables or cards clearly identified by their special application.

A deviation rose makes it easy to determine the course to be steered without making calculations. Glue one compass rose inside another and draw lines from the uncorrected magnetic courses on the inner ring to the corrected compass courses on the outer one. For example, steer 063° to make good 060° and 267° to make good 270°.

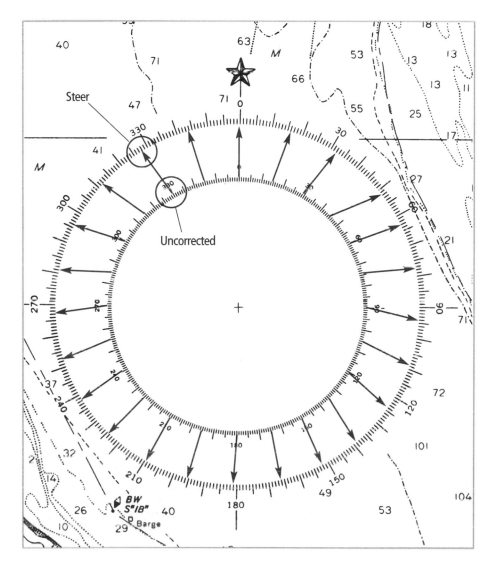

Correcting Compass Error

When we convert compass courses to magnetic courses using a deviation table or card, we are correcting a compass. But when we convert from magnetic to compass, we are said to be *uncorrecting*. The most correct course or heading is the true one, the next most correct is the magnetic course (after taking account of variation), and then comes the least correct course: the compass course, determined after adding or subtracting deviation. As we work away from true toward compass, we are uncorrecting. As we work back toward true, we are correcting.

Anybody doing celestial navigation uses true bearings and directions and later converts them into magnetic. And small-scale charts require calculations in true degrees for the simple reason that they do not have magnetic roses. With those few exceptions, true degrees and the true compass rose are abstractions for the navigator.

Still, correcting and uncorrecting to and from true degrees is sometimes necessary. There are several important rules

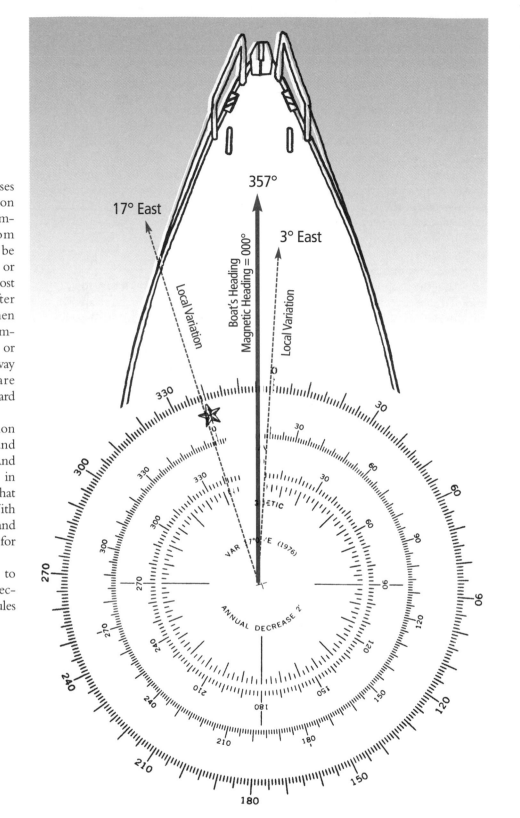

This diagram shows the relationship between true ("most correct"), magnetic ("less correct"), and compass ("least correct") degrees. The inner ring shows magnetic, the middle true, and the outer compass. The local variation is 17°, which means that the earth's magnetic field pulls magnetic headings 17° east (right) of true headings. The compass deviation at this heading is 3° east, which means that the boat's own magnetic field pulls compass headings 3° east (right) of magnetic headings. Therefore, when the compass reads 357°, the boat is sailing on courses of 000° magnetic and 017° true. These calculations may be done mathematically following the rules of thumb "correcting, add east" and "uncorrecting, east is least."

of thumb. We've already mentioned two of them:

1. *When correcting (from compass to magnetic to true)*, easterly errors are added, westerly errors are subtracted.

2. *When uncorrecting (from true to magnetic to compass)*, easterly errors are subtracted, westerly errors are added.

The rule is summarized in an easily remembered bit of doggerel:

Correcting, add east.

Uncorrecting, east is least.

Earlier we converted both ways using variation and deviation errors. Here's another example:

On chart 5142 (San Pedro Channel), the true course from the middle entrance of San Pedro Bay to the Fl 4sec whistle buoy is 147°T (true). We know that local variation is 14°40' east. We also know that our boat's compass has 4° west deviation on the course she is on.

First we must determine which of the two rules of thumb applies. We are converting from true to magnetic to compass course, which means that we are uncorrecting — working away from the most correct course. "Uncorrecting, east is least." So we subtract east variation and east deviation, and add west variation and west deviation.

One computation problem: we cannot use an electronic decimal calculator to solve this problem unless we convert minutes into fractions of degrees. Since 40' is two thirds (.67) of 60', the decimal equivalent of 14°40' is 14.67°. To solve this problem with a calculator:

147.00° T (true course)
-14.67° variation
132.33° M (magnetic course)

Now convert 147° to a more usable number: 146° 60'. Then:

146° 60' T
-14° 40' east variation
132° 20' M (magnetic course)

Next the magnetic course must be uncorrected with the deviation. Which rule applies? We're still uncorrecting, working away from true, so "Uncorrecting, east is least" is our guide. The deviation is westerly, and therefore it's added:

132.33° M (magnetic course)
+ 4.00° west deviation on this course
136.33° M (compass course)
or 136° 20' M (compass course)

Communicating a Course Change. After the course is calculated, the navigator says to the steerer, "steer one-three-six." The steerer acknowledges by repeating, "one-three-six," and alters course. When the course is reached, the steerer reports, "one-three-six," and centers the helm to hold that course. The navigator acknowledges, "one-three-six," and in the log book writes the time (using the 24-hour clock format), the speed, and the course: "1525, San Pedro Entrance, 6 knots, change course to 136°M for Fl 4sec whistle."

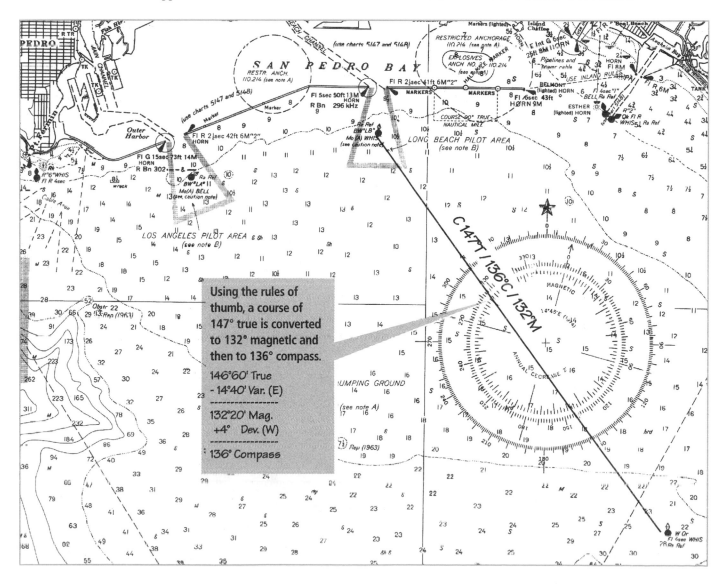

Using the rules of thumb, a course of 147° true is converted to 132° magnetic and then to 136° compass.

146°60' True
- 14°40' Var. (E)

132°20' Mag.
+4° Dev. (W)

136° Compass

Correcting Compass Error

This means that at 3:25 PM the boat cleared the entrance, and at a speed of 6 knots altered course to 136°, headed toward the buoy.

To some people, this sequence of verbal repetitions of the course and the written log entry may seem unduly militaristic. But having so many checks and double-checks makes it almost impossible for the steerer to steer the wrong course. The written record allows the crew to backtrack if they get into trouble later on. In time these routines become habitual. Most piloting errors are caused by careless memories and communication, not lack of technique.

The "Timid Virgins" Rule. We have just followed a logical process that is summarized in the foolish statement "Timid Virgins Make Dull Companions." The first letters of each word stand for True, Variation, Magnetic, Deviation, and Compass, which we calculated in that order:

"Timid" = 147° true course

"Virgins" = 14° 40' east variation

"Make" = 132° 20' magnetic course (true° − variation° = magnetic°)

"Dull" = 4° west deviation

"Companions" = 136° 20' compass course (magnetic° + deviation° = compass°)

HANDS ON: Steering by the Compass

Turn the boat until the desired course is directly under the forward lubber's line. The compass card will appear to move as the boat turns, but in fact the card is stationary and the lubber's lines are in motion. Once she's on course, the boat will unavoidably make minor swings to either side as she heels, pitches, rolls, and is nudged by waves. To compensate for these swings, bring her back to course by pushing the tiller in the opposite direction or turning the steering wheel in the same direction.

If you are sitting to the side and can't read the number under the forward lubber's line easily, use a side lubber's line after subtracting or adding 90° or 45° from or to the compass course.

Do not stare at the compass. The lubber's line and card will quickly mesmerize you and you'll lose all feel for the boat and probably wander off course. Rather, glance periodically at the compass and try to sensitize your body to the tug of the helm and the angle of the wind when the boat is on course. A reliable steering technique is to steer by (be guided by) a landmark on shore or a star in the sky that corresponds to the correct compass course. Regularly check the landmark or star against the compass. Very few steerers are good enough to keep a boat to within 2° of course in smooth water; in rough weather, steering errors of 5–10° are common. If conditions force the boat off course for more than a few minutes, notify the navigator. The steerer should not make arbitrary course changes, no matter how good the reasons for them may be, without consulting the navigator, checking the chart, or evaluating the consequences of the change. This is especially true in unfamiliar, tricky waters and in periods of limited visibility.

Every boat has her own steering characteristics. Dinghies, racing boats, and light-displacement boats will readily yaw, or wander off course. By the same token they may be easily brought back to course with a minor helm change. Heavy boats with long keels have excellent directional stability, which means that it will take muscle to turn them. This also means that a heavy boat must usually be oversteered to initiate a course change, and that the helm must be checked before she has reached the new course so she does not keep swinging. Only experience will tell how quickly or slowly she will maneuver.

Remember that no boat can be steered unless she has steerageway. Slow-moving, heavy boats steer ponderously. Rapidly moving light boats maneuver quickly unless the rudder is too small. Don't expect any boat to respond promptly if she's just drifting along at 2 knots.

The letters are reversed for correcting, leaving the silly saying "Companions Dull Make Virgins Timid."

The logical order is:

"Companions" = compass course

"Dull" = deviation (add if east, subtract if west)

"Make" = magnetic course (compass° ± deviation° = magnetic°)

"Virgins" = variation (add if east, subtract if west)

"Timid" = true (magnetic° ± variation° = true°)

Remember that when correcting — working from compass to magnetic to true — "Correcting, add east."

Steer at the object or use a hand-bearing compass when taking important or difficult bearings. Otherwise, cut bearings over the cockpit compass using the edge of your hand. Take three bearings, average them (throwing out erratic ones), and remember them with care.

HANDS ON: **Taking Bearings**

One of the essential skills of piloting is taking accurate compass bearings on landmarks and aids to navigation in order to fix the boat's position. The most reliable way to take a bearing is to aim the boat right at the object and then read the heading at the forward lubber's line. Since this usually takes her off course, sailors instead take most bearings over the compass.

To take a bearing using a built-in compass, stand behind it facing the object — a buoy, a landmark, or another boat. Close one eye and extend a hand sideways, little finger down, over the compass dome, pointing at the object. This sighting hand should be directly over the pivot post. Now read the bearing on the compass card on the far side of the pivot post and under your little finger. With practice you should be able to cut a bearing (as this procedure is called) with an accuracy of 5°. If a lubber's line lies under your sighting hand at a 90° or 45° angle to the boat's heading, the accuracy should be even better. Remember that the bearing is the compass direction toward the object sighted. The reciprocal bearing, which is 180° different, is the compass direction from the object.

When cutting bearings:

1. Be sure that you have an **unobstructed view** of both the compass and the object you are sighting.

2. **Remove your watch** or other ferrous or magnetic objects.

3. **Keep your "cutting" hand straight and vertical.**

4. Before reading the compass, **sight down your hand** to guarantee that it's aimed directly at the object.

5. **Take three bearings and average them.** In rough or foggy weather, you may have to discard any bearings widely different from the average. Reliable bearings will fall within 5° of each other.

6. To avoid memory lapses, **remember the bearing as a three-digit number** (35° should be remembered as "zero-three-five degrees") followed by the name of the object ("red nun number 4," "nearest tower," "large green bell," and so on). Keep reciting the bearing and the object's name until they're written down.

7. When recording bearings in the ship's log or a notebook, **include the time of the sighting and the reading of the distance log,** a mechanical device like an automobile's mileage gauge. The log entry might read, "1135 hours, Annapolis entrance green flasher number 1 bears 330°, log 221.4 miles."

Bearings may also be taken with hand-bearing compasses, which are easy to use but may not be compensated. If there is any error, be sure to correct it before logging the bearing.

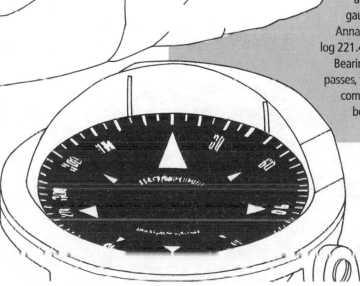

CHAPTER 11

Plotting and Position Finding

Coastal piloting is the art and science of finding your boat's position and calculating safe courses near land using the navigation aids and tools described earlier: buoys, lighthouses, charts, and the magnetic compass. In this chapter we'll see how these and other aids and tools help the navigator (pilot) accomplish three crucial tasks — plotting the dead reckoning position, calculating courses to be sailed, and plotting positions using compass bearings and lines of position.

The navigator's main responsibility is to know the boat's position while keeping her from running aground on the shore (sometimes called by sailors "the bricks," "the flats," or "the beach," depending on local geology). There have always been tricks for helping to keep a boat in deep water. Old-time sailors favored "barking dog navigation" and "potato navigation." In the first, keep sailing until you hear a barking dog on shore, then change course quickly and abruptly. In the second, heave potatoes

ahead and when you no longer hear a splash, turn even more quickly and abruptly. Those quirky navigation skills are behind us, yet the occasional sailor still carries a sounding pole slightly longer than the keel is deep and posts a crewmember on the bow to poke the bottom.

Most sailors would prefer to know that land is looming well before it can be reached with a potato or a stick, and so they rely on more sophisticated tools

and skills, the most advanced of which today are electronic positioning devices. GPS (Global Positioning System) and Loran-C can provide a quick, accurate fix of the boat's position.

But no seaworthy navigator ever relies on a single system of navigation. Electronic equipment sometimes is inaccurate or unreliable, and for that reason it must be regularly checked against the traditional piloting concepts and disciplines that we will describe here.

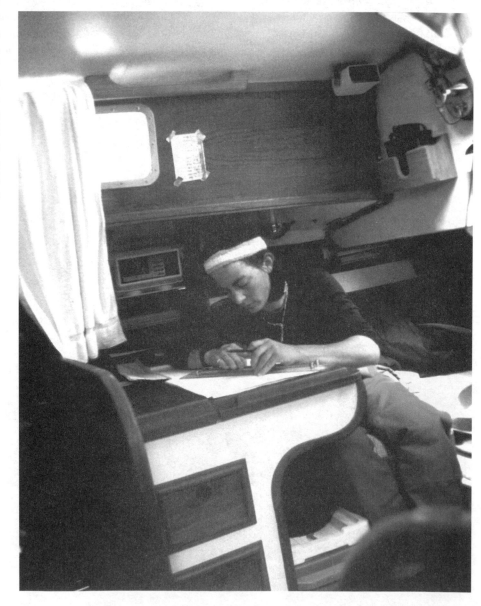

A good navigator's station does not have to be large or complicated. The navigator should have a comfortable, secure seat and be able to easily see and work with all her tools and instruments without disruption. If the station is like this one and near the companionway, communication between the navigator and the cockpit crew is clear and quick.

A Navigator's Tools

A navigator's basic kit, stored in a chart table or drawer, should include the following:

Charts for all areas you are likely to visit, including harbor charts for all ports that you might possibly call at in case of emergency. Charts are best stowed flat or rolled with their numbers and areas of coverage clearly noted on their backs and corners. Or use a chart book covering the areas where you sail. Carry the most recent editions.

Reference books for the area, including tide tables and tidal current tables and charts for saltwater areas for the current year, plus the *Coast Pilot,* the *Light List,* and a commercial cruising guide.

A log book for recording the vessel's business.

A small notebook and scratch paper.

Pencils (plenty of them) plus erasers and a sharpener. At least one pencil should be red so you can emphasize important features, such as a lighthouse's range of visibility.

A fine-tip pen for marking changes to aids to navigation on charts.

A stopwatch or wristwatch with a stopwatch function.

Binoculars, either 7 x 35 or 7 x 50. Any magnification greater than 7 restricts field of view and causes sighted objects to jump around excessively in rough weather. The second number indicates the size of lens; the larger, more expensive 50-mm lens gathers more light than the 35-mm lens. Binoculars encased in rubber are less susceptible to damage if dropped. Binoculars should be handled carefully with the strap around the user's neck, and should be stored, preferably in the cabin, in sturdy cases. Clean the lenses with eyeglass tissue and fresh water.

An electronic calculator. Some manufacturers market programmed (or programmable) calculators specifically for navigators and pilots. Stow the calculator in a box or plastic bag with a gel sack to absorb moisture.

A protractor for measuring angles on the chart.

Dividers for measuring distances. Dividers are similar to a drawing compass except that both legs are pointed. (A **drawing compass,** helpful in other ways, can be used, but the pencil may mark up the chart.) Some dividers have crossed legs so they can be adjusted with one hand.

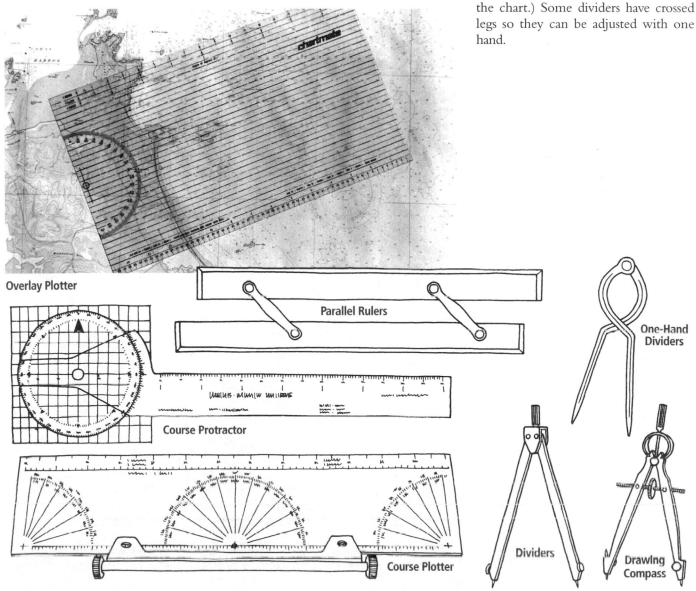

Overlay Plotter

Parallel Rulers

One-Hand Dividers

Course Protractor

Course Plotter

Dividers

Drawing Compass

A Navigator's Tools

A plotter is used to mark bearings or courses on the chart. There are several types of plotter. Every pilot and navigator prefers one type and swears by it. With each, the chart is spread out with geographical north at the top.

One of the most popular types, parallel rulers, consists of two plastic or wood straightedges linked and held parallel by metal hinges. It allows the pilot to transfer courses and bearings between the chart's compass rose and other parts of the chart. After the original alignment is made, the rulers are "walked" across the chart by alternately spreading and bringing together the straightedges, keeping one straightedge immobile while the other is moved. This way, a line can be drawn at one corner parallel to a line at another corner. The surface under the chart must be absolutely flat and the pilot must have plenty of elbow room so that the rulers can be walked across the sheet without losing parallelism. Some navigators prefer to use two draftsman's right triangles instead of parallel rulers, laying their hypotenuses against each other and then sliding the triangles in turns across the chart to transfer bearings and courses.

A disadvantage with parallel rulers and triangles is that their reference point must be a compass rose on the chart, which often is far from the line to be measured. This is why some navigators like to mount on the chart table a draftsman's drawing machine, whose long arms make an easy job of transferring bearings.

Another type of plotter is a combination straightedge/protractor called a course protractor or course plotter. It transfers courses and bearings using as a reference not the compass rose but the chart's latitude-longitude grid. A straightedge is laid over a parallel of latitude or a meridian of longitude — which on Mercator charts run exactly east-west and north-south — in order to determine true directions or bearings of courses or bearings. Then a device like a compass rose on the plotter is adjusted to the local variation to indicate the magnetic directions.

The following equipment found elsewhere in the boat will also help produce accurate DR plots and fixes:

A compensated magnetic compass in the cockpit and another at the navigator's station below.

A hand-bearing compass for taking accurate bearings.

A reliable depth-sounding device

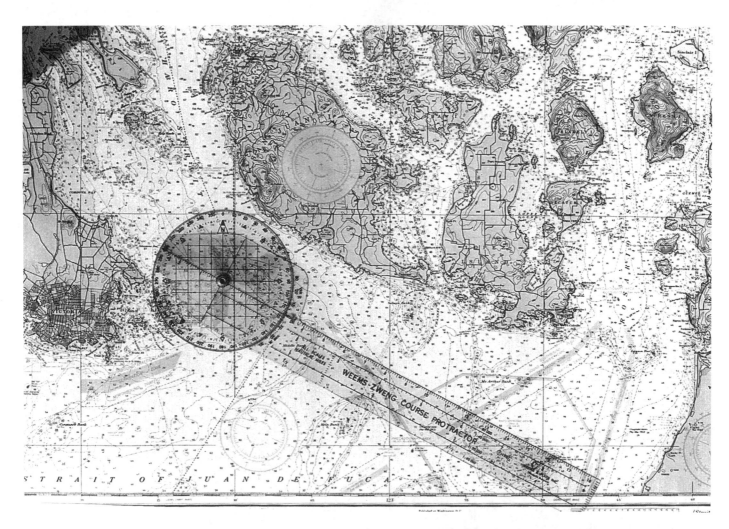

The course protractor is laid over the latitude-longitude grid rather than the compass rose. You must adjust either the protractor or your calculations for variation.

that determines and displays the depth of water under the hull. Today the most commonly used sounder is electronic and shows depths in graphic or digital displays. A readout in the cockpit gives the steerer quick warning of shoal areas, while a repeater readout below is visible to the navigator.

An electronic speedometer, preferably with an odometer or distance-run indicator. A repeater readout below assists the navigator. You may not need a speedometer if you carry a good GPS or Loran-C instrument, which calculates and displays speed and distance.

A reliable, accurate timepiece.

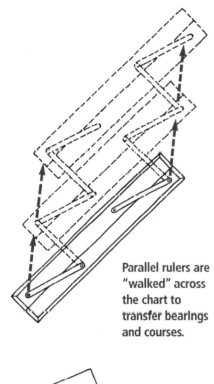

Parallel rulers are "walked" across the chart to transfer bearings and courses.

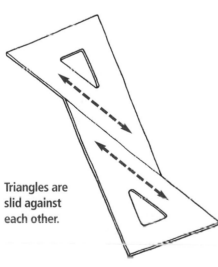

Triangles are slid against each other.

Magnetic or True?

Once she has chosen her tools, every new navigator must make an important decision about using them. Should calculations be made in true degrees or in magnetic degrees? There are good arguments on both sides, with all authorities agreeing that once you choose a style, you should stick with it.

The experts who recommend making all calculations in true degrees generally are offshore celestial navigators who use true degrees when computing azimuths before eventually "uncorrecting" from true to magnetic to come up

with a compass course. You may also choose to use true degrees if you are using small-scale charts that do not have magnetic roses (due to the frequent changes in variation over their vast area), or if you enjoy the convenience of using the latitude-longitude grid as a reference for your course protractor.

On the other hand, few coastal navigators, sailing within sight of land, ever take a sun sight, and the only bearings they take are over the card in a magnetic compass. Most plotters work as well with the compass rose as with the grid.

And most important, if a pilot uses magnetic degrees, she'll be computing in the same language that the steerer uses. Piloting is complicated enough without two meanings of the word "degree." This is why we prefer to use magnetic degrees throughout. The one irreducible constant on a boat is that "north" on the compass card will aim at magnetic north.

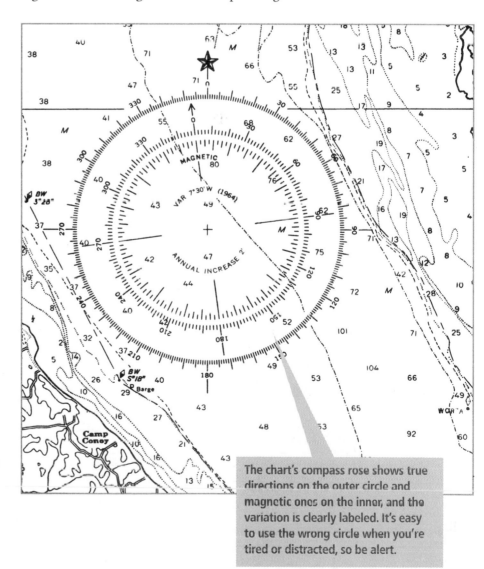

The chart's compass rose shows true directions on the outer circle and magnetic ones on the inner, and the variation is clearly labeled. It's easy to use the wrong circle when you're tired or distracted, so be alert.

The Log Book and SOP

The log book or log is the boat's official diary. It's a written record of the boat's progress and events, with notations for courses, speeds, and other important navigation information. By referring to this written record, the navigator can double-check calculations as well as backtrack out of difficult situations. The log is a handy place to record weather observations such as barometer readings and wind directions and velocities so the crew can keep track of and anticipate long-term weather developments. The log book also serves as a communication medium between sailors standing different watches who may not have another opportunity to

This is a page from a log book that the author designed, *The Norton Boater's Log*. Note the columns for navigational information and weather, the blank column for data of temporary concern, the large spaces for weather and comments, and the easily read graph form for recording barometer readings.

HANDS ON:
The SOP (Standard Operating Procedure)

Although most of us take to the sea to shed shore-side routines, we must accept the fact that system and procedure play an important role in piloting. In the short run, taking every step the same way and with the same routine will save time and worry (especially when exhaustion crimps the memory). In the long run, establishing and following a standard operating procedure (SOP) will guard against mistakes and perhaps a disaster. The busy world of a sailboat is a greenhouse for Murphy's Law. Consider, for example, how difficult communications can be in the noise of wind and waves. Instructions and reports about courses and bearings must be clearly enunciated by the speaker and just as clearly acknowledged by the listener.

"The greatest hazard to navigation is a bored navigator," observes Hewitt Schlereth in his excellent piloting manual, *Commonsense Coastal Navigation*. Carefully observed procedures minimize the opportunities for tedium and mistakes. Never make a calculation without consciously considering all relevant factors. They include variation, deviation, tide, current, leeway (side-slippage), the skill of the steerer, the eyesight of the person who took the bearing, the possibility of confusion between sighted objects — and, perhaps most important, the clarity of instructions and other communications among the crew. When providing a course for a steerer, be as clear as possible. Explain the factors that went into your calculations; otherwise he may think it is his responsibility to compensate for, say, leeway and arbitrarily alter course.

Checking and plotting the dead reckoning position regularly is an important SOP, even when the GPS seems to be behaving well. In fine weather and open, familiar waters, every 60 minutes may be sufficiently frequent, but if the conditions are challenging and the waters unfamiliar, you should check at 30-minute or even 15-minute intervals. The faster you're sailing and the more ground you're covering, the more frequently should you check. Calculations should be done on paper, preferably in a special notebook, and positions should be clearly marked with a pencil on the chart and in the log book along with the times.

In the log book, note course and weather changes and the appearance or passing of key buoys or landmarks. If you make a mistake in the log or when doing calculations, don't erase them or throw the paper away. Just cross them out with a line so they are still legible; your "mistake" may turn out to be correct. Keep in mind the chance that you (or somebody else, in case you are incapacitated) may have to backtrack through your plot and calculations if the boat gets lost.

In addition, describe in the log any unusual or potentially dangerous occurrences in the unlikely event that you're involved in a Coast Guard inquiry, and log all radio transmissions.

Night sailing especially requires a routine. The skipper or navigator may ask to be awakened whenever another boat is nearby or when the course or wind changes. And the pilot should carefully brief the crew about upcoming hazards, buoys, and course changes, especially in restricted visibility. The navigator's job is a specialized one but not sacred. He or she should never feel above explaining it to shipmates.

FROM Catalina   TO Santa Barbara
DEPARTURE DATE May 11   ARRIVAL May 12
CREW JR
Leah R.
Chuck Hawley
Charlie Barn

DATE	TIME	GIVEN COURSE	COURSE STEERED	SPEED	LOG	engine hours	WEATHER	COMMENTS
5/11	0800	095°	095	6k	0	1,100	foggy, calm	- clear harbor under power
	0845	330°	335°	7k	0	1,101	"	- set sail; cut engine
	1000	330	335	7k	8	—	Wind W, 10k	
	1100	335	335	7.3	15	—	" " 12k	fast reach in clearing weather.
	1200	335	335	7.5	23		building; spray	- sun's out!
	1400	335	335	8	31		Wind WSW, 12k	- lunch — Chowder and capsize pie!
	1600	335	339	7.8	55			15k
								- reef at 1530

BAROMETER   0900   1200   1400   1600

30.2/1023									
30.1/1019									
30.0/1016									
29.9/1012									

TIDES
High: 0838
Low: 1850

alert their shipmates to problems such as damaged gear and nearby ships. In legal proceedings, the log is an official document admissible as evidence.

Besides serving as the official record book of a cruise, the log is a handy agent of morale building. Here is where the crew can make observations about informal events on board — for example, a good joke or a tasty meal.

THE DR

The dead reckoning position (the DR) is where the pilot thinks the boat is located based solely on the boat's distance run over a known course. The dead reckoning plot, also called the DR, shows a boat's progress over time from dead reckoning position to dead reckoning position. No bearings — taken either with a compass or an electronic device — are required for a DR. This is where the DR differs from the estimated position and the fix. If there is a single

bearing on a charted object, where it crosses the boat's track is the estimated position (EP). If there are two or more bearings, where they cross is the a fix. While an accurate fix or estimated position is desired, it often is not attainable because each requires one or more cross-bearings, which are not always available.

Until then, there is the DR — your best estimate of your position based on the undisputed facts at hand. The DR has the unique virtue of being derived solely from data available on the boat herself, right in front of the pilot's eyes: course, speed, and distance run.

Distance Run. To compute distance covered or run, you need to know how fast the boat has been going for how long. If you sail at 5 knots for 45 minutes, you can quickly calculate that you have covered 3.75 miles. If the boat has a sum log (a distance-run dial, like an automobile's odometer), then the math

may already be done for you. Just read the dial when you start out and read it again when you want to know where you are. But sum logs often are inaccurate, especially in waves when they record the boat's vertical as well as horizontal travels. This is where keeping track of speed and time do the job.

A simple way to determine distance run is to time how long it takes to run a known distance between two charted objects (A and B) and keep going at the same speed for an equal amount of time. Then plot the next DR (C).

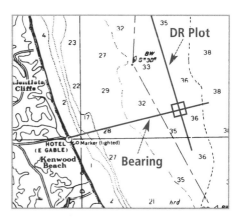

The estimated position (square) is the crossing of a single bearing and the dead reckoning plot.

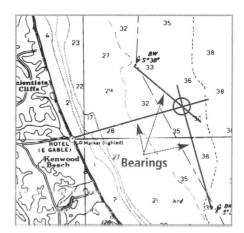

The fix (circle) is the crossing of two or more bearings. It is the most reliable position.

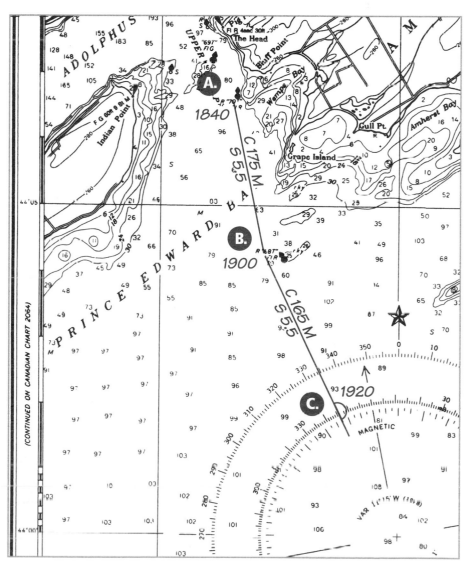

251

The DR

When you start out or pass a charted object or make a fix, note and log the time. When you want to make a DR plot, note the time again and factor it against the speed. Since knots are based on 1-hour increments (a knot is 1 nautical mile per hour), these calculations will be simple if the time intervals are in multiples of 6 minutes, which is ⅒ of an hour — for example, 18, 30, and 54 minutes. You also need to know your average speed during that time interval, and that calculation may itself be fairly complex.

Determining Speed. The average speed used by the pilot is often the steerer's estimate of the average of the readings on the boat's speedometer or the GPS or other electronic navigation device. But sometimes the boat may not have a speedometer, or if she does, it may not be trustworthy. (Speedometers may be less accurate at very low and very high speeds than at moderate speeds between 4 and 8 knots, and like any electronic device they are vulnerable to malfunctions.)

A steerer who knows his boat well can estimate speed about as accurately as a speedometer once there is another frame of reference. One is hull speed, which we discussed in chapter 1. Hull speed (a displacement boat's maximum speed) is equal to the square root of the waterline length in feet, multiplied by 1.34. A boat with a waterline length of 25 feet has a hull speed of 6.7 knots. She may exceed it when pushed by big waves, but that is about the fastest she will sail. At hull speed, a boat sails in the hollow between two waves, one at the bow and the other at the stern. The hollow extends between the bow and stern along the windward side. But if there also is a crest about amidships, the boat is moving at approximately one-half hull speed; if there are two crests, she's moving at about one-third hull speed. Therefore, if you know your boat's

waterline length, you can estimate speed by looking over the windward side and counting the waves alongside at the waterline.

Another frame of reference for speed is the appearance of the passing water. We started the 1972 Transatlantic Race from Bermuda to Spain with a broken speedometer. We measured our boat's speed by timing how quickly she passed objects that we threw into the water at the bow. Soon the helmsmen's estimates of speed were so accurate that our DR was extremely close to positions determined by the sextant.

We used the Speed/Time/Distance formula for measuring speed: To find speed (S), multiply distance (D) by 60, and divide the product by time in minutes (T); or

$$S = \frac{60 \times D}{T}$$

For example, let's say that your boat is 30 feet long. When her bow is directly alongside a buoy, start the stopwatch. As soon as the buoy is alongside the stern, stop the watch. It takes this boat 3 seconds to clear the buoy. The problem can be stated this way: "If it takes 3 seconds for a boat to go 30 feet, how fast is she sailing?" Here's the solution:

**T (time) =
3 seconds = ³⁄₆₀ minute = .05 minute**

**D (distance) =
30 feet = ³⁰⁄₆₀₇₆ (nautical mile)
= .005 nautical mile**

Therefore,

$$\frac{60 \times .005 \text{ mile}}{.05 \text{ minute}} = \frac{.3}{.05} = 6 \text{ knots}$$

If the distance is in statute miles, the speed will be in miles per hour, and if the distance is in nautical miles, the speed is in nautical miles per hour, or knots. A knot is 1.15 statute miles. (The speed is usually called a "knot," although before the 20th century mariners also said "knots per hour.")

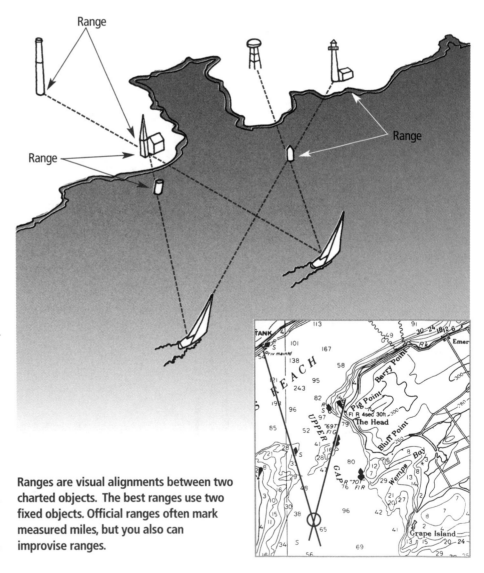

Ranges are visual alignments between two charted objects. The best ranges use two fixed objects. Official ranges often mark measured miles, but you also can improvise ranges.

Any measured distance may be used to determine speed. You may run between ranges shown on charts or between two buoys or lighthouses a known distance apart This calculation is more accurate using fixed objects, since buoys swing about on their anchor rodes, but whatever objects are used, they must be indicated on the chart so you can calculate the distance and course between them.

The Coast Guard and other agencies have erected ranges to indicate measured miles at various places along the coastline. The ranges and the true course along the measured mile are shown on charts. When running a measured mile, start your stopwatch at the first range and stop it when you reach the second range. Be sure to sail the indicated course in order not to go too far. If it takes a catamaran 4 minutes 22 seconds to run 1 mile, calculate speed as follows (after converting seconds into decimals):

$$S = \frac{60 \times 1}{4.37} = 13.7 \text{ knots}$$

Measured miles and other known distances can be helpful in other ways. Auxiliary sailboats and powerboats can run them at several RPM settings to provide data for a speed table. Combined with fuel consumption figures — which can usually be calculated with an accurate fuel gauge — you can determine optimum fuel-efficient cruising speeds. In every boat there is a point at which increased throttle brings only a small jump in speed along with a large leap in fuel consumption.

In salt water, be sure to add any favorable current (in knots) or subtract any contrary current to find the speed made good. We'll say more about current in the next chapter.

You may also use the logarithmic scale printed on many nautical charts to solve for speed when running over measured distances. Place one divider point on miles run and the other on minutes run, then lift the dividers without adjusting them and place the right point on 60. The left point will show the speed.

Determining Distance. Once you know your boat's speed and the time she has been underway, you can move on to calculate the distance run. The Speed/Time/Distance formula can be used, this time solving for distance. Let's assume that our boat has been averaging 5.5 knots for 35 minutes. What is the distance run? Use this version of the Speed/Time/Distance formula:

$$D = \frac{S \times T}{60}$$

Here, enter these values: speed (S) = 5.5 and time (T) = 35. Therefore,

$$D = \frac{5.5 \times 35}{60} = \frac{192.5}{60} = 3.2 \text{ miles}$$

Again, you can use the logarithmic scale printed on many charts.

Steering the Course. For the DR you must be able to chart the direction in which the boat has sailed since the last plot or fix. Since no boat can stay precisely on course for very long, this is necessarily an average of all the small meanders. Only the steerer can tell you what that average is. Unfortunately, the natural human desire to please often gets in the way of an honest report, and the steerer may simply parrot back the course that the navigator told him to steer. This course may not be the accurate average because of steerer error, wind shifts, obstructions, or other factors. The skipper and navigator must strongly encourage helmsmen to be truthful in their reports. A 6° mistake will put the boat off course by 1 mile every 10 miles.

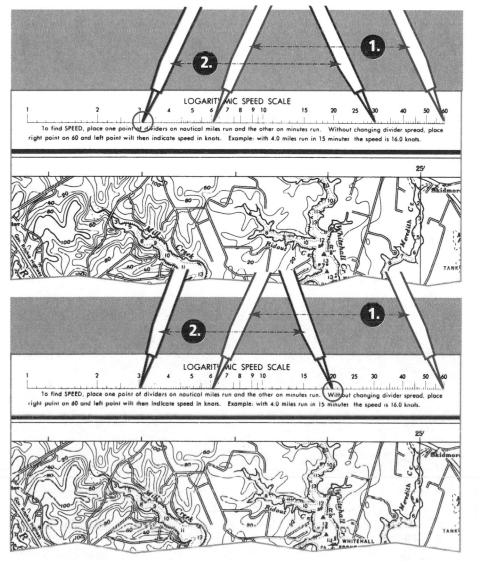

A chart's logarithmic scale can be used with dividers to solve for speed, distance, or time underway. Instructions are printed under the scale. To solve for distance, place one point on 60 (1) and the other on the number corresponding to speed, then lift the dividers and, without adjusting the spread, move the right point to the time intervals and read the number under the left point (2). To solve for time, place one point on 60 and the other on speed, then move the left point to the distance.

The DR

Plotting. When the distance run and course are known, the navigator can plot the DR from the last DR or the last fix. If using parallel rulers, she lays one straightedge over the course on the compass rose nearest to her position — being careful to use the inner, magnetic rose. Then she "walks" the rulers across the chart until a straightedge lies over the last position. The navigator draws a light line from the position approximately the distance the boat has run. If she's using a course protractor, the navigator makes certain that the correct amount of variation has been added or subtracted before turning the arm to the desired course. Then she aligns the protractor with a meridian of longitude or a parallel of latitude, with the arm over the last position, and draws the line. (On Great Lakes Polyconic projections, use only the center meridian on the chart as the others are slightly curved.)

Plotted courses are labeled with the direction in degrees and the average speed. The direction goes above the line, the speed below. For example, the steerer reports an average course of 165° and an average speed of 5.5 knots. The pilot converts the compass degrees to magnetic, if necessary. (If there is no deviation, the compass course is the same as magnetic.) The label reads:

$$\frac{C\ 165\ M}{S\ 5.5}$$

"C" stands for compass course, "M" for magnetic degrees, "S" for speed in knots or MPH. If there is deviation and the navigator has not corrected it, "C"(compass) replaces "M." Likewise, if true degrees are used, "T" is used in place of "M."

Now we know the direction of the course line and can plot the distance run, here 3.2 miles. Two distance scales are available on the chart. One is on the chart's margin; it shows the average of all

distance scales on the chart. Place the right leg of the dividers on 3 and the left leg on the .8 point on the tenths scale, to the left of 1. The dividers now span 3.2 miles at the chart's average scale. Lift the dividers and place one leg at the departure point and the other leg on the course line, where a small pencil mark is made. Enclose the mark in a half-circle

arcing above the line. Label the arc with the time in the 24-hour clock, without the word "hours." For example, 1910 is 7:10 PM and 0940 is 9:40 AM.

The other, more accurate distance scale is the latitude scale on the sides of the chart. Be sure to use the latitude directly alongside the course line you are measuring. On Mercator and Polyconic

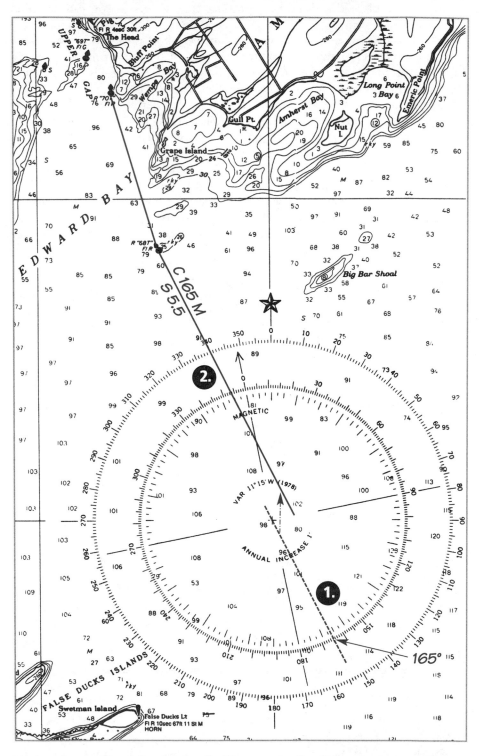

To plot a course, (1) use the plotter to find the compass direction on the rose and (2) transfer it as a parallel line running through the departure point, labeling it. Reverse the steps to find the direction of a course already plotted.

charts, latitude increments vary from the top to the bottom of the chart.

If the distance measured is greater than the span of the dividers, set the dividers at 5 or 10 miles and "walk off" the distance, keeping track mentally. The last bit may be less than the 5- or 10-mile increment, so may be measured on the margin scale.

Now print "D" and the distance to the right of the "S" notation below the course line.

A DR plot will look like this:

$$C\ 165\ M$$
$$\overline{}$$
$$S\ 5.5\quad D\ 3.2$$

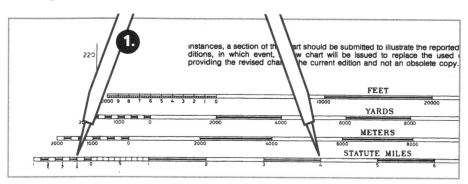

To plot the distance on a plotted course, (1) spread the dividers over the distance using the chart's margin scale (above) or the latitude scale (below) and (2) transfer the distance to the chart with one leg on the departure point. Label the DR.

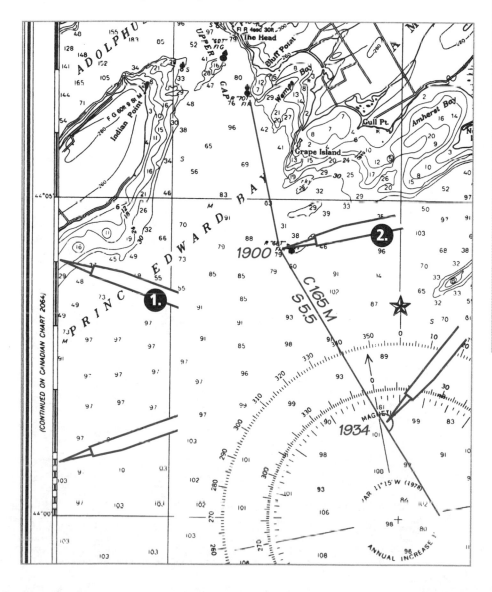

The DR

Choosing the Speed. Occasionally a navigator must calculate how fast (or slow) to go in order to reach the destination. For example, he may want to arrive at a channel before the tide becomes unfavorable or after it becomes favorable. In those cases he wants to know the optimum efficient speed.

The 6-minute rule can be used to quickly solve this problem. For instance, in 48 minutes the strong tide becomes favorable at a narrow channel 5.5 miles ahead. That means that you want to arrive no sooner than 48 minutes from now, since if you get there when the tide still runs against you, you're wasting time and energy. What should your maximum speed be? Using the 6-minute rule, the navigator first divides 48 by 6 to get 8, which he divides into 5.5. The result, 0.7, is the distance he must cover every 6 minutes, or 0.1 hour. The optimum maximum speed, then, is 0.7 x 10, or 7 knots. The Speed/Time/Distance formula also works, solving for Speed (S) as shown earlier.

"Running Out Your Time." Sometimes you'll need to know how long it will take to cover a known distance at a known speed. Our old friend the Speed/Time/Distance formula can be used to solve this problem. In this case, you solve for Time (T):

$$T = \frac{60 \times D}{S}$$

For example, heading out of a Maine harbor in a dense fog, the navigator takes her departure from (passes) a buoy at 1032 hours (10:32 AM) and sets a course for another buoy 4.1 miles distant. Anticipating that she will never be able to see the second buoy through the pea soup fog, she wants to know how long it will take to reach the buoy at a speed of 6.3 knots. She uses the Speed/Time/Distance formula to solve for time:

$$T = \frac{60 \times 4.1}{6.3} = \frac{246}{6.3} = 39 \text{ minutes}$$

It will take 39 minutes to cover the distance.

Adding 39 minutes to 1032 hours, the navigator determines that the boat will pass the second buoy at 1111 hours (11:11 AM). (The chart's logarithmic scale can also be used to solve for time.) By running out your time, you may hopscotch from buoy to buoy without even seeing them. Experienced navigators use stopwatches when running out their time in poor visibility, when an error of a few seconds can be dangerous. An example of this method is the way that submarines avoided underwater shoals in the book and film *The Hunt for Red October.*

Speed/Time/Distance Calculators. If you lack the interest or mathematical confidence needed to tackle these formulas, buy a Speed/Time/Distance calculator at your chandlery. This is nothing more than an old-fashioned circular slide rule. In addition, some electronic calculators have been programmed to solve these problems with the push of a couple of buttons.

"Running out your time" is an excellent tactic for staying in the channel and making turns at buoys in poor visibility. Figure how long it will take to run the distance, keep track of the time with a stopwatch, and steer a straight course.

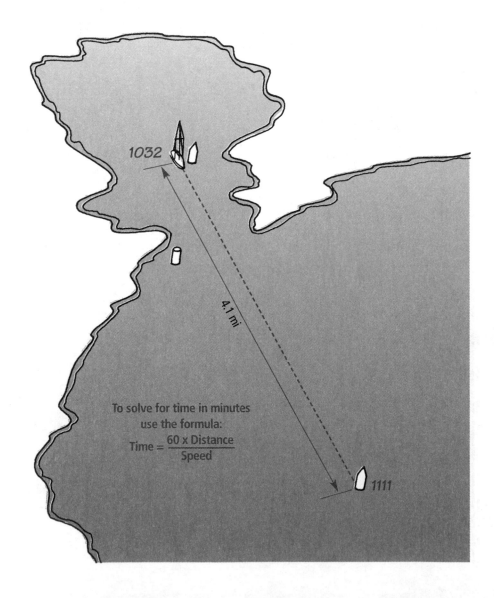

1032

4.1 mi

To solve for time in minutes use the formula:
$$\text{Time} = \frac{60 \times \text{Distance}}{\text{Speed}}$$

1111

Setting the Course

When the navigator figures the course from the present position to the destination, he lays the edge of the plotter between the two points, and using the chart's compass rose, computes its magnetic angle. This is called the rhumb-line course or track (abbreviated TR). The navigator tells the steerer to sail the TR and, presumably, the boat eventually reaches her destination without deviating from it.

That, at least, is what happens in the best of all possible worlds when the steerer steers with pinpoint precision and when there are no natural forces pushing the boat to one side or another of her TR. But this is rarely the case. Waves, wind, tidal current, leeway, and steerer error can pull or push the boat far off the TR. Very rarely can a TR longer than 5 miles be set without the need to compensate for one or more of these forces.

Besides establishing the TR, the navigator must estimate what these forces will be and how to compensate for them. The job has at least four considerations:

1. The navigator must precalculate a compass course that takes natural forces and errors into account.

2. While the boat is underway, he must plot a DR based solely on speed and heading.

3. When possible, he must estimate the boat's position based on single bearings.

4. And when possible, he must fix the boat's position by crossing two or more bearings.

While this may seem complicated, actually it's quite simple. Between fixes — the most reliable type of position determination — the navigator keeps track of the boat's position using the DR and estimated positions, and constantly reevaluates the course, making corrections as necessary. As we saw earlier, the DR is important because it's based on the only known indicators sitting right there in front of the navigator's eyes: the

boat's course and the boat's speed, which when factored against time compute the distance run. The estimated position (EP) is a continuous check on the DR until a fix can be taken. And all courses and positions are plotted relative to the TR, the straight line between the departure and destination.

The major forces are leeway, steerer

The DR plot is a pictorial account of the boat's progress between fixes based on regular DR (half-circle) and EP (square) plots and positions.

error, and current. When calculated with the track, they produce the course made good (CMG) — the course that the boat effectively sails. These forces are relatively simple to calculate. Sometimes they take the form of an angle and at other times they are shown as vectors, or force arrows.

Leeway is side-slippage due to the wind and waves pushing against the windward side. If a buoy that you expect to see on your leeward side appears on the windward side, you are making leeway. While keels, centerboards, and rudders absorb or redirect

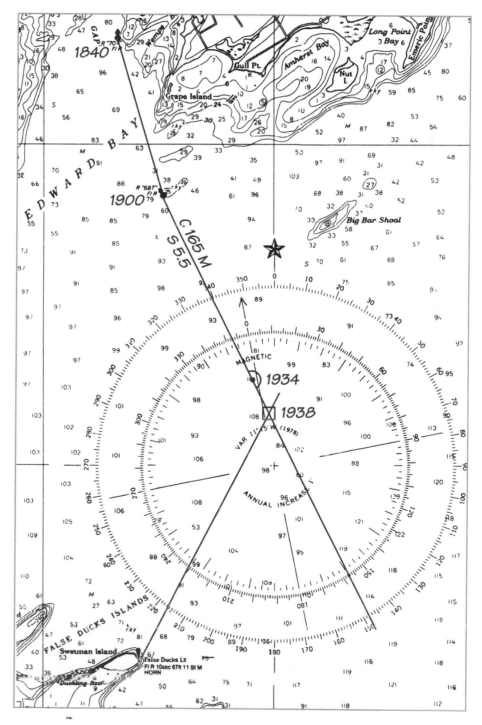

Setting the Course

most of the side force, there usually is some leeway. It ranges between 2° for highly efficient racing boats sailing in smooth water to 20° for cruising sailboats in a gale. If the navigator has not compensated for this large side force, he should be notified immediately. If leeway is to port, it is subtracted from the TR; if to starboard, it is added to it.

Steerer or helmsman error may be minimal with an America's Cup skipper, but most of us are not that competent. If the steerer is distracted by talking, eating, sightseeing, or daydreaming, the boat will wander and his meandering wake will tell the navigator that the calculated course is not being sailed. Perhaps a gentle reminder will bring the steerer back to his responsibilities, or maybe somebody else who is more attentive should steer. If factors other than boredom are driving the boat off course, a good steerer will report them to the navigator. Helmsman error can be to either side of the TR.

Current takes two forms, tidal and wind-driven, and is present on almost all bodies of salt water and large lakes. Unlike leeway and steerer error, current can reliably set the boat forward and backward as well as to the side.

The navigator reduces these errors to degrees and applies them to the TR. For example, the rhumb line course, or TR, is 168° and the boat is on the port tack. From experience the navigator is aware that leeway is 3° (to starboard, since the boat is on port tack). He predicts that the steerer will tend to oversteer about 4° upwind (to port). And the navigator, after reading the tidal current chart, estimates that the boat will be set 4° to starboard.

The total effect is 3° to starboard because the two 4° errors cancel each other out. Because it is to starboard, it is added to the TR (a port effect is subtracted) to produce an effective course made good (CMG) of 171°. To compensate, the navigator has the boat steered 3° the other side of the TR, or 165°. While this course seems to aim the boat to port of her destination, the various forces involved will actually take her there.

Updating the DR. Having calculated the compass course (or course through the water) that, combined with the forces and errors, will result in a course made good (or course over the ground) identical to the TR, the navigator now must keep track of the boat's position. Until he can take a fix,

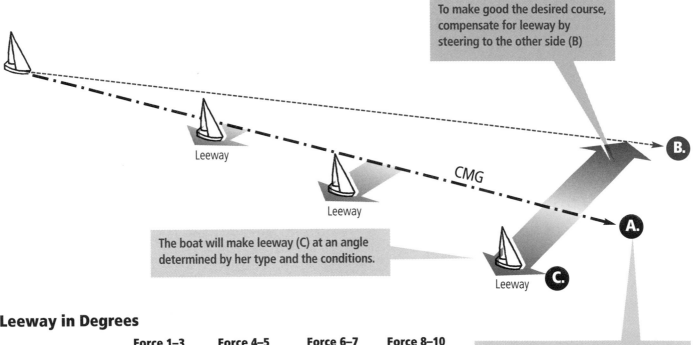

To make good the desired course, compensate for leeway by steering to the other side (B)

Leeway

Leeway

CMG

The boat will make leeway (C) at an angle determined by her type and the conditions.

Leeway

B.

A.

C.

The course made good (A) is the sum of all the forces affecting the heading, including the rhumb line course, leeway, steerer error, and current.

Leeway in Degrees

Boat Type	Force 1–3 3–10 knots		Force 4–5 11–21 knots		Force 6–7 22–33 knots		Force 8–10 34–55 knots	
	Beat	Reach	Beat	Reach	Beat	Reach	Beat	Reach
Cruiser (shallow draft)	10°	5°	8°	4°	12°	10°	20°	12°
Cruiser-racer (deep keel)	6°	4°	4°	2°	6°	4°	12°	6°
Very large cruiser	10°	4°	8°	4°	12°	12°	20°	15°

This table shows typical leeway angles for different types of cruising boats in varying conditions. Under power in force 1–5, leeway is slightly less than when under sail; in force 6–10, it is about the same. Table adapted from Bruce Fraser, *Weekend Navigator* (De Graff, 1981). "Beat" indicates a close-hauled or close-reaching course. "Reach" is a beam or broad reach.

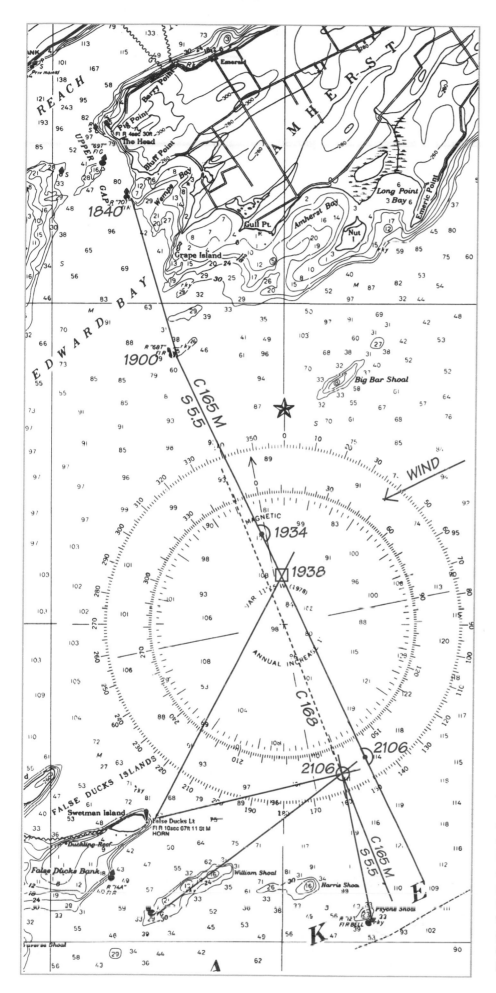

the DR is the most reliable and important plot.

In our example, the DR should be on a line running at 165°, 3° to the left of the TR, even though the navigator is pretty sure that the various side forces are pushing her along on the TR. The navigator regularly brings the boat's DR position up to date using the distance run since the last plot.

Anticipating steerer error, current, and leeway with a total effect of 3° to starboard, the navigator orders a compass course of 165°, or 3° to port of the rhumb line of 168°. He updates the DR (half-circle) and takes an EP (square), using the compass course until he can get a fix (circle). The fix shows that his predictions were correct and that the course made good was 168°. From this new point of departure, the course remains 165° because the side effects still apply.

The EP and LOP

A navigator can plot an **estimated postion (EP)** by adding one bit of external, charted evidence to the onboard evidence undergirding the DR. A helpful piece of external evidence is a depth sounding of water under the boat. If the sounding is 20 feet, and the chart shows a narrow stretch of 20-foot depths surrounded by shoals of 5–10 feet, the boat's approximate position is obvious. While the sounding may not tell the navigator exactly where the boat is, it tells him where the boat is *not* located — and knowing where you are not may be as valuable as knowing precisely where you are when trying to avoid running aground.

More exact information is provided by a compass bearing on a charted object, such as a buoy or a lighthouse. This bearing is called a **line of position (LOP)**. Being on a line of position is like standing on a long road that has no identifiable cross-streets: you know you're

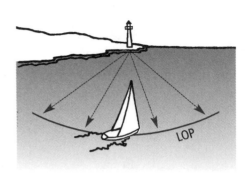

A circle of position (COP) is an arc that has a known radius from a charted object. This radius could be the range of visibility to a lighthouse. Arc B, with a radius of 4.5 miles, is a COP in the chart segment below.

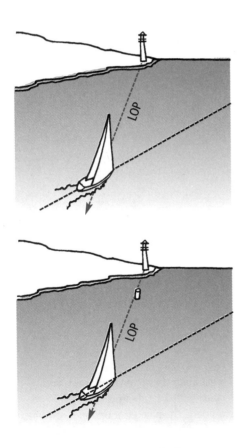

A line of position (LOP) is a single compass bearing to a charted object — for example, a range line. On the chart segment (right) line A is an LOP.

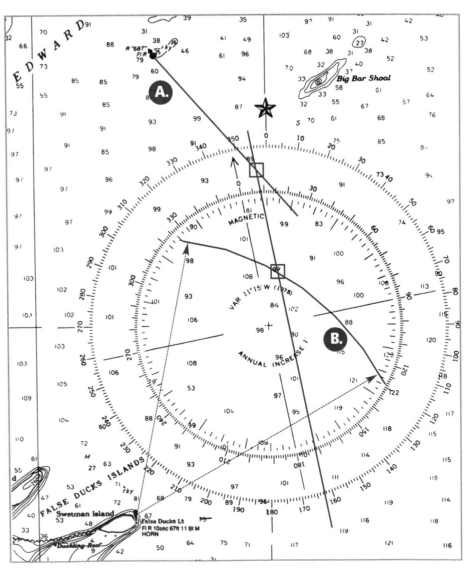

somewhere on the road, but not whether you're at its beginning, its middle, or its end. Once you discover a cross-street, you're on the equivalent of two lines of position, and so are fixed, assuming that this intersection is mapped.

An LOP may be straight — typically, a compass bearing to or from a buoy, lighthouse, or charted landmark, or a range between two charted landmarks. An LOP may also be curved — a circle of known distance from an object — and therefore is called a circle of position (COP). The LOP or COP must be based on an angular or distance measurement from a charted object (preferably a fixed object, like a lighthouse or smokestack, rather than a buoy). An LOP is labeled with the time of sighting above the drawn line and with the magnetic bearing below the line. Don't draw the line all the way across the chart; simply show which object the LOP is based on and make the line long enough to cross your estimated position.

After taking the bearing and marking the LOP on the chart, update the DR plot. Sometimes the bearing and the DR position intersect. If so, draw a small square around the intersection to indicate an estimated position (EP). Conceivably, the boat is on the LOP

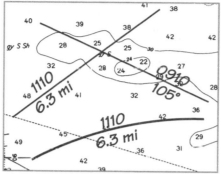

LOPs and COPs usually are labeled, but if the charted object is clearly indicated, they are left without labels.

either above or below the DR, but the rule of thumb is to locate estimated positions as near as possible to dead reckoning positions. If the LOP crosses the track behind or ahead of the DR position, the EP square is drawn on a line at a right angle to the DR position. (A protractor is helpful with this plot.)

Whatever the evidence and its effect on the estimated position, the navigator is faced with a dilemma if the EP is far off the DR. Is there a new rhumb line to the destination? Should she change the compass course? Or should she stay with the original compass course and keep the DR and discard the EP based on this evidence? Since an EP is based on only one bearing, nobody should place too much faith in it. In a strong wind and current and limited visibility, the navigator should stick to her guns and the original course unless she has lost all faith in the DR. The reason why the EP is not entirely reliable is that it is based only on a single bearing, which is not perfectly reliable. Even with an accuracy of ±5°, which is fairly good in many conditions, an LOP only indicates an area of location.

So it's generally good seamanship to base your piloting decisions on your DR using the EP as a guide until you can take a fix. Still, the EP can be an extremely helpful tool. Not only does it help a navigator find out where the boat is not, but there are many opportunities for EPs since only one object and bearing are required.

Whenever you are lost or confused, you should not hesitate to slow or even stop the boat, calmly look around and reevaluate the situation, or even turn around and backtrack to the last buoy.

If the DR and the EP coincide, simply draw a box and label it with the time (A). If the EP falls ahead of or behind the DR, draw a box around the LOP where it is closest to the DR (B). This will be where a line from the DR meets the LOP at a right angle. Here the LOPs are not labeled since the charted object is obvious.

The Fix

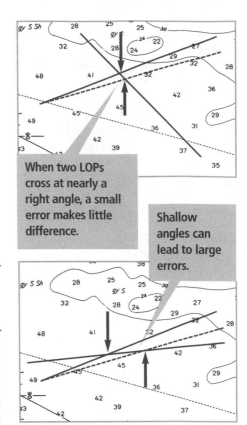

When two LOPs cross at nearly a right angle, a small error makes little difference.

Shallow angles can lead to large errors.

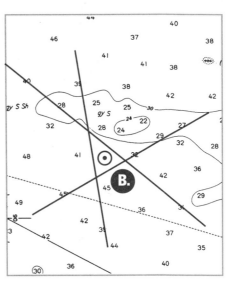

If the EP is where you think you *might* be based on one piece of external evidence, a fix is where you *probably* are based on two or more pieces of external evidence. If your boat is tied up to the only wharf in a harbor next to a light-house, and both are charted, her position is fixed. If she's sailing, the position is fixed if two or more lines of position are plotted using bearings to the end of the wharf, to the lighthouse, to a chimney, or to a buoy — so long as the objects are charted and the bearings cross.

Bearings used to compute a fix should be taken as near to simultaneous-ly as possible on objects at least 30° apart, using the cockpit compass or a hand-bearing compass. In rough weather or poor visibility, a bearing that is cut (taken) over a cockpit compass may be inaccurate by as much as ±5°. Even in ideal conditions, a 5-inch compass can-not be read more accurately than ±2°. A hand-bearing compass is more accurate in all conditions so should be used when taking important "make or break" bear-ings. Otherwise, take the bearing by steering directly at the object (sighting it down the centerline) and reading the heading on the cockpit compass's for-ward lubber's line.

Bearings should be as broad as possi-ble since narrow intersections can cause large errors. The larger the angle of intersection, the less the damage if the bearing is off by a few degrees. The min-imum crossing angle between the two bearings is 30°. The optimum is 90°. If you're fairly sure of your approximate position before taking bearings, pick out objects on the chart that will give you the broadest angles of intersection and then take the bearings. But if you're not

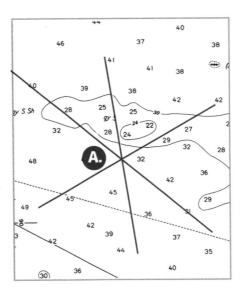

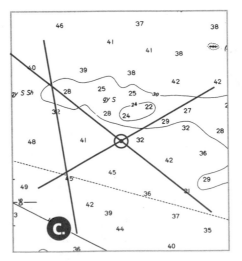

Rarely will three bearings intersect at a point (A). More likely they will outline a triangle called a "cocked hat" (B). If the hat is small and the bearings are equally reliable, draw the fix circle in the middle. If the cocked hat is large, throw out the least reliable bearing (C) — for example, the one on the most distant object.

sure of your position, it's better to look around and find objects that make good angles, take bearings, then locate them and plot the LOPs on the chart.

Ideally, three or more cross bearings should intersect at a point, but usually they form a small triangle (sometimes called a "cocked hat"). If the triangle is larger than about ½ mile, the bearings should be considered untrustworthy and taken again. If the triangle remains large, consider it an area of uncertainty rather than a fix. Plot the course using the two most reliable bearings rather than the center, as you would with a small triangle of intersection.

The label for a fix is a circle around a dot, with the time of the fix using the 24-hour clock. If the fix is based partly or wholly on radio bearings, write "RDF Fix" next to the circle and time. If it's based on GPS or Loran readings, write "GPS Fix" or "L Fix." If based on radar bearings, write "Rad Fix."

The Running Fix

The standard fix that we have just described is based on two or more near-simultaneous bearings crossing at a broad angle. Frequently, though, only one object is in sight to take a bearing on. In that case the navigator uses a technique called "advancing the bearing" to take a special type of fix called the running fix. What he does is take successive bearings on the same object, then move them along his track so that, in effect, LOPs from the same object are crossed. Though not as reliable as the standard fix, the running fix is valuable.

To advance a bearing after plotting it on a chart, draw a line parallel to it through the boat's DR track, making the distance between the first LOP and the advanced LOP equal to the distance run. Label the advanced LOP with the times both of the original bearing (for ready reference) and of the advancement, and with the compass bearing in degrees. When advancing a bearing for a running fix, be sure to compute for course changes and current.

Simply advancing the LOP provides a bearing for a new EP on the DR track. To turn this EP into a running fix, take another bearing on the original object and cross it with the advanced LOP. Circle the intersection and label it "R Fix." Alternatively, cross the advanced LOP with a bearing on a second charted object; again label the intersection "R Fix."

A running fix's accuracy lies somewhere between the near-certainty of a standard fix and the mixed reliability of an estimated position.

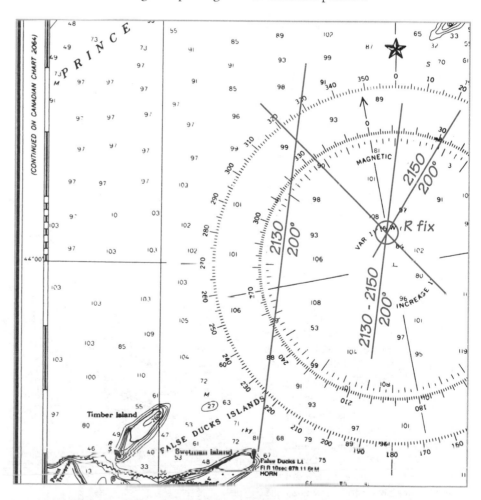

Label the fix with a circle and the time.

To take a running fix, take an LOP from a recent bearing (A) and advance it along the track by the distance run (B). Then take a new bearing (C) either on the same object or on another object.

Indirect Courses

So far we've been talking about direct courses from departure to destination — the straight rhumb line and track on which the steerer makes only small course changes. Sometimes, however, the wind isn't very cooperative and forces you to zig-zag. You may have to beat to windward to your destination on a series of legs, and at no time will you be sailing directly at your destination. There also are times on a run when a light or strong wind makes it ineffective or dangerous to sail square before the breeze. In those conditions it is better to sail on a broad reach, jibing from time to time to stay near the rhumb line.

Keeping track of your position on indirect courses is no different from normal piloting, so long as the plot is updated at every tack or jibe. In undemanding conditions, keeping a DR plot and figuring an estimated position (EP) just before each tack or jibe should be sufficient. When estimating leeway and steerer error, remember that both are greatest when sailing close-hauled or in waves. However, if the visibility is limit-

On an indirect course, first sail the longest leg, the one aiming closest to the destination. Here, to get from A to B when beating to windward, the boat first sails on a long port tack (1). If the wind backs (shifts counterclockwise), she is lifted up to the mark and sails the shortest possible distance (2). If the wind veers (shifts clockwise), she tacks on the header toward the destination, again sailing the shortest distance (3). A boat starting out on starboard tack, however, will sail the same distance only if the wind does not shift; otherwise, she will waste all the distance she covers on starboard tack before the shift.

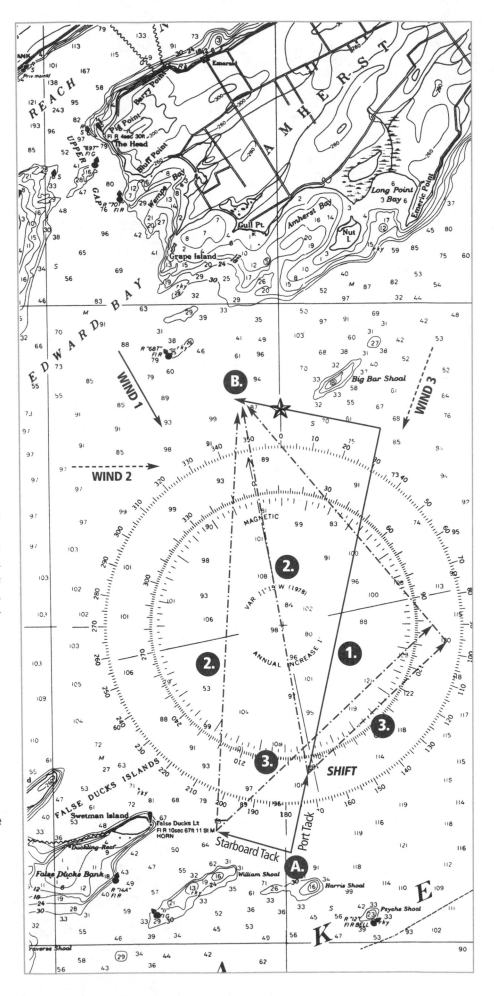

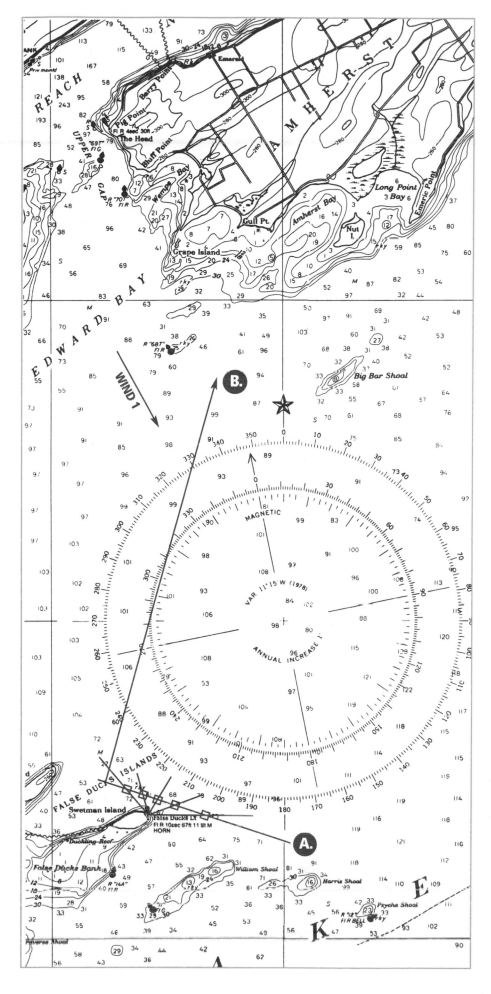

ed, the wind and sea are fierce, or the waters are dangerous, do not alter course until you have made a reliable fix, if at all possible.

When the destination is dead to windward or leeward, limit the variables by sailing an equal time or distance on each tack so you stay roughly the same distance from the rhumb line on either side.

Sail the Longest Leg First. If the course is indirect but not a dead beat or square run, the boat will sail on one tack longer than on the other. A sound rule of thumb for this situation is to sail the longest tack first. This will take you closest to your destination and will minimize the effects of a shift in wind or wave direction.

An important exception to this rule is in poor visibility: take the shortest tack earliest if it presents the opportunity for a fix. In this condition, knowing where you are is a higher priority than sailing an efficient course.

An exception to the rule of sailing the longest leg first is that in poor visibility, in fog or rain, the highest priority often is to know where you are. Sail within sight of aids to navigation (here a lighthouse) as long as you can.

Solve plotting problems on the charts printed here, using a plotter on the compass rose and dividers on the latitude scale on the left margin of the chart on the facing page. Courses and bearings are in magnetic degrees, distances are in nautical miles, and speeds are in knots. Answers may be found at the end of the book, following the Index.

1. What is the magnetic course from False Ducks Lt. (at the bottom of the chart on Swetman Island) to buoy R"70T" FlR (off Bluff Point near the top of the chart)?

A. 358°
B. 009°
C. 189°

2. A boat sails from False Ducks Lt. to buoy R"70T" FlR and then back to False Ducks Lt. On the first leg she averages 5.5 knots and reaches the buoy in 1 hour 50 minutes. She makes the second leg in 2 hours 15 minutes. What is the approximate distance between the two objects? What is the average speed on the second leg?

A. 11 miles; 5 knots
B. 10 miles; 4.4 knots

3. A boat on a course of 176° passes buoy R"70T" FlR at 1842 hours (6:42 PM). At 1900 hours, she passes buoy R"68T" FlR. What is her average speed?

A. 8.7 knots
B. 5.5 knots
C. Not enough information is available

4. In a fog, a boat making 4 knots on a course of 345° passes buoy R"68T" FlR at 1003 hours. At what time should she pass the buoy off Indian Point (on the west side of Upper Gap, at the top of the chart)?

A. 1103 hours
B. 1054 hours

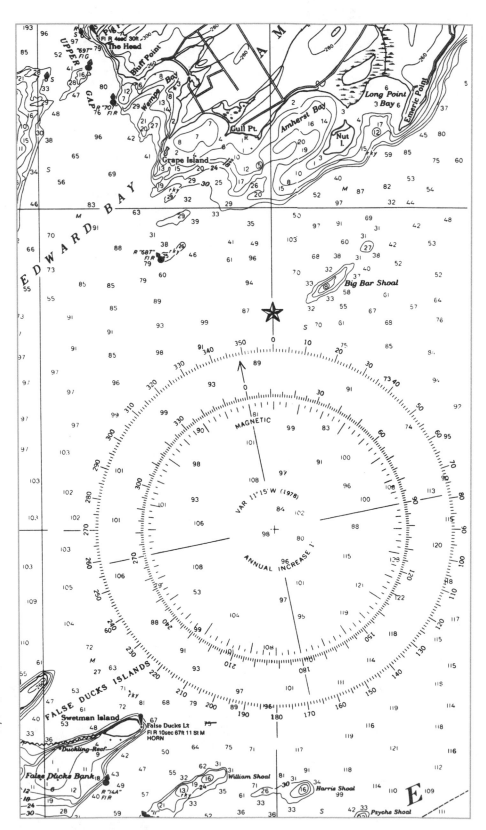

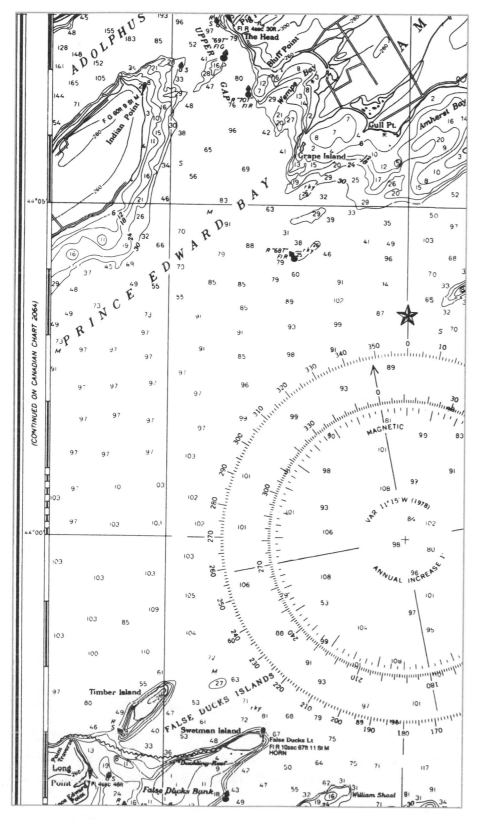

5. A shallow-draft cruising sailboat under sail passes buoy R"69T" FlG on a course of 180°, which will take her 1 mile east of Swetman Island. However, a 25-knot east wind quickly comes up. How much leeway, and in which direction, should her navigator anticipate? What course should be sailed to compensate for leeway.

A. *10–12° leeway to the west; compensated course 168°*

B. *10–12° leeway to the east; no compensation*

6. What type of position is shown at 1920 on page 251? What type would it be with an LOP to False Ducks Lt.? If there were an LOP to False Ducks and another to Indian Point Lt.?

A. *An estimated position, a fix, and a dead reckoning position*

B. *A dead reckoning position, a fix, and an estimated position*

C. *A dead reckoning position, an estimated position, and a fix*

7. From R"68T" FlR, your boat sails at 6 knots on a course of 230°. At 1400 False Ducks Lt. bears 180°. At 1412 hours, it bears 170°. How could you fix your position without taking another bearing? From the 1412 position, what are the bearing and range to the Fl 4sec lighthouse on Prince Edward Point?

A. *This position can only be estimated; bearing 205°, range 6.2 miles*

B. *With a running fix; bearing 200°, range 5.3 miles*

8. Beating into a south-southeast wind, you sail out of Upper Gap late in the afternoon. Your destination is False Ducks Lt. Which tack should you sail on first?

A. *It doesn't matter*

B. *Starboard tack*

C. *Port tack*

CHAPTER 12

Special Piloting Techniques

Anybody who has sailed through a thick fog, across a swift tidal current, or along a rocky, irregular shoreline guarded by few aids to navigation knows the meaning of the word "anxiety." While many of us go to sea in quest of adventure, there are times when we would prefer less of it and more certainty. From moment to moment, navigators (pilots) in these tricky situations may not know where they are, much less where their course will take them. The GPS or Loran-C electronic device may provide a little comfort, but only if the navigator is certain it is accurate and only if it is backed it up by careful piloting using traditional skills. The worst mistake any navigator can make is to bet the boat's safety on a single skill or object.

It's in testing times like these when good navigators earn their keep. They must stay calm while examining all available evidence: taking bearings, reading electronic instruments, making and checking calculations, and attempting to reduce each of the many variables down to the narrow edge of probability. Navigators should keep up the dead reckoning plot assiduously and not turn down any chance for taking bearings and getting a fix. While they should present a mien of confident optimism to shipmates, posturing and egotism have no place on board when the navigation becomes uncertain. It is much healthier for a navigator to stop the boat or turn around rather than allow false pride to run her up on a reef.

This chapter will describe some handy skills beyond the basics that the navigator can use. We'll show several ways to estimate and fix your position using only one buoy, and how to calculate course alterations to avoid hazards ahead or to compensate for currents.

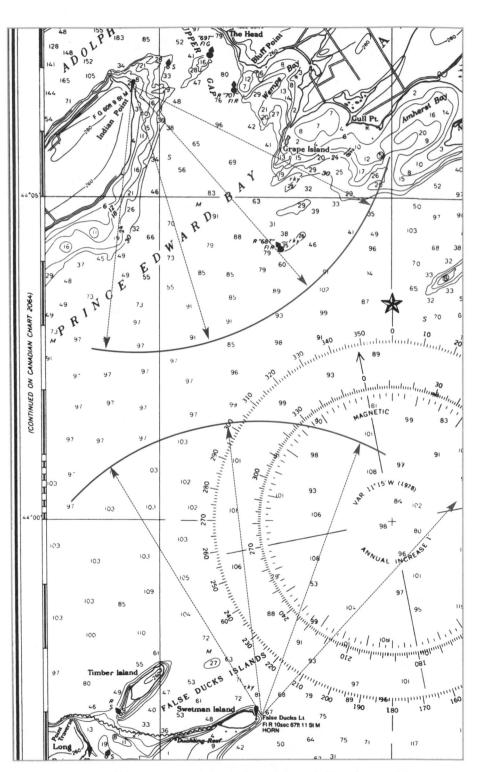

A circle of position, linking points equidistant from a charted object, is one of the ingredients of a successful fix using only one aid to navigation. Be sure to use the distance scale at the same latitude.

Position Finding with One Aid: Distance-Off

We have seen how to make a running fix by using two bearings taken on the same object at different times, advancing the first LOP along the boat's track until it intercepts the second. There are several other ingenious ways to find your position using only one aid or landmark. They fall under the general category of distance-off. By using simple geometry (in almost every case already precalculated), you can convert a single bearing and your distance run into a number that shows how far offshore you are sailing — that's the distance-off part

— and, more important, into a reliable estimated position or fix. The feature common to all these techniques is the concept of the circle of position, which we have already introduced.

Circle of Position (COP). A line of position (LOP) is a compass or range bearing to or from a charted object. As the name suggests, it's a straight line. Every object on it has the same compass direction to the object. Serving the same purpose but with a different shape is a circle of position (COP). Every object on its circumference is equidistant from the center. That distance is the distance-off.

Using any of the techniques described below, determine the distance-off from the sighted object either by taking a series of bearings on it, by measuring a vertical angle with a sextant, or by some other means. The distance-off is the radius of the COP. Spread your drawing compass a distance equal to the distance-off on the chart's side latitude

scale exactly left or right of the object. Then place the point of the compass on the object and draw an arc of the COP near your DR position. If you are completely lost you may have to draw the entire circle, or at least an arc sufficiently large to cover the body of water.

Doubling the Relative Bow Bearing. This method for finding distance-off and making a one-aid fix requires you to take two bearings on the aid as you approach it on a steady course. These are relative bearings, or angles between the bow and the aid, taken using the side lubber's lines on any accurate compass. At the moment when the second bearing is exactly twice the first bearing, the distance-off (from the boat to the sighted object) equals the distance run between the times of the two bearings. This is because the distance run, the distance-off, and the distance from the object to the boat at the moment of the first bearing form three sides of an isosceles triangle, whose two equal sides are the distance-off and the distance run.

The easiest pair of relative bearings to work with is 45° and 90° since they can readily be taken using the two side lubber's lines on the normal sailboat compass. When the aid bears 45° off the bow, start your stopwatch or read the log. When the object is dead abeam at 90° relative, stop the watch and, using the Speed/Time/Distance formula, calculate the distance run, or read the log. At that moment the boat is on a circle of position from the object, its radius equal to the distance run. Where the COP crosses the DR track, you have an estimated position. A 45°/90° combination is called a "bow and beam" bearing.

To fix your position using this method, take a compass bearing on the object when the bearing is doubled. That compass bearing forms a line of position. Where the LOP and the COP cross, you have a fix.

When taking the first bearing, make it as wide as possible — preferably between 30° and 45° (meaning that the second bearing will be 60° to 90°). Any error will have a greater effect if the relative angle is shallow.

Predicting Distance Off. A serious drawback of most doubled bearings is that they tell you only the distance off at the time of the second bearing. You may want to predict distance-off before

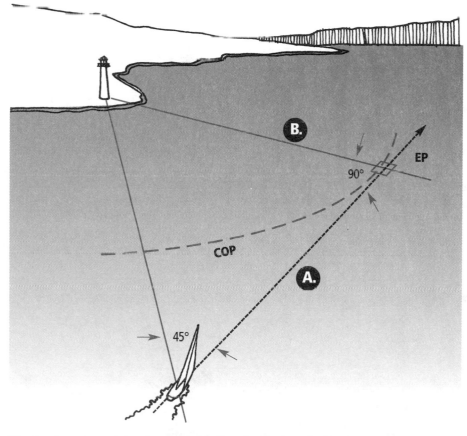

The simplest way to determine distance-off and a COP is to double the relative bow bearing. When the second bearing (2) is twice the first one (1), the boat's distance from the object (D) equals the distance run between the two bearings (A). Where the COP crosses the DR, there is an estimated position (box). As you run between the bearings, don't change course; steer a straight compass heading. Be sure to factor in current when making your calculations for distance run. "Bow and beam bearings" taken over lubber's lines are the easiest combination to use, but 40°/80°, 35°/70°, and other doubled pairs also work.

Position Finding with One Aid: Distance-Off

you reach the object because you're worried about being too close to it. Many lighthouses stand on rocky points of land that should be given a wide berth (passed at a distance).

Certain combinations of relative bearings (including a few doubled bearings) can be used to predict distance-off when the object is abeam. In each case the distance-off is equal to the distance run between each of these two bearings. You need not compute distance run between the second bearing and when the object is abeam. Again, don't alter

course between bearings. As listed by Frederick Graves in his fine book *Piloting*, these pairs are:

20°/30°, 22°/34°, 25°/41°, 26½°/45°, 27°/46°, 29°/51°, 32°/59°, 35°/67°, 37°/72°, 40°/79°, 43°/86°, 44°/88°, 45°/90°

The ⁷⁄₁₀ Rule and the ⁷⁄₈ Rule can also be used to predict distance-off when the sighted object is abeam:

In the ⁷⁄₁₀ Rule, if the first relative bearing is 22½° and the second is 45°, the distance-off when the object is abeam is 0.7 the distance run between the first two bearings.

In the ⁷⁄₈ Rule, the two bearings are 30° and 60°. When the object is abeam, the distance-off is 0.875 the distance run.

Relative Stern Bearings. So far we've been talking about bow bearings made while the boat is approaching a charted object like a buoy, a lighthouse, a water tower, or a waterfront smokestack. Bow bearings allow you both to calcu-

late your present distance-off (at the time of the second bearing) and to predict your distance-off when the object will be abeam.

Sometimes you must calculate distance-off by taking two bearings on an object you are passing or have already passed. For example, a landmark may be obscured by a hill as you approach it but be visible once it's abaft the beam. Or you may want to plot a series of estimated positions or fixes while the landmark is visible, before you sail into a fog bank. To figure the distance-off to an object you have passed, take relative stern bearings using any of the techniques already described — except that instead of doubling a bearing, cut it in half. The first bearing will be the broader one. When the relative bearing to the object is exactly half the first bearing, compute the distance run and the distance-off, which will apply to the moment when the first bearing was taken. Using paired

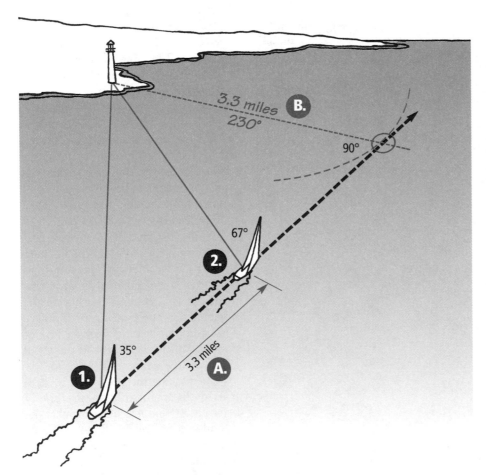

Several pairs of relative bearings listed in the text can be used to predict distance-off when the charted object will be abeam. Here, the distance run between the first and second bearings (A) equals the eventual distance-off (B). If the navigator takes a compass bearing on the object when abeam, the intersection of the LOP and the COP is a fix.

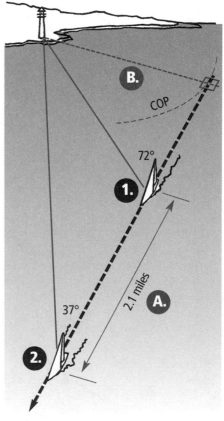

Paired stern bearings can be used to determine distance-off at a previous time. Take the broadest bearing first. The distance run between the two bearings (A) equals the previous distance-off (B).

bearings or the 7/10 or 7/8 Rules, you can work backward to find out how far off the object you were when it was dead abeam, at a relative bearing of 90°.

Bobbing the Horizon. As we saw in chapter 9 in the section on lighthouses, if you know the height of an object and the height of your eye above the water, you can calculate the range of visibility between you and it. In the case of lighthouses this method is used to determine how far away the light's flash can be seen.

To review, calculate range of visibility using these steps:

1. Find the object's height. Charts and the *Light List* show the heights of lighthouses and other objects, such as bridge spans. *The Coast Pilot* provides the heights of these and other objects from base to top. Read this number carefully. Often the height shown is not the height of the top of the lighthouse itself but that of its light, which may be several feet below the structure's top.

2. Find the object's geographical range of visibility:

Range (nautical mi.) = 1.144 √height
Range (statute mi.) = 1.317 √height.

3. Determine the height of your eye above the water, and using either formula determine your own range of visibility.

4. Add the two ranges of visibility (the object's and yours). The result is the mileage you must be from the object to first see it.

The geographical range of visibility is the radius of a COP around the object. To see if you are on that COP, use a technique called bobbing the horizon. If the light or top of the lighthouse or light tower is visible on the horizon, stand or sit in the position used in step 3 above. Then bob your head a foot. If the object disappears, the boat probably is on a COP whose radius is the range of visibility. If the object stays in sight when you bob your head, you're inside the COP.

Lighthouses showing alternating lights of different colors can have two ranges of visibility — one for a white light and another, 25 percent shorter in radius, for a green or red light.

Using the Sextant to Determine Distance-Off. Used chiefly in celestial navigation, the sextant also can be a handy tool when piloting, and especially for determining distance-off a tall object by measuring its vertical angle. A sextant is an adjustable sighting device used to determine angles to elevated objects — usually the sun and the stars, but also to the tops of lighthouses and tall buildings of known height. Since the sextant can't be used unless there is a clear horizon line, the system we will describe is helpful only in good visibility.

Using the sextant, find the vertical angle between the top of an object of known height and the high-tide mark on shore (which usually is indicated by a change of color or a line of weed). Using tables, correct the sight for "dip," or height of eye. Read the angle on the sextant. Then enter the corrected angle into the following formula to determine distance-off in nautical miles:

**Distance-off in nautical miles =
object height x 0.566
corrected angle in minutes**

To convert to statute miles, multiply by 1.15.

This technique can be used to determine your distance from any object of a known height — another boat's mast, a skyscraper, a church steeple, or a bridge span. Tall objects have wider ranges of visibility than short ones.

Besides measuring vertical angles, a sextant can be used to measure the included horizontal angle between two visible objects. Once you know the horizontal angle, you can draw a circle of position whose circumference passes through both objects and your own position. Hold the sextant on its side and adjust it. Read the angle. Using the plotter or a protractor, duplicate the angle on the chart, one side passing through each object, and then draw a COP through it with a drawing compass. (Later we'll see how this COP and the sextant can be used to help you stay away from rocks or shoals.)

Determining a COP with vertical and horizontal angles may be quicker than taking bearings, but also less accurate.

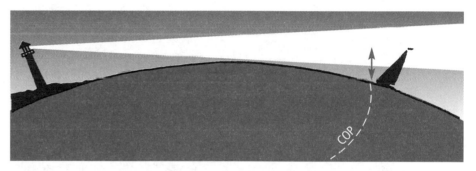

Near the perimeter of a lighthouse's geographical range you may be able to determine distance-off by bobbing your head until the light drops behind the horizon.

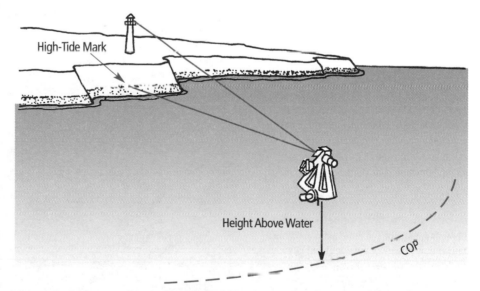

High-Tide Mark

Height Above Water

COP

A sextant sight on an object of known height can provide approximate distance-off. Measure the angle between the high-tide mark and the object's top and compensate for your height of eye with the "dip" correction.

Position Finding with One Aid: Distance-Off

Uses for Distance-Off and Circles of Position. As we've already suggested, there are three important uses for circles of position. Before we move on, let's review them.

First, by calculating distance-off using relative bow or stern bearings or sextant angles, you can plot an estimated position. The circle of position is considered a single bearing, and the EP is where it crosses the track nearest to the DR position.

Second, by combining a circle of position with a compass bearing to the same charted object, you can plot a fix. That is where the COP and the LOP cross. Therefore, by using a series of bearings on a single charted navigation

HANDS ON: Estimating Distance-Off

Besides calculating distance-off and circles of position using bearings and angles, you can estimate them quickly and with reasonable accuracy using several techniques demanding almost no mathematical figuring.

One method is **navigation by sound.** Sound travels at a speed of 5 seconds a nautical mile. When you see a lightning flash or a cannon's smoke, start counting seconds. The time interval until you hear the thunder or boom is divided by 5, and the quotient is the distance to the lightning or cannon in nautical miles. When near a bluff or cliff, blow a horn and time how long it takes for the echo to return. Divide the interval by 10 (since the sound has had to travel there and back). The quotient is your distance to the hill in nautical miles. (Unfortunately, navigation by sound does not work well in fog, which diffuses noises in unpredictable patterns.)

The eye blink method exploits the fact that almost everybody's arm is 10 times longer than the span between the two eyes. Stretch out your right arm and raise a finger (or hold a pencil or stick). Then, closing your left eye, line the finger up against a tree or landmark on shore. Now open your left eye and close your right eye. Using the chart, estimate the number of feet, yards, or miles your finger has apparently moved against the land and multiply that number by 10. The product is the distance-off in the same units.

Counting trees can give a rough estimate of distance-off. In this technique, passed along by Hewitt Schlereth in his book *Commonsense Coastal Navigation,* look at the shore with your naked eye. If you can count individual trees, you're about 1 nautical mile offshore. If you can count windows on waterfront houses, the distance-off is about 2 nautical miles. And if you can see the junction line between land and water, you're about 3 nautical miles away.

The hand-span method of determining distance-off is used when you can see two objects on shore that are a known distance apart — such as a lighthouse and a water tower shown on the same chart. Hold your hand up with the palm facing shore and move it toward or away from your face until it just covers the ground between the two objects. (You may have to

To estimate distance-off, stretch out your hand (A), blink your eyes (B), and estimate how far the object has apparently moved (C). The distance-off (D) is 10 times that distance.

If you know the distance between two objects on shore (A), hold your hand up and move it until it covers them (B). Multiply the ground distance by the distance from hand to eye (C) and divide by your hand's width to determine distance-off.

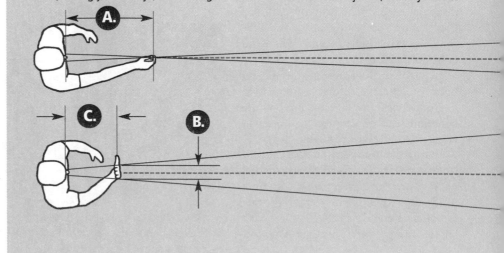

aid you can keep a careful plot as you pass it. This may be helpful when you are sailing along a lonely, rocky shore in unpredictable currents.

Third, distance-off and COPs can keep you from getting too close to shore. Some people are naturally able to judge distance accurately; most people are not and need all the help they can get.

spread or fold down some fingers). Now measure the span of your hand covering the ground as well as the distance from your face to your hand. The ratio of the two distances is equal to the ratio of the distance between the two objects to the distance-off. Use this formula to calculate distance-off:

Distance-off =
(face to hand) x (ground distance)
hand span

For example, if the hand span is 6 inches, the face-to-hand distance is 9 inches, and the ground distance between objects is 2 miles, the solution is:

$$\text{Distance-off} = \frac{9 \times 2}{6} = 3 \text{ miles}$$

While not as reliable as taking bearings or using a sextant, these enjoyable, helpful "quick and dirty" tricks may keep you from piling up on shore.

Another interesting hand-span trick tells you how much more daylight you'll have to get where you're going. Hold your hand sideways at arm's length with the thumb tucked in, and estimate the number of palm widths between the horizon and the sun. Each palm width represents an hour until sundown. Add half an hour for dusk if you're sailing in temperate latitudes.

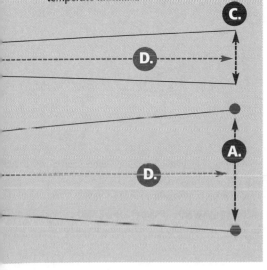

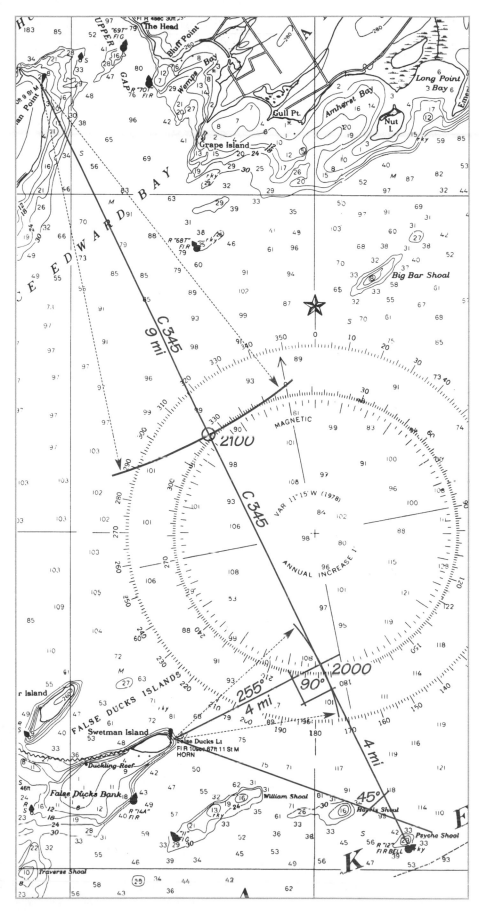

You can make a fix using only one aid by drawing a COP based on bow and beam bearings (A) or bobbing the horizon (B), and crossing the COP with an LOP to the same charted object.

273

Danger Bearings and Circles

When sailing near shore, the navigator may precalculate and plot lines and circles of position to help keep the boat away from rocks and other hazards. These LOPs and COPs are called danger bearings and circles. When plotted on charts, they can be used the way a driver uses the curb and centerline in a road.

Danger Bearings. An aid to navigation may include a danger bearing. For instance, some lighthouses show a white or green light over safe water and a red light (called the red sector) over shoals. The line on the chart between the two colors is a type of danger bearing. On one side a boat is safe; on the other side she risks trouble.

Another kind of charted danger bearing is a range consisting of two or more daybeacons or landmarks that, when aligned one behind the other, indicate a safe course. If the steerer keeps them aligned, the boat is in safe water, but if she steers either side (so that one object

moves to the left or the right of the other), the boat is in danger.

When approaching a hazard such as a reef or sunken boat, the navigator should plot a danger bearing to an adjacent charted object or to the edge of the hazard itself. The bearing is the minimum safe course that avoids the hazard — an LOP that, assuming the boat stays on it or to the safe side, will take her clear of danger. Once the navigator has identified the danger bearing, this safe LOP, she should plot it on the chart and clearly mark its dangerous side with a red pencil. If the danger is to starboard of the bearing, she writes "NLT" and the bearing on the LOP. This means that the bearing to the charted object must be *no less than* the one marked. For example, "NLT 072" means that the boat is in danger if the bearing to the object is 071° or less. But if the danger is to port, "NMT" and the bearing are written on the LOP —to indicate that the bearing

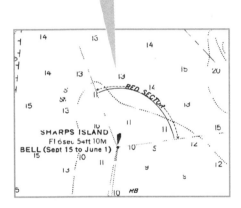

A lighthouse's red sector is a type of danger bearing. It is a fixed red light shining over shoal water.

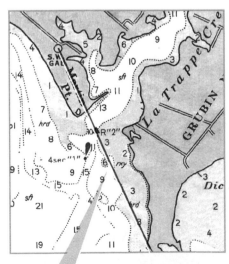

It may be dangerous to steer at a solitary object since the boat may be swept to the side even though headed directly at it. A range using two charted objects is a much better guide.

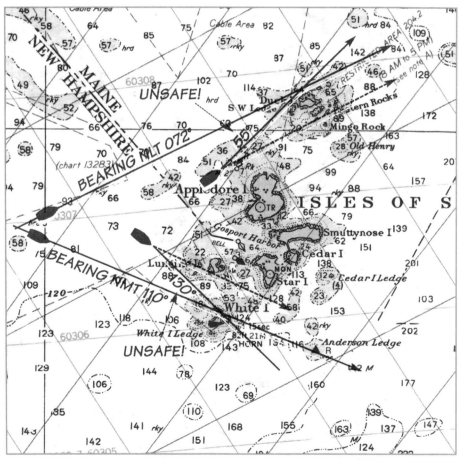

Lacking a range, set a course around a hazard but also establish danger bearings — courses or bearings that provide the minimum safe berth. If a bearing labeled "NLT" decreases or one labeled "NMT" increases, you are being sucked toward the hazard. Danger bearings are particularly helpful at night, when it's usually difficult to estimate distance-off.

to the charted object should be not more than the bearing noted. Thus "NMT 072°" means that the boat is at risk if the object bears 073° or more. If the boat is exactly on the danger bearing or to the other side, she is safe.

How this information is communicated to the steerer (helmsman) is crucial. The navigator must use the simplest, least ambiguous language possible. If the danger bearing is 072° and she has written "NLT 072°" on the chart, she can say, "Don't let the bearing to that buoy get below 072°," or "We're safe if that buoy bears more than 072°." Since "below" and "more" may cause confusion, the navigator may use land terminology ("Don't steer any more to the left") and show the steerer the chart and use hand signals. The navigator could also give the steerer a safe course using an improvised range: "Keep that church steeple in front of that water tank."

When there is tidal or wind-driven current, or when sailing in very strong winds, it's a mistake to instruct the steerer to steer directly at a solitary buoy or landmark. Current or leeway may well drag the boat toward the shoal area even while the steerer obediently keeps the bow pointed at the buoy.

Whatever instructions the navigator gives, she should go on deck and explain the situation to the steerer, pointing out the hazard and any buoys or landmarks, and asking if there will be any difficulty sailing the safe course. It's all well and good for a navigator to tell a steerer to steer 072°, but if the boat can't sail that course because it means running dead before the wind in a dangerously wild sea, then the navigator must give other instructions. Boats have been lost because the pilots buried their heads in the charts and lost touch with the practical problems on deck.

Danger Circles. If you can enclose a hazard in a circle and then find a way to stay outside it, you'll keep out of trouble. This is another area where the sextant can be handy. First, draw an arc around the hazard with a drawing compass. Then, using the plotter or a protractor, plot bearings from various points on the circumference to landmarks or buoys that the circle passes through and calculate the included angle. Mark the hazardous area with red lines and label the circle "NMT" and the minimum

safe included angle between the objects. Set the sextant to the angle and take horizontal sights as you sail by the hazard. Whenever the angle between the two objects is greater than the computed angle, you're inside the danger circle. Whenever it's smaller, you're outside it. If you don't have a sextant, use relative bearings sighted through a pelorus or an improvised viewfinder, or take compass bearings.

Another way to make sure you're safe is to locate an object on or near the center of the plotted danger circle, such as a daybeacon or an oyster stake, and keep it dead abeam. By doing this, you'll sail around the circumference of the circle.

HANDS ON: The Rule of 60

A navigator frequently must calculate a safe course around a hazard that lies at a distance dead ahead. An extremely helpful method, called the Rule of 60, quickly computes the necessary course alteration with good accuracy. All you need to know is, first, how far ahead the hazard lies and, second, how far to one side you want to pass it. The Rule of 60 formula is:

$$\text{Course alteration} = \frac{60 \times \text{desired distance-off}}{\text{distance ahead}}$$

For example, sailing on a course of 185°, the boat is headed right at a reef 12 miles ahead. The safest passage around the reef is 4 miles to the side from its center. So,

$$\text{Course alteration} = \frac{60 \times 4}{12} = 20° \text{ course alteration}$$

So the safe course around the reef is 20° either side of the present course — either 165° or 205°.

The Rule of 60 is accurate to within 2 degrees and works only when short distances are involved. However, even if off by a couple of degrees, it provides an extremely quick solution to one of piloting's most difficult problems.

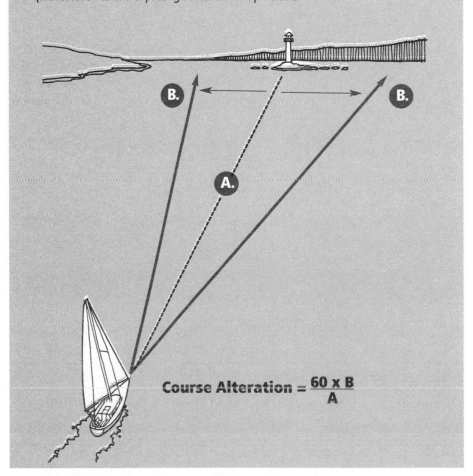

$$\text{Course Alteration} = \frac{60 \times B}{A}$$

Piloting with Soundings

We've seen how position determination depends on reference to visible, charted objects using the magnetic compass and up-to-date charts. Nautical charts also contain information about objects that are invisible from the boat but that can be verified, measured, or identified using electronic equipment. Among these are electronic or radio signals like those used in GPS navigation. Another important set of data printed on charts is soundings, or water depth. Charts show soundings in feet, in fathoms (multiples of 6 feet), or in meters

(the scale is clearly indicated on the chart border). In saltwater tidal areas, soundings are at Mean Lower Low Water, which is the average of the lower of low tide levels and, therefore, a good prediction of the lowest tides. The National Ocean Service *Tide Tables* and privately published publications derived from it show the range between mean low water and mean high water and the range for spring and neap tides for every day of the year. Most charts show tidal ranges for a few places in the area they cover. Therefore, you can convert the charted depth to depths for times other than that of MLW.

On charts, soundings are printed at intervals, and dashed or dotted contour lines are drawn to make it easier to distinguish water of different depth. Bodies of especially shallow water are shaded light blue. The delineations for these contour lines and shaded areas vary from chart to chart and area to area.

Using these aids, the navigator can easily reduce hundreds of individual soundings into several relatively clear blocks of water.

Sounding Instruments. There are two types of depth sounder: the lead line and the electronic sounder. Until 1950 most soundings were made with lead (pronounced "led") lines. These are long lengths of narrow-diameter rope with a lead weight at one end and marked at regular intervals with plastic, leather, or painted indicators using a variety of colors or numbers to show depth. The traditional sounding lead had on its bottom some soft tallow to pick up a small sample of the sea's floor. An experienced fisherman would know not only the depth of water near his home port but also the location of spots with mud, sand, rock, or weedy bottom. (According to one old New England tale, a mate tested his skipper's skill at navigating by smearing some shore dirt from his boots

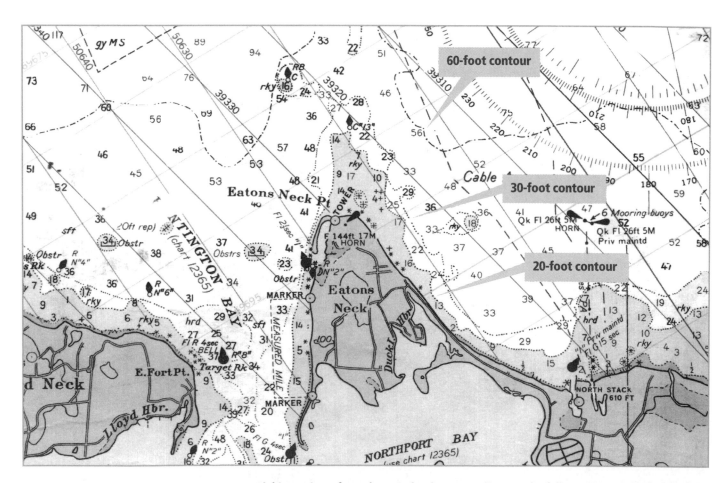

Linking points of equal water depth, contour lines can be followed by a navigator. On this chart, where soundings are in feet, dashed and dotted lines mark 60-foot, 30-foot, and 20-foot contours. These are the water depths at Mean Lower Low Water. Using the chart and depth sounder, the navigator can carefully and safely follow contour lines around hazards and into harbors.

onto the tallow. The old man inspected it carefully and announced with horror that the nearby island had sunk and they were fogbound over a chicken coop.)

To use the lead line, stand on the bow with the boat going slow ahead and heave the lead forward. Let the line run out. When the bow passes near the line, pull until the line is vertical and read the

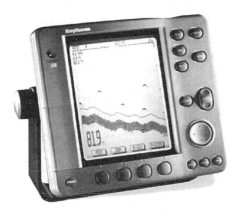

Determining depth with a depth sounder (above) or lead line (below), the navigator slowly feels his way along contour lines, staying in safe water while navigating around hazards (right top). Depth soundings can also be used to estimate positions when fog shrouds buoys over shoaling areas (right bottom).

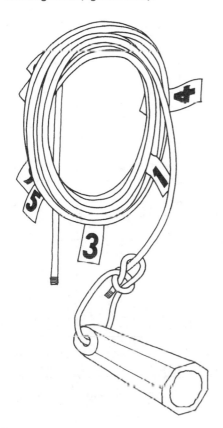

tag nearest the water. Be sure to retrieve the line before it tangles in the propeller or rudder. Before heaving the lead again, coil the line carefully.

This slow procedure is difficult to repeat more than once every minute or so. Today, electronic depth sounders are much faster, and in most cases more accurate. The depth sounder is sometimes called a "Fathometer" after the trade name of the first of its type, developed by the Raytheon Company, or an "echo sounder," which accurately describes how it works. A sound signal is sent out through a transducer installed in the boat's bottom. It travels through the water until it bounces off an object, and its echo is received by a hydrophone located near the transducer. An instrument converts the time lag between the sending and reception of the signal into a visual indicator. In older depth sounders, a blip of light is shown on a graduated scale. In newer instruments,

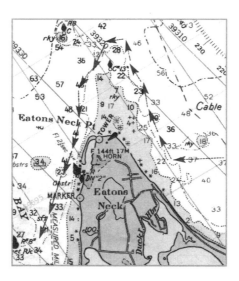

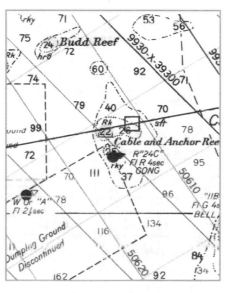

the depth is shown digitally in feet, fathoms, or meters. When reading the depth sounder, you should know how deep in the water the transducer is. Most depth sounders have an alarm that can be set to go off when the sounding is less than a specified depth (often the boat's draft plus a few feet).

The depth sounder provides a continuous display of soundings. (Some sounders also provide a printed summary of readings over a set period of time.) Because its signals are echoed by any object underneath, the sounder will momentarily pick up a large fish or school of fish. You will be more than mildly surprised the first time a tuna triggers a 15-foot spot in water that your chart shows is 100 feet deep, but you'll eventually become less alarmed by such fluctuations.

The Depth Sounder and Piloting. The depth of the water below is one more piece of information that a good navigator uses to find a position. Rarely will a sounder pinpoint your position precisely, but it will help you estimate your position. You can use the sounder's reading much like a single bearing on a landmark to provide a good EP. If there is only one area where the depth is 30 feet and the sounder reads 30 feet, the boat is in that area. While most soundings won't tell you exactly where you are, they will help you determine generally where you are and are not.

Because water depth may vary on several sides of a deep channel or hazard, you can judge which way you are approaching by the sounder's reading. There are times, too, when you can follow (trace) a contour line clearly shown on a chart right around a hazard and into a harbor without ever seeing a buoy or land. When tracing a contour, keep the speed down and post one crew member to watch the display (or heave the lead) and another to keep a lookout. It's all too easy to become mesmerized by the sounder and lose touch with other aids.

Tide and Current

Tide (the rise and fall of water) and current (the horizontal motion of water due mainly to tidal changes) are key considerations for any navigator on salt water. It's important to be able to predict tide changes and current direction and velocity. Remember, though, that tide tables are only *predictions* of tidal behavior. Due to local conditions, tides may be higher or lower and currents may be faster or slower than predicted. Rarely do they stick exactly to schedule.

Government tide publications use Standard Time. Be sure in summer to add an hour for Daylight Saving Time to synchronize the tables with your watch.

Determining Tide Levels. Tides change on a semidiurnal (twice-daily) or diurnal (once-daily) schedule in regular patterns, depending on the relative position of the moon and the local geography. Whatever the schedule, it is described in the National Ocean Service publication *Tide Tables,* which provides

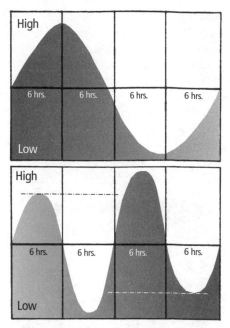

There is one tide change a day in a diurnal schedule (top), and there are two (with tides at different levels) in a semidiurnal schedule (above).

A tide table shows times of high and low tide. Here, the second low tide on July 18 is at 3:16 PM, according to the table. Adding an hour for Daylight Saving Time, change that to 4:16 or 1616 hours. The height, or range between low and high tides, is listed under high tide.

Day of Month	Day of Week	JULY HIGH a.m.	Ht.	p.m.	Ht.	JULY LOW a.m.	p.m.	Day of Month	Day of Week	AUGUST HIGH a.m.	Ht.	p.m.	Ht.	AUGUST LOW a.m.	p.m.
1	S	8 20	6.3	8 36	7.2	2 14	2 23	1	T	9 24	6.4	9 37	7.2	3 19	3 29
2	S	9 08	6.3	9 21	7.2	3 03	3 11	2	W	10 03	6.6	10 16	7.2	4 01	4 11
3	M	9 51	6.4	10 03	7.3	3 46	3 55	3	T	10 42	6.7	10 54	7.2	4 37	4 49
4	T	10 32	6.5	10 41	7.3	4 27	4 36	4	F	11 17	6.9	11 30	7.2	5 14	5 26
5	W	11 09	6.6	11 20	7.2	5 05	5 14	5	S	11 53	6.9	. . . . .	. . .	5 48	6 03
6	T	11 47	6.7	11 56	7.2	5 43	5 52	6	S	12 06	7.2	12 28	7.0	6 24	6 40
7	F	. . . . .	. . .	12 22	6.7	6 18	6 30	7	M	12 41	7.1	1 05	7.1	6 59	7 18
8	S	12 33	7.1	12 59	6.8	6 54	7 07	8	T	1 20	6.9	1 45	7.1	7 35	7 58
9	S	1 10	7.0	1 38	6.8	7 31	7 47	9	W	2 03	6.8	2 27	7.1	8 13	8 45
10	M	1 51	6.9	2 19	6.8	8 08	8 29	10	T	2 49	6.6	3 14	7.1	9 01	9 38
11	T	2 32	6.7	3 01	6.9	8 48	9 19	11	F	3 41	6.4	4 09	7.1	9 51	10 37
12	W	3 19	6.5	3 49	6.9	9 33	10 10	12	S	4 40	6.2	5 08	7.1	10 49	11 41
13	T	4 10	6.4	4 42	7.0	10 24	11 06	13	S	5 45	6.2	6 13	7.2	11 55	. . . . .
14	F	5 06	6.3	5 38	7.1	11 19	. . . . .	14	M	6 50	6.4	7 15	7.4	12 44	1 01
15	S	6 08	6.3	6 36	7.3	12 06	12 19	15	T	7 53	6.6	8 17	7.6	1 46	2 04
16	S	7 10	6.4	7 35	7.5	1 06	1 19	16	W	8 51	7.0	9 15	7.8	2 44	3 03
17	M	8 09	6.6	8 33	7.8	2 06	2 20	17	T	9 47	7.3	10 11	7.9	3 39	4 01
18	T	9 07	6.9	9 29	8.0	3 02	3 16	18	F	10 40	7.6	11 03	7.9	4 32	4 54
19	W	10 04	7.2	10 24	8.1	3 58	4 12	19	S	11 31	7.7	11 55	7.8	5 22	5 46
20	T	10 58	7.4	11 18	8.1	4 50	5 08	20	S	. . . . .	. . .	12 22	7.7	6 12	6 38
21	F	11 51	7.5	. . . . .	. . .	5 42	6 03	21	M	12 45	7.5	1 12	7.6	7 02	7 31
22	S	12 12	7.9	12 43	7.6	6 33	6 57	22	T	1 36	7.2	2 03	7.4	7 52	8 23
23	S	1 05	7.7	1 36	7.5	7 26	7 55	23	W	2 29	6.8	2 55	7.2	8 43	9 20
24	M	2 01	7.3	2 32	7.4	8 19	8 50	24	T	3 25	6.4	3 50	6.9	9 37	10 18
25	T	2 56	6.9	3 28	7.2	9 14	9 50	25	F	4 22	6.1	4 46	6.7	10 34	11 15
26	W	3 57	6.5	4 25	7.0	10 11	10 50	26	S	5 21	6.0	5 45	6.6	11 32	. . . . .
27	T	4 56	6.2	5 24	6.9	11 07	11 51	27	S	6 19	6.0	6 42	6.6	12 14	12 30
28	F	5 57	6.1	6 21	6.9	. . . . .	12 07	28	M	7 14	6.1	7 35	6.8	1 09	1 23
29	S	6 56	6.0	7 16	6.9	12 49	1 03	29	T	8 04	6.3	8 22	6.9	1 59	2 14
30	S	7 49	6.1	8 07	7.0	1 44	1 56	30	W	8 51	6.5	9 05	7.0	2 45	2 59
31	M	8 39	6.3	8 55	7.1	2 34	2 47	31	T	9 31	6.8	9 47	7.2	3 26	3 42

When tides exceed average rise in height, expect a corresponding drop in low tide.

the time and range of high and low tides for every day of the year for thousands of locations. In each case the point of reference is the datum Mean Lower Low Water level.

Tides are rarely the same from change to change, since the rapidly varying orbit of the moon, whose gravitational pull is mainly responsible for the tides, pulls the mound of water that is the tide wave along under it. In a semidiurnal tidal pattern, one tide will be slightly higher or lower than the other. The more overhead the moon is, the greater the range will be. Another major effect on tide level is the relative position of the moon and the sun. Their combined gravitational pull when they are aligned at full and new moons causes higher and lower tide levels. These are spring tides. (See chapter 4.)

The *Tide Tables* indicate when the tide is high and low, and what the level is at those times. They don't tell you what the level is at other times, but there are ways to predict intermediate levels.

The Rule of Twelfths says the following about semidiurnal tides: the tide usually will rise or fall approximately $\frac{1}{12}$ of its range after hour 1; $\frac{1}{4}$ after hour 2; $\frac{1}{2}$ after hour 3; $\frac{3}{4}$ after hour 4; $\frac{11}{12}$ after hour 5; and its entire range after hour 6. Note that half the tidal rise and fall occurs during the middle of the tide, during hours 3 and 4, when the tidal currents are swiftest. These are approximate figures, since on a semidiurnal schedule the tide changes about every 6 hours, 12 minutes, and since the environment may affect the tide schedule.

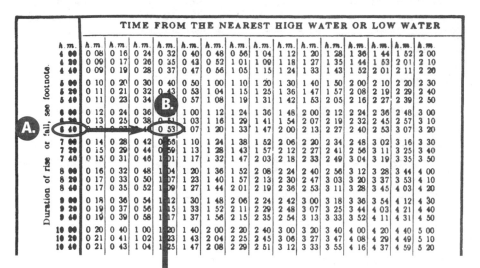

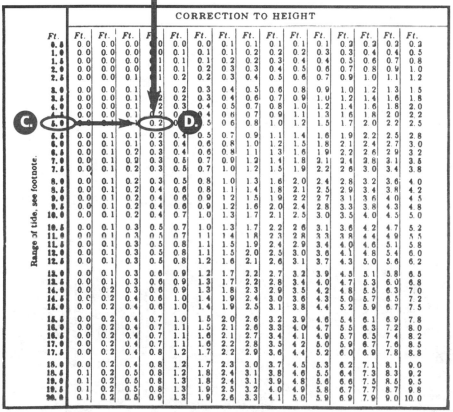

To estimate depths for times between low and high tides, first find the time closest to the interval between low and high (A), then go across that row until you reach the column under the number closest to the interval between the desired time and the nearest tide change (B). Run down this column to the row headed by the number most closely corresponding to the tide range (C). The intersection between the row and column (D) is the height above mean low water at the desired time.

Tide and Current

Determining Tidal Currents. Not only are water levels subject to calculation and prediction, but tidal current — the speed and direction of the water flooding in and ebbing out — must be considered when planning a course. The slower the boat, the more current affects her progress, yet even high-speed multihulls can be delayed or thrown off course by strong contrary or side currents. A tidal stream as slow as 1 knot can double the size of wind-driven waves if current and wind are contrary, and 2- or 3-knot currents running against a force 7 wind can set up mammoth breaking waves. So it's valuable and sometimes vital to be able to predict the direction and speed of any upcoming tidal currents.

Some general principles apply about currents. They tend to run swiftest in constricted channels between two large bodies of water. Still water does not run deep; current is most rapid in deep channels, not shallow areas. When water swings around a bend, the current usually runs swiftest on the outside of the turn and most slowly on the inside. And current may be created or accelerated by strong, steady winds. The greatest current of all is the Gulf Stream, which acts as a kind of drain for immense quantities of water shoved into the Gulf of Mexico by the Atlantic's trade winds.

Tidal current tables, published by the government in CD-ROM format and by various publishers in printed format, list times of slack water and times, direction, and speed of maximum current for reference stations and thousands of subordinate stations. Tidal current charts show how currents flow at intervals between high and low tide. Don't expect these tables and charts to be perfectly accurate. Onshore winds may shorten and delay the ebb (outgoing tide) and weaken ebb currents. Offshore winds may dampen and delay the flood tide. The best indicator of tidal current is not

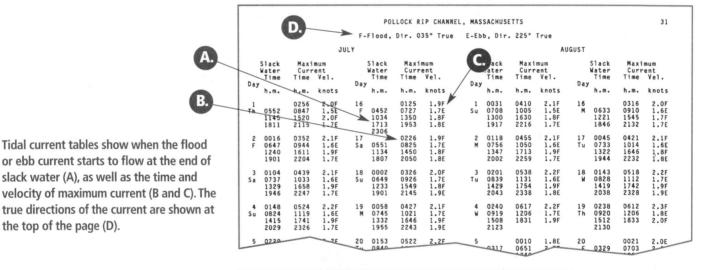

Tidal current tables show when the flood or ebb current starts to flow at the end of slack water (A), as well as the time and velocity of maximum current (B and C). The true directions of the current are shown at the top of the page (D).

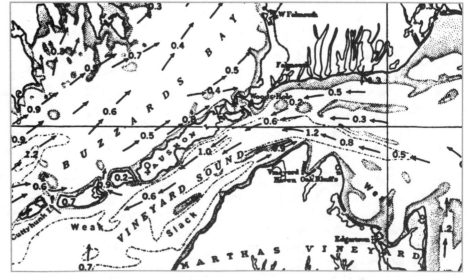

You can draw your own current charts or use ones published for a few areas. Here, using the current wisely can add up to 1.5 knots if you run with the current on the north side of Naushon Island rather than run into the 1-knot flow on the south side. Remember that tide tables and charts aren't much more than highly educated guesses at tidal activity. Pay as much attention to local indicators as you do to the printed publications.

an entry in the tables but a buoy leaning downstream, ripples streaming off a pier's piling, or the way your own boat is held stern to the wind when she's at anchor. If a fix puts you 2 miles ahead of your DR position after an hour of sailing, you have 2 knots of favorable current — even if the tables indicate otherwise.

Slack Water. The times of high and low tide given in the *Tide Tables* indicate when the water level has reached its apex and nadir. However, the reference time for tidal current is that of slack water, when the current is flowing very slowly (at a speed of ½ knot or less). The times of high or low and slack water aren't always the same. The water may keep flowing into an area even when the rise has stopped, since it may be moving along to another body of water.

Then, too, slack water varies in duration depending on the local current. In places where the maximum current is weak, it lasts for quite a while. But where the maximum current runs strong, slack water is short-lived. If the maximum current is 1–3 knots, slack water may lasts for 2 hours down to 38 minutes — one-half before and one-half after the time given in the tables. With maximum currents of 4–6 knots, slack water lasts for 29 minutes down to 19 minutes. A 10-knot current has only 11 minutes of slack water between the end of the flood and the start of the ebb, and vice versa.

Predicting Tidal Currents. Set is the direction in which current pushes the boat. Drift is the velocity. Although a GPS will calculate them while you're under way, if you want to predict currents before choosing your day's sail and heading out (and experienced sailors always do), the job is up to you. It's not hard, and often there's a lot to lose or gain. A 3-knot head (contrary) current will cut a 6-knot boat's speed by half. A 3-knot favorable current, on the other hand, will increase her speed by half. Few cruising sailboats are so fast that their pilots can choose courses without taking current into account.

To translate tidal current velocities and directions into helpful piloting aids, first try to visualize the relationship between the current and the boat's course. It helps to sketch the course on a sheet of paper and then draw vectors, or force arrows, at the appropriate angles. The following rules of thumb are help-

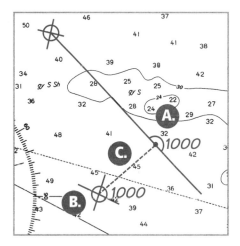

ful when you predict current effect on the boat:

When a current is running approximately parallel to the boat's course, the set is ahead or astern and the drift is equal to the current. A head current decreases speed made good (the speed over the bottom) by a number equal to its velocity. A stern current increases her speed made good by its velocity.

When a current is beam-on (from the side), the set is to the side and only the course made good is affected.

A current at a 45° angle to the course affects the boat in two ways: half its force increases or decreases the speed made good over the bottom, and the other half pushes the boat to the side.

A tidal current force arrow will have a length equal to the drift in knots, and its direction will represent the set. Since the effect of drift and set is measured in terms of the length of time that the current strikes the boat, when planning a

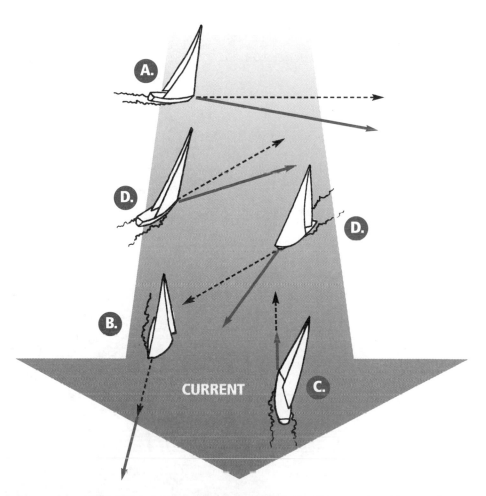

A beam current (A) affects only the course made good over the ground, and bow and stern currents (B and C) only the speed made good. Currents at a 45° angle to the bow and stern (D) affect course and speed, one-half their velocity for each.

Tide and Current

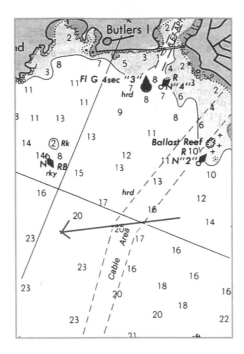

The length and direction of a vector (force arrow) indicate the current's set and drift. When drawing vectors, use the same scale.

course calculate how many hours you will be under way between your departure and destination. Start by figuring how long the passage would take with no current: divide the distance by your anticipated speed; the quotient is the passage time in hours.

If the vectors indicate that the current will be contrary all the way, multiply its velocity by the passage time and add the product to the passage time. What you're doing is calculating how much you will be set back for the duration of the passage. If the current is favorable, subtract the product from the passage time. Here you're figuring how much you will be advanced for the duration of the passage.

A simple way to predict the current's effect on speed is to subtract (or add) average current velocity from (or to) your anticipated speed to find a speed made good over the bottom, and then divide that speed into the distance to find your passage time.

Once you have predicted the total set and drift for a leg or passage (B) you know how far you should head on the other side of the rhumb line (A) to compensate. Determine the course alteration in degrees using the Rule of 60.

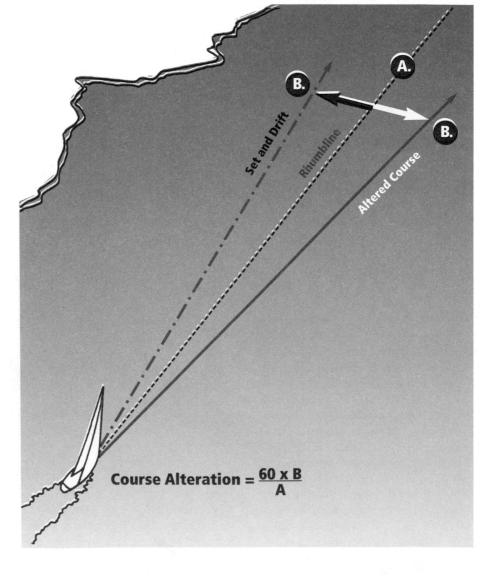

$$\text{Course Alteration} = \frac{60 \times B}{A}$$

With a beam current, multiply the average velocity by the passage time to see how far the boat will be pushed to one side during the trip. An accurate course, then, will be sailed toward a point that same distance up-current. Using the Rule of 60 formula (used earlier to calculate course alternations around an object ahead), you can figure how far to compensate for current. This formula is:

Course alteration =
$$\frac{60 \times \text{desired distance change}}{\text{distance ahead}}$$

If the Current Changes Direction.

Those predictions are fairly easy to make if the current runs consistently in the same direction. But what if the tide changes during the passage or you alter course?

If these changes are predictable, break your long passage down into a series of short legs and precalculate the set, drift, passage time, and course alteration for each leg. If the tide changes halfway across, at mid-passage, you may well find that the flood and the ebb cancel each other out so the rhumb-line course can be sailed without corrections. On the other hand, you may not be able to anticipate set and drift with 100 percent accuracy. If you are unsure about tidal current and are in a vulnerable situation, quickly fix your position. Then try to estimate the actual set and drift and make your calculations for the next leg or legs.

Wind-Driven Current. The wind causes surface currents of its own. A wind that has blown from a steady direction for several hours kicks up a current of about 2 percent of its speed. A 25-knot wind may create a ½-knot current. In the Northern Hemisphere, the wind-driven current runs at a slight angle to the right of the wind's direction (for instance, an east wind will create a current flowing northwest). In the Southern Hemisphere, the angle is slightly to the left. In bodies of shallow water with weak tides, such as Chesapeake Bay, wind-driven currents are frequent in fresh to strong winds. On large lakes, a strong wind will pile up water on a shore, stimulating a strong current called a seiche. The effect of wind-driven current is figured like that of tidal current, but is more difficult to predict since there are no tables.

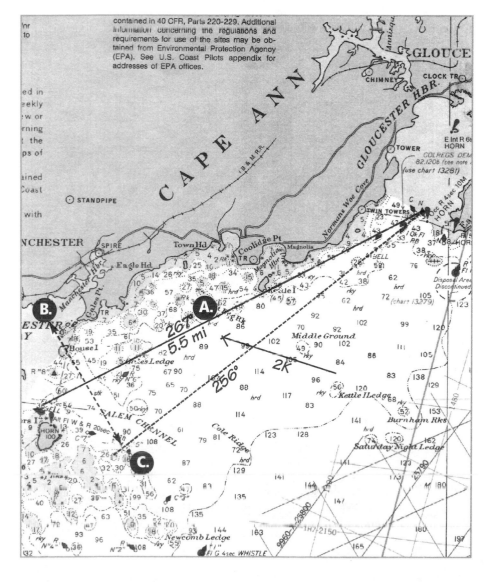

In this example, the navigator estimates that at 4.5 knots, with one-half the 2-knot 45° current working in his favor, it will take 1 hour to sail from Gloucester to the Salem Channel bell buoy. Since the other half of the current's velocity will push the boat to starboard at a drift of 1 knot (B), he must set a course 1 mile to port through the water (C). The rhumb line is 5.5 miles long (A). How many degrees should he alter course? Using the Rule of 60, Course Alteration = 60 x 1 mile ÷ 5.5 miles = 11°. The rhumb line course is 267°, so he alters course 11° to port to 256°.

Tide and Current

HANDS ON: **Cheating the Tide**

By cleverly taking advantage of the tide and local geography, you may find the most favorable currents and also cheat the tide — sail where a contrary current is unusually weak or where there are back eddies (favorable local currents). Good candidates are small coves near shore and tide races (tide rips) where currents run in different directions (for example, out of a harbor and around a point of land) and meet in swirls and rough water. Some of the strongest races and most complicated currents are found at tidal bars — sand bars and other shoals where currents clash. Sailors who love sailing in shallow waters find that cheating the tide can be as rewarding as winning a race or crossing an ocean.

Try to maximize the amount of time you sail in favorable stern currents and minimize the time you sail in unfavorable bow currents. This may mean getting under way earlier or later than you would normally wish, but you'll end up saving time under way. Remember, too, that currents tend to run faster in deep water and around points of land than in shoal water and in shallow indentations in the shore.

In rough weather, a current contrary to the wind, even if on your stern, will slow

Currents alongshore may turn back on themselves in back eddies. If you play them right, you can turn a contrary current into a favorable one.

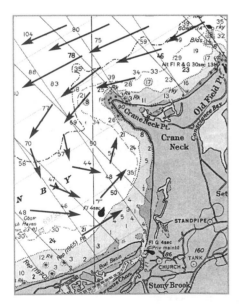

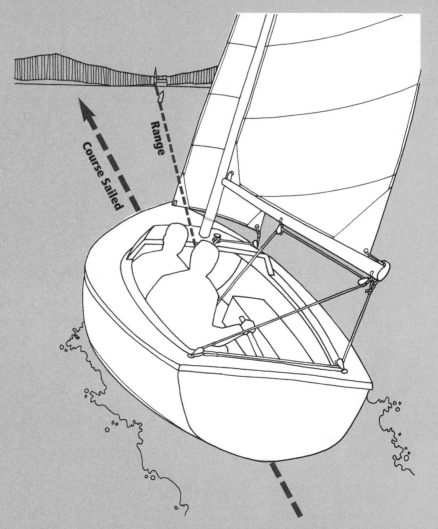

A range between two fixed objects in alignment will tell you if you are being carried to one side or the other. If the two objects stay aligned, you are correctly compensating for the current no matter what your heading may be.

you down because of the large breaking seas it creates. You often will sail faster, safer, and more comfortably in a current running with the wind and waves rather than against them.

If you have a choice, save your fastest point of sail (almost always a reach) for sailing into an unfavorable current and your slowest point of sail (normally a run) for going with a favorable current.

When sailing in a beam current, steer by a range on the shoreline. This might be two buildings or big trees in alignment. When the range is steady, you know you're steering in a way that compensates for the current. If the near object moves up-current, you're being set down; if it moves down-current, you're overcompensating.

Back eddies, or local counter currents, may form off piers or wharfs or inside indentations in the shore. They will set your boat contrary to the normal current.

When beating in a beam current on the leeward side, pushing the boat upwind, you'll make the best speed over the ground if you foot (sail fast without pinching).

Contrary to popular belief, if you're beating into a head current there's no advantage to pinching up so the current hits the bow on its leeward side. Called "lee bowing the current," all this does is slow you down since the boat will be carried along no matter what her heading is. A much more effective way of handling a head current is to foot and sail fast so you get out of it as soon as possible.

Keep your eye out for any indicator of current velocity and direction — a lobster pot's buoy, a drifting object, or the water around an oyster stake or piling all will signal water motion.

When sailing on a long leg in current, take advantage of every opportunity to take a bearing to estimate your position, or two or more bearings to fix it. A fix is the best possible measure of the current's set and drift. Between fixes, keep a careful DR plot.

Guidelines for Safe Piloting

Don't make assumptions and don't cut corners when the visibility is poor or the sea is rough. Observe all buoys, giving them a wide berth. Stay well outside shoal areas.

Make the most difficult passage on a reach, when you have speed, comfort, and maneuverability. Try to avoid beating out of a small harbor with few aids to navigation. Sailing close-hauled and tacking require much more concentration than reaching — concentration that should be available for piloting in a challenging situation.

Plot your course toward the most visible object if you have doubts about your piloting ability or the visibility. A lighted buoy is more visible than a can or nun, a lighthouse is more visible than a lighted buoy, and in daylight a steep, rocky cliff may be more visible than a lighthouse. Once you've seen the object, set your course toward another highly visible aid or landmark.

Preplot your course and any alternatives, including danger bearings, danger circles, and lighthouse ranges of visibility.

Make your passage a series of short legs of precomputed duration, which you keep track of using a stopwatch and the Speed/Time/Distance formula.

Keep a good lookout for other boats, land, and aids to navigation. Assign your most conscientious crew to this crucial job.

Assign the best steerer to the wheel or tiller in tricky situations and the most knowledgeable, experienced navigator to the chart table. Make clear who is in charge.

Use all your senses: if you smell pine trees, you're probably approaching shore. If you see a buoy leaning, there's current flowing in the direction of the tilt. If you feel rougher water, a shoal is nearby. The best way to tune your senses is to stop the boat, quiet the crew, and concentrate.

At night, avoid using white lights; otherwise night vision will disappear and not return for 10 or 15 minutes. Use red lights or at least paint a flashlight or light bulb red with a marking pen.

Stay away from lee shores. If the wind is blowing onshore (toward the land) stay much farther offshore than you would in an offshore wind blowing toward the water. Even if you aren't in danger of being blown onto shore, the wind will be unpredictable up to a mile to windward of a lee shore as it begins to rise over the land.

Alcohol and navigating don't mix. Even a can of beer will scramble a pilot's calculations.

Don't panic. Keep your head. Trust your DR plot until an estimated position or a fix tells you otherwise. Rely on basics and your boat's SOP. This is why you established it to begin with. When in doubt, stop or heave-to and think things through.

Reaching a Surprise Destination. Sometimes a navigator will get a fix and find himself located several miles from the DR position for no apparent reason. His first reaction should be to get another fix immediately. If this fix confirms the first one, there may be some backtracking to do, since the discrepancy must be explained and understood. Among the errors he could have made are that he forgot to account for deviation, leeway, or steerer error, or one of those was larger or smaller than anticipated. Or when he calculated the course he either overcompensated or undercompensated for current.

To help analyze the error or errors, first calculate how far off the DR actually is. Measure the distance and magnetic direction from the DR position to the fix and compute the tide drift and set since the last fix. If they are large (2 knots and more than 10 degrees) and the visibility is poor or night is approaching, the wisest thing to do is to stop or heave-to while you and your shipmates try to solve the problem. Look around the compass for a piece of metal, double-check your course and current calculations, and try to reconstruct the events since the last fix — perhaps one steerer wandered off course. In the short run these meanders are easily corrected, but if their cause is serious, in the long run they can be dangerous.

Introduction to Celestial Navigation

Despite great advances in electronic navigation, one of the most reliable techniques for finding your way when out of sight of land remains the skill that Americans call celestial navigation and the British call astro-navigation. This is the science of gauging your position using the sun, moon, planets, and stars as reference points. Even if the detailed techniques of celestial are no longer vital, they remain important and enjoyable skills to learn. Electronics can break down, but celestial bodies are always there (albeit at times obscured by clouds and fog).

In a general book there isn't room to do justice to every aspect of celestial navigation. The best we can do is introduce the fundamental equipment and skills, and encourage readers to go on from there. Many planetariums, maritime museums, and colleges offer courses on the subject, and there are good instructional manuals, some of which are listed in our bibliography.

Basic Principles and Tools. The tools of celestial navigation are the sextant (which takes "sights," or vertical angles to the celestial body), the chronometer (to take the exact time of a sight), and tables (for calculating the position from the sight and time).

In basic theory, celestial navigation and piloting share some common features. For example, they both use the DR as a starting point. The navigator takes bearings on objects whose positions are known and charted. Those bearings are lines of position (LOPs), and where LOPs cross is a fix. The difference is that where bearings in piloting are compass angles to stationary objects on or near the water's surface, bearings in celestial navigation are vertical angles to objects in the sky that are moving or appear to be in motion. Those angles are measured with a sextant.

In piloting, the navigator uses a chart to locate the objects on which bearings

are taken. In celestial navigation, the navigator uses printed or computerized astronomical tables that pinpoint the positions of bodies for every second of the year. To make sense of the tables, the navigator needs to know not only what the angle to a celestial body is but when the sight was taken. This is why the chronometer is needed.

To illustrate celestial's concepts, construct a simple model from an apple, a pencil, a thumbtack, and some string. Celestial navigation texts use more complicated models when teaching theory, but this will do for an introduction. Anywhere on the side of the apple, push the pencil point into the core, leaving the eraser several inches above the skin.

The apple represents the globe and the eraser represents the celestial body (the sun, star, or moon). The spot where the pencil pierces the apple's skin represents what is called the celestial body's geographical position (GP), or the position on the earth's surface between the center of the earth and the body.

Next, tack the end of the string to the tip of the eraser. Stretch the string down to the apple and swing a circle around the GP. That circle is a circle of position (COP). From every point on that circle, the altitude, or vertical angle, to the celestial body is the same. For a

In this simple model, the apple is the globe, the pencil eraser tip is a celestial body, the string is the sight through the sextant, and the inscribed angle between the string and the surface is the altitude to the body as measured by the sextant. The GP is where the pencil pierces the apple and the COP is the circle defined by the altitude. For a given altitude, you're somewhere on the COP. If you know exactly when the sight was taken, you can determine the COP using tables that show the positions of the celestial body.

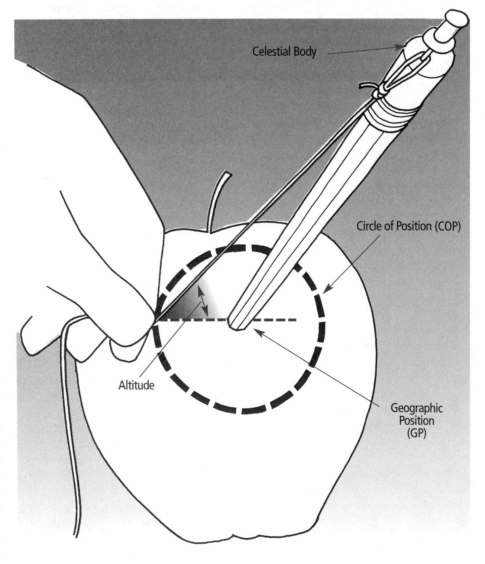

Celestial Body

Circle of Position (COP)

Altitude

Geographic Position (GP)

given altitude you're somewhere on a circle like this one. While a full-size COP is not straight, it is so large, with a radius thousands of miles long, that the part of the circle used to plot positions on a chart is represented as a straight line of position (LOP). Cross this LOP with the boat's track since the last fix and you have an estimated position (EP). Cross it with another LOP (for example, from another celestial body) and you have a fix. Cross it from a previously used LOP and you have a running fix.

Because it uses the dimension of altitude, celestial navigation has an advantageous position-finding technique that is impossible with piloting. It's called the noon sun sight. The noon sun sight is used when the sun has risen as far as it will rise, which happens within a few minutes of noon, local time. A noon sun sight gives the boat's longitude. Cross this longitude with an LOP advanced from a star or sun sight taken earlier in the day and you have a fix.

The Sextant. The sextant measures the altitude (or vertical angle) to the celestial body, using the horizon as the base line. For calculating positions, the most reliable altitudes are between 30° and 60°. Since a clear, steady horizon is the frame of reference for taking altitudes, celestial navigation may be impossible in bad weather due either to instability because of the boat's wild rolling or to poor visibility (navigators speak of times when there is "no horizon" because it blends into the sky). While "bubble" sextants with artificial horizons may work on aircraft, the bubble may be too unstable for use on pleasure boats. The range of sextants is broad, from inexpensive plastic ones designed for lifeboats to high-precision metal instruments.

The Chronometer. A chronometer is an extremely accurate timepiece such as a quartz crystal watch set to Coordinated Universal Time, known as Greenwich Mean Time (GMT or Z), which is the time at zero degrees longitude passing through Greenwich, England. Chronometers should be checked against atomic clocks or the

time tick on shortwave radio stations. Another way to take time is to set a stopwatch off the time tick and then record the time when the sight is taken. In practice, it's a good idea to do sights with two people, one to take the sight and read the angle off the sextant and the other to write down the time of the sight. Be accurate: an error of less than 5 seconds can lead to a mistake of 1 mile. Take several sights and either choose the best one, throwing out the ones that fall out of a pattern, or average the readings and the times.

The Calculations. Once the sight is taken and its time (exact to the second) is noted, the navigator refers to tables in two publications, *The Nautical Almanac* and the sight reduction tables. The data found there (or in programmed calculators or computers) are used in calculations that produce a position.

The almanac is used to figure the position of the celestial body at the time of the sight and to make small corrections in the sight based on the navigator's height above the water and other factors. It contains tables that show the geographical positions of celestial bodies for every second of every day of the year covered by the edition. Sight reduction tables are then used to figure the boat's position, using as a point of reference the boat's assumed position, which is based on her dead reckoning or estimated position. Different types of sight reduction tables are used in the various systems of making calculations.

Relying on this data — the boat's DR, the sextant angle, the time, the almanac, and the sight reduction tables — the navigator calculates the boat's position mathematically either by hand or using a computer or calculator. The end result is two numbers: the azimuth, or true bearing to the celestial body, and the intercept, or distance down the azimuth. The LOP is a line passing through the intercept at a right angle to the azimuth.

Celestial navigation may sound complicated, and it is at first. But the complications have more to do with learning the steps than with mastering astronomical theory or calculus. Much more than mathematical genius, what's needed is attention to detail.

A good sextant is easily adjusted and has clear indicators. There should be several filters to protect the eye when taking sun sights.

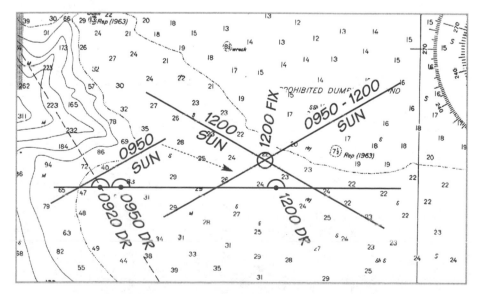

Although a celestial plot uses many piloting concepts and skills, running fixes play a more important role in celestial navigation than in piloting.

Review Quiz

Solve plotting problems on the chart here by using a plotter on the compass rose and dividers on the latitude scale on the left margin. Courses and bearings are in magnetic degrees, distances are in nautical miles, and speeds are in knots. Solutions may be found following the Index.

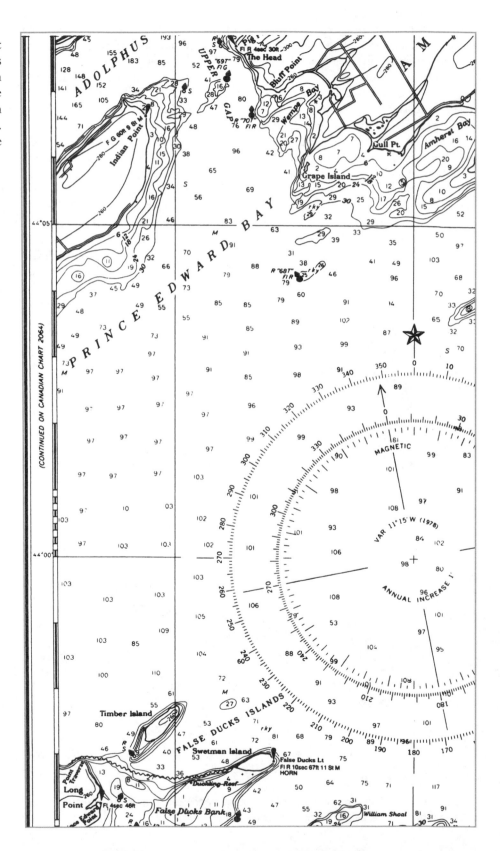

1. You are sailing at a speed of 5 knots on a course of 180°. At 1300 hours (1 PM), False Ducks Lt. bears 045° off the starboard bow at 225°. At 1336 hours, the light is directly abeam at 270°. What is your position at 1336?

    A. The light bears 315° and is 3 miles away

    B. The light bears 270° and is 3 miles away

    C. There's not enough information

2. When you stand up in a rowboat, you see the light on False Ducks lighthouse. When you sit down, the light disappears behind the horizon. Approximately what is the distance to the lighthouse?

    A. 10.8 miles

    B. 9.4 miles

    C. 11 miles

3. You are next to the buoy off Long Point (just above "4 sec") and heading in a northerly direction out into Prince Edward Bay. What are the approximate danger bearings for clearing Timber Island (including the buoy at the 9-foot spot)?

    A. Not less than (NLT) 200° on the buoy and not more than (NMT) 230° on the northeast tip of the island

    B. NLT 020° on the buoy and NMT 045° on the tip of the island

    C. 030° on the center of the island

4. The course from R "68T" FR, south of Grape Island, to the middle of Timber Island is 210°. What approximate courses must the boat steer to pass by the island with a safe berth of 0.3 mile?

    A. 204° to pass to the east and 216° to pass to the west

    B. 175° to pass to the east and 220° to pass to the west

5. If you had to enter Upper Gap from Prince Edward Bay using your depth sounder to find your way, on which of the following routes would your equipment serve to best advantage?

    A. Up the middle of the channel

    B. Up the eastern side of the channel

    C. Up the western side of the channel

6. You will need only scrap paper for this problem. You are sailing at 6 knots on a course of 045°. The current chart indicates that the tidal current's set and drift are 090° and 2 knots respectively. Estimate your approximate speed made good (SMG) and approximate course made good (CMG).

    A. SMG 4 knots, CMG 045°

    B. SMG 5 knots, CMG 030°

    C. SMG 7 knots, CMG 060°

7. At night, you pass "69T" FG, off The Head, at 2130 at a speed of 5 knots. You steer 188° in order to keep False Ducks Lt. dead ahead. A friend in another boat tells you over the VHF/FM radio that there is a current with a set of 270° and drift of 1 knot. Which course should you steer to compensate for this set and drift?

    A. 200°

    B. 176°

CHAPTER 13

Electronic Navigation and Radiotelephones

In this chapter, we will look at electronic instruments used on today's boats. These include the speedometer and other performance instruments, Loran-C, radar, the Global Positioning System (GPS), the radio direction finder, and the radiotelephone. (The depth sounder was described in chapter 12.) Electronic devices are in a state of constant improvement if not revolution, and therefore there is no way that any book can be completely up to date concerning them. This chapter must not be regarded as a substitute for instrument owners' manuals.

Which instruments should you carry? Sailors who want quick, reliably accurate, repeatable navigational assistance both in their home port and on the oceans and seas will want to have a GPS receiver. The older Loran-C, which may be phased out, remains an excellent tool for navigation near North America. Radar, properly used, is an excellent coastal navigation instrument as well as a safety device in traffic or fog. Radio direction finders, while not as accurate as GPS, Loran-C, and radar, can be helpful if radio beacons are nearby.

Radiotelephones provide instant access to nearby boats, weather forecasts, shore-based telephones, and the Coast Guard and other services. While computerized, multi-function speed, wind, and other performance indicators probably will appeal only to racing sailors, most owners will want to have a speedometer and a wind strength and direction indicator so they can gauge performance relative to the wind strength and angle.

All those instruments are available and very helpful, but with their advantages come expense and maintenance problems. The best advice is to buy only the instruments that you really need, and then use those instruments both well and with caution. The accuracy, compactness, and seeming simplicity of electronics can be distracting if not downright hypnotic. It's all too easy to assume that a GPS receiver is precisely correct 100 percent of the time and therefore to forget to keep a systematic dead reckoning plot. Not only do electronics make mistakes, but navigators can interpret and plot their readings erroneously.

Never rely entirely on only one navigation aid or system. If the GPS is the belt of your vessel's navigational trousers, use the DR plot as suspenders. In rough weather, tide-swept waters, poor visibility, or other difficult conditions, take advantage of every possible navigation aid, electronic or visual, but consider the DR to be your baseline.

Performance Instruments. Devices that measure and indicate the boat's speed and the wind's strength and direction help you plan and sail safe, accurate courses. Since these devices were developed for racing boats, they are called performance instruments, but cruising sailors can also take advantage of them.

Speedometers (also called knot-meters) measure straight-ahead speed through the water. The paddlewheel or electronic sensor on the outside of the hull that measures speed should be kept clean, and the instrument should occasionally be calibrated during timed runs over known distances using the Speed/Time/Distance formula (see chapter 11). A good speedometer can compute and display the average speed over a period of time ranging from a few seconds to a minute. Speedometers can be connected to devices called sum logs, or recording logs, which show the distance run in miles.

Speed and distance run may also be calculated by and displayed on GPS and Loran-C instruments, although in those cases the information includes the effect of tidal current and other current. In other words, these instruments show the speed and distance over the bottom rather than through the water, as a speedometer does. Many skippers will want both types of information. Still, the ability to measure speed without having to install a speedometer is appealing.

Apparent-wind indicators (AWI), consisting of a wind vane and sensors at the top of the mast and an electronic readout in the cockpit, indicate the direction and speed of the apparent

A hand-held GPS (top), a performance instrument showing tacking angle and wind direction (middle), and an electronic chart plotter (bottom) can be found in many well-equipped boats.

wind. At the least, these instruments allow the crew to determine the most effective sailing angle and also indicate when they should reef or shorten down to smaller sails. Sailing at night without an AWI can be very inefficient. Some AWIs have integral computers that can calculate true wind speed and direction and help the crew determine the point of sail on a new course.

Velocity-made-good (VMG) indicators combine the input of a speedometer and AWI to calculate the boat's progress and optimum course. Upwind, the VMG tells the crew how to balance close-windedness against straight-ahead speed; downwind, it helps the crew decide on the fastest, shortest course. A computer may be programmed to compare this information with data from a velocity prediction program (a mathematical prediction of a boat's speed and VMG for each point of sail and wind strength). The computer then calculates and displays a number that tells how efficiently the boat is being sailed. In this way the vague "feel" that tells sailors when their boat is going well can be quantified.

Radio Direction Finder (RDF)

The most elementary electronic navigation device is the RDF. Less accurate than GPS, Loran-C, and radar, but still found on many boats, RDF receivers take bearings on radio beacons on lighthouses, airport towers, AM radio transmitters, and other facilities that send out long-wave radio signals. If the beacon is charted, a line of position (LOP) can be drawn. NOS charts show the locations, frequencies, and Morse code call signals of marine beacons and aerobeacons.

The RDF is tuned to the frequency of a nearby beacon until its Morse code call signal is heard clearly. Then the RDF is swung horizontally or its antenna is rotated. When the signal is loudest, the antenna is at a right angle to the LOP to the beacon. When it is silent, the instrument is aimed directly at or away from the beacon. This point of silence is called the null. The null can be translated into a bearing using a magnetic compass or a compass rose on the RDF. Aiming the antenna to find the null is like pointing your hand directly at a buoy or a light-

house, except that the "sighted" beacon may be 30 to 200 miles distant. The use of earphones may make identifying radio signals easier, while protecting your shipmates from the brain-numbing repetition of high-frequency dots and dashes.

Because many beacons are located at entrances to major harbors, an RDF is often used to home-in on a port by following the radio path.

RDF bearings are rarely accurate to less than about 5°. Operator error will increase that margin of error significantly. Because of this predictable inaccuracy, radio bearings are plotted with special labels — "RDF bearing," "R bearing," or "Rfix." LOPs using radio beacon bearings should cross at or near right angles. Some accuracy is gained by using hand-bearing RDFs.

Since radio waves are affected by metal, an RDF must be calibrated to the individual boat, much like a compass, by taking test bearings on familiar objects at different headings. The usual problem is the lifeline. If there is an all-metal loop around the deck, the RDF may be inaccurate. Break the loop by securing the lifelines to the pulpits with sturdy lengths of line rather than shackles.

Most US radio beacons are expected to be dismantled in the early years of the 21st century.

On a chart a radio beacon is shown by a circle, the letters "R Bn," the frequency, and, often, the Morse code dot-dash identifier.

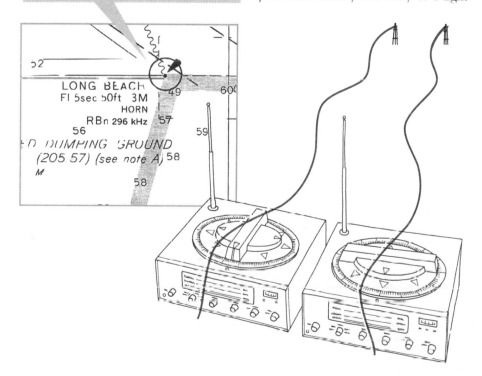

The most modern RDFs, like this one demonstrated by the author, are completely self-contained and easily aimed.

Reception is weakest at the null, when the rotating antenna points at or away from the beacon, and strongest when the antenna is at a right angle to the signal.

Loran-C

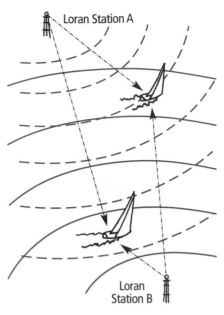

Loran, the dominant electronic navigation device from the 1970s into the 1990s, is easier to use and more accurate than an RDF. Loran today means Loran-C, the second generation of Long Range Navigation systems developed during World War II. Pairs of transmission stations send out pulsed signals simultaneously over a low frequency. The onboard receiver-computer tuned to those stations receives the signals. If the boat is exactly halfway between the two stations, on what is called the center line, there will be no time difference (TD) between the reception of the two signals. If she is anywhere else between the stations, one signal will be received before the other one. The TD in microseconds will be computed by the receiver. The receiver usually computes TDs for two or more pairs of stations, called chains, each with its own distinctive pulse group repetition interval (GRI). Most TD lines are curved like hyperbolas, which is why Loran is called a hyperbolic navigation system.

To fix a position, the navigator can plot the displayed TD lines on the chart or program the instrument to convert TDs into more easily read latitude and longitude and then plot them. Loran instruments can convert the raw data of TDs into other data, including the boat's speed over the bottom, her set and drift due to current, and the bearing and distance to a destination (called a waypoint) whose location is programmed into the instrument by the navigator. A waypoint can be the position of a buoy, harbor, racing mark, or fishing ground. A good Loran set can be programmed with dozens of waypoints. If waypoints, course, and speed data can be shown in the cockpit on a remote display called a repeater, the steerer can keep track of the boat's progress and adjust course without having to depend on someone below to monitor the Loran set.

In addition, the instrument can keep an anchor watch by setting off an alarm whenever the boat moves beyond a set distance. Loran-C can also interface with radar and computerized charts so waypoints are shown on radar scopes and computer screens.

A Loran receiver is tuned to signals sent simultaneously by pairs of stations. It displays the time difference (TD) in reception and the pilot plots the position using a chart (below) printed with corresponding TD lines or with latitude and longitude.

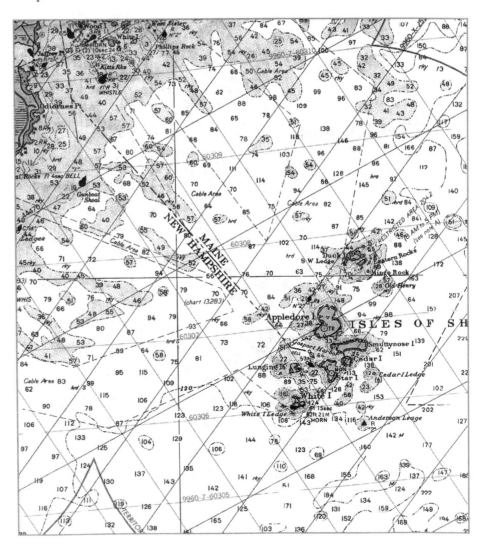

Global Positioning System (GPS)

GPS, a satellite system, succeeded Loran-C as the dominant navigation device in the 1990s. It is the world's first global electronic navigation system.

A prime benefit to mariners of the post-Sputnik era has been the use of orbiting satellites in electronic navigational systems. The first was Transit (sometimes called SATNAV), a US system developed first for submarines. By the 1980s SATNAV was found in many pleasure boats. SATNAV used a total of 10 satellites in orbit, but because of gaps in coverage, an hour or more would pass between opportunities for fixes. The government then developed another satellite navigation system with greater coverage called the Global Positioning System, with 24 satellites on six different orbital planes so that at any time, at every spot on the globe, at least three satellites are above the horizon and therefore can be used to take a fix. When GPS became fully operational in 1996, SATNAV was taken out of service.

Satellite navigation works on a principle similar to that of celestial navigation: if you know the exact location of a celestial body and can measure your relationship to it, you can calculate your own position. In celestial navigation, the relationship is measured in angular degrees above the horizon, and a circle of position results. Cross two circles of position and you have a fix.

With GPS, the relationship is the distance from the boat to the satellite measured in the change in the wavelength of a radio transmission between the two. The change is the Doppler shift. An example of how it works is the variation in pitch of a train's whistle as it approaches. The boat's receiver hears and times a satellite's radio signal (which includes the satellite's position) and, with its self-contained computer and an internal clock, factors the change in wavelength, the boat's speed and course, and the satellite's position, speed, and course

against each other to arrive at the boat's position. The satellite's own position is calculated and fed to the satellite by four ground monitoring stations. For military reasons, a filter called selective availability keeps signals sent to military users more accurate than those sent to civilian receivers. The first can pinpoint a position to within about 50 feet, the second

to about 300 feet. Selective availability may be circumvented through a system called differential GPS, which works only close to North America.

Anything Loran-C can do, GPS can do. It automatically displays positions, calculates boat speed and heading, figures distance and bearing to hundreds of waypoints, stands anchor watch, interfaces with radar, and so on. GPS's repertory is constantly being expanded. A popular use of GPS is in a course plotter, which displays the local chart and the boat's position on the GPS screen or the radar.

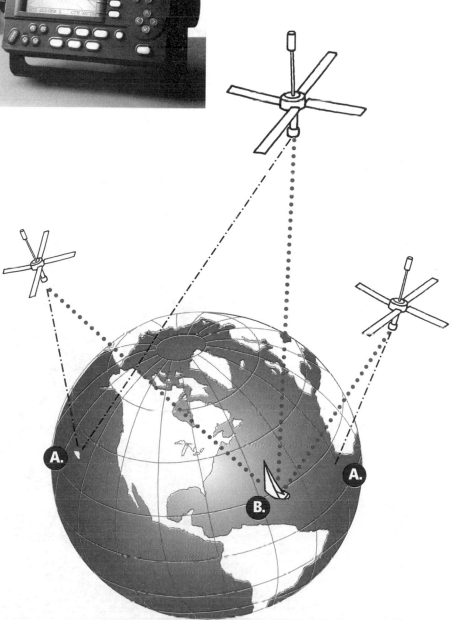

With GPS a monitoring station (A) gives the satellite its position. At any time anywhere on the globe three of the 24 satellites in the system are visible. The boat's receiver (B) picks up a signal from each satellite and calculates the distance to each on its internal computer to produce a fix. Many GPS devices are hand held.

Radar

Radar scanners used to be found only on ships and large yachts, but now they appear on boats as small as 20 feet. When operated and interpreted with care, radar is an extremely valuable tool for navigating near shore as well as a fine safety feature.

In radar, a radio pulse is transmitted through a rotating antenna called a scanner. If the pulse hits a reflective target (the best reflections are made by wide, vertical, sharp-edged metal objects), it bounces back to be received by the scanner before another pulse is transmit-ted. A device converts this information into a visual display on a screen called a scope. The display is a point of light called a pip or blip.

The theoretical radar range in nautical miles is 1.22 times the square root of the height of the scanner. Thus, a scanner 16 feet above the water has a range of almost 5 miles. Tall targets like the bridge of a large freighter may be seen beyond that range, assuming that the radar is powerful enough to send the pulses that far. Rain and other precipitation considerably shorten the range and may even make radar ineffective, and fog slightly shortens the range. (The benefit of this sensitivity to precipitation is that radar is a useful detector of approaching bad weather.)

Scope Displays. Three different types of scopes are found on pleasure-boat radar sets. Each has a 360° azimuth around the perimeter to indicate relative courses and bearings.

The display seen on most pleasure boat scopes is Relative Presentation/ Ship's Head Up, which shows the boat in the center of the scope and displays the boat's heading as a line running straight up. When the boat turns, the land is seen as moving around her; when the scope is switched to short ranges, this motion can be dizzying. Another problem is that the scope's display is oriented differently from most charts, which are north up. It takes some practice to be able to move confidently and easily from the scope to the chart and back again.

Another display, True Presentation/ North Up, is oriented like a chart. The boat is in the center and true north is straight up. On the third type of scope, a True Motion display, true north is also straight up but the boat need not be placed at the center. True Motion displays can interface with GPS and Loran-C to display waypoints, range, and bearing on the scope.

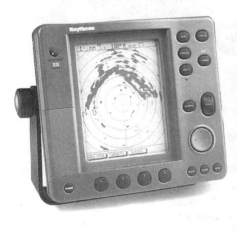

A radar set sends out pulses through a scanner (above), which then receives echoes bounced back by objects, whose locations are shown as pips on the scope (right and below). Clarity of reception varies with the object and the weather.

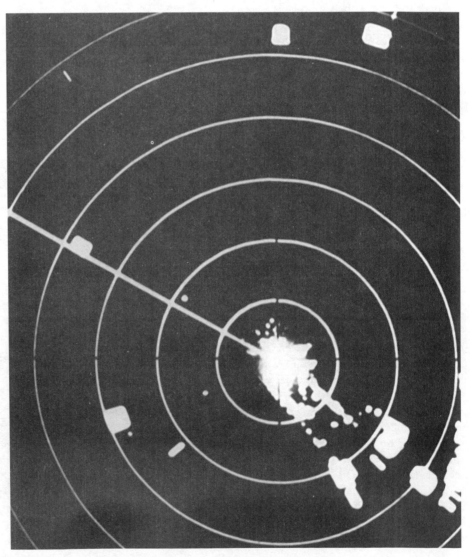

The set's range (the mileage scale on the scope) can be quickly adjusted to change the display from long ranges (showing large areas) to short ranges (showing small areas). A good practice is to start with a medium range like 4 miles in order to get oriented to your general position, and then to shift down to short ranges like 2 or even ½ miles to identify targets. Ranges (distances) to targets in miles are calculated using fixed range rings and the adjustable variable range marker (VRM). The distances in miles between range rings and between the boat and the VRM are displayed on the scope.

Bearings to targets in degrees are taken with the adjustable electronic bearing line (EBL). The bearings are displayed on the scope, usually in relative degrees.

Tune the set to the strongest possible signal. Signal strength and reception change as the set warms up and as ranges are changed, so keep an eye on tuning gauges. Set the gain control so there is a very faint background of white dots, or "sea clutter" (the reflection off waves). If the accuracy of ranges and bearings seems in doubt, slightly reduce the gain and switch to a shorter range. If nearby targets appear fuzzy it may be due to too short a range, or to sea clutter.

A problem inherent with sailboats is a blind spot caused by a mast, boom, or other on-board reflective object that may screen targets. To check to see if your boat has built-in blind spots, go out in a light rain or moderately rough sea and adjust the rain and sea clutter controls to show some clutter, which is shown as white dots. Wherever the clutter disappears on the scope, there is a blind spot.

Radar Navigation. When sailing near buoys and distinctive landmarks, navigators with a choice of equipment may prefer to find their way with radar ranges, radar bearings, or both. To make a fix with radar ranges, first determine your range to each of two or more known charted objects (preferably lighthouses or headlands) using the range rings or the variable range marker (VRM) in a distance-off calculation. The range in miles is displayed on the scope. On the chart, spread the legs of a drawing compass to the range in miles, using the chart's mileage or latitude scale. Place the compass's sharp point on

the charted object and, without changing the spread of the legs, draw an arc near your dead-reckoning position. That arc is a circle of position (COP); you are somewhere on it. Repeat these steps with another fixed charted object. Where the COPs cross is a fix.

While radar ranges generally are more accurate than radar bearings, bearing fixes can be made using the electronic bearing line (EBL) much the way that they are made with a compass or radio direction finder. Be sure to convert the relative bearing displayed on the scope to a magnetic bearing.

Range-and-bearing fixes can be made with just one charted object. At the same time, determine both your range and relative bearing to a charted object. Convert the relative bearing to a magnetic one and plot it as a line of position (LOP).

Lay off the range using a drawing compass and plot a circle of position (COP). Where the COP crosses the LOP is the fix.

Label these fixes "Radar fix" so you have a record of how you arrived at them in case you later discover that electronic interference or some other factor has made your instruments unreliable.

Collision Avoidance with Radar. The main reason most people outfit their boats with radar is to help them avoid collisions with other objects.

Identifying Targets. Accurate target identification is one of the most difficult aspects of radar use. Targets sometimes seem to appear and disappear, enlarge and shrink, and even multiply in number. Reliable target identification comes with experience, but there are some helpful rules of thumb. First we'll look at the problem.

Radar "sees" only those objects that reflect its pulses. This means that the display on the scope can be misleading. The size of a target has little to do with its

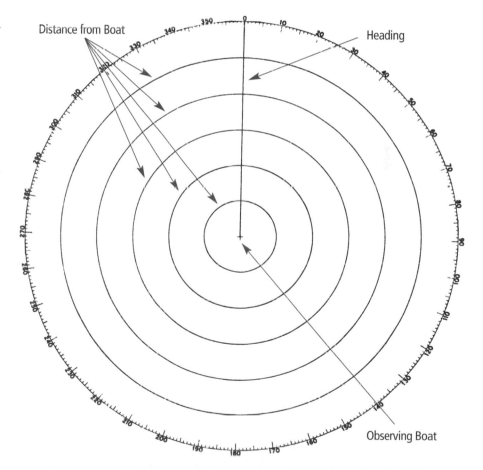

A Relative Presentation/Ship's Head Up display like this one is found on many pleasure-boat radar scopes. The observing boat is shown at the center of the scope and the line straight up is her heading. The circular range rings show distance from her at equal intervals. On most scopes, the heading in magnetic degrees, the range (or distance to the outer ring), and the interval between the rings are clearly displayed.

Radar

reflectibility; shape and composition are everything. Metal reflects and wood does not: at short range, a floating soft drink can may seem as large as a 20-foot wooden boat. Vertical surfaces reflect and horizontal ones do not: where a waterfront beach slopes gradually back to a hill, the radar will pick up the hill but not the beach, encouraging the navigator to plan a course that will take the boat right onto the beach. Another problem is that a large target like a ship or an island screens smaller targets behind it.

Most buoys and other government aids to navigation are exceptionally reflective. Some are equipped with small radar reflectors called ramarks, which transmit a dot-dash signal, or racons, which respond to radar pulses by transmitting their own signal in order to enhance the echo. Even buoys without these special devices reflect very well because their angular structures offer plenty of metal faces to catch and throw back pulses.

Add reflection off the water and you see a lot of pips on the scope. Which one is a target to worry about? Is it stationary or moving? If stationary, is it a buoy or a vessel dead in the water? If moving, which direction is she heading and at what speed? Identifying targets may sound simple, but it is not. One reason is that you the observer are also moving. In other words, the view on the scope is not the same kind of steady bird's eye view that we get when doing dead-reckoning or any other kind of navigation.

What this means is that on a moving boat the display on the radar scope is not a true representation of reality. Things that seem to be in motion are actually dead in the water, and vice versa. If that sounds strange, compare a buoy with a boat paralleling your course at your speed. The anchored buoy appears on the scope as moving in a course opposite

to yours at a speed equal to yours. Meanwhile, the moving boat seems to be stationary.

Because radar can be misleading, people who buy radar sets should be aware that their legal or insurance liability in case of a collision may well depend on their proving that they accurately interpreted the display. According to Rule 7 of the Navigation Rules, "Proper use shall be made of radar equipment if fitted and operational, including long range scanning to obtain early warning of risk of collision and radar plotting or equivalent systematic observation of detected objects." A radar textbook summarizes court opinions this way: "Failure to interpret correctly what your radar shows, or can be made to show, is held by the courts to be culpable negligence." So, if you have radar, learn how to use it, and use it well.

The Relative Motion Line. To identify and keep track of potentially dangerous moving targets, military and merchant mariners use a technique called Rapid Radar Plotting. Using vector analysis, the observer first determines the other vessel's speed and course, then calculates what course or speed changes his or her own boat must make in order to avoid a collision. This work is done with a grease pencil right on the scope. Rapid Radar Plotting does take special training. Coast Guard districts can provide the names and addresses of nearby schools offering courses in all aspects of radar.

There is another way to identify and avoid targets that, while less accurate than Rapid Radar Plotting, is simpler to learn and use. This is the technique of keeping track of the target's relative motion line (RML). There are two ways to keep track of the target's RML, one "quick and

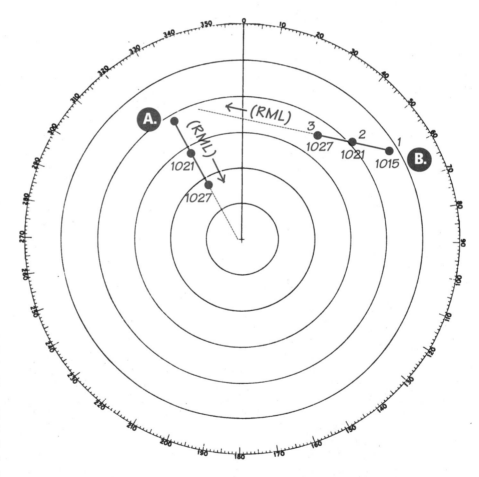

Once a pip appears on the scope, keep track of it to see if a collision threatens. Using a straightedge (like a short, narrow piece of cardboard) trace the target's motion from position to position. The line that results is called the relative motion line (RML). If you do this every 6 minutes (which is one-tenth of an hour) you can easily convert distance into speed by multiplying by 10. Here the RML for target A indicates a collision will occur unless one of the boats turns, while the other RML shows you will clear target B.

dirty" and the other more involved.

The radar operator takes range and bearing fixes on a nearby vessel every few minutes. The faster you and the vessel are closing on each other, the more frequent the fixes should be. Remember that the course and speed shown on the scope are relative. The other vessel's actual course and speed are different. Again, if you want to be sure of her actual course and speed, stop your boat and take radar or compass bearings on her.

Whenever possible, back up an RML plot with visual bearings on the other vessel. If there is any chance of collision, call her on VHF/FM radiotelephone channel 6, 9, 13, or 16 to identify yourself and talk the situation over. Alter course with care. There are many stories of crews that turned into targets' actual courses while thinking that they were dodging them. Keep track of the analysis by plotting it on a standard ship's plotting sheet (available at special navigation instrument outlets) or on a sheet of paper with range rings drawn on it.

Here's how to keep an RML plot on a target:

1. From the center, lay out your course, mark it OC ("own course"), and note your speed.

2. Using the range and bearing to the target as shown on the scope, plot the target's position. Label it "1" and note the time.

3. At regular intervals, take new range and bearing fixes on the target and plot them, labeling them "2," "3," etc., and noting the time. Draw a line between the positions. That line is the RML. It represents the target's apparent speed and course taking into account your boat's speed and course.

4. Compare the positions. If position 2 is closer to you than position 1, you and the target are closing on each other.

5. Calculate the object's relative speed. With dividers, measure the distance the target traveled between position 1 and position 2 on the RML. With the plotting sheet's scale, estimate the distance, then estimate the object's speed. (If the plots are 6 minutes apart, simply multiply the distance by 10 to get the speed.)

6. Compare the target's relative speed with your boat's actual speed. If the target's relative speed is greater than your speed, the target is another vessel coming

at you. If the target's relative speed is less than your speed, the target is another vessel headed away from you at a speed slower than yours. If the two speeds are equal and the two positions are on a line paralleling your course, the target actually is stationary. It may be a rock, a buoy or a boat dead in the water. Finally if the target's two positions are the same, it is another vessel heading on the same course as yours at the same speed as yours.

7. If the RML is aimed at you and the target is getting closer, a collision or very close call is likely. An RML pointed at you means that the bearing to the target is not changing. Either you must alter course or you must talk the situation over with the other vessel and ask her to alter course.

Radar Reflectors. Making sure your own boat is visible on other vessels' radar scopes is as important as spotting them on your own scope. The best reflector is a metal object with a lot of faces at sharp angles. A round aluminum mast may not provide enough reflectibility on its own, but stuff it with crumpled-up aluminum foil and it will stand out beautifully on other vessels' radar scopes.

Tests of commercial radar reflectors have shown that one of the best is a folding device hung off the backstay or a halyard. An electronic radar detector can also be useful; while it won't make you more visible on another vessel's scope, it may pick up her radar pulses and give enough warning to get out of the way.

A good radar reflector provides many sharp angles.

HANDS ON: "Quick and Dirty" RML Use

The "quick and dirty" RML radar method is to lay a straightedge on the scope along the line of the target's relative motion in order to see if the target is on a collision course with your boat. The straightedge can be a strip of paper or cardboard. When you first see the target on the scope, mark it with a grease pencil. A couple of minutes later, place the edge of the paper on the target's new position and turn the edge until it cuts through the first position. As you continue to track the target, adjust the straightedge to compensate for changes in the target's relative course. Back up these observations with visual bearings on the target. If you are confused by the scope, you can stop your boat in order to track the target's actual course (which unlike the RML is based solely on her speed and heading). But don't stop when you're near another moving boat, whose crew may be misled by your action.

If the straightedge aims toward the center of the scope, you and the target will collide unless one or both of you take action. Carefully monitor the situation on the scope and on deck, and don't change course impulsively.

Radiotelephones

Several types of radio systems are used to link one vessel to another, a vessel to the Coast Guard and the marine police, a vessel to shore, and a vessel to weather and emergency services. Among these are satellite phone systems, used often on the high seas, and citizens band (CB) and ham radio. The most popular systems afloat are very high frequency/FM (VHF/FM) and single-sideband (SSB) radiotelephones. VHF/FM provides a sharp signal over many channels within a short range of about 50 miles, using inexpensive transmitter-receivers. SSB is more expensive and complicated to use, but has a range of more than 1,000 miles.

Very High Frequency/FM (VHF/FM). As anyone who owns an AM/FM radio knows, FM (frequency modulated) stations provide the sharper reception by far. Unfortunately the price paid for this excellent reception is a fairly wide signal. To make room for the large number of FM channels required by the growing

Offshore, the single-sideband (SSB) radiotelephone provides a range of 1,000 miles or more. Like VHF/FM, SSB sets have a distress frequency.

population of sailors, the very high frequency band must be used. The higher the frequency of radio transmissions, the shorter is their range, and the frequencies normally used by marine VHF/FM systems have a range limited to less than about 50 miles, although a temperature inversion or other atmospheric irregularity may increase the range.

Channels are reserved for special purposes. The most important one, and the one found on all receivers, is channel 16:

Channel 16 is the distress channel continuously monitored by the Coast Guard and other agencies; it also is used to initiate communications, which are then quickly switched to other channels. Channel 16 must not be used for prolonged conversations.

Channel 6 is for ship-to-ship transmissions concerning safety.

Channel 9 is for ship-to-ship communications and may be used to initiate communications.

Channel 12 is for traffic advisories in port operations

Channel 13 is for ship-to-ship communications.

Channels 14 and 65-A are for ship-to-ship and ship-to-shore communications concerning port operations.

Channel 22-A is for Coast Guard and maritime safety information broadcasts and communications with the Coast Guard after initial contact on channel 16.

Channels 24, 26, and 28 are for public telephone calls through a marine operator.

Channel 67 is for commercial ship-

The very high frequency/FM radiotelephone is the standard tool for communicating when sailing near shore, where its limited range is not a problem.

to-ship transmissions, except on Puget Sound where it may be used for non-commercial ship-to-ship transmissions.

Channels 79-A and 80-A are for commercial ship-to-ship and ship-to-shore transmissions, except on the Great Lakes where they may be used for non-commercial ship-to-ship transmissions.

Channel 70 is a distress and safety channel for vessels with Selective Digital Calling.

Channels 68, 71, 72, and 78-A are for non-commercial use, ship-to-ship or ship-to-shore.

Channel 83-A in some areas is used by the Coast Guard Auxiliary.

Channels WX-1, WX-2, and WX-3 (reception only) are for weather broadcasts.

A valuable option when sailing in crowded waters is a scanner, which automatically receives any transmission it picks up over the channels. Without a scanner you may miss an important message or a distress signal from another boat, the Coast Guard, or the marine police.

What to Look for in a VHF/FM. Technology and advertising hype can be misleading, and a VHF/FM purchaser may end up with more or less equipment than needed. A standard 25-watt set is sufficiently powerful for most needs, but the variety of antennas available presents a choice that is much less simple. The typical antenna is a wire protected by a long fiberglass whip. Generally speaking, the longer the antenna, the greater is its power — or "gain." High gain tends to narrow and focus the radiation pattern of the radio waves, which increases effective range. But this arrow may be so sharp that it aims far above other boats as the transmitting vessel rolls and pitches in rough weather. The "fatness" of a low-gain transmission will cover a deeper though shorter range in the same conditions. The decision about which antenna to

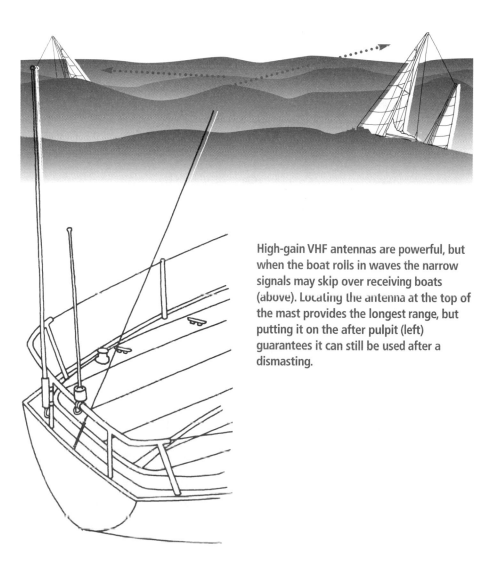

High-gain VHF antennas are powerful, but when the boat rolls in waves the narrow signals may skip over receiving boats (above). Locating the antenna at the top of the mast provides the longest range, but putting it on the after pulpit (left) guarantees it can still be used after a dismasting.

Radiotelephones

Though limited in range, a hand-held VHF provides backup and contact directly from a cockpit or life raft.

buy often has more to do with the boat's size than with any other factor. An 8-foot antenna would be extremely awkward on a boat small enough to roll violently in a seaway, while it would fit nicely on a large vessel stable enough in rough weather to effectively use a high-gain antenna.

On sailboats, VHF/FM antennas are often placed at the masthead. This increases the range and locates the antenna far out of the way of crew members (who could break one on the rail simply by leaning on it), but the long cable to the antenna may cause power loss. More significant, the receiver will be useless if the mast breaks unless a replacement antenna can be installed on deck. There's the same risk if the permanent backstay is used as the antenna, as is also common. The best place for the antenna is far aft, where it will be out of the way of normal deck activity. Most VHF/FM equipment can be readily installed by the operator.

An extremely valuable type of VHF/FM radiotelephone is the hand-held version that many smart skippers carry in their cockpits and put in abandon ship bags. Though their low power allows them a limited range, these handy receivers, used properly, can help you get out of potential collision situations. In a crowded harbor or channel, or when near freighters or other large ships, you can use the hand-held VHF to talk to captains of other vessels to alert them of your position and intentions. After you abandon ship, this radio may attract rescuers' attention. And with a hand-held, you can go off in the dinghy and communicate with the boat over the main radiotelephone. Hand-helds are battery-powered, so check the batteries often.

Licensing. The Federal Communications Commission requires that all marine-band equipment and operators be licensed. Equipment licenses are issued by the FCC, 1270 Fairfield Road, Gettysburg, PA 17325-7245; (800) 322-1117.

Regulations. Although marine radio frequencies are often the nautical equivalent of the backyard fence, the system is not intended for gossip and chitchat. Transmissions should not be made unless necessary; in particular, channel 16 must be reserved for initiating calls and for distress calls. Certain FCC regulations govern marine-band transmissions. In summary, these regulations say the following:

Any transmissions (made or overheard) concerning marine safety — including distress calls — must be logged, and the log entries must be signed.

Profanity may not be used during transmissions.

Attempts to contact another boat over channel 16 may take no longer than 30 seconds and be repeated no more frequently than every 2 minutes. After the third failed attempt, a delay of 15 minutes (or 3 minutes, if transmissions from other boats will not be interrupted) must ensue before another try is made.

Once contact is successfully completed on channel 16, you must switch to another channel within two minutes.

Transmissions must be made with the minimum necessary power. (A switch on VHF/FM sets allows power reduction from 25 watts to 1 watt.)

Conversations must be as brief as possible, and messages must be truthful.

Identification using the boat's name and her call sign is required by all parties at the beginning and the end of a conversation but not at the start and end of each exchange during the conversation. If they talk long enough, the parties must identify themselves at least once every 15 minutes.

Overheard information is considered privileged and may not be divulged — except in cases of emergency. A radiotelephone channel works like a big telephone party line and, by law, the privacy of exchanges must be respected.

Violations of these and other regulations can lead to warnings, revocations of licenses, and fines.

Single-Sideband (SSB). Although single-sideband (SSB) radiotelephones are licensed like VHF/FM equipment and their use and rules of operation are the same, they are quite different in other ways. A high-frequency (12- to 22-MHZ), high-power (75- to 150-watt) system, SSB is much better suited for offshore use than its very-high-frequency, low-power, limited-range cousin. Its range can be more than 1,000 miles. SSB antennas are large and complicated; they and the receivers must be installed and tuned by professionals. An SSB station license will be approved only if the boat also has a VHF/FM receiver.

The name "single-sideband" is derived from the way in which the radio waves are transmitted, which in turn is a variation on AM (amplitude modulation) transmission. An AM signal includes a "carrier" on which two bands that contain the same information are transported. Since these bands lie either side of the carrier, they are called sidebands; old AM radiotelephones were called "double sidebands." SSB replaced AM in the early 1970s, suppressing the carrier, eliminating one of the sidebands, and focusing all the saved energy into the remaining sideband. The resulting signal is narrower and takes up less space — allowing more channels.

Operating an SSB radiotelephone is more difficult than handling a VHF/FM. Propagation tables ease the chore of selecting the right channel for the conditions, but the operator's experience and "touch" are equally important.

Every SSB receiver must have the distress frequency, 2182 kHz; 1670 kHz is used to contact the US Coast Guard.

HANDS ON: How to Make a Call

To contact another boat, first turn on the VHF/FM set and turn to channel 16. When the frequency is clear of all other conversations, state the following message into the microphone:

"[Boat called], this is [sending boat and call sign]. Over." State the boats' names slowly and accurately. Use the military alphabet when saying the call sign (for example, WS 3838 is "Whiskey Sierra three-eight-three-eight"). Since "nine" and "five" can sound alike, say "niner" for "nine."

The contacted boat should respond:

"[Sending boat], this is [boat called and call sign]. Over." Then the sending boat names another channel to switch to. When the two boats are on that channel, the conversation resumes.

To end a coversation, say "out" in place of "over."

You can use the radio as a telephone and place calls to shoreside phones through a marine operator on designated channels. (In 1999 AT&T announced it would eliminate its high seas service.) Marine operators are cheerful, competent, and concerned people who often will go to great lengths to help a caller. But they cannot solve the problem of paying for the call. When you place the call, you will be required to call collect or charge it to your telephone credit card, home phone, or a special account. A collect call is far better than using a credit card, whose number may be overheard by anybody on this open channel. Many credit card numbers have been stolen this way. Increasingly, boaters are relying on satellite communications for ship-to-shore communications, using cellular telephones for voice transmissions or laptop computers for electronic mail.

The Mayday Call

Press the alarm signal on the transmitter (if it has one) for 30–60 seconds. This will alert people monitoring the frequency that a distress call is imminent.

Slowly and clearly say "Mayday" three times, then the name of your boat three times. Give your VHF/FM or SSB call sign (printed on the license). Report your position either as latitude and longitude or as a bearing and distance from a charted object. The rescuer should be able to quickly enter your position as a waypoint on the GPS or Loran.

Describe your situation briefly; for example, "Dismasted and drifting southeast at 2 knots onto Catalina Island 3 miles downwind. Require tow."

Describe your boat's most important features, emphasizing her rig, length, and color. Say how many people are aboard.

Keep repeating the above four steps until somebody acknowledges your call.

CHAPTER 14

Anchoring

Ground Tackle

When you're "dropping the hook," whether for a brief lunch stop in a quiet cove or for a stay of several months in a tropical port, you are engaged in what many sailors consider to be the quintessential seaman's act. Anchoring properly requires familiarity with some specialized equipment and skills, as well as careful planning and alertness to weather and current.

A lightweight anchor exhibits the parts found on most anchors.

Rode Rode

Shackle

Chain Rode

Shank

Fluke

Crown

The equipment used when anchoring, called ground tackle, is divided into two categories: the anchor (the "hook") itself and the rode, a length of rope or chain (and sometimes a combination of the two). Larger boats also require windlasses (electric winches on the foredeck) to pull up the ground tackle, which can be heavy.

There is no perfect anchor or rode. Each of the types available has its strengths and weaknesses. For this reason an experienced skipper, even on short cruises, carries at least two types of anchors and rodes so the boat is prepared for different harbors and weather conditions. Long-distance cruisers may carry four or five anchors of varying types and weights, plus one 200-foot all-chain rode and two 300-foot nylon rodes, each with 60–100 feet of chain. In areas like coastal Alaska, where depths often are over 80 and even 100 feet, many boats carry at least one rode longer than 500 feet.

Anchors. The anchor is the boat's insurance policy, and like insurance policies anchors come in many types and sizes. The key factors are shape, size, and weight. While they differ in many respects, all types of anchors have four things in common.

First and most obviously, anchors are nonbuoyant, made of galvanized steel, stronger high-tensile steel, or aluminum.

Second, anchors are connected to the boat by a rode several times longer than the water is deep.

Third, anchors have one or two flat surfaces called flukes that set (grab or dig) into the bottom. The shape and sharpness of the flukes determine whether the anchor does better in soft bottoms (like mud and sand), in hard bottoms (gravel, grass, weed, or hard clay), or in foul bottoms (rocks or abandoned anchors, rodes, wrecks, and other man-made items discarded in an anchorage). Coral also is a foul bottom, but boats should not anchor in coral because their anchors damage it.

Fourth, running between the flukes and the rode in all anchors is an arm called a shank, whose length and angle help the flukes dig in. In addition, many anchors also have a device that keeps the anchor from tripping (lifting out of the bottom, dragging, and not resetting) when the boat shifts position due to a wind or tide change or a swing to one side in a gust. This swinging, or sailing around the anchor, might cause the anchor to trip and drag until (the crew hopes) the hook resets itself. On some anchors the anti-tripping device is a horizontal bar called a stock; on others it is a hinge where the shank meets the flukes. The stock or hinge might catch or be jammed by a rock, shell, or other object on the bottom. Anchors without stocks and hinges have unusually large flukes that grab a large part of the bottom and can hang on even when the rode is at an oblique angle.

Some anchors are good for some situations, others for others. For example, while the bottoms of many Atlantic Coast ports are relatively shallow and sandy or muddy, Pacific Ocean anchorages often are deep or littered with rocks and coral. Just where, when, and how certain anchors work best is the subject of perpetual speculation and occasional testing. People analyze anchors' underwater performance endlessly, much as psychologists reflect on the inner workings of the mind. When selecting ground tackle, a good rule of thumb is to follow the example of experienced sailors in your area.

Anchor weight is recommended by manufacturers or can be determined by various tables. Alternatively, observe the caution laid down for equipping a long-distance cruiser by Linda and Steve Dashew in their excellent *Offshore Cruising Encyclopedia* (2nd edition): "Look at the average size of anchor in use for boats of your type, and double the size. After doing this, if you think you can swing it, add another 50 percent." Weight is in part relative. An anchor for a 50-footer will weigh far more than for a 25-footer. But there is one absolute concerning anchor weight: 60 pounds is about the maximum weight that a fit person can handle without a windlass and without risking back strain or other injury.

There are three families of anchors:

The **working anchor** (primary anchor) is an anchor of medium weight — in the middle range of the guidelines for your boat — used for regular overnight anchoring in conditions other than a gale or storm. A good cruising boat carries two working anchors: a primary for the typical bottoms in the cruising area (for example, a hard bottom), and a secondary for other bottoms (a soft bottom, for instance). Two popular combinations are the plow and the lightweight, and the Bruce and the lightweight.

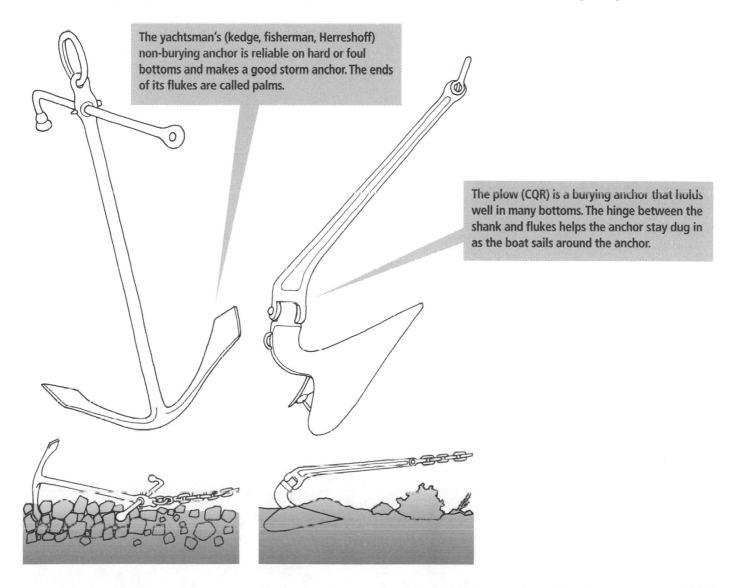

The yachtsman's (kedge, fisherman, Herreshoff) non-burying anchor is reliable on hard or foul bottoms and makes a good storm anchor. The ends of its flukes are called palms.

The plow (CQR) is a burying anchor that holds well in many bottoms. The hinge between the shank and flukes helps the anchor stay dug in as the boat sails around the anchor.

Ground Tackle

A **storm anchor** is an unusually heavy anchor of any type used mainly in heavy weather, sometimes in tandem with the working anchor on two rodes.

A **lunch hook** is a very lightweight anchor suitable only for short stops during the day when the crew stays on board and can keep an eye on things.

Anchor Types. Each of those three families includes two design types. **Non-burying** anchors hook onto rocks and hard bottoms and must rehook themselves when the boat changes position. **Burying** or deep-burying anchors dig deep into soft bottoms and usually hold when the boat swings. Some anchors function in both a non-burying and burying way (for instance, the plow anchor).

Here we'll describe the five most popular types of anchor. The weights recommended here are conservative ones for normal cruising in protected waters by a typical modern, light- to moderate-displacement 35-foot cruiser-racer. Larger boats, long-distance sailors, and boats anchoring in unusually difficult cruising grounds will want bigger anchors according to manufacturers' recommendations.

The traditional **yachtsman's anchor** (known also as the kedge, fisherman, and Herreshoff) is a non-burying anchor and the heaviest and largest of these types. It is little used today. A safety-conscious skipper of a 35-footer would choose a yachtsman's weighing 60 pounds. As a non-burying anchor, it succeeds because of its weight and its ability to grab a rock or another underwater protrusion with the palm-shaped tips on its flukes. It is one of the few anchors that can be relied on to grab in thick grass and weed, but because the flukes are narrow, it does not hold well in soft mud. Due to its size and awkwardness, it is rarely used as the working anchor. But it is carried for use as a storm anchor, especially for rocky or

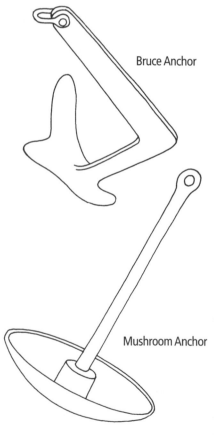

Bruce Anchor

Mushroom Anchor

The Bruce (top) and the mushroom (above) are popular anchors for different purposes. The Bruce is a working anchor, the mushroom is used in moorings because it is hard to break out.

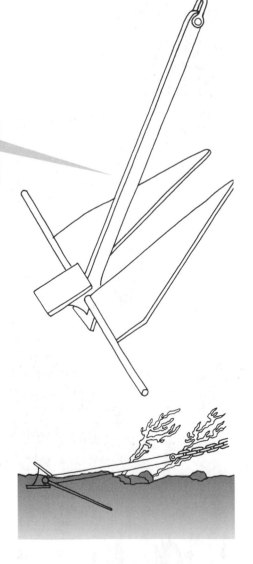

Easy to handle, the lightweight is a burying anchor that holds well in a soft bottom but can skip across a hard one.

grassy bottoms. It cannot be stowed unless first disassembled.

The **plow anchor** (known also by the trade name CQR — "secure") is far more popular and less awkward to handle than the yachtsman's, and because it is a burying anchor it can be lighter. A 35-footer would carry a plow weighing at least 35 pounds. Many experienced sailors make the plow the primary working anchor. In a reader survey in the magazine *Blue Water Sailing* in 1997, the plow ranked highest both as the working or primary anchor and as the anchor to have if for some reason there's only one on board. Widely respected for its holding power under large loads, it is used as a storm anchor in heavy weights. While the plow may not be best for all bottoms, it generally holds well in most of them, although the flukes may slide over grass or weed and slice through soft mud. A swivel allows the shank to swing over so the anchor digs in when the boat is off to one side. A plow is often stowed on a short sprit on the bow with a roller for the rode.

The **lightweight anchor** (also known by such trade names as Danforth, Fortress, and West Performance), as the name suggests, is unusually light. A steel lightweight used as a working anchor on a normal 35-footer should weigh at least 20 pounds, and an aluminum lightweight at least 16 pounds. In the *Blue Water Sailing* survey, the lightweight ranked as the most popular secondary anchor, or the one to use if the primary drags. Most lunch hooks are lightweights, as are anchors used for kedging-off (pulling a grounded boat into deep water).

The lightweight requires greater scope (more rode in proportion to the water depth) than other anchors. It's a burying anchor, with unusually wide, sharp flukes and a stock. Once dug into mud, lightweights generally hold extremely well under great loads, and some long-distance sailors carry large ones as storm anchors for those bottoms, complementing a plow or yachtsman's anchor. But lightweights may skip over grass, weed, and hard clay, and may not grab large rocks (which may bend these anchors). Clay, shell, or gravel may jam them. When dropped into the water, lightweights may not fall straight but instead "sail" to the bottom.

The aluminum Fortress type is unusually light (a 35-footer might carry a 16-pound Fortress) and holds well. Its shank can be adjusted to optimum angles of 32° for sand and 45° for mud, and some Fortresses can be disassembled to ease the problem of stowage in a small boat. Lightweights can be stowed flat on deck in brackets.

The relatively new and increasingly popular **Bruce anchor** (and other claw-like anchors like it) is a burying type with no moving parts. A cautious skipper of a typical 35-foot cruiser-racer would carry a 35-pound Bruce. The Bruce is widely respected for its ability to quickly set itself (dig in) when the boat first anchors, and to resist being tripped (pulled out without resetting itself) when the wind or tide change. Because it is unusually effective on foul bottoms and at short scope (when relatively little rode is let out), many skippers prefer it for anchoring in crowded harbors. It holds well in most bottoms, including rock, sand, and grass (which deflects most other anchors). But the Bruce may grab loose rocks and not dig in, and has a reputation for dragging under extremely high loads. It can be stowed conveniently on a bow roller.

Also relatively new is the **Delta anchor,** which looks like a plow without a hinge but comes in lighter weights. A 35-footer would carry a Delta weighing at least 22 pounds. The Delta was the second most mentioned primary anchor in the 1997 *Blue Water Sailing* survey. It holds in a wide range of bottoms, excepting large rocks and weed. It also can be stowed on a bow roller.

These are the most well known and widely used anchors. Other familiar anchors include the **mushroom,** used usually in a mooring because it holds well but is hard to retrieve; the **Northill,** a lightweight burying type that has a tendency to snag on underwater objects; and the **grapnel,** a very lightweight multi-pronged anchor used chiefly as a lunch hook or for grabbing objects below the water. A number of other anchors designed along the plans of the lightweight and plow have small, dedicated followings.

Anchor Rode. The anchor is one part of ground tackle. The other is the rode — the length of rope, chain, or combination of the two that links the anchor to the boat. It must be strong and long enough for expected loads and water depths. It must also absorb the sudden shocks of a boat jerking in rough weather, for otherwise the anchor will be pulled right out of the bottom. And the rode should sag in order to permit the pull on the anchor's shank to be as close to horizontal and parallel to the bottom as possible so the flukes dig in instead of lifting up and pulling out.

A rode made of nylon line satisfies the first two requirements quite well, for nylon is both strong and stretchy. Dacron rope stretches only slightly, polypropylene resists chafe hardly at all, and natural fibers like manila and cotton are weak and will rot. Stretch is an important consideration when choosing the rode's diameter. Although the rode must be strong enough to take the load, it should not be so large that it doesn't stretch. Under a given load, a smaller line will stretch more than a large one. A rode that is too big will not stretch enough to absorb jerks as the boat rises and falls in waves and pulls back in hard wind gusts.

Besides strength and stretch, the third consideration is sag. Any rope suspended between two points has a natural sag, called catenary. But it may not be enough for an anchor rode, which near the anchor should lie at an angle of 8° or less to the bottom. With this nearly horizontal pull, the flukes will dig in. At a broader angle, the rode will lift the shank and, with it, the flukes, causing the anchor to pull out and drag. It may reset itself if the angle narrows; otherwise the anchor is useless.

There are several ways to increase horizontal pull. One is to let out more rode and thereby increase scope. Scope is the ratio between the length of rode let out and the vertical distance from the boat's deck to the water's bottom directly below. With a scope of 3:1, 30 feet of rode is let out in an area where the water depth and freeboard total 10 feet. This

scope is low and may be suitable for extreme calm conditions only. At night the scope should be 5:1 or more (50 feet of rode), and in strong winds it should be at least 7:1 (70 feet of rode).

Another way to increase horizontal pull is to have a rode made of a denser material than rope. Steel chain, which weighs about 10 times more than nylon, is the material of choice, either as a lead (a 6-foot or longer length at the bottom of the rode) or as much or all of the entire rode. Chain has other advantages: while it won't stretch, a chain rode is so heavy that it will take a gale to straighten it out; and, unlike rope, it won't be cut or abraded by rocks. Yet an all-chain rode is hard to handle. Most weekend cruisers (who anchor frequently in safe, relatively shallow harbors) use only a short chain lead (pronounced "leed") at the bottom of the rode. Most long-distance cruisers use an all-chain rode.

The rule of thumb with rode, as with

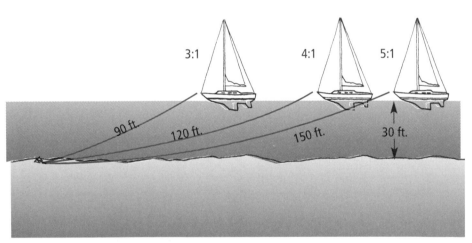

Scope is the ratio between the amount of rode let out and the distance from the deck to the water's bottom (or the freeboard plus water depth). The higher the ratio, the more rode is veered out (veered, let out) and the more horizontal the rode is under water.

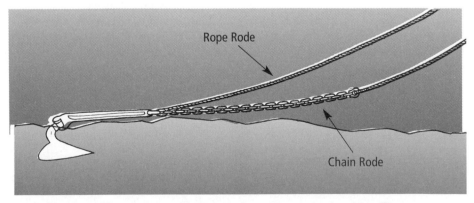

A rode that is all- or part-chain will sag more than a rope rode, thereby pulling horizontally instead of lifting the shank. Unlike rope, chain is not chafed by a rocky or otherwise foul bottom.

the anchor itself, is this: "The more challenging the anchorage, the heavier the equipment." When the harbor is deep and exposed to the sea or lake, and when the bottom is rocky and the weather unpredictable and rough — that's when you require heavy ground tackle, including an all-chain rode. But a nylon rode with a short chain lead ususally is very satisfactory in mud-bottomed, shallow, protected harbors in stable, normal weather.

One good reason for a rope rode in normal cruising is its ease of handling. On a typical cruise in sheltered waters, when you anchor once or twice daily, you don't want to have to wrestle with hard, slippery chain. Rope can be easily coiled on deck and stowed in a portable container there or passed through a deck hole to a locker below. You can winch a rope rode using a standard sheet or halyard winch and cleat it on a normal cleat. The only maintenance you need to

perform on nylon is to hose it off periodically with fresh water and check for chafe, trimming off the worn ends.

Chain is nowhere near as easy to use. First off, it's much heavier: 200 feet of rode weight about 35 pounds if nylon but 350 pounds if chain. When stowed below in the bow, a pile of chain throws the boat out of balance and digs the bow into waves (for this reason it should be stowed amidships). Chain cannot be securely cleated, and it is very tough on the hands; gloves should be worn. Long lengths of chain must be handled on windlasses, which are special winches with drums called wildcats that have notches for chain links and brakes that, when tightened, secure the chain. Chain also requires careful maintnance. From time to time it must be untwisted and regalvanized to prevent rust.

A major problem with an all-chain rode is that, unlike nylon rope, it does not stretch. In all but strong winds, the cate-

nary absorbs shock loads that might pull the anchor out, but in a blow the line may straighten. To put some give back into the rode, rig an elastic snubber. This is a length of heavy nylon line tied to the chain with a rolling hitch and cleated on deck. Tie the hitch, veer out (veer, let out) several feet of chain and line, then cleat the line, leaving the chain above the hitch without tension. The more nylon is veered out, the more stretch there will be. On some boats, a metal hook is used in place of the rolling hitch, though the hook might weaken the chain.

Have at least a 6- to 10-foot chain lead on a nylon rode. The rode needs weight near the anchor. If for some reason you do not have a few feet of chain near the bottom (or if there isn't enough chain), you can increase the sag by running a kellet (sliding weight) down the rode on a sentinel (traveler) made of a block, shackle, or loop of line. Attach a 20–50 pound weight such as a small anchor to the sentinel, then attach a long control line and let the kellet slide down most of the way.

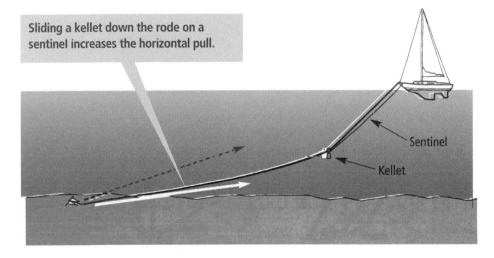

Sliding a kellet down the rode on a sentinel increases the horizontal pull.

Sentinel

Kellet

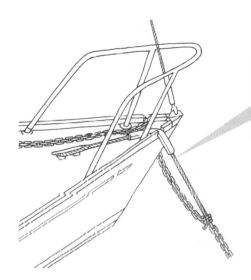

Since chain does not stretch, to put some give into the rode attach a nylon shock absorber to an all-chain rode, using a rolling hitch or steel hook.

Ground Tackle

Choosing Ground Tackle. Ground tackle has to resist the loads on the boat, which are functions in part of her displacement but largely of her windage (wind resistance) due to her exposed area. Because an anchored boat usually is headed into the wind, the main factor is the boat's beam. But since she will also sail around the anchor, presenting one side and then the other to the wind, length also is important. So are freeboard, rig, and hull type (multihulls can present portions of two or three hulls to the wind). Table 14-1 is a conservative estimate of loading. Again, the key factor is beam. Table 14-2 provides some general guidance in determining minimum anchor and rode sizes.

Splices and Shackles. The weak link in ground tackle is the attachment point. Knots and splices, properly done, hold well. Line may be spliced directly to the end of chain so the rode passes easily over the bow roller and windlass wildcat. Shackles should be at least one size larger than the chain. The working load limit should be stamped on the shackle. Shackles made of soft metals like bronze and high-tensile galvanized steel often are preferred for anchor duty since they will flex and bend slightly under great loads and not fracture the way that a hard stainless steel shackle might. Grease the threads so the pin can be removed easily. Secure knots and shackles by seizing or mousing them with stainless steel wire or strong synthetic cord.

If you anticipate switching the rode, or if you want the flexibility of being able to spread the load occasionally, tie the rode to the anchor or chain. The fisherman's (anchor) bend (top) is excellent, but a bowline (bottom) will also do if the bitter end is seized with light line to the standing part. Also mouse the shackle pin.

Table 14-1: Estimated Horizontal Loads on Anchored Boats (In Pounds)

Boat Length	Boat Beam	Approximate Wind Speed		
		15 knots	30 knots	42 knots
20'	7'	90	360	720
30'	9'	175	700	1400
35'	10'	225	900	1800
40'	11'	300	1200	2400
50'	13'	400	1600	3200
60'	15'	500	2000	4000

These are conservative estimates. In some conditions the loading may be less. Since the most important factor is beam, refer first to that column. To calculate the load at 60 knots, multiply the figure at 30 knots by 4. (Source: American Boat and Yacht Council)

Table 14-2: Anchor and Rode Selection Guide

	Working Anchor (Wind to 30 knots)						
	Anchor (pounds)				Rode (diameter)		Lead Range
Boat Length	Light-weight	Plow	Bruce	Yachts-man's	Nylon	Chain	Chain
20'	5	15	11	25	⅜"	¼"	6–33'
30'	12	20	17	35	⁷⁄₁₆"	¼"	16–46'
35'	12	25	22	45	½"	⁵⁄₁₆"	11–40'
40'	20	35	33	55	½"	⁵⁄₁₆"	18–48'
50'	35	45	44	75	⅝"	⅜"	21–46'
60'	60	60	66	100	¾"	⁷⁄₁₆"	27–44'

These are minimums. The right-hand columns show the ranges of recommended minimum lead, the chain inserted between a rope rode and the anchor. The lower number is the length for the lightest anchor, the higher number for the heaviest anchor. (Source: Earl Hinz, *The Complete Book of Anchoring and Mooring*)

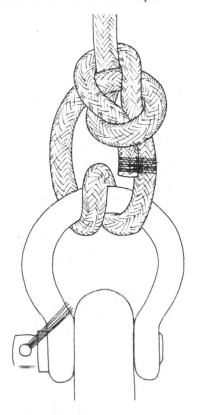

Here are a few rules of thumb for buying rode.

Nylon rode should be ½ inch in diameter for every 9 feet of boat length overall.

In calculating the rode's length, find the deepest harbor you may anchor in and multiply its depth at high tide by at least 8. Add some more length. Buying a rode that's exactly the right length is a false economy since you will have to trim some chafed sections from the ends every year or so.

If you have two anchors (as you should), also have two rodes of equal length and strength and at least one long length of chain. Someday you may have to set both anchors in a storm, or a rode may break, or one anchor may be so inextricably tangled in an underwater cable or rock that you won't be able to recover it and will have to cut the rode.

"The deeper the bottom, the heavier the rode."

The total weight in the rode should be at least equal to the anchor's weight.

In a chain-rope rode, the chain should be one-half the diameter of the nylon.

If you anticipate switching the rode, or if you want the flexibility of being able to spread the load occasionally, tie the rode to the anchor or chain. The fisherman's (anchor) bend (top) is a excellent, but a bowline (bottom) will also do if the bitter end is seized with light line to the standing part. Also mouse the shackle pin.

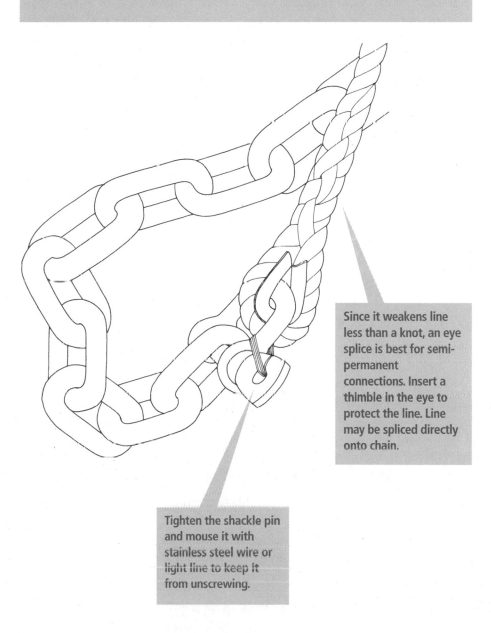

Since it weakens line less than a knot, an eye splice is best for semi-permanent connections. Insert a thimble in the eye to protect the line. Line may be spliced directly onto chain.

Tighten the shackle pin and mouse it with stainless steel wire or light line to keep it from unscrewing.

Ground Tackle

Deck Equipment. In storms, many boats that go adrift do so not because their anchors drag but because the deck gear has broken or the rode has chafed through. Install the largest chocks that will fit on the bow, one on either side of the stem. If you use a roller for the rode, it must be firmly bolted to the bowsprit or bow so it is not bent or ripped off by the rode's hard pull. Nylon anchor rodes are cleated on large through-bolted cleats abaft the chocks.

Chafe (rubbing) is a major worry everywhere on a boat, and especially

with anchor rodes. Often the lead is fairest when the rode crosses the deck to the cleat on the side opposite the chock. The cleats must be angled about 15° to the side so the rode doesn't jam in them. On a windlass, the wildcat notches must match the size of the chain links; otherwise the chain will slip while it's being retrieved or

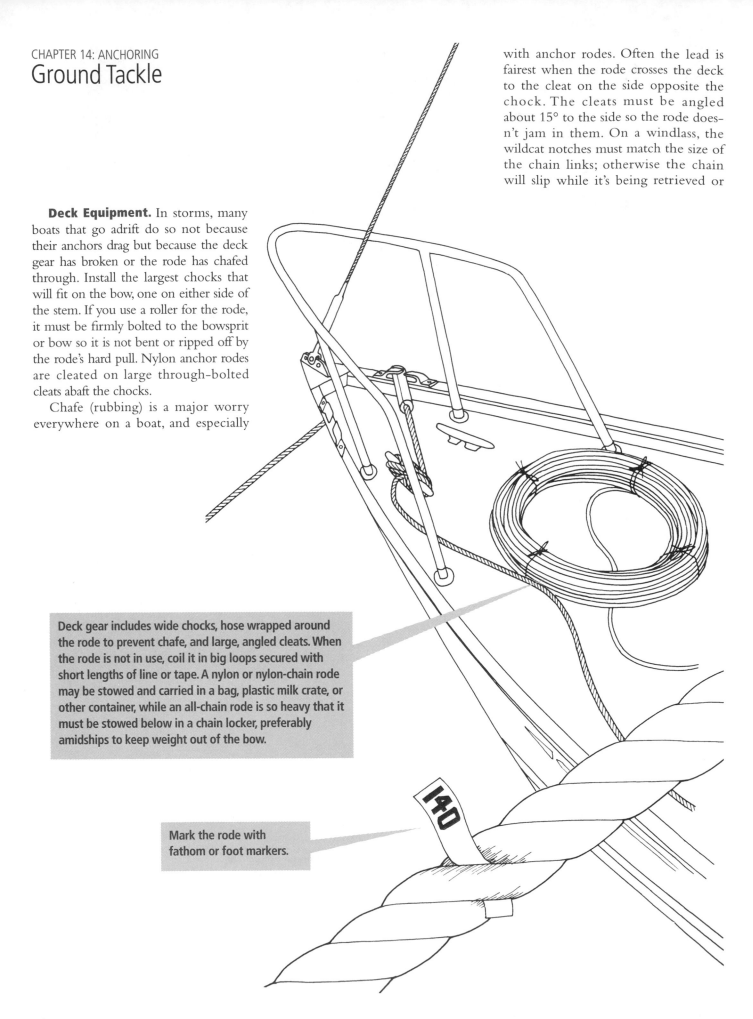

Deck gear includes wide chocks, hose wrapped around the rode to prevent chafe, and large, angled cleats. When the rode is not in use, coil it in big loops secured with short lengths of line or tape. A nylon or nylon-chain rode may be stowed and carried in a bag, plastic milk crate, or other container, while an all-chain rode is so heavy that it must be stowed below in a chain locker, preferably amidships to keep weight out of the bow.

Mark the rode with fathom or foot markers.

when the boat tugs on the rode.

As the rode and anchor come aboard, clean off mud that comes along. Some boats carry saltwater deck pumps to provide a stream of water for this purpose. If mud gets on deck, it will foul up your shoes and clothes, and perhaps the sails as well. If mud gets below, it will make a terrible stink before it dries, and then flake off and clog the bilge limber holes, which allow water to flow to the bilge pump.

Rode Maintenance. The bitter end of the rode must be secured to the boat before you drop anchor. It's embarrassing as well as unseamanlike to let the whole rode slip overboard. If you stow the anchor and rode on deck or in a portable container, tie the bitter end around the mast with a bowline. If the rode is stowed in a chain locker below, tie the bitter end to a padeye bolted to the locker or to a strong beam. The bitter end of an all-chain rode should be tied with a line that can be cut in an emergency. Any rope or chain rode will twist and kink. From time to time untie the bitter end, haul the rode on deck, shake out the twists, recoil or restow the rode, and then resecure the bitter end.

Once a year, cut the worn end off a nylon rode and retie or resplice it to the shackle. If the line or chain is worn in any other area, turn it end for end, with the old bottom now at the top, to spread the wear. To minimize chafe, rig rubber hose (a piece about 2 feet long slit from end to end with light lines attached) around the vulnerable part of the rode, or place a thick rag or a piece of leather between the line and the chock or other chafe point. Since nylon is highly elastic, check for wear 2 feet either side of any fitting. While at anchor in rough weather, let out or pull in the rode a couple of feet every few hours to keep chafe from being localized on a single spot on the rode.

Sometimes an anchor may be bent by a rock. If the damage appears to compromise the anchor's design and strength, have a welder straighten it out. Welding at stress points may weaken the anchor, however.

You will want to know exactly how much rode you have paid out, so mark the line or chain. You can paint chain links or whole sections with different colors. Paint doesn't adhere well to rope, but colored markers and flags may be sewn or twisted into line.

This plow anchor is stowed on a bow roller, and the windlass takes both chain and rope. The chock, though suitably large, is not open at the top, which means that the docking line must be threaded rather than quickly dropped in. The U-bracket in the pulpit allows the crew to haul in the rode hand-over-hand. The lead is not perfectly fair: note how the rode has abraded the tape on the headstay turnbuckle.

How to Anchor

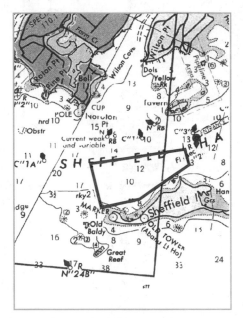

When the wind is in the prevailing southwest, the area outlined on this chart is an ideal anchorage since it is protected by Sheffield Island and its reef and is well out of the channel. But this is no place to anchor in a strong north wind.

Anchoring properly requires you to do more than simply heave the hook overboard. It takes planning, teamwork, and a weather eye.

Choosing an Anchorage. The first problem is to pick a safe anchorage, which means one that is not too crowded, is protected by land from onshore wind and large waves, and has good holding ground (a bottom that your anchor will dig into). Crowded harbors rarely allow enough elbow room for sufficient scope. If a squall comes up in the night, chances are that at least one boat will drag her anchor and be blown down on her neighbors. You also don't want to be forced to anchor so far out that you're faced with a 30-minute row just to get ashore.

One solution to crowding is excellent protection. In most sailing areas there is choice of protected anchorages, although in a given wind or tide, some may be more appealing than others. Have an anchorage in mind as your destination when you get under way in the morning, but also consult the chart, *Coast*

Pilot, and cruising guide for one or two fallbacks in case the weather deteriorates or your plans change. You need shelter from wind and waves. Few harbors are so snug that they offer protection from strong winds in all directions, so you usually must try to match the anchorage to what you think the weather will be. Listen to the National Weather Service forecasts on the VHF/FM radio, watch the sky, and be sensitive to the wind's direction. Look to the west and gauge the coming weather.

A protected anchorage generally is one where an onshore wind does not blow unimpeded. But an offshore wind can be dangerous, too. A hard blow may blast powerful gusts called williwaws down a bluff, hill, or mountain. But as a general rule, except in calm weather, avoid anchoring unless there is a point of land, an exposed reef, or a shallow underwater sand bar to protect you against the wind and waves of an onshore breeze.

While studying the chart, try to antic-

There is an abundance of coves and harbors in Muscongus Bay, on the mid-Maine coast. Anchorage (A) offers shelter except in a northeasterly, (B) is well protected except to the east, (C) is sheltered from all directions except the south once you get in close to Cranberry Island, and (D) offers protection in an easterly. Besides wind direction the skipper takes tidal current, water depth, the bottom ("rky" means a rocky bottom), and possible crowding into consideration.

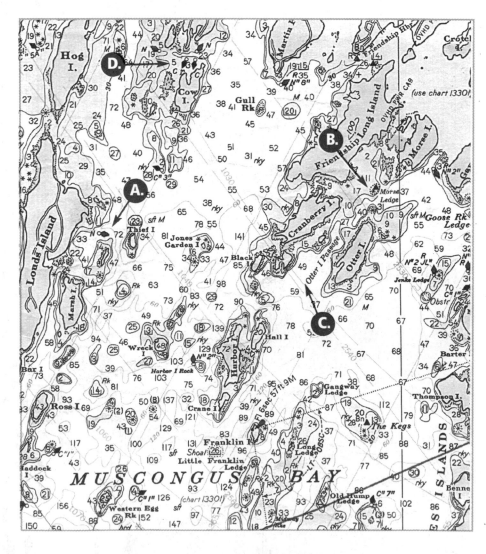

ipate tidal flow in and around possible anchorages. Current deep in a harbor usually is weak. Near the mouth and in channels it may flow strong and at oblique angles, depending on the state of the tide. In confused currents an anchored boat may lie with her bow into the current and her side facing the wind — a combination that inevitably leads to rolling and sailing around the anchor. A line of foam usually indicates a tide rip or a tide line on either side of which currents run in different directions. And when you're near a channel, you probably will experience a lot of rolling in the wakes of passing boats. (It's illegal to anchor so your boat obstructs a channel.)

The anchorage should offer good holding ground — a bottom that your anchor can grab. The bottom type is usually indicated on the chart. Given a choice between a rocky bottom and a mud bottom, a crew with only a lightweight anchor at hand should choose the mud bottom. Avoid weedy and grassy bottoms whenever possible, no matter what type of anchor you're carrying. Some harbors are notoriously bad anchorages. For example, the bottom of the main harbor on Nantucket Island in New England is full of grass. There are a few sandy spots that provide good holding, but only until the wind rises or shifts and the anchor trips and tries unsuccessfully to reset in grass. A boat can be safely anchored in Nantucket for a week until a wind shift rips out the anchor and sends her dragging. So, rent a mooring or a slip at the marina.

Carefully examine the chart for underwater snags, such as cables and wrecks. While your anchor will grab them tightly, you may never see it again.

Special Anchorages. The Coast Guard sets aside areas for mooring and anchoring called special anchorages. The holding ground may be no better in a special anchorage than in some isolated cove (it may actually be worse, in fact, since the bottom may be fouled by old anchors and rodes waiting to trip your own hook). But special anchorages usually offer conveniences such as slips, moorings, and shore-boat (launch) service (for a fee) provided by a local marina or yacht club. Ashore there will be fuel, laundries, and grocery stores. Since anchoring in a special anchorage may be risky, the few dollars' rent for a mooring will bring peace of mind.

Be wary about picking up a private mooring without permission early in the afternoon, for its owner may return from his daysail with little charity in his heart. Don't leave the boat to go ashore until you're sure the mooring is safely yours for the night.

Approaching the Anchorage. If the anchorage is unfamiliar, approach it cautiously with the chart in hand and the *Coast Pilot* or a cruising guide nearby. Be alert to the confusing effects of a change in scale from a relatively small-scale coast chart to a large-scale harbor chart. What seemed like a short distance on the former can seem like a long one on the latter. As you enter the harbor, orient yourself visually to the buoys and land

Even a crowded anchorage may have a hole. However, before dropping the hook there, try to find out if other skippers have avoided it for a reason, like a bottom that is covered with weed or fouled with old anchor chains.

How to Anchor

marks shown on the chart. Study the shore and estimate how the wind and water will flow around it. A steep bluff may create williwaws, and a point of land may be surrounded by strong current. Check the water depth on the chart and your depth sounder. Gradual shoaling usually means there are no especially tricky tidal currents to worry about, but a steep shoaling may mean nasty current. If anchored boats are bunched together, try to figure out why. Perhaps there's less wind or a better bottom there. But if they're rafted together and are flying the same burgees (yacht club flags), they're friends enjoying a cruise in company and tied up side by side.

Project a disaster scene on your mental movie screen. When a dangerous squall blows in, how will the boats lie? Where will the gusts come from? Which boat is likely to drag first? What's the quickest way out of the anchorage if you have to leave?

Anchoring Etiquette. Cruise around the harbor for a few minutes with your senses alert. Without being hypercritical, evaluate your neighbors. A big powerboat with closed windows probably has her air conditioning on, which means her noisy generator will run all night. A boat smothered by children won't be any quieter. A boat that looks unkempt may well be the one whose crew is least skilled (but then again, many brave, successful long voyages have been made in boats that look less like yachts than tramp steamers).

The fundamental rule of etiquette in anchoring is first come, first served. If boats swing together, the blame is on the vessel that anchored later. Yet it seems that no matter how much elbow room you have when you drop your hook, the neighborhood always is crowded when the wind or current changes direction. This is because the boats have varying amounts of rode veered out (let out) and

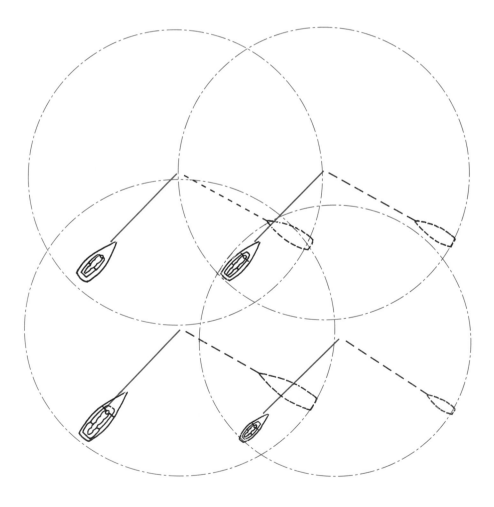

In wind shifts, boats often will sail around their anchors in the same pattern. The greater the scope, the better the chances that they will collide. If you expect a wind shift, anchor on what will be the fleet's windward side.

they therefore swing on radiuses of different lengths. Your main concern is with swinging room, which is how much space your boat will have to swing freely around the anchor as the wind and current shift. Since long boats take up more room than short ones, it's a good idea to anchor near boats your size. If you expect a major wind shift, anchor on what will be the fleet's windward side.

There are other factors: Boats with large rigs usually will lie fairly steadily to the wind, while those with small rigs may be more influenced by the current. Light boats with high freeboard and the mast well aft may sail around their anchors with the unpredictability of puppies on a leash. But the most important factor is the amount of rode that other boats have veered out. You can predict another boat's swinging room by looking closely at her anchor rode. The shallower the angle it makes to the water, the greater the scope and, there-fore, the farther the boat will swing. If the angle is very steep, the boat probably is on a mooring, which means her swinging radius is short. A cocktail of moorings, anchors, and a radical wind shift often leads to serious trouble.

To estimate your own swinging radius, use this formula:

$$\text{swinging radius} = \text{length} + \sqrt{(\text{rode})^2 - (\text{depth} + \text{freeboard})^2}$$

First, take the footage of rode let out and square it. Second, add the water depth at the anchor to the freeboard of the bow and square the sum. Third, from the result in the first step subtract the result in the second step. Fourth, calculate the square root of the remainder and add it to the boat's total length, including projections astern (for example, a dinghy hanging off a painter). The result is the swinging room with the rode fully extended.

Preparing to Anchor. While the skipper is choosing a spot for anchoring, one or two crew members are on the foredeck preparing the ground tackle. Everything may be almost ready, with the anchor lying on a bow roller. Just check that the rode is clear to run without snagging (pulling out about 50 feet), untie the lashings holding the anchor down, and cleat the rode taut to keep the hook from dropping over until you need it. If the rode is all-chain, lead it over the wildcat with the windlass brake on.

Otherwise the anchor and rode must be led properly under the lifelines and through the chock. Bring the ground tackle on deck (if necessary), and tie the rode's bitter end to the mast. Then carry the anchor forward, slip it under the lifelines or pulpit (a restraining assembly of pipes on the bow), and either leave it there or, if it might bang against the hull, pull it back aft over the lifelines and pulpit. Inspect the shackles. Take a wrap of the chain or nylon around a cleat to keep the anchor from sliding overboard. Now overhaul and fake the rode to work the hockles (kinks) out.

Once the skipper knows where she wants to anchor, she should notify the foredeck crew and everybody else on deck, pointing to the spot and announcing the water depth. If it's very deep, more rode must be pulled out.

On small cruisers and boats with small crews, the anchor may be dropped from the cockpit, where it is stored in a locker. Lead the rode at the bow through the chock and then aft around the stays and over the lifelines to the cockpit. Tie or shackle the rode to the anchor. If the other end of the rode is led aft from the bow to the cockpit, nobody must go forward when anchoring (but you'll probably need a crew forward to weigh, or raise, the anchor).

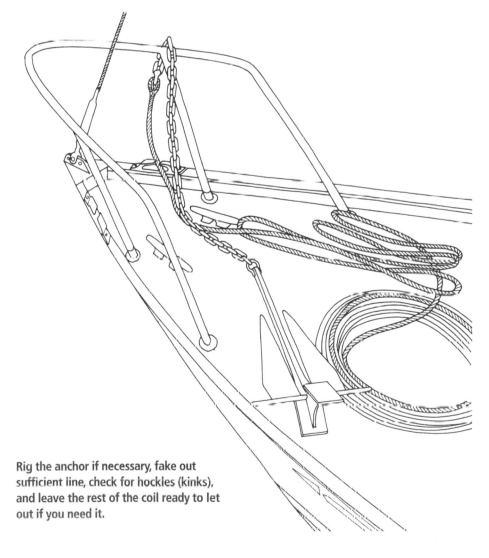

Rig the anchor if necessary, fake out sufficient line, check for hockles (kinks), and leave the rest of the coil ready to let out if you need it.

How to Anchor

Dropping the Anchor. Steer the boat into the wind toward the chosen spot (or, in a calm, into the current), allowing her to slow and then stop. You should not drop the anchor until she is stopped dead or making sternway (going backwards). If the boat is making forward progress, the flukes will dig in the wrong way. As a guide, use a range on shore or a floating object like a buoy, or spit in the water, to determine if you've stopped.

Drop the hook. When anchoring in very deep water, just before dropping the anchor fix the boat's position on the chart using compass bearings, GPS, Loran-C, or radar. Most of the time this fix won't be needed, but someday when you're having trouble getting the anchor up because you don't know where it is and what direction its flukes are dug in, you will want to be able to return to this exact position. On the skipper's command or hand signal, the foredeck crew drops the anchor over. With the engine in slow reverse or the mainsail backed (pushed out against the wind), the boat begins to make sternway (sail backward) away from the anchor while the crew veers out rode.

Setting the Anchor. Now set the anchor. The first job is to make the rode lie at a shallow angle to the bottom. This requires initially veering out plenty of rode. In normal weather, with an all-rope rode, veer out about 10 feet of rode for every foot of water depth below. With a rope rode that has at least 12 feet of chain, the initial scope can be about 7:1. With an all-chain rode, it can be about 5:1. In strong winds or rough seas, this initial scope should be higher. These large scopes are only temporary.

Once the rode is out, the crew cleats the rode (if it is rope) or tightens the brake on the windlass (if it is chain). Back the boat down hard against the rode. If there is any time a cruising boat needs a reverse gear, it's now. Light-displacement, high-sided boats may swing to one side, so try to steer the bow into the wind.

You'll know if the anchor is set if the bow suddenly dips and swings toward the rode. If it doesn't, veer out more rode. If the boat continues to slide astern, the anchor has picked up a shell or is skimming across grass. Pull up the anchor, clean off any rocks or shells, refake the rode, and try again. If the anchor is clean, try another spot.

Keep the engine in reverse a little longer, gauging the boat's position against other boats, a range, or spit in the water. Once you're sure the rode is set, it's time to decrease scope by taking in line. In normal conditions, with a light to fresh wind and moderate waves, once you are sure the anchor is dug in securely, decrease the scope slightly to about 7:1 for a lightweight anchor and about 5:1 for other anchors. In rough weather, 10:1 and 7:1 may be needed. A rode with lots of chain can be set with lower scope.

Anchoring Under Sail. Though less challenging to seamanship than anchoring under sail, anchoring under power is safer and more reliable. Still, successfully anchoring under sail, without the engine

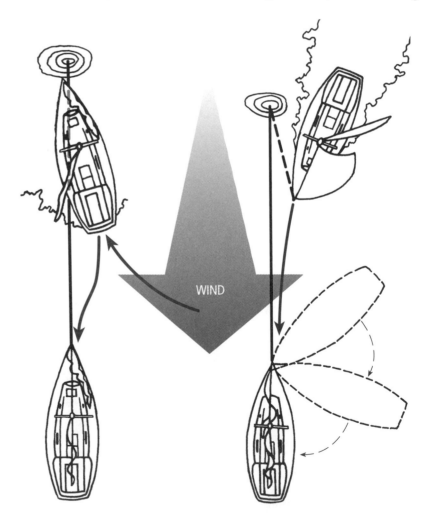

WIND

Drop the anchor when the boat is stopped and back down while veering out rode.

Anchoring under sail, drop the hook on a run to dig it in quickly.

in gear, is a soul-satisfying mark of good seamanship. By definition a good anchorage is fairly calm, so you may have to work hard to keep her sailing comfortably under mainsail alone.

If you're anchoring under sail, you may set the anchor by dropping it while sailing on a run dead before the wind. Drop the anchor over the side or stern, veer out enough rode (as above), and cleat the rode securely. When the anchor grabs and sets, the bow will swing right up into the wind — help it along with the helm while leaving the main sheet eased entirely. Once she's headed into the wind's eye, find a range and make sure the rode is set, as we have described.

Anchoring Multihulls. "The notion that multihulls somehow require only tiny anchors has no credibility with me," writes Chris White, an experienced multihull designer and sailor, in his book *The Cruising Multihull.* There is nothing special about multihulls' ground tackle.

Even though they are lighter than monohulls, multihulls can pull hard on anchor rodes. They are wider, higher, and have more hulls, which means they present much more windage. The load may be especially large if the multi lies at an angle to the wind, with all her windward hull and a portion of her second (and, if a trimaran, third) hull exposed to the wind. Therefore, multihulls should use at least the same weight anchors that similar-length keel boats use.

In order to spread the loads to their two hulls, catamarans may secure the anchor rode to or through a bridle rigged between the two bows. The bridle consists of two long, heavy nylon lines leading from the two bows at a broad angle to a meeting point several feet forward of the mast. Once the scope is about correct, the rode is tied to the meeting point and further adjustments are made using the bridle. Trimarans may secure the rode at the center hull.

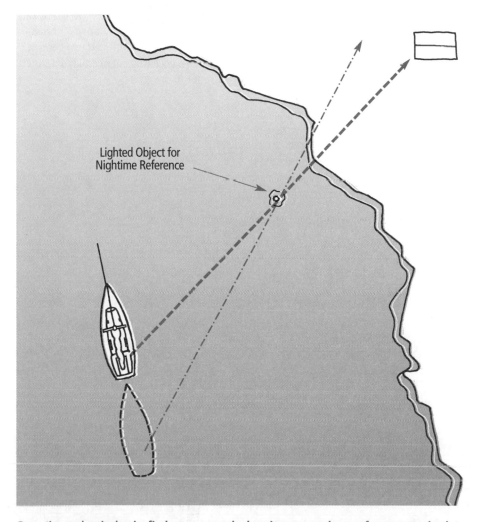

Lighted Object for Nightime Reference

Once the anchor is dug in, find ranges or take bearings so you have references to check to see if you're dragging. One range should include a lighted object.

How to Anchor

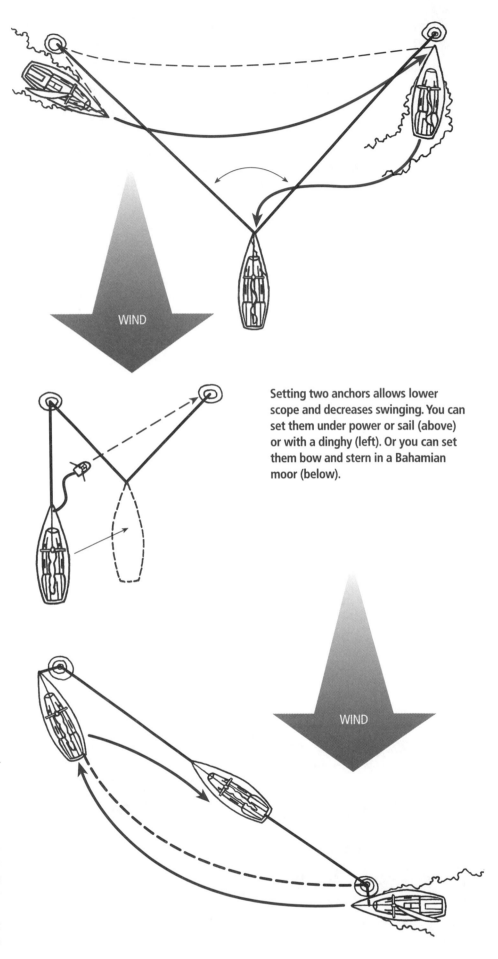

Sailing Around the Anchor. After the anchor is set, if you find your boat sailing around it, first to one side and then the other, consider trying two solutions. One is to set a riding sail — a small sail far aft that catches the wind and pushes the bow into it. The riding sail can be a mizzen on a yawl or ketch. On a sloop, try setting the storm jib or another small jib on the backstay, hoisting it by the main halyard with the clew pointing forward, and sheeting the sail flat amidships.

Another possible solution to the problem of sailing around the anchor is to secure the anchor rode slightly to the side instead of directly over the bow (being careful to protect against chafe). This off-center attachment exposes a side of the hull to the wind and may steady the boat. If the wind comes up hard, the rode should be led back to the centerline or a centerline bridle in order to reduce the exposed area.

Cleaning Up. The skipper should inspect the foredeck to make sure that the correct scope is set, the rode is properly cleated and coiled, and chafing gear is installed. Douse and furl the sails, tying them securely with sail ties. Pull halyards away from the mast with lines or lengths of bungee cord called gilguys so they don't clank and disturb people on neighboring boats.

When you drop the hook in an area that is not marked "special anchorage" on the chart, Rule 30 in the Rules of the Road specifies that you identify yourself with special signals that warn off other boats. The anchor light is a 360° all-round white light either hung off the headstay or lit at the top of the mast. (Do not use a strobe light, which people will interpret as an emergency signal.) During the day, the rules say, a black ball must be hung over the foredeck, although few pleasure boats show this signal.

Once the boat is settled down, fix the boat's position for future reference

Setting two anchors allows lower scope and decreases swinging. You can set them under power or sail (above) or with a dinghy (left). Or you can set them bow and stern in a Bahamian moor (below).

WIND

WIND

with bearings on fixed objects, with the GPS, or with a range (for example a house lined up behind a wharf). At night, try to find a lighthouse, street lamp, or other fixed light on shore to use as a reference. Check these references every now and then. Later you'll refer to them if you wake up at night with normal skipper's anxiety. Leave the applicable harbor and coast charts open on the chart table for quick reference, and make sure some flashlights are handy in case you have to work on deck in the dark. While everybody's starting to relax, point out the boat's position to one or two trusted crew members who may have to take charge if you're not around for some reason.

Many GPS and Loran-C sets have anchor watch alarms that sound when the boat moves away from a position programmed into the machine.

Using Two Anchors and Other Techniques. A level of security is provided by using two anchors on two rodes either laid at an angle to the bow or over the stern and bow. To drop two anchors off the bow, first set one to port of where the boat should lie, then sail or power across the wind, letting out rode (keeping it clear of the propeller), to drop the second anchor. Set both anchors and adjust the rodes until the boat hangs balanced between them with an included angle of 30°–60°. (Another way is to run the second anchor out in a dinghy or other small boat.) Some skippers use this system to spread the load between two anchors, requiring lower scope. Others do it to pin the boat in a tidal stream to restrain swinging. Less scope is needed with two anchors.

In narrow tide-swept anchorages where there is very little swinging room, two anchors may be set bow and stern in the Bahamian moor. Powering ahead, drop one anchor over the stern, cleat it there, and dig it in as you power on until the scope is about 8:1. Drop the other anchor over the bow, cleat it there, and fall back until the boat is halfway between, with 4:1 scope on each rode. The boat should lie with her bow or stern into the current. If the current is on the beam, she will swing aound or her anchors will trip.

In some harbors boats use anchors to help them moor at wharves, with the anchor over the bow and the stern against the wharf. Crews board and leave over the stern on planks. This is called a Mediterranean moor or Med moor.

Anchors may also be used to keep boats from blowing down onto piers or floats in rough weather. The anchor is run out in a dinghy and dropped abeam of the yacht.

Sometimes several boats will hang off a single anchor in temporary or overnight raft-ups. The center boat (usually the largest one) drops her heaviest anchor. When it's firmly dug in, the other boats tie up on either side, using fenders and full sets of spring, bow, and stern lines to keep the boats from sliding forward and aft and the masts from tangling if the boats should roll. The

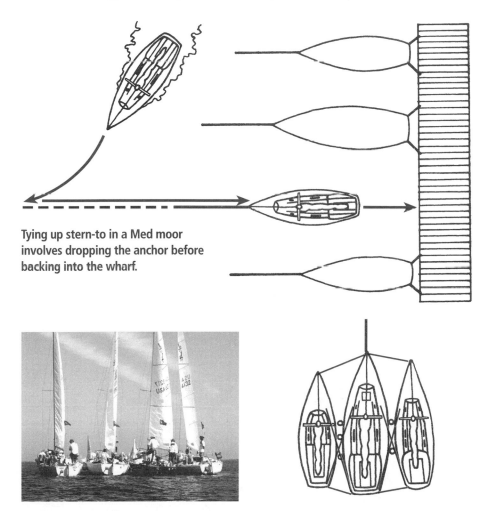

Tying up stern-to in a Med moor involves dropping the anchor before backing into the wharf.

Rafting-up requires one heavy anchor and full sets of docking lines so rigs don't tangle.

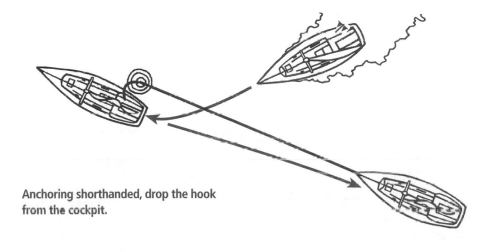

Anchoring shorthanded, drop the hook from the cockpit.

How to Anchor

scope should be greater than if a single boat were anchored. Each boat must be prepared to leave the raft quickly if the anchor drags, and overnight raft-ups should be limited to two or three boats.

If you're sailing singlehanded or shorthanded and plan to anchor, you can drop the hook without going onto the foredeck. Before entering the anchorage, heave-to; lead the rode properly through the chock; carry the anchor aft outside the pulpit, lifelines, and all rigging; and lay it in the cockpit. Cleat the rode on the foredeck so there's sufficient scope for the anchorage. When you've found your spot, back down and drop the anchor from the cockpit. Then adjust the rode.

KEDGING-OFF

If you have run aground, you might be able to use the anchor to pull yourself off into deeper water. This is called kedging-off. If the tide is falling or the wind is blowing you out shore, you'll have to move fast.

Get out a lightweight anchor and in a dinghy row the anchor and rode into deeper water (or tie it to a life jacket or fender and swim it out). Set the anchor, lead the rode to a winch, and take a hard strain. The lead must be fair and people must stay well away, since the full weight of the boat will soon come on the rode. As waves bounce the boat up, the strain on the rode pulls her out a little more into deeper water. Keep tightening the rode as she moves.

Alternatively, you can winch the boat off with the help of the engine as the crew sits to leeward to heel her and decrease draft. If you are backing out, keep the helm centered so the rudder's resistance is as low as possible. Be absolutely sure that the rode is clear of the propeller before you shift into gear. You could also lead the rode to the bow and, hauling in, spin the boat on her keel until she's aimed back toward safe water. When the bow is pointed directly at the anchor, try to power off the shoal.

Warning: Kedging-off places tremendous strains on ground tackle. Rodes may be stretched to the breaking point. Never stand over or behind a rode while kedging-off. The backlash of a broken rode may cause serious injury.

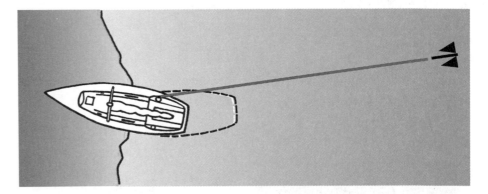

If you run aground and can't sail off, first try kedging-off stern-first, leading the rode to a powerful sheet winch.

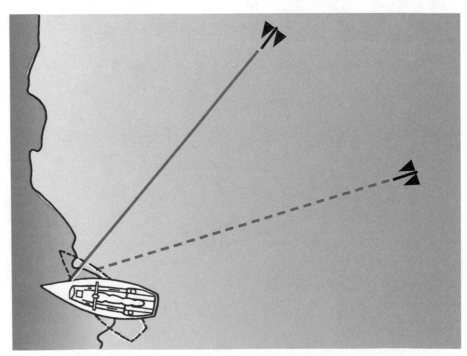

A fin-keel boat may often be spun off by leading the rode through a block on the bow, resetting the anchor if necessary.

Weighing Anchor

When it's time to weigh (raise) anchor, go into forward gear and power toward it as a crew member hauls in the slack rode. To guide the steerer, the crew points in the direction of the rode, which is hidden from the view of those in the cockpit. When the bow is directly over the anchor, the crew says, "Straight up and down" (or signals by holding a hand straight up). The steerer shifts into neutral gear as the taut rode is cleated on the bow cleat.

When the crew signals that the rode is secure, the steerer puts the engine into forward gear. Moving slowly forward, the boat pulls the anchor shank up, trips the anchor, and pulls the flukes out of the bottom opposite to the way they went in. When the anchor is freed, the boat accelerates and the bow bobs. The steerer goes dead slow while the crew retrieves the rode and anchor either hand-over-hand or with the windlass.

When the anchor breaks the surface, if it's clean the crew hauls it up on deck, but if it's dirty he may signal to go slightly faster so the bow wave scours the chain and hook with the help of a mop or long-handled brush. He may also bounce the anchor up and down in the bow wave by hauling on the rode, being careful not to pull the sharp flukes into the topsides (looping the bight of a line under the flukes helps keep them from spinning against the sides). Then the anchor can be pulled into the bow roller or on deck. Put away the rode.

Weighing anchor under sail is a satis-fying piece of seamanship best tried by a maneuverable boat with an all-rope rode, in a light or moderate wind, and in an uncrowded anchorage. Set the main-sail and start sailing on a close reach as you veer out rode so it is slack. When you have about 2 knots of speed, head up and tack, pulling on the rode to accelerate. Veer out rode on the new tack and get going again. Keep swooping to one side, then another, sailing close-hauled when you can and gaining a few feet on the rode with each tack. After several tacks you'll sail over the anchor with come slack in the rode (so it is not straight up and down). Sail beyond the anchor and cleat the rode. Your headway will trip the anchor. It can help to lead the rode through a block shackled on the stem or pulpit.

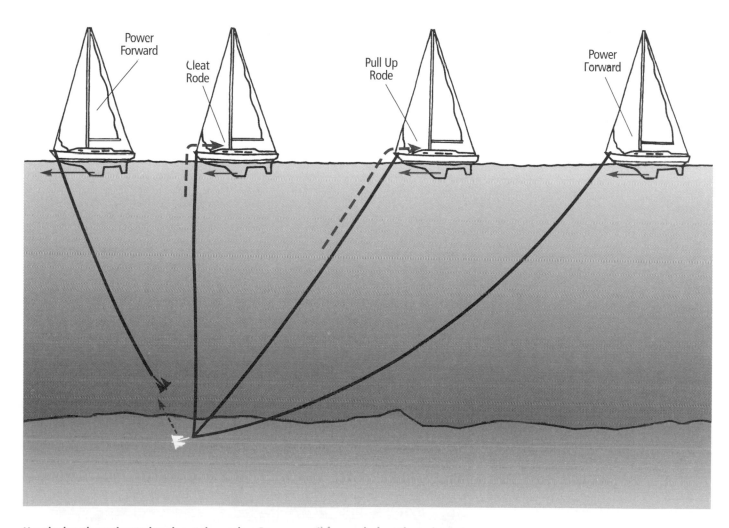

Use the boat's motion to break out the anchor. Power or sail forward, cleat the rode, and head in the direction opposite to the one in which the flukes are dug to trip the anchor.

Weighing Anchor

If It Doesn't Break Out. Sometimes an anchor will become stuck in very thick mud, behind a rock, or under an obstruction like a cable or a length of chain. Simply pulling on the rode in the direction away from the flukes will not be sufficient. Such problems often can be anticipated. A bottom marked "rky" may well be a maze of rocky ledges and cracks that can snag flukes. A special anchorage may cover a rat's nest of old rodes and anchors. If you're anchoring in such places, buoy the anchor by rigging a trip line — a long length of strong nylon tied to the crown (the point where the shank meets the flukes) with a buoy at the other end. Anchor as usual, throwing the trip line and buoy in afterwards. Later, if the anchor doesn't break out, veer out enough rode so you're sure the shank is lying on the bottom, power forward to the buoy, and pull up on the trip line. It will pull the anchor opposite to the direction it's dug in. To allow the

boat to move around freely, you may have to buoy the anchor rode itself, disconnecting it from your boat and leaving it behind tied to a dinghy or buoy while you work on the trip line. Alternatively, tighten the rode and run a kellett down it as far as it will go. Then veer out much of the rode, power ahead, and pull forward and up on the sentinel.

Some anchors are made so the rode itself can serve as a trip line, with the shank cut away to make a slot to allow the shackle at the end of the rode to slide all the way down to the crown. After you sail beyond the anchor, pull up on the rode to lift the crown.

Sometimes you may have to move the obstruction itself. It may be a chain rode leading to a mooring or another anchored boat. Once you've located the obstruction, fish for it with a grapnel or boat hook. If one of its ends can be found (say, at a nearby mooring), lift it with line and pull out your rode. Be

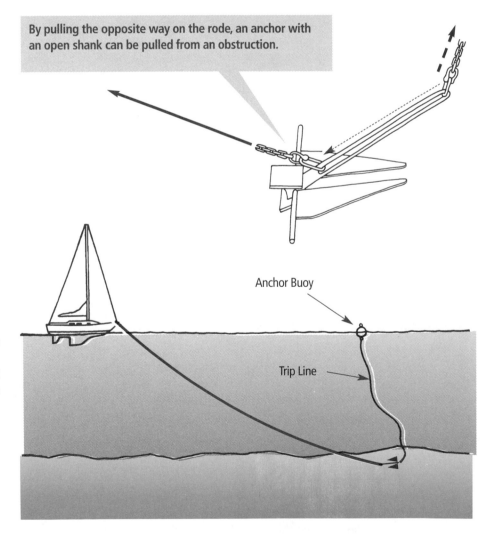

By pulling the opposite way on the rode, an anchor with an open shank can be pulled from an obstruction.

Anchor Buoy

Trip Line

If you anticipate a recovery problem, buoy the anchor. To do this, tie a trip line to the crown and connect it to a cushion or buoy. When it's time to leave, pull the anchor up by the trip line.

patient; in a crowded harbor you may have to lift many chains.

Making a Mooring. A good mooring is more secure than any anchor you could carry on board. You can safely use it with scope of 2:1. This reduced swinging room allows many moored boats to use a harbor. You can construct your own mooring using a heavy object (like an old engine block) or a large mushroom anchor, very heavy chain, a length of heavy nylon rope to use as the pendant (pulled on deck), and a buoy to hold the pendant at the surface where it can be retrieved. The chain and rope should be attached below the water surface with a swivel, which will prevent twisting and kinking. Make sure the swivel's own breaking strength is at least double the load in a storm anchor in a gale. The pendant should have a large eye and be protected against chafe, inspected regularly, and replaced of ten.

HANDS ON: **Anchoring Hints**

Safe anchoring depends as much on cautious, alert seamanship as it does on strong ground tackle. You should have an anchor big enough for your boat (plus some), a nylon rode in good condition that is long and stretchy enough for the anticipated water depth and strains, and sufficient chain to keep the rode low to the bottom. Use all your senses to determine if the hook is holding: bearings on landmarks; the sound of waves splashing dead on the bow and on the sides; the bounce-bounce as her stem rises and falls when she's secure and when she's dragging.

If there are three irreducible rules of thumb for safe anchoring they are: avoid lee shores like the plague; don't anchor too close to other boats; and when in doubt, let out more rode. All too many sailors can tell hair-raising stories about boats dragging down on them and, eventually, onto shore in the midst of a midnight thunder squall.

It is land, not the sea, that is a ship's greatest enemy, and if you plan to avoid a run-in with land, choose and use your ground tackle wisely.

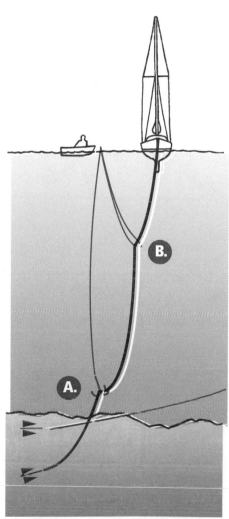

To recover your rode from under another, fish with a grapnel (A) or pull the other rode up with a weighted line (B).

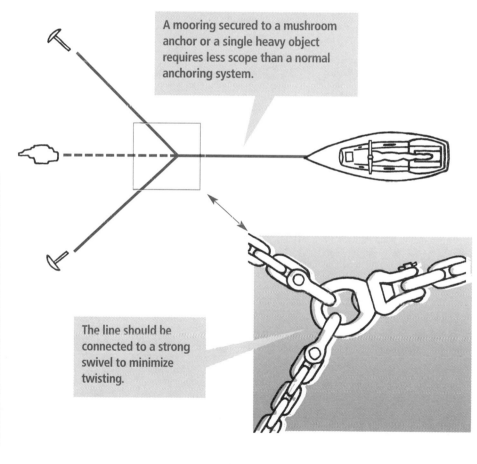

A mooring secured to a mushroom anchor or a single heavy object requires less scope than a normal anchoring system.

The line should be connected to a strong swivel to minimize twisting.

CHAPTER 15

Sailing in Heavy Weather

The power of the wind increases exponentially. That's the first of three important things to remember when the wind pipes up. A force 6 (22–27 knot) strong breeze is about twice the speed of a force 4 (11–16 knots) moderate breeze, but it's eight times more powerful. A force 9 (41–47 knot) strong gale — survival conditions — is another eight times more powerful than a force 6.

The second thing to remember is that "heavy weather" is not just an absolute wind speed but also a relative condition depending on the boat and crew. Heavy weather is when you risk losing control of your boat. In a force 6, a sturdy 60-foot, 40,000-pound traditional cruising yawl typically is sailing "as steady as a church" (as sailors used to say) and going where her steerer aims her. Yet this same force 6 may make life very uncomfortable aboard a modern 30-foot, 6,500-pound cruiser-racer. With less stability and a smaller keel, she is knocked far over by puffs and struggles to make a destination upwind. A 20-foot daysailer or 14-foot dinghy may never even head out in a force 6 — or in a force 4.

The third thing to remember is that while loss of control is instantaneous, the worsening conditions that cause it often sneak up on you. An especially strong afternoon sea breeze, a thunder squall, a weather front, a microburst dropping out of the clear sky — every one of them can kick up a 25-knot wind in a matter of minutes on any summer day. Sailors are most often taken by surprise when sailing before the wind on a run or reach. A big wind increase is hard to ignore when you're sailing closehauled because you're banging into the building breeze and steepening waves. But off the wind, a gust may seem neither obvious nor a bad thing because its danger is masked by the thrill of higher boat speed.

"Be aware of your environment," is the rule of Chay Blyth, the great British round-the-world sailor.

Once the wind builds to the point where the boat heels on the verge of being out of control, merely flattening and luffing the sails is not enough. Now you're in a whole new realm. Everything is different in heavy weather, every job more difficult. Chores like changing clothes, going forward to lower a sail, and cooking become major challenges. Gear is constantly under strain and subject to wearing chafe. When the wind shrieks through the rigging, even being heard is a serious problem.

For beginning sailors, willingly venturing out into very rough weather is a bad idea unless an experienced hand is aboard. But as you gain confidence, when the wind blows gather a good crew, take a deep breath, and head out there. The more you sail in heavy weather, the more you'll learn about your boat and the quicker your seamanship skills will grow. The knowledge that you can survive it will someday help you get through a sudden squall or storm. So both respect heavy weather and practice sailing in it.

A deeply reefed 35-foot sloop runs under control before a force 8 gale in the middle of the Atlantic Ocean, en route to the Azores. She and her crew of four made their destination safely.

Crew Preparation

In cold weather the crew will be especially thankful to have warm clothes, plenty of rest, and a settled stomach. Here the author steers down the face of a wave during the 1979 Fastnet Race storm. The air and water temperatures were in the 60s, and the wind speed was dropping from 60 knots.

Before it gets rough, sailors who are prone to seasickness should watch their diet and take medication that they know works for them. This is not a time to experiment with new pills. Nor is it the time to take a macho attitude about on-deck safety. When footing becomes uneasy, each crew member must wear the clothing and personal safety equipment described in previous chapters: a foam or inflatable life jacket and/or (in a larger boat) a safety harness. Put this gear on before coming on deck. Pulling on a life jacket or safety harness requires two hands, and on deck in rough weather you will need at least one hand simply to hold on.

In June 1998 one of the world's greatest sailors, the Frenchman Eric Tabarly, a giant in ocean voyaging for almost 40 years, a man of remarkable skill and courage, was at sea off the coast of Wales preparing for heavy weather when his gaff-rigged boat rolled and the gaff knocked him overboard. Wearing neither a life jacket nor a safety harness, Tabarly drowned. His body was found weeks later by fishermen. The loss of such a sailor under easily avoidable circumstances is doubly tragic and a lesson to us all about wearing basic personal safety gear.

Crew Organization. The skipper must lay out the chain of command and specify who should perform such duties as steering, sail handling, cooking, and navigating. While some organization is always required, clear crew structure is especially important in rough weather, where teamwork and decisive action are fundamental to safety.

Assign duties appropriate to the crew members' strengths and weaknesses. For example, the cook should have an iron stomach. In heavy weather the most qualified steerer on any boat may well be a good dinghy sailor. This is because the typical dinghy sailor has had more experience with demanding conditions than most big-boat sailors. While dinghies can be overpowered in winds as light as 15 knots, which blow frequently, most big boats don't begin to lose control until the wind is over 25 knots, a rare occurrence in many areas.

During the day in heavy weather and whenever the boat is sailing for more than 12 hours, spread the personnel load and keep people rested by breaking the crew up into sub-crews called watches, which change at regular intervals. Each watch should have its own organization. The head, the watch captain, should be the most experienced, knowledgeable sailor regardless of his or her age, familiarity with the boat, and relationship to the boat's owner. Besides being an experienced sailor, a good watch captain also is a good leader. While individual watch members must be prepared to perform any necessary task, the watch captain should appoint them to specific jobs according to their individual skills and aptitudes.

There is a well-tested set routine to the change of the watch. The members of the new, ongoing watch are roused by the old, offgoing watch in time for them to get dressed, have a cup of coffee or a snack, and get on deck with a few minutes left over so they can get a feel for the conditions and be briefed about the boat's position, nearby vessels, the weath-er, and the status of the running rigging. All this usually takes at least 20 minutes in bad weather (when foul-weather gear and safety harnesses must be put on) and 10 minutes in good weather. You don't do the other watch a favor by letting them sleep a little longer if it means that they have to rush to get on deck in time. It is rude to your shipmates to be late getting on deck. It is dangerous and rude for the offgoing watch to leave important chores (like changing sails) to the oncoming watch, whose coordination and alertness will revive slowly.

Regardless of the weather, as soon as the new watch is settled down they should inspect the sails and recoil and recleat all halyards and sheets to make sure there are no kinks in the lines. The new watch should never assume that the old watch made no mistakes.

The windier, rougher, wetter, and colder the conditions, the shorter the watches should be and the fewer people should be on deck. There should always be some people assigned to be on call ready to come on deck for a sail change or other maneuver. They may be the next watch according to the schedule, or they may be people who for one reason or another don't stand scheduled watches, for example, the cook or navigator, who are busy at their stations, night and day.

Crew Preparation

Hand Signals

Heavy weather is usually so noisy that effective verbal communication is impossible. The following hand signals, introduced earlier, are commonly used as commands:

Head up: Point to windward.

Head off: Point to leeward.

Pull the line: Point toward the crewmember holding the line.

Ease the line: Point away from the crewmember holding the line.

Hoist or pull up: Point up.

Lower or pull down: Point down.

Stop, "made": Open palm toward the crewmember.

Cleat the line: "OK" sign (circle with index finger and thumb).

Here are four successful watch systems using a six-person crew as an example:

Two three-person watches, 4-on/4-off. Each watch usually is on deck for 4 hours then below for 4 hours before coming back up (called "4-on/4-off"). At night or in rough weather, the watches can be 3-on/3-off. Once a day they dog the watch (stand 2-on/2-off) to change the pattern, usually at 1600 and 1800 hours in the 24-hour clock that's used afloat, or 4 and 6 PM. An alternative in good weather is to stand 6 hours each in the morning and afternoon watches to allow the off-watch more time to sleep.

Two three-person watches, Swedish system. The Swedish watch system also splits the crew in half but uses an irregular schedule. Beginning at 1900 hours (7 PM), the watches run 5 hours, 4 hours, 4 hours, 5 hours, and 6 hours. The shortest watches are in the darkest part of the night, the longest during the day and evening. This system dogs itself automatically.

Three two-person watches. Each watch is on deck for 2, 3, or 4 hours, with 4, 6, or 8 hours off. Splitting the crew into thirds is successful in bad weather because a minimum number of people are on deck for relatively short periods. It's also good for long passages when not much sail handling is called for.

Individual rotations. Three people are on watch at all times, but instead of changing as a group, a single fresh body comes on deck each hour. Each crewmember is on deck for 3 or 4 hours and then is relieved and goes below. This system provides a broader variety of sociability and less crowding below at the watch change. A disadvantage is the possibility of confusion during sail changes and other maneuvers.

Boat Preparation. The cautious worst case psychology that the navy calls "forehandedness" is always a healthy state of mind in a boat, but never more so than when thinking ahead to heavy weather. Plan for the time when the waves will be so high that they will break on deck, and when the boat will roll or pitch so violently that gear flying around below can hurt someone.

Keeping water out of the boat is crucial. Downflooding (taking a wave through a hatch or companionway) can fill the bilge and radically demoralize the crew. When the first hint of rough weather appears, shut and dog (lock) all hatches and ports. Install washboards (companionway slats) in the companionway. These are sturdy wooden or plexiglass slats that fill the gap and should be fixed in place with locks, dead bolts, or other devices to prevent them from falling out if the boat rolls over. Most boats have two or three small washboards to provide the option of leaving one out in good weather to allow air and light to come below. In bad weather each washboard should be in place. Boats have been sunk by two or three large waves pouring down even small holes.

Because of the danger of downflooding and holing, every boat must have at least one big manual pump that can be operated from the cockpit. An electric pump is not reliable in emergencies because the batteries or wiring may short out. A mesh screen secured across the pump intake will prevent gurry from clogging the mechanism. Carry buckets for bailing in emergencies.

As for loose gear flying around below, a skipper of a boat that had been caught in a gale reported that the boat rolled so wildly that "Even cottage cheese was lethal." Stow gear to keep it in one place not only when the boat is level but also when she rolls or pitches at steep angles. Be especially alert to heavy objects such as tools, cutlery, pots, and canned goods. Stow them low in well-secured drawers or lockers (the best ones have dead bolts or other strong latches) or in the bilge, or tie them down with strong line. Before placing canned goods in the bilge, remove their paper labels and mark the cans with indelible pens; the paper will wash off and clog bilge pumps. Refrigerator lids must be locked down, as should floorboards (the slats in the cabin sole or floor) and storage batteries, which, if they capsize, may leak acid into the bilge, creating noxious fumes that will drive the crew onto deck.

Shortening Sail

When the wind blows so hard that depowering techniques (see chapter 3) aren't enough to control heel, you must make the sail plan both smaller and lower by shortening sail (shortening down). This means lowering or reefing a sail or setting a smaller sail. Small sails have less heeling force than large ones, and sails set low in the rigging exert less leverage than ones set high.

You can simply lower a sail. Most boats sail capably in fresh or strong winds under mainsail alone, with the traveler eased down to cut weather helm. But except in smooth water, it is not a good idea to sail under jib alone or (in a yawl or ketch) under mizzen and jib. This is because the mainsail provides considerable fore-and-aft support for the mast, controlling mast bend and pumping (bending alternately forward and aft in the middle of the mast). Since pumping may throw the mast out of column and break it when the boat falls off a wave, the mast must be as straight and stiff as possible in rough weather. Tensioning running backstays led partway up the mast stiffens the mast. Temporary running backstays may be rigged by leading a spare jib or spinnaker halyard aft under a spreader to a strong attachment point amidships and then tightening the halyard — although this places loads on the spreader.

Larger boats, sailed well under shortened sail, should be able to make headway into winds up to what are called survival conditions — a force 8 (34–40 knot) gale and above. If you are unable to make headway, at least keep plugging along under deeply reefed mainsail. Even a small sail set steadies a boat dramatically. A reliable technique is to motor-sail under the reefed mainsail with the engine on. Under power, keep the boat sufficiently upright so the engine's water intake is in the water. If the boat heels too far for too long, the engine will overheat and burn out. And

if the fuel tank is not clean, pitching and rolling will stir up dirt that may clog the fuel lines. A fuel filter that can be cleaned or replaced quickly is extremely valuable in rough weather.

Reefing. Most boats larger than about 20 feet can be reefed by lowering the mainsail (or sometimes a jib) a few feet and securing the excess sail cloth. The typical cruiser-racer's mainsail can be reefed twice, with each reef equal to 15–25 percent of the sail's area (less in light-air regions, more in heavy-air regions and offshore, where a third reef is a good idea). Two reefs will cut the sail area by as much as one-half, and three reefs by almost three-fourths. Smaller, lighter boats should be reefed earlier, faster, and deeper than large, heavy ones. The exception to this rule is the racing boat, which depends on crew weight on the windward rail for a large part of her stability; she may be reefed later. If she does not sail offshore, a dedicated racing boat may have only one reef plus a flattening reef, which, more an outhaul than a reef, flattens the mainsail while decreasing its area only slightly.

Reefing Equipment. There are two types of reefing systems: tie-in and roller reefing.

Tie-in reefing is by far the most common system because it is faster and more efficient. It's also called jiffy reefing (because it's quick) and slab reefing (because the sail is tied down in slabs).

To tie in a reef, you must have a mainsail equipped with two cringles (heavy metal eyes) at approximately the same height above the boom, one in the sail's luff and the other in its leech. After the halyard is lowered, the cringles are pulled down and secured to the boom with luff and leech reefing lines (also called earings). The luff reefing line pulls and holds the luff down (the luff line may be dispensed with and its cringle is secured to a hook at the gooseneck). The leech reefing line pulls the leech out and down; it should bisect the angle at the clew. The lines may be led through blocks to the deck so they can be conveniently tightened and let out by the crew using winches. (A single-line reefing system has been developed to somewhat simplify the procedure.) The loads on these lines can be high and so they should be Dacron or some other

HANDS ON: When Should You Reef?

If you're even thinking about shortening sail, you probably should have done it already. "When in doubt, reef her," is a reliable maxim. Another is, "Reef early and reef deep." Three reliable signals that it's time to reef are a steep heel angle, breakneck speed, and discomfort.

Extreme heel. When sailing upwind or on a beam or close reach, keel boats should be permitted to heel no more than 25° and centerboarders 15°. When the boat heels that far or more ("on her beam's end," as sailors say) she goes out of balance and then quickly out of control. An inclinometer secured to a visible place in the cockpit is a worthwhile investment.

High speed. If you hear the whooping and hollering of an excited crew, consider slowing the boat. When a non-racing monohull or multihull is sailing unusually fast on a reach or run, it's usually time to reef. High speed can be exhilarating, and in expert hands a boat sailing very fast is a joy. But in other hands (or in the hands of a tired or distracted expert), high speed can be dangerous. The boat may jump waves, falling into the trough with great force, or broach with tremendous violence and then capsize or be dismasted.

Discomfort. A boat can be uncomfortable in several ways. She may be hard to steer, heeling sharply, pounding into waves, or digging her bow and leeward side into waves. If you feel insecure not only on your feet but when sitting down, and if steering is a fight, it's time to slow her down and level her off. As Rod Stephens, the American yacht designer and sailor, put it, "Nothing makes a boat more comfortable than taking 2 knots off her speed."

Shortening Sail

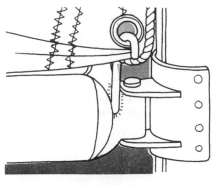

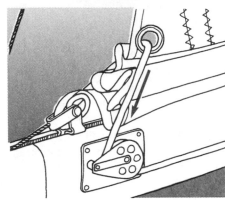

Secure the luff cringle at the gooseneck with the luff reefing line or a hook (top) before tightening the halyard and tensioning the leech cringle (right). The leech reefing line should pull the cringle out and down equally.

low-stretch material almost the size of the main sheet. It's a good idea to have a spare 6-foot length of heavy Dacron for doubling-up on the leech cringle.

Running between the cringles, to gather up the extra sail cloth after the sail is reefed, is a row of short lines called reef points or a row of grommets (small metal eyes) through which light line or sail stops (sail ties) are led.

Any boat heading offshore should be equipped with at least two permanently led leech reefing lines. Otherwise, except in areas of predominantly light wind, at least one leech line should be rove permanently so a reef can be quickly tied in on any point of sail.

Alternatively, a messenger can be rigged. This is a light line (about ¼ inch) that snakes a heavy line through a remote fitting. Here, it runs continuously between the cringle and the clew. It has a short tail that is tied into an eye splice at the end of the leech line. When the mes-

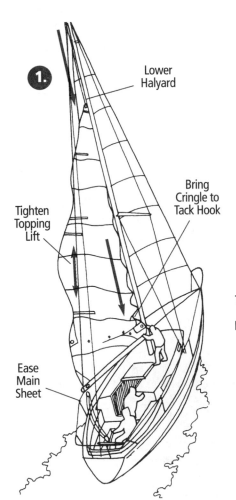

1.

Lower Halyard

Bring Cringle to Tack Hook

Tighten Topping Lift

Ease Main Sheet

Before tying in a reef, tighten the topping lift, ease the main sheet, and lower the halyard until the cringle is at the tack.

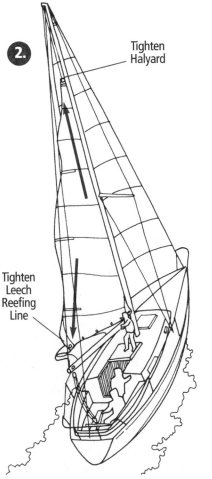

2.

Tighten Halyard

Tighten Leech Reefing Line

Secure the luff cringle, tighten the halyard, and tighten the leech line until the leech cringle is on the boom.

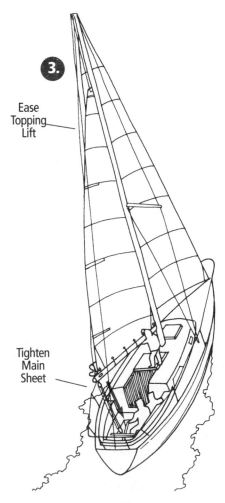

3.

Ease Topping Lift

Tighten Main Sheet

Finally, ease the topping lift, trim the sheet, and tie up the loose sail with reef points or light line.

senger is pulled, it hauls the reefing line up to and through the cringle and then down to the boom, where the crew secure it with a knot (a buntline hitch is good for the purpose). Because the boom must be over the deck for a messenger to work, this system is slow when the boat is on a reach — which is another reason to rig leech reefing lines permanently.

Jibs may be reefed using the tie-in system if they have cringles and grommets. The sail is lowered until the luff cringle is hooked into the jib tack fitting, and a new jib sheet is led to the upper leech cringle. The excess sail is bunched up inside lacings passed through the grommets.

Roller reefing works by rolling the sail up around the boom or headstay. Roller reefing is rarely used in mainsails, but is often found in jibs as a part of the roller-furling system. The gear must be strong and there should be foam inserts in the sail's luff that flatten the sail as it is rolled up; otherwise, a roller-reefed jib will be baggy. To roller-reef a jib, ease the sheet until the sail luffs partially and turn the roller-furler until a sufficient amount of sail has been rolled up. Proceed with care; the loads are high.

How to Reef. A reef can be tied in the mainsail singlehanded, but the job is faster with at least two crew.

1. If there is a topping lift for the boom, tighten it to keep the boom from falling into the water when the halyard is eased. (A spring-loaded boom vang will also do this job.)

2. Ease the main sheet and boom vang to luff the sail.

3. Lower the main halyard and pull the luff cringle down to the gooseneck. Secure it there with the luff reefing line or a hook. This step will be quick if there is a paint, tape, or wire reference mark on the halyard so you know exactly how far to lower it.

4. Tighten the halyard until there is a tension crease running from the tack to the head. Cleat the halyard.

5. With the sail still luffing, haul down on the leech reefing line until the leech cringle is lying on the boom. (If the vang is loose, the sail will rise to the sail, speeding up the reef and easing the load.) The steerer has the best view and should tell the crew when to stop pulling. Cleat the line. In hard conditions, double up by tying a strong line through

the cringle and around the boom.

6. Trim the main sheet until the sail fills, ease the topping lift, and neaten up the reef with reef points (use a reef knot, or square knot with a loop on the final turn) or a long length of light line passed through the grommets and under the foot or around the boom. Coil the reefing lines so they're ready to run when the reef is shaken out (let go).

If the mainsail is rigged for roller reefing, perform steps 1–3, then turn the boom with the crank until enough sail area has been rolled up. Finally, tighten the halyard.

Storm Sails. A cruiser-racer's sail inventory should include a very small (number 4) working jib for fresh winds to be set with a single- or double-reefed mainsail. If heading offshore or into areas known for heavy weather, she should also have a provision for a third mainsail reef and storm sails, which include the storm trysail and storm jib. These sails may seem ridiculously small when set in anything but survival conditions of force 8 and above. But because the wind's power increases so rapidly, they will be plenty large for hard conditions.

The storm trysail is a low jib-like sail about one-fourth the size of a mainsail, with no battens. On offshore boats, the trysail should run up and down the mast on its own track so it can be set quickly, using the main halyard after the mainsail is lowered. A traditional trysail is trimmed to the deck with a sheet secured to the clew, and the boom is lowered so it does not fly around. But some trysails are set on the boom, like a small mainsail, with the clew at the outhaul.

The storm jib is a tiny jib, smaller even than the number 4, that should be set on an inner stay called the forestay (sometimes, inner forestay).

Storm sails should be set near the middle of the boat to keep the center of effort of the sail plan over the center of lateral resistance of the hull. This helps the boat to balance well at different heel angles. Practice setting storm sails and leading their sheets before heading out.

Sailing in Large Waves. "It wasn't the wind — it was the waves!," survivors of storms have reported about the greatest threat they encountered. The most damaging waves usually are not the long, fast-moving swells of mature offshore storms that have been blowing for many

hours. While those waves can be dangerous, worse still are the short, breaking waves found in shallow water, in rapidly shifting winds, when current runs against the sea, and in the early part of a storm.

A breaking wave can destroy a boat by heaving onto her tens of thousands of pounds of water at a speed of 30 knots. Sailing or powering into breakers (when beating or reaching) or with them (when running) at high speeds can be dangerous. The boat may jump over the crest to smash down — literally, "fall off a wave" — with a crash that can dent or fracture the boat's bottom and heave the crew around with rib-cracking violence. And being caught beam-to the wave invites being rolled over or stove in by the breaker and filled with water. The trick for the steerer is to dodge the crest and steer toward the flat spots to the sides.

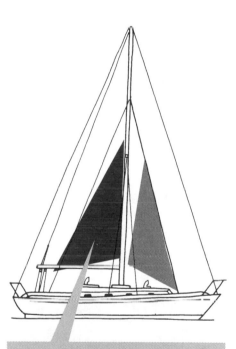

A storm trysail is a very small sail set in place of the mainsail.

Boat Handling

Waves on the Bow. Sailing into a big blow and a roaring head sea has sometimes been called "a hard chance," and for very good reason. It is fraught with difficulty and risk. If caught in such a situation — say, when trying to work your way off a lee shore into the teeth of a gale — you must steer skillfully.

When heading into waves, steer for flat spots around and between waves (which usually come in groups of three). Keep speed manageable while maintaining healthy steerageway. Hitting a wave head on or changing tacks clumsily may leave the boat dead in the water. The next wave might smash her, spin her either way, or force her backward. Sternway (sailing backward) may force the rudder hard over and either jam or break it. Before tacking in a rough sea, head off slightly to increase speed and then come around in a relatively flat spot. After the boat falls off on the new tack, be careful not to trim the main sheet too hard and point too close to the wind until speed has returned.

Waves usually run with the wind, but the wind may shift and the "new sea," as sailors call it, may take a while to replace the old one. For a period of time the sea may be extremely confused, with waves coming from both directions and meeting to form small breakers. Such a mixed sea is extremely difficult to steer in. If

the wind happens to decrease (and it often does so during a major wind shift), the sails may not steady a sailboat and she may slat (rock violently). Strains on rigging, gear, and crew may be greater in slatting conditions than in a strong wind. To steady the boat's motion, increase boat speed and alter course to find a more favorable angle to the confused sea. The agitation will eventually die and in time will leave a single wave train running with the wind.

Waves on the Stern. Running before the wind in waves presents the dangers of broaching and pitchpoling. You want to keep the stern toward waves while controlling speed and sailing in flat water. The main problem is uncontrolled speed. The steep, breaking waves of new storms repeatedly push the boat faster. As the storm matures, the waves lengthen and carry everything on them at tremendous velocity. Surfing is exhilarating and also risky.

Broaching occurs when the steerer loses control of the helm and the boat heads up into the wind radically. On a run or reach, she will round up until her side is exposed to the waves, which may then smash and even capsize her. As the boat runs down the face of a wave, she may go out of her normal trim: the bow drops and the stern lifts, moving the center of lateral resistance forward and creating sudden, extreme weather helm. Sail the boat almost level. Some good helmsmen sailing downwind in heavy weather concentrate not on the compass but on the foredeck, steering it parallel to the horizon. Steer for flat spots, aiming partly across waves and looking for "runways" to land on either side of the crest ahead.

All this may be easier said than done. The speed of a lightweight monohull or a multihull may double as she surfs down the face of a large wave. As the speed increases, the boat's tolerance of steering error decreases. Mariners talk of "forgiving" and "unforgiving" boats, and of "seakindly" hulls. A forgiving, seakindly vessel will seem to make her own way through rough weather, tolerating all but the most flagrant mistakes at the helm. But an unforgiving, high-performance boat — like a 200 mile-per-hour race car in the hands of a beginning driver — can be a dangerous weapon if her steerer does not respond instantly to changes in

A confused sea can cause severe pitching upwind, so try to steer around bad waves.

In this force 7 (28–33 knot) blow, the mainsail has been roller-reefed to about one-half its size, and a preventer (dark line leading from end of boom) holds the boom out. The object dragging in the water is a reaching strut used on the after guy on reaches.

speed, course, and balance.

The safest thing to do if your boat threatens to go out of control when running in rough weather is to slow down. Keep enough steerageway to climb up the back of waves, but shorten sail and, if necessary, run out drogues (which we will describe soon) to keep her from accelerating wildly.

Pitchpoling is worse yet than a broach. As a boat accelerates down the face of a steep wave she may develop so much momentum that instead of leveling off in the trough, she plunges bow-first into the back of the next wave, suddenly stops, and somersaults over her stem. The forces created by this somersault are immense.

Jibes and the Preventer. Any jibe, whether an accidental one or an uncontrolled intentional one, is a worry because the boom slamming across can smash sailors and rigging. The boom must be controlled by both careful sailing and a preventer, a line that keeps it from swinging across the boat. This crucial piece of safety gear, which belongs on every boat larger than a daysailer, is described in chapter 5.

The best protection against an accidental (all-standing) jibe is to avoid sailing on a dead run square before the wind. A broad reach is much safer than a run because the wind is slightly on the side, the boat heels to leeward just enough to stop rolling, and you must head off many degrees before she will jibe. As a guide, use heel angle, the feel of the helm (which should have a little weather helm), the feel of the boat under your feet (there should be little or no rolling), and three wind indicators — the masthead fly (wind arrow) at the masthead, the telltales in the windward shrouds, and your neck. Electronic apparent wind indicators may be helpful, though the display in the cockpit may be slightly delayed. Another good guide to wind direction is the jib, which on a broad reach fills on the same side as the boom. If it hangs unfilled over the foredeck or fills on the side opposite the boom, you're on a run, not a broad reach.

The danger of a square run is that it often evolves into sailing by the lee, with the wind coming over the leeward quarter. The wind then catches the mainsail on the wrong side and violently throws it and the boom across in a wild jibe. All it takes is a wind shift of just a few degrees, a wave slapping the bow, or a quick roll to windward to catch the steerer unawares. The steerer must be extremely alert as there is no steady "feel" on a run. With the wind pushing straight ahead, the helm is neutral and vague, with no pressure to serve as a ref-

erence point. The steerer may be caught by surprise by small changes in wind or wave and the boat rounds off (heads off sharply).

A roll to windward induces lee helm that the steerer may not be quick enough to catch. Rolling is common on dead runs in heavy weather due to big waves and also to the phenomenon of hull speed. When displacement boats (ones other than planing boats and multihulls) can't go any faster, they roll. Then comes the dangerous accidental jibe.

In heavy weather, even an intentional jibe can be risky. If the boom is not held down by a boom vang or taut main sheet, there may be a goosewing jibe, where the boom lifts and bangs into the permanent backstay and the sail and battens snag the upper rigging and spreaders. Goosewing jibes have dismasted boats and broken booms. (This unfortunate maneuver gets its name because the spars assume the awkward angle of a goose's wing.)

When jibing intentionally in strong winds, do it when sailing fast down the face of a wave rather than when climbing slowly up the back of one. The apparent wind will be less and the boom will slam across with less force. Put the strongest crew member on the main sheet. As the preventer is eased, trim the sheet quickly and as much as you can without creating excessive weather helm. The steerer tells everybody where the boom is, since all must be wary of it as it passes. When the steerer shouts, "Boom coming across," everybody ducks a couple of feet, even hugging the deck. After the boom jibes, the steerer heads off a couple of degrees to counter the bow's swing and keep the boat flat. Ease the sheet very quickly as the preventer is tightened on the new leeward side. It is crucial that the sheet be free to run out easily, without kinks.

Sometimes an intentional jibe may seem too risky, and the only alternative is to wear about (tack while sailing off the wind). Do this carefully. Don't lose headway or the boat will hang in irons at the mercy of the waves.

Squalls

Heavy weather generally appears either as a local, fast-moving, and unpredictable squall or line of squalls or as a large, relatively well-anticipated gale created by a depression. Squalls may be more dangerous than gales because they spring up rapidly, often with little warning. Towering, fierce and black, kicking up steep waves with 50-knot gusts, then flattening those same waves with hammers of rain before sweeping on, a thunder squall can pass in 20 minutes and scatter fleets of boats across large bodies of water.

Squalls often occur on exceptionally hot, humid afternoons. They may be at the cutting edge of a new weather front, or they may be purely local in origin. The calling card is a steep pile of dark, thick cumulonimbus clouds and, below it, ragged swirls — the kind that in a Hollywood film announces the arrival of witches and extraterrestrial beings. When you see a black cloud approaching, take a moment to analyze it. The sharper, darker, and lower the front edge of the cloud, the more trouble you can expect, so sail away from it if you have the chance. Another cause for alarm is vertical turbulence between layers in the cloud as indicated by ragged scud.

The distance in miles to the approaching storm may be estimated by timing the interval between the flash of lightning and the sound of the thunderclap and dividing by 5. Squalls move as rapidly as 30 or 40 knots, so don't waste too much time in this exercise.

Preparing for a Squall. Plot your position using every available aid. If you're near a harbor and are sure you can reach it before the squall hits, you may want to run for shelter. But getting close to land may invite being thrown up onto a lee shore. If you have any doubt about your chances of reaching a safe harbor before the squall hits, stay far away from land and shoal spots.

When you see this, prepare for a squall: hand out life jackets and safety harnesses, shorten sail, close hatches, secure gear, decide on your strategy, and fix your position.

Whether or not you decide to head for shore, make your vessel safe for rough weather. Here are some important preparation steps:

1. **Put on your foul weather gear,** life jacket, and safety harness, and instruct your crew to do the same.

2. **Douse the jib** or set a small one. Be prepared to quickly take two or three reefs in the mainsail. Overhaul halyards and sheets to be sure they will run out without kinking.

3. **Shut and dog (bolt down) hatches** and ports and install washboards in the companionway.

4. **Secure deck gear,** personal items, food, dishes, and other objects in lockers, which must be shut tight.

5. **Determine your strategy** for handling the squall and discuss it with your crew. Don't overdramatize the situation, but don't underestimate it, either.

6. To the crew, **point out the location of the essential gear** and be sure some-

As the squall approaches, prepare the boat as you try to sail away from it. Unless you can get into a harbor immediately, stay well away from land so you're not blown ashore.

one knows how to work it. This gear includes the bilge pumps, radiotelephone, engine, flares, and life raft.

7. **Assign the most experienced steerer to the helm.**

If there are children on board, make sure someone is firmly in charge of them. When the squall first hits, they should be below. If the situation warrants, you may later allow them on deck to watch the spectacle — a rousing thunder squall is one of God's wonders.

A squall may hit first with a sharp wind gust knocking the boat well over on her side and then quickly become tame, perhaps leaving you feeling a bit disappointed after all your preparations. But if the gusts are preceded by rain, be prepared for a long, hard bash. Two traditional mariner's sayings set the scene:

When the wind before the rain,
Let your topsails draw again;
When the rain before the wind,
Topsail sheets and halyards mind.

And:

The sharper the blast,
The sooner it's past.

If you haven't reefed, you may have to ease your sheets and luff your sails in this first gust, but don't let them flog or a batten will break. If you douse a sail, don't worry too much about a neat furl. Just make sure the sail won't blow off the boom or foredeck and that there are no lines dragging overboard to tangle in the propeller in case you use the engine. If the mainsail is down and the boat is rolling, save a cracked head by tightening the preventer.

Lightning. While lightning rarely hits boats, when it does it can cause considerable damage. Crews should not become fatalistic about being fried. Don't panic, and do take precautions. Try to get below, but if you must be out in the open, don't touch metal objects, especially the stays and mast.

If lightning does strike, it probably will damage the boat and her equipment more than the crew. Through-hull fittings have been blown out through bilges, antennas have been melted, electronic instruments have been destroyed, and compasses have lost their magnetism. The best protection is a good grounding system. This includes a lightning rod at the top of the mast, a ground of heavy copper wire running from the base of the mast to the keel bolts, and

grounded chain plates and other through-hull and through-deck metal objects. Such a system is standard on most pleasure boats (many boats built before 1980 in California, where there is little lightning, are not grounded). The mast will attract the energy from direct hits and transfer it to the water through the ground. If your boat is hit by lightning, immediately inspect her for damage and her instruments for inaccuracies. You or your insurance company should hire a professional surveyor and a professional compass adjustor.

In the Squall. Other than strong wind and the steep waves it kicks up, your main problem will be poor visibility, for thick rain or hail may make it impossible to see the bow and even the compass. This is why it's so important to be certain of your position at the time the squall hits. Keeping a close eye on the chart and GPS, try to gauge your changing relationship to aids to navigation and your heading relative to the shore. If the wind allows, sail parallel to or away from shore. Keep a sharp lookout, especially in channels, where boats may be bunched dangerously as they try to make harbor. If you do come across another boat, don't automatically assume that her crew has her under control or is alert to the niceties of the Navigation Rules. Give her a wide berth.

The squall may pass after an exciting half hour or so, leaving in its wake sunshine and decks scrubbed clean by hard rainfall. There may be a fresh northwest wind or, then again, there may be a flat calm. If you're sure that another squall is not looming on the horizon, open the hatches to air the cabin out, pump out the bilge — water may have seeped below — and check halyards and sheets for chafe before getting under way again. Look around for capsized boats that you can help rescue or report to the Coast Guard.

Gales

Gales are depressions, so wind circulates around them predictably. When your back is to the wind your extended left hand will point at the center of the storm.

Part of a deep low-pressure weather system, a gale is usually (but not always) predicted. It may be too compact and moving too fast for forecasters to keep up with. At sea, indications of an approaching gale are a falling barometer, ground swell (long waves) running across the waves caused by the local or prevailing wind, plus a dense, dark cloud mass, usually to the west. Prepare as you would for a squall but with the knowledge that the bad weather will last much longer. The checklist for squall preparation should be followed, with these additions:

1. **Cover all large windows** with storm shutters — wooden or plastic coverings screwed to the cabin over windows to protect the glass from shattering in breaking waves. Cover every window no matter what the wind direction.

2. **Do your cooking** before the sea gets rough. Fill Thermos bottles with hot drinks, soup, and stew. If you must cook when the boat is rolling and pitching,

wear your foul-weather gear to protect your body from spilled hot food.

3. **Establish a watch schedule** and assign steerers.

4. **Pull out the storm sails** and inspect them.

5. If there are few hand rails below or on deck, **rig lines** between sturdy attachment points to facilitate moving around.

6. If you have longstanding worries about your equipment, end them now either by **replacing the weak fitting** or fixing it (if you have time).

7. **Keep crew morale up,** but not at the level of euphoric exuberance. Cautious optimism is the best state of mind.

Storm Strategy. Try to predict the path of the low-pressure system and how it will affect you. Use the forecasting tools covered earlier in chapter 4. One is Buys-Ballot's Law: when the wind is on your back, low pressure is to your left and high pressure is to your right. The other is the crossed-winds rule: when your back

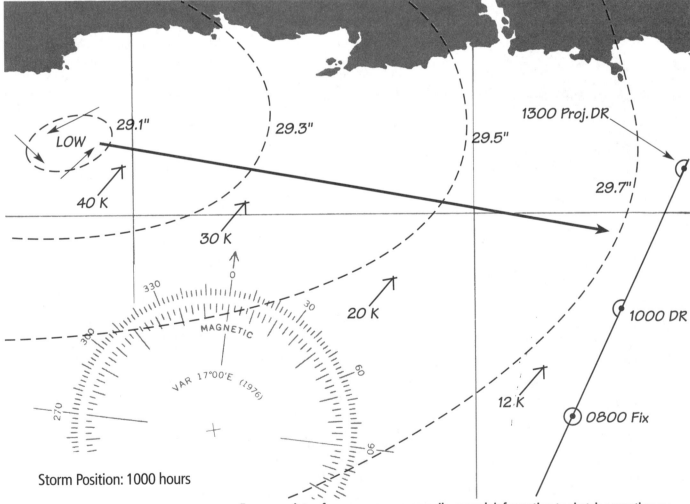

From a variety of sources you can compile enough information to sketch a weather map showing the approaching storm and the wind and isobars around it.

is to the wind, if the air flow aloft is from your left, the weather probably will deteriorate in the next few hours.

Using recent barometer readings taken on board and from broadcasts, and recorded faithfully in the log, sketch a weather map on which you should include nearby land and shoals. Estimate the storm's rate of advance and its force. A shallow depression with a minimum atmospheric pressure of 30 inches (1016 millibars) that is moving relatively slowly at 15 knots will probably have force 5–7 (17–33 knot) winds that shift gradually. But a deep depression with a pressure of 29 inches (984 millibars) that's racing over the ground at 30 knots will contain force 8–10 (34–55 knot) winds that shift drastically.

The danger also depends on how the storm hits you. If its backside just grazes you, consider yourself lucky. But you will have major problems if its front side, called the dangerous semicircle (and especially its front right side, sometimes called the dangerous quadrant) hits you squarely. On your sketch, draw the wind arrows as they circulate counterclockwise around the storm, then plot the route of fastest escape. If the storm aims to catch you in the maw of its dangerous semicircle, you must try to get as far from the center of the depression as you can by sailing fast at a right angle to the storm's track. This means sailing either on a starboard-tack close reach to get to the left of the approaching depression or on a port-tack run or broad reach to get to the right of it. With a storm approaching from the west, this means sailing south or north — whichever takes you fastest away from the path of the gale. If the barometer rises, you're succeeding; if it falls rapidly, however, you're either sailing toward the center or are being enveloped by the gale.

If you have serious worries, call the Coast Guard on VHF/FM channel 16 or single sideband frequency 2182, describe your situation, and schedule regular status reports.

Storm Tactics, Drogues, and Sea Anchors. If you can't dodge a gale, you must sail through it under shortened canvas or storm sails. If the storm is coming at you from land and there's plenty of open sea around you, stay there. If you're trapped against a lee shore, you'll have to fight to work your way out to sea. Sometimes it's blowing too hard to sail toward your destination, and you must change your priorities to concentrate on survival or at least comfort.

Sailors have evolved several tactics for surviving bad storms. Most involve carrying sail and putting out drag devices for slowing or stopping the boat. As Victor Shane writes in his essential book on storm tactics and survival gear, *Drag Device Data Base: Using Parachutes, Sea Anchors, and Drogues to Cope with Heavy Weather,* "Boats have to be forcefully

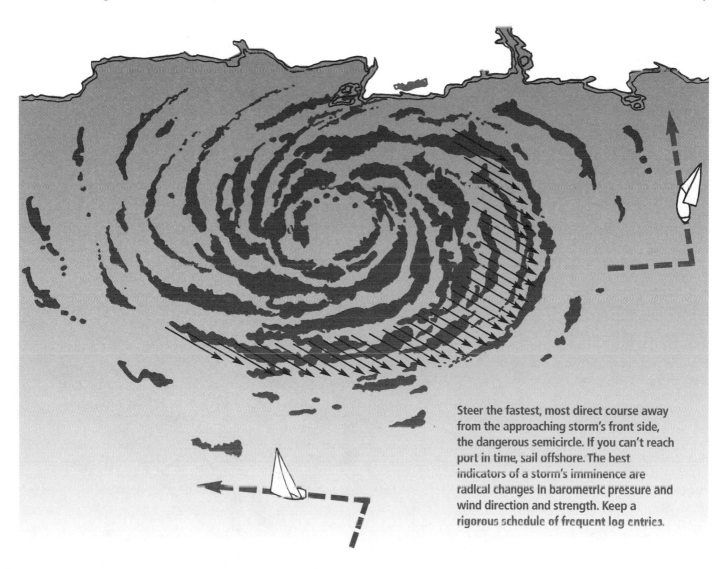

Steer the fastest, most direct course away from the approaching storm's front side, the dangerous semicircle. If you can't reach port in time, sail offshore. The best indicators of a storm's imminence are radical changes in barometric pressure and wind direction and strength. Keep a rigorous schedule of frequent log entries.

Gales

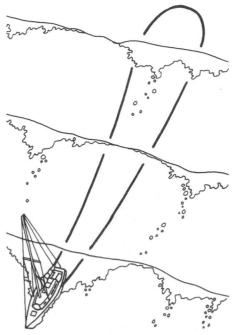

brought into alignment by some clever, auxiliary means." There are two types of parachute-shaped drag devices set either astern (in which case they are called drogues) or ahead (sea anchors, para-anchors). They are set on 100–300 foot lines, such as anchor rodes, that are attached to the boat at a single strong point or, with catamarans and sometimes with monohulls, using bridles. These devices are set so they dig deep into the water on the back of the second or third wave astern or ahead.

Discussions of storm tactics often stray into debates about these two families of drag devices. In their quest for absolute answers, many participants in these heated arguments choose one device and damn the other, studiously ignoring the fact that there is nothing absolute even about a storm at sea. Conditions are constantly changing as the gale starts, matures, and eventually dies. Different tactics and gear work best at different stages and on different types of boats. This is why less strident, more flexible skippers carry both types, and often two or more versions of each.

Here are the usual storm tactics:

Running before it on a run or broad reach, with or without towing a drogue, has been called an "active" storm tactic because the boat is steered in order to get around steep breaking waves. This often is an excellent tactic in the early stages of a storm, before the seas have become regular. Just enough sail is carried for steerageway when the boat is sailing "uphill" on the backs of waves.

The challenge is to control speed on the downhill side, when surfing down a wave's face. In breaking seas, the speed down waves should be high enough so you can stay ahead of white water and not be pooped (smashed on the stern by breakers, which might cause damage or

To slow a boat when running before it, tow a drogue — either warps (above) or a dedicated drogue like the Galerider (right).

fill the cockpit), yet not so high that the steerer loses control and the boat broaches, pitchpoles, or plows into the back of the next wave. Modern light-displacement keel boats and almost all multihulls can be driven much too fast in these conditions. Another problem with running before it is that constant, careful steering is demanded; when an exhausted

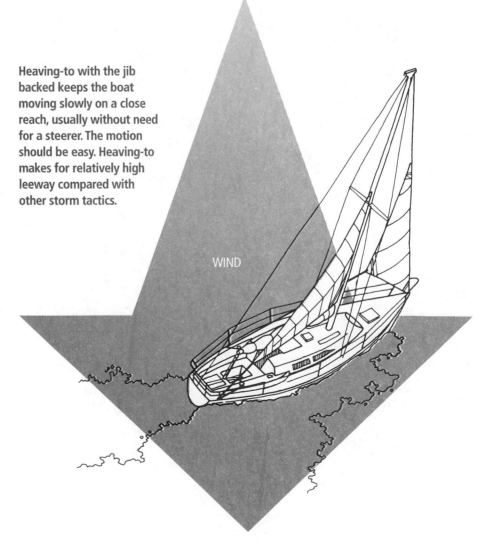

Heaving-to with the jib backed keeps the boat moving slowly on a close reach, usually without need for a steerer. The motion should be easy. Heaving-to makes for relatively high leeway compared with other storm tactics.

WIND

To keep the bow into the wind and seas, set a sea anchor. Long-distance cruisers should carry both a drogue and a sea anchor so they are prepared for changing conditions.

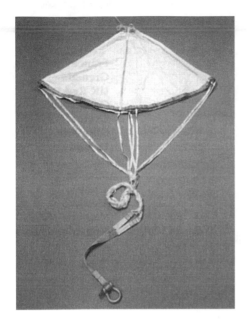

Heaving to with a sea anchor, set on a bridle for easy adjustment, creates a slick to windward and may cut leeway to less than 1 knot.

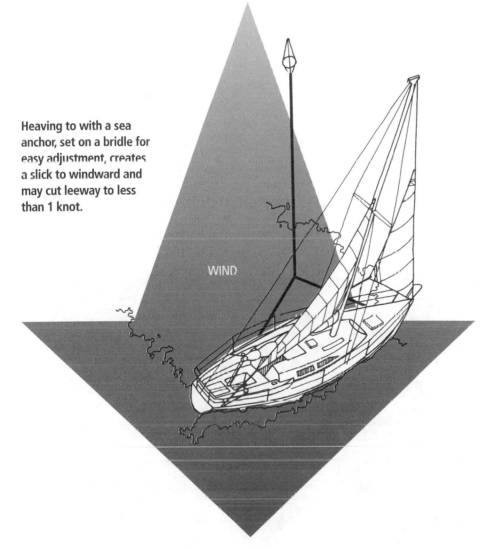

WIND

steerer makes a mistake, even a conservative heavy boat may broach. A third problem is that running with it may take a boat rapidly toward a lee shore.

Towing a drogue is a proven way to control speed when running before a big sea. The boat still will make several knots, perhaps as much as 75 miles a day, toward a lee shore, but in much better control. The simplest drogue is a warp — a long length of heavy rope or chain (like an anchor rode) in a bight, with each end tied to the boat. There also are dedicated drogues with parachute-shaped drag devices. Some have a single drag, like the 3–4 foot diameter Galerider, which is made of heavy webbing. Others use many drags: the Jordan Series Drogue is a set of more than 100 5-inch-diameter cones secured at intervals to a 300-foot line. Dedicated drogues may be towed astern from a single point (which obviously must be strong) or from two points on a bridle, which may be adjusted to

change the angle and affect steering. Warps and dedicated drogues may be weighed by anchors, chain, or other objects to increase resistance or help them dig into the water.

Heaving-to under sail keeps the bow near the wind and the boat more or less in the same place and does not require a steerer (this is why it is called a passive tactic). We looked at heaving-to in chapter 2, but a review may be helpful. To heave-to, get on a close reach, back the jib (trim it to windward), and adjust the main sheet (or storm trysail sheet) and the helm until the boat is sailing at about 2 knots. Lash the helm where the boat sails comfortably. The boat will sail herself in a series of swoops, coming off to about 60° to the apparent wind and then coming up to about 40°, all the while making about 2 knots of leeway, about 50 miles a day. You want to make leeway in such conditions since sideslippage leaves a slick of relatively smooth water to windward that breaks waves before they reach the boat. To increase leeway, decrease side resistance by partially raising an unballasted centerboard or daggerboard. (Ballasted boards, which help stability, should be left fully down).

A hove-to boat will be heeled enough to steady her motion and may be going fast enough to avoid being trapped by steep waves. The crew may rest and eat without having to bother with the helm (though a lookout should be kept and the running rigging should be checked periodically for chafe). Since heaving-to leaves a boat vulnerable to very steep breaking waves, it is not the best tactic early in the storm or in an exceptional storm.

Lying to a sea anchor is another passive tactic, with the bow into the wind and no sail set but with a sea anchor set out over the bow. A sea anchor (sometimes called a para-anchor) is a sturdy fabric parachute set at the end of an anchor rode or other long line and sometimes weighted so it rides deep. Much larger than the typical drogue (the recommended diameter is 35 percent of the boat's overall length), it creates far more resistance, with two effects. First, it holds the boat in position without risk of sailing too fast, pitchpoling, or being

Gales

pooped; there is very little drift down-wind with a sea anchor. Second, the sea anchor holds the boat's sharpest portion, the bow, into the wind and waves. Many multihull sailors favor this storm tactic; catamarans should set sea anchors off bridles, just as they do regular anchors. A light trip line may be included to collapse the sea anchor for ready retrieval. One risk of a sea anchor is that a violent surge aft may damage the boat's rudder. Another is a breaking wave.

Heaving-to with a sea anchor on a bridle, as used by the circumnavigators Larry and Lyn Pardey in their heavy-displacement boats, is a variation on two themes. The boat is hove-to under deeply reefed mainsail or storm trysail and the sea anchor is set on a bridle so the boat lies at about 50° to the wind. The sea anchor and boat leave a slick that smooths the water to windward. Drift to leeward is less than 1 knot.

Lying ahull is the most passive tactic as it leaves the boat under bare poles (with no sail set) and no special equipment, such as a sea anchor, set out. Monohulls may drift as fast as 2 knots to leeward, multihulls 4 knots. This tactic's big risk is that it leaves the boat lying still and fully exposed to the waves as she lies beam-to — a very dangerous situation in breaking seas. All the other tactics turn the boat's ends to the waves.

Tying-Up in Heavy Weather. Hurricanes and gales are extremely dangerous to moored, anchored, and docked boats. If a storm watch is in effect (indicating that the blow may arrive within a day or so), haul the boat out of the water or take her far up a local "hurricane hole" — a well-protected creek or cove that has historically served as a haven for boats in storms. Well away from other boats and land, set out and dig in at least two anchors, including a storm anchor, in the direction expected to be to windward when the worst hits.

Sailing in heavy weather can exhaust even the most experienced crews. Try to rest when you can, to stay as dry and warm as possible, to keep yourself hydrated and well fed, and to wear and clip on safety harnesses (left).

Before any hard blow, carefully inspect and prepare the boat. Start with the lines holding her in place. Rig back-up mooring pendants or docking lines, securing them separately to strong cleats, winches, or the mast. Be sure you can cast them off quickly in case you have to get away in a hurry. Carefully protect these lines and anchor rodes at the chocks and other abrading spots with chafing gear (hoses or rags).

It is crucial that you eliminate all the windage you can. A boat with furled sails on the headstay and boom or a dodger set over the companionway always sails around her anchor, mooring, or dock far more aggressively than a boat that has been stripped. This leads to broken rodes or docking lines and collisions with other boats and piers. Before a gale, therefore, remove and stow below or ashore all non-fixed gear, including sails, dodgers, covers, sheets, small spars, flags, small boats, and anything else that adds to the boat's exposed area. If possible, remove the boom and spinnaker pole and replace the halyards with messengers (light Dacron or nylon line).

You must also secure objects in cabins and batten down (securely close) all hatches, ports, and companionways. Hang all your fenders (rubber bumpers) over the bow and sides to fend off the float and other boats that may go adrift and bear down on you.

If sails and dodgers are exposed on nearby boats, go aboard and remove them, leaving a note of explanation. Since the other boat may well drag down on you, the favor is both yours and the other skipper's. Preparing for a storm is one time when boaters in an area must come together in mutually supportive community.

While staying aboard is possible in a minor gale, think carefully about doing it in a major storm. If you are tempted to stay on board, balance the few hypothetical advantages against the many sure risks. While you might be able to help your vessel by running the engine to ease the load on lines, for instance, you also will put your life in the path of danger. The Coast Guard always urges people to stay ashore, and for good reason.

Morale in Heavy Weather. Heavy weather and survival conditions can be extremely demoralizing. Every effort must be made to resist lethargy in the face of these conditions. Start by keeping up the normal shipboard and living routines. The cabin must as neat and dry as possible, with wet clothes and foul-weather gear kept well away from bunks, whether in the head, in waterproof bags, or in a special locker near the companionway. Hot food must be served, and if it can't be eaten seasick crews should nibble on salt-free crackers or other bland nourishment. The crew must also try to sleep; if that is impossible due to the boat's motion, simply lying still for a couple of hours can be refreshing. At least every hour, the bilges must be pumped and running rigging and sails must be checked for chafe. Navigation must be kept up, as must a lookout for other vessels and for land.

Routine may not be enough to maintain morale. Under strong, calm, cheerful, purposeful leadership, many crews have avoided passivity and survived terrible storms on the faith that something better was awaiting them at the other side. Thoughts of family and friends ashore usually provide sufficient motivation to keep sailing, as does loyalty to shipmates and the vessel.

Some survivors are driven by religious or mystical faith. Consider how an especially distressed boat survived one of the worst storms of the late twentieth century, the 1994 Queen's Birthday Storm (it came at the time of Queen Elizabeth II's official birthday) in the South Pacific. A crew of inexperienced sailors in a catamaran made it through appalling conditions largely because they shared a belief that most of us would think bizarre. They were mystically convinced that, if they survived, they would rendezvous with aliens whose space ship would gather them up and take them to a higher realm. That belief was motivation enough for the owner to steer actively for almost a day in force 12 (64-knot-plus) hurricane winds and huge waves that would easily have flipped the boat had the crew given up and laid ahull. With a drogue towed astern to keep the boat's speed under some control (although at times she went fast enough to fly a hull), he steered using the helm and bursts on the boat's two engines. In time the crew was rescued (against their will) by a fishing vessel.

The lesson from this story (as well as many other accounts of survival in appalling conditions, both at sea and near shore) is not obscure. While a good boat, basic seamanship skills, and an understanding of weather are important to riding out a tough storm, the human element may sometimes be the one crucial factor in survival at sea.

If you get badly seasick, you may have to stay on deck. Be sure to hook on your safety harness.

CHAPTER 16 Emergencies

Sailors should not overly sentimentalize the sea and boats by regarding their inherent risk as romantic, uncontrollable, or inevitable. When someone drowns at sea, too often is it said, "He would have wanted to die that way." What "he" really wanted, of course, was to live to sail another day. It is far healthier to mourn deeply the loss of a friend and try to learn from his mistakes. While we cannot control the sea, we can improve our skills and equipment so the tragedies of the past do not repeat themselves.

Taking seriously the possibility of emergencies requires the cautious state of mind known as "forehandedness." A helpful rule of thumb, long laid out by the United States Navy, is that "The price of safety is eternal vigilance." In chapter 7 we looked at the personal safety of the individual sailor. Here we will examine situations that may put the boat at risk.

The Float Plan. An important safety practice is to make sure that other people know where you are on the water. Before heading out, leave a float plan with a friend and your yacht club or marina. A float plan is a written itinerary of your planned trip that includes contacts and the times when you plan to return. If you change your schedule later on, check in and alter the float plan. Instruct your contact at home to notify the Coast Guard if you do not call or appear on schedule.

Other Notification. If you must abandon your boat for another vessel, your fellow mariners will conduct time-consuming, possibly risky searches unless they know you are safe. Leave a note indicating where you have gone and notify the Coast Guard or police. If you deploy safety gear while being rescued or making a rescue, retrieve it from the water so other boaters who come across it are not alarmed.

"Formula for Disaster." "Why did all those people get into such terrible trouble?" As the author of "*Fastnet, Force 10*," a book about the most murderous storm in the history of pleasure boating, the 1979 Fastnet Race, I'm often asked that question. Fifteen sailors died, 24 yachts were abandoned, and five yachts sank in a vicious gale in the waters between Ireland and England. It was the worst single disaster in the history of pleasure sailing. I sailed in the race, and while the boat I was in suffered no major damage, I would not want to go through a storm like that again.

What happened? There are several answers, few of them unambiguous. While some of the boats in the race were not fit for storm conditions, not every boat that got into trouble was poorly designed, built, or sailed. Crew injuries, gear damage, and bad luck all played their part, but most important was the brutal, unseasonal violence of the storm itself.

Still, close study of the 1979 Fastnet storm and other storms reveals repeated patterns of human behavior in catastrophe that can be summarized as the

His 34-foot sloop lying disabled in 50-knot winds and 30-foot breaking waves, a sailor prepares to jump overboard so he can be rescued by a military helicopter during the 1979 Fastnet Race storm.

Formula for Disaster. The formula consists of seven factors that appear time and again in major emergencies.

Factor 1. A rushed, ill-considered departure is first on the list because it turns up in almost every bad accident. While the demands of jobs, families, and racing schedules often dictate when we go out on the water, none of these imperatives bears any relation to the schedule that counts the most in good seamanship. That schedule is nature's cycle of tide and wind.

Every sailor should be able to identify the sailing conditions in which she or he is comfortable, and say "No!" when that comfort zone threatens to be exceeded. A cautious risk-analysis approach is used by an experienced offshore sailor, Steve Dashew: "A five percent or even two percent chance of a severe blow should be enough to keep one in port until the situation is clarified." This requires reading weather forecasts with a worst-case scenario firmly in mind, since most meteorologists (to avoid being alarmists) may delay forecasting heavy weather until there is a greater degree of certainty.

Factor 2. The route is dangerous because it passes through predictably risky waters. This doesn't automatically mean deep water. It can be more hair-raising to sail a 20-foot daysailer through a narrow channel crowded with high-speed powerboats than to pound into a Gulf Stream gale in a 40-foot cruising boat. Sometimes a route suddenly becomes dangerous because conditions change. For example, you may choose a route because the tidal current is favorable there, but you'll wish you were somewhere else when the wind shifts dead ahead and kicks up steep waves as it blows against the contrary current. Other dangerous routes take a boat away from protected waters, toward a lee shore, or into waters frequented by sudden storms.

Factor 3. The route has no alternative where the crew can "bail out." Many crews have gotten into serious trouble because they set courses far from intermediate harbors of refuge. Plan ahead for times when you will need to find nearby shelter in order to deal with a small problem (such as a torn sail or a tired crew) that, if not addressed, may lead to a big emergency.

Factor 4. The crew is unprepared. Sailors who come aboard without foul-weather gear and warm clothes are candidates for hypothermia. Some people do not have the basic sailing skills and experience to handle themselves and the boat. Old salts can be just as vulnerable if they don't know where to find and how to use equipment. Sailors who have not practiced such procedures as bending on storm sails and handling crew-overboard recoveries will be at least two steps behind. The crew can also be too small. For example, two people sailing a boat in rough weather over a long distance may become exhausted and make mistakes. Singlehanded sailors face this hazard all the time. The controversial practice of solo sailing has been defended as the ultimate in man-against-the-sea self-sufficiency, and even as an expression of "the triumph of the human spirit." While we're also romantic about sailing (see the preface), there are limits — as well as many other ways for the human spirit to find fulfillment without facing the perils inherent in sailing alone. The Navigation Rules sensibly require crews to keep a "proper lookout," which a sleeping singlehander obviously cannot do while the automatic pilot does the steering. At the far end of the pastime are solo racers taking unstable, fragile boats into predictably stormy latitudes. These skippers are, in fact, not very self-sufficient. This is demonstrated by the long narrative of breakdowns, groundings, and sinkings during around the-world races, followed by rescues by others putting their own boats and lives at risk.

Still, many able singlehanded sailors do cruise carefully in seaworthy boats, taking special precautions near shipping lanes and land. The bottom line is that solo long-distance sailing should be approached with the greatest respect and care, and ventured into only by skilled, fit sailors in good vessels.

Factor 5. The boat is unprepared. Major damage can occur because the crew, when preparing the boat, did not have the healthy caution known as a worst-case state of mind. The results can be dangerous. To cite a few simple examples: when charts are missing, boats can't find refuge; when flashlights don't have batteries, nobody on deck can see at night; when knives are dull, lines can't be cut; when life jackets are waterlogged, they won't provide buoyancy; when the boat's batteries aren't tied down, they may capsize and leak noxious acid into the bilge and force the crew on deck.

Factor 6. The crew panics after an injury. A shipmate's injury or illness always threatens to distract the crew from good seamanship. In order to get the injured person to assistance, people may make well-meaning but poor decisions that put the boat and her whole crew at risk — like sailing toward a lee shore in a gale or abandoning ship though the boat is floating. Even when the injury or illness is treated competently on board, crew discipline can break down unless the skipper and watch captains assert strong leadership. The hard truth that the individual must sometimes give way to the good of the whole may seem out of place in a pastime that usually is relaxed and enjoyable, but there are times when it must be the governing principle.

Factor 7. Leadership is poor. Vague, weak leadership can cause low morale and lead to mistakes. Poor leadership often results from an excess of testosterone. Macho skippers unable to admit their personal limitations may lose the respect of their crews. A skipper who does not wear a life jacket or safety harness in rough weather sets a poor example, and one who does not assign a clear line of authority may cause a leadership vacuum. A good skipper knows when to defer to the judgments of more talented people and also whom to appoint in a chain of command. This structure may seem too rigid to people who prefer to think of sailing as an escape from the disciplines of work life ashore, but it's necessary in tough conditions and emergencies.

An Example. Those are the seven factors. Here's an extreme example of how all seven can come together.

Despite pessimistic weather forecasts and a falling barometer, a boat sets out on an overnight delivery trip because the skipper has a business meeting the next afternoon (Factor 1). The first part of the route is across a patch of shoal water that is notoriously rough in even a capful of wind (Factor 2). While beating off a lee shore (Factor 3), she is caught by a building wind that quickly develops into a gale. The small crew, who were up partying the night before, collapses in seasickness and exhaustion (Factor 4).

Preparation

The main halyard (which the skipper has been meaning to replace for weeks) snaps and the boom falls, hits the skipper in the head, and knocks him out (Factor 5). The crew spends an hour arguing about what to do next (Factor 6) because the skipper did not designate a second in command (Factor 7). They finally decide to get the injured man ashore and head into a tricky harbor for which there is no chart on board since the owner never anticipated calling there (Factor 4 again).

From there on, blind luck is their only salvation. It is poor seamanship to have to fall back on luck.

Four Rules of Preparation. The lessons of the Formula for Disaster can be boiled down to four rules of preparation. Each covers a small family of concerns on sailboats of all types. Write down step-by-step standard operating procedures (SOPs, or what the navy calls billets) to cover equipment and job assignments. Type the SOPs in duplicate and bind both sets in brightly colored notebooks. Put one notebook in the chart table and the other in the emergency pack described below under Rule 1.

In an emergency, turn to the relevant SOP and read it out loud to the assembled crew. If the reading does nothing else, it will calm the crew by forcing them to focus on specifics.

Rule 1: Prepare the Boat. With a worst-case state of mind, inspect your boat and gear. Look at furnishings and equipment below, asking, "What will happen when the boat is rolled over?" With that point of view you'll find yourself being seriously concerned about many gear items you might otherwise take for granted. For example, you will lock in washboards so they will not fall out if the boat rolls and see to it that lockers and drawers won't fly open.

Check that safety gear is aboard, in good shape, and instantly accessible. Look at safety equipment, asking, "Can

we get to it fast in an emergency? Will it work?" Fire extinguishers must be charged and handy to the cook. Flares must be dry and easy to locate, the life raft should have received an annual checkup from a certified inspector, and safety harnesses, flashlights, foul-weather gear, emergency rations, heaving lines, crew-overboard gear, and other important equipment must be ready for use. Emergency gear must be set aside in an abandon ship bag. On an overhead drawing of the boat, such as the designer's accommodation plan, chart the location of all important gear, and post the drawing over the chart table.

Finally, examine the boat, asking, "Will it work in rough weather?" Perhaps the hull and sails are not up to the challenge. A boat heading out into the ocean must have been designed and built with the heavy loads and special needs of seagoing in mind. If the boat is suitable and you are headed offshore, install and maintain large manual bilge pumps with screens over their intakes, plugs to drive into holes left by broken through-hull fittings, strong storm sails, and sturdy steering gear, spars, and rigging.

For detailed recommendations on the design, construction, and rigging of cruising boats, there are two excellent publications, both listed in the bibliography, that contain detailed analysis and checklists of suitable gear: *Desirable and Undesirable Characteristics of Offshore Yachts* and *Safety Recommendations for Offshore Sailing*.

In their concern about big equipment, sailors often ignore the small items that hold all these pieces (and many others) together. In other words, don't lose your kingdom for the want of a horseshoe nail. Nautical horseshoe nails are shackles, clevis pins, cotter pins, and other fastenings.

One last concern: make sure all your sails go up and down easily and the engine starts without special treatment or magical incantations.

Rule 2: Prepare the Crew. Introduce the crew to the workings of the sailing gear, engine, plumbing, pumping, and electronic equipment. They must be shown safety and heavy-weather gear and given the opportunity to practice with it in drills in which roles are alternated. Hold a crew meeting where jobs will be assigned and a chain of command

established. If the boat will be out overnight or longer, make up and post watch schedules (described in chapter 15), and insist that people stick to them so there are no misunderstandings. Be explicit about rules for personal safety devices. On well-managed boats, safety harnesses and life jackets are worn at night and in rough weather. Make sure everybody has proper clothing and personal gear, including non-skid shoes, foul-weather gear, and warm clothes for damp, cool weather. Assign priorities and tasks for preparing for heavy weather, among them cooking hot food and heating water before the sea gets too rough for working at the stove. It is essential that the crew be rested. In rough weather, shorten watches and make them smaller in order that as few people as necessary are exposed to the elements.

Rule 3: Choose a Safe Route. When you plan your cruise or voyage, be sure to identify and be prepared to enter backup ports between your departure point and ultimate destination. You'll need plenty of charts plus relevant tide tables, cruising guides, and the *Coast Pilot*. On the charts, locate and mark especially risky or crowded areas such as race courses, shoals, tide races, and narrow channels. Also mark highly visible landmarks and aids to navigation. In poor visibility, you'll want to avoid the risky spots while steering for the highly visible ones. You may want to highlight potentially dangerous areas on the chart using an indelible pen with purple ink, which is highly visible under the red light used in the navigator's station to preserve night vision.

Rule 4: Prepare for Emergencies. Your goal is to be able to solve the problem quickly and efficiently, without crew panic. Practice the basic sailing skills, including sailing to windward both in strong and light winds, as well as the procedures that are directly or indirectly important in emergencies. These latter include crew-overboard rescue with everybody taking different roles, pumping the bilge, reefing the mainsail, changing a jib, setting the storm sails, lighting a flare, hauling the life raft on deck, working the fire extinguisher, going aloft in the bosun's chair or sling, starting the engine, using the radiotelephone, and reading the position from the GPS or Loran-C instrument.

Running Aground

Running aground can be a minor annoyance, a catastrophe, or something in between depending on the situation. When a centerboarder runs up on a shallow sand or mud bottom, it's no problem: raise the centerboard, turn the boat around, and sail back the way you came. If the centerboarder fetches up hard on gravel, however, the centerboard trunk may be jammed and you may not be able to raise or lower the board. If she bangs into a rock, the centerboard or rudder may be bent or broken.

Running aground in a keel boat pre-sents a more difficult problem, since the keel cannot be raised. If the tide is rising, you'll eventually float off. Otherwise you must kedge off with the anchor, sail or power off, arrange for a tow, or wait for the tide to change.

You may be able to jump into the water and push her off, or sail or power off. Usually you must first decrease the boat's draft by heeling her. Move the crew as far to leeward as possible and trim the sails. Sometimes rocking the hull side to side breaks the suction of the bottom on the keel. You may even be able to shove her off with the spinnaker pole, or by jumping overboard and putting your shoulder to her bow. If that doesn't heel her sufficiently, run a hal-yard out to an anchor or boat and pull hard. Be aggressive and don't give up until you're absolutely sure she's stuck.

If you must wait for the tide to flood and lift you off, and if there's an onshore wind, set out an anchor in deeper water to restrain the boat from being blown farther up the shore. You can use this anchor to pull yourself off (see chapter 14). If the shoal will dry out (be exposed) at low tide, hang fenders along the low side to protect it from scratch-ing. Then sit and wait.

In a strong onshore wind pushing the boat higher onto the shore or reef,

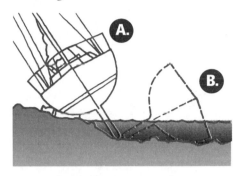

A grounded boat should be allowed to lie on the side away from the water (A), otherwise she may be flooded by the incoming tide (B).

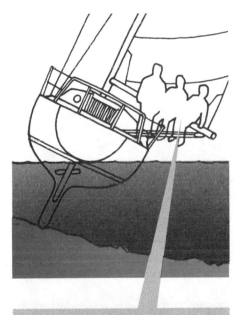

If barely aground, heel and rock the boat or try to spin her away from the shore by backing the jib or kedging off.

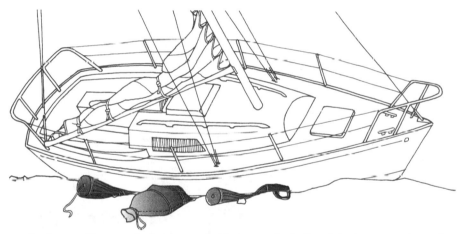

Lay fenders, cushions, and other protection between the hull and the bottom to keep the topsides from being badly scratched. Put out an anchor and wait for the tide to rise unless a strong onshore wind is blowing, when you must call for help.

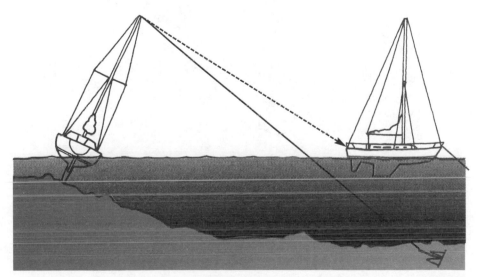

To induce heel, lead the main halyard to an anchor or moored boat.

Running Aground

quickly arrange a tow off as soon as you can, calling the Coast Guard or a commercial towing service on the radiotelephone or a cellular phone.

If you ran up on a rock at high speed, the impact may have loosened the keel bolts and she may be leaking. Check the bilges right away, and if you find water coming in, start pumping.

TOWING

There may be times when you must request or accept a tow from another boat — for example, if you're hard aground, if your boat is leaking badly, or if the engine has broken down and another emergency requires that you get to shore quickly. One reason that does not usually justify an emergency tow is running out of gasoline or diesel fuel when there's plenty of wind to sail home to an easily accessed harbor. Another is having to beat to windward. Of the many thousands of expensive and some-

times dangerous missions conducted each year by the Coast Guard and commercial towing services, many are to "rescue" crews that have panicked in conditions and situations in which a boat should be self-sufficient.

But there are times when a tow is appropriate. In any situation when a boat offers a tow, before passing her your line tactfully ask her crew if they will charge for their service. They may be insulted (in which case apologize). Then again, this question may save you a lot of money. If a Coast Guard vessel arrives, she may give you a tow unless a commercial vessel is available. To protect yourself from salvage claims that might leave the boat in the hands of the towing crew, stay on board.

The tow line should be strong and long; the anchor rode is ideal. On a small boat it can be tied to the mast (but not one stepped on deck). On a large boat, secure it to a large, through-bolted bow

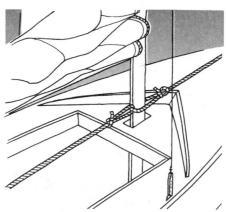

Tie the lines of towed and towing boats through each other at the mast using bowlines in order to spread the loads.

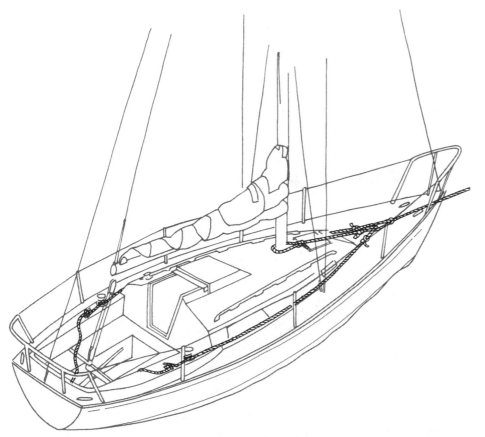

When towing, spread the load by leading backup lines to winches and the mast (do not use the mast if it is stepped on deck). Protect against chafe.

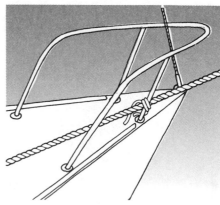

If there is no bow chock or if the towing line is too big for the chock, rig a temporary fairlead.

cleat. When there are large strains (such as when being hauled off a shoal), pull the excess line aft to the largest sheet winch, take several wraps, and grind most of the stretch out of the line in order to back up the cleat or mast. The tow line must be led through a chock at the stem, using split hose, rags, or other chafing gear to protect the line. If the chock makes for an unfair lead, rig a large block or a short length of line as a fairlead.

Before getting under way, tell the tow boat's skipper how fast your boat will safely go, and, if she's aground, how deep into the bottom she's imbedded. Agree on hand signals and a VHF/FM channel to be used to transmit instructions. If the other fellow appears to be careless and unseamanlike, you may decide to cast off the tow and fend for yourself.

Start with the tow line short, then lengthen it as you increase speed. The tow should start slowly to gradually pull the stretch out of the line. Stay away from the line. If it snaps, the backlash could break your leg. Gauge your progress against a range of trees or buildings on shore. If she doesn't move soon, try pulling in the other direction. Be cautious about pulling her off backward; the rudder might break. Don't force a boat. If she doesn't want to come off, wait for a higher tide.

Once under way on a tow, find a safe speed where the two boats are in wave troughs and on crests at the same time. The steerer on the towed boat should keep the tow line from rubbing against the headstay and the boat from wandering out to the sides of the wake. If another boat wants a tow, take her line and secure it where your own tow line is cleated or tied so the two loads balance each other.

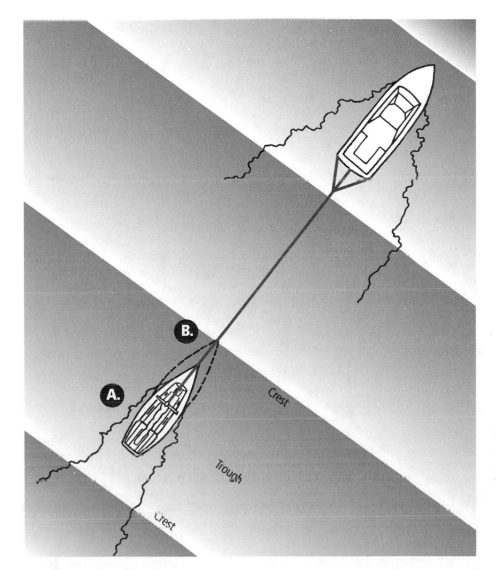

Keep the tow line long with the towed boat riding easily in the trough of a wave (A), not climbing up its back (B). Steer carefully and use hand signals or the radio to communicate between the two boats.

Steering Failure

know how it works before heading out.

Replacing a broken steering mechanism is one thing, but jury-rigging a damaged rudder can be very difficult. If the rudder post breaks or the rudder hits a floating object and falls apart, you've lost the major component of the steering gear. An emergency rudder for a small boat can be an oar on the side,
canoe fashion, or an oar or object over the stern. An oar is too weak for a boat larger than about 20 feet, but applying the same principle will lead to a long combination tiller-rudder created from a spinnaker pole or other long metal tube and plywood sheets screwed to its end. The hinge is the problem. Once the strains build, the emergency rudder can

If the tiller, wheel, or steering cable breaks, you'll have to make emergency repairs. You might be able to fix the cable with nicopress clamps or bulldog clamps (adjustable wire clamps), or splice the tiller with light line and a piece of hardwood or stainless-steel tubing. Replacing a broken steering wheel and its gear is a more difficult proposition. Most sailboats equipped with wheels also have an emergency tiller that can be installed on the rudder post; be sure you

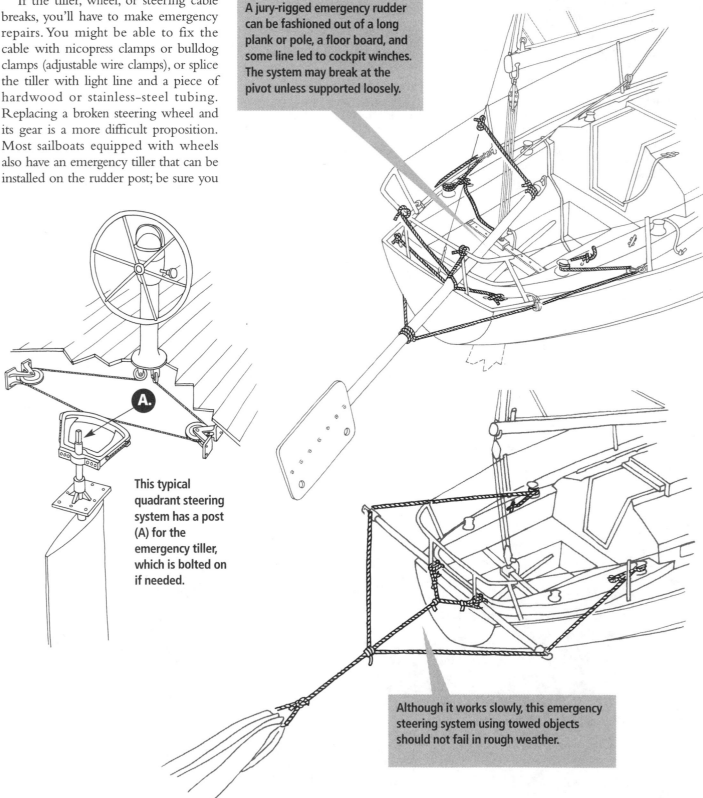

A jury-rigged emergency rudder can be fashioned out of a long plank or pole, a floor board, and some line led to cockpit winches. The system may break at the pivot unless supported loosely.

This typical quadrant steering system has a post (A) for the emergency tiller, which is bolted on if needed.

Although it works slowly, this emergency steering system using towed objects should not fail in rough weather.

snap in half at its pivot. To allow give in the system, use a loose hinge made of rope suspended from the backstay.

Providing less positive steering but a more reliable structure is a drag towed astern — a bucket, spinnaker pole, or fender — from a set of lines. Pulling the object to one side will slowly force the boat to head to that side.

HANDS ON:
Steering with the Sails

A rudderless sailboat can be steered with her sails either with or without emergency equipment. By adjusting the fore-and-aft location of the sail plan's center of effort, using the farthest forward and far-thest aft sails, a crew can create weather or lee helm. A divided rig can be steered fairly well under "jib and jigger." A sloop may require a small jib set on the backstay.

"Jib and Jigger"

Temporary Mizzen

Dismasting

Although ocean racers often suffer mast failures due to hard use of extremely slender spars, the normal cruiser-racer's mast should outlive its owner — assuming that its owner treats it with reasonable care. There are two common causes of dismasting. One is allowing the mast to bend too far, either sideways or fore and aft. If the mast is not straight, it goes out of column and loses much of its integrity. In rough seas, the mast must be as straight as possible and running backstays should be used to keep it straight. The second and by far most frequent cause of mast failure is a broken fitting — a collapsed spreader, a snapped shroud, or a parted turnbuckle.

The crew's first response to a dismasting will be shock, but as soon as they recover they must spring to the broken spar and keep it from holing the hull. In rough weather, the mast will be jack-knifed over the leeward rail and every wave will slam the boat down onto it. If

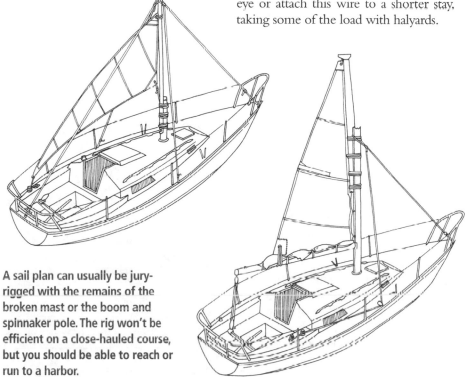

A sail plan can usually be jury-rigged with the remains of the broken mast or the boom and spinnaker pole. The rig won't be efficient on a close-hauled course, but you should be able to reach or run to a harbor.

possible, drag the mess back on board. Otherwise you'll have to pull or cut the sails off, cut the halyards, pull the cotter and clevis pins out of any remaining turnbuckles, and allow the mast to sink before it holes the boat. In the next chapter we'll show how to rig cotter pins so they can be pulled out quickly in emergencies.

You may be able to save the sails without their being torn too badly and later use them on a jury-rigged (impro-vised) mast. You can set a sail either from the top of the mast's stump or from a spinnaker pole or boom stepped as an emergency mast. Some sailboats have made long passages under jury rigs.

Broken Stay. Should a shroud, the headstay, or the backstay break but the mast not collapse, immediately cast off all sheets to luff the sails and alter course so the broken stay is to leeward. A halyard might be rigged as a temporary stay, leading it over the end of the spreader if it replaces a shroud. Tighten the halyard as much as possible. Nurse the boat along gently since the replacement is weaker than the original stay. Some modern-day rope is as strong as wire and can be used for this purpose.

It's a good idea to carry a spare stay as long as the longest stay in the rigging with a terminal (eye) installed at one end plus a spare, large turnbuckle. Using bulldog clamps, you can fashion another eye or attach this wire to a shorter stay, taking some of the load with halyards.

Capsize

All kinds of boats can and do capsize, but this accident is less likely with keel monohulls than with dinghies, centerboard daysailers, and small to medium-size multihulls. When these boats sail too fast, broach, or are hit by a sudden gust of wind just after a tack or jibe, and the crew is unable to quickly ease sheets, they will go over on their side with no keel to stop them. Their low range of positive stability (90° or less) may lead to a capsize. The best prevention is a combination of an alert crew and a system for very quickly easing sheets. On all dinghies and even large catamarans and trimarans, sheets are cleated in quick-release cam cleats within reach of the steerer.

If you do capsize in one of these lightweight boats, you can count on her staying afloat unless she is holed badly. Dinghies and other boats with a small cockpit (or no cockpit at all) can be righted immediately. Swim around the boat or climb over the windward rail and pull down on or stand on the centerboard to lever the hull back upright. Make sure the sheets are cast off, for otherwise she can tip right over again once the sails are filled. Climb back aboard and sail off.

If the boat can't be righted, either because she has swamped (is full of water) or because you're too tired to pull her up, don't leave the boat. Stay with the capsized boat with your life jacket on and wait for rescue. Some open daysailers may be bailed out after being swamped, but many must be towed to shore. When the tow boat comes alongside, get the sails down and secured, tie the tow line to the mast, and as the two boats slowly gather way, hang off the transom. Water will flow aft and over the stern, and soon you may be able to hail the powerboat to stop the tow and then climb aboard and bail out the rest. Great strains are put on a hull and rig when a swamped boat is towed, so try to make the tow slow and brief.

A dinghy or catamaran that has turtled (turned completely over) may resist righting by her crew. In that case you may have to swim — cautiously — under the boat, lower the sails, and hand the main halyard to a powerboat crew, who can pull the mast up.

When a small catamaran capsizes, she may well turtle unless the crew is very quick. Many small catamarans are rigged with special righting lines that, when pulled by the crew, pull the boat

(Above) If your small boat can't be righted, or if you're too tired, stay with her and await rescue. (Right) Otherwise, stand on the centerboard and lever her back upright. Be sure to free all sheets first so that the sails do not fill when the boat becomes upright. If you abandon your boat for a rescue boat, notify the Coast Guard and leave a note indicating that you are safe and where you may be found. Otherwise, people may conduct a long search that may bring them into danger.

upright before turtling. These boats often have foam in their sails to keep the mast from sinking.

Larger catamarans and trimarans can capsize and turtle, but they won't sink unless they are holed. In fact, one good argument for choosing a multihull is that, unlike a keel boat, it is its own life raft. Good offshore cruising multihulls are equipped so that, should they capsize and turtle, they become what designer Chris White calls "inverted homes" where crews can live safely and fairly comfortably until help arrives. These boats have permanent escape hatches in their bottoms that can be opened to allow an exit, light, and air. Self-righting systems using gin poles and counterweights have been developed for capsized multihulls. Otherwise, a turtled cat or tri must await the arrival of a rescuing ship or an especially lucky combination of large waves that can roll her back upright.

Boats with keels can capsize and survive without sinking. In the 1979 Fastnet Race, about 90 boats were rolled over beyond their range of positive stability and many stayed turtled for a minute or more. All but four of these boats recovered and were sailed or towed to port, but only after the crews spent hours bailing out tons of water. On another 20 boats, the crews mistakenly believed that their boats were sinking or became (understandably) frightened by broken, loose fixtures and fittings flying around in the cabins, so they abandoned ship for life rafts. Five sailors later died in or near their life rafts as the yachts they had abandoned survived the gale.

A boat is far less likely to stay upright when dismasted than if her rig is still standing, since the mast increases the moment of inertia. So do everything you can to keep her mast up. This means sailing cautiously to keep the mast clear of the water. A quick, hard knockdown may smash a mast.

Life Rafts

The rule of thumb about using life rafts is "Don't get in one until you have to step up." In other words, the boat is the best place to be until she sinks. But boats do sink, and any crew heading offshore should carry an inflatable life raft or dinghy with a tested capacity equal to or greater than the size of the crew. Because the manufacturer's claimed capacity may be optimistic, fit the raft to the crew.

There are three families of life rafts:

The rescue platform and **rescue pod,** for use when rescue is almost immediate, are little more than especially sturdy swimming rafts that keep people out of the water without shelter from the elements. They may be equipped with signaling devices and other survival equipment.

The coastal raft, intended for emergencies where rescue will be quick and when the conditions are not too hostile, has only one buoyancy tube. This low wall provides some but not much shelter.

The offshore raft, aimed at sustaining life for extended periods of time and in very demanding climates, has two buoyancy tubes and a canopy shelter.

In addition, inflatable rubber dinghies can be used as life rafts, although they may be less stable than dedicated rafts.

Optional design features in some or all of these rafts include a double or inflatable bottom (for insulation), a canopy (for protection from the elements), and ballast bags (to provide stability against rolling and capsize). Most inflation systems are manually operated, while some rafts may inflate automatically. Life rafts may be stowed in plastic canisters permanently mounted on deck, in deck lockers, and or in fabric valises that can be quickly carried on deck. However it is stored, the raft should be deployable within a very few minutes.

Every life raft, its inflation system, and its gear should be inspected by a manufacturer's authorized inspection facility at least every two years.

Abandon Ship Gear. Each raft should be carrying a number of vital gear items when it parts company with

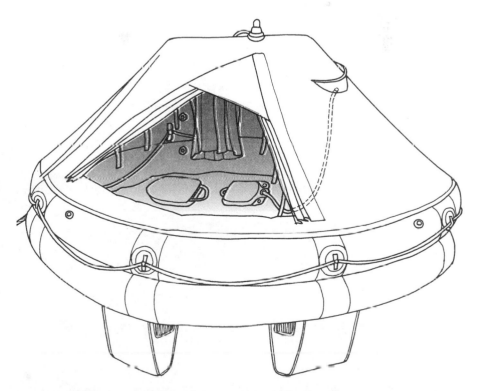

This offshore life raft, with two buoyancy tubes, a canopy, and ballast bags, is the type usually carried on offshore voyages and when cruising in cold or lonely waters. The emergency gear should be custom-tailored to the boat and crew.

Life Rafts

Leaks and Sinking

the boat. Since only some of this equipment may be provided by the manufacturer, each crew should carefully chose the items that are stored in the raft or carried in the abandon ship bag (ditch bag) — a waterproof sack (for example, a kayaker's bag) ready to be taken when the crew leaves the sinking boat.

This gear includes flares, the emergency position indicating radio beacon (EPIRB, to be covered later in this chapter), a handheld VHF/FM radio, flashlights, emergency rations, water, a watermaker for converting salt water to fresh, rope, tape, and other items that would be damaged by the dampness inside a life raft's container. In the life raft you can stow some water, a signaling mirror, a first-aid kit, a sharp knife with a ground-down point, a sea anchor, handholds, a strong painter, fishing gear, cups or other containers for food and water, space blankets, seasickness medication, and special equipment needed by crew members (for example, prescription medication and reading glasses).

A lot of water can be taken aboard a keel boat before she sinks — much more, in fact, than is needed just to fill the bilges. If the boat is so low that water is splashing over the rail, she's probably going down, but keep pumping and bailing until then.

Often the amount of water in the cabin after a capsize or a holing may cause a crew to panic and abandon a boat that is later found safely afloat. Perception has a great deal to do with your faith in the vessel. While a heavy-displacement boat with deep bilges can take a considerable amount of water aboard before it is even visible above the cabin sole (floor), in a light-displacement boat with a shallow bilge and no sump (recessed area to hold bilge water), almost every drop that comes aboard as spray or rain will be noticed.

Minor Leaks. You should pump the bilges on a regular, frequent schedule so as not to be caught by surprise by a new leak. If you are taking on a couple of strokes of water every few hours, inspect the bilge and then the deck. In the bilge, the keel bolts may be weeping; they will have to be tightened when the boat is next hauled out. Look, too, at the stuffing boxes, which keep large amounts of

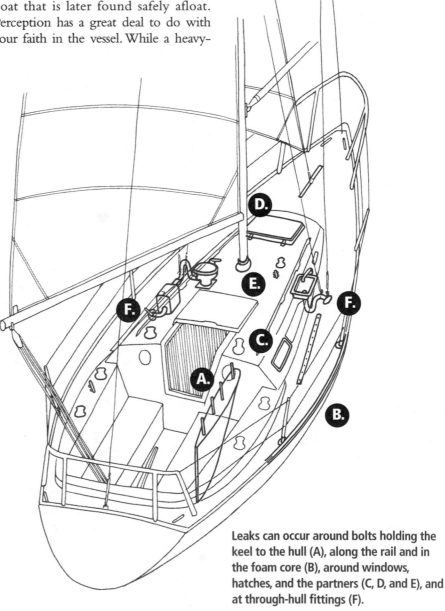

Leaks can occur around bolts holding the keel to the hull (A), along the rail and in the foam core (B), around windows, hatches, and the partners (C, D, and E), and at through-hull fittings (F).

water from coming in through the propeller shaft and steering gear. They should leak only very slightly.

Cracks, holes, and other minor leaks in the hull, deck, or equipment may be repaired very satisfactorily using Marine-Tex or another of the easy to use, quick-setting repair putties that are on the market. A can or tube of one of these putties should be carried in the boat.

Spray and solid water may be coming through the deck. Check the partners (the deck hole around the mast), window frames, and fastenings for deck fittings, such as cleats. A leaky window can be caulked using putty or even chewing gum. The partners often are the culprit. They must be covered by a mast boot — a rubber or fabric cover, often with two or more layers, that is carefully secured to the deck and the mast using hose clamps or other devices. The best time to construct a mast boot is before you leave port, and it (and the entire deck) should be checked for leaks by spraying with a hose.

Another source of relatively minor leaks is the wooden or foam core in the hull. Water may enter the core in the bilge, and when the boat heels, travel up the sides and seep into a locker or (if you're really unlucky) a bunk. Such a mysterious leak may take a long time to track down and fix.

If a leak is large, inspect the through-hull fittings — the intake and outlet holes for water and waste that are opened and closed with sea cocks (valves controlled by levers or faucet-type handles). The sea cock may be corroded or cracked, the hull around it may have opened up slightly, or the tube or pipe led to the fitting may be loose. If a sea cock or other through-hull fitting is leaking badly, you will know about it quick enough. A 2-inch hole that is 1 foot below the waterline allows in almost 50 gallons per minute, faster than the typical electric bilge pump can handle. If this hole were 3 feet below the waterline, it would allow in more than 80 gallons per minute. You must close the hole. Start with a tapered wooden plug. Sets of these plugs, made from soft pine, should be carried on board with a hammer to drive them home. Match a plug to a hole and secure it to the through-hull fitting with a length of string.

To cover a hole above the waterline,

nail, screw, or tie on sheets of plywood that support bunk mattresses. Repairing a hull holed below the waterline is more difficult. A good temporary patch can be made by tying a sail or a mattress over the outside of the hole with lines that pass under the boat. Then plug the hole from the inside with cushions, sail bags, clothing, or some other object. If

possible, heel the boat so the hole is above water.

Meanwhile, keep pumping and bailing. Sometimes the freshwater pumps in sinks can be adapted to pump out the bilge alongside the bilge pumps. Somebody should be delegated to keep the bilge free of small objects that might clog the pumps. Most bilges are divided

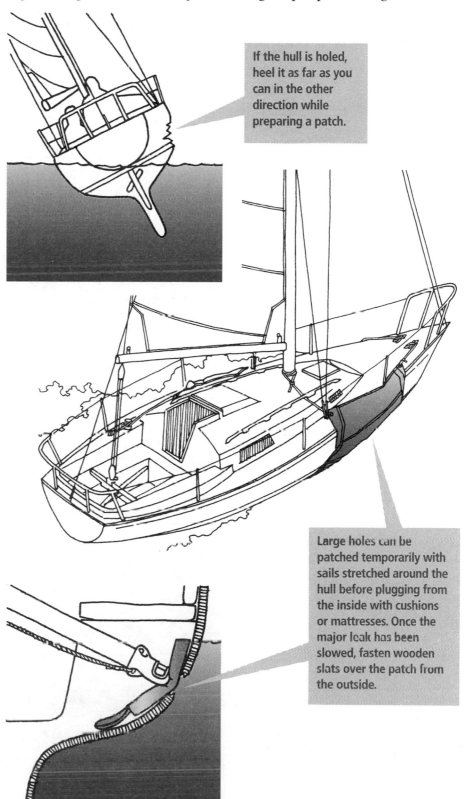

If the hull is holed, heel it as far as you can in the other direction while preparing a patch.

Large holes can be patched temporarily with sails stretched around the hull before plugging from the inside with cushions or mattresses. Once the major leak has been slowed, fasten wooden slats over the patch from the outside.

Leaks and Sinking

into compartments by the frames used to keep the hull rigid. Small holes in the frames called limber holes allow water to pass to the sump, or lowest point in the bilge, where the pump's intake is normally located. The limber holes may be clogged with paint, dirt, or other gurry. A limber hole chain — a light chain that runs fore and aft through all the holes — can be pulled to clear the limber holes. In boats not equipped with limber hole chains, regularly clean out these small drains with a marlinspike or a screwdriver.

The Coast Guard and commercial rescuers carry high-capacity engine-powered pumps that can be dropped to you from an airplane or helicopter or brought out in a boat.

FIRE

Besides sinking, the greatest regular threat to any vessel is fire. Preparation is crucial.

Several types of fire extinguishers are available and in some cases required by federal law. Extinguishers should be placed in easily accessible locations near stoves, engines, grills, and other devices where fires are likely to occur. They must not be placed where you have to reach through flames to get to them. All extinguishers should be checked and, if necessary, recharged at least once a year.

Minimum legal requirements are that every boat with an engine (except open boats smaller than 26 feet with outboard engines) must carry at least one approved Class B portable fire extinguisher. Class B extinguishers are designed to put out fires of flammable liquids, including gasoline, diesel fuel, paint, tar, and the cooking fuels alcohol and kerosene. They come in two sizes — I and II (small and large). These minimum requirements are laid out in greater detail in appendix I, but here is a summary: boats smaller than 26 feet must carry one B-I extinguisher; 26–40 footers must carry one B-II or two B-Is; and 40–65 footers must carry one B-II and one B-I or three B-Is. Adjustments to these minimums for portable extinguishers may be made if the boat has an inboard engine with a fixed, permanent-

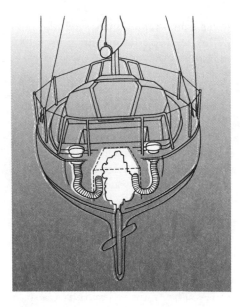

A boat with a gasoline engine must have a bilge blower; one with a diesel engine should have one.

HANDS ON: **Preventing an Alcohol Fire**

If the boom is the most dangerous object on a sailboat, the alcohol stove comes a close second. Though theoretically less destructive than a fire involving propane gas, which can explode, an alcohol fire is far more likely to occur. A flare-up of liquid alcohol due to incomplete preheating (which turns the liquid into a gas) can create a jet of flame that can scorch the boat's ceiling, burn the cook's face, and ignite the entire boat if the liquid alcohol spills and spreads when the boat rolls. To avoid a flare-up you must

Locate a fire extinguisher near the stove but not where the cook must reach through flames to get at it.

be attentive and systematic. This is not a job for untrained beginners.

Make sure that the alcohol tank is at least half full and fully pressurized so that the flow to the stove is steady. Have a pot of water and an extinguisher handy.

During the preheating process, allow a small amount of liquid alcohol into the burner (the cup should be about half full at most) before turning off the valve and striking a match. Keep an eye on the flame. At this stage, the burning alcohol is heating the jet so that the subsequent flow of alcohol is a gas, not a liquid. As soon as all the liquid alcohol is burned off from the cup, carefully reopen the valve and listen. You should hear the hiss of gas, not the gurgle of liquid. If you hear the hiss, immediately light the gas before the jet cools. If you hear a gurgle, preheating was not finished. Turn everything off and mop up all liquids before trying again.

Don't allow wind to blow down the companionway onto the stove. It may extinguish the flame during preheating. If the flame blows out without the cook's knowledge, he or she may well assume that preheating is complete and then open the valve to light what turns out (too late) to be a large puddle of liquid alcohol that is likely to spill into the oven or onto the floor. It helps to observe the burner from the side, where the flame is most visible.

ly mounted extinguishing system.

To use a fire extinguisher, aim at the base of the flame, pull the handle, and apply the foam or other extinguishant with a sweeping motion.

Fighting Fire. The typical fire in a pleasure boat is a liquid one involving cooking fuel (alcohol or kerosene) or, more rarely, engine fuel (gasoline or diesel oil). Your first response should be to immediately cut off the fuel supply from the tank so the fire is not fed. The ignition key shuts off the engine's fuel pump. Stoves should have shutoff valves that are handy so as to not require you to reach through flames to use them.

Then an **alcohol or kerosene fire** can be extinguished with a Class B extinguisher or with water. Many cooks keep a pot of water on the stove for this purpose. A **gasoline, diesel oil, or grease fire** should be attacked with a Class B extinguisher. Do not use water, which will only spread the flames.

An **engine fire** is fought with a fixed extinguisher or a portable Class B extinguisher aimed through the smallest possible access hole to the engine compartment so the extinguisher does not blast the flame into the rest of the boat.

An **electrical fire** should be fought with a Class C fire extinguisher designed specifically for this purpose, although a heavy dousing with water may work if an extinguisher is not available.

Sniffers and Blowers. While not active firefighters, sniffer-type alarm systems are superb fire-prevention aids for boats with engines fueled by gasoline or stoves by heavier-than-air propane. Fumes from these fuels may settle in the bilge and be unnoticed by crew members unless the sniffer alarm goes off. An open flame may ignite the fumes with the force of a bomb. If there is propane in the boat, light no matches and do not start the stove or a gasoline engine. Open up all the hatches and floorboards and vent out the gas by blowing air through the boat, pushing it along by waving a towel or blanket. You can literally bail out the fumes with a bucket; since these gases have distinctive pungent odors, a quick sniff will tell you if you're bailing gas or air. Keep testing using the bilge sniffer.

For the same reason, the engine's blower helps vent fumes through ducts required on most boats by federal law.

Distress Signaling

Federal law and the Navigation Rules require that certain equipment and signals be used by distressed mariners to attract attention. Before using any of them, the skipper must honestly ask herself if a life-threatening emergency actually exists on board, since sending out an SOS or flare will trigger a sequence of events that will cost others time, effort, and perhaps physical risk. Even coming alongside a disabled boat in a rough sea can do considerable damage to both vessels and crews.

So reflect. Can the boat possibly make her way to port under sail if the engine has been disabled, or under jib alone if the mainsail has blown out? Does the crew's burned hand really demand immediate hospital attention? Are you truly in distress because the GPS navigation device's batteries have run dry or the engine won't start? Obviously, a severe head injury to a crew member or a major hole below the waterline or a broken mast is a major emergency, but each demands different levels of attention: the head wound should be treated immediately, while the holed boat may be able to make her way to harbor and the dismasted boat's crew can anchor and clean up.

Approved and Recognized Distress Signals. Here is a summary of minimum legal requirements for distress signals on all boats in US waters. Do not use distress signals in jest. By law, they may be displayed only when a life is in danger.

With the exceptions of rowboats, boats smaller than 16 feet, boats participating in races, and open, engineless sailboats smaller than 26 feet, all pleasure boats must carry day-use, night-use, or combination distress signals. The excepted boats must carry night signals when out at night.

Day-use signals include three orange smoke signals and an orange flag with a black square and black circle.

Night-use signals include a bright flashlight signaling SOS (dot-dot-dot, dash-dash-dash, dot-dot-dot) and three Coast Guard–approved red flares that are either handheld or capable of being fired into the sky. (Note: In some states, flare guns must be registered as firearms.)

Day/night signals meeting both requirements are three Coast Guard–approved red flares.

Obviously, a good solution is to carry a minimum of three flares, at least a couple of which should be parachute-type rockets. Because they show higher, they are visible over longer ranges than other flares.

The best flares (parachutes and handhelds alike) are the ones made to the standards of the international Safety of Life at Sea Convention (SOLAS). SOLAS flares (almost all of which are Coast Guard–approved) usually are brighter, show longer, have longer hang times, and have longer lives than non-SOLAS flares, often remaining effective beyond the 42-month expiration period demanded by law. They are more expensive, but since lives are at stake this is a small price to pay. SOLAS flares are required for many racing boats.

Flares may lose their power with age and dampness. One way to check that flares are in operating condition is to test

The best flares are parachute-type rockets made to SOLAS standards. Store all your flares in a waterproof container that can be found quickly.

Distress Calling

nication, say **"Silence Distress."** If a crew can help by relaying the Mayday message, it prefaces the message by announcing **"Mayday Relay."** The end of radio silence is announced by the operator with the words **"Silence Fini"** ("seelonce feenee" — silence ended).

Crews hearing the original call should immediately determine if they

one flare from a set during the annual Fourth of July celebration. Another is to have a group test along with other boat-owners after receiving permission from your local Coast Guard district headquarters.

The Navigation Rules include the following as acceptable distress signals: continuous sounding of a foghorn; firing a gun or other explosive device; rockets throwing stars of any color and fired at short intervals; a rocket parachute flare or a red hand flare; orange smoke; flames (such as a fire in a bucket); a square flag above or below a ball; code flags "NC"; "S-O-S" sent by any means; "Mayday" spoken over a radio telephone; and a person repeatedly raising her or his arms.

Unofficial but widely recognized distress signals include: waving an orange or orange-red flag; flying the national flag or yacht ensign upside-down; a rapidly flashing strobe light and dye marker in the water.

Stow distress signals in dry, accessible, and clearly marked lockers in the cabin near the companionway. Under the Coast Guard rules, flares have expiration dates because they absorb moisture, so you must purchase new ones. Save the old ones for backup and practice. Make sure everybody on board knows how to work a flare before heading out on a long passage. When sailing at night, have a very bright battery-operated flashlight handy to shine on your sails if another vessel approaches.

To make radio transmissions absolutely clear, use the phonetic alphabet when spelling names. In addition, the numeral 9 should be spoken as "niner" to prevent confusion with "five."

Radio Distress Calls. Most calls for assistance are sent out verbally over radiotelephones (either VHF/FM channel 16 or single-sideband frequency 2182 kHz) or by code using on-board satellite-based systems, such as EPIRBs. The international Morse Code system of signaling "S-O-S" was shut down in 1999. When making radiotelephone calls, you must first indicate what kind of help you require. There are three categories:

"Mayday" precedes a request for immediate assistance by a dangerously distressed vessel. This is the English version of the French word *m'aidez* — help me.

"Pan-pan" (pronounced "pahn-pahn") repeated three times precedes a request for assistance by a boat that is not distressed.

"Securite" (pronounced "saycuri-tay") precedes a warning to other vessels of danger.

Once one of these is transmitted with the distress message, you or officials may order radio silence on the channel or frequency with the words **"Silence Mayday."** ("Silence" is given the French pronunciation, "seelonce.") To clear the channel of all non-emergency commu-

The Phonetic Alphabet

A	Alfa
B	Bravo
C	Charlie
D	Delta
E	Echo
F	Foxtrot
G	Golf
H	Hotel
I	India
J	Juliet
K	Kilo
L	Lima
M	Mike
N	November
O	Oscar
P	Papa
Q	Quebec
R	Romeo
S	Sierra
T	Tango
U	Uniform
V	Victor
W	Whiskey
X	X-ray
Y	Yankee
Z	Zulu

HANDS ON: The Mayday Call

1. Press the alarm signal on the transmitter (if it has one) for 30–60 seconds. This will alert people monitoring the frequency that a distress call is imminent.

2. Slowly and clearly say "Mayday" three times, then the name of your boat three times. Give your VHF/FM or SSB call sign (printed on the license). Report your position either as latitude and longitude or as a bearing and distance from a charted object. The rescuer should be able to quickly enter your position as a waypoint on the GPS or Loran.

3. Describe your situation briefly; for example, "Dismasted and drifting southeast at 2 knots onto Catalina Island 3 miles downwind. Require tow."

4. Describe your boat's most important features, emphasizing her rig, length, and color. Say how many people are aboard.

Keep repeating steps 1 through 4 until somebody acknowledges your call.

RADIO LOG				
DATE	TIME	VESSEL	CALL	MESSAGE
11/8/98	1415	R.H. Dana	KX1111	S.O.S. fire. Pos 6 miles
				East of Miami
	1416	call R.H. Dana	"	Asknowledge SOS
	1417	called USCG	16	Report SOS and
				Dana position
	1420	USCG		Informs standing by
				Dana. No help needed.
	1440	R.H. Dana	KX1111	Informs fire out...
				no injury.

can help by plotting their and the distressed boat's positions. If they cannot help, they should say nothing. If they can help the boat, they address the distressed boat by name, give their own boats' names and call signs, acknowledge the distress call, say they are proceeding toward her, and give course, speed, and estimated time of arrival.

Distress calls must not be made unless there is a legitimate emergency threatening the boat or her crew. It is illegal to knowingly transmit a fraudulent or false distress signal.

EPIRB. An excellent way to call for help is to use an emergency position-indicating radio beacon (EPIRB). This is a small, buoyant radio transmitter that sends out a signal that is picked up by satellites, aircraft, or ships, which then notify rescuers who can home in on the signal. There are three types of EPIRB. The oldest is the 121.5 MHz frequency type, both Class A (automatic activation) and Class B (manual activation). The position of both can be located with only modest accuracy and they also have a history of triggering false alarms. A small version of the Class B EPIRB, the Mini B, can be carried by sailors. If they fall overboard and activate the device, a boat can home in on them with a special device. If many 121.5 devices are triggered (for example in the

1998 Sydney-Hobart Race storm), rescuers may be confused by the plethora of signals.

Far superior is the 406 MHz EPIRB, also available in automatic and manual versions. It sends a coded signal to satellites that includes a message (pre-programmed by the owner) that identifies the owner and boat and provides contact numbers ashore so rescuers can check on the boat's status and location. Because the signal is personalized, there is a far less chance of false alarms with the 406 than with the older Class A and B devices.

The third type is an improvement on the 406. Called the GPIRB, it contains a global positioning (GPS) navigational device that automatically includes the boat's exact position in the coded signal sent to satellites. This adds to the precision and speed of the rescue effort.

A boat heading out into deep water should carry a GPIRB or 406 in the cabin or the abandon ship bag to take in a life raft.

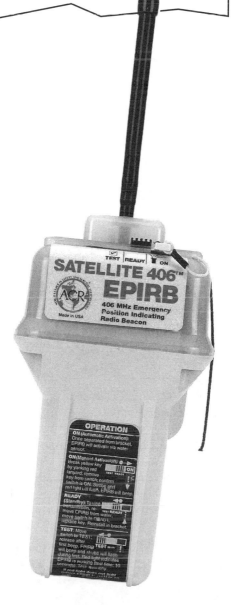

Evacuation

Using data from radio and EPIRB transmissions and its own AMVER (automated mutual-assistance vessel rescue) system, the Coast Guard often is able to provide quick search and rescue service to distressed vessels within about 200 miles of the coast. If the Coast Guard itself cannot send one of its 44- or 47-footers or another vessel, it (or your own distress call) will attract the attention of ships. Crews can be rescued either by other boats or by helicopters. The larger the rescuing vessel and the closer she is to the distressed boat, the greater the risk. The best tactic often is for the ship to lie dead to windward a distance away to provide a lee, calming

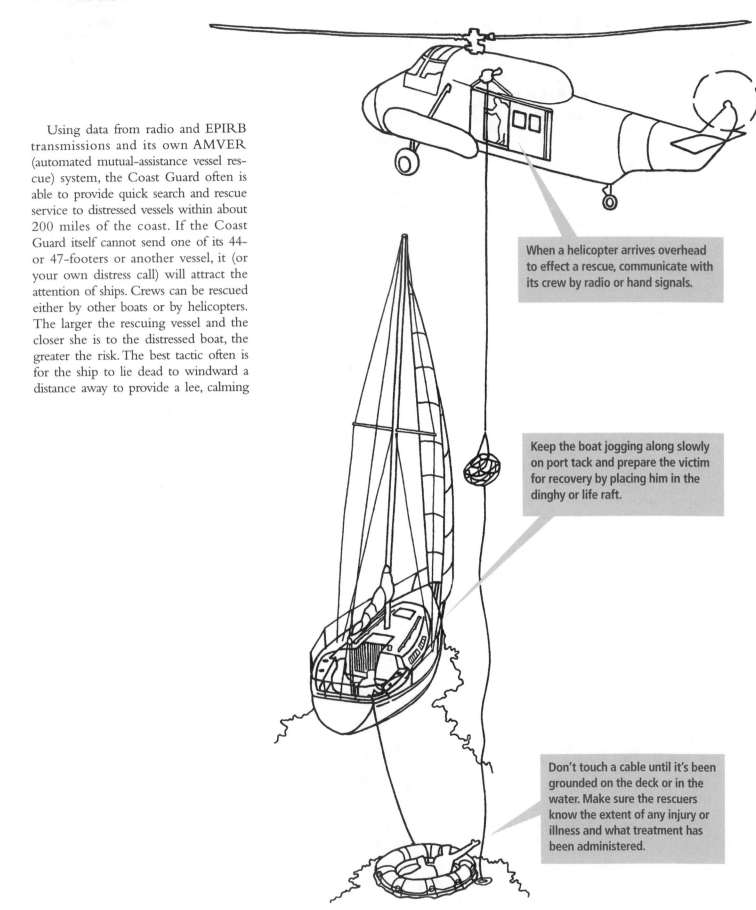

When a helicopter arrives overhead to effect a rescue, communicate with its crew by radio or hand signals.

Keep the boat jogging along slowly on port tack and prepare the victim for recovery by placing him in the dinghy or life raft.

Don't touch a cable until it's been grounded on the deck or in the water. Make sure the rescuers know the extent of any injury or illness and what treatment has been administered.

the seas. She then sends down a small boat or heaves a line that can be attached to the distressed boat's life raft or the crew themselves, who should be wearing life jackets, safety harnesses, and survival suits. People can be hoisted on deck by their safety harnesses.

The Coast Guard relies heavily on rescue helicopters, which are able to drop pumps and people to the boat and also pick up injured crew members using litter baskets. If somebody on board must be evacuated and you see or hear the helicopter approaching, clear the cockpit and deck of all unnecessary rigging and gear, then bring the casualty on deck in a life jacket.

The pilot is in charge of the operation. Follow his or her orders. In most helicopters, the pilot is on the starboard side. Therefore, unless otherwise ordered, keep the boat on port tack to provide him or her the best possible visibility. Communicate with the helicopter using the VHF/FM radio or hand signals. Because of obstructing rigging, many rescues of sailors are made from life rafts or dinghies towed astern of the boat. The downdraft from the helicopter rotor will be loud and powerful, making it difficult to hear and even stand. Be extremely careful when handling the equipment dropped from the helicopter. A wire cable will give off a strong shock if it's touched before being grounded on deck or in the water. A rope, however, may be handled as it drops, but don't cleat it or the helicopter will be tethered.

Tape or pin a detailed account of the victim's injury or illness, and of any treatment you've given, to his clothes so that doctors ashore will know the background.

If the entire crew must abandon ship, leave a note with your name, probable destination, and contacts.

HANDS ON: **Preparing for Emergencies**

After storing emergency gear, locate it on a plan of the boat and post the plan on a bulkhead. Before getting under way, talk through all emergency procedures, show how to use flares and the life raft, and take newcomers on a thorough tour of the boat.

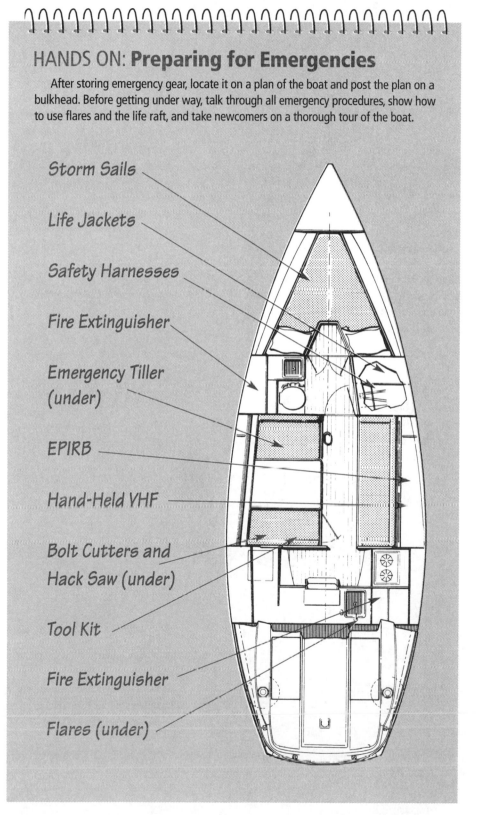

Storm Sails

Life Jackets

Safety Harnesses

Fire Extinguisher

Emergency Tiller (under)

EPIRB

Hand-Held VHF

Bolt Cutters and Hack Saw (under)

Tool Kit

Fire Extinguisher

Flares (under)

CHAPTER 17

Equipment and Maintenance

Here we'll look at ways to keep the boat in good condition. Our focus will be on maintaining the running and standing rigging and the engine, and on making cosmetic repairs. Concerns about the integrity of the hull and spars should be addressed by marine surveyors, who can be located in the yellow pages for areas near popular sailing areas.

RUNNING RIGGING

Chafe is the main cause of broken sheets and halyards, so keep your eye peeled for flat or worn spots and broken fibers or wire strands. Cut off worn ends of lines and turn sheets, docking lines, and rope halyards end-for-end once a year so the strains are equally distributed. This is why when you buy new sheets and halyards, you should cut them more than long enough to do the job and have some line left over.

Find the cause of the chafe. It may be due to a line rubbing against the cabin, a stanchion, a stay, or another fixed object. In that case, move the lead. Or chafe could be caused by a block that either is too small for the rope or wire or does not properly spin or swivel. Make sure the blocks and their swivels work as they should. Disassemble blocks and clean off any salt deposits or dirt with a rag dampened with solvent. Then rub or spray a little light waterproof lubricant on the center pin (heavy grease will clog it and light oil will wear off quickly) before reassembling the block.

At mid-season have a couple of friends hoist you aloft on a bosun's chair to lubricate halyard sheaves and blocks. While you have the lubricants out, lightly grease the main sheet travel-er car. Keep a rag handy to clean up any excess lubricant before it drips onto the deck or sails.

Sails. We looked at sail repairs in chapter 3. A repair kit will include heavy-duty shears, rolls of "sticky back" cloth for quick patching, Dacron cloth for sewing on patches, small shears for ripping seams, a sewing palm for pushing needles through the cloth, a variety of needles, waxed thread, Ripstop tape for spinnakers and other light sails, tubular webbing (like sail ties), and rubbing alcohol (for removing glue).

Winches. Salt and dirt will quickly

Keep winch pawls (right) and bearings free of dirt and salt with frequent hose-downs. Tear them down regularly and lubricate them with light oil and grease.

Swiveling blocks usually provide a fair lead, but the swivel must be strong. Wash out salt deposits with fresh water and put light oil on the pins and swivels.

gum up winches. Regularly hose them down and, a couple of times every sailing season, tear them down, pulling off the drums and gears. Clean off the old lubricant with a paper towel soaked with solvent and repack the roller bearings and pawls with light grease and oil. Be careful not to use too much or too heavy lubricant, which might gum up the bearings and make the winch hard to turn. Carry spares for the important winches.

The Steering System. Regularly crawl below and inspect the steering gear, whether or not it feels stiff. Grease

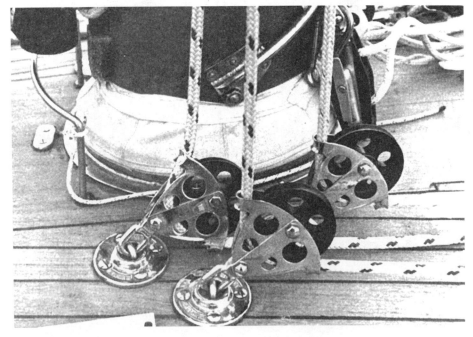

the system regularly using the grease cap located on or near the rudder post. Check for fair leads and examine and lubricate the blocks for the steering cables, replacing them if they're cracked or loose, and make sure the cables themselves are tight and not frayed. Tighten the stuffing box around the rudder post where it enters the hull, leaving it to leak only very slightly, and replace the gasket if it leaks badly.

Stanchions and Lifelines. The stanchions and lifelines should be inspected regularly for bending, chafe, and loose fittings due to the vibration and friction of sheets rubbing against them and sailors grabbing them. Because lifeline wire may gather water under its plastic coating, some experienced owners prefer to leave them bare; either way, inspect them for rust.

Set screws in stanchion bases must be tight, as should lock nuts and cotter pins on turnbuckles, which should be taped. Turnbuckles should be tight enough so that the lifelines are taut. All clevis pins should be exactly the right diameter for their holes. If there is a gangway (opening) in the lifelines, make sure the pelican hooks used to open and shut it are not bent, and tape them when the gangway is closed.

Tuning the Mast. The mast must be straight athwartships when you're sailing close-hauled in about 12 knots of wind. Tuning the mast (adjusting the rigging so the mast is straight) is done before and while you are underway.

Before heading out, tighten the upper shrouds and head- and backstays so they are taut and the mast is straight when you look up the mast track or groove on its aft side. To make sure it's not tilted to one side, use the main halyard as a guide. Lower the halyard so it's taut when the shackle is on the chain plate (deck eye) of the starboard upper shroud. Then, without adjusting the halyard, take it over to the port side. The shackle should be in the same position against the chain plate. If not, the mast is canted. Keep adjusting the upper shrouds until the halyard measurement shows the mast is straight. Tighten the other shrouds so they're slightly tighter than the uppers.

Then go sailing in a moderate wind in smooth sea. Look up the mast track on both tacks. If the tip of the mast falls off, the upper shroud is too loose or the lower shroud on that side is too tight; if it cants to windward, the upper is too tight or the lower too loose. On boats with two sets of spreaders, the intermediate shroud running from the tip of the lower spreader to the base of the upper spreader controls the upper part of the mast along with the upper shroud. An overly tight intermediate can lead to mast failure in rough seas since, because it is shorter, it stretches less than the upper shroud and may pull the mast to windward while the mast tip sags off.

When sailing, don't adjust shrouds when they're on the windward side; the job will be hard if not impossible. Tack so that shroud is loose, pull the cotter pins out of the appropriate leeward turnbuckle (or loosen the locknuts), and using a wrench, a screwdriver, or a marlinspike, tighten or loosen the turnbuckle two or three turns. Then tack back and look at the mast. With a simple, one-spreader rig, tuning can be quite quick, but it becomes increasingly complicated with more complex rigs, so be patient. Keep going through these steps until the spar is straight, but never stop examining the rig in different conditions. When it looks right, record in the log the number of threads visible on each turnbuckle.

In a moderate wind or stronger, the windward upper shrouds will be very taut and the lowers will be moderately taut. The leeward shrouds will be less taut unless they are made of low-stretch rod, when they will seem quite slack.

Fore-and-aft tuning affects the mast's rake and bend. If the boat has lee helm or not enough weather helm (you want a tug when sailing close-hauled in light or moderate wind), rake the mast aft a little. To do this, remove the rubber or wooden mast blocks (shims) from the partners (the mast hole in the deck), then unwind the headstay turnbuckle several turns and tighten the backstay turnbuckle. Then replace the blocks so the mast is straight (this usually involves shifting a block from behind the mast to forward of the mast). If there is a hard pull of weather helm, pull the mast forward a little by reversing this process. If the boat has forward and aft lower shrouds, they may have to be adjusted. Masts stepped on deck have no mast blocks to adjust.

If you tune only in light air, you may rake the mast too far aft. This is because

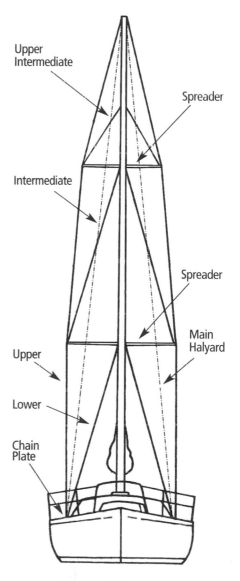

This double-spreader rig is held up by upper, intermediate, and lower shrouds. To check if a mast is tilted, pull the main halyard shackle to one chain plate, cleat the halyard, and take the shackle over to the other chain plate. It should touch the chain plates at the same point.

Running Rigging

modern boats tend to have small mainsails and so do not develop optimum weather helm of about 3° until they are heeled fairly far over. Enough rake to provide weather helm in light air will cause too much helm in moderate or fresh air. Remember that in light air you can always induce weather helm by pulling the traveler car up until the main boom is over the centerline.

Mast bend, which flattens a mainsail, is induced by pulling the top of the mast back with the permanent backstay and allowing its mid and bottom sections to bow forward. (The bow should always be forward, never aft.) Mast blocks at the partners can be moved aft to encourage bend or forward to limit it. If the boat has running backstays, ease the windward one to induce bend and tighten it to straighten the mast. Tension on the after and forward lowers also affects bend.

With all this plus powerful adjustable backstays, it can be easy to overbend the mast. This is a bad idea in rough seas, when a straight mast is mandatory. If your boat has a flexible mast, go sailing with your sailmaker or boatbuilder to get sound professional advice on handling it without breaking it.

While working on the mast, go below, pull up the sole near the mast, and with a flashlight inspect for corrosion at the mast step. Water can accumulate there if drain holes are clogged. The mast should be removed every few years and carefully inspected from end to end.

Stays and Their Equipment

A mast and stay are no stronger than their spreaders, turnbuckles, chain plates, clevis pins, and tangs (metal straps on the mast to which stays are connected). Make sure the upper and intermediate shrouds are secured in the ends of spreaders with a pin or wire, and that the spreader tips are taped or padded with leather to minimize sail chafing. Turnbuckles must be hefty enough for the load, with a large safety factor. Regularly inspect them and the clevis pins attaching them to the other parts for wear and bend. The pins must exactly fit their holes — any smaller and they will bend and snap.

Turnbuckles with open barrels that allow you to see the threads are better than close-barreled fittings. Turnbuckles that are locked with cotter pins are more secure than those with locknuts, which can vibrate loose unless they're glued down with silicone sealer. Turnbuckles must be lubricated lightly so they can be easily adjusted. Anhydrous lanolin, available at pharmacies, is an excellent lubricant. Carry several spare turnbuckles and a variety of clevis and cotter pins.

Tangs and chain plates must be aimed along the line of the stay, and their eyes should not be worn. If there is any wear or elongation in a tang or its clevis pin, replace it immediately. Check terminals (ends) of stays for kinks or cracks and spread silicone sealer over any gaps between them and the wire so water doesn't get in and corrode from the inside out.

The stays and their fittings must be allowed to find their ideal position and angle when they are both taut on the windward side and loose on the leeward side. Otherwise, they will fatigue and break. Toggles between the stay's eye and the turnbuckle and between the turnbuckle and the deck are mandatory.

Never secure a line under load to a turnbuckle or toggle, or the fitting may bend.

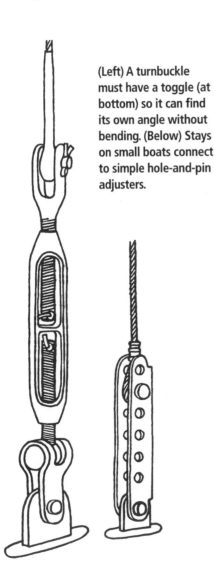

(Left) A turnbuckle must have a toggle (at bottom) so it can find its own angle without bending. (Below) Stays on small boats connect to simple hole-and-pin adjusters.

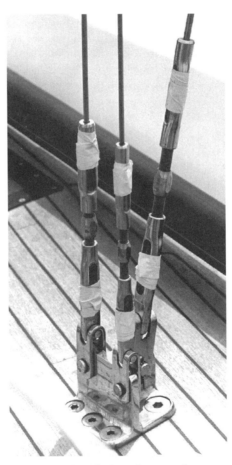

Make sure that clevis and cotter pins are the right size for the holes. Wrap a couple of layers of tape around the turnbuckle cotter pins. Inspect often for wear and damage.

HANDS ON: **How to Use a Cotter Pin**

Cotter pins hold the rig together. They keep a turnbuckle from unwinding, a shackle from opening, and a sheave pin from pulling out of a block. Either because they're small and inexpensive, or because they don't appear to take a load, they are often taken for granted. Here is good advice on using them from Rod Stephens.

The standard straight cotter pin that looks like a bobby pin should fit snugly into the hole in the fitting and project beyond it a distance one-half the width of the fitting — just enough so that it can be locked in place simply by spreading the two sides slightly. If the pin is too long, it will have to be doubled back sharply, and that will make it very hard to remove quickly.

Being able to pull a cotter pin easily is extremely important when clearing away a broken mast. Modern standing rigging is so hard to cut, even with hacksaws and bolt cutters, that the only way to take a rig apart on short notice is to disassemble the connectors, which means first removing the cotter pin and then driving out the clevis pin with a hammer or winch handle.

Once you've found or made a cotter pin the right length, stick it through the hole in the fitting, and with the tip of a screwdriver gently spread the sides enough so the pin will not fall out. Put a drop of silicone sealer on the pin to hold it in place, and then, to protect sails and skin from it, take two wraps of plastic tape (also called rigging tape) around it. Plastic tape is more waterproof than duct tape. You should file down the pin's sharp ends. You'll have to replace the tape from time to time, which provides a good excuse for a thorough inspection.

Some people cover turnbuckles with plastic boots to protect sails from cotter pins, but while that goal may be satisfied, they're also hiding the turnbuckles from a critical eye.

Besides straight cotter pins, there are circular cotter pins (ring-dings). They do not project from the fitting, and they're easy to install — which, unfortunately, also means that they come undone easily. A capsize, vibration, or a chafing sail or line can unscrew one of these little pins with amazing efficiency. If you use them, tape them carefully.

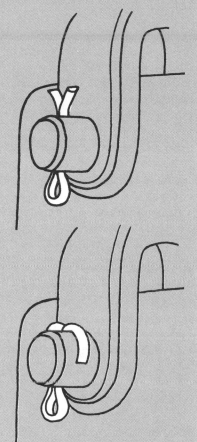

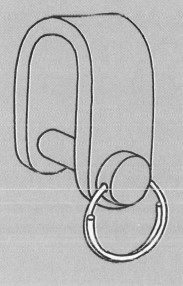

A cotter pin should fit snugly, project only one-half the fitting's width, and be spread only slightly (top). It doubled back on itself, it will be nearly impossible to remove quickly in an emergency (above). Hold the pin in place with sealer and tape it.

With the proper equipment, going aloft to inspect or repair rigging should not be a problem at anchor or the dock, or even when under way in smooth water. (Only in big emergencies should anyone go aloft in rough conditions, when wild swinging can cause seasickness and severe injuries.) The seat the crew rides on is the bosun's chair (bosun's sling). The bosun (the pronunciation of "boatswain") is the crew member assigned to do maintenance. The traditional bosun's chair was a wooden slat, but today it's more likely to be a Dacron sling, which is more comfortable and almost impossible to fall out of.

A good bosun's sling has side pockets and a strap to secure the seated sailor.

Going Aloft

The person going aloft in the sling or chair should wear long pants, since legs will rub against the mast and halyards. He or she should also wear a safety harness or short tether to secure to the mast or stays to stop swinging when the boat rolls, and to serve as a backup support should the halyard break. Tools, fittings, oil, and tape are carried in pouches in the chair or in a canvas bag dangling from the seat, or are tied to the chair with light lines.

One or more crew members can pull the halyard with the aid of a winch or electric anchor windlass. Attach two halyards (a primary and a backup) to the chair. Use a wire, Dacron, or other low-stretch halyard; with a nylon line, the person will bounce unsteadily as the line stretches and compresses. On some boats there is a special line for pulling crew aloft called the gantline. Rigged outside the mast through a large block at the masthead, the gantline also serves as a backup main halyard.

Secure the halyard to the chair with a screw-in shackle or a bowline or fisherman's bend. Snap shackles may open when they rub against the rigging or mast. If there's no way to avoid using a snap shackle, wrap the pin and lanyard with several layers of tape.

Lead the halyard to the biggest cockpit winch or the windlass. The winch should be well away from the mast so the haulers won't be hit by objects accidentally dropped by the person aloft. Use blocks to make the lead fair, with the line coming up to the winch drum at an angle so there are no overrides to jam each other. Attach a long line to the bottom of the chair and lead it through a block on deck well away from the mast and from there back to the cockpit; this is a downhaul to hold the person away from the mast if he or she swings about as the boat rolls in waves.

Here's how to pull a person up. With one person tailing on the primary halyard from a position that allows a clear view aloft, and with another person grinding on the winch, steadily haul on the halyard. Pause every few feet to tension and cleat the backup halyard on its own winch. When the boat rolls, stop hauling and take a strain on the downhaul. To avoid confusion, communications should be only between the tailer and the person aloft, and every command should be clearly acknowledged before any action is taken.

The person going up may be able to help by pulling on the stay or halyard, but he or she should concentrate on not banging against the mast or tangling in the rigging. Whenever there's a pause to do some work, the person aloft should loop the tether around the mast or rigging. When the person aloft is at the desired height, the haulers cleat the halyards and label them (for example by wrapping sail stops around the winches and cleats) to remind other people not to touch them. Avoid walking under the person aloft.

To lower the person, sit behind the winch with your feet braced against it, facing the mast. Take all but three or four turns off the winch. With large-diameter rope you may need three turns; with wire or small-diameter rope you'll need more turns. Working your arms in a motion like a long, steady swimming stroke, let the halyard out so the person comes down in a slow but continuous drop. Short bites are no good because the person drops in uncomfortable jerks. If necessary, brake the halyard by pushing the sole of your foot against the turns on the winch. Let off the backup halyard to keep up with the primary halyard.

The person going up can also pull him- or herself aloft. The advantage is that you are free to adjust your position without assistance. You'll need a sturdy 3:1 or 4:1 tackle with enough line in it so the blocks can be spread at least one-half the length of the mast; if the normal line in the tackle is too short, temporarily replace it with a long Dacron line like a jib or spinnaker sheet (don't use a stretchy nylon line). Secure the tackle between the chair and the two halyards using screw shackles or lines. If the tackle has a cam cleat, put it at the bottom end near the chair. Pull the halyards until the top tackle block is as far aloft as possible when the chair is a couple of feet above the deck. Carefully cleat the halyards, put on the tether line or safety harness, gather your tools and fittings, and get into the chair. Then pull yourself up with the tail of the tackle. Put the line in a sack or bucket attached to the bosun's chair so it does not snag below and keep you from lowering yourself.

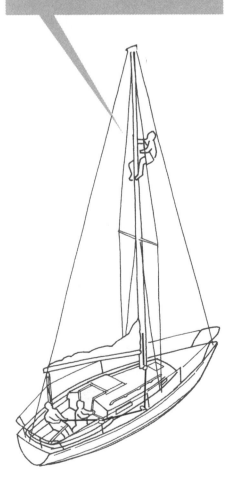

When pulling a crewmember aloft, lead the halyard to the biggest winch through one or more turning blocks. Nobody except the person aloft should give instructions. Additional gear can be hauled aloft in a bucket hooked to another halyard. Lowering, let the line out with a smooth, easy motion to minimize jerking.

The Hull and Interior

If the boat is to remain in the water for extended periods of time, her bottom must be painted with an anti-fouling paint known to be effective in her local waters. Some of these paints can be easily applied with a roller. If you intend to race, spend some time smoothing the bottom with special wet sandpaper, starting with a rough grade and working down to smooth grades. Take a swim every week or so and scrub scum off the waterline, bottom, and propeller.

The topsides can be cleaned with special fiberglass cleansers and then waxed and polished. After a while a fiberglass hull's gel coat will start to fade and craze, and the usual solution is to paint it. Modern polyurethane paints will provide a long-lasting, glossy finish; they should be applied by professionals. While the boat is out of the water, examine the keel, rudder, and the outside of through-hull fittings for cracks and loose fits. Look carefully at the bottom for osmotic blisters. These are pox-like bumps where water has got under the gel coat. They will have to be removed by professionals who grind down and replace the gel coat.

Down below, inspect the fuel line to the stove for cracks and kinks, and make certain the shutoff valve works easily. If you anticipate cooking while under sail, rig a strong strap that can be snapped around the cook's waist to keep him safely in the galley even in rough weather. In the same conditions, people may want to sleep in bunks on the windward side. To restrain them, rig 8-inch-high wooden bunk boards or Dacron lee cloths along the inboard edge of the bunks.

Locker doors and drawers must stay closed when on the windward side. Magnetized latches aren't strong enough. Install positive snap latches accessible through finger holes. Stow tools and other heavy objects as low as possible, and put emergency gear in a special clearly marked locker.

If salt water gets below, wipe it off with a chamois or soft rag damp with fresh water. Keep water off the electrical panel, but if you can't, spray it with silicone before it gets wet and shorts out.

Many new boats are delivered without any grab rails or ventilation ducts. Buy and bolt in enough grab rails to allow a crewmember to go forward to the mast both on deck and below. The best vent is the Dorade, in which a rubber or plastic cowl is screwed into a box that contains a baffle to restrict water, but not air, from getting below (unless there's considerable solid water on deck). The head (marine bathroom) should have a vent, as should the galley. In hot weather, a cloth air scoop may be hung through the forward cabin's hatch.

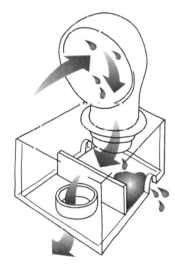

A Dorade vent allows air below while its baffle blocks incoming spray. In rough water, however, turn the cowl aft.

Deadbolts are the best method for securing a drawer or a companionway washboard.

The Engine

The best guide to engine upkeep is the owner's manual, which describes scheduled maintenance, troubleshooting, and minor repairs that can be performed by owners. Still, there are some general rules of thumb for maintaining engines.

Use clean fuel. According to a diesel equipment manufacturer, 90 percent of engine troubles are caused by dirt or water in the fuel. The fuel should be clean; if you have any questions, use a filter when fueling-up. In any case, there should be two fuel filters installed in inboard engines. One is a sediment-type filter for separating out water located between the onboard tank and the pump that lifts fuel from the tank. Drain the bowl on this filter periodically. The other fuel filter, between the lift pump and injection pump, has a fine-mesh paper filter for catching dirt. Clean or replace this filter regularly. If dirty fuel is a steady problem, the tank should be cleaned out. A related fuel problem is an air lock caused by air bubbles in the line, usually when a tank runs dry. Remove an air lock by opening petcocks in the fuel line and hand-pumping fuel through until no bubbles show.

Lubricate the engine. High-speed modern diesels depend on good lubrication. Nigel Calder, in his book *Marine Diesel Engines*, reports that over one-half of bearing failures are due to dirty oil or lack of oil. Use the correct grade of oil, change it on schedule, and run the engine often at fairly high speeds to keep oil well distributed. The pleasure of handling a boat under sail often distracts sailors from this duty.

Attend to the cooling system. Alongside dirty fuel and poor lubrication, inadequate cooling is one of the three main reasons for breakdown in inboard engines. In most boats, the engine is cooled by raw water that is pulled in through a seacock by a pump and then pumped through the engine

The Engine

jacket and thrown out in the exhaust. When you start the engine, look over the stern at the exhaust to see if cooling water is splashing out. If it is not, or if the engine temperature gauge reads high, immediately shut off the engine and inspect the cooling system. The seacock may be closed, the pump's strainer may be blocked by weed, or the pump may be broken. Carry spare impellers.

Keep the battery charged. Make sure its connections are tight and clean. Cruising boats should carry two or more heavy-duty batteries with a master switch that allows one or all to be used. By reserving one battery for starting the engine, you will always be able to get the engine going, and once it is running all the batteries can be charged. A testing system (either a voltmeter or a lamp connected to a wire) measures engine charge and traces down juice-draining short circuits.

Keep water from backing into the engine. There should be a loop in the exhaust pipe to stop this from happening, but even if there is a loop, a big following wave may shove water up the pipe. A pine plug on the end of a lanyard can be inserted in the pipe, but remember to pull it out before starting up.

In outboards and other gasoline engines, use clean spark plugs. Outboard gasoline engines are subject to many of the same problems as diesel inboards — bad fuel, poor lubrication, and inadequate cooling — plus electrical ignition failure. The spark plugs must be clean. Carry the proper size wrench to remove plugs, an emery board to clean the points, and some spare plugs. Use the correct oil-gas mixture to keep the engine properly lubricated. If an outboard falls into salt water or dirty fresh water, immediately rinse it off with clean fresh water, dry it off, remove the spark plugs, and squirt light engine oil into the cylinders. Replace the plugs and try to start it.

Drains, intakes, and other through-hull fittings can cause serious problems if they malfunction. You must be able to shut them off quickly with seacocks, which should be well lubricated and clearly marked at the open and closed positions. Ideally, any pipe leading overboard will loop above the waterline so that water does not siphon back, but this isn't always the case.

Keep sea cocks lubricated, and shut them off when you leave the boat. If a hose breaks when a sea cock is open, the boat may sink.

WINTERIZING

Many of the maintenance problems surrounding boats can be pinpointed during an inspection while the boat is prepared for the off-season, whether or not she is hauled out. This is the time to look for the strains of a long summer and, in a northern area, prepare the boat for a brutal winter ashore.

Once the boat is hauled out, the first job is to clean her, starting with the underbody. With a high-powered hose, a scrub brush, and (if necessary) a putty knife, get all the marine growth off before it dries and cakes onto the paint. Wear old foul-weather jacket, pants, and boots for this wet, messy job. Once the growth is completely removed and the underbody and waterline are dry, give them a thorough sanding with rough sandpaper to smooth the paint and knock off any loose chips in preparation for the next paint job.

A good winter project is to remove the sea cocks, winches, and blocks and take them home for thorough cleaning and lubricating. Also take the sails home or to the sailmaker's for repair and cleaning. And remove the sheets, halyards, cushions, awnings, and other fabric objects. Rinse them off, dry them, and store them in a cool, dry part of the house along with the sails.

If the mast and standing rigging are pulled out, lay them on sawhorses and inspect them carefully for wear, cracks, loose fastenings, and enlarged screw and clevis pin holes. A worn main halyard sheave (or loose strands on the halyard itself) indicates that the lead may not be fair. At the least, replace the sheave. You may also have to angle it slightly to improve the lead.

Below, wipe down the cabin with a damp rag, for any salt left behind will breed a generation of mildew. Clean out the toilet and sinks, and remove the door to the head so it will be ventilated. Pump out and clean the bilge. Electronic

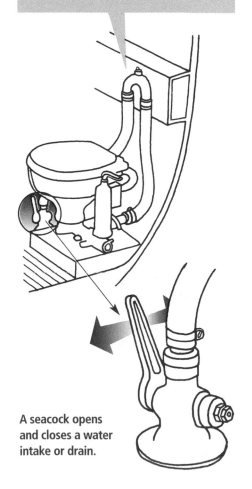

Loops above the waterline keep water from siphoning in through water intakes and drains.

A seacock opens and closes a water intake or drain.

instruments are sensitive to condensation caused by the extreme rise and fall of temperature and humidity that come with winter, so take them home. Charts and other paper items —books, toilet paper, notepads — should also be taken off so they don't mildew and rot. Anchors and rodes should be thoroughly washed, then dried and either taken home or put below.

Drain all water lines. If you think that water remains in a U-joint or other low spot, pour a cup of vodka into the line. Regular antifreeze is poisonous, and vodka's relatively mild taste will not offend anybody but teetotalers on your first cruise next spring.

Carefully follow manufacturer's instructions for winterizing the engine. For safety reasons, empty all gasoline tanks; a diesel tank should be left topped-off so there's no space for condensation to occur. Batteries may either be taken home or left on board with their cables disconnected.

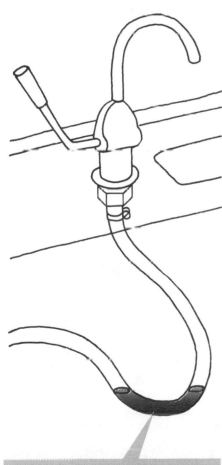

When winterizing, drain all pipes and pour some vodka as anti-freeze into U-joints where moisture might collect.

Tools, Tape, and Lubricants

Every valve, screw, and nut on board should be adjustable by a suitable tight-fitting wrench or screwdriver in the tool chest. Don't rely on pliers, since they provide limited grip and can mangle a recalcitrant nut. Adjustable locking pliers are powerful and useful tools, as are crescent wrenches, but every boat larger than 25 feet also deserves a present of a set of socket wrenches. (Before you make this sizable investment, check whether your fittings are secured with metric- or English-gauge fastenings.)

Have on hand a good supply of a variety of stainless-steel clevis and cotter pins of the right sizes, and stainless and bronze wood, sheet metal, and machine screws (with the right-size nuts for the latter). Secure them tightly in plastic jars (carefully labeled) stored in a sturdy, water-resistant box. Before buying the extra fastenings, determine what gauge and length are needed for your most important fittings.

A hammer or small sledge is a handy tool on board. You will drive few nails but you will have to loosen corroded or stuck fittings. A strong hacksaw, bolt cutters, and a small ax may help clear broken rigging away, although pulling clevis pins usually is fastest except on very small boats. If your pocketbook can stand it and if you sail on salt water, buy one each of the most important tools in stainless steel or bronze. Otherwise inspect your tools for corrosion and give them a light coating of Vaseline or oil.

Carry a variety of lubricants and tapes. Silicone sprays are especially useful since they can lubricate without leaving a greasy film. Lanolin is an excellent lubricant, too. In another container have a variety of rolls of tape. Duct tape is exceptionally handy for short-term uses because it's strong, though not waterproof. Electrician's tape is stretchy and strong, and comes in many colors, which are helpful when you must label different wires or lines.

Spare line can be classified as a tool — especially light line that serves a wide variety of needs. Marline is one of these, and there are strong, small-diameter nylon braids (sometimes called flag halyard rope) and shock cords that will do many jobs. Make sure, too, that there is at least one sharp sailor's knife on board to cut these lines.

An excellent way to protect yourself against crippling breakdowns is to standardize your fittings and fastenings so that backup parts can be versatile. Few problems can be more irritating than trying to turn a Phillips-head screw with a slot-head screwdriver without destroying the head, or wondering how to replace a broken main halyard screw shackle with a spare snap shackle half its strength. If every screw and shackle has five uses, then you not only need fewer types of spares, but also are secure in knowing that you're self-sufficient. Versatility, flexibility, and practicality always go hand-in-hand on the small independent island that is a boat.

A well-sharpened rigging knife, with a marline spike that locks in place, should be in every cockpit. The spike opens knots that are jammed. Experienced sailors carry their own knives and wear them on a lanyard when on deck.

CHAPTER 18 Traditions and Courtesies

The pastime of pleasure boating, traditionally called "yachting," is more than 300 years old — far older than baseball, golf, tennis, and almost every other outdoor sport. In all those years, sailors have developed many traditions that not only add a touch of ceremony but also provide guidelines for safe, courteous behavior on crowded waterways. Although nobody has to subscribe to all these traditions and courtesies to sail a boat competently, they can make sailing more rewarding and enjoyable.

Sailing Etiquette. There are two fundamental and seemingly contradicto-

ry principles of sailing etiquette: privacy and mutual aid. Sailors must respect each other's right to privacy and independence, yet, in the tradition of seafarers, must always be ready to come to each other's aid in emergencies. As with farmers and other battlers against the elements, there is a common bond among all mariners that inevitably brings both mutual respect and mutual support.

Courtesies at Rest. When moored, anchored, or docked, don't infringe on other boats' air and physical space. Here's a rule of thumb for when you are anchored: the longer you have to

From the Pacific to the Atlantic, opening day at American yacht clubs often is celebrated by a flag-raising ceremony presided over by uniformed commodores.

run your engine or your charcoal grill, the more numerous are your children, the louder is your voice, or the more you want to play your radio (in short, the more disruptive you are), then the farther downwind you should be from your neighbors. This basic tactfulness isn't any different from simple courteous behavior ashore, where the golden rule "do unto others as you would have them do unto you" works so well.

In the marina (just as at home), don't impose on your neighbors' privacy and patience any more than you have to. If you must cross boats when they are raft-ed-up (tied up side-to-side), walk across their yards (their foredecks), not through their living rooms (their cockpits). Rig your docking lines so you can adjust them yourself on your own boat. When finished with equipment belonging to the marina and intended for common use, put it back where it belongs. Do not leave hoses, electrical cords, and docking lines strewn around underfoot.

Crowded docks and harbors demand both respect of others' privacy and concern for mutual safety.

Under Way

Sailors who like to party should not assume that everybody else does, too. Many people go out in boats in order to find a place for quiet reflection that is rarely available on shore. There is an etiquette to determining whether a neighbor is open to an invitation to socialize. Go over to the other boat and stop a courteous 6 feet away. Engage in some wheel-greasing small talk (compliments about the boat's design and appearance are always welcome). Judge from the tenor of the conversation whether an invitation

would be welcome. If you do ask the other people over to your boat, don't be offended if they express their need for solitude by politely turning you down. While it is not a breach of courtesy to reject a social invitation, no true sailor will turn away a request for advice concerning weather, navigation, or anchoring, or help with rigging, the engine, and first aid.

When you do go aboard another boat, your hosts may solicit your opinions about her. This is tricky territory. No matter how strongly the owner protests that your most frank and objective evaluation will be welcome, treat the situation as delicately as you would a parent's request for an opinion about his or her children. Most boat owners believe in their heart of hearts that their boats are beyond criticism, and those few who believe otherwise would prefer not to have their doubts echoed by a visitor.

Flag Etiquette

Flags are fun, and most sailors know it since they fly lots of them in a number of patterns. They might enjoy it more by learning the simple, traditional rules of what is called flag etiquette — the flying of flags in certain specified locations and patterns. These flags include the ensign (the national flag), the burgee (the flag of a boating organization that the boat's owner belongs to), and the private signal (the owner's unique identifying flag).

The Ensign. For most people on boats, flag etiquette begins and ends with the problem of which ensign, or

Daysailers and cruisers should avoid interfering with racing boats, which stand out because they are sailed with intensity in large groups.

HANDS ON: Courtesies Under Way

Your behavior when under way should be guided by respect for the letter of the Navigation Rules combined with a sensitivity to other people's concerns. This respect will guide you in many ways.

Leave a float plan (a copy of your planned itinerary) with friends and save them needless worry if you're late.

Observe speed limits posted in harbors not just because it's the law but because the golden rule suggests that other crews are no more interested in rolling around in your big wake than you would be in theirs.

Give boats engaged in fishing a wide berth. You are required by the Navigation Rules to alter course. Pass well upwind of them to avoid scaring away the fish and forcing them to reel in their lines to avoid tangling with your keel and rudder.

When cruising near racing boats, stay well away. Racing boats are not hard to identify: they don't fly the ensign (national flag), they sail in clusters toward or away from powerboats flying a blue flag with "RC" (for race committee), and they are being sailed with great intensity (if most of the crew is looking at the sails, the boat is probably racing). While it is written nowhere in the Navigation Rules that a racing sailboat has the right of way over a non-racing sailboat, cruising and daysailing sailors usually are pleased to relinquish the right of way temporarily if they are asked to in a nice way. When racers wave their fists and shriek, "We're racing!," they seem arrogant and selfish. So do cruisers who barge through a fleet of racers.

national flag, to fly and where to fly it. Sailors and all other boating people who are United States citizens may choose between two flags. One is the usual 50-star national flag known as the ensign. The other is a special flag called the yacht ensign that, in place of the 50 stars standing for the states, has a fouled anchor on a field of 13 stars.

The story of these two ensigns is an interesting one. In the early to mid–19th century, most yachts looked like fishing boats and other commercial vessels. At that time, each port charged a local duty to visiting commercial vessels, whose skippers often attempted to convince customs officials that they were pleasure sailors. The officials ignored those claims and collected fees from all entering boats, including yachts. Under pressure from yachtsmen, the American and British governments independently approved special national flags to be flown only from yachts. In the United States, the yacht ensign was designed by the officers of the New York Yacht Club in 1848. It remains a legal national flag for pleasure boats in US waters.

By law, the only pleasure boats *required* to fly the yacht ensign in US waters are ones that are documented, or registered with the federal government and not a state. Every other US boat *may* fly either the yacht ensign or the standard national ensign (except in foreign waters, where a US-registered boat may fly only the 50-star flag). Still, many yacht clubs require members to fly the yacht ensign.

The size of the ensign is determined by the size of the boat that flies it. On the fly (the flag's horizontal measurement), there must be a minimum of 1 inch of flag for every 1 foot of the boat's overall length. The hoist (vertical measurement) is two-thirds the length of the fly.

The ensign or yacht ensign may be flown from either of two locations. The purpose is to make the flag highly visible from off the boat while presenting it in a respectful manner so it is not damaged.

One of these locations is a flagstaff on the stern, customarily just to starboard of the centerline. Wooden staffs of various lengths are available at many marine equipment outlets. Choose a staff long enough to fly the flag free of the boat's equipment and engine exhaust. The other position, the most traditional one, is the leech of the aftermost sail. The flag may be sewn permanently to the sail or (to allow lowering in bad weather) hoisted on a small halyard led through a leech cringle or small block. On a boat with a Bermudian (Marconi) rig, the position is two-thirds of the way up from the clew. On a gaff-rigged boat, it is flown just below the gaff. The leech position is not a good one if the boat has a permanent backstay, which will quickly damage the flag when it bangs against the wire. For this reason, very few boats other than a few gaff-riggers fly ensigns on their sails today. Many boats fly their ensigns from the backstay, where they tend to droop without distinction.

Whichever ensign is used and wherever it is flown, show the flag from morning colors (8 AM) to evening colors (sunset) whether you are under way or not under way, under sail or under power. There are three exceptions to this rule. First, the ensign is not flown on a boat sailing in a race. Second, to prevent wear and tear, the flag need not be flown when out of sight of other vessels. Third, the flag is flown while entering or leaving a port, even at night, and then is lowered after anchoring or leaving the port.

At morning colors, the ensign is hoisted rapidly before other flags. At evening colors, the ensign is lowered slowly and with ceremony after other flags.

Traditionalists salute dignitaries by dipping (briefly lowering and then raising) the ensign. It is dipped when passing ships in the US and foreign navies; when passing another yacht (with the most junior skipper initiating); when anchoring, mooring, or docking near a flag officer (commodore) in the skipper's yacht club; and when a senior flag officer anchors, moors, or docks nearby. After the ship or yacht being saluted returns the salute, the flag is hoisted again.

Except when the boat is racing, fly the ensign from 8 AM to sunset on the stern or from the leech of the aftermost sail.

Flag Etiquette

The Burgee. The burgee is a small swallow-tailed flag displaying the symbol of the owner's yacht club or other sailing organization. Although it may be flown day and night, in order to save wear and tear many owners lower it when they leave the boat. The burgee's dimensions are, on the fly, approximately ½ inch for each 1 foot between the water and the top of the tallest mast; and on the hoist, two-thirds the length of the fly. The burgee is usually flown at the top of the mast (the forwardmost mast in a divided rig).

The Private Signal. A private signal is a small, custom-designed flag that carries symbols standing for the owner. For example a man of strong personality named Page with a boat named *Pageant* has a private signal that shows a ceremonial trumpet. The signal is sized according to the rule for burgees. It may be flown day and night, but not when another sailor is in command. (The private signal

and the burgee follow the sailor, not the boat.) On a two-masted boat, the private signal is flown at the top of the aftermost mast. On a single-master, it may go either in the starboard rigging on a flag halyard or on a staff forward.

Flagpoles. A yacht club or other boating organization is traditionally considered to be a ship facing the water. This is why the flagpole often looks like a gaff-rigged mast without the sail or boom but with the gaff and spreaders. Therefore, the ensign is flown from the gaff below the yacht club's burgee, which is at the top of the flagpole. This is not disrespectful to the national flag but, rather, reflects traditional usage on a ship.

Half-Masting. The ensign is half-masted (hauled down halfway and left there) from morning colors to 1200 on Memorial Day and other days of mourning. It is full-masted (hoisted all the way) before half-masting as well as before being lowered all the way.

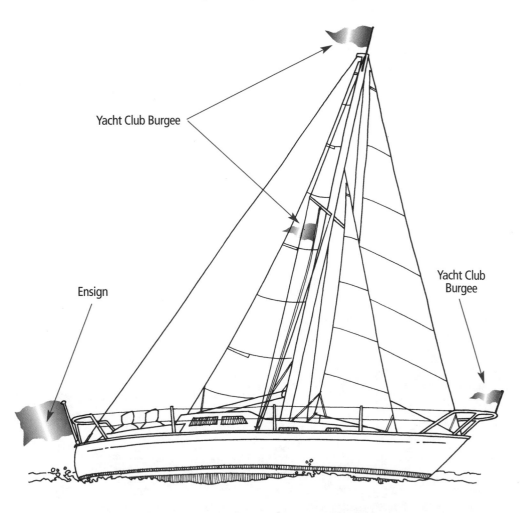

Yacht Club Burgee

Ensign

Yacht Club Burgee

Traditionally, the yacht club burgee is flown at the masthead on a pig stick hoisted on a light flag halyard (top), but it may be flown from the starboard spreader or a jack staff. The ensign is usually flown at the stern but may be flown from the leech of the after sail.

Other Flags. Traditional flag etiquette also includes a number of other flags.

The union jack is a rectangular blue flag with 50 stars flown from the jack-staff by boats at anchor or in the marina on Sundays and holidays and when dressing ship.

A courtesy flag is the flag of the host country flown in the starboard rigging of a visiting vessel after pratique (health and customs clearance) has been issued. Port officials have been known to take great offense at a visiting vessel that does not fly the courtesy flag.

A race committee flag is flown by a boat used to start and finish races. It is blue and shows a fouled anchor between the letters "R" and "C."

An officer's flag is issued by many yacht clubs and boating organizations to each top club official with the title of commodore. Like navy admirals, these officials are called flag officers. Typically, the officer's flags take the place of the burgee or the private signal.

Owner absent (blue flag) and **guest present** in the absence of the owner (blue with white stripe) flags may be flown from the lower starboard spreader.

Meal pennants, seen usually on large yachts with professional crews, announce that the owner (white flag) or the paid crew (red flag) is eating. The owner's flag is flown from the lower starboard spreader, the crew's flag from the lower port spreader. (The sides are reserved in other ways: the owner and guests board the boat on the starboard side, with the owner boarding first and leaving last, and the paid crew board on the port side.)

HANDS ON: The Pig Stick

The burgee should be flown from the top of the mast unless it is badly obstructed by antennas and wind instruments. Up there, the flag is carried on a small pole called a pig stick that is hoisted on a continuous light halyard called a flag halyard. If the block is especially large and strong, the flag halyard can be used as a messenger to carry a larger line through it to be used as a back-up halyard.

The pig stick is a wooden or aluminum rod with a swivel for attaching the flag and two eyes or grooves for securing the halyard. The halyard is either tied to the eyes with bowlines or secured to the grooves with clove hitches. The ends of the flag halyard must be tied together to make it a continuous loop. Hoist the stick quickly but carefully so it doesn't foul in the rigging; it's best to pull the stick up on the leeward side when sailing on a reach. Then pull down hard to steady and straighten the pig stick. The halyard may be cleated on the mast (at the risk of

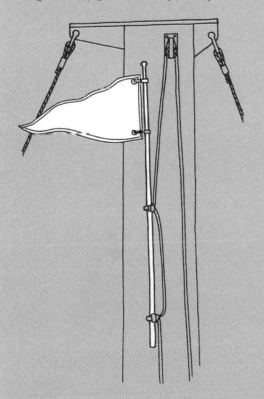

clanging against it) or to a cleat on a shroud. It may also be tied to a toggle or turn-buckle at the bottom of a shroud.

Carrying the burgee at the masthead is difficult on the many modern boats that have masthead radio antennas and wind-direction indicators, which the flag may knock off. You can use an especially long pig stick (for example, two ski poles jammed together) or rearrange the equipment aloft (which may be impractical). Many skippers choose to fly the burgee in the starboard rigging from the outboard side of the lowest spreader on a flag halyard there. While this practice is decried by purists, it is a reasonable adaptation of an old and good tradition of making the starboard rigging a position of honor. Another possibility that is permitted by flag etiquette but rarely used is to follow the lead of powerboats and fly the burgee from a short spar forward — in the case of a sailboat, on a pole called a jackstaff standing on the bow pulpit.

(Top to bottom) The race committee, guest present, and owner absent flags.

Flag Etiquette

Code Flags and Dressing Ship. Even in this day of radiotelephones, signaling with code flags still occurs. Each flag stands for a letter of the alphabet, a number, or a repetition of a letter or number. Many flags have special meanings. For example, the red "B" flag generally signals danger, whether dangerous cargo on a ship or, in a race, a protest that another crew has violated the racing rules.

On the Fourth of July, yacht club opening days, and other times specified by authorities, pleasure boats not under sail dress ship by hanging code flags from their masts in lines stretching from the water below the bow to the water below the stern. Only code flags are used in the hoist; the ensign, burgee, private signal, and union jack fly in their usual places. A recommended flag sequence that produces a colorful display is: AB2, UJ1, KE3, GH6, IV5, FL4, DM7, P0, Third Repeater, RN, First Repeater, ST Zero, CX9, WQ8, ZY, Second Repeater.

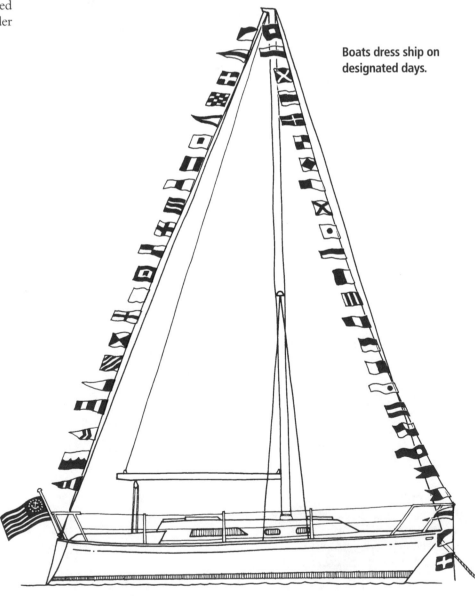

Boats dress ship on designated days.

Clothing

Any sort of clothing will do in a boat so long as it is appropriate for the weather, but there are some traditional outfits for social occasions.

Daytime Clothing. When many people think of sailing, one of the first things to come to mind is a version of the naval officer's hat called the "yachtsman's cap." When worn without any other formal clothing, it's meant to tell the world that the wearer is a capable, nautical character. While it may be traditional, this hat is impractical on the head of a busy sailor. To many experienced sailors it means that the person wearing it is either a rookie or a powerboater. Even mild physical labor is impossible with this hat on. It flops over the eyes and eventually falls right off. (As we will see in a moment, this hat is suited for formal occasions.)

For normal activity in a boat or around a yacht club or marina, the only

The blue blazer is standard wear at sailors' functions like awards ceremonies. If made of synthetic materials, it will survive a stay in a crowded onboard locker without wrinkling.

uniform needed is comfortable shirt and pants plus a hat for keeping sun off your face. Many sailors who care about tradition favor khaki or Breton red pants and navy blue or white shirts.

Semiformal and Formal Dress. The jacket for semiformal dress around boats, for both men and women, is the blue blazer, a descendant of the first uniforms used in the British Royal Navy. At relatively informal occasions, it may be worn with an open-collared shirt over trousers or a skirt. At more formal occasions, the blazer often is worn over khaki or gray trousers or skirt with the official tie, scarf, or pin of a boating organization. White trousers and skirts add another level of formality. A blazer pocket patch may carry the insignia of the wearer's yacht club or other primary boating organization. The yachtsman's cap finds its place in formal uniforms prescribed by yacht clubs and other boating organizations.

A sensible sailing outfit includes sunglasses, a brimmed hat, and loose-fitting clothes. A shirt collar protects the neck from the sun. Long-sleeve shirts offer additional protection; many sailors wear their old dress shirts.

Yachting History

While men and women have been sailing for thousands of years, for most of that time they did so for commerce or war, and the idea of going to sea for fun is fairly new. The first systematic pleasure sailing took place in the Netherlands in the 16th century. The traditional word for pleasure boat, "yacht," is a Dutch word — derived from *jaght,* meaning "fast." A *jaght schip* was a quick, maneuverable boat. When King Charles II left Amsterdam in 1660 to return to England after a long exile, he brought along his own yacht. Of Charles, a fanatical sailor, it was said that "two leagues' travel at sea was more pleasure to him than 20 by land." Before long, his brother James also had a yacht. The inevitable occurred, and the first yacht race recorded in history was sailed on May 21, 1661 (Charles won). Charles bought more than 25 yachts during his 25-year reign and encouraged much experimentation with rigs and hulls. His biggest mistake was to make fun of the first Western multihulled sailboat, a catamaran named *Innovation* built by Sir William Petty. It wasn't until after about 1980 that multihulls were taken seriously by large numbers of sailors.

If pleasure sailing was a sport of kings, it also was a sport of admirals, or at least of navies. The naval influence comes down in many ways besides the blue blazer and the yachtsman's cap. We see it in one of the two traditions for naming a boat, one romantic and the other naval.

The romantic tradition, dating back to the ancient Egyptians, is that a boat is (or represents) a woman who brings luck to the crew. For many centuries eyes were painted on the bow, and male sailors believed that if they brought a woman on board they risked angering the jealous goddess who was the spirit of the boat. Women now sail freely, but this ancient tradition of giving a vessel a personality, and a female one at that, survives in the use of the pronouns "she" and "her" to refer to the boat, which remains a living thing. Sailors speak and write the boat's name as they would a human name — for example, *Mary, Elixir,* and *Cunizza.*

The naval tradition is different. A boat or ship is not a person but an institution, an "it" and not a "she." The name is prefixed with the article "the," for example, "the *Enterprise.*" Both usages are accepted and widely used. This author, preferring the romantic tradition, uses "she" and does not use the prefix "the."

The America's Cup. Not only kings but commoners also took to the water at the dawn of pleasure sailing. The first yacht club was the Water Club of the Harbour of Cork, founded in Ireland in 1720. While the members occasionally sailed their yachts in choreographed processions similar to those used in the Royal Navy, the club was mostly a social

The most famous pleasure boat in history is the schooner *America*. In 1851 she won the trophy that came to be named after her and that is still being raced for.

Joshua Slocum's *Spray* completed the first singlehanded circumnavigation in 1898 (below). Since then, many solo sailors and families have sailed around the world, including the Kuhners (bottom), who did it twice.

organization. One of its rules required that any member who was caught talking about sailing during a banquet would be fined. Today, that rule would empty the dining room of any self-respecting yacht club.

There is some dispute about the identity of the first American yacht club; good cases have been made that clubs were founded in Detroit, Boston, and New Orleans in the 1830s. But it took a New York yacht to spur the growth of the sport in America. The yacht was the 101-foot schooner *America*, owned by a syndicate of members of the New York Yacht Club (founded in 1844). On August 22, 1851, she won a race off Cowes, England, against the fleet of England's most prestigious yacht club, the Royal Yacht Squadron, and with it a trophy called the Squadron Cup. The syndicate gave the trophy to the New York Yacht Club for use in international competition. It soon came to be called the America's Cup, and in 24 matches between 1870 and 1980 the club's boats successfully defended it against chal-

lenges from Britain, Canada, Australia, France, Sweden, and Italy.

The greatest boat in America's Cup competition was the 1903 winner, *Reliance*. At 143 feet from bow to stern she was the world's largest singlemasted sailboat until 1998. *Reliance* was designed and built by a man who stands next to Alexander Graham Bell and Thomas Edison in the pantheon of American technological geniuses. This was Nathanael G. Herreshoff, the great "Captain Nat" of Bristol, Rhode Island. Other than the sailboard and the winged keel, there are few concepts in sailing today that he did not think up or develop in his long lifetime between 1848 and 1938.

The America's Cup, the oldest trophy for regular international competition, finally changed hands in 1983, when *Australia II* with her innovative winged keel took it to the Southern Hemisphere. Four years later, the cup was taken back to America by the San Diego Yacht Club. After three contests there, it was won by New Zealand in 1995.

Sailing Today

The Second Golden Age of Sail.

Racing has often been the laboratory where yacht designers work out their ideas. Some of the most important technological advances were first tried on the race course. Yet for most sailors the emotional satisfactions are more memorable than technology. When J. P. Morgan (reportedly) advised an acquaintance who wanted to buy a yacht, "If you have to ask how much it costs, you can't afford it," he might well have been saying that pleasure sailing offers emotional rewards that far outweigh its financial cost.

For most people, sailing means cruising and daysailing in relatively small boats. One of the most famous of them was *Spray*, a tubby 36-foot converted fishing sloop that a grizzled fisherman, Joshua Slocum, sailed around the world between 1895 and 1898. His cheerful book about this, the first singlehanded circumnavigation, *Sailing Alone Around the World,* has inspired generations of cruising sailors.

Besides inspiration, sailors also require practical advice. Early on, the most important of them was Thomas Fleming Day, who became the editor of the boating magazine *The Rudder* in 1890 and spent 26 years assuring people of the radical idea that they could go out there in small boats without spending a fortune and without dying the grim deaths that skeptics and professional mariners predicted for them. "The danger of the sea for generations has been preached by the ignorant," Day wrote. "Small vessels are safer than large, providing they are properly designed, strongly built, thoroughly equipped, and skillfully manned." The backbone of good seamanship is "confidence in yourself, confidence in your craft, confidence in your crew."

While Day may have gone a little bit overboard here, nobody would go sailing for pleasure without sharing at least some of his sunny spirit and his demythologization of the sea. The idea that our own confidence and abilities will fend off the sea's power lies at the very heart of the pastime of pleasure sailing and motivates the writing of books like this one. Inspired by Tom Day and other writers and sailors, people began to go out there in increasing numbers at the same time that the great golden age of commercial sailing was drawing to a close. It is no exaggeration to say that the rush of amateur, pleasure-seeking men and women to the sea has created the Second Golden Age of Sail.

After World War II, the boating industry developed ways to build boats relatively inexpensively and in large numbers out of fiberglass, which requires little of the time- and cash-absorbing maintenance work that old wooden boats did. By the 1980s almost every sailboat was built of fiberglass or a combination of it and high-tech, strong, lightweight materials. By then, the 1979 Fastnet Race storm and other gales were

The variety of boats and experiences is as great as the types of people who enjoy them. The pastime can be enjoyed by children racing Optimist prams (top) as well as by families cruising on large boats (left and opposite). Modern multihulls (below right) and around the world racers (below) provide new levels of speed and thrills for sailors of all ages.

stimulating the healthy reevaluation of safety equipment and boat design that forms a central theme in this book. While the spirit of confident pioneers like Charles II and Tom Day remains strong, it is now tempered healthily by the more realistic standards of modern seamanship.

Small Boats. Many new sailors are introduced to the sport in cruising boats and large one-design keel boats. This does not mean that small-boat sailing is dead. New types of small boats appeared after 1960, most notably sailboards and catamarans, and older designs that have been around for many decades (including the Snipe, Thistle, and Lightning) have, if anything, gained in popularity since they made the transition from wooden hulls and cotton sails to fiberglass and Dacron. Today, thousands of youngsters learn to sail and compete in Optimists, Blue Jays, and other small boats in yacht club sailing programs that can be as intense as Little League. Many of those young sailors survive the rigors of those programs and grow up to be lifelong sailors. Adult sailing instruction also takes place in boats smaller than 25 feet whose quickness and speed make them excellent schools for mastering the pastime's basic skills.

One of the strengths of the pastime is its diversity. In almost every sailing area, people can choose a boat that suits their athletic ability, skills, and ambitions. There literally are different boats for different folks. At a recent Olympics, a gold medal in a dinghy class was won a young man from Seattle named Carl Buchan, and one in a keel-boat class was won by his father, Bill, who at 49 was at an age that would have disqualified him from topflight competition in most other sports.

In their wake come generation after generation of people of all ages who dream (as do you and I) about the sea and boats.

Required Equipment

Safety Requirements. Below is a summary list of mandated safety equipment and other requirements set by Federal law and enforced by the United States Coast Guard (USCG) and by state and local agencies. The equipment listed here is described and evaluated in the main text in the chapters on personal safety, rules of the road, and emergencies. (Lengths given here are lengths overall.)

The equipment lists are minimum requirements as required by law. They do not address many circumstances and situations. Excellent advisories for larger inventories of equipment are provided by two organizations:

The United States Coast Guard Auxiliary recommends valuable gear beyond what is required by law and also provides free courtesy examinations of boats on request. Local Coast Guard Auxiliaries are located in most boating areas and are listed in telephone directories.

The Offshore Racing Council addresses the needs of sailors going out into deep water, whether racing or cruising. Its valuable booklet *Safety Recommendations for Offshore Sailing* lists standards that, besides serving as rules for offshore racing, are reliable advisories for any cruising boat. This publication is available from the United States Sailing Association (US Sailing), whose address is in appendix II.

Boat and Operator Licenses. Boat registration: All states require registration of boats with engines, and may require it of sailboats.

Operator licensing: Many states require that operators of pleasure boats be licensed by taking boating education courses or passing an examination on the Navigation Rules and boating safety. Information may be obtained from state police, departments of natural resources, or other agencies. The Coast Guard requires that operators of all boats used commercially be licensed. Standards vary with the vessel's size. Your local Coast Guard station or district headquarters will provide more information.

PFDs. Most boats are required to carry one wearable USCG-approved Personal Flotation Device (PFD, life jacket) of the appropriate size for each crewmember plus one throwable PFD. So long as these requirements are satisfied, non-approved PFDs may be worn. The USCG has five PFD types, each with a unique design. Detailed descriptions and evaluations may be found in chapter 7. Approved wearable PFDs (Types I–III and V) must be "readily available." Approved throwables (Type IV) must be "immediately available." Each USCG-approved PFD is clearly labeled with its type and capacity in pounds. The Coast Guard requires that all PFDs be kept in serviceable condition.

Boats 16 feet or shorter must carry one USCG-approved wearable PFD for each person on board. The PFD must be the correct size for its wearer.

Boats longer than 16 feet must carry one USCG-approved wearable of the correct size for each person, plus one throwable Type IV device in the boat.

Some small craft (including sailboards, canoes, rowing shells, and kayaks) are exempt from these rules, but some states do not recognize these exceptions.

Sound Signals. Boats are required to carry whistles or horns to make sound signals specified by the Navigation Rules.

Boats up to 39 feet must carry any sound signal that makes "an efficient sound signal."

Boats 39–65 feet must carry a signal with a range of at least ½ mile, plus a bell. Boats 66–240 feet must carry a signal with a range of at least 1 mile, plus a bell. Sound signals on larger boats must have a range of 2 miles or more.

As range increases, the pitch of the sound signal becomes lower.

Visual Distress Signals. Most pleasure boats must carry signals approved for use in emergencies at day, at night, or at both day and night.

These signals include lights, flares, and smoke signals. The exceptions to this rule are a few types of boats that need not carry day signals when out during the day, but must carry night signals when out after sunset. These exceptions are: boats smaller than 16 feet; boats participating in organized events such as races or marine parades; open sailboats without engines that are smaller than 26 feet; and manually propelled boats.

The following signals are approved:

Day signals only: Floating orange smoke signals (three must be carried); hand-held orange smoke signals (three); orange flag with black square and circle (one).

Night signals only: An electric light, such as a bright flashlight.

Combination day-night signals: Self-propelled rocket parachute red flares (three must be carried); aerial pyrotechnic red flares (three); hand-held red flares (three); pistol-projected parachute red flares (three, the pistol may be subject to state or local firearms laws).

Fire Extinguishers. Most boats equipped with engines must carry at least one USCG-approved portable fire extinguisher of a specified size. Exempted are boats smaller than 26 feet that do not carry people for hire and do not have cabins or compartments in which flammable vapors can be trapped.

Class B extinguishers are for fires of gasoline, diesel fuel, alcohol, and other flammable liquids. Class A extinguishers are for combustible solids. Class C extinguishers are for electrical fires.

Portable extinguishers come in two sizes: I and II (small and large).

The minimum requirements for boats with and without fixed fire extinguisher systems are as follows:

Boats smaller than 26 feet without a

fixed system must carry one B-I extinguisher. No portable extinguisher is required if there is a fixed system.

Boats 26–39 feet without a fixed system must carry two B-I extinguishers or one B-II extinguisher. One B-I is required if there is a fixed system.

Boats 39–66 feet without a fixed system must carry three B-I extinguishers, or one B-II and one B-I. If there is a fixed system, the requirement is two B-Is or one B-II.

Gasoline Engines. Because gasoline and its fumes are explosive, gasoline engines must have special equipment:

Backfire flame arresters are required on boats with gasoline inboard engines.

Natural ventilation using ducts and vents is required in boats with inboard gasoline engines or with outboard gasoline engines where gas fumes may be contained in the bilge or a compartment such as a locker containing a fuel tank. Under the law, the size of the ducts and vents is determined by the volume of the compartment to be ventilated. An electric exhaust blower may also be installed; a sign concerning its use must be posted.

Navigation Rules. A boat larger than 39 feet must carry a printed copy of the Navigation Rules.

Navigation Lights. The Navigation Rules specify navigation lights to be used at night. They are covered in detail in chapter 8. To summarize:

Boats smaller than 23 feet under sail or oars must be prepared to show a white light if they do not carry navigation lights.

Larger boats under sail must show red and green sidelights and a white sternlight. These lights may be shown on deck or in a tricolor light at the top of the mast (but not in both places). If the boat is smaller than 39 feet, sidelights must be visible 1 mile away and the sternlight 2 miles. If the boat is larger, all three must be visible 2 miles away.

Boats under power must carry sidelights, a sternlight, and a white masthead or steaming light that shines through the same arc as the sidelights and above them. (A sailboat under power must not use the tricolor.) If the boat is smaller than 39 feet, the stern and masthead lights must be visible 2 miles away and the sidelights must have a range of 1 mile. If the boat is 39–66 feet, the ranges are 3 miles for the masthead light and 2 miles for the stern and sidelights.

Capacity Plates. The Coast Guard calculates maximum capacity for many boats smaller than 20 feet. A plate showing the calculated capacity in persons, weight, and engine horsepower must be affixed to the hull.

Discharge Placards. A placard warning against disposal overboard of garbage must be posted conspicuously in any boat larger than 26 feet. A placard warning against disposal overboard of oil or oily water must be conspicuously posted near the engine compartment of boats larger than 26 feet.

Marine Sanitation Devices (MSDs). Disposal overboard of untreated human waste is prohibited. The Coast Guard has approved a number of devices for treating waste and for storing waste so it may be pumped out at shoreside and other harbor stations.

The Coast Guard and Other Boating Organizations

Many government and volunteer organizations are concerned with pleasure boating.

The United States Coast Guard (USCG). The Coast Guard is the agency of the Department of Transportation assigned to (among many other services) enforcing federal boating laws, approving boating safety equipment, maintaining aids to navigation, investigating boating accidents, and conducting search and rescue (SAR) missions. Coast Guard personnel have authority to stop, board, and inspect vessels and to impose citations and fines, arrest crews, and seize vessels for violations of safety and other laws.

The Coast Guard has several districts and many stations in the United States and its territories. Locations of and contacts for district headquarters are listed in National Ocean Service nautical chart catalogs and on the Coast Guard's helpful Web site on the Internet. Telephone directories also list USCG stations and district headquarters. Notify your local station or district headquarters to report an accident or hazard to navigation (after reporting it over VHF/FM channel 16). Each USCG district publishes *Local Notice to Mariners*, a periodical announcing changes in buoyage and other aids to navigation, regattas and marine parades, and anything else that might affect safe navigation locally. It is available in chart outlets and on the Internet.

The Canadian Coast Guard provides many of these services in Canadian waters.

State and Local Agencies. They delegate boating regulation to one or more of several agencies, including the police and the departments of natural resources, fisheries, conservation, or parks and recreations. Many towns appoint harbor masters who supervise the waterfront, moorings, anchorages, and other boating areas.

Volunteer Organizations. Tens of thousands of volunteers work through several national organizations for better, safer boating.

The United States Sailing Association (US Sailing) is sailing's national governing body. Membership is open to all. While historically concerned mostly with racing (it still publishes the racing rules, sponsors national championships, and organizes Olympic teams), US Sailing today provides a number of valuable programs and publications for all sailors. One of its most important activities is developing rules for safety equipment. Another is training: US Sailing establishes standards for sailing instruction and trains instructors. US Sailing may be reached through its Internet site and at PO Box 1260, 15 Maritime Drive, Portsmouth, RI 02871.

The United States Power Squadrons (USPS) is a national organization with hundreds of local bodies (called Squadrons) that teach boating courses. The USPS is a private organization in which membership is available only by invitation. Despite its name, the Power Squadrons has many sailing members. The Internet and the telephone directory will help you contact the national organization and local Squadrons.

The Coast Guard Auxiliary (USCGA) is the civilian volunteer arm of the United States Coast Guard. Membership is open to all who own at least a 25 percent share in a boat. Hundreds of local bodies (Auxiliaries) conduct boating instruction, inspect yachts, patrol waterways, and provide other valuable services. Auxiliaries may be found through telephone directories or the Internet.

In Canada: The Canadian Yachting Association (CYA) is the equivalent of US Sailing. The Canadian Power and Sail Squadrons (CPS) offers many of the services provided by the USCGA and USPS. The Canadian Marine Rescue Auxiliary (CMRA), a volunteer arm of the Canadian Coast Guard, furthers boating safety and responds to search and rescue calls.

Sailing and Yacht Clubs. Across America are thousands of local members-only organizations of sailors. Some clubs have facilities not much larger than a shack and charge very low dues. Others have elaborate marinas and restaurants and impose dues in the thousands of dollars. Most clubs fall between these two extremes. Most clubs with waterfront facilities monitor radiotelephone emergency channels and will provide assistance to any boat.

ABYC. The American Boat and Yacht Council is a nonprofit agency that sets and publishes recommended standards and practices for boat and equipment design, construction, and repair. For example, it has reliable guidelines for lightning protection. These standards, drawn up by engineers, are used by marine surveyors when evaluating boats and will also assist any boat owner. ABYC's address is 3069 Solomons Island Rd., Bowie, MD 20715. Names of marine surveyors may be found in telephone directories and on the Internet.

Cruising and Racing

For every 10 people who sail, five probably hope to cruise around the world and three hope to win a national racing championship. Of course, not all of them fulfill their ambitions. Most end up happily joining the remaining two sailors in pleasant daysailing with an occasional cruise or race. But dreams of great adventure live on wherever there are wind, water, and sails.

As we saw in chapter 1, cruising and racing boats can be very different. There also are differences in the ways they are sailed. Where cruising sailors set their sails to produce the most comfort in the wind gusts, racing sailors usually set enough sail to produce the best speed in the wind lulls. To put it another way, most cruisers usually sail in a comfortable low or middle gear, while racers usually are in a hard-driving high gear.

Here we will say a word or two about those great lures of new sailors, cruising and racing, and about how to get involved with them.

Learning How to Sail. The basic skills of boathandling under sail must be mastered if boating is to be more than powering around in calms with the engine on. The best way is to learn how to sail in a small boat under trained instructors at a community or commercial sailing school. Dinghies and keel daysailers are the most effective boats for learning because they reward good technique and punish mistakes more quickly than big boats.

Once you've learned the basic skills, the next step is to try sailing under the tutelage of an experienced friend or an instructor who can tutor you in the basic skills, including anchoring, docking, and navigating. Many charter companies lease boats with sailing instructors on board.

Chartering. You don't have to own a boat in order to go cruising. Many people who love cruising but who don't have the time, energy, and money to bother with upkeep are happy chartering (renting) boats. For the price of the annual upkeep of a 35-foot boat, you should be able to charter a boat of comparable size for two or three weeks in almost any of the world's desirable sailing grounds. Big charter companies can offer boats not only in such popular American areas as the Maine coast, Chesapeake Bay, the Florida Keys, Lake Huron, and Puget Sound, but also in Tahiti, the Caribbean, Greece, New Zealand, Scotland, and other fine places.

The northern areas are available only in the summer, but most others have excellent all-year sailing. The Virgin Islands, for example, may be warmer during the summer than the peak winter season, but summer winds are reliable there and charter fees are lower in July than February.

Boats may be chartered either with paid professional crew (typically a captain and cook) or "bare-boat," without paid crew. The former appeals to people who want instruction and help with heavy loads. The latter is attractive to people who can handle a boat alone.

There are two types of charter operators. The simplest is the individual boat owner who cannot use her boat every week and wants to recoup some expenses. The other is a company that owns a fleet of boats for full-time charter duty, usually in resort areas. Chartering from a fleet operator may be more expensive but usually guarantees prompt service on the water should you require repairs in a hurry.

Boats for charter are listed in advertising and classified sections of many boating magazines, some of which also publish evaluations of charter companies.

Bare-boat charters usually cannot be arranged unless the charterer is a qualified sailor with experience in basic seamanship and sailing, including the skills of steering effectively to windward, reefing, anchoring, and docking. Owners and managers of charter boats usually require prospective charterers to prove their sailing competence by submitting a résumé of their experience or passing a test.

Boat Ownership. Chartering may not be sufficient to satisfy a sailor's appetite. People choose boats to purchase for many reasons, good and poor. Everybody wants a good-looking vessel, but smart prospective boat owners place higher priorities on the boat's cost, ease of handling, speed, stability, and seaworthiness using factors that we examined in chapter 1.

A common mistake is to purchase too large a boat for the owner's pocketbook, physical strength, and sailing ability. Two guidelines here are helpful: first, annual maintenance of a fiberglass boat costs about 10 percent of the purchase price (and much more for a wooden boat); second, the largest sail that a fit person can handle is about 600 square feet. These are two reasons why so many sailors own boats in the 30–38 foot range.

Used boats may appear to be bargains, but anybody looking at a used boat should be alert to hidden structural problems that only a careful inspection by a professional marine surveyor will turn up.

Types of Cruises. One of the pleasures of sailing is its variety. The general cruising categories are, first, coastal (or alongshore) cruising for people who anchor at night and, second, long-distance (or ocean) cruising for those who do not.

In good weather, a well-built, well-handled cruising boat larger than about 25 feet can sail overnight to find a new coast to cruise along. People who have never sailed overnight or longer without stopping have missed out on the wonderful experience of waking up on a boat that is under way. But much can also be said for "gunkholing" (exploring small coves and waterways). Plenty of adventure can be found near shore, and

Cruising and Racing

nothing quite relaxes a mind exhausted by shoreside worries as returning to a favorite harbor in just the right vessel.

Racing. Wherever there are sailors there is sailboat racing. Every weekend and on many weekday evenings throughout the year, winter and summer, hundreds of thousands of sailors aged eight to 80 compete in sailboats of all sizes. You can have just as much fun banging about a lake in a Sunfish as racing on the high seas in a $5 million ocean racer. Besides offering enjoyment and an outlet for competitive spirit, racing is one of the best ways to learn how to steer and trim a sail well.

Until the 1990s, almost all racing was by amateurs, but there now is a band of professional sailors racing for pay in the America's Cup and other contests.

One-Design Racing. The most popular kind of racing is one-design competition, which gets its name from the fact that all the boats in the race have the same shape and sail area, and so they are potentially equally fast. This leaves winning up to the skipper and crew, although the hull, rigging, and sails must be carefully refined, too. One-designs sail relatively short day races, lasting between 30 minutes and 3 hours.

Few competitive sports offer as much choice as one-design racing. When choosing a class, first figure out how much money, time, and energy you can afford to expend, then look around for local classes that fit your requirements. Some extremely ambitious, skilled sailors are attracted to the highly competitive Olympic classes.

Handicap Racing. Besides one-design racing between equal boats there is also handicap racing between different types and sizes under rules intended to allow boats of all sizes a chance to win. Again there are choices. All-out ocean racers built solely for competition, with almost no cruising amenities, usually race under complex international rules like the International Measurement System (IMS), which calculates handicaps based on a boat weight, sail area, and measurements. Then, for cruiser-racers, there are rules like the Performance Handicap Racing Fleet (PHRF) rule, which assigns handicaps through evaluations of the boat's performance rather than her measurements.

How Races Are Conducted. Most races start between a buoy and a boat called the committee boat. A series of signals indicate the time left to the start, and boats maneuver to get the best position on the starting line when the start signal appears. They then sail around a course defined by buoys called marks (turning marks) until they reach the finish line. Small one-designs may sail a 3-mile course while cruiser-racers and America's Cup boats may cover 25 or more miles in a day. The winner of a one-design race is the first boat to finish; in a handicap race it is the boat with the lowest corrected time, after handicaps are computed.

Distance races are started the same way. Some are finished in the same location after the boats sail around a buoy or island and back, but long-distance races of 300–2,500 miles may run from one port to another — for example, from Los Angeles to Honolulu; Newport, Rhode Island, to Bermuda; and Chicago to Mackinac Island, Michigan.

The Racing Rules. Written rules keep racing fair and boats from colliding. In most sports the rules are enforced by referees, but in sailboat racing the rules usually are enforced by the competitors themselves (although referees may also be used). Racing sailors are encouraged to acknowledge rules violations. The penalty is to stop and sail two complete circles (thereby losing distance) before racing on. But if one boat "protests" another, claiming that the second boat violated a rule, and the second boat does not take the penalty, a post-race hearing may lead to the imposition of a lower finish position or even disqualification. The following four right-of-way rules often apply. Note that the first three are similar to the rules of the road.

Port tack keep clear: When boats are on different tacks, a boat on the port tack must keep clear of a boat on the starboard tack .

Windward boat keep clear: When boats are on the same tack and are overlapped, the windward boat must keep clear of the leeward boat.

Overtaking boat keep clear: When boats are on the same tack and not overlapped, the boat astern (overtaking) must keep clear of the boat ahead.

Do not tack or jibe too close: A tacking or jibing boat must keep clear of other boats.

Other rules: (1) Boats changing course or acquiring right of way must give other boats a chance to keep clear. (2) At marks or obstructions, outside boats must give inside boats room to pass. (3) The penalty for hitting a mark is to sail one circle. (4) Boats crossing the starting line before the start signal must turn back and recross the line.

The United States Sailing Association (US Sailing) publishes and distributes the complete *Racing Rules of Sailing* as well as a handy summary of the rules and an excellent guide by David Perry. Contact US Sailing through its Internet site and at PO Box 1260, 15 Maritime Drive, Portsmouth, RI 02871.

Racing Organizations. The official national governing bodies of sailboat racing in North America are the United States Sailing Association, or US Sailing, and the Canadian Yachting Association, or CYA (1600 James Naismith Drive, Suite 504, Gloucester, Ontario K1B 5N4). They publish the racing rules and instructional manuals, manage handicap systems, and run training and other programs that concern racers and all other sailors.

Children and Sailing

While there is no best age for learning how to sail, it is a fine thing to be able to start out in childhood, when the senses are wide open and the mind is relatively uncluttered by prejudices accumulated over the years. Here are some thoughts on easing children into sailing by someone who has had long on-the-water experience both as a child and as a parent.

Begin by teaching swimming and rowing to acquaint children with the water. Then move on to basic sailing skills. Theory can wait until kids have taken some science courses at school. Put children in boats small enough so the strains can be easily managed, like the Optimist Pram or Blue Jay. Or in a large boat, assign a child a job with a relatively light load, like casting off a sheet. Encourage the child to steer.

Cautiously introduce racing. While kids will enjoy informal tests of speed that are part of fun drills (like sailing backwards and without a rudder), serious racing should be postponed until they have sailed at least two years. Failure in competition can discourage love of sailing much too early in life.

Encourage playful "messing around in boats," as Kenneth Graham wrote in *The Wind in the Willows*. Sailing and especially racing can get so serious that they constipate the flow of enjoyment. In a boat as well as a Little League team, drilling skills into a child's skull can easily be overvalued by concerned parents and coaches. Encourage kids to take reasonable chances, to play, and to explore in their boats. An on-the-water game of tag with a tennis ball can be a joyous event.

Encourage children to learn about the world of water. Most kids are fascinated by the shore, lakes, the sea, natural marine life, and the weather. Whatever children learn about them will increase their pleasure and respect for the environment. Most areas near water have nature centers.

Sailing Schools. Sailing is taught in public community programs, private sailing schools, and yacht club junior programs. A sailing school (for children and also adults) should meet the standards set by the United States Sailing Association.

Here are some basic concerns: The school must exhibit a strong concern for safety, and Coast Guard–approved life jackets must be required for all sailors. Boats for children must be self-righting and self-rescuing. The instructors must be certified by US Sailing, the American Red Cross, or another respected authority, and must be trained in first aid.

Safety Tips for Children.

Teach children to swim early. The earlier they know how to swim, the more they will respect and enjoy boats and the water.

Protect against sunburn. Children must be lathered with high-SPF sun lotions and protected by hats and long-sleeve shirts. A bad sunburn early in life can discourage a child; it surely makes a melanoma much more likely later in life.

Use safety equipment. Put kids in life jackets and/or safety harnesses and keep them there. Install netting in the lifelines to keep young children on deck. Older children may be cautiously taken out of life jackets once they have proved their swimming ability and endurance.

Impose limits. Point out such danger areas as the boom, a sheet that is under load, and a spinning steering wheel. Make sure the child knows who is in charge on deck, and what the boundaries of wandering are. As at home, develop a tone of voice that says, "Listen to me! This is serious!"

Know where children are. Have them check in regularly with the steerer. It helps to have each child wear clothing of a distinctive color.

Glossary of Sailing Terms

Here are definitions of the most commonly encountered boating terms. Other definitions may be found in the text, using the index. For more on this fascinating and often complex language, see the author's *The Illustrated Dictionary of Boating Terms* (1998), which defines more than 2,000 terms.

aback. With sails trimmed to windward.

abaft. Behind.

abeam. At right angles to a boat.

aboard. On a boat.

adrift. Unsecured.

afloat. Floating.

aft, after. Toward the stern.

aground. Stuck on the water's bottom.

aid to navigation. A buoy, lighthouse, or other channel marker.

air. Wind.

alee. To leeward, away from the wind. "Hard a-lee" is the command for tacking.

aloft. In the rigging above the deck.

alongside. Beside.

amidship(s). In the middle of the boat.

angle of attack. The angle between the sail and the apparent wind or the rudder, keel, or centerboard and the water flow.

apparent wind. The wind felt on the moving boat.

appendage. A rudder, keel, centerboard, or skeg.

astern. Behind the boat.

athwartships. Across the boat.

auxiliary. A sailboat that has an engine.

aweigh. Describes an anchor unhooked from the bottom.

B

back. (1) To trim a sail to windward; (2) counterclockwise shift in wind direction.

backstay. A stay running aft from the upper part of the mast, either permanent or running (adjustable).

backwind. Wind flowing from a forward sail into the leeward side of an after sail.

bail. To remove water with a bucket.

bailers. Sluices in the bilge of a small boat to remove water.

balance. The degree to which all the forces on a boat are symmetrical so she sails with slight weather helm.

ballast. Weight in the keel or bilge on the windward side that restrains the boat from heeling too far.

Barber hauler. A sail control that changes the athwartships lead of the jib sheet.

batten. A wooden or plastic slat inserted in the leech of a sail.

batten down. Secure in preparation for heavy weather.

beam (BM.). A boat's greatest width.

beamy. Wide.

bear away. To head off, away from the wind.

bearing. The angle from the boat to an object.

beat. A close-hauled course.

below. Beneath the deck.

bend on sails. To install sails on the boom and headstay.

Bermudian (Marconi) rig. A three-sided mainsail.

berth. (1) A boat's position when tied to a pier or float; (2) a wide berth is a large margin of safety; (3) a bed in a boat.

bight. Any part of a line between its ends.

bilge. The lowest part of a boat's hull.

binnacle. A support or pedestal for a compass.

bitter end. The end of a line.

blanket. To come between the wind and a sail so the sail is not full.

block. A pulley on a boat.

board. (1) Centerboard; (2) to go on a boat; (3) a leg or part of a course.

boat. A vessel small enough to be put aboard a ship.

boat hook. A pole with a hook on its end.

boat speed. Speed through the water.

boltrope. The rope along the luff or foot of a sail.

boom. The spar that extends and supports the foot of a mainsail.

boom vang. A tackle or rod that restrains the boom from lifting.

boot top. The painted band on the boat's topsides at the waterline.

bottom. (1) The submerged land; (2) the boat's hull under the water, or underbody.

bow. The most forward part of the boat.

breeze. Wind.

broach. For a boat to go out of control and head up or off sharply.

broad off, broad on. About 45° from the bow or stern.

bulkhead. A wall below that provides athwartships support for the hull.

bunk. A bed in a boat; also berth.

buoy. A floating object marking a channel, an obstruction, or a mooring.

buoyancy. The upward force that keeps a boat floating.

by the lee. Sailing on a run with the wind coming over the leeward quarter.

C

cabin. A room in a boat.

calm. Little or no wind. A flat calm is totally devoid of wind.

canvas. Sails or sail area.

capsize. To turn over.

cardinal points. North, east, south, and west. The intercardinal points are northeast, southeast, southwest and northwest.

carry away. To break.

cast off. To let a line go.

catamaran (cat). A multihull with two hulls.

cat boat. A wide, shallow boat with a large mainsail and no jib.

cat rig. A single- or two-masted boat with no jib.

caught aback. With the sails backed, or trimmed to windward.

centerboard. A retractable appendage in the keel or hull.

center of effort. The point in the sail plan that is the balance point for all the aerodynamic forces.

center of lateral resistance. The point in the hull's underbody that is the balance point for all the hydrodynamic forces.

centerline. An imaginary line that runs down the middle of the boat from bow to stern.

chafe. Abrasion or wear.

chain plate. A strap on the hull to which stays are secured.

channel. Water sufficiently deep to sail in, often marked by aids to navigation (channel markers).

chart. A nautical map.

charter. To rent a boat.

chine. The intersection between the topsides and the boat's bottom. A hard chine makes a sharp turn.

chock. A fairlead for the anchor rode and docking lines.

chop. Short, steep waves.

chord. An imaginary line drawn between the luff and leech of a sail. The chord depth is the deepest part of the sail.

circumnavigation. A voyage around something, often the world.

cleat. A wooden, plastic, or metal object to which lines under strain are secured. There are two kinds of cleats, horn and quick-action.

clevis pin. A large pin that secures one fitting to another.

clew. The after lower corner of a mainsail, jib, or mizzen, and either lower corner of a spinnaker.

close-hauled. Sailing as close to the wind as is efficient; also beating, on the wind.

coaming. A low wall around a cockpit.

Coast Guard. United States Coast Guard (USCG).

coastal. Near shore.

cockpit. A recessed area in the deck containing the tiller or wheel.

coil. To arrange a line or rope in easily manageable loops so it can be stowed.

COLREGS. The international Navigation Rules.

companionway. Steps leading down from the deck to the cabin.

compass. A magnetized device oriented to the globe's magnetic field that indicates directions and bearings in compass degrees on the compass card.

compass rose. A duplicate of the compass card printed on a chart.

confused. Describes a sea with waves from many directions. *See* slop.

cotter pin. A small pin used to secure a clevis pin and to keep turnbuckles from unwinding.

course. (1) The compass direction that is steered; (2) the sequence of buoys rounded in a race.

cradle. A frame that supports a boat when she's hauled out of the water.

crew. Everybody who helps sail a boat.

cringle. A large reinforced eye in a sail.

cruise. Two or more days spent living on a boat that is underway, with stops for the night.

cruiser-racer. A boat comfortable enough for cruising and fast enough for racing. Also racer-cruiser.

cruising boat. A boat used mostly for cruising.

Cunningham. A line controlling tension along a sail's luff.

current. Horizontal movement of the water caused by tide or wind.

custom boat. A boat built specifically for one client, as against a stock boat.

cut. The shape or design of a sail.

cutter. A single-masted boat that flies two jibs at a time.

D

daggerboard. A centerboard that is retracted vertically rather than hinged.

danger sector. The fixed red part of a lighthouse's light shining over shoals.

daysailer. A boat without a cabin that is used for short sails or racing.

dead. Exactly.

dead-end. To secure an end of a line to an object.

dead reckoning (DR). the calculation of a boat's position based on course and distance run.

deck. The lid on a hull.

depower. To lessen heeling forces by making sails less full.

deviation. A compass error caused by metal objects on board.

dinghy. A small, light boat.

displacement. A boat's weight — more accurately, the weight of the water she displaces.

displacement boat. A relatively heavy boat that cannot plane.

dock. (1) The water next to a float or pier; (2) to bring a boat alongside a float or pier.

docking line. A line securing a boat to a float or pier.

dodger. A fold-up spray shield at the forward end of the cockpit.

double bottom. A watertight compartment between the bottom and the sole, or floor.

douse. To lower.

downhaul. A line that holds an object down.

downwind. Away from the direction from which the wind blows.

draft (draught). (1) The boat's depth below the water; (2) the amount and position of fullness in a sail.

drag. (1) Resistance; (2) when an anchor breaks out and skips along the bottom.

drift. A current's velocity.

drifting. In a calm, to be carried by the current.

E

earing. A reefing line.

ease. (1) To let out a sheet, (2) to reduce pull on the helm.

ebb. The dropping, outgoing tide.

Glossary of Sailing Terms

eddy. A circular current.

end-for-end. To reverse a line.

estimated position (EP). A best estimate of a boat's position based on her dead reckoning plot and one bearing.

eye. A loop.

eye of the wind. The precise wind direction.

F

fair. Without obstruction.

fairlead. A fitting through which a line passes so chafe is avoided.

fairway. The middle of a channel.

fair wind. A reach or run.

fake. To make large loops on deck with a line in order to eliminate kinks.

fastening. A screw or bolt.

feel. The steerer's sense of how well the boat is sailing.

fender. A rubber bumper hung between the boat and a float or pier.

fend off. To push off.

fetch. (1) To sail so the boat clears a buoy or other object; also lay; (2) the distance to the windward shore.

fitting. A piece of gear.

fix. A position based on two or more crossed bearings.

float. A floating platform to which boats may be tied.

flood. The rising, incoming tide.

fluky. Unpredictable and weak.

following sea. Waves from astern.

foot. (1) The bottom edge of a sail; (2) to steer slightly lower than close-hauled in order to increase boat speed.

force. A measurement of wind speed and sea state in the Beaufort Scale.

fore. Prefix indicating location toward the bow.

fore and aft. Everywhere on the boat.

forereach. To carry way while heading almost into the wind.

foresail. A jib.

forestay. A stay running from the foredeck aft of the bow to the mast, on which a small headsail is set.

foretriangle. The area bounded by the mast, foredeck, and headstay.

forward. Toward the bow.

foul. (1) Tangled; (2) a violation of a racing rule.

foul-weather gear. Water-resistant clothing and boots.

founder. To swamp or sink.

fractional rig. A rig whose headstay goes partway up the mast.

free. (1) On a broad reach or run; (2) a freeing wind is a lift, or a shift aft.

freeboard. The distance from the deck to the water, or the height of the topsides.

fresh air, wind. Wind of about 16–22 knots.

front. The approaching edge of a high-pressure or low-pressure system.

full. Not luffing.

full sail. All sails set.

furl. To roll up and secure a sail to a boom or stay.

G

gadget. A specialized piece of gear.

gaff rig. With a four-sided mainsail; the top edge is supported by a spar called a gaff.

galley. A boat's kitchen.

gangway. An opening in the lifelines to facilitate boarding from a float or another boat.

gasket. A sail tie.

gear. Equipment.

genoa. A large jib whose clew overlaps the mast and mainsail.

gilguy. A line or length of shock cord that holds a halyard away from the mast.

gimbals. Supports that allow a compass or stove to remain level as the boat heels.

give. Stretch.

give-way vessel. The vessel that does not have the right of way.

gooseneck. The fitting securing the forward end of the boom to the mast.

grommet. A small metal ring set into a sail.

ground tackle. The anchor and anchor rode.

gunwale (pronounced "gun'l"). A boat's rail at the edge of the deck.

gust. A strong puff of wind.

guy. A line controlling the position of a spinnaker pole; the after guy pulls the pole back and eases it forward and the foreguy restrains it from lifting.

H

halyard. A line or wire rope that hoists a sail and keeps it up.

hand. (1) A crew member; (2) to lower.

hank. A small snap hook that secures the jib luff to the headstay.

harden up. To head up.

hard over. As far as possible in one direction.

hatch. An opening in a deck, covered by a hatch cover.

haul. To veer, or shift direction clockwise.

haul in. To trim.

haul out. To pull out of the water.

head. (1) The top corner of a sail; (2) a boat's bathroom.

headboard. The reinforcement in the head of a sail.

header. A wind shift requiring the steerer to head off.

heading. The course.

head off. To alter course to leeward; also bear off.

headroom. A cabin's height. Standing headroom allows a person to stand.

headsail. A jib.

head sea. Waves from ahead.

headstay. The stay running from the bow to the mast.

head-to-wind. With the bow heading dead into the wind.

head up. To alter course to windward; also harden up.

headway. Forward motion.

heave. To throw.

heave-to. To nearly stop a boat under sail.

heavy air, wind. Wind of gale force, stronger than 28 knots.

heavy weather. Rough seas and strong winds.

heel. A boat's athwartships tilt.

helm. (1) The tiller or steering wheel; (2) the boat's tendency to head off course: with weather helm, she tends to head up, with lee helm, to head off.

helmsman. See steerer.

high. (1) Several degrees beyond the required course; (2) too close.

high cut. With the clew high off the deck.

high performance. Fast.

hike. To lean over the windward rail to counter the heeling forces on the sails.

hiking strap. A strap in the cockpit that restrains a hiking sailor's feet.

hockle. A kink.

holding ground. The bottom in a harbor.

hounds. The location of the jib halyard block on a mast.

house. The roof of a cabin extending above deck.

hull. A boat's shell, exclusive of appendages, deck, cabin, and rig.

hull speed. A boat's theoretical maximum speed.

I

inboard. In from the rail.

inflatable. A life jacket, life raft, or other safety device that must be inflated.

in irons. Head-to-wind with no headway or sternway.

J

jackline. A line, wire, or strap on deck onto which safety harness tethers are clipped.

jackstay. A short stay running from the foredeck to the mast; also babystay.

jib. A sail carried on the headstay or forestay; also headsail, foresail.

jibe. To change tacks by heading off until the sails swing across the boat.

jigger. Mizzen.

jumper stay. A short stay on the forward side of the mast, held out by a jumper strut.

jury rig. An improvised replacement for damaged gear.

K

kedge off. To use an anchor to pull a grounded boat back into deep water.

keel. An appendage or fin on the boat's bottom that provides deep ballast and lateral area.

ketch. A two-masted boat whose after mast, the mizzenmast, is shorter than the forward mast, the mainmast, and is also located forward of the rudder post.

kink. A twist in a line; also hockle.

knockdown. A drastic increase in the angle of heel.

knot. (1) Turns in a line to form a loop or secure it to another object; (2) 1 nautical mile per hour.

L

land breeze. A wind blowing from the shore to the water.

landmark. A highly visible object on the shore.

lanyard. A short line.

lash. To tie.

launch. (1) To move a boat into the water from land; (2) a ferry between land and a moored boat; also shore boat.

lay. To sail a course that will clear a buoy or shoal; also fetch.

layout. The arrangement of gear on deck or of furniture in the cabin.

lead (pronounced "leed"). (1) A block for a sheet; (2) to pass a line through a block or fairlead; (3) a short length of chain at the bottom of an anchor rode.

lead (pronounced "led") **line.** A length of rope with a weight at the end used to determine water depth.

lee, leeward. Downwind.

leech. The after edge of a mainsail, jib, or mizzen, and both sides of a spinnaker.

lee helm. A boat's tendency to head off, away from the wind; opposite of weather helm.

leeway. Side-slippage to leeward.

leg. A portion of a passage or race.

length. Length overall (LOA) is the boat's length from bow to stern on deck. Length on the waterline or waterline length (LWL) is the boat's length at the water's surface.

lie ahull. For a boat that is underway to sit with no sails set.

life jacket. A buoyant device that keeps its wearer afloat; also PFD.

lifeline. A coated wire above the deck that restrains the crew.

life raft. An inflatable boat for use in emergencies.

lift. A wind shift allowing the steerer to head up.

light. (1) Describes a sail that is luffing; (2) an illuminated aid to navigation or a boat's navigation light.

light air, wind. Wind less than 8 knots.

light line. Line ¼ inch in diameter or smaller.

light sails. Spinnakers and mizzen staysails.

line. Any length of rope that has a particular use.

low cut. With the clew near the deck.

lubber's line. A post in a compass used to determine the course or a bearing.

luff. (1) The forward edge of a sail; (2) bubbling or flapping in a sail.

M

magnetic. Relative to magnetic north, as against true.

mainmast. The mast, or the tallest of two masts.

mainsail (pronounced "mains'l"). The

Glossary of Sailing Terms

sail hoisted on the after side of the mainmast.

make fast. To cleat a line.

Marconi rig. Bermudian rig.

marina. An area of piers and wharfs where boats tie up.

mariner. Someone who goes out in a boat or ship.

mark. A buoy used in a race course.

marline. A general-purpose tarred light line.

marlinspike. A pointed tool on a sailor's knife used to pry open knots, start holes in wood, and accomplish other jobs.

mast. A wooden or aluminum pole supported by standing rigging from which sails are set.

masthead. The top of the mast.

masthead fly. A wind direction indicator at the masthead.

masthead light. A white light illuminated when powering at night, located not at the top of the mast but about two-thirds of the way up the mast; also steaming light, bow light.

mast step. The support for the bottom (heel or butt) of the mast.

mizzen (jigger). The small, aftermost sail on a ketch or yawl, set on the mizzenmast.

moderate air, wind. Wind of about 9–15 knots.

monohull. A boat with one hull.

mooring. A permanently set anchor with buoy for tying up.

motor sailer. A sailboat with an especially large engine.

multihull. A boat with two hulls (a catamaran) or three hulls (a trimaran).

N

nautical mile. 1.15 statute miles; 1 knot is 1 nautical mile per hour.

Navigation Rules. The United States inland and the international (COLREGS) rules for preventing collisions; also rules of the road.

No-go zone. The angle to the wind at which the sails do not fill.

O

ocean racer. A boat used for racing overnight or long distances.

offshore. (1) Out of sight of land; (2) from the land toward the water.

off the wind. Reaching or running.

on board. On a boat.

onshore. From the water toward the land.

on the beam. Abeam.

on the bow (stern). To one side of the bow (stern); also off the bow (stern).

on the wind. Close-hauled.

one-design. A single design to which many sister ships are built.

open boat. A boat without a deck.

outboard. (1) Out toward and beyond the rail; (2) a retractable engine mounted at the stern.

outhaul. A sail control that secures the clew of a boomed sail, and adjusts tension along its foot.

overhang. The distance the bow and stern extend beyond the waterline.

overhaul. (1) To clear or inspect a line; (2) to overtake.

overlap. Alongside of.

overpowered. Heeling too far, difficult to steer.

overstand. To lay or fetch a buoy or shoal with room to spare.

overtake. To come up on from astern.

P

padeye. A metal loop to which blocks and shackles are secured.

painter. A bow line on a dinghy.

part. (1) To break; (2) one of the sections of line in a tackle.

partners. The deck opening for the mast.

passage. Some time spent under way.

pay out. To ease.

pendant (pronounced "pennant"). A short length of wire or line used as an extender for a halyard, tack, or mooring.

PFD (personal flotation device). The official term for life jacket and other flotation.

pier. A platform on posts that sticks out from the shore.

piloting. Navigation within sight of land.

pinch. To sail too close to the wind when close-hauled.

pitchpole. To somersault on a wave.

plane. To skip up and across the water at high speed.

play. (1) To trim a sheet assiduously; (2) a loose fit in a fitting.

plot. To draw a boat's course and position on a chart.

point. To sail close to the wind.

points of sail. Close-hauled, reaching, and running.

pooped. Smashed by a wave breaking over the stern.

port. (1) The left side when facing forward; (2) a small window; (3) a commercial harbor.

porthole. A small round window; also port.

protected water. A body of water partially surrounded by land.

pound. To smash down heavily on waves.

preventer. A line that restrains the boom from swinging.

puff. A quick, local increase in wind velocity.

pulpit. A stainless-steel guardrail around the bow or stern.

Q

quarter. The side of the boat near the stern.

R

race. (1) An especially strong current; (2) an organized competition.

rail. The outer edge of the deck.

rake. The forward or after tilt of a mast.

range. (1) The difference in water level between high and low tides; (2) the full extent of a light's visibility; (3) two objects that, when aligned, indicate a channel or the course of another vessel.

reach. (1) To sail across the wind; (2) a channel between the mainland and an island.

reef. (1) To decrease a sail's size; (2) a shoal composed of rocks or coral.

reeve. To lead a line through a block or cringle.

regatta. A series of boat races.

render. To run easily through a block.

rhumb line. The most direct course between two points.

rig. (1) The spars, stays, sails, etc.; (2) to get a boat ready for sailing or prepare a sail or piece of gear for use.

rigging. The gear used to support the rig: standing rigging supports the mast, running rigging controls the sails.

right of way. The legal authority to stay on the present course under the Navigation Rules.

roach. The sail's area aft of the line running between its head and clew.

rode. The anchor line.

roller furl (reef). To stow or reef a sail by rolling it up.

rudder. An underwater flap adjusted by the helm to steer the boat. It pivots on the rudder post.

rules of the road. The Navigation Rules.

run. (1) A course with the wind astern; (2) distance covered.

running lights. Lights on a boat illuminated when under way at night.

S

safety harness. A body harness that is hooked to the boat to prevent falling overboard.

sail control. A line that shapes or holds a sail.

sail handling. The hoisting, trimming, and dousing of sails.

sail tie (stop). A strap for securing a furled sail; also gasket.

schooner. A boat with two or more masts, the forwardmost of which, the foremast, is shorter than the aftermost, the mainmast.

scope. The ratio between the amount of anchor rode let out and the depth of the water.

scow. A fast, flat-bottomed, blunt-bowed daysailer raced on lakes.

scull. To propel a boat by swinging the helm and rudder back and forth.

scupper. A deck or cockpit drain.

sea. (1) A wave; (2) a large body of salt water.

sea boot. A rubber boot for using on board.

sea breeze, lake breeze. A wind blowing from the water to the land.

seacock. A valve opening and closing a pipe through the hull.

sea condition. The size and shape of the waves.

seakindly. Comfortable in rough seas.

sea room. Enough distance from shore and shoals for safe sailing.

seaway. Rough water.

seaworthy. Able to survive heavy weather.

secure. To fasten or cleat.

self-bailing. Automatically draining.

self-steering. Automatically steering without a steerer.

set. (1) To raise a sail; (2) a current's direction.

set up. To rig.

shackle. A metal hook that secures a line to another object.

sheave (pronounced "shiv"). The roller in a block.

sheer. The curve of the rail.

sheet. The chief sail control, it pulls the sail aft and down.

shifty. Frequently changing direction.

ship. A vessel large enough to hold a boat.

shoal. Dangerously shallow water.

shoot. To head directly into the wind.

shorten sail. To reef or set a smaller sail.

shorthanded. With a small crew.

shroud. A side stay.

singlehanded. With only one person on board.

SSB. Single-sideband radiotelephone.

sister ships. Boats of the same design.

skeg. A small, fixed fin attached to the underbody near the stern.

skipper. The person in charge of a boat.

slack. (1) Not moving; (2) loose; (3) to ease.

slat. To roll in a calm with the sails slapping back and forth noisily.

slicker. A foul-weather jacket.

slip. A dock between two floats in a marina.

sloop. A single-masted boat that flies one jib at a time.

slop. An especially confused seaway.

slug. A fitting on a sail's luff or foot that attaches it to the mast or boom by being inserted into a groove.

snap hook (shackle). A spring-loaded hook or shackle.

snub. To wrap a line once around a winch or cleat so most of its pull is absorbed.

sole. A cabin or cockpit floor.

sound. To measure depth.

spar. Any mast, boom, gaff, or spinnaker pole.

speed made good. A boat's speed relative to land; also velocity made good (VMG).

spinnaker. A light, ballooning sail used when sailing off the wind.

splice. To make an eye in the end of a line or link two line ends together by interweaving strands.

spreader. An athwartships strut holding shrouds out from the mast and providing lateral support.

stanchion. A metal post supporting lifelines.

stand-on vessel. The boat with right-of-way.

Glossary of Sailing Terms

starboard. The right side, facing forward.

stay. A wire supporting the mast.

staysail. A small jib tacked down partway back from the headstay.

steer. To aim a boat.

steer by. Use as a guide when steering.

steerageway. Enough speed through the water to allow efficient steering.

steerer. The person who is steering; sometimes a helmsman.

stem. The forward edge of the bow.

step. To install a mast.

stern. The aftermost part of the hull.

sternway. Motion astern.

stiff. Resists heeling, not tender.

stock boat. A boat with many sister ships built by the same manufacturer from the same design.

stow. To put in the proper place.

strong air, wind. Wind of about 23–30 knots.

surf. To slide down the face of a wave.

swamp. To be filled with water.

swell. Long waves; also groundswell.

T

tack. (1) With the wind coming over one side or the other; (2) to change tacks by heading up until the sails swing across the boat; (3) the forward lower corner of a sail.

tack down. To secure the sail's tack.

tackle, block and tackle (pronounced "taykle"). A system of line and blocks that increases hauling power.

tail. To pull on a sheet or halyard behind a winch.

tang. A metal strap on a spar to which a stay or block is secured.

telltale. A piece of yarn or ribbon in the shrouds or on the sail to help the crew determine wind direction and sail trim.

tender. Heels quickly, not stiff.

thimble. A metal or plastic eye worked into an eye splice to protect the line or wire against chafe.

tide. The rise and fall of salt water due to the moon's and sun's gravitational pull.

tide rip. A line of rough water where two tidal currents meet.

tied-in reef. A reef secured by tying cringles to the boom, as against roller reef.

tight. Pulled hard or straight.

toggle. A hinged metal fitting in the standing rigging that keeps the stay and turnbuckle from bending.

topping lift. A line or wire that holds up a boom or spinnaker pole.

topsides. The outer sides of the hull.

trailerable. Describes a boat that can be placed on a trailer and towed behind a car.

transom. The athwartships-running surface at the stern.

trapeze. A wire hanging from a racing dinghy's mast, from which a crew member is suspended in order to counteract heeling forces.

traveler. An athwartships-running track for the main or jib sheet.

trim. (1) To pull in (a sheet); (2) the set of a sail; (3) the bow-up or bow-down attitude a boat assumes when she's at rest.

trimaran (tri). A multihull with three hulls.

trip. To break loose.

true. Relative to true north, as against magnetic.

true wind. The wind's direction and strength felt by a stationary object.

tune. To adjust the standing rigging until the mast is straight.

turnbuckle. A threaded fitting used to adjust a stay's length.

twist. The amount that a sail's leech sags off relative to the imaginary straight line between the clew and head.

two-block. To raise all the way.

U

under bare poles. With no sail set.

underbody. The part of the hull that is underwater.

under power. With the engine on.

under rigged. With not enough sail set; also undercanvassed.

under way. Moving.

unreeve. To remove a line from a block or cringle.

unrig. To remove or disassemble gear after it is used.

upwind. Toward the direction from which the wind blows.

USCG. United States Coast Guard.

US Sailing. United States Sailing Association, the governing body of sailboat racing in the US.

V

vang. The boom vang.

variable. Unsteady in strength and direction.

variation. The local difference in degrees between true and magnetic directions.

veer. A clockwise shift in the wind direction.

veer out (veer). To let out an anchor rode.

vent. A ventilator.

vessel. Any boat or ship.

VHF/FM. Very-high-frequency radiotelephone.

voyage. A long passage.

W

wake. The water turbulence left behind by a moving boat.

washboard. A removable slat in a companionway.

waterline. The boat at the water's surface.

way. Headway.

weather. (1) General atmospheric

conditions; (2) wind; (3) upwind; (4) to survive a storm.

weather helm. A boat's tendency to head up, into the wind; opposite of lee helm.

weigh anchor. Raise the anchor.

williwaw. A gust of wind down a hill.

winch. A geared drum used to pull lines.

windage. Wind resistance.

windlass. A winch for the anchor rode.

windward. Upwind.

wing-and-wing. With the jib and mainsail set on opposite sides when sailing on a run or broad reach.

working sails. The mainsail and smaller jibs.

Y

yacht. A well-built pleasure boat of a larger size.

yaw. To aim one side or another of the course.

yawl. A two-masted boat whose after mast, the mizzenmast, is shorter than the forward mast, the mainmast, and is located aft of the rudder post.

YC, yacht club. A club for pleasure sailors.

A Sailor's Library

Listed below are the titles of approximately 70 publications that a sailor should know about. Most of the books are in print, meaning that they may be ordered through bookstores and online book services. Others may be available in public libraries or from used-book services.

General. Badham, Michael, and Robby Robinson, ed. *Sailors' Secrets* (Camden, ME: International Marine, 1997). Practical tips for better sailing by a number of authorities, including the author of *Annapolis*.

Maloney, Elbert S. *Chapman Piloting, Seamanship and Small Boat Handling* (New York: Hearst Marine Books, 1996). "Chapman's" is a standard reference on many aspects of boating.

Rousmaniere, John. *The Illustrated Dictionary of Boating Terms* (New York: W.W. Norton, 1998). Over 2,000 terms in today's boating language.

Vigor, John. *The Practical Mariner's Book of Knowledge* (Camden, ME: International Marine, 1994). A collection of helpful tips.

Boat Design and Types. Brewer, Ted. *Understanding Boat Design,* 4th ed. (Camden, ME: International Marine, 1994). A relatively non-technical guide to how boats of all kinds are designed.

Killing, Steve, and Dougas Hunter. *Yacht Design Explained* (New York: W.W. Norton, 1998). An exceptionally clear, thorough survey of yacht design and how designers work.

Marchaj, C. A. *Seamanship* (Camden, ME: International Marine, 1996). A highly technical analysis of cruising boat design.

Rousmaniere, John, ed. *Desirable and Undesirable Characteristics of Offshore Yachts* (New York: W.W. Norton, 1986). A standard manual on choosing and rigging a monohull to take out in the ocean.

White, Chris. *The Cruising Multihull* (Camden, ME: International Marine, 1990). An excellent survey of cruising catamarans and trimarans and the skills used to handle them.

Cruising. Dashew, Linda and Steve. *Offshore Cruising Encyclopedia,* 2nd ed. (Tucson, AZ: Beowulf Publishing, 1997). A guide to every step of buying, preparing, and handling a boat offshore.

Hood, Jeremy R. *Safety Preparations for Cruising* (Dobbs Ferry, NY: Sheridan House, 1997). A manual on cruising seamanship that concentrates on safety.

Equipment and Maintenance. Calder, Nigel. *Boatowner's Mechanical and Electrical Manual,* 2nd ed.(Camden, ME: International Marine, 1996), *Marine Diesel Engines* (Camden, ME: International Marine, 1987). Two of the best books on their topics.

Hinckley, Henry R., III. *The Hinckley Guide to Yacht Care* (Camden, ME: International Marine, 1998). An excellent guide to first-class boat maintenance.

Hinz, Earl. *The Complete Book of Anchoring and Mooring,* 2nd ed. (Centreville, MD: Cornell Maritime Press, 1994). A fine book on anchoring.

Taylor, Roger. *Knowing the Ropes: Selecting, Rigging, and Handling Lines Aboard,* 2nd ed. (Camden, ME: International Marine, 1993). Knots and ropework, modern as well as traditional.

United States Sailing Association. *Safety Recommendations for Offshore Sailing; Safety Recommendations for Cruising Sailboats* (Portsmouth, RI: US Sailing Association, annual). Two excellent guides to equipping a cruising boat.

West Marine Master Catalog (West Marine, annual). The catalog of America's largest mail-order boating supply outlet includes much solid how-to advice.

Heavy Weather. Coles, K. Adlard, and Peter Bruce. *Heavy Weather Sailing,* 4th ed. (Camden, ME: International Marine, 1992). A bible of heavy weather seamanship.

Dashew, Steve, ed. *Defensive Seamanship* (Tucson, AZ: Beowulf Publishing, 1999). A collection of advisories by several writers (including the author of this book) on offshore and heavy-weather seamanship.

Farrington, Tony. *Rescue in the Pacific* (Camden, ME: International Marine, 1995). A force-12 storm in the South Pacific and how several crews survived it.

Pardey, Lin and Larry. *Storm Tactics Handbook* (Salt Lake City: Pardey, 1995). A manual by a thoughtful circumnavigating couple.

Rousmaniere, John. *"Fastnet, Force 10"* (New York: W.W. Norton, 1980). The story of the 1979 Fastnet storm, with many seamanship lessons.

Shane, Victor. *Drag Device Data Base: Using Parachutes, Sea Anchors, and Drogues to Cope with Heavy Weather,* 4th ed. (Summerland, CA: Para-Anchors International, 1997). Storm tactics, sea anchors, and drogues; essential reading for anyone thinking of going offshore.

Navigation. Blewitt, Mary. *Celestial Navigation for Yachtsmen* (Camden, ME: International Marine, 1996). This little book probably has launched more celestial navigators than any other manual.

Coote, John O. *Yacht Navigation My Way* (New York: W.W. Norton, 1989). An excellent review of basics and an experienced navigator's tricks.

Dunlap, G. D. and H. H. Shufeldt. *Dutton's Navigation and Piloting,* 14th ed. (Annapolis, MD: Naval Institute Press, 1985). A standard text; encyclopedic.

Eyges, Leonard. *The Practical Pilot* (Camden, ME: International Marine, 1989). A thorough survey.

Schlereth, Hewitt. *Commonsense*

Coastal Navigation (New York: W. W. Norton, 1982). One of the best surveys of the basics of piloting.

Racing. Conner, Dennis, and Michael Levitt. *Sail Like a Champion* (New York: St. Martin's Press, 1992). A manual by one of the most successful skippers of his time.

Jobson, Gary, and Jay Kehoe. *The Winner's Guide to Optimist Sailing* (New York: Simon & Schuster, 1997). An introduction to racing the standard boat for youngsters.

Perry, David. *Understanding the Racing Rules of Sailing* (Portsmouth, RI: US Sailing Association, 1997). An excellent guide.

Walker, Stuart H. *Advanced Racing Tactics* (New York: W. W. Norton, 1992). One of many good manuals by a keenly observant skipper.

White, Rick, and Mary Wells. *Catamaran Racing for the 90s* (Key Largo, FL: Ram Press, 1997). A manual on racing small catamarans.

Sails and Sail Trim. Marchaj, C. A. *Sail Performance: Techniques to Maximize Sail Power* (Camden, ME: International Marine, 1996). The most complete book on sailing theory; highly technical.

Whidden, Tom, and Michael Levitt. *The Art and Science of Sails* (New York: St. Martin's Press, 1990). The best book on modern sailmaking and sail trim.

Traditional Boats and Skills. Cunliffe, Tom. *Hand, Reef, and Steer* (Dobbs Ferry, NY: Sheridan House, 1992). Traditional rigs and boats and the special skills needed to sail them.

Toss, Brion. *The Complete Rigger's Apprentice* (Camden, ME: International Marine, 1998). Exactly what the title says. Encyclopedic in scope.

Weather. Dashew, Steve and Linda. *Mariner's Weather Handbook* (Tucson, AZ: Beowulf Publishing, 1999). A manual for analyzing and forecasting weather and for choosing weather tactics.

Kotsch, William J. *Weather for the Mariner*, 3rd ed. (Annapolis, MD: Naval Institute Press, 1983). A standard technical guide to weather theory and forecasting for mariners.

Lee, Albert. *Weather Wisdom* (New York: Doubleday, 1976). The source of some of the useful weather rhymes in our chapter on weather.

Rubin, Louis D., Sr., and Jim Duncan. *The Weather Wizard's Cloud Book* (Chapel Hill, NC: Algonquin Books, 1989). How to predict weather by looking at the clouds; lively and direct.

Watts, Alan. *The Weather Handbook* (Dobbs Ferry, NY: Sheridan House, 1994). A guide to marine weather for the average sailor.

History. Rousmaniere, John. *The Golden Pastime: A New History of Yachting* (New York: W. W. Norton, 1986); a history of pleasure boating. *The Low Black Schooner: Yacht America* (Mystic, CT: Mystic Seaport Museum, 1987); a biography of the most famous pleasure boat in history. *A Picture History of the America's Cup* (Mystic, CT: Mystic Seaport Museum, 1988); a handsome history of the America's Cup.

Some Classics. Many wonderful writers have been sailors, and vice versa. Here are some of the author's favorite stories about cruising and racing.

Childers, Erskine. *The Riddle of the Sands* (1903). The only great spy story whose solution lies in a tide table; made into a good movie.

Griffiths, Maurice. *The Magic of the Swatchways* (1932). Charming stories of cruising in shoal waters by the long-time editor of *Yachting Monthly*.

Howland, Llewellyn. *Sou'West & by West of Cape Cod* (1947). Sailing life in southern Massachusetts at the turn of the last century.

Loomis, Alfred F. *The Hotspur Story* (1954). A loving history of a sailing family and their boat, by the best American boating writer of the 1920–1950 era.

MacGregor, John. *The Voyage Alone in the Yawl Rob Roy* (1867). The first great cruise story.

Mitchell, Carleton. *Passage East* (1953). One of the very best sailor-writers lyrically describes life aboard a boat making an ocean voyage.

Rosenfeld, Morris and Stanley. *A Century Under Sail* (1988). A brilliant collection of the greatest sailing photographs.

Roth, Hal. *Two Against Cape Horn* (1978). A nearly fatal cruise to the Horn described by the skipper, a great adventurer-writer.

Slocum, Joshua. *Sailing Alone Around the World* (1900). The first solo circumnavigator's colorful story.

Smeeton, Miles. *Once Is Enough* (1959). The story of a wild voyage in the South Pacific, told brilliantly.

Starr, Donald. *The Schooner Pilgrim's Progress* (1997). A circumnavigation in a schooner in the early 1930s, told warmly and humorously.

Thompson, Winfield M., and Thomas W. Lawson. *The Lawson History of the America's Cup* (1902). A beautiful history of the early days of the America's Cup.

Magazines. Here are the more popular boating magazines with national readerships, many of them of general interest to the broad community of sailors. In addition, many boating areas have their own local newspapers and magazines.

Blue Water Sailing. Offshore sailing.

Cruising World. General interest, instruction, boat and gear evaluations.

Multihulls. Catamarans, trimarans, instruction.

Ocean Navigator. Navigation, offshore sailing.

Practical Sailor. Tests of boating gear and boats.

Sail. General interest, instruction, boat and gear evaluations.

Sailing. General interest, excellent photographs.

Sailing Canada. General interest, Canadian boating news.

Sailing World. Racing, instruction, boat evaluations.

Seahorse. The international magazine of sailboat racing, published in England.

Soundings. Boating news, extensive brokerage listings.

WoodenBoat. Traditional boats, wooden construction.

Yachting. General interest, sail and power, large boats.

Yachting Monthly. An English cruising publication.

Index

Index

Index

Index

Review Quiz Answers

Chapter 11

1. *B. 009°.* The direction in true degrees is 358°, and the reciprocal course is 189°.

2. *B. 10 miles; 4.4 knots.* Use two versions of the Speed/Time/Distance formula to solve these problems. First solve for distance, then for speed.

3. *A. 8.7 knots.* There are two ways to solve this problem. Each requires you to start with the distance run of 2.6 miles, which can be found with dividers on the latitude scale. The simplest way is to use the 6-minute rule: if the boat took 18 minutes to go 2.6 miles, then (dividing by 3) in 6 minutes she went 0.87 mile. Since 6 minutes is 0.1 hour, multiply 0.87 by 10 to find the speed, 8.7 knots. You could also use the Speed/Time/Distance formula to solve for speed.

4. *B. 1054 hours.* This is an example of running out your time. First use dividers to find the distance to the buoy, 3.4 miles. Then use the Speed/Time/ Distance formula to solve for time under way: multiply 3.4 by 60, divide the product by 4 to arrive at 51 minutes, and add 51 to 1003 hours to find the arrival time.

5. *A. 10–12° leeway to the west; 168° compensated course.* A boat like yours will make 10–12° leeway in these conditions. Since an east wind blows from the east and pushes boats to the west, the compensation must be to the east, so subtract 12° from the original course to find the new course.

6. *C. A dead reckoning position, an estimated position, and a fix.* A DR (half-circle) has no LOPs, an EP (box) has one, and a fix (circle) has two or more.

7. *B. With a running fix; bearing 200°, range 5.3 miles.* Using a running fix, draw a line parallel to the first bearing on False Ducks Lt. through the intersection of the boat's track and the second bearing on the light.

8. *C. Port tack.* Since your course is to the south and the wind is from the southeast, you will spend more time on the port tack than on the starboard tack. As a rule of thumb, sail the longest leg first so you can be in a position to take advantage of wind shifts. In this case, another advantage of starting out on the port tack is that you will sail faster toward the long-range visibility lights on False Ducks and Prince Edward Point. These lights will provide assistance at night.

Chapter 12

1. *B. 270° and 3 miles.* Solve this problem using the system of doubling the relative bow bearing. In the 36 minutes between the 45° and 90° bearings, at 5 knots you travel 3 miles according to both the Speed/Time/Distance formula and the 6-minute rule. Since the distance run equals the distance off, you know that you are 3 miles off the light on the LOP of the beam bearing.

2. *B. 9.4 miles.* You are bobbing the horizon. Use the formula for determining geographical range in nautical miles: multiply 1.144 times the square root of the lighthouse's height, 67 feet, to arrive at 9.36 nautical miles. This geographical range is a little more than 1.5 miles shorter than the light's nominal range of 11 miles (which is included in the chart label). From a higher platform you should be able to see the light out to its nominal range.

3. *B. NLT 020° and NMT 045°.* A danger bearing is a minimum bearing that guides the navigator in avoiding a hazard. Here, the bearing from the buoy off Prince Edward Point to the Timber Island buoy is about 020° and the bearing to the northeast side of Timber Island is about 045°. If the boat ever gets into the cone between those bearings, then the boat is sailing into the area between the buoy and the island tip and risks running aground. This will be the case if the bearing to the buoy is a num-ber lower than 020° (for example 015°) and the bearing on the island's northeast tip is a number higher than 0450 (for example 050°).

4. *A. 204° to pass to the east and 216° to pass to the west.* Use the Rule of 60 to calculate the necessary course alteration. Here, to clear the island by approximately 0.3 mile, the boat must alter course so she passes approximately 0.7 mile either side of the island's center. Therefore, the desired distance off is 0.7 mile. The distance ahead to the island is about 7 miles. Multiply 0.7 by 60, and divide the product by 7. The resulting course alteration to either side is 6°, which is subtracted from or added to 210° to come up with the new, safe courses.

5. *C. Up the western side.* All things being equal, following a long, fairly straight contour like the 30-foot contour on the western side is less confusing than working with no contours (as in the middle) or working with a circuitous one (as on the eastern side).

6. *C. SMG 7 knots, CMG 060°.* Current set (in contrast with wind direction) is the direction toward which the flow is moving. Here, the current is from off the boat's port quarter and is pushing the boat forward and to starboard. A vector diagram would provide the most accurate measurement, but as a rough estimate the SMG is about 7 knots and the CMG is about 60°.

7. *B. 176°.* Use the Rule of 60. Since the distance to the light is 10 miles, at a speed of 5 knots you will sail for 2 hours. Therefore the 1-knot current will push you to the west a total of 2 miles. Compensate by steering 2 miles to the east of the point. Multiply 2 (the course change in miles) by 60, then divide the product by 10 (the distance ahead). The result is 12°. Since the course change is to port, it is subtracted from 188° (the original course) to come up with 176°. If the course change were to starboard, it would be added, to come up with 200°.

Acknowledgments and Credits

Everyone who opens this book quickly becomes aware of Mark Smith's genius. Only I can testify to his contribution as friendly collaborator in every step of an innovative and complex project that began more than 20 years ago. The illustrations have been selected in order to show a range of older and new boats that are available, the types of boats found in a typical marina or in the advertisements and brokerage listings in a boating magazine. Pictures of recent boats and equipment have been provided by several people and companies named to the right. I want especially to thank Captain Henry Marx of Landfall Navigation. Herb McCormick kindly helped gather some pictures.

Harvey Loomis edited this edition with his characteristic care. Chapters have been helpfully reviewed by Dick Goennel, Chuck Hawley, Dick McCurdy, Bill Robinson, Leah Robinson Rousmaniere, Will Rousmaniere, and Hewitt Schlereth. At Simon & Schuster, Fred Hills and Janice Easton unfailingly encouraged us and provided the freedom to shape new ideas; Patricia Bozza and Peter McCulloch astutely managed the copyediting and production. Tina, Stephanie, Natalie and Cristina Smith — the Craw Avenue production squad — labored long, hard, and well on what must have seemed like an endless flow of words and pictures. Many readers have taken the time to comment on the book and recommend changes, many of which have been made.

I have been lucky to work at safety-at-sea seminars alongside John Bonds, Kelsey Burr, Chuck Hawley, Dick McCurdy, Hal Sutphen, Wayne Williams, and others who taught me as much as they did our audiences. Cornell Maritime Press and John de Graff Inc. granted permission to use tables from Earl Hinz's *The Complete Book of Anchoring* and Bruce Fraser's *Weekend Navigator*, respectively. Bob Bond of the Royal Yachting Association is responsible for the helpful concept of the "No-Go Zone."

In almost 50 years of sailing, I have been taught and encouraged by many shipmates, whose voices and faces remain vivid with me long after we last sailed together and, in many cases, years after their passing to that bay where the wind is always abaft the beam and all boats are seakindly. The list leads off with James Ayer Rousmaniere, my father, who has always been at the helm, and then proceeds with Dana, Will, and Leah Rousmaniere. I think also of Ward Campbell, Steve Colgate, John Coote, Bill Cox, Jim Crane, Skip Dashew, Dick Deaver, Tom Dykstra, Clayton Ewing, Hod Fuller, Hazard Gillespie, Lindsay Hewitt, Larry Huntington, Sherry Jagerson, Bruce Kirby, Harvey Loomis, Jim and Sheila McCurdy, Angus McIntyre, John and Mike Mooney, the Dave Noyeses, Susan Noyes, Arthur and John Page, Bill Rothschild, Donald Starr, David Storrs, Sam Stout, Eric Swenson, and Owen Torrey.

May you be so lucky with your shipmates.

John Rousmaniere
Stamford, Connecticut

PHOTO CREDITS:
Bahamas News Bureau: 75 (bottom), 77 (top), 78, 87, 95, 330, 348 (bottom)
Peter Barlow: 125, 127, 332
Diane Beeston: 331
Ellen Bentsen: 106
Escape Sailboats: 32 (top)
Bermuda News Bureau: 141 (bottom right)
Tyler Carder: 44 (middle left), 45 (all), 294 (top left), 360, 369 (top)
Corsair Marine: vii (bottom), 19 (top), 37 (all)
John Coursen: 172
Dan Devine: 21, 35 (top)
Guy Gurney: 18 (bottom right), 248
Robert Hagan: 7 (all), 33 (middle and bottom left), 34 (bottom), 44 (middle and bottom right), 79 (top left), 82 (bottom), 178 (top)
Steve Henkel: 164 (top), 186, 287, 336, 358 (top), 373 (right)
Hinckley Yachts: 141
Louis Kruk: 38
Landfall Navigation: 177, 180, 236 (left), 337, 353, 355
Leslie Lindemann: 103
Long Beach News Bureau: 107
Harvey Loomis: viii (middle), 324
Millie Rose Madrick: 175 (bottom), 177 (top)
Stephen Mason: 57
Wendy Morgan: 375
National Oceanographic and Atmospheric Administration: 110, 114, 123, 124, 125
Dan Nerney: 178 (bottom), 366
New York Times: 122, 124
National Oceanographic and Atmospheric Administration: 122, 124, 133 (all)
North Sails: v (top), 16 (left and bottom), 28 (top), 29 (top), 33 (right), 79 (top right), 80 (all), 81 (bottom four), 82 (top), 83 (bottom), 87, 88 (all), 93, 102, 105 (all), 108 (top), 109 (all), 111, 141 (bottom left), 319, 369 (bottom), 377, 377 (bottom)
Nick Noyes: 325
Karina Paape: 5
Pacific Seacraft: 29 (bottom)
Neil Rabinowitz: 376
Raytheon Marine Company: 277, 294 (bottom left), 298 (bottom), 300
Robin Hood Marine: 83 (top)
Leah Robinson Rousmaniere: x, 377 (middle right)
John Rousmaniere: vi (middle), 9, 18 (top), 25, 32 (bottom left), 44 (top right), 49, 51, 55, 57 (top), 61, 62, 73, 79 (bottom), 97, 103, 104 (all), 106, 108 (bottom three), 112, 113, 134, 141 (top), 142, 145, 147, 154 (all), 155, 158, 159, 161, 162, 166, 175 (top), 181, 182, 185 (bottom), 246, 297, 311, 313, 338 (bottom), 339, 348 (top), 358 (bottom), 363, 373 (bottom left), 377 (middle left)
Royal Navy: 340
Gail Scott Sleeman: 367
Barry Tenin: 291
West Marine Products: 176, 184, 187, 290 (all), 293, 298 (top), 338 (top)